TEXTS AND STUDIES

CONTRIBUTIONS TO

BIBLICAL AND PATRISTIC LITERATURE

EDITED BY

J. ARMITAGE ROBINSON D.D.

HON. PH.D. GÖTTINGEN HON. D.D. HALLE

CANON OF WESTMINSTER

VOL. VII.

No. 3. CODEX 1 OF THE GOSPELS AND ITS ALLIES

CODEX 1 OF THE GOSPELS AND ITS ALLIES

BY

KIRSOPP LAKE M.A.

LINCOLN COLLEGE OXFORD
CURATE OF S. MARY THE VIRGIN OXFORD

Wipf & Stock
PUBLISHERS
Eugene, Oregon

Wipf and Stock Publishers
199 W 8th Ave, Suite 3
Eugene, OR 97401

Codex 1 of the Gospels and Its Allies
By Lake, Kirsopp
ISBN: 1-59244-836-4
Publication date 8/26/2004
Previously published by Cambridge, 1902

MATRI

ET

SORORI

CARISSIMIS

PREFACE.

THE following pages are an attempt to represent in a convenient form the text of a group of minuscule manuscripts of the Gospels, which have long been known to be remarkable for many important and probably ancient readings.

It is not quite certain what is in general the best method of editing the text of a group of manuscripts which closely represent a common archetype. The late Professor Ferrar in his edition of the manuscripts which are usually called after him attempted to reconstruct the text of the archetype. He was probably justified in doing so, because the manuscripts with which he was dealing were, with one exception, of the same date, and did not differ greatly from one another in value. But I have not followed his example in the present case, because cod. 1 is both older and better than any of the others. It has seemed preferable to print continuously the text of cod. 1, and to give the readings of the other manuscripts in an *apparatus criticus*, adding for convenience the readings of the Received Text; and in the Introduction to indicate those readings in which it is possible that cod. 1 does not preserve the text of the archetype so faithfully as the other manuscripts.

A point which, though of small importance in itself, often causes inconvenience to the student of the Text of the New Testament, is the absence of any short method of quoting groups of manuscripts which are known to represent a common original, such as the Ferrar group, or the present group. It is very cumbrous to have to write

13—69—124—346—543—788—826—828

every time that one wishes to quote the consensus of all the Ferrar MSS. I have ventured to make a slight addition to the usual critical notation in order to reduce this inconvenience, and in the Introduction have used *fam*[13] to express the Ferrar group which is headed by cod. 13, and *fam*[1] to express the group headed by cod. 1. By these symbols I do not mean to imply that all the manuscripts comprised in the group are in agreement, but merely that there is no doubt as to the reading of the archetype which they represent.

The work here offered is based on my own collations of all the manuscripts of the group. I have compared my collation of cod. 1 with that of Tregelles, checking both by a second study of the manuscript itself.

I have to thank the Trustees of the Revision Surplus Fund at Oxford for a generous grant in 1898, which enabled me to go to Basel, Venice and Rome, and the Librarians at Basel and Venice for kindly allowing codd. 1 209 to be sent for my use to the Bodleian Library. I also owe a debt of gratitude for much valuable help to the Editor of this series, to Dr Sanday, and to Dr Rendel Harris. I am also especially grateful to Mr F. Crawford Burkitt for revising and adding to my references to the Syriac Versions, and to my old school friend Mr G. A. Wathen for collating part of cod. 209 at Venice, when for a few days I was ill and unable to go to the Library.

KIRSOPP LAKE.

ST CROSS COTTAGE, OXFORD,
Easter, 1902.

TABLE OF CONTENTS.

ERRATA VEL CORRIGENDA.

Page 10 Mt vii 24 ὁμοιωθήσεται αὐτὸν: *dele* αὐτὸν
„ 48 Mt xxvi 36 n. Γεθσημαινη: *lege* Γεθσημανη
„ 111 Lc vii 11 ἐν τῷ: *lege* ἐν τῷ ἑξῆς
„ 120 Lc ix 61 οἴκῳ: *lege* οἴκῳ μου
„ 166 Jo v 35 ἀγαλλιασθῆναι: *lege* ἀγαλλιασθῆναι
„ 166 Jo v 35 n. αγαλλιασθηναι: *dele*

INTRODUCTION.

CHAPTER I.

DESCRIPTION AND HISTORY OF THE MANUSCRIPTS OF THE GROUP.

Cod. Evan. 1 (*Basel A. N.* IV 2).

The technical description of this manuscript given by Dr Gregory is as follows:

1. (Ac 1 P 1) Basil. bibl. Univ. A. N. IV 2, olim B VI 27 saec X (Burgon XII vel XIII) 18·7 × 11·6, membr, foll. 297 (non 306), col. 1 (13·6 × 6·8), ll 38; litt mai aur; disp et lin usit; litt infra lin; ι adscriptum et ita τωι; prol, capp, titl, sect (Mt 352 xxviii 1 Mc 236 xvi 12 Lc 340 xxiv 36 Ioh 227 xxi 15), (non can), syn (lect et ἀναγνώσεις Mt 116 Mc 70 Lc 114 Ioh 67 m sec), pict (man Ioh Proch); Act Cath Paul habent apparatum Euthalii (init, ἀναγν m ser): *Evv Act Cath Paul* (Phm Hebr) Act autem et epp praemisit bibliopegus evangeliis; in evangeliis insignis est textus qualem fere repraesentat Origenis in Mt commentarius; item cum codd 118 (cf. Griesbach. *Symb. crit.* 1, p. CCII—CCXXIII) 131 saepe consentit saepius cum cod 209 (cf. WH *Intr.* par. 211) adult sub finem Ioh.

There is but little addition to be made to this description, but the following points are worth mentioning.

Dean Burgon was probably right in ascribing the manuscript to the XIIth century. This is the date which M. Henri Omont gives in his *Catalogue des manuscrits grecs des bibliothèques de Suisse* in the *Centralblatt für Bibliothekswesen* for 1886, nor did any of the various scholars who recently saw the manuscript while it was in the Bodleian feel inclined to support an earlier date. I believe that Wetstein was the first to date it as belonging to the xth century: his reasons, so far as they were not palaeographical, are given and discussed below in connection with the picture of St John which is reproduced in the frontispiece.

The *second hand*, which added the lectionary marks and the *ἀναγνώσματα* in red ink, may safely be ascribed to the xiiith century, and is that of a monk named Malachi (v. Jo xxi 25 note).

A late hand has added at the beginning of the manuscript some extracts from Jerome; but it is almost certainly so late as to belong to a scribe at Basel in the xvth century. A late scribe has also added on f. 305 (really f. 296 as the 'foliator' has passed from 290 to 300 in his numeration) the Orphic hymn *εἰς Δία θυμίαμα στύρακα*, which begins

Ζεῦ πολυτίμητε Ζεῦ ἄφθιτε κ.τ.λ.

and a still later hand has scribbled a few extracts from Cosmas and Dionysius. But these hands are quite late, and must, I think, be those of scribes who worked on the manuscript after it had passed into the library at Basel.

The only picture which survives is that which stands before the Gospel according to St John. An interesting history attaches to its interpretation.

It will be seen from the frontispiece that the picture consists of two parts, with an iambic couplet at the bottom. The lower and larger part is the usual representation of John dictating his Gospel to Prochorus, while the hand of God proceeds from a cloud in the right-hand corner. There has never been any question about this, but an interesting though unwarrantable theory was based by Wetstein on the upper medallion and the iambic couplet at the foot of the picture. As this theory has been (so far as I know) more or less accepted by all scholars who have dealt with the manuscript, it will be best to give it in Wetstein's own words as they are found on pp. 55—6 of the 1730 edition of his Prolegomena.

Singulis evangeliis praefixae fuerant olim picturae, sed quae a tribus prioribus evangeliis jam una cum quattuor aliis foliis recisae sunt: in

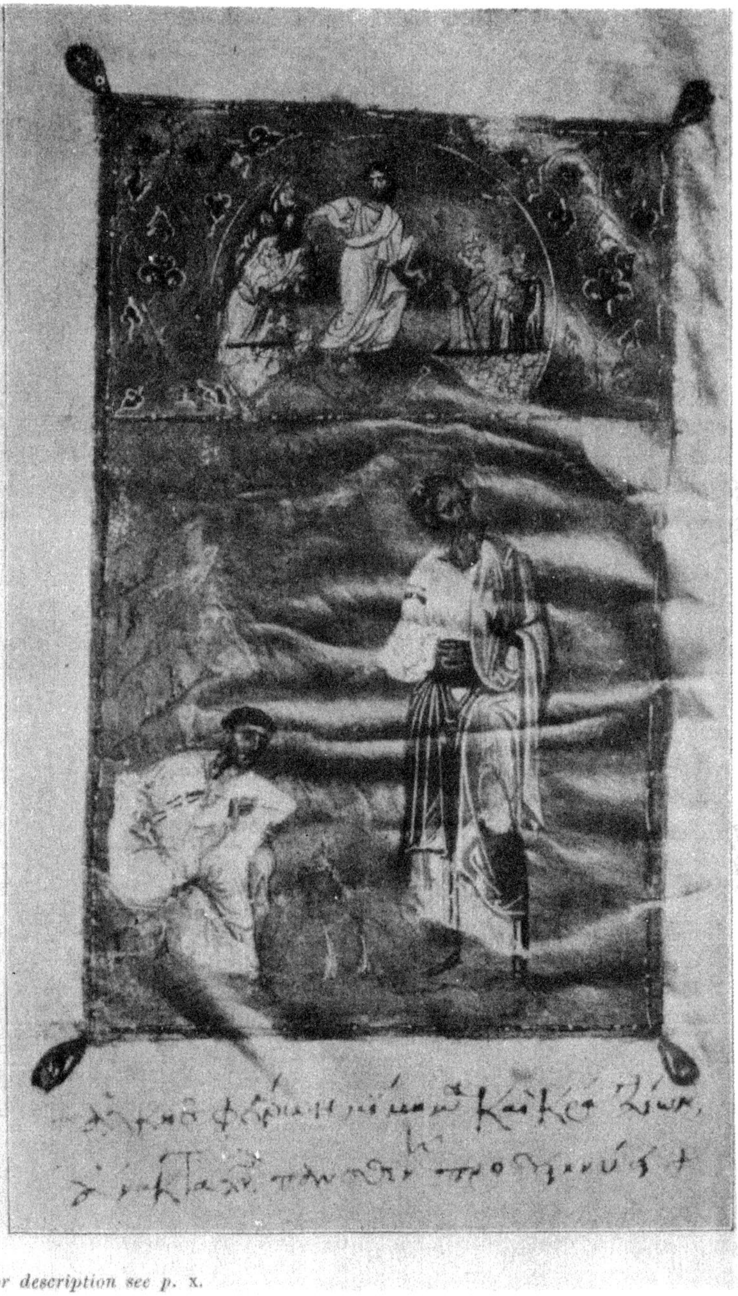

For description see p. x.

fronte evangelii Joannis vero depictus conspicitur Christus, sinistra tenens crucem duplicem, dextram vero duobus viris porrigens, quorum prior veste caerulea indutus barbaque candida insignis capite obvelato conspicitur, posterior vero vultum praefert juniorem, vesteque purpurei coloris indutus est; ad pedes Christi jacet Clavis; ad sinistram ejus stant duae personae, quarum altera amplectens crucem, coronam auream gestat in capite, indutaque pallio est caerulei coloris auro distincto, barba crinibusque canis; altera junior videtur veste purpurascente coronaque aurea insignis, cum hac epigraphe adjecta, †ἡ ἀνάστασις† duobusque Jambis

Ἀλκῆς φέρων μίμημα καὶ κράτους Λέων
Ἄνακτα Χριστὸν πανσθενῆ προδεικνύει.

Unde conjicimus duas istas figuras exhibere Leonem Sapientem cum filio Constantino Porphyrogenneto; alluditur quippe ad nomen Leonis, quod et Imperatorem et animal fortissimum et ipsam fortitudinem denotat, teste Clemente Alex. *Strom.* v p. 413 ubi de signis Aegyptiorum hieroglyphicis scribens eadem fere verba habet: ἀλκῆς μὲν καὶ ῥώμης σύμβολον αὐτοῖς ὁ Λέων: simul etiam alluditur ad Resuscitationem Lazari, Joann. Cap. VI. expositam, et ad templum memoriae hujus resuscitationis ab ipso Imperatore Leone dicatum, cujus rei testis est Codinus de Officiis cap. 16, κατὰ τὴν Ἀνάστασιν τοῦ ἁγίου Λαζάρου εἰς τὴν ἐπ' ὀνόματι αὐτοῦ τιμωμένην σεβάσμιον μονήν, et Leo Grammaticus: ἔκτισεν ὁ Λέων εἰς τοὺς λεγομένους τόπους τὸν ἅγιον Λάζαρον κατασκευάσας μονὴν ἀνδρεῖαν εὐνούχων ἔνθα καὶ τοῦ ἁγίου Λαζάρου σῶμα καὶ Μαρίας τῆς Μαγδαληνῆς ἀνακομίσας ἀπέθετο ποιήσας καὶ τὰ ἐγκαίνια τῆς αὐτῆς ἐκκλησίας. Similes occurrunt versus inter Opera Theodori Studitae a Sirmondo edita, p. 170,

Λέων σὺν υἱῷ τῷ νέῳ Κωνσταντίνῳ.

Item p. 199, Οἱ τὸ κράτος λαβόντες ἐκ θεοῦ μόνου
Λέων τε Κωνσταντῖνος οἱ στεφηφόροι &c.

Quare Imperatoris fuisse Codicem fortassis inde etiam conjici potest quod et τίτλοι Eusebiani omnes aureis literis scripti, et primae singulorum paginae Distinctiones aureis punctis notatae sunt, instar Codicis Gallicani XIII[1].

Concessit postea in usus alicujus ecclesiae ut videtur quo tempore manus imperitior et junior principium et finem Ἀναγνώσεων margini adscripsit una cum hac praecatiuncula: κύριε συγχώρησον τὴν ψυχὴν τοῦ δούλου σου Μαλαχίου ἱερομονάχου τὸ τοῦτο γράφοντος.

This attractive theory involves the following propositions.

(1) The two figures in the medallion are emperors.

[1] Cod. Evan. 14.

(2) The iambic couplet refers to a man named Leo, and not to a lion.

(3) The date of the manuscript is the tenth century.

All three are probably wrong: Dr M. R. James, to whom sent a photograph of this picture, at once identified the scene as the usual representation of the *Harrowing of Hell*. The description which Dr James gives of the whole picture is as follows.

The lower part of the picture represents St John dictating to the Deacon Prochorus. In the medallion above is the Harrowing of Hell. Our Lord, in the centre, holding a small cross in his left hand takes the hand of Adam, who with Eve is emerging from an enclosure on the left. Below our Lord's feet are the broken gates of Hell. On the right of these lies the key. On the right, in an enclosure like that on the left, stand two men whom I take to be David and another prophet who predicted the event represented.

This description is confirmed by the following extract from Didron's *Guide de la Peinture* (p. 199), which is the highest authority on the subject, as it is a translation of a Greek manuscript on Mt Athos embodying the rules for illuminating manuscripts which were faithfully followed for so long by Byzantine artists.

La descente aux enfers.

L'enfer comme une grotte obscure, sous des montagnes. Des anges resplendissants enchaînent Béelzébuth, le chef des ténèbres; ils frappent d'autres démons, et en poursuivent d'autres avec des lances. Plusieurs hommes nus et enchaînés regardent en haut. Un grand nombre de serrures brisées. Les portes de l'enfer sont renversées; le Christ les foule aux pieds. Le Sauveur prend Adam de la main droite et Ève de la gauche. A gauche du Sauveur, le Précurseur le montrant du geste. David est près de lui, ainsi que d'autres rois justes avec des couronnes et des nimbes. A gauche, les prophètes Jonas Isaie et Jérémie; le juste Abel et beaucoup d'autres personnages avec des nimbes. Tout autour, une lumière éclatante et un grand nombre d'anges.

Accordingly our upper medallion is a somewhat simple form of the picture described by Didron. I have since found it in cod. evan. 113 as a separate picture: the general arrangement is the same, but St John the Baptist is added. I have also been told that a similar arrangement is found in the famous mosaic at Torcelli.

There is then, in the picture, no reference to Leo the Wise or to Lazarus, or to the monastery of the Ἀνάστασις: and consequently there is no reason for referring the Λέων of the iambic couplet to a man named Leo, or for assigning the manuscript in spite of its palaeographical appearance to the tenth century.

An interesting problem is however raised by the iambic couplet:

Ἀλκῆς φέρων μίμημα καὶ κράτους λέων
Ἄνακτα Χριστὸν πανσθενῆ προδεικνύει.

The meaning clearly is that the lion is the symbol of St John because the Fourth Gospel sets forth the royal strength of Christ. But this is an unusual statement in Greek documents. It is found in a good many Latin sources which are examined in Dr Lawlor's *Book of Mulling*; but I only know of one Greek manuscript which has preserved the tradition, though it is probable that when attention is directed to the matter it will be found in more. The manuscript in which I have found it, cod 113 (B. M. Harl. 1810), does not preserve the iambic couplet, but it has the tradition in the form of a prologue which is an extract from the *Quaestiones* of Anastasius Sinaita, which in turn are derived at this point from Irenaeus *Haer.* III xi 8.

The text of cod. 113 is quite ordinary and shows no connection with the family of cod. 1. It would be precarious to suggest a connection between Anastasius and cod. 1; and I have not been able to find any other facts which throw light on the matter.

The result of this investigation is therefore disappointing. I began my work with the impression that, as the Abbé Martin had shown that the *Ferrar group* was immediately connected with Calabria or Sicily, so Wetstein had shown that cod. 1 was connected with the monastery of the Ἀνάστασις in Constantinople; but a closer examination has destroyed his argument, and has left the *provenance* of cod. 1 an open question.

The history of the MS therefore is certain only as far back as the middle of the 15th century. At that time it was in the possession of John of Ragusa in Dalmatia, who was sent in 1433 by the Council of Basel on a mission to the Greeks. He was at that time Principal of the order of the Dominicans at Basel. He was made Cardinal in 1440 by Pope Felix V, and probably died in 1443. He bequeathed his library, which included cod. 1, to the Dominicans of Basel. The MS remained in their possession until the dissolution of the monastery, with the exception of thirty years, during which it was lent to Reuchlin for the use of Œcolampadius, who was helping in the correction of Erasmus's edition. In 1559 it passed with the rest of the books of the Dominicans into the library of the University, to which it still belongs.

Cod. Evan. 118 (*Oxon. Bodl. Auct. D. inf.* 2—17).

Dr Gregory's description is as follows:

118. Ox. Bodl. Misc. 13. Saec XIII, in 4, membr, foll. 256 (sect m ser Mc 234 xvi 9), lect, init, ἀναγν, (syn et men m post.): *Evv*; man ser suppl (chart) Mt i 1—vi 2 (membr) Lc xiii 35—xiv 20 et xviii 8—xix 9 (chart) Ioh xvi 25—xxi 25. Olim Marshii (24) archiepisc. Armachani (†1713). Grsb. diligenter cont. *S. c.* 1, p. CCII—CCXXIII. Textum plurima bonae notae cum 1 209 131 habere testantur W. H. *Intr.* par. 211.

This description is accurate; but the following points may also be noticed.

The size of the parchment leaves is 19·9 × 14·4, and the average size of the column of writing on each page is 15·2 × 10·4.

The writing is ordinary, and typical probably of the later rather than the earlier part of the thirteenth century. There are some places where the scribe has deliberately refrained from finishing a word, and others where he has inserted an alternative reading. The importance of this fact is the light which it throws on the relations of 118 to the other members of the group (v. p. xxvi).

It is stated in Scrivener's Introduction (ed. 4, Miller) that 118 contains the ῥήματα and στίχοι. This is not the case. The ῥήματα are not given; and στίχοι are found only in Lc and Jo. In Lc they are added by a late hand (probably the third), and in Jo they are on the supplementary paper leaves which were added probably by the fourth hand.

It is stated in the same book, and also in Coxe's catalogue, that the MS is a palimpsest. It is hard to be certain whether this is so or not. The facts of the case are these:—(1) The supplementary leaves, which are conjugate, containing Lc xiii 35—xiv 20 and Lc xviii 8—xviii 29, are undoubtedly palimpsest. Mr Burkitt in 1896 identified part of the under-writing as Ps. xviii (xix); if it were necessary, probably the whole could be deciphered. The character of the script is a large formal minuscule, which may perhaps belong to the XIIth century. (2) The other supplementary leaf, containing Lc xviii 29—xix 9, is quite clearly not palimpsest. (3) On f. 162 a blank has been left in order to begin St Luke's Gospel on a fresh quaternion; and there certainly seem to be a series of almost entirely obliterated lines in a small minuscule hand, running perpendicularly from about an inch and a half from the bottom edge to the extreme top of the page. But I have failed to read with certainty a single word: only an occasional letter is at all plain. On f. 155, the conjugate leaf of f. 162, there are probably similar traces of under-writing; but it is impossible to speak with certainty. The same is true of most pages in the MS. There seem to be traces of under-writing, but they are very faint, and in many cases may equally well be discolorations of the parchment.

118 was left to the Bodleian by Narcissus Marsh, Archbishop of Armagh, who died in 1714. Beyond the fact that it is a codex which he obtained through Dr Halifax, about the year 1699, nothing is known of its previous history. But as Dr Halifax was chaplain at Aleppo from Jan. 1687–8 to Nov. 1695, it is probable that he brought it from the East.

It is however possible to trace from the internal evidence a few facts of its history.

Originally it contained at least 25 quaternions. This is shown by the signatures on the vellum; the quaternion beginning Mt vi 2, the first of those which now remain, is signed $\bar{\gamma}$; and the last which remains is signed $\overline{\kappa\gamma}$. This implies that the MS contained some additional material (probably the tables of Eusebian canons, a synaxarion and perhaps a menology) in the first and in the greater part of the last quaternions; for Mt i 1—vi 2 would fill up quaternion $\bar{\beta}$, and Jo xvi 25—end would not fill up more than quaternion $\overline{\kappa\delta}$ and two folia of $\overline{\kappa\epsilon}$. Not very long after it was finished, perhaps in the early part of the XIVth century, the first and last leaves of the 17th quaternion were lost; the MS was taken to pieces, and the place of the missing leaves was filled by two new ones, viz. a conjugate pair of palimpsest folia, taken from a XIIth century Psalter (v. supra). At the same time the loss of another leaf, viz. the 1st leaf of the 18th quaternion, was supplied by the same scribe (the second hand), who however did not again make use of his old Psalter, but took a clean piece of vellum, and sewed it neatly on to the narrow "guard" of the last leaf of the quaternion, which had not fallen out when the first leaf was lost. This fact suggests that no great interval elapsed between the loss of these leaves, and the substitution of others in their place.

At some date after this the first menology was added, by the third hand, on page 74, which had been left blank in order to begin St Mark with a fresh quaternion. It gives a full but (judged by the usual dates) inaccurate menology for April and the first week of May, and can hardly have been written earlier than the end of the XIVth century. On the whole it is the ordinary Constantinopolitan menology, but many of the saints are put a day or two earlier or later than usual, and there are a few who really belong to other months. No saints of a very late date are mentioned: the latest by far is Cosmas of Chalcidice, who was killed by the iconoclasts in the VIIIth century. The same scribe also added the *στίχοι* to St Luke.

After this it would seem that the MS lay neglected for some time in a place infested by mice, and that it was lying on its side. For the middle of the outside has been nibbled away in a large semicircle to a depth of about an inch. If it had been standing up, it would have been nibbled at the bottom corner; and if it had been in use, and therefore occasionally moved, it would have been nibbled more equally all over.

About the same time during or after this period of neglect it lost the first two and last quaternions, and these lacunae were filled on paper by a scribe, who does not seem to be later than the XVth century (the fourth hand). He also added a synaxarion and menology of an ordinary type, at the beginning of the MS, and the *στίχοι* to St John at the end of the Gospel.

After this, but not long after, another, the fifth hand, added an ἐκλογάδιον, an ordinary menology, and the tables of the Eusebian canons; while the same, or possibly a contemporary hand, also added the Gospels for Holy week.

While in this condition the manuscript passed into the possession of a certain παπᾶς, or parish priest of the Greek Church, named Φίλιππος ὁ Κούσολος[1]. He died, according to a note which is given twice (viz. on what were then the first and last pages of the MS), in 1654. The remainder of the existing volume—a few scraps of psalms and lections in a late hand (the sixth)—was most probably added after the book had passed in 1699 (approximately) into the hands of Halifax and Marsh.

The latter has added on the first page what is supposed to have been his motto, "πανταχῇ τὴν ἀλήθειαν." The binding of the MS has tooling which is found on several MSS in the Bodleian, and it was therefore probably bound by the Library authorities.

There is a mutilation on ff. 120—1 which seems to be recent. The leaves have been torn diagonally across, so that the top lines are almost entirely missing but the bottom ones are intact (v. p. 190 f.).

Cod. Evan. 131 (*Rom. Vat. Gr.* 360).

Dr Gregory's description is as follows:

131. (Ac 70 P 77) Rom. Vat. Gr. 360. saec XIV vel XV (Birch XI) 23·5 × 17·5, membr, foll. 233, coll. 2 (15·4 × 4·8: 2 coll. = 11) ll 37, litt mai rubr; membr crass, disp usit. sed foll. 10 in fascic; lin inusit, atr subnig; Carp, Eust.-capp. t, sect (Mc 234: xvi 9), (non can), (lect, init m sec) syn, men, subscr, στιχ, vers; Euth: *Evv Act Cath Paul.* (Hebr. Tim); m pr multa correxit; textus bonae notae, cf. WH *Intr.* par. 211. Aldus Manutius Pauli filius codicem bibliothecae Vat, Sixto V papa (a 1585—1590), dono dedit. Concluditur ex consonantia textus cum editione *N. T. Gr.* Aldina anni 1518 hunc codicem in eam editionem edendam adhibitum esse. Birch. cont evangelia. Ex errore Scholz. quarto loco "Ap. 66" designavit, deest vero Apoc.

There is little to add to this description, but the following points may be noticed.

[1] Κούσολος or Κούζολος is a modern Greek word meaning (i) humpbacked, (ii) half-witted. Here it is presumably the former.

The date is almost definitely fixed by the following note, which comes at the end of St Luke:

ἐπὶ ἔτους ,ςωια ἰνδικτ. ᾱ ἐγίνετο χειμέριος καιρὸς πάνυ· καὶ ἐχιώνησεν ὅλος ὁ μωρέας ἰουναρίω εἰς τὴν ζ̄ καὶ ἐπεκράτησεν ὁ χιὼν ἡμέρας β̄ καὶ μετὰ ταύτην ἔπεσεν λαῦρος ὑετὸς καὶ ἐγίνετο θνῆσι ἄπειρος εἰς τὰ κτῆνι.

This shows that the manuscript was in existence in the year 1303. The hand by which this note was written was not the first hand: I thought myself that it was almost contemporary; Dr Mercati, however, thinks that the first hand is considerably earlier.

The menology throws no light on the *provenance* of the manuscript. It is not very full and is of the ordinary type. There are a few names scrawled on blank pages of the manuscript, in the usual formulas, as follows:

(1) before St Matthew:

μνήσθητι κε̅ τὰς ψυχὰς τῶν δούλων σου παρασκεβου, μαρίας κε των(?) εγγετερων

(2) before the *κεφάλαια* to St Luke:

μνήσθητι κε̅ τὴν ψυχὴν τοῦ δούλου σου στα. ματ. καὶ ιω̅ ηρίνι καὶ συγχώροσον αὐτῶν ἐν ἡμέρᾳ κρίσεως

(3) before St John:

μνησθήτω κε̅ τὴν ψυχὴν τοῦ δούλου σου κηριώκη ἅμα σιρίας καὶ τὸν τέκνων αὐτοῦ ἐν ἡμέρᾳ κρίσεως.

Dr Mercati thinks that these names were scrawled before the time of Aldus. This seems to show that the book was not in a monastery, as men, women and children seem to be mentioned.

I am indebted to Dr Rendel Harris for pointing out to me that the connection with the Aldine edition of 1518 is an unwarrantable conjecture made by Birch.

Birch says:—"Mirum hujus codicis cum Aldi editione in lectionibus singularibus consensum observavi, cujus rei nonnulla exempla hic afferam," and then after giving a list of eighteen readings, which it is unnecessary to repeat here, he concludes "Quae omnia cum eodem modo in Aldina editione reperiantur facile adducor ut credam Aldinum hic nostrum secutum esse neque ut multi opinantur solam Erasmi editionem expressisse."

It will scarcely be believed that all the eighteen readings which Birch cites as peculiar to 131 and the Aldine edition against Erasmus are nevertheless found in the first edition of Erasmus.

There is therefore no reason for thinking that Aldus made use of this manuscript in preparing his edition of the New Testament. It may be well to add that the actual possession of the codex by Aldus is undoubted, for on the first leaf is inscribed "Sixto V. P. O. M. Gulielmo Sirletto S. R. E. Card. Praeside Bibliothecae Vaticanae, Aldus Manucius, Pauli F. Aldi N. D. D."

Cod. Evan. 209 (*Ven. Marc.* 10).

Dr Gregory's description is as follows:

209. (Ac 95 P 108 Ap 46) Ven. Marc. 10. saec XIV (al XI vel XII) et XV, 19·5 × 12, membr, foll. 411, col 1, ll 27, prol. capp-t, capp (et capp Latt. m. nov.), titl, sect (Mc 236), (non can), lect; Euth. in Cath, Paul; *Act Cath Paul* (Phm Hebr) *Evv Apoc* (Apoc est saec XV ll 24, scriptura Evv 205 similis); Plurima bonae notae in Evv habet cum Evv 1 communia, multa cum 118, 131; codicis 205 fortasse parens. Olim Bessarionis qui in Conc. Flor. a. 1439 secum habebat. Birch. Engelbreth. Fleck. Burgon. (*Guardian* a. 1873, p. 1229) perl. cf. W. H. *Intr.* par. 211.

To this description it may be added that this manuscript is one of those in which the symbol στ (sometimes surrounded by a circle) is found at intervals, throughout the four Gospels. It is probable that the sign means στάσις, and is connected with some form of lectionary use; but as I do not certainly know what this use may be, and can find no book which deals with the point, I give a list of the verses to the end of which it is affixed in 209.

Mt	ix 8	στ $\bar{α}$
	xii 8	στ in a circle
	xvii 13	στ in a circle
	xxiv 3	στ in a circle and στ $\bar{γ}$

Mc	v 34	στ in a circle
	vi 29	στ $\bar{\alpha}$
	vii 37	στ in a circle
	x 45	στ in a circle
	xi 33	στ $\bar{\beta}$
	xiv 2	στ in a circle
Lc	v 7	*στάσις* $\bar{\alpha}$ written apparently by the same hand as the στ $\bar{\alpha}$ series
	viii 21	στα $\bar{\beta}$
	xi 28	στα $\bar{\gamma}$
	xv 32	στα $\bar{\delta}$
	iv 42	στ $\bar{\alpha}$
	vii 13	στα $\bar{\beta}$ in a square
	x 16	στα $\bar{\gamma}$ in a square
	xiii 30	στα $\bar{\delta}$ in a square.

These divisions do not seem to correspond to any lectionary use with which I am acquainted. But Father Chrysostom of the Laura on Mt Athos told me that they refer to the long lessons which were read in Holy week, though the modern lessons are much shorter.

There are also marked the ordinary *εὐαγγέλια* and *ἑωθινὰ* for Holy week, but no other lections are noted.

The chief difficulty in connection with this manuscript is the determination of its date. The opinions which have been given in the past vary from the fifteenth century, suggested by Birch and supported by Zanetti's Catalogue at Venice, to the twelfth, suggested by Burgon. Several palaeographic experts who recently saw 209 while it was at Oxford, were unanimous in placing it in the fourteenth century, and this, as we have seen, is the view of Gregory. On palaeographical grounds this opinion is no doubt sound, but on textual grounds I think there is a great deal to be said in favour of the thirteenth century. The reason is a simple one. It is difficult to repress the suspicion that 118 is a copy of 209. (1) There is a long list of passages in which 118 209 differ both from the text of 1 and from the Received Text. Some of these are probably cases where 1 does not represent the family text, but many of them must be mistakes in the archetype of

118 209, or in whichever of the two is the original of the other. (2) There are also many cases in which 118 209 have the received text against 1. (3) There are many cases in which 1 209 agree against 118. (4) There are no cases of importance (and only 27 altogether) in which 1 118 are found against 209 ς. These facts require one of two explanations; either 118 is a copy of 209; or 118 209 are copies of the same archetype, 118 having been made carelessly, and 209 with care. I think that the facts (3) and (4) make the former alternative the more probable; and since 118 is clearly a thirteenth century codex, I think that it is possible in spite of the palaeographical evidence that 209 belongs to the 13th century and is earlier than 118.

The matter may be put as a balance of probability thus. Which is more likely, that 209 is an abnormally written manuscript which has deceived palaeographical experts, or that of two manuscripts both copied from the same original, 118 should be frequently unfaithful to the archetype, and 209 never, *except where* 118 *is also unfaithful*?

The question admits of doubt, but as all the readings of 118 209 are given, individual scholars may easily judge for themselves.

There is nothing remarkable about the appearance of the manuscript except that the Latin chapter-numbers have been added by a late scribe who explains in a note written in Greek that they have been added for convenience in finding references when disputing with Latins. The same hand wrote at the beginning of the volume:

ἡ νέα διαθήκη πᾶσα δηλόνοτι αἱ πράξεις τῶν ἀποστόλων, αἱ ἑπτὰ καθολικαὶ ἐπιστολαὶ, αἱ ιδ̄ τοῦ ἁγ. Παύλου, δ̄ εὐαγγέλια καὶ ἡ ἀποκάλυψις· ἐστὶ δὲ τὸ βιβλίον ἐμοῦ Βεσσαρίωνος καρδινάλης τοῦ τῶν Τούσκλων.

This is presumably Bessarion's own writing: and it is legitimate to guess that the disputations with the Latins were those of the Council of Florence.

I can find nothing at all to throw any light on the history of the manuscript before it passed into the possession of Bessarion.

It may be well to add here a note on 205. I was convinced

when I studied the question at Venice that 205 was a copy of 209. An hour's work only revealed two or three differences between the manuscripts, and those clearly accidental. It is for this reason that no further notice has been taken of 205. It would be interesting if the scribe of 205 were shown to be the same as the one who added the Apocalypse in 209, but the impression formed on my mind in 1898 was adverse to this suggestion.

CHAPTER II.

THE RELATIONS SUBSISTING BETWEEN 1 118 131 209.

The genealogical relations which subsist between any given MSS can be deduced, in the absence of direct information, by studying the variations from the standard text which they share in common. This is another and slightly more accurate way of enunciating the old rule that "community of error implies unity of origin." It is slightly more accurate because in dealing with late MSS the familiar text, the presence of which calls for no explanation, is not the true text, but the late ecclesiastical or *Syrian* text, which is perhaps better named the *Antiochian* text, and it is deviation from this in any considerable degree which indicates community of origin.

To determine therefore the genealogical relations of the MSS under discussion it is sufficient to compare them with the standard of the *Antiochian* text, and not with any supposed "true" text. This is an easy task because the text of Stephanus (the T.R.) as reproduced by Scrivener or Lloyd is a sufficiently accurate presentation of the *Antiochian* text to serve all practical purposes; and the few places where Stephanus has an unusual reading can be easily noted, when any real result is affected.

For the sake of clearness I shall now give at once the results which have been obtained by such a comparison of the text of 1 118 131 209 with the text of Stephanus, and shall then proceed to justify these results one by one.

(1) 1 118 131 209 have a common ancestor *W*.

(2) Either 118 209 have a common archetype *X*, or 118 is a copy of 209.

(3) 209 is more faithful to *X* than is 118.

(4) 118 was written by an eclectic scribe who was acquainted with *X*, and sometimes hesitated between the text of *X* (or of 209) and the *Antiochian* text.

(5) *X* was copied from two MSS *Y* and *Z*, of which *Y* belonged to the same family as 1, and was probably an ancestor of it, and *Z* to the *Antiochian* family. Probably *Y* was mutilated.

(6) 131 is in Mc i—v and in Lc i—xxiv descended from another MS of the same family as 1, which was neither *X* nor 1 nor *Y*.

(7) The immediate archetypes of 1 118 131 209 were probably minuscule MSS.

These results may be illustrated by a diagram thus:—

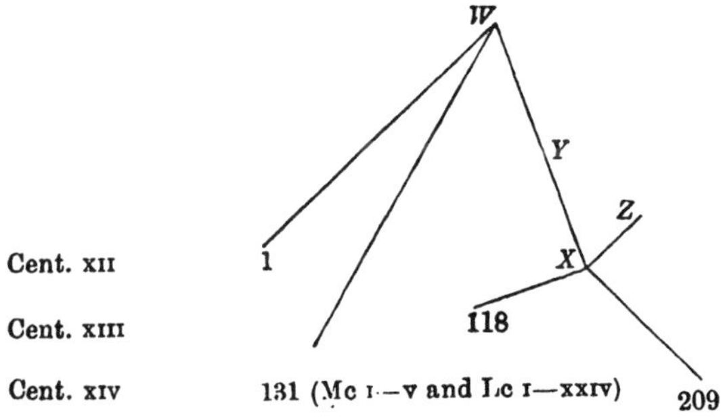

(1) 1 118 131 209 *have a common ancestor* W.

A comparison of the texts of these MSS with each other and with the text of Stephanus shows that in the sections comprising Mt i—x, xxii—Mc xiv, Lc iv—xxiii, Jo i—xiii, xviii there are in 1 2243 variants from the text of Stephanus; 1731 of these are found in 118 209, and 214 more in 209, though not in 118.

Similarly for the sections comprising Mc i—v Lc i—xxiv there are in 1 1188 variants from the text of Stephanus; 804 of these are found in 131, which elsewhere agrees very closely with the text of Stephanus.

This would be sufficient to suggest a common ancestry for 1 118 131 209 in the sections mentioned even if none of the variants were singular or subsingular, but since on the contrary some of them are attested by no other Greek manuscripts and many of them by only a few others, it is certain that in the sections in question 1 118 131 209 represent a common ancestor which may be called *W*. The only alternative theory is that 118 131 209 are copies of 1, but this possibility is excluded by facts which are mentioned in the following sections.

(2) 118 209 *have a common ancestor X.*

It has been already shown from 1, that 118 and 209 in certain sections agree closely with 1. Similarly it may be shown that in the other sections the texts of the two MSS are largely identical, agreeing in 238 variants from the T. R., and differing from each other in only 33.

This affinity cannot be explained by supposing that 209 is a copy of 118; for, in the former sections, when one of the two MSS agrees with 1, and the other with the T.R., in nearly 300 places it is 209 which agrees with 1, and only once is it 118.

It might be explained by supposing that 118 is a copy of 209 if it were not for the verdict of all the palaeographers who have seen the manuscripts together, that 209 is later than 118. I have expressed in Chapter I my feeling that it is possible that after all 209 is an abnormally written manuscript which deceives palaeographers, but I do not feel at liberty to build on that feeling, and therefore in this chapter I must exclude the possibility that 118 is a copy of 209. Excluding, then, this possibility, it is obvious that this close affinity between 118 and 209 can only be explained by the theory that they have a common ancestor in the sections which are not faithful to the 1 type, as well as in the bulk of the Gospels, where they resemble 1.

It is also shown by these facts that 1 is not directly the ancestor of either 118 or 209. Because, if it were so, it would be necessary to suppose that 118 was written by an eclectic scribe who used 1, as a rule, but at intervals preferred to follow another copy, and that 209 was afterwards written by another scribe who was also eclectic, and whose eclecticism led him to make in nearly every case exactly the same divergences and agreements with 1 as the scribe of 118 had made. Such a coincidence in eclecticism is barely conceivable in a few instances, but in the case of a large number, as in the present, it is quite out of the question. Therefore it is certain that the immediate ancestor of 118 and 209 was some MS now lost which may be called *X*, and which was composed by some eclectic scribe out of two MSS, one of the same type as 1 which may be called *Y*, and the other of a type nearly approaching the T. R. which may be called *Z*.

(3) 209 *is more faithful to X than is* 118, *and* (4) 118 *was written by an eclectic scribe who was acquainted with X, and sometimes hesitated between the text of X and the Antiochian text.*

This is proved by the fact mentioned above that in 379 cases 209 has the reading of 1, while 118 has the reading of the T. R., but in only 27 cases are the relations reversed. And it is for this reason that the palaeographical judgment that 118 is older than 209 is open to suspicion.

It is not however difficult to account for the markedly less faithful character of 118, for it is certain that the scribe of 118 was eclectic in his copying. This might be guessed from the number of places where he reverts to the T.R., and it seems to be proved by the long list of passages in which he either leaves a blank, doubting what words exactly to copy, or puts an alternative reading above the word he has actually written. An appendix on p. xxxvii gives those which are clearly due to the hesitation of the scribe between the reading of 209 (as best representing the archetype *X*) and the T.R. The remainder are to be found in the critical notes. Griesbach in his *Symbolae Criticae* regarded these passages as a proof that 1 was known to the scribe of 118. It will however be seen in the list given that they can be explained equally well by a knowledge of 209 (or of the lost MS which is best represented by 209); and, as it has been shown that 118 is not directly descended from 1, it is obvious that Griesbach's theory must be amended in the manner indicated.

(5) *X was copied from two manuscripts Y and Z, of which Y belonged to the same family as* 1 *and Z to the Antiochian family. Y was probably mutilated.*

It has been already mentioned that 118 209 agree so closely with 1 in Mt i—x, xxii—Mc xiv, Lc iv—xxiii, Jo i—xiii, xviii that the three manuscripts must have a common ancestry in these sections, and it has also been shown that the agreement between 118 and 209 is equally significant in the remaining sections, so as to suggest that they have a common ancestor *X*. These facts imply that the scribe who produced *X* made use of two sources, (*a*) a manuscript belonging to the same family as 1, which may be called *Y*, and (*b*) a manuscript belonging to the Antiochian family, which may be called *Z*.

It is obvious that the eclecticism which led him to follow sometimes *Y* and sometimes *Z*, may have been due to necessity or choice. That is to say, he may have abandoned the use of the MS of the type of 1 because it was mutilated or illegible, or he may have done so simply because he disliked the reading of his exemplar and preferred to use another copy.

It is not possible to say with absolute certainty that either of these alternatives is excluded or demonstrated by any available evidence. But there are certain facts which raise a presumption that the scribe was influenced by both reasons in his occasional abandonment of the text of the type of 1.

In considering this point it must be remembered that mutilations in MSS generally take the form of the loss either of complete quires, usually of course quaternions, or of conjugate leaves. If therefore a MS which had been mutilated in several places was used as an archetype by the scribe who used a MS of a different type to fill up the lacunae, it ought to be possible to trace definite proportions in the length of the passages where the secondary type of text is followed, and by using this as a standard of measurement to reconstruct conjecturally the mutilated archetype, showing what quires and what leaves were missing when it was used. If this cannot be done, then the probability is that the change of type is due to a deliberate eclecticism on the part of the scribe. If it can be done in some places, but not so as to explain the phenomena in others, then it is probable that the scribe was in some cases deliberately eclectic, and in others was compelled to desert his original exemplar, because it was mutilated.

It is to this last class that the facts belong in the case of the archetype of 118 209. In the Fourth Gospel there is a series of four passages where the sudden abandonment of the text of the type of 1, and the use of another, can be explained on the theory that the MS of the former type was one which contained on each page 18—19 lines of the same length as the lines in Lloyd's Greek Testament, and that two conjugate leaves, a single inserted leaf, and a complete quaternion were missing when the MS was used by the scribe of the archetype of 118 and 209. The facts which go to make this probable are as follows.

There are four passages in the Fourth Gospel where 118 and 209 leave the 1 type of text:—

(1) viii 28—viii 43.

(2) x 4—x 18.

(3) xi 33—xi 48.

(4) xiii 34—xviii 3.

The lengths of these four passages stated in lines of Lloyd's Greek Testament are:—

(1) 36 lines.

(2) 36 lines.

(3) 36 lines.

(4) 292 ($=8 \times 36\frac{1}{2}$) lines.

The lengths of the three passages which intervene between these four are:—

(1) viii 43—x 4 $=146$ ($=4 \times 36\frac{1}{2}$) lines.

(2) x 18—xi 33 $=111$ ($=3 \times 37$) lines.

(3) xi 48—xiii 34 $=219$ ($=6 \times 36\frac{1}{2}$) lines.

We are thus led to suggest that the composition of the MS in this part of the Fourth Gospel was

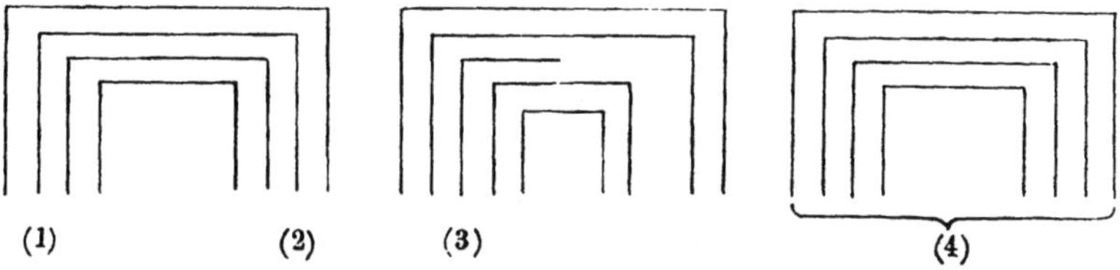

that the four passages mentioned above were contained on the leaves indicated by the figures, and that they were lost before the MS was used by the scribe of the archetype of 118 and 209.

So far as it goes, this is fairly satisfactory. But it does not go nearly far enough to prove that mutilation of his exemplar will explain the eclecticism of the scribe of the archetype of 118 209. For these four passages are not the only places in the Fourth Gospel which seem to desert the MS of the type of 1, on the contrary the whole of the remainder of the Gospel after xx 1 is slightly less faithful to 1 than it is to the other type. But that this cannot be explained by any theory of a mutilated archetype can be seen by noting the coincidences with and differences from 1.

Coincidences with 1.	*Number of differences from* 1 *which follow each coincidence.*
Jo xx 1	1
xx 11	2
xx 14	—
xx 14	—
xx 15	3
xx 20	4
xx 28	—
xx 28	—
xx 28	—
xx 29	1
xx 31	1
xxi 3	5
xxi 8	1
xxi 11	3

Coincidences with 1.	*Number of differences from* 1 *which follow each coincidence.*
xxi 15	3
xxi 17	—
xxi 17	3
xxi 19	7

This looks very much like deliberate eclecticism; and there is certainly one other instance which seems to point the same way—the case of the *Pericope adulterae.* In 1 this is added with a note at the end of the Gospel. But in 118 209 it comes in the ordinary place, without any note; and the text is different from that of 1. It looks as though the archetype of 118 209 had deliberately inserted the passage from another MS. But it would not be well to press this point, as the differences of 118 209 in this place from the T.R. are perhaps barely sufficient to make it certain that the *pericope* was found in their archetype.

In the case of the other Gospels there are several passages where the type of 1 is deserted, but none where any case in support of the theory of a mutilated archetype of 118 209 can be made to appear as probable as it does in the case of the Fourth Gospel.

It may be well to discuss these, if only to give the negative result.

(1) Mt x 34—xxi 46.
(2) Mc xvi 9—xvi 20.
(3) Lc i 1—ii 43.
(4) Lc iii 7—iii 20.
(5) Lc xxiv 19—xxiv 34.

It seems difficult without distorting the facts to account for the phenomena of these passages by a theory of mutilation. The questions which have to be asked in this connection in each case are:—

(i) Is there any reason for supposing that in these passages there is any use at all of the text of the type of 1?

(ii) Supposing that this question can be answered in the negative, can any explanation be given which will be consistent with the composition of the codex suggested by the passages in the Fourth Gospel?

In attempting to answer the first question, it becomes necessary to remember in the first place that, although the T.R. is a fair representative of the Antiochian text, it is not an absolutely accurate one; and therefore there may be readings in which 1 118 209 agree together, not because of the peculiar element in the family text, but because the T.R. has adopted some reading which is not really characteristic of the Antiochian text: and, in the second place, that there is hardly any MS known which has not got a few peculiar readings, and therefore that it is possible that the MS of the type of the T.R. used by the archetype of 118 209 may have occasionally coincided, in variants from the Antiochian text, with the MS of the type of 1.

It is therefore necessary to examine the readings of the type of 1 found in the five passages mentioned above.

(1) Mt x 34—xxi 46.

In this passage there are 310 variants from the T.R. found in 1, and of these 41 are also found in 118 209. The question is whether these 41 readings imply that a MS of the same type as 1 was used, or not. Twenty-six out of the 41 may be dismissed as readings which belong either to the genuine Antiochian text, or to a text so common as obviously to need no explanation, i.e. they are readings which Tischendorf quotes as found in more than 50 MSS, or even in a greater number.

The following remain:—

xii 14 *ἐξελθόντες δὲ* c. ℵBCD al[7].
xiii 16 *ἀκούουσιν* c. ℵBCDMX al[35].
xiv 13 *ἀκούσας δὲ* c. ℵBCDLZ al[15].
xiv 22 *om. ὁ Ἰησοῦς* c. ℵBC*DIPΔΘ al[25].
xv 5 *om. καὶ* c. ℵBCDT^c 33 al[3].
xv 5 *om. αὐτοῦ* c. "al."
xv 14 *πεσοῦνται εἰς βόθυνον* (*ι. βόθρον.*) c. (D)LZ 124 (346).
xv 31 *ἐδόξαζον* c. ℵL al plus[35].
xvi 25 *οὗτος σώσει αὐτὴν* c. 33.
xvi 28 *ἑστώτων* c. ℵBCDLSU 13—124. 22. 33. 157. al plus[20].
xviii 15 *om. καὶ* c. ℵBD 33 al plus[30].

xix 24 τῶν οὐρανῶν. c. Z 33 124 157 48[evv.]
xix 24 *om.* εἰσελθεῖν c. ℵLZ 33 al pauc.
xx 10 πλεῖον c. BCNZ al[8].
xx 23 *om.* καὶ c. ℵBDZ al[5].
xxi 46 ἐπεὶ c. ℵBDL 22. 33.

It will be seen that only in one case (xv 5, 2nd) is there a variant which is confined, according to Tischendorf, to this family, and in that case, as it is merely the omission of a pronoun, it is difficult to feel any degree of certainty either way.

This is not a matter that can be argued at length with advantage. Either these readings have been due to the use of a MS of the type of 1, which was only used at intervals in this passage, but was elsewhere the habitual exemplar; or they may be due to accidental coincidences between 1 and the MS which was to fill up the lacunae in the MS of the type of 1, which was used by the scribe of the archetype of 118 and 209.

It remains to see whether this passage can be accounted for as due to the loss of complete quaternions of the size suggested by the investigation of the passage in the Fourth Gospel. Those passages suggested a page of 18—19 lines (or a leaf of 36—38 lines), i.e. a quaternion of 288—304 lines. Therefore Mt x 34—xxi 46 ought, if the lacunae be due to the loss of several quaternions, to be more or less exactly a multiple of some figure varying between 288 and 304.

But Mt x 34—xxi 46 contains 1056 lines in Lloyd's Greek Testament; and this does not correspond to any definite number of quaternions, though it is only 2½ lines short of 29 leaves of 36½ lines each. Therefore, even if it is assumed that there was no use made in this passage of the MS of the type of 1, still there is no evidence of a positive kind to suggest that the archetype was mutilated.

(2) Mc xvi 9—xvi 20.

In this passage there are five variants from the T.R. in 1, and a note. The note is found in 209 (not in 118) and so in the first of the five variants, viz. xvi 9 *σαββάτων* for *σαββάτου*, but this is found in KΠ al[60], so that it proves little. It may, however, with the note, be the end of the passage agreeing with 1. There are not enough variants in this passage to make it possible to form any judgment. Its length is not sufficient for it to have filled a complete leaf of the suggested archetype by itself; but perhaps it has to be taken together with the next passage.

(3) Lc i 1—ii 43.

In this passage there are in 1 67 variants from the T.R., and of these 10 are found in 118 209. But of these 10 only the following are important—

i 61 *om.* *ὅτι* c. y$^{scr.}$ al^{4}.
i 63 *ἔσται pro ἐστι* c. CU al^{35}.
i 77 *ἡμῶν pro αὐτῶν* c. ACMO^{ahdf}RU 28 c$^{scr.}$ al^{10}.
ii 31 *om.* *τῶν* ante **λαῶν**, no other authority (not 209)—

the six others being found in at least 60 other MSS. It is also obvious that the first and last of the four quoted are the most important, and if the last were not so easy to explain as haplography of the last syllable of *πάντων* it would be very strong evidence.

The length of this passage measured as before is 264 lines. This is short of one complete quaternion of the size suggested by about 24 lines, and this deficiency would be almost exactly supplied by the last 12 verses of Mark, if it is supposed that the MS had no tables of *κεφαλαῖα*.

It is therefore possible that this passage and the preceding one taken together point to the loss of a complete quaternion from the MS of the type of 1 used by the scribe of the archetype of 118 209.

(4) Lc iii 7—iii 20.

This passage in 1 contains 11 variants from the T.R., none of which are found in 118 209. It is separated from the preceding passage by 39 lines, i.e. by one leaf of the suggested archetype (the first leaf of the succeeding quaternion), and itself contains 39 lines, i.e. is the second leaf of the quaternion. But there is no trace of alteration of type further on to suggest the loss of the conjugate leaf.

(5) Lc xxiv 19—xxiv 34.

Here there are in 1 nine variants from the T.R., and none of them are in 118, 209. The length of the passage is 37 lines—the right length, but again unsupported by any evidence as to the loss of the conjugate leaf.

It is, therefore, now possible to summarise the answer to the two questions suggested above as follows:—

(1) There is no convincing evidence that there was any use of the MS of the type of 1 in the passages where it seems to be generally deserted, though there are a few places which may be very well explained by such a use.

(2) The evidence derived from a consideration of the length of the apparent lacunae in four cases out of the five is favourable to the theory of mutilation, and in no case is at all opposed to it.

On the whole therefore the balance of evidence is slightly in favour of the theory that *Y* was a manuscript which had a page containing the same amount as 18—19 lines of Lloyd's Greek Testament, and that it had been mutilated to some degree in each Gospel before it was used by the scribe in question. It is probable that this scribe was also occasionally eclectic and emended the text he was copying; and it is possible, though not probable, that this eclecticism may explain the passages which have been ascribed to the mutilation of the MS of the type of 1.

It is probable that *Y* is an ancestor of 1, and not 1 itself or a descendant of 1, because (*a*) 1 is not mutilated, (*b*) there are a number of readings in 118 209 (in places where the text shows no signs of the use of any other MS) in which 1 agrees with the T.R. against 118 209 (v. Chap. III, where the list of these readings is given). These are explained most naturally as places where the habitual use of the Antiochian text exercised its usual effect and made the scribe of 1, perhaps unconsciously, desert the text of his exemplar, which is preserved in 118 209.

(6) 131 *is in Mc i—v and in Lc i—xxiv descended from another MS of the same family as* 1, *which was neither X nor* 1 *nor Y.*

131 only preserves the text of the family of 1 in Mc i—v and Lc i—xxiv; elsewhere it has a text which in the main is Antiochian though it has a certain number of variants. In these two sections

it does not agree exclusively either with 1 or with 118 209. The list of readings in which it differs from 1 as well as from the Antiochian text is given in Chapter III. Many of them are no doubt merely mistakes due to the scribe of 131 itself, but some must belong to its archetype.

These make it quite certain that 131 is not a copy of *X*. *X* has been shown to have been made by following sometimes *Y* and sometimes *Z*. In Lc i 1—ii 43, and again in Lc iii 7—iii 20, it followed *Z*, but in these passages 131 is following the text of the family of 1, to which *Z* does not belong.

It is hardly less certain that 131 did not use *Y*; there are very few places where 118 131 209 agree together against 1 and ς; the most important are,

Lc ii 38 *add.* ἐν *ante* Ἱερουσαλήμ.
v 19 πῶς *pro* ποίας.
xv 20 αὐτοῦ *pro* ἑαυτοῦ.
xvi 6 ὁ δὲ εἶπε *pro* καὶ εἶπε.
xx 17 *om.* αὐτοῖς 1°.

The remainder (v. p. xli) are usually accidental coincidences in spelling. There are, it is true, a considerable number of readings where 118 131 209 ς agree against 1, but there are many more where either 131 or 118 209 support 1 against the Antiochian text.

The archetype of 131 was therefore neither *X* nor *Y*. It is very improbable that it was 1 itself. 131 is full of misspellings which it is difficult to believe could have been made if the scribe had been using a beautiful manuscript like 1. There are also many readings in 131 which are not found in 1. I think it would be difficult to prove from these that 131 is not a descendant of 1 with one or more ancestors intervening, but it is more likely that 131 and 1 are descendants of the same ancestor, 1 being far the more faithful copy, but occasionally, as in Lc xvi 6 (ὁ δὲ εἶπε 118 131 209, καὶ εἶπε 1 ς) reverting to the Antiochian text when 131 remained true to its archetype.

(7) *The immediate archetypes of* 1 118 131 209 *were probably minuscule manuscripts.*

In the case of well-written manuscripts such as 1 118 209 and, to a less extent, 131, it is very difficult to form any opinion as to the script used in their exemplars.

Dean Burgon in a letter to the *Guardian* referred to the ancestor of 209 as probably an uncial manuscript, but apparently he merely based his opinion on general probabilities.

In working through the text of these manuscripts I have found nothing to support the theory of an uncial original. On the other hand, though I have not found much to suggest a minuscule, the following passages seem to me to point clearly in that direction.

(*a*) Mc viii 34: 1 has *διενέχθησαν* for *διελέχθησαν*, from confusion between a minuscule ν and a minuscule λ, which are sometimes very hard to distinguish.

(*b*) Mt viii 12: 118 209 have *ἐμβληθήσονται* for *ἐκβληθήσονται*, from confusion between a minuscule μ and a minuscule κ.

(*c*) Lc viii 22: 131 has *ἀνεύη* for *ἀνέβη*, and similarly in Lc ix 38 it has *ἀνευόησε* for *ἀνεβόησε* and in Lc xi 38 *εὐαπτίσθη* for *ἐβαπτίσθη*, probably from confusion between a minuscule β and a minuscule υ: but this may be due to pronunciation, as *ἀνεύη* and *ἀνέβη* would be practically identical in the spoken language.

It is possible that there may be other variants in these manuscripts which throw light on this point, but I have not noted any. So far as they go, they point to minuscule rather than uncial ancestors for 1 118 131 209.

APPENDIX TO CHAPTER II.

List of readings[1] *in which the scribe of* 118 *seems to have hesitated between two readings, viz. the reading of* 209 *and that found in the Textus Receptus* (v. p. xxvi).

		Reading of 118	Reading of 209	Reading of ς
Mt	vii 14	om *τι* spat. rel.	*και*	*οτι*
	viii 10	*ουδενι* praem. spat.	*παρ ουδενι*	*ουδε εν τω Ισραηλ*
	x 19	*παραδω* spat. rel.	*παραδωσι*	*παραδιδωσιν*
	xv 32	*ημερ* spat. rel.	*ημεραι*	*ημερας*
	xvii 5	*φωτ* spat. rel.	*φωτος*	*φωτεινη* (sic 1)
	xviii 19	*μων* praem. spat.	*ημων*	*υμων* (sic 1)
	xxii 14	om *εισι* spat. rel.	*εστι*	*εισι* (sic 1)
	39	om *σου* 2° spat. rel.	*σου* post *εαυτον*	*σεαυτον* pro *εαυτον σου*
	xxiv 31	om *μεγαλης* spat. rel.	*μεγαλης*	*φωνης μεγαλης*
	xxv 22	praem. spat. ante *ειπε*	*ειπε*	*λαβων ειπε*
	32	*αφορ* spat. rel.	*αφορισει*	*αφοριει*
	xxvi 7	*τ κεφαλ* spatt. rell.	*της κεφαλης*	*την κεφαλην*
	71	*Ναζ* spat. rel.	*Ναζαρηνου*	*Ναζωραιου*
	xxvii 29	*επι την δεξιαν* *εν τη δεξια*	*εν τη δεξια*	*επι την δεξιαν*
	xxviii 3	*ωσ* spat. rel.	*ως*	*ωσει*
	4	*ω* spat. rel.	*ως*	*ωσει*
Mc	i 20	*μισθ* spat. rel.	*μισθιων*	*μισθωτων*
	29	*υς* *ευθεως*	*ευθυς*	*ευθεως*
		ων *εν* *εξελθοντες ηλθον*	*εξελθων ηλθεν*	*εξελθοντες ηλθον*
	35	*α* *εννυχον*	*εννυχα*	*εννυχον*

[1] **This list might have been made longer by adding those readings in 118 which seem to be due to a knowledge of 209 and some text other than ς, but it seemed better to mention here only cases which are quite clear. The remainder may be seen in the notes.**

	Reading of 118	Reading of 209	Reading of ς
Mc i 44	αυτ spat. rel.	αυτης	αυτοις (sic 1)
ii 27	primum scripsit εγενετο, tum erasit, denique rescripsit	εκτισθη	εγενετο
iii 7	εις προς	εις	προς (sic 1)
27	om αλλ spat. rel.	αλλ	om αλλ
vi 4	συγγεν σι	συγγενευσι	συγγενεσι
11	ος η οσοι αν μη δεξονται υμας μηδε ακου μηδε ακουσωσιν	ος αν μη δεξηται υμας μηδε ακουση	οσοι αν μη δεξωνται υμας μηδε ακουσωσι
25	ειπε θελωεγουσα θελω	ειπε θελω	ητησατο λεγουσα θελω
28	εδωκ spat. rel.	εδωκε	εδωκεν αυτην
vii 8, 9	ανθρωπων κβαπτισμους ξεστων και ποτηριων και αλλα παροιμια ταυτα πολλα ποιειτε και ελεγεν	ανθρωπων και ελεγεν	ανθρωπων βαπτισμους ξεστων και ποτηριων και αλλα παροιμια ταυτα πολλα ποιειτε και ελεγεν
23	ταυτα εσω τα πονηρα εσωθεν	ταυτα εσωθεν	ταυτα τα πονηρα εσωθεν
viii 1	πα spat. rel.	παλιν πολλου	παμπολλου
10	om Μαγδαλα spat. rel.	Μαγδαλα	Δαλμανουθα
23	primum scripsit αυτ, tum erasit et του τυφλου rescripsit	αυτου	του τυφλου
ix 7	φω (delet.) θε φωνη	φωνη	ηλθε φωνη
35	spat. rel. ante διακονος	διακονος	εσχατος και παντων διακονος
xi 2	ευρησετε m. p. del. ε 2° et spat. rel.	ευρησητε	ευρησετε
23	αρθη spat. rel.	αρθηναι	αρθητι
	βληθη spat. rel.	βληθηναι	βληθητι
32	praem. spat. ante αν	αν	αλλ εαν [αλλ tantum 1]
xiv 15	ανωγε spat. rel.	ανωγεων	ανωγεον
32	ε ερχονται	ερχεται	ερχονται (sic 1)
Lc iv 43	απεσταλ spat. rel.	απεσταλην	απεσταλμαι
viii 45, 46	αποθλιβουσιν ο (eras.) και λεγεις τις ο αψαμενος μου ο δε Ιησους	αποθλιβουσιν ο δε Ιησους	αποθλιβουσιν και λεγεις τις ο αψαμενος μου ο δε Ιησους
54	εγειρ spat. rel.	εγειραι	εγειρου
ix 5	ξ δεχωνται υμας	δεχωνται	δεξωνται υμας
xi 15	Βεε βουλ spat. rel.	Βεεζεβουλ	Βεελζεβουλ

		Reading of 118	Reading of 209	Reading of ς
Lc	xxi 4	*αυτο* spat. rel.	*αυτων* (v. p. 145)	*αυτοις*
	xxii 34	*μ* *ειδεναι* spat. rel.	*με ειδεναι*	*μη ειδεναι με*
	59	*ἀλλ ὅστις*	*ἄλλός τις*	*ἄλλος τις*
Jo	i 42	ο *πρωτον*	*πρωτον*	*πρωτος*
	iv 27	ζ *εθαυμασαν*	*εθαυμαζον*	*εθαυμασαν*
	vi 39	rel. spat. post *με*	*με*	*με πατρος*

It will be observed that the scribe's interest in the text he was copying grew fainter as he reached the end of his task, until in St John there are hardly any instances of his hesitating between two readings.

CHAPTER III.

THE RECONSTRUCTION OF THE ARCHETYPE.

It has been shown in the previous chapter that in Mc i—iv and in Lc i—xxiv we have three independent representations of the archetype of this family of manuscript, viz. 1 118-209 131 (though 118-209 desert us in Lc i—ii and xxiv). In the rest of the Gospels we have two independent representations, 1 and 118-209 (though 118-209 sometimes fail, notably in Mt xi—xxi).

On what principles, then, is it best to attempt to reconstruct the text of the archetype?

In considering this question it must be remembered that in dealing with late MSS the influence exercised upon the scribes by the Antiochian text can hardly be over-estimated. They probably were at least as well acquainted with the Gospels as the monks of to-day in the convents on Mt Athos; and the amount which these know by heart, and the quickness with which they detect any mistakes in quotation, are well known to all who have had the privilege of talking with them and have endeavoured to quote the Greek Scriptures to them. Therefore in reconstructing an archetype from two late MSS it is generally right to adopt that reading which differs from the Antiochian text. It is more doubtful whether in the case of three MSS it is right to follow one against two which have the Antiochian text. It is of course necessary to consider each reading on its merits, but in the case of MSS of equal value I believe that we should generally follow the single manuscript unless there is reason for regarding its reading as merely a slip. In the present instance however this is a point which is not so important as it is in the case of the Ferrar group, since it is impossible to regard the MSS as of equal authority. Cod. 1 is undoubtedly both the oldest and the best; and, apart from obvious slips, I do not think that anywhere I should prefer the reading supported by 118-209 131 ς to the reading found in 1.

Three other combinations remain to be considered.

(1) 118-209 131 against 1 ς.
(2) 118-209 „ 1 131 ς.
(3) 131 „ 1 118-209 ς.

There are only 21 readings in which 118-209 131 agree against 1 ς.

These are:—

		Reading of 1 ς	Reading of 118-209 131
Mc iii	7	προς	εις (προς^{εις} 118)
iv	38	μελει	μελλει
Lc ii	38	Ιερουσαλημ	εν Ιερουσαλημ
v	19	ποιας (δια ποιας ς)	πως
viii	22	ενεβη	ανεβη (ανευη 131)
	54	εγειρε (εγειρου ς)	εγειραι (εγειρ spat. rel. 118)
xi	53	λεγοντος δε αυτου	om αυτου (sed non 209)
xii	27	περιεβαλετο	περιεβαλλετο
xiii	21	ενεκρυψεν	εκρύψεν
xv	15	αγρους αυτου	om αυτου (sed non 209)
	20	εαυτου	αυτου
xvi	6	και ειπε	ο δε ειπε
xix	29	Βηθφαγη (Βηθφαγην ς)	Βηθσφαγη (Βηθσφαγην 118 209^2)
xx	1	ειπον	ειπε
	17	εμβλεψας αυτοις	om αυτοις
xxi	3	εβαλεν	εβαλλεν
	4	αυτοις	αυτων
		εβαλον	εβαλλον
		εβαλεν	εβαλλεν
xxii	30	καθησεσθε (καθισεσθε ς)	καθισεσθε
	35	υστερηθη (υστερησατε ς)	υστερηθητε

This is a surprisingly short list; and from it some deductions may at once be made. For no stress can be laid on the readings in Mc iv 38, Lc xii 27, xxi 3, xxi 4 (2nd and 3rd), as they are probably due to the well-known tendency of scribes to put λλ instead of λ; or on the readings in Lc viii 54 and Lc xxii 30, which are merely itacisms; or on the reading in Lc ii 38, which is really the Antiochian reading; while it is doubtful whether πῶς in v 19 ought not to be regarded as a natural emendation for the difficult ποίας. The remainder may be regarded as probably the readings of the archetype of *fam*[1].

This striking witness to the superiority of the text of 1 naturally influences the judgment which is to be passed on the remaining combinations. Therefore although I think that all readings of 118-209 or of 131, which differ from 1 ϛ, deserve consideration, and many of them ought probably to be regarded as the readings of the archetype, yet they cannot be allowed the same prominence as they would undoubtedly have deserved if it had been found that where we have three independent witnesses to the text, 118-209 and 131 more often supported each other against 1 ϛ.

It is therefore not easy to give a list of readings found in 131 or 118-209 which probably ought to be regarded as those of the archetype. I have thought it best to be content with giving, in the two lists which follow, all the readings in which 118 209 or 131 differ from 1 ϛ. I have only excluded (*a*) readings which come in passages where (as was shown on pp. xxvii—xxxiv) 118-209 either represent an archetype *Z*, which did not belong to the family of 1, or have been much altered by an eclectic scribe; (*b*) mere variations of spelling; (*c*) readings which are practically identical with the Antiochian text; (*d*) those which are really Antiochian though not followed by ϛ. It is quite certain that many of those readings which I give have no claim to be considered as the probable readings of the archetype; but, as any attempt to make a selection would necessarily be based on very uncertain and subjective criticism, I have thought it best to be content with giving lists in which scholars may conveniently find the material for making their own choice.

		[1] Reading of 1 131 ϛ	[2] Reading of 118-209
Mt	i 11	Ιωακειμ	Ιακειμ
	ii 1	εν ημεραις Ηρωδου του βασιλεως	om
	v 45	ουρανοις	τοις ουρανοις

[1] 131 only in Mc i—v and in Lc i—xxiv.

[2] 118 is missing until Mt vi 3.

		READING OF 1 131 ς	READING OF 118-209
Mt	vi 17	*προσωπον σου*	om *σου*
	viii 20	*κλινη*	*κλῖναι* (hoc accentu)
	31	*ημας* 2° (*ημιν* ς)	om
	33	*παντα και τα*	*παντα τα κατα*
	ix 5	*τι γαρ*	om *γαρ*
	x 34	*επι την γην· ουκ ηλθον βαλειν ειρηνην*	om[1]
	xxii 46	*αυτω αποκριθηναι*	*αποκριθηναι αυτω*
	xxiv 6	*θροεισθε*	*θροηθητε*
	xxvi 24	*ο μεν υιος*	*και ο μεν υιος*
	xxvii 2	*παρεδωκαν αυτον*	om *αυτον*
	46	*λαμα σαβαχθανει* (*σαβαχθανι* ς)	*λιμας αβαχθανη*
	60	*εθηκεν*	*εθετο*
	63	*εκεινος ο πλανος*	*ο πλανος εκεινος*
Mc	ii 8	*διαλογιζονται*	*λογιζονται*
	10	*αφιεναι επι της γης*	*επι της γης αφιεναι*
	22	*ο οινος ο νεος*	*ο νεος οινος*
	iii 28	*τοις υιοις των ανθρωπων*	*τοις ανθρωποις*
	iv 21	*ο λυχνος*	om *ο*
	v 14	*εξηλθον*	*ηλθον*
	vi 5	*ουδεμιαν*	*ουδε μιαν*
	13	*εξεβαλλον*	*εξεβαλον*
	45	*εως*	*εως ου*
	vii 33	*απολαβομενος*	*επιλαβομενος*
		εβαλε	*εβαλλε*
	viii 9	*ως*	*ωσει*
	35	*απολεση την ψυχην αυτου*	*απολεση την εαυτου ψυχην*
	x 11	*ος εαν...μοιχαται* (sed 1 post vers. 12 habet et *και* pro *ος*)	om[2] 209 (118 sicut ς)
	xi 32	*αλλ ειπωμεν* (*αλλ εαν ειπωμεν* ς)	*αν ειπωμεν*
	xii 44	*εβαλεν*	*εβαλλεν*
	xiii 4	*ταυτα παντα* (*παντα ταυτα* ς)	om *παντα*
	7	*ακοας πολεμων*	*ακαταστασιας*
	xiv 9	*λαληθησεται εις μνημοσυνον αυτης*	*εις μνημοσυνον αυτης λαληθησεται*
	32	*ερχονται*	*ερχεται*
	44	*δεδωκε*	*εδεδωκει*
	53	*αρχιερεα*	*αρχιερεα Καιαφαν*
	56	*κατ αυτου*	*κατ αυτου λεγοντες*
	71	*ανθρωπον τουτον*	om *τουτον*
	xv 23	*εδιδουν*	*εδιδου*

(1) Homoioteleuton.

(2) Homoioteleuton?

	Reading of 1 131 ς	Reading of 118-209
Mc xv 34	εβοησεν	ανεβοησεν
	λαμα (λαμμα ς) σαβαχθανει (-θανι ς)	λιμας αβαχθανη
xvi 9	αναστας δε	αναστας δε ο Ιησους
Lc iii 28	Αδδει (Αδδι 131 ς)	Αδειμ
32	Ωβηδ	Ιωβηδ
	Βοοζ	Βοοσζ
33	του Αλμει του Αρνει (om ς)	του Ιωραμ
iv 4	ρηματι θεου	ρηματι εκπορευομενω δια στοματος θεου
38	η πενθερα δε (η δε πενθερα 131)	πενθερα δε
v 19	εισενεγκωσιν	ενεγκωσιν
36	το επιβλημα (om το ς)	om
vi 10	αποκατεστη (αποκατεσταθη ς)	απεκατεστη
17	αυτων	αυτου
20	του θεου	των ουρανων
44	εκαστον γαρ	om γαρ 209 (118* deest)
49	οικιαν	την οικιαν
vii 8	πορευθητι	πορευου
32	ουκ εκλαυσατε	ου συνεκλαυσατε
viii 3	Σουσαννα	Σωσαννα
29	παρηγγελλε γαρ	και παρηγγειλε (cf. παρηγγειλε γαρ 131)
41	υπηρχε	απηλθε
x 36	πλησιον γεγονεναι	γεγονεναι πλησιον
xi 5	μου	om
7	ηδη η θυρα	η θυρα ηδη
	εις την κοιτην	επι της κοιτης
10	ανοιγησεται	ανοιχθησεται
33	το φως βλεπωσιν (το φεγγος ς)	βλεπωσι το φως
48	αρα...αυτους	om
xii 28	χορτον	χορτον του αγρου
41	ταυτην	αυτην
xv 29	ειπε τω πατρι	ειπεν αυτω, πατερ
xvi 11	ει ουν	om ουν
xix 8	τετραπλουν	εις το τετραπλουν (118 hiat)
11	αυτων ταυτα	ταυτα αυτων
13	δουλους εαυτου	δουλους αυτου (om αυτου 131)
48	και οι πρωτοι του λαου	om
xxi 16	συγγενεων (και συγγενων 131 ς)	om
xxii 66	εαυτων	αυτων
xxiii 30	αρξονται	αρχονται
56	υποστρεψασαι δε	om δε
Jo i 27	Βηθαβαρα	Βηθανια

		Reading of 1 131 ς	Reading of 118-209
Jo	iv 49	πριν	πριν η
	vi 37	εκβαλω	εκβαλλω
	43	ο Ιησους	om ο
	vii 12	αλλοι δε	om δε
	22	περιτεμνετε ανθρωπον	περιτεμνεται ανθρωπος
	30	αυτον πιασαι	πιασαι αυτον
	32	οι αρχιερεις και οι φαρισαιοι (tr. ς)	om
	viii 27	ουκ	και ουκ
	52	τον λογον μου	μου τον λογον
	x 22	εγενετο	εγενοντο
	37	πιστευετε	πιστευητε
	42	εκει (ante εις αυτον ς)	om
	xi 30	εις	προς
	xii 5	τριακοσιων	διακοσιων
	18	τουτο	τουτον
	xiii 10	αλλ εστι καθαρος ολος	om 209 (non 118)
	xviii 7	παλιν ουν	[1]om ουν 209
	15	συνεισηλθε	συνηλθε
	xix 20	της πολεως ο τοπος	ο τοπος της πολεως
	26	ιδου	ιδε
	28	μαθητης	μαθητης εκεινος
	31	η ημερα	om η
	34	ευθυς	ευθεως
	35	αυτου εστιν η μαρτυρια	εστιν η μαρτυρια αυτου
	38	Ιωσηφ	ο Ιωσηφ

		Reading of 1 118 209 ς	Reading of 131
Mc	i 29	Ιακωβου και Ιωαννου	Ιωαννου και Ιακωβου
	ii 26	συν αυτω	μετ αυτου
	iii 6	εξελθοντες	ελθοντες
	15	αποστελλη	αποστελει
	20	συνερχεται	συνερχονται
	iv 1	συνερχεται (συνηχθη 118 ς)	συνερχονται
	26	εγειρηται (εγει^{η}ρεται 118)	εγειρεται
	v 3	μνημειοις	μνημασι
Lc	i 35	γεννωμενον	γενομενον
	41	της Μαριας	om
	61	εν τη συγγενεια	εκ της συγγενειας
	ii 1	αυτη η απογραφη	αυτη απογραφη

(1) 118* stops at Jo xvi 25.

		Reading of 1 118 209 ς	Reading of 131
Lc ii	7	και ανεκλινεν αυτον	om
	8	φυλακας	τας φυλακας
	28	Θεον	Θεον Ισραηλ
	37	απο του ιερου	om απο
	47	ακουοντες	ακουσαντες
	52	Ιησους	ο Ιησους
iii	1	ετει δε	om δε
	2	του Ζαχαριου	om του
	15	παντων	απαντων
		περι Ιωαννου (του Ιω. 118 209 ς)	om
	18	τον λαον	τω λαω
	28	Ελμωδαμ	Εσλωδαν
	32	Σαλμαν (Σαλμων 118 209 ς)	Σαλμαναν
iv	11	οτι	om
	14	περι αυτου	αυτου
	18	την καρδιαν	τη καρδια
	41	αυτα	αυτω
v	36	επιβλημα (1°)	om
vi	5	αυτοις	αυτοις ο Ιησους(1)
vii	6	ο εκατονταρχος φιλους	φιλους ο εκατονταρχος
	21	εχαρισατο	εδωρησατο
	22	κωφοι	και κωφοι
	44	σου εις την οικιαν	εις την οικιαν σου
viii	2	πονηρων	ακαθαρτων πονηρων
	5	αυτου	αυτων
	22	εγενετο δε (και εγενετο ς)	εγενετο
	24	και επαυσατο (επαυσαντο ς)	om
	25	που	πως
	31	απελθειν	εισελθειν
	36	αυτοις	om
	41	ηλθεν	προσηλθε τω Ιησου
ix	33	μη ειδως ο λεγει	om
	47	τον διαλογισμον	τους διαλογισμους
	54	Ιακωβος	και Ιακωβος
x	11	ημιν	om
	22	γινωσκει	επιγινωσκει
	25	ποιησας	ποιησας ινα
xi	1	καθως	ως
	3	ημων	om
	5	μου	om
	27	ειπεν αυτω	om αυτω
	46	δυσβαστακτα	βαρεα και δυσβαστακτα

(1) Perhaps a dittography of οις.

	Reading of 1 118 209 ς	Reading of 131
Lc xii 4	φιλοις μου	om μου
9	αρνησαμενος με	om με
30	τουτων	τουτων απαντων
31	ταυτα παντα	om παντα
37, 38	ους ελθων...εκεινοι	om
42	οικετιας (θεραπιας 118 209 ς)	οικιας
xiii 2	ειπεν αυτοις	om αυτοις
xiv 14	ανταποδοθησεται δε (γαρ ς)	om δε
21	και παραγενομενος...ταυτα	om 131
28	θελων	ο θελων
xv 1	οι αμαρτωλοι	om οι
12	της ουσιας	om
22	πατηρ	πατηρ αυτου
	αυτου 1°	om
xvii 4	αμαρτη	αμαρτηση
23	η ιδου	om η
36	σωμα	πτωμα
xviii 29	η γονεις η αδελφους	η αδελφους η γονεις
xix 11	παραχρημα μελλει η βασιλεια του θεου αναφαινεσθαι	η βασιλεια του θεου παραχρημα μελλει φαινεσθαι
30	αυτον	om
36	αυτων	εαυτων
48	ακουων	ακουειν
xx 6	καταλιθασει	καταδικασει
9	την παραβολην ταυτην	παραβολην
xxii 15	παθειν	απελθειν
21	παραδιδοντος με	om με
36	το ιματιον	τα ιματια
53	η ωρα και η εξουσια	η εξουσια και η ωρα
58	ιδων αυτον	αυτον ιδων
59	αυτου	αυτων
63	προσωπον	προσωπον ετυπτον αυτον και
64	προφητευσον	προφητευσον ημιν Χριστε
65	εις	προς
xxiii 52	τω Πιλατω	om τω
54	ημερα ην	ην ημερα
xxiv 4	και ιδου	om και
20	εις κριμα θανατου	om

CHAPTER IV.

THE CHARACTER OF THE TEXT OF THE ARCHETYPE.

It is never quite easy to establish the textual affinities of late manuscripts. There is so large an amount of mixture and of assimilation to more ordinary types that the real character of the text is obscured. The manuscripts of this group offer a sufficient example of this fact. Ultimately all four represent a common original, but not one of them has escaped mixture with the ordinary type of text; in the case of 131 it is only in St Luke and a few chapters of St Mark that the original archetype seems to have been followed, while in 118 we have a most interesting example of the way in which a scribe sometimes deserted the text of the manuscript which he was copying and sometimes doubted which of two readings he would adopt.

The first and obvious deduction from this fact is that for our present purpose it is useless to consider those readings in which 1 118 131 209 agree with the Antiochian text. Some of them are probably the original readings of the archetype, some are due to contamination; but it is impossible to determine which are due to each of these causes.

A second deduction is that not much can be learnt from readings which are non-Antiochian, but otherwise almost or quite universal. It is interesting, for example, to find that *fam*^{1} preserves the short form of the Lord's prayer in St Luke; but as this form is probably the correct one in this Gospel and has such wide attestation, the fact does not throw light on the special affinities of the text of *fam*^{1}, beyond showing that it represents a non-Antiochian original. That this is true of *fam*^{1}

may easily be seen by noticing the number of readings in which the *apparatus criticus* shows that it differs from the Textus Receptus; but I have also added at the end of this chapter a short list (A), which contains the readings in Mt i—v and Mc i—iv which are found in all or almost all the earliest authorities but not in the Antiochian text.

It is the study of subsingular readings, to adopt Dr Hort's phrase, which may be expected to be more fruitful. For this purpose I have prepared other lists (BCDEF) which are appended to this chapter. It does not seem necessary to attempt the very tedious task of making them exhaustive, and they only deal with illustrative sections from each Gospel, viz. Mt i—vii and xxvi —xxvii, Mc i—x, Lc ix—xi, Jo iii—vi. Four of these lists (BCDE) contain readings which may be assigned to some definite family; B giving readings which are characteristic of the Old Latin, C those characteristic of the Old Syriac[1], E those characteristic of the text found in אB and the allied MSS, while in D I have after some hesitation inserted those which are found in both Old Latin and Old Syriac. In the last instance I am not sure whether I have done right, for at first sight it appears that readings found in both Old Latin and Old Syriac can scarcely be called subsingular; but I have so acted in deference to the theory (though I do not hold it myself) that the Old Latin version was first made in the East: if this be true, readings found in Old Latin and Old Syriac may properly be regarded as subsingular. List F contains subsingular readings which cannot be identified as characteristic of any generally recognized type, and list G readings which seem to be peculiar to *fam*[1]. It has sometimes been difficult to assign readings to their proper list, and in several cases no doubt other scholars might have made a different distribution; but the value of this kind of evidence is cumulative, and does not depend on the absolute certainty with which each reading can be classified; so that although various items in each list may be doubtful I do not think that the general result is much affected.

[1] I am deeply indebted to Mr Burkitt for taking much trouble in the revision of my references to Syriac authorities.

The Text of Fam[1] *in St Mark.*

It will be seen at once from these lists that the text of *fam*[1] in St Mark differs from that in the other Gospels in two points. It has a more definite connection with the Old Syriac, and it has a greater number of readings which cannot be classified as belonging to any generally recognized family.

The second point is particularly striking: lists BCDE contain 98 readings in all, list F contains 107 readings. A closer examination of the lists throws light on this curious fact. There is a common element in all the lists; more than three-fourths of the readings are supported by some or all of the following: *fam*[13] 22 28 565 700. So far then as St Mark is concerned we have to recognize a close connection between *fam*[1] and *fam*[13] 22 28 565 700. This connection admits theoretically of two explanations:—(1) some one of the group may represent the original archetype of a lost family, and the variations of the other manuscripts may be due to mixture with different types of text: (2) no one of the group may be a faithful representative of the original text, but all may have suffered mixture with the more ordinary types. I regard the latter as by far the more probable explanation. Assuming then that this group represents a common original, which is not reproduced perfectly by any one of the extant manuscripts, the explanation which may be given of this noteworthy relationship will depend on the view taken of our knowledge of Pre-Antiochian texts. If it be supposed that we have even a partial knowledge of all the types of text which obtained before the Antiochian text became dominant, probably all this group of minuscules must be regarded as representing a lost recension which was based on a knowledge of all the early types of text and has been preserved in several late forms, all of which have been mixed with the Antiochian text. In other words it must be a recension which stands in the same relation to the early texts as the Antiochian text does, since it implies a knowledge of them all and an eclectic criticism which followed sometimes one and sometimes another.

But it is just this accurate knowledge of the early texts which is not possessed.

The only types of text of undoubted antiquity of which we have certain knowledge are:

(1) The text represented by the two Old Syriac MSS, but no Greek MSS.

(2) The text represented by D and the Old Latin MSS.

(3) The text represented by ℵB and the Bohairic version.

Of these three types, and of these alone, a fair knowledge may be claimed. But although our knowledge does not go much further than this with any certainty, there is yet evidence to show that there were other types, whose existence can be proved, if their character cannot be clearly defined. Such is the text represented by Clement's quotations, and that represented by $ℵ^c$, which seems to be a Caesarean text of which there are more representatives in the Epistles than in the Gospels.

So far therefore from allowing us to think that we have an adequate knowledge of the early texts, the evidence indicates that our knowledge is limited and unequal.

In fact, in trying to restore the early texts, we are in much the same position as a geographer who tries to map out a submerged continent from an archipelago of islands; except indeed that the geographer can judge by accurate soundings (and the textual critic can only speculate) as to the nature of the ground beneath the sea.

The bearing of these facts on the problem presented by the group of minuscules under discussion (*fam*^{1} *fam*^{13} 22 28 565 700) is that we are led to the question whether the connection is really so close as it might at first seem. It is not necessary to suppose that they represent a definite lost MS or a definite lost recension produced by an eclectic criticism (the two things are almost the same in the end); for they may represent one ancient local text, which has suffered different degrees of corruption from mixture with the Antiochian text; or they may even represent more than one local text, *fam*^{1} for instance coming from one neighbourhood, *fam*^{13} from another, and so on. But if this last hypothesis be true, it is at least probable that the neighbourhoods in question were not widely separate, otherwise the similarity of text would be hard to explain.

The points, then, which seem to stand out are these:

(1) *Fam*[1] represents a text earlier than the Antiochian, though it has been mixed with it.

(2) Its closest relations are with *fam*[13] 22 28 565 700.

(3) The large group *fam*[1] *fam*[13] 22 28 565 700 might represent a pre-Antiochian recension in variously corrupted forms; but it more probably represents either one local text or several local texts; and, if the latter hypothesis be taken, the localities in question were probably neighbouring.

The questions therefore which remain are, (1) Is there any method which may help us to decide between the hypotheses of one local text and several local texts? (2) In what region is it probable that this locality or these localities ought to be sought?

(1) The only clue which I can suggest is a *consideration of mixed variants*, that is, those variants where some members of the group have one reading and others have another. The value of the consideration of mixed variants lies entirely in the theory of mixture and is so far quite hypothetical. This theory may be stated thus:—The tendency of scribes must always have been to assimilate texts to the most popular standard. At any time since the sixth century, and perhaps since the fourth, this popular standard was the Antiochian text. Therefore we expect to find early texts mixed with the Antiochian text. If we possess two representatives of an early text we expect to find that one has been mixed in one place, the other in another, and we reconstruct the archetype by following as a rule that copy which in any given instance has the non-Antiochian text. Supposing this rule always to hold rigidly (which of course it does not), if several MSS really represent the same ancient text mixed in different ways with the Antiochian text, there will only be two elements to consider, and there will be binary but not ternary variation, as the latter cannot be produced without a third element. This, then, gives a clue in investigating the point at issue. It will be found worked out for a selected chapter on pp. lxxiii—lxxvi, in a tabular form to which a few words of comment are added. It will be seen that as a rule there is binary and

not ternary variation, but there are exceptions, such as Mc i 16, where we get the following variants.

(*a*) *ἀμφιβάλλοντας τὰ δίκτυα, fam*[13] 565.

(*b*) *ἀμφίβληστρα βάλλοντας, fam*[1].

(*c*) *ἀμφίβληστρον βάλλοντας*, 700.

(*d*) *βάλλοντας ἀμφίβληστρον*, 28 ϛ.

This kind of reading would be decisive against the theory of a single locality if the rule just enunciated were rigidly true. But it is not rigidly true: mixture is not strictly confined to mixture with the Antiochian text, and, even if it were, there are variants in the Antiochian text itself. So that in readings like the above it is always difficult to decide exactly what weight ought to be given to the evidence. My own opinion is that the evidence as a whole does not point clearly to a single locality, though it does not exclude it; and further that it does definitely exclude localities widely separate.

(2) There is very little evidence as to the direction in which this locality ought to be sought. Such as there is can be given shortly.

Fam[1]. As was shown in Chapter I, there is no sufficient reason for connecting any one of the MSS of this family with a definite locality. Palaeographically they are not South Italian, and may be Constantinopolitan. Codex 1 seems to have used the same arrangement of symbols for the Evangelists as did Anastasius of Sinai, but this really proves nothing.

Fam[13]. All the MSS of this group, except cod. 69 which is later, come from Calabria, and probably from the same monastery. But there is no reason for supposing that their archetype was (or was not) Calabrian. The only evidence is that they possess a stichometric reckoning of *ῥήματα*[(1)] which occurs in a series of Syriac MSS, the oldest of which is cod. Sinait. 10, a ninth century MS of miscellaneous contents.

Codd. 22 28 700 give no clues at all so far as I am aware.

Cod. 565 comes from Houmisch Khan in Pontus and has an important colophon at the end of Mark, *ἐγράφη καὶ ἀντεβλήθη ὁμοίως ἐκ τῶν ἱεροσολυμῶν ἀντιγράφων*.

(1) See Dr Rendel Harris' *Origin of the Ferrar Group*, Cambridge, 1893, and a note by Mr Burkitt in the *Journ. of Theol. Studies* for 1901, p. 429 ff.

This "ὁμοίως" refers the colophon back to a series found in Λ and some other MSS, of which the important sentence is:—*τὸ εὐαγγέλιον κατὰ Ματθαῖον ἐγράφη καὶ ἀντεβλήθη ἐκ τῶν [ἐν] Ἱεροσολύμοις (?) παλαιῶν ἀντιγράφων τῶν ἐν τῷ ἁγίῳ ὄρει ἀποκειμένων.*

In a note in the *Journal of Theological Studies*, vol. I p. 445, I drew attention to the fact that this *ἅγιον ὄρος* can hardly mean anything except Mt Sinai, as the title was not used of Jerusalem and the colophon is too early for it to mean Mt Athos. It therefore means that the MSS which possess it represent older MSS which came from Jerusalem and were copied on Mt Sinai.

This is all the external evidence that bears on the question at issue. It does not go far. The only striking point is that in every case something has brought Mt Sinai into the question. This is curious: but it is not enough to build upon.

The evidence from the character of the text is not much more helpful. The lists of readings at the end of this chapter speak for themselves. Probably no one would like to build confidently any theory upon them. But the effect on my own mind of producing these lists has been to emphasize the points of resemblance with the Old Syriac, which seem to be often of a very striking character. Mr Burkitt has strengthened this impression by pointing out to me that many of the subsingular readings in list F are of such a nature that it is quite possible that they are the Greek which underlies the Old Syriac version, as the method followed by the Syriac translator makes the distinction between them and the ordinary readings to disappear.

Further than this it seems impossible to go at present. The conclusion which we have reached may be stated thus: (1) fam^{1} in St Mark seems to form part of a larger family of which the most certain members are fam^{13} 22 28 565 700; (2) this larger family seems to represent a local text or local texts which were current in a comparatively limited region in the East; (3) the only definite localities which there is any reason to suggest are Jerusalem and Sinai, and even for these the evidence is insufficient to justify confident assertion.

The Text of Fam[1] *in the other Gospels.*

It is far more difficult to say anything about the character of the text in the other Gospels, as the phenomena are by no means so clearly marked. The list of subsingular readings, which are found in none of the generally recognized types of text, is much reduced in size, and is not much longer than the list of readings supported by ℵB, which, especially in St Matthew and St Luke, are more prominent than in St Mark. The list of distinctly Old Syriac readings is much reduced in length, and I doubt whether any of the readings which I have placed in the list are sufficient to prove a definite point of connection between *fam*[1] and the Old Syriac. The most striking of these readings is in Mt xxii 16 f. Ἰησοῦν Βαραββᾶν: but although it is true that this is apparently characteristic of the Old Syriac text, the evidence of Origen goes to show that it was a reading widely known in early times and omitted from later texts owing to religious sentiment.

There is no reason for supposing that *fam*[1] forms in these Gospels part of a larger family containing *fam*[13] 22 28 565 700. There are, it is true, a considerable number of readings where the text of *fam*[1] agrees with one or more of these manuscripts; but I do not think that the amount[(1)] is sufficient to justify any deduction.

We have, therefore, in *fam*[1] a text which as a whole stands alone. It has many points in common with the text of ℵB, some points in common with the Old Latin text, a considerable number of readings which cannot be classified, and only a few which are shared with the Old Syriac.

An element akin to ℵB and a Western (geographically speaking) element are therefore the most noticeable features. The same description would be true of the text in use at Alexandria in the days of Clement. But there is no special closeness of connection between Clement's text and the text of *fam*[1], and therefore we cannot say that the text of *fam*[1] seems to represent in

(1) It is perhaps worth notice that it is greater in St John than in St Matthew or St Luke.

these Gospels the pre-Origenic text of Alexandria. At the same time this is not an impossible suggestion. Our knowledge of the pre-Origenic text depends on Clement's quotations, which are often free and by no means cover the whole text.

The reason of the difference in type between the texts of St Mark and the other Gospels.

It is a remarkable feature in the text of the New Testament that St Mark's Gospel contains more variants than the other Gospels, and that several manuscripts contain interesting texts of St Mark but ordinary texts of the other Gospels. In connexion with this fact two points may profitably be remembered. (1) As Victor of Antioch remarks, St Mark's Gospel was not often commented upon by early writers. Therefore it escaped much of the levelling process which the text of the other Gospels had to endure. Ultimately it succumbed, but not soon enough to prevent the survival of comparatively unrevised texts in many copies such as ΔΨ 28 565, which have more ordinary texts elsewhere. This fact explains, at least partially, the number of variants in St Mark's Gospel.

(2) In the earliest period of their history the Gospels circulated as separate books. During this stage St Mark's Gospel was naturally less used than the others: indeed, as Mr Burkitt has remarked in *Two Lectures on the Gospels*, it was almost lost, and although it was ultimately preserved by inclusion in the fourfold Gospel it had by that time been mutilated at the close. "As part of the fourfold Gospel Canon, a new lease of existence, happily for us, was assured to it; but it had entered into life maimed." This implies that its text was spared much of the levelling and assimilating process that falls to the lot of manuscripts of popular works which are not protected by literary fame or religious scruple. In this way we have in some of our old copies of St Mark texts which are rougher and more careless than the texts of the other Gospels.

It is perhaps not out of place to suggest that the importance of this early stage of the history of the Gospels has been somewhat under-estimated by students of the Synoptic problem. One of the most difficult features of that difficult question is the "Secondary features" of St Mark, that is to say those passages where St Matthew and St Luke agree against St Mark. The explanation offered has usually been either (i) that an Ur-Marcus lies behind the Canonical Gospel, (ii) that in these passages the compiler of the second Gospel has been using the (so-called) *Λόγια* of St Matthew, (iii) that the author of the third Gospel was acquainted with the first.

Without attempting to discuss the merits of these theories I would suggest that many of the passages in question may be due to the fact that the scribes of manuscripts during the period before the formation of the fourfold Gospel were acquainted with the first and third Gospels, though often ignorant of the second, and emended their copies accordingly. In other words, that assimilation took place between the first and third Gospels while the second remained unaffected. This implies that the scribes of the first period were much freer in their methods than those of a later date, and that the text of the first and third Gospels is sometimes corrupt in all extant manuscripts; such a conclusion is not without other support, and is one to which Patristic evidence often leads the student of the text of the Gospels.

APPENDIX TO CHAPTER IV.

Lists of Illustrative Readings (v. p. xlix).

These lists have been compiled from Tischendorf's *apparatus criticus* and other editions of manuscripts and versions. I have received much help in this connection from Mr Burkitt.

As I have used some symbols which are not found in the *apparatus* of Tischendorf I give a list of those which are not self-explanatory.

71 = Tischendorf's g^{scr}.
470—475 = Tischendorf's a^{scr}—f^{scr}.
476—479 = Tischendorf's h^{scr}—l^{scr} (1).
480—489 = Tischendorf's n^{scr}—w^{scr}.
565 = Scrivener's 473 = Tischendorf's 2^{pe} = WH's 81.
700 = Scrivener's and Hoskier's 604.
fam^{13} = the Ferrar group (13—69—124—346—543—788—826—828, the three last being at present uncollated).
Syr S = the Sinaitic Syriac.
Syr C = the Curetonian Syriac.
Syr-pesh = the Peshitto.
Syr-pal = the Palestinian Syriac.
Syr-hkl = the Harkleian Syriac.
Syr-Diat = the Diatessaron of Tatian.

It will be seen that in the notation of the minuscules I strictly follow Dr Gregory. I feel sure that this is the best course to adopt, as his catalogue is (in the German edition) fuller than Scrivener's, and it is known that it will be even fuller in the next edition, which is being prepared.

List A.

Readings which are found in most ancient authorities but not in the Antiochian text.

Mt i 7, 8 Ασαφ pro Ασα ℵBCD^{lucae} 700 k q c g_1 g_2 sah boh aeth syr-hkl^{mg} Diat $^{arab (cod. A)}$ arm Epiph

18 γενεσις ℵBCPSZΔ syr-hkl (de versionibus non liquet) Eus^{dem} Ps-Ath Max

(1) Tischendorf also calls 477 i^{cant} (v. Scrivener's Cod. Augiensis).

Mt i 18 om *γαρ* ℵBC*Z 700 latt syrr sah boh Iren^{lat}

19 *δειγματισαι* ℵ$^{a\ vel\ b}$BZ syrr^{vid} (cf Col ii 15 et Heb vi 6)

22 Κυριου sine *του* ℵBCDZΔ 33 127*

25 *υιον* sine addit ℵBZ 33 a b c g_1 k sah boh syr SC Amb

ii 3 *ο βασιλευς* Ηρωδης ℵBDZ 124 157 latt^{vid} Eus^{dem}

8 *εξετασατε ακριβως* ℵBC*D 33 124 latt sah boh syr-hkl

9 *εσταθη* ℵBCD 33 Orig Eus^{dem}

11 *ειδον* (ℵ)BCD al pler a f k q syrr sah boh arm Orig Eus^{dem}

18 om *θρηνος και* ℵBZ 22 latt sah boh syr-pesh-pal (? Just^{tr})

19 *φαινεται κατ οναρ* ℵBDZ latt syrr sah

iii 3 *δια* pro *υπο* ℵBCD fam^{13} 33 157 700 latt Iren^{lat}

4 *ην αυτου* ℵBCD

6 add *ποταμω* ℵBCMΔ al$^{plus\ 30}$ sah boh syrr Orig

8 *καρπον αξιον* ℵBCEKMSVΓΠ fam^{13} 565 700 al pler latt sah boh syr-hkl Orig

16 *ευθυς ανεβη* ℵB 108 127 243 435 700 latt syr C

iv 3 *προσελθων ο πειραζων ειπεν αυτω* ℵB fam^{13} 33 157 700 k syr S

5 *εστησεν* ℵBCDZ 33 sah syr S latt (*statuit*) Eus^{dem}

16 *φως ειδε μεγα* ℵBC fam^{13} 33 latt pler Orig Eus^{dem} Chr Cyr^{es}

18 om *ο* Ιησους ℵBCDKMΠ al pler b k f q vg syrr

v 25 *μετ αυτου εν τη οδω* ℵBDL fam^{13} 28 33 a b c g_1 h q syr C-pesh boh

om *σε παραδω* post *κριτης* ℵB fam^{13} k arm aeth Epiph Chr Hil Arn

30 *απελθη* ℵB 21 22 33 157 latt syr C boh aeth

31 om *οτι* ante *ος* ℵBDL fam^{13} 33 127 al pauc latt Chr

32 *πας ο απολυων* ℵBKLM al pler f vg syr-pesh arm aeth

μοιχευθηναι ℵBD fam^{13} 22 33 Orig Chr

44 *αγαπατε τους εχθρους υμων και προσευχεσθε υπερ των διωκοντων υμας* sine addit. ℵB 22 k syr SC Orig Iren^{lat} Cyp

47 *εθνικοι* ℵBDZ 22 33 al^{15} latt syr C boh Cyp Lucif

το αυτο ℵBDMUZ al^{30} syr pesh arm aeth Cyp Lucif Aug

48 *ως* ℵBF^{a}LZ fam^{13} 33 225 Clem^{bis} Orig^{bis} Eus^{dem} Ath

ο ουρανιος ℵBD^{b}EF^{a}LUZ al^{30} a f vg syr-hkl arm aeth Clem Orig Ath Basil Chr Cyp

Mc i 2 *εν* Ησαια *τω προφητη* ℵBDLΔ 22 700 1071 al pauc latt syrr boh

11 *εν σοι* ℵBD^{gr}LPΔ fam^{13} 22 28 33 565 700 al^{25} latt boh syr-pesh

14 om *της βασιλειας* ℵBL 28 33 69 b e ff_2 t syr S

19 om *εκειθεν* BDL 28 124 565 a b ff_2 g_1 boh syr S-pesh

27 om *οτι* ℵBL 33 565 syr S-pesh

39 *εις τας συναγωγας* ℵAB unc pler fam^{13} 157 238 435 565 al

45 *παντοθεν* ℵB unc pler 33 157 238 1071 al^{20}

ii 5 *σου αι αμαρτιαι* sine *σοι* ℵBDGLΔ 33 69 al^{10} (cf b e)

17 om *εις μετανοιαν* ℵBADKLΔΠ 22 28 435 700 al^{40} b e f ff_2 vg boh syr-pesh-hkl (syr S hiat)

20 *εκεινη τη ημερα* ℵABCDLKSΔ fam^{13} 28 33 157 al^{60} syrr arm

Mc ii 21 om *και* ante *ουδεις* ℵABCKLSΔ fam^{13} 28 33 700 1071 al^{50} latt syrr boh arm

24 om *εν* ℵABCDKLMΔΠ fam^{13} 700 al^{30} latt

iii 7 *ανεχωρησε* post *αυτου* ℵBCDLΔ fam^{13} 33 700 al^{10} latt boh pesh *ηκολουθησε* ABGLMPSΓΠ 700 al^{40} f vg boh Vict^{ant}

11 *εκραζον* ℵAB unc pler fam^{13} 33 al$^{plus 50}$

27 *αλλ* ℵBCLΔ fam^{13} 28 33 700 1071 a d ff$_2$ boh arm syr-hkl^{mg}

32 *περι αυτον οχλος* ℵ^{c}ABCKLMΔΠ fam^{13} 28 33 700 al^{50} latt

33 *και* pro *η* ℵBCGLUVΔ al$^{plus 50}$ latt syr S-pesh

35 om *μου* post *αδελφη* ℵABDLΔ fam^{13} 28 33 700 al^{20} c f ff$_2$ q arm

iv 1 *πλοιον* sine *το* ℵBCLKMΠ al pler syr S

4 om *του ουρανου* ℵABCL unc^9 fam^{13} 22 700 al^{100} b c e vg boh syr S-pesh-hkl arm aeth

9 om *αυτοις* ℵAB unc^{15} 22 700 al pler latt syrr boh

19 om *τουτου* ℵBCDLΔ (565 700) al^6 b c e i vg arm

21 *ερχεται ο λυχνος* ℵBCDLΔ 33 al pauc latt boh syr-pesh-hkl aeth

22 om *τι* BDHKUMΠ* fam^{13} 28 700 al^{80} b e ff$_2$ i q aeth

32 *μειζων* ante *παντων* ℵBCDLΔ 28 33 al^{12} latt syrr boh arm aeth

37 *μεγαλη ανεμου* ℵ*^{etc}BDLΔ fam^{13} 28 565 700 b c ff$_2$ vg syr-pesh arm aeth

και τα κυματα ℵBCDLΔ fam^{13} 28 565 700 1071 latt boh syr-pesh arm aeth

List B.

Readings for which the Old Latin version is the chief ancient authority.

Matt iii 5 add *πασα* ante *Ιεροσολυμα* al^4 a k l mm (cf b c q) aeth

v 36 *ποιησαι* ante *μιαν τριχα* D k Clem Cyp Aug

37 *τουτου* pro *τουτων* k Tert$^2/_2$

46 *τουτο* pro *το αυτο* latt

vii 11 *αγαθα δοματα* a b c f g$_1$ h k q Cyp (syrr non liq)

xxvi 15 *στατηρας αργυριου* D a b q Eus^{dem} Orig (sed haec om *αργυριου*)

29 om *οτι* ℵBDZ fam^{13} 33 116 241* a b c h q vg arm aeth Clem Eus Orig Cyr Iren^{lat} Cyp

44 om *εκ τριτου* ADKΠ 157 al^4 a b

xxvii 23 *λεγει αυτοις ο ηγεμων* DL al pauc latt boh syr-pesh aeth

43 *ει πεποιθεν* D a b h l sah boh arm aeth Eus^{dem}

49 *και σωσει* D a b c e ff$_2$ h l q Orig^{lat} (syr S *και σωζων* vel *και σωζει*)

Mc ii 17 om *αυτοις* D a b c ff g$_1$ q (hiat Syr S)

iii 4 *απολεσαι* LΔ 22 124 565 700 al pauc latt syr-pesh arm (syr S legi non potest)

29 om *εις τον αιωνα* D 22 28 565 700 a b e ff$_2$ g$_1$ q Ath Cyp

31 *και ερχεται* ℵDG 565 al^2 a b e ff$_2$ g$_1$ q

34 *τους κυκλω* (D) fam^{13} 28 700 latt

iv 5 *τα πετρωδη* ℵD 33 565 al^5 b c d e f l vg

Mc iv 26 ως ανθρωπος οταν c (*quomodo homo cum*)
39 τη θαλασση και ειπε D 565 700 b c e ff$_2$ i q (hiat syr S)
v 26 om παρα D (Φ) 28 68 220 565 700 (non exprim latt (exc c) syrr)
27 om εν τω οχλω al pauc e (hiat syr S)
28 εν εαυτη DKΠ 33 565 700 al$^{plus 30}$ a c e ff$_2$ i q arm (hiat syr S)
37 αυτου pro Ιακωβου DGΔ 565 al pauc a syr-hkl (hiat syr S)
vi 7 προσκαλεσαμενος et om και D 565 al^{5} (a b c ff$_2$ i q)
15 om ελεγον ℵ 28 565 700 a b c ff$_2$ syr-pesh arm
31 υμεις sine αυτοι (D) 28 565 700 b f q vg boh arm (non liq syrr)
33 om αυτον BD 28 700 al pauc a b i
47 παλαι D 28 251 a b i g$_2$
55 φερειν DM (565 700) a b ff$_2$ i boh (non liq syrr)
vii 6 ειπεν pro γεγραπται D 565 a b i arm (syr S=*as it is written that he said*(1))
25 om αυτης ℵDΔ fam^{13} 28 565 al^{8} latt (non liq syrr)
28 λεγουσα D 69 565 al^{5} a f n i q
29 υπαγε ante δια D 565 a b c f g$_1$ i q n syr-pesh (non syr S)
30 om αυτης D 28 b ff$_2$ i n q
ix 7 om(2) ηλθε k
11 Ηλειαν sine οτι D 108 al^{5} k b i ff$_2$ q
19 και pro ο δε D fam^{13} 28 565 al^{2} a b c i k f q boh aeth
38 om οτι ουκ ακολουθει ημιν DX fam^{13} 28 al^{4} latt arm
48 τελευτησει a b c ff$_2$ i q
x 39 om αυτω post ειπον D 28 565 700 al pauc a b c ff$_2$ i k q
42 μεγαλοι sine αυτων N al pauc k (*majores*)
Lc ix 14 ανδρες ωσει D 218 477 a e f
56 om γαρ UΓΛ fam^{13} 22 477 al^{20} a e syr-hkl Antioch
59 πρωτον απελθειν AKΠ fam^{13} al^{25} a b e q vg Orig Bas(3)
62 την χειρα sine αυτου B al^{3} a b q arm Valentt ap Iren Orig Bas Tert Cyr
x 14 εν τη κρισει ανεκτοτερον εσται a b q
27 εν ολη καρδια D 157 a b c ff$_2$ i l q aeth
34 ηγαγεν sine αυτον 488 al pauc latt boh
xi 22 διαδωσει b c f ff$_2$ g$_1$ i q vg
34 εσται (2°) KLMXΠ fam^{13} 28 33 al^{20} b e f q vg syr-pesh arm
37 add αυτον ταυτα fam^{13} 477 al^{10} c e f ff$_2$ g$_1$ i (*cum loqueretur haec*)
Jo iv 3 Ιουδαιαν γην D fam^{13} 106 al^{25} a b e ff$_2$ l arm aeth
51 om αυτου (2°) ℵDL a b c e vg
v 2 λεγομενη DV 33 al pauc a b d e ff$_2$ l q Chr

(1) Syr S perhaps represents Tatian's combination of Mt and Mc. F. C. B.

(2) The Syriac evidence is confused. Syr S has φωνη ηλθε, agreeing with fam^{13} 28, but omits λεγουσα; syr-pesh has λεγουσα but not εγενετο, some codices of syr-pesh add εγενετο to φωνη but none prefix it. F. C. B.

(3) Syr SC-pesh seem to represent πρωτον απελθοντι, but it may be a translation of πρωτον απελθειν. F. C. B.

List C.

Readings for which the Old Syriac version is the chief ancient authority.

Mt	iv	2	om τεσσαρακοντα νυκτας al^{10} syr C-Diat (non S)
	v	22	add τω αδελφω αυτου ante μωρε L fam^{13} 78 108 700 1071 ff_1 syr SC arm boh
	vi	6	om τω ante εν τω κρυπτω D fam^{13} 232 syr SC Aphr
	xxvi	44	om παλιν U^{txt} ? 346 al pauc a syr S
	xxvii	16	Ιησουν Βαραββαν 241^{2} 299^{2} syr S-pal arm
		17	Ιησουν τον Βαραββαν 22* 241^{2} 299^{2} syr S-pal arm Orig^{lat} (cf B et scholia ap S codd gr pauc)
Mc	i	13	om εν τη ερημω ΚΠ 69-124 565 700 al^{15} syr S arm
		17	om γενεσθαι fam^{13} 28 700 1071 al pauc b syr S-pesh aeth pers
	ii	27	εκτισθη 700 syr S-pesh (non Diat)
	iii	8	om απο της Ιδουμαιας ℵ* 258 472 c ff_2 syr S arm
	iv	15	om ευθεως syr S arm
	v	1	Γεργεσηνων LUΔ 28 33 565 700 1071 al^{20} boh syr S-hkl^{mg} arm aeth arr Epiph
		40	ο δε Ιησους M 124 238 271 syr-pesh-hkl c* (S hiat)
	vi	23	om οτι ο εαν...δωσω σοι et tr και ωμοσεν αυτη post βασιλειας μου syr S
	vii	21	κλοπαι φονοι 33 700 syr-pesh arm
	viii	29	λεγει αυτοις sine και αυτος 28 syr S arm aeth
		31	τη τριτη ημερα fam^{13} 28 33 565 al^{5} d g_1 syr S arm aeth
	ix	21	add ο Ιησους 28 124 a c f syr S-pesh
		39	om Ιησους fam^{13} 28 syr S arm
		43	om εις την γεενναν 28 435 syr S
	x	11	om επ αυτην 228 262 565 syr S-pesh arm
		14	add επιτιμησας fam^{13} 28 565 syr S-hkl^{mg} arm
		20	εποιησα 565 syr S Aphr^{392}
Lc	ix	13	βρωματα ante εις παντα syr SC-pesh
		33	Ηλια μιαν syr SC-pesh Tert
	x	35	om εγω ℵ syr SC arm Chr Amb Aug
	xi	27	φωνην post οχλου ΚΠ al pauc syr SC (non pesh)
		33	om ουδε υπο τον μοδιον LΓΞ 69 syr S arm^{zoh}
		49	εξ αυτων sine και AKUΠ al^{10} d syr SC-pesh-hkl
Jo	iii	2	om α συ ποιεις 1 syr S
	iv	9	om ουν ℵ*V* 61 229* 565 al^{15} syr SC$^{(1)}$-pesh arm boh Cyr
		42	add παρ αυτου ℵΠ^{2} fam^{13} syr C-pal arm

(1) ουν is generally omitted by syr SC in St John unless it really means 'therefore' as in i 25. F. C. B.

List D.

Readings which are found in both the Old Latin and Old Syriac versions, but not in ℵB *or in the Antiochian Text.*

Mt i 16 om Ιησους 64 b d syr C (sed hi om ο λεγομενος)
vi 15 om τα παραπτωματα αυτων ℵD 22 a h k vg syr-pesh (syr S hiat) Aug Cyr Hesy
20 και pro ουδε ℵ a b d f g_1 h q vg syr C Cyp Aug Chrom
25 om και τι πιητε ℵ 4 22 codd ap Hier a b k vg syr C aeth pers[w] (?Clem) Ath Bas Chr Hil
xxvi 10 om γαρ ℵ[ca] al pauc a vg sah syr S-pesh arm aeth
28 om γαρ C[3] 22 700 al pauc a c syr S-pesh aeth Chr Iren[lat]
70 add ουδε επισταμαι DΔΘf a b n syr S-pal
73 om και συ D b c h l n[2] q syr S Orig[lat]
xxvii 26 παρεδωκεν αυτοις ℵ[ca]DFLN al pauc latt syr S-pal aeth Aug
Mc i 28 om ευθυς ℵ* 28 33 435 565 700 latt syr S boh arm
ii 3 φεροντες παραλυτικον CDG fam[13] 565 700 al[10] latt syr-pesh-hkl arm
15 om και D 28 al[5] latt syr-pesh
19 om οσον...νηστευειν DU 33 235 248 700 1071 a b e i syr-pesh aeth
24 add οι μαθηται σου DM fam[13] 28 565 700 latt syr S-pesh aeth
iv 16 om ομοιως D fam[13] 28 565 700 al[5] a b c ff_2 i syr S-pesh arm
33 om πολλοις C*LΔ 28 33 700 al[20] b c e syr-pesh boh aeth
41 οι ανεμοι ℵ[ca]DE 33 435 565 700 1071 al[10] b c ff_2 i syr-pesh boh aeth
v 4 πολλας πεδας κ.τ.λ. D 22 28 251 365 700 latt syr S
21 om εν τω πλοιω D 28 565 700 al[5] a b c e i syr S arm
vi 22 θυγατρος sine αυτου b c f syr S-pesh arm boh aeth
25 ειπε sine addit DΔ 28 565 a b i ff_2 syr S-pesh arm
27 om ο βασιλευς D 28 251 565 700 latt syr S
44 om τους αρτους ℵD 28 565 700 latt syr S arm
45 αυτον D fam[13] 28 40 565 700 al[15] latt syr S-pesh arm boh Orig
51 om λιαν[(1)] D[gr] 28 700 (non 565 ut ap Tisch) b syr S (sed syr S om εκπερισσως)
53 om και προσωρμισθησαν D 28 565 700 latt syr S-pesh arm
vii 9 στησητε 28 latt syr S-pesh arm go Hier Cyp Zen
viii 7 και αυτα ευλογησας MNW[d] 28 124 565 al pauc latt syr S-pesh arm

[(1)] The text of this verse is remarkably confused. We have apparently two distinct conflations, one connected with λιαν and the other with εξισταντο, so that we get

(1) λιαν εν εαυτοις εξισταντο ℵBLΔ
(2) περισσως εν εαυτοις εξισταντο D fam[1] 28 700 (with small variations)
(3) εθαυμαζον tantum syr S
(4) λιαν εθαυμαζον και εν εαυτοις εξισταντο syr-pesh
(5) λιαν εκπερισσου εν εαυτοις εξισταντο· και εθαυμαζον ς. F. C. B.

Mc viii 10 *Μαγδαλα* (D) fam^{13} (28) 271 (565) (latt) (syr S)

15 om *ορατε* D 2 565 latt syr S arm

21 *ουπω* ℵCLKΔΠ 127 565 al^{10} k syr S

24 om *οτι* et *ορω* DM^{mg} 565 700 al pauc latt boh syr S-pesh-hkl arm

ix 10 *οταν εκ νεκρων αναστη* D fam^{13} latt syr S-pesh

12 om *μεν* DL 28 565 latt syr S-pesh-hkl^{mg} arm aeth

22 om *και* (2°) DI fam^{13} 565 al pauc latt boh syr S-pesh

39 om *ταχυ* F* 28 a b c d ff$_2$ i k syr S arm

x 1 *περαν* sine *δια του* DGΔ fam^{13} 28 565 al^{25} latt syr S-pesh arm

21 *αρας τον σταυρον* ante *δευρο* G fam^{13} 28 al^{5} a syr S-pesh arm aeth Iren

24 add *αυτου* post *μαθηται* DΔ 565 al^{5} a b c ff$_2$ k syr S

38 add *αποκριθεις* D fam^{13} 28 91 565 a b ff$_1$ i k q

Lc ix 18 *μαθηται αυτου* MU fam^{13} al^{20} a f sah boh syr SC-pesh-hkl arm aeth go

32 *και διαγρηγορησαντες* b ff$_2$ q vg syr SC-pesh

39 add *και ρησσει* ℵD 166 477 latt boh (syr S)-pal

48 *το παιδιον τουτο* D al pauc latt syr C-hkl Cyr

x 20 *δαιμονια* D 157 237^{schol} 565 e f syr SC-pesh boh Eus Bas Cyr Thdrt Orig Amb

23 *ειπεν αυτοις* D e syr S boh

xi 1 om *και* ante *Ιωαννης* ℵ^{a}Δ 12 69 a b c f i l q syr SC boh

7 om *μου* C*M 71 157 al pauc b c ff$_2$ g$_1$ i l m q syr SC-hkl aeth

11 *υιος αυτου* 124 al^{5} b f ff$_2$ q syr SC-pesh-hkl^{txt} arm aeth Dial

Jo iii 31, 32 om *επανω παντων εστι και* ℵ*D 22 565 a b e f ff$_2$ l syr C (syr S legi non potest) arm Tert Hil Quaest

32 om *τουτο* ℵD 22 28 a b e ff$_2$ l boh syr C (?syr S)-pesh arm aeth Orig^{lat} Eus Hil Quaest

iv 1 *Ιησους* pro *κυριος* ℵDΛ 22 565 al^{20} a b c e vg syr C$^{(1)}$-pesh-hkl^{txt} boh arm Chr

6 om *ουτως* fam^{13} a b e ff$_2$ syr SC$^{(e\ spat)}$-pesh-pal arm aeth

47 *ηλθε* ℵ*C fam^{13} 33 a b e ff$_2$ l Syr C (S hiat) arm aeth Chr

49 om *μου* D b e ff$_2$ l syr C (S hiat)-pesh Chr

v 9 add *εγερθεις* ℵD fam^{13} a b e ff$_2$ syr S-pesh-hkl c* arm (sed ℵ latt potius *ηγερθη και* transferre videntur)

15 *με* pro *αυτον* DΛ^{2} 29 40 357 a e ff$_2$ l q syr C (non S) pesh$^{cod\,41}$ boh arm

List E.

Readings for which ℵB *are the chief ancient authorities.*

Mt i 20 *Μαριαν* BL Eus Chr Cyr

24 *εγερθεις* ℵBCZ Epiph

(1) The evidence of syr S cannot be adduced for two reasons: (1) it is not legible, (2) in this section "our Lord" has been constantly substituted for *Ιησους*. F. C. B.

Mt ii 22 om επι ℵB fam^{13} 33 127 565 700 al pauc arm Eus^{dem} (syrr non exprim cf Lc iii 1)
iii 11 υμας βαπτιζω ℵB 33 700 vg
iv 9 ταυτα σοι παντα δωσω ℵBC*Z 33 al pauc vg Orig Chr
vi 12 αφηκαμεν ℵBZ syr-pesh-hkl Orig Bas
28 αυξανουσιν...κοπιωσιν...νηθουσιν ℵB 4 33 Ath Chr
32 επιζητουσιν ℵB 4 fam^{13} 22 Max
vii 4 εκ pro απο ℵB fam^{13} 28 33 235 al^{5}
21 τοις ουρανοις ℵBC*Z 33 124 al pauc Cyr
24 ομοιωθησεται ℵBZ fam^{13} 22 33 al^{8} a b vg (sed non k f h q m) sah syr-pesh-hkl^{mg} arm aeth Orig
αυτου την οικιαν ℵBCZ 33 Orig
26 αυτου την οικιαν ℵBZΣ 700
28 ετελεσεν ℵBCZΓ fam^{13} 33 al^{15} Orig Chr
xxvi 26 δους ℵBDLZ fam^{13} 33 boh
42 om το ποτηριον ℵABCILΔΠ* 33 b ff$_2$ q sah syr-hkl aeth Orig Eus Chr Ambr
60 om ψευδομαρτυρες ℵBL 124 sah boh syr-pesh-pal aeth Orig
63 om αποκριθεις ℵ^{c}BGLZ fam^{13} 33 vg boh aeth Orig Cyr
xxvii 12 om των ante πρεσβυτερων ℵBLXΓ 69 al^{25} Orig Chr
21 τον Βαραββαν ℵBL 33 122
33 κρανιου τοπος λεγομενος ℵ^{*etcb}BL 33 157 ff$_1$ Ps-Athan (om syrr pro more)
61 Μαριαμ ℵBCLΔ
Mc i 2 καθως ℵBLKΔΠ 33 565 700 1071 Orig
23 add ευθυς ℵBL 33 boh Orig
27 διδαχη καινη αυτη (ℵBL 33) 565
31 om ευθεως ℵBCL 28 33 700 e boh arm
34 add Χριστον ειναι ℵ^{c}BCGLM fam^{13} 28 33 435 700 al^{60} syr-hkl c*
iii 31 καλουντες ℵBCL fam^{13} 28 565 700
iv 12 om τα αμαρτηματα ℵBCL 22 28* 251 340 b boh arm Orig
v 2 εξελθοντος αυτου ℵBCLΔ fam^{13} 33 565 700 al^{10} b f
12 om παντες οι δαιμονες ℵBCLΔ fam^{13} 22 28 251 boh aeth
41 κουμ ℵBCLM 33 271 1071 al^{20} ff$_2$
vi 15 om εστιν ℵBC*LΔ 28 33 565 Orig
43 κοφινων πληρωματα ℵBLΔ fam^{13}
vii 5 κοιναις ℵBD 28 33 565 700 i q vg boh arm
8 om βαπτισμους...ποιειτε ℵBLΔ 251 boh arm (syr S om vers. 8)
27 τοις κυναριοις βαλειν ℵB 28 q
29 το δαιμονιον post εκ της θ. σου ℵBLΔ boh
x 32 οι δε pro και ℵBC*LΔ 565 boh arm
34 αποκτενουσιν sine αυτον ℵBLΔ 565 al pauc b c arm
37 αριστερων BLΔ
43 μεγας γενεσθαι ℵBCLΔ fam^{13} 565 al pauc (f ff$_2$ q)
Lc ix 8 τις ℵBCLXΔΞ fam^{13} 33 al^{15} go arm

Lc	ix	12	αγρους sine τους ℵBEX fam^{13} 700
		15	κατεκλιναν ℵBLΞ fam^{13} 33 700
		16	παραθειναι ℵBCX 700 al^{15}
		18	οι οχλοι λεγουσιν ℵBLRZΞ boh sah
		20	πετρος δε αποκριθεις ℵBCLΞ boh sah
		27	αυτου ℵBLΞ Cyr
		37	τη εξης sine εν ℵBLS fam^{13} 477 q
		49	εν ℵBLXΔΞ fam^{13} 33 61^{mg} 700 al^{6} boh
		51	προσωπον sine αυτου BLΞ 239 700 c
		54	μαθηται sine αυτου ℵB 157 700 e arm Antioch
	x	20	εγγεγραπται ℵBLX 33 Eus Bas Cyr Thdt
		27	εν ολη τη διανοια ℵBLΞ 157 boh
		32	om γενομενος ℵ^{c}BLXΞ 33 700 boh arm aeth
		39	Μαριαμ ℵB^{3}C*LPΞ 33 boh
		42	ολιγων δε εστι χρεια · η ενος (ℵ)BC^{2}L 33 boh syr-hkl^{mg} aeth Orig Bas Cassian
	xi	12	om εαν ℵBL fam^{13} 33 al^{6} Dial
		14	om και αυτο ην ℵBA*L al^{7} boh arm aeth
		25	add σχολαζοντα ℵ^{c}BCLRΓ al^{12} f l boh syr-hkl c* aeth Orig
		37	om τις ℵBL fam^{13} 157 700
		49	διωξουσιν ℵBCLX al^{12}
		54	om και ζητουντες ℵBL 239 boh
Jo	iii	17	om αυτου ℵBLT^{b} 22 262 Cyr
	iv	25	απαντα ℵBC Orig
		34	ποιησω BCDKLT^{b}Π al^{8} Clem Orig Cyr Chr
		36	om και post ινα BCLT^{b}U 33 67 e g_1 boh syr-hkl-pal arm Orig Heracl Cyr
		52	ειπον ουν BCL 33 al arm
		53	εκεινη sine εν ℵBC vg Chr
	v	36	δεδωκε ℵBLΓ fam^{13} 33 157 565 al^{40} Ath Cyr
		38	εν υμιν μενοντα ℵBL fam^{13} 33 b c vg syr-pal aeth Ath Cyr Hil

List F.

Readings which are supported by a few other manuscripts, but cannot be identified with any authority generally recognized as primary.

Mt	i	6	Σαλομων pro Σολομωντα ℵ* (latt) (Σολομων 700) cf LXX
		7	Σαλομων pro Σολομων 33 700 latt (Σαλωμων ℵ^{b}) cf LXX
	ii	12	την εαυτων χωραν pro την χωραν αυτων ℵ 157
	iv	24	εξηλθεν ℵC 33 al mu (?) syr hkl^{mg} boh Orig
	v	33	κυριω sine τω LΔ al pauc
		39	om σου post σιαγονα ℵ 33 127 157 435 al^{50} a f h Bas Chr Orig
	vi	1	ουρανοις sine τοις ℵ*D 33 Chr
	vii	13	εισπορευομενοι (ℵ^{b}) 157

Mt vii 27 *προσερρηξεν* CM al pauc Bas
28 *παντες* Δ Orig (Eus^{dem} *παντες* pro *οι οχλοι*)
xxvi 27 om *και* (2°) CLZΔ 33 157 252* q arm (non liq syrr)
29 *καινον μεθ υμων* CLZ 28 33 al^{2} aeth Eus Chr
34 *αλεκτοροφωνιας* L a Orig (cf xxvi 75)
36 *εως αν* DLKM^{2}ΓΔ al^{13} Chr^{txt}
39 om *μου* LΔ al pauc a (hiant k e) vg codd. opt. Orig Eus Ath Did Bas Cyp$^{2}/_{2}$ Hil
40 om *ουτως* Δ
42 add *ο Ιησους* L fam^{13} al pauc arm
53 *δοκει σοι* C* 700 al^{5} syr-hkl^{mg} Orig
54 *εδει* C 28 al^{3} Orig
61 om *αυτον* B 69 700 arm aeth Orig
67 add *αυτον* DG 700 syr[1]-pesh-hkl
xxvii 3 *ο Ιουδας* Orig
17 *των δυο* Δ Orig (sed hi habent *των δυο* ante *απολυσω*)
23 *λεγοντες* KΠ* al^{10} a b sah Chr
29 *εθηκαν* KNΠΔ fam^{13} 33 al^{10}
41 *ομοιως και* BK fam^{13} 33 al^{5} a c d f syr-pesh boh arm Eus Orig
56 *Μαριαμ* CLΔ
57 *εμαθητευθη* ℵCD 33 700
Mc i 9 *εν τω Ιορδανη υπο Ιωαννου* 28
13 *επι ημερας* fam^{13} 28 565 700
21 *εισπορευεται* 6 22 71 Orig$^{1}/_{2}$
30 *του Σιμωνος* LMΔ fam^{13} 565 700 al^{25}
36 *ο τε* KΠ fam^{13} 28 565 700 al pauc
40 om *αυτον* (3°) ℵL 300 565 al pauc e arm
41 om *αυτω* post *λεγει* ℵ*c ff$_{2}$ syr-pesh
ii 14 *ηκολουθει* C* 28 258
20 *νηστευουσι* D*FUΠ al^{6} go
iii 2 *παρετηρουντο* AC*DΔΣ 10 67 238 565 700
4 add *τι* E 700 al pauc
13 *ανεβη* P al pauc
17 *Ιακωβον* sine *του* CKSΔ fam^{13} 700 al^{15}
20 *οχλος πολυς* 61 aeth
31 *εστηκοτες* C^{2}GL 124 700
33 *απεκριθη* sine *και* 28 122 433 565 700
και λεγει fam^{13} 28 122 433 700 (cf ℵB)
iv 5 *εξεβλαστησε* fam^{13} 28
8 *επι* pro *εις* C 28 124 565 700 al^{15}
11 *τα μυστηρια* G al^{12} syr-hkl arm^{zoh}
15 *εις αυτους* B fam^{13} 28

[1] Syr S has '*were slapping his cheeks*' so that the Greek represented by it is uncertain. F. C. B.

Mc iv 16 δεχονται al pauc

18 om ουτοι εισι fam^{13} 28 700 al arm

21 add ινα ante υπο (2°) fam^{13} 28 565

22 ει μη ινα (1°) fam^{13} 28 565 700

ει μη ινα (2°) 13 (ap Tisch sed non in coll Ferrar) al pauc

24 λεγει pro ελεγεν 7

37 βυθιζεσθαι G 33 al^{16}

38 om το ante προσκεφαλαιον 28 235 565 700

40 ουτως ante δειλοι fam^{13} 28 arm

41 αυτω υπακουει ℵ*CΔ fam^{13} 28 al pauc

v 7 om Ιησου 33 700 al pauc

10 παρεκαλουν AΔ 28 565 al^{10} c ff$_2$ g$_1$ g$_2$

11 om προς τω ορει 33 (?)

27 add του κρασπεδου M 33

33 αιτιαν (fam^{13}) 28 (fam^{13} αιτιαν αυτης)

37 παρακολουθησαι D 28 124 565 700

42 ως 33 238 565 700

vi 7 προσκαλεσαμενος D 565 al^{5} (cf latt syrr)

11 ος αν...δεξηται C* (cf ος αν τοπος ℵBLΔ fam^{13} 28 al)

τους λογους 106 syr-hkl

20 om και αγιον al^{5}

22 ο θελεις D 238 565 al pauc

26 ηθελεν Π* al pauc

33 εγνωσαν B*D

35 om αυτου A 28 261 282 c arm (cf fam^{13})

η ωρα ηδη πολλη 569 (ap Tisch 7^{pe})

36 κωμας και αγρους al (?)

καταλυσωσι 22*

37 om αυτοις AL 33

45 πλοιον sine το ℵ 33 253 565

εις pro προς 28 565 700 Orig

54 οι ανδρες του τοπου εκεινου AGΔ fam^{13} 28 33 565 700 al pauc syr-pesh arm

55 εστιν εκει 28 700

56 om η αγρους L*g$_2$ syr-pesh [(1)]

ηψαντο sine αν ℵDΔ fam^{13} 33

διεσωζοντο N fam^{13} 700

vii 1 om οι 565 700

13 πολλα τοιαυτα ℵM* fam^{13} 700 al^{6}

17 επηρωτησαν 33

19 om τον ante αφεδρωνα S 700

(1) κωμη and αγρος are habitually rendered by the same word in syr SC-pesh. Here syr S has a transliteration of αγρος, which is however a naturalized Syriac word, cf Zech ii 4. F. C. B.

Mc vii 23 om τα πονηρα 565 700 al pauc
26 om εκ L fam[13] 565 700 al[6] q
27 om αυτη 28 90* c fuld
28 om αυτω fam[13] 565 al[5]
37 υπερεκπερισσως DU 435 (cf 69 υπερ· περισσως spat rel ut vid)
viii 4 ωδε ante τις 28 565 (700)
10 om το ante πλοιον L fam[13] 28 33 700 al[10]
14 ενα μονον αρτον εχοντες 28 565 700 (cf fam[13] ενα μονον εχοντες αρτον)
15 απο (2°) GΔ fam[13] 28 (cf a f q)
Ηρωδιανων G fam[13] 28 251 565 i arm
16 εχουσι B 28 565 700 c g_2
23 αυτου 565 700
και (3°) G fam[13] 28 al pauc
ix 5 ελεγε fam[13] 28
9 διεστελλετο C
11 επηρωτησαν A fam[13] 28 33 al[5]
13 ηλθε C 700 al pauc
14 om πολυν 28 arm
17 ειπεν αυτω I fam[13] 565
18 om αν ℵ* 127 al pauc
26 πολλα και Δ 565 al[10]
28 ηρωτων D al pauc
31 εγερθησεται fam[13] al pauc
33 διελεχθητε 28
προς εαυτους fam[13] 28 565
35 om παντων εσχατος και al pauc
36 om αυτο 28 565 arm
λεγει al pauc
39 εν pro επι fam[13] al pauc
45 απελθειν 28
50 αρτυθησεται K 14 91 255 299
x 1 συμπορευεται fam[13] 28 al[5]
4 ενετειλατο 299 477
16 τιθων fam[13] 28
19 om μη φονευσης Γ 300 f (cf D k quae om μη φονευσης sed pro eo habent μη πορνευσης)
20 om διδασκαλε KΠ al[6] Clem
25 πλουσιον post του θεου 299
27 om παντα...θεω ΔΨ 69 157 al[10] l arm[zoh] Clem
28 ηρξατο αυτω λεγειν ο Πετρος 124 (ηρξατο λεγειν αυτω ο Πετρος 28 565)
36 ποιησω pro ποιησαι με CD fam[13] 565 al[5]
40 add υπο του πατρος μου ℵ*[et cb] al[5] a syr-hkl[mg]
41 ηγανακτησαν A al pauc g_2 q

Mc	x	42	om *αυτους* 238 299
		44	*υμων ειναι* D 565 al pauc
		49	*θαρρων* fam^{13} 28
			εγειρου fam^{13} 28
Lc	ix	2	*ασθενεις* ℵADLΞ al^{5}
		4	*ὃ αν* MXΓ 700
		7	*γενομενα* AX fam^{13} al^{15}
		13	*μη* Λ 262
		19	add *αλλοι δε Ιερεμιαν* fam^{13} 251 syr-hkl c*
		22	*υπο* D
			om *και γραμματεων* Orig
			αναστηναι ACDF^{w}KΠ 69* 157 al^{20} Orig Dial
		29	*προσευξασθαι* ℵ*
		35	*εγενετο φωνη* al^{10}
		46	om *το* ante *τις* 28 254
		54	*εκ* CD 700 go Bas Chr
		55	*ποιου* D 700 al^{10} Chr Antioch
		61	*εν τω οικω* Valentt ap Iren Antioch
	x	1	*εαυτου* H al pauc
		17	*ημιν υποτασσεται* Λ 237 al pauc e
		19	*πατειν* sine *του* Orig Caes Epiph Cyr Antioch Thdrt
		31	om *εν* B
		38	*αυτον* pro *αυτους* 157 d syr-pal arm^{mss}
	xi	34	add *ολον* ante *το σωμα* 2° ℵ^{ca}X al^{4} f boh syr C (non S) aeth
		41	*εσται* DXΓ al^{12} a aeth Tert Bas
		46	*επι* C
		48	*ταφους αυτων* (fam^{13}) 157 Chr Lcfr (fam^{13} ante *οικοδομειτε*)
		53	*οι νομικοι και οι φαρισαιοι* i syr-hkl^{mg} (cf D latt)
			add *αυτω* post *ενεχειν* al^{5}
Jo	iii	19	*μαλλον οι ανθρωποι* al pauc
		20	*αυτου τα εργα* AKΠ al^{10} Chr
		24	*φυλακην* sine *την* E*M 22 235 473 565 Orig Eus
		26	*Ιωαννην* sine *τον* 106 485
			ιδου D
		28	*εμοι* 124 al pauc
	iv	5	*οὗ* pro *ὃ* C*DLMS 28 33 157 700 al^{25} Chr
		16	*Ιησους* sine *ο* ℵ*AΠ* al pauc
		23	om *και γαρ...αυτον* 22
		35	om *ιδου λεγω υμιν* 22 108 124 301^{txt} Orig$^{3}/_{7}$
		37	*αληθης* 22 al pauc Chr
	v	19	*λεγει* 485
			ουδε εν 565 Orig
		25	*ακουσωσιν* ℵL 33 69 157 565
		26	om *ουτως δεδωκε...εαυτω* ℵ* (? homoiotel)
		44	*πιστευειν* AL 22 33 249 565 Chr Cyr

List G.

Readings which appear to be peculiar[1] *to fam*[1].

Mt xxvi	45	om ιδου et add γαρ post ηγγικε (cf BE syr S arm sah ιδου γαρ)
		ωρα μου
	55	om διδασκων
	70	ο pro τι
	73	add παλιν
	75	αλεκτοροφωνιας (cf xxvi 34)
xxvii	10	καθως
	13	κατηγορουσιν
	58	add ουν
Mc i	20	μισθιων
ii	2	οχλοι πολλοι
iii	8	και απο Ιεροσολ. και απο της Ιουδαιας
	31	η μητηρ και οι αδελφοι αυτου
iv	1	συνερχεται
		παρα
	17	om η διωγμου δια τον λογον ευθεως (homoiotel)
	18	λογον μου
	20	om σπαρεντες
	21	λεγει
	26	την γην
	29	τοτε pro ευθεως
	30	τινι ομοιωματι
v	16	πως εσωθη ο δαιμονισθεις
	39	om εισελθων
	42	δεκαδυο
vi	4	om αυτοις
	7	αποστελλειν αυτους
	18	εχειν post γυναικα
	27	απολυσας pro αποστειλας
	32	πλοιαριω
		ιδοντες
	33	συνεδραμον και ηλθον εκει[2]
	37	om αυτω
	42	παντες post εχορτασθησαν

[1] Itacisms are not included in this list, as they are not noted by most collators, are found in many MSS, and have no critical value.

[2] 209 omits *και ηλθον*. This is one of the passages where it is difficult to feel certain about the text of the archetype.

Mc	vi	46	*ανηλθεν*
		48	*εναντιος ο ανεμος* sine *αυτοις* (cf ℵA)
			επι της θαλασσης περιπατων
		49	*φαντασμα εδοξαν ειναι*
		51	*εξεπλησσοντο*
		56	*οποτε*
			ασθενεις
	vii	13	*την εντολην*
	viii	2	*ημερας ηδη*
		6	*επι την γην*
		21	*ειπεν*
		38	om *των αγιων*
	ix	17	*εκ του οχλου εις*
		25	add *πολυς*
			om *τω ακαθαρτω*
		34	*διενεχθησαν* (v. p. xxxvi)
	x	1	*οχλος πολυς*
		2	*επηρωτησαν αυτον οι Φαρισαιοι*
		13	*φερουσιν*
		37	om *εις*
Lc	ix	10	*τοπον πολεως*(1)
		15	*αυτους* pro *απαντας*
		32	*συνεστωτας* sine *τους*
		35	*εκλεκτος*
		47	*γνους*
	x	15	*ἢ...υψωθηση*
		31	om *αυτον*
	xi	34	*σωμα* 1° sine *σου*
Jo	iii	23	*ο βαπτιζων*
	iv	8	*απελυθεισαν*
		12	*του Ιακωβ*
		18	*ο ανηρ*
		23	*τω πνευματι*
		39	*των Σαμαρειτων εις αυτον*

(1) Syr S has ܠܬܪܐ ܕܡܕܝܢܬܐ, but ܠܐܬܪܐ ܕܡܕܝܢܬܐ would represent the text of fam[1]; it is better, however, not to press this, as the affinities of text in this passage are so obscure. F. C. B.

Table to illustrate the mixture of the text of the group fam^{1} fam^{13} 22 28 565 700 with ς (v. p. lii).

The following table is not intended to *prove* that this group has a common origin. That this is so is shown, so far as it can be, by *List F.* The table is meant to illustrate the fact mentioned on p. lii that when the members of this group do not support one another, they usually have the reading of ς. To show this I have given on the left of the table the readings in which the members of the group differ from ς, and on the right the readings of ς, while I have shown the agreement of each member of the group either with the family text or with ς, viz. the symbols *fam* and ς. It will be noticed that the degree of mixture with ς, tested in this somewhat rough and ready method, differs considerably—565 seems to be the least, and 22 the most mixed, for *fam*^{1} has 31 variants from ς, *fam*^{13} 30 variants, 22 11 variants, 28 26 variants, 565 48 variants, 700 30 variants. It is also worth noticing that *fam*^{1} has 4 variants unsupported by any other member of the group, *fam*^{13} has 3, 22 has 1, 28 has 2, 565 has 4, 700 has 8. This, too, seems to suggest that 565 is the purest member of the group. As it is also the only codex which says anything about the origin of its archetype (v. p. liii) this fact is especially important.

	Reading of some member of the large group	fam^{1}	fam^{13}	22	28	565	700	Reading of ς
Mc i 1	Ιησου Χριστου sine addit	ς	ς	ς	fam	ς	ς	Ιησου Χριστου υιου του θεου
2	καθως	fam	ς	ς	ς	fam	fam	ως
	εν Ησαια τω προφητη	fam	ς	fam	ς	fam	fam	εν τοις προφηταις
	αποστελλω	ς	ς	ς	fam	fam	ς	εγω αποστελλω
4	εν τη ερημω βαπτιζων	ς	ς	ς	fam	ς	fam	βαπτιζων εν τη ερημω
5	εξεπορευοντο	ς	ς	fam	ς	ς	ς	εξεπορευετο
	παντες εβαπτιζοντο	ς	fam	ς	fam	fam	ς	εβαπτιζοντο παντες
	Ιορδανη sine addit	ς	ς	ς	ς	fam	fam	Ιορδανη ποταμω
6	ο Ιωαννης	fam	ς [1]	ς	ς	fam	fam	Ιωαννης

(1) 69 reads ο Ιωαννης, but has no support in the other members of *fam*^{13} so far as they have been collated.

	Reading of some member of the large group	FAM^{1}	FAM^{13}	22	28	565	700	Reading of ϛ
Mc i 7	οτι ερχεται	ϛ	ϛ	ϛ	ϛ	fam	ϛ	ερχεται
	ικανος λυσαι	ϛ	ϛ	ϛ	fam	fam	ϛ	ικανος κυψας λυσαι
8	υμας βαπτισω	ϛ	(fam)[1]	ϛ	ϛ	fam	ϛ	εβαπτισα υμας
	υμας βαπτισει	ϛ	fam	ϛ	ϛ	fam	ϛ	βαπτισει υμας
9	ο Ιησους	ϛ	fam	ϛ	fam	ϛ	ϛ	Ιησους
	εν τω Ιορδανη υπο Ιωαννου	fam	(fam)[2]	ϛ	fam	(fam)[2]	(fam)[2]	υπο Ιωαννου εις τον Ιορδανην
10	εκ	ϛ	fam	ϛ	fam	fam	ϛ	απο
	εις αυτον	ϛ	fam	ϛ	ϛ	ϛ	ϛ	επ αυτον
11	ιδου φωνη εκ των ουρανων ηκουσθη	ϛ	ϛ	ϛ	fam	fam	ϛ	φωνη εγενετο εκ των ουρανων
	εν σοι	fam	fam	fam	fam	fam	ϛ	εν ω
12	ευθεως	ϛ	ϛ	ϛ	ϛ	ϛ	fam	ευθυς
13	ην εκει sine addit	fam	?[3]	ϛ	fam	fam	fam	ην εκει εν τη ερημω
	επι ημερας	fam	fam	ϛ	fam	fam	fam	ημερας
	τεσσαρακοντα, και νυκτας τεσσαρακοντα	ϛ	fam	ϛ	ϛ	ϛ	ϛ	τεσσαρακοντα sine addit
14	Ιησους	ϛ	ϛ	ϛ	ϛ	ϛ	fam	ο Ιησους
	ευαγγελιον του θεου	fam	ϛ	ϛ	fam	fam	ϛ	ευαγγελιον της βασιλειας του θεου
15	πεπληρωται	fam	ϛ	ϛ	ϛ	ϛ	ϛ	οτι πεπληρωται
16	του Σιμωνος	fam	fam	(ϛ)[4]	ϛ	fam	(fam)[5]	αυτου
	αμφιβαλλοντας τα δικτυα	(ϛ)[6]	fam	(ϛ)[6]	fam	fam	(ϛ)[6]	βαλλοντας αμφιβληστρον
	εις την θαλασσαν	ϛ	fam	ϛ	fam	fam	ϛ	εν τη θαλασση

[1] *Fam*^{13} reads υμας εβαπτισα, apparently owing to a partial assimilation to ϛ, altering βαπτισω to εβαπτισα, but preserving the order of the words.

[2] Here also there seems to be a case of partial assimilation: all the MSS except 22 agree in the order, placing υπο Ιωαννου last, but *fam*^{13} 565 700 have altered εν τω Ιορδανη to εις τον Ιορδανην agreeing with ϛ.

[3] The evidence of *fam*^{13} is obscure. 69 124 read ην εκει, 13 346 543 788 826 828 read ην εν τη ερημω. I am inclined to think this is an instance of assimilation to a well-known text which differed from ϛ. The omission of εκει is found in ℵABDL *fam*^{13} 33 al pauc latt boh aeth go Orig Eus[dem], but the omission of εν τη ερημω only in KΠ* *fam*^{1} 69-124 al[11] syr[sin] arm. The curious disagreement between 69-124 and the rest of *fam*^{13} raises an interesting problem as to the relations of the MSS of *fam*^{13} to each other; both 69 and 124 often have peculiar readings, and at present it is very hard to give any satisfactory reason for this.

[4] 22 has a conflation of the family text and ϛ—αυτου του Σιμωνος.

[5] 700 has Σιμωνος without του.

[6] The text of this verse is obscure. Probably the true reading is αμφιβαλλοντας without any addition. This seems to have been found a difficulty, and the attempts at expansion or modification fall into two groups, (1) the addition of δικτυα, found in D *fam*^{13} 28 565, (2) the addition of αμφιβληστρον or αμφιβληστρα, αμφιβληστρον being adopted by perhaps the majority of MSS. When αμφιβληστρον was inserted there was no reason for preserving the αμφι in αμφιβαλλοντας, and so βαλλοντας

	Reading of some member of the large group	fam[1]	fam[13]	22	28	565	700	Reading of ς
Mc i 17	αλιεις	fam	fam	ς	fam	ς	fam	γενεσθαι αλιεις
18	λινα[1]	ς	ς	ς	ς	ς	fam	δικτυα
	δικτυα	ς	fam	ς	ς	fam	fam	δικτυα αυτων
19	προβας	fam	fam[2]	ς	fam	fam	ς	προβας εκειθεν
	κατασκευαζοντας	ς	ς[3]	ς	fam	ς	ς	καταρτιζοντας
20	δικτυα. και αφεντες	ς	ς	ς	ς	fam	ς	δικτυα. και ευθεως εκαλεσαν αυτους· και αφεντες
	μισθιων	fam	ς	ς	ς	ς	ς	μισθωτων
21	εισπορευεται	fam	ς	fam	ς	ς	ς	εισπορευονται
	ευθυς	fam	ς	ς	fam	fam	fam	ευθεως
	σαββασιν	ς	fam	ς	fam	fam	ς	σαββασιν εισελθων
	εδιδασκεν αυτους	ς	ς	ς	ς	ς	fam	εδιδασκεν
23	και ευθυς ην	fam	ς	ς	ς	ς	ς	και ην
24	λεγων τι	ς	ς	ς	ς	fam	ς	λεγων εα τι
25	απ	ς	ς	ς	ς	ς	fam	εξ
27	εαυτους	fam	fam	fam	fam	ς	fam	αυτους
	τουτο; διδαχη καινη αυτη	fam	(ς)[4]	ς	ς	fam	(fam)[5]	τουτο; τις η διδαχη η καινη αυτη
	κατ εξουσιαν	fam	ς	ς	ς	fam	ς	οτι κατ εξουσιαν
	και εξηλθε	ς	ς	ς	ς	ς	fam	εξηλθε δε
28	ακοη αυτου	fam	ς[6]	ς	fam	fam	fam	ακοη αυτου ευθυς

is the reading of ς, but there are many variations in order, and the text does not seem to have settled down to *βαλλοντας αμφιβληστρον* for some time. Hence we have *αμφιβληστρα βαλλοντας* in *fam*[1], *αμφιβαλλοντας αμφιβληστρα* in 22, and *αμφιβληστρον βαλλοντας* in 700, all of which are clearly akin to ς and may easily represent different attempts to emend the unfamiliar use (in this passage) of *δικτυα*.

[1] *λινα* is not found here in any MS except 700; it is not found elsewhere in this sense in the N.T., but it is found in the *Gospel of Peter* in the last line but one, *εγω δε Σιμων Πετρος και Ανδρεας ο αδελφος μου λαβοντες ημων τα λινα απηλθαμεν εις την θαλασσαν.* This passage has been marked in some editions of the *Gospel of Peter* as a reminiscence of Jo xxi 2 f. But I think that Mr F. C. Burkitt is probably right in the suggestion which he has made on p. 32 of his *Two Lectures on the Gospels*, that the author of the *Gospel of Peter* is using the lost conclusion of S. Mark. If so, this is evidence for the Marcan use of *λινα*; it is not of much value, but it is sufficiently interesting to be worth noting.

[2] 124 omits *εκειθεν*.

[3] 124 reads *κατασκευαζοντας*.

[4] *Fam*[13] reads *τουτο; τις η διδαχη καινη αυτη;*

[5] 700 reads *τουτο; καινη διδαχη*.

[6] *Fam*[13] also adds *πανταχου* to *ευθυς*. The text of this passage is very complicated and interesting. There are four variants:

(1) *ευθυς* but not *πανταχου* ADΓΔΠ unc[9] al pler syrr-pesh-hkl.

(2) *πανταχου* but not *ευθυς* b e q boh.

(3) both *ευθυς* and *πανταχου* ℵ[c]BCL *fam*[13].

(4) neither *ευθυς* nor *πανταχου* ℵ* *fam*[1] 28 565 700 c ff_2 syr S arm aeth.

Reading of some member of the large group	fam[1]	fam[13]	22	28	565	700	Reading of ϛ
Mc i 29 ευθυς	fam	fam	ϛ	fam	fam	ϛ	ευθεως
εξελθων ηλθεν	fam	fam	fam	ϛ	fam	fam	εξελθοντες ηλθον
30 του Σιμωνος	fam	fam	ϛ	ϛ	fam	fam	Σιμωνος
31 πυρετος	fam	ϛ	ϛ	fam	fam	fam	πυρετος ευθεως
32 παντες προς αυτον παντας	ϛ	fam	ϛ	fam	fam	ϛ	προς αυτον παντας
33 ην συνηγμενη	ϛ	fam	ϛ	ϛ	fam	fam	επισυνηγμενη ην
34 αυτον (τον) χριστον ειναι	fam	fam	ϛ	fam	fam	fam	αυτον
35 εννυχα	fam	ϛ	ϛ	fam	ϛ	ϛ	εννυχον
και αναστας	ϛ	fam	ϛ	ϛ	ϛ	ϛ	αναστας
36 κατεδιωξεν	ϛ	ϛ	ϛ	ϛ	ϛ	fam	κατεδιωξαν
ο τε Σιμων	fam	fam	ϛ	fam	fam	ϛ	ο Σιμων
37 σε ζητουσι	ϛ	fam	fam	ϛ	fam	ϛ	ζητουσι σε
38 λεγει	ϛ	ϛ	ϛ	ϛ	ϛ	fam	και λεγει
39 εις τας συναγωγας	fam	fam	ϛ	ϛ	fam	ϛ	εν ταις συναγωγαις
40 γονυπετων	fam	ϛ	ϛ	ϛ	fam	ϛ	γονυπετων αυτον
θελησης	ϛ	ϛ	ϛ	ϛ	fam	ϛ	θελης
41 λεγων	ϛ	fam	ϛ	ϛ	fam	ϛ	και λεγει
λεγει	fam	ϛ	ϛ	ϛ	ϛ	ϛ	λεγει αυτω
42 και ευθεως	ϛ	ϛ	ϛ	ϛ	fam	ϛ	και ειποντος αυτου ευθεως
44 ειπων	ϛ	ϛ	ϛ	ϛ	fam	fam	και λεγει αυτω
μηδενι ειπης	ϛ	fam	ϛ	ϛ	fam	fam	μηδενι μηδεν ειπης
45 δυνασθαι αυτον	ϛ	ϛ	ϛ	ϛ	ϛ	fam	αυτον δυνασθαι
εις πολιν φανερως	ϛ	ϛ [1]	ϛ	fam	fam	ϛ	φανερως εις πολιν
επ ερημοις	ϛ	ϛ [2]	ϛ	fam	fam	ϛ	εν ερημοις
παντοθεν	fam	ϛ	ϛ	ϛ	fam	ϛ	πανταχοθεν

[1] 124 reads *εις πολιν φανερως*.

[2] 124 reads *επ ερημοις*. It is worth noting that in this chapter we have five instances of 124 preserving what seems to be the text of the original family, against the rest of *fam*[13]. Cod 124 is certainly different in many passages from the rest of *fam*[13]. It has been supposed to be the least valuable, but it is possible that the MSS of *fam*[13] fall into two groups, one consisting of 124, the other of 13-346-543 and possibly others of the uncollated MSS 788 826 828. If this were so it would give 124 an increased value, in spite of its well-known carelessness and assimilations to ϛ, and would explain those readings in which it seems to have preserved the family text of the larger group better than the other MSS in *fam*[13].

ΑΓΙΟΝ ΕΥΑΓΓΕΛΙΟΝ ΚΑΤΑ ΜΑΤΘΑΙΟΝ

I. Βίβλος γενέσεως Ἰησοῦ Χριστοῦ, υἱοῦ Δαβίδ, υἱοῦ Ἀβραάμ. ᾱ
2 Ἀβραὰμ ἐγέννησε τὸν Ἰσαάκ· Ἰσαὰκ δὲ ἐγέννησε τὸν Ἰακώβ· Ἰακὼβ δὲ γ
3 ἐγέννησε τὸν Ἰούδαν καὶ τοὺς ἀδελφοὺς αὐτοῦ· Ἰούδας δὲ ἐγέννησε τὸν
Φαρὲς καὶ τὸν Ζαρὰ ἐκ τῆς Θαμάρ· Φαρὲς δὲ ἐγέννησε τὸν Ἑσρώμ·
4 Ἑσρὼμ δὲ ἐγέννησε τὸν Ἀράμ· Ἀρὰμ δὲ ἐγέννησε τὸν Ἀμιναδάμ·
5 Ἀμιναδὰβ δὲ ἐγέννησε τὸν Ναασσών· Ναασσὼν δὲ ἐγέννησε τὸν Βοὸζ
ἐκ τῆς Ῥαχάβ· Βοὸζ δὲ ἐγέννησε τὸν Ὠβὴδ ἐκ τῆς Ῥούθ· Ὠβὴδ δὲ
6 ἐγέννησε τὸν Ἰεσσαί· Ἰεσσαὶ δὲ ἐγέννησε τὸν Δαβὶδ τὸν βασιλέα. Δαβὶδ
7 δὲ ἐγέννησε τὸν Σαλομὼν ἐκ τῆς τοῦ Οὐρίου· Σαλομὼν δὲ ἐγέννησε τὸν
Ῥοβοάμ· Ῥοβοὰμ δὲ ἐγέννησε τὸν Ἀβία· Ἀβιὰ δὲ ἐγέννησε τὸν Ἀσάφ·
8 Ἀσὰφ δὲ ἐγέννησε τὸν Ἰωσαφάτ· Ἰωσαφὰτ δὲ ἐγέννησε τὸν Ἰωράμ·
9 Ἰωρὰμ δὲ ἐγέννησε τὸν Ὀζίαν· Ὀζίας δὲ ἐγέννησε τὸν Ἰωάθαμ· Ἰωάθαμ
10 δὲ ἐγέννησε τὸν Ἄχαζ· Ἄχαζ δὲ ἐγέννησε τὸν Ἐζεκίαν· Ἐζεκίας δὲ
ἐγέννησε τὸν Μανασσῆ· Μανασσῆς δὲ ἐγέννησε τὸν Ἀμώς· Ἀμὼς δὲ
11 ἐγέννησε τὸν Ἰωσίαν· Ἰωσίας δὲ ἐγέννησε τὸν Ἰακείμ, Ἰωακεὶμ δὲ
ἐγέννησε τὸν Ἰεχονίαν καὶ τοὺς ἀδελφοὺς αὐτοῦ ἐπὶ τῆς μετοικησίας
12 Βαβυλῶνος. μετὰ δὲ τὴν μετοικησίαν Βαβυλῶνος Ἰεχονίας ἐγέννησε
13 τὸν Σαλαθιήλ· Σαλαθιὴλ δὲ ἐγέννησε τὸν Ζοροβάβελ· Ζοροβάβελ δὲ
ἐγέννησε τὸν Ἀβιούδ· Ἀβιοὺδ δὲ ἐγέννη τὸν Ἐλιακείμ· Ἐλιακεὶμ δὲ

1 Δαβιδ] Δα̅δ per compendium cod. et sic passim
8 in marg. εν τη τριτη των βασιλειων Ασα sed nunc evanuit

Titul. Το κατα Ματθαιον αγιον ευαγγελιον 209 ϛ — 209 ϛ
1 Ἀβρααμ ϛ **2** Ἀβρααμ ϛ **4** Αμιναδαμ bis 209, Αμιναδαβ bis ϛ **5** τον Βοοζ] pr τον Σαλμων· Σαλμων δε εγεννησε ϛ **6** Δαβιδ δε] + ο βασιλευς ϛ Σολομωντα ϛ **7** Σολομων ϛ Ασα ϛ **8** Ασα ϛ et in marg. 209 m. ut vdr. prim. add. εν τη τριτη των βασιλειων ασα **10** Αμων bis ϛ **11** om τον Ιακειμ...εγενν. ϛ Ιακειμ pro Ιωακειμ 209 μετοικεσιας 209 ϛ **12** μετοικεσιαν 209 ϛ **13** εγεννησε 209 ϛ

ἐγέννησε τὸν Ἀζώρ· Ἀζὸρ δὲ ἐγέννησε τὸν Σαδώκ· Σαδὼκ δὲ ἐγέννησε 14
τὸν Ἀχίν· Ἀχὶν δὲ ἐγέννησε τὸν Ἐλιούδ· Ἐλιοὺδ δὲ ἐγέννησε τὸν 15
Ἐλεάζαρ· Ἐλεάζαρ δὲ ἐγέννησε τὸν Ματθάν· Ματθὰν δὲ ἐγέννησε τὸν
β̄ Ἰακώβ· Ἰακὼβ δὲ ἐγέννησε τὸν Ἰωσὴφ τὸν ἄνδρα Μαρίας, ἐξ ἧς ἐγεν- 16
ι νήθη ὁ λεγόμενος Χριστός.

Πᾶσαι οὖν αἱ γενεαὶ ἀπὸ Ἀβραὰμ ἕως Δαβὶδ γενεαὶ δεκατέσσαρες· 17
καὶ ἀπὸ Δαβὶδ ἕως τῆς μετοικεσίας Βαβυλῶνος γενεαὶ δεκατέσσαρες· καὶ
ἀπὸ τῆς μετοικεσίας Βαβυλῶνος ἕως τοῦ Χριστοῦ γενεαὶ δεκατέσσαρες.

γ̄ Τοῦ δὲ Ἰησοῦ Χριστοῦ ἡ γένεσις οὕτως ἦν. μνηστευθείσης τῆς 18
ε μητρὸς αὐτοῦ Μαρίας τῷ Ἰωσήφ, πρὶν ἢ συνελθεῖν αὐτοὺς ηὑρέθη ἐν
δ̄ γαστρὶ ἔχουσα ἐκ Πνεύματος Ἁγίου. Ἰωσὴφ δὲ ὁ ἀνὴρ αὐτῆς, δίκαιος ὢν 19
ι καὶ μὴ θέλων αὐτὴν δειγματίσαι, ἐβουλήθη λάθρα ἀπολῦσαι αὐτήν.
ταῦτα δὲ αὐτοῦ ἐνθυμηθέντος, ἰδού, ἄγγελος Κυρίου κατ' ὄναρ ἐφάνη αὐτῷ, 20
λέγων, Ἰωσήφ, υἱὸς Δαβίδ, μὴ φοβηθῇς παραλαβεῖν Μαρίαν τὴν γυναῖκά
σου· τὸ γὰρ ἐν αὐτῇ γεννηθὲν ἐκ Πνεύματός ἐστιν Ἁγίου· τέξεται δὲ υἱόν, 21
καὶ καλέσεις τὸ ὄνομα αὐτοῦ Ἰησοῦν· αὐτὸς γὰρ σώσει τὸν λαὸν αὐτοῦ ἀπὸ
τῶν ἁμαρτιῶν αὐτῶν. τοῦτο δὲ ὅλον γέγονεν, ἵνα πληρωθῇ τὸ ῥηθὲν ὑπὸ 22
Κυρίου διὰ τοῦ προφήτου, λέγοντος, Ἰδού, ἡ παρθένος ἐν γαστρὶ ἕξει καὶ 23
τέξεται υἱόν, καὶ καλέσουσι τὸ ὄνομα αὐτοῦ Ἐμμανουήλ, ὅ ἐστι μεθερμη-
νευόμενον Μεθ' ἡμῶν ὁ Θεός. ἐγερθεὶς δὲ ὁ Ἰωσὴφ ἀπὸ τοῦ ὕπνου 24
ἐποίησεν ὡς προσέταξεν αὐτῷ ὁ ἄγγελος Κυρίου· καὶ παρέλαβε τὴν
γυναῖκα αὐτοῦ, καὶ οὐκ ἐγίνωσκεν αὐτήν, ἕως οὗ ἔτεκεν υἱόν· καὶ ἐκάλεσε 25
τὸ ὄνομα αὐτοῦ Ἰησοῦν.

Α′ II. Τοῦ δὲ Ἰησοῦ γεννηθέντος ἐν Βηθλεὲμ τῆς Ἰουδαίας ἐν ἡμέραις
ε̄ ζ Ἡρώδου τοῦ βασιλέως, ἰδού, μάγοι ἀπὸ ἀνατολῶν παρεγένοντο εἰς
Ἱεροσόλυμα, λέγοντες, Ποῦ ἐστιν ὁ τεχθεὶς βασιλεὺς τῶν Ἰουδαίων; 2
εἴδομεν γὰρ αὐτοῦ τὸν ἀστέρα ἐν τῇ ἀνατολῇ, καὶ ἤλθομεν προσκυνῆσαι
αὐτῷ. ἀκούσας δὲ ὁ βασιλεὺς Ἡρώδης ἐταράχθη, καὶ πᾶσα Ἱεροσόλυμα 3
μετ' αὐτοῦ· καὶ συναγαγὼν πάντας τοὺς ἀρχιερεῖς καὶ γραμματεῖς τοῦ λαοῦ 4
ἐπυνθάνετο παρ' αὐτῶν ποῦ ὁ Χριστὸς γεννᾶται. οἱ δὲ εἶπον αὐτῷ, Ἐν 5
Βηθλεὲμ τῆς Ἰουδαίας· οὕτω γὰρ γέγραπται διὰ τοῦ προφήτου, Καὶ σύ, 6
Βηθλεέμ, γῆ Ἰούδα, οὐδαμῶς ἐλαχίστη εἶ ἐν τοῖς ἡγεμόσιν Ἰούδα· ἐκ σοῦ
γὰρ ἐξελεύσεται ἡγούμενος, ὅστις ποιμανεῖ τὸν λαόν μου τὸν Ἰσραήλ.
ϛ̄ ι τότε Ἡρώδης λάθρα καλέσας τοὺς μάγους ἠκρίβωσε παρ' αὐτῶν τὸν 7

7 μαγους] αγους cod. per incuriam deauratoris

209 14 Αζωρ 209 ς Αχειμ bis ς 16 εγεννηθη] + Ιησους 209² ς
ς 18 γεννησις 209 ς της] pr γαρ ς om 209* sed spat. rel. in quo 209² γαρ
της scr. ευρεθη 209 ς 19 παραδειγματισαι 209 ς 20 Μαριαμ ς
22 του κυρ. 209 ς 24 διεγερθεις ς 25 τον υιον αυτης τον πρωτοτοκον 209 ς
1 om εν...βασιλεως 209* ins. 209² in marg. 3 Ηρωδης ο βασιλευς 209 ς

8 χρόνον τοῦ φαινομένου ἀστέρος, καὶ πέμψας αὐτοὺς εἰς Βηθλεὲμ εἶπε,
Πορευθέντες ἐξετάσατε ἀκριβῶς περὶ τοῦ παιδίου· ἐπὰν δὲ εὕρητε,
9 ἀπαγγείλατέ μοι, ὅπως κἀγὼ ἐλθὼν προσκυνήσω αὐτῷ. οἱ δὲ ἀκούσαντες
τοῦ βασιλέως ἐπορεύθησαν· καὶ ἰδού, ὁ ἀστήρ, ὃν εἶδον ἐν τῇ ἀνατολῇ,
10 προῆγεν αὐτούς, ἕως ἐλθὼν ἐστάθη ἐπάνω οὗ ἦν τὸ παιδίον. ἰδόντες δὲ
11 τὸν ἀστέρα ἐχάρησαν χαρὰν μεγάλην σφόδρα· καὶ ἐλθόντες εἰς τὴν οἰκίαν
εἶδον τὸ παιδίον μετὰ Μαρίας τῆς μητρὸς αὐτοῦ, καὶ πεσόντες προσεκύ-
νησαν αὐτῷ, καὶ ἀνοίξαντες τοὺς θησαυροὺς αὐτῶν προσήνεγκαν αὐτῷ δῶρα,
12 χρυσὸν καὶ λίβανον καὶ σμύρναν. καὶ χρηματισθέντες κατ' ὄναρ μὴ ἀνα-
κάμψαι πρὸς Ἡρώδην, δι' ἄλλης ὁδοῦ ἀνεχώρησαν εἰς τὴν ἑαυτῶν χώραν.
13 Ἀναχωρησάντων δὲ αὐτῶν, ἰδού, ἄγγελος Κυρίου φαίνεται κατ' ὄναρ
τῷ Ἰωσήφ, λέγων, Ἐγερθεὶς παράλαβε τὸ παιδίον καὶ τὴν μητέρα αὐτοῦ,
καὶ φεῦγε εἰς Αἴγυπτον, καὶ ἴσθι ἐκεῖ ἕως ἂν εἴπω σοι· μέλλει γὰρ
14 Ἡρώδης ζητεῖν τὸ παιδίον τοῦ ἀπολέσαι αὐτό. ὁ δὲ ἐγερθεὶς παρέλαβε τὸ
15 παιδίον καὶ τὴν μητέρα αὐτοῦ νυκτός, καὶ ἀνεχώρησεν εἰς Αἴγυπτον, καὶ ἦν
ἐκεῖ ἕως τῆς τελευτῆς Ἡρώδου· ἵνα πληρωθῇ τὸ ῥηθὲν ὑπὸ Κυρίου διὰ
16 τοῦ προφήτου, λέγοντος, Ἐξ Αἰγύπτου ἐκάλεσα τὸν υἱόν μου. τότε Β'
Ἡρώδης, ἰδὼν ὅτι ἐνεπαίχθη ὑπὸ τῶν μάγων, ἐθυμώθη λίαν, καὶ ἀποστείλας
ἀνεῖλε πάντας τοὺς παῖδας τοὺς ἐν Βηθλεὲμ καὶ ἐν πᾶσι τοῖς ὁρίοις αὐτῆς
ἀπὸ διετοῦς καὶ κατωτέρω, κατὰ τὸν χρόνον ὃν ἠκρίβωσε παρὰ τῶν μάγων.
17 18 τότε ἐπληρώθη τὸ ῥηθὲν ὑπὸ Ἱερεμίου τοῦ προφήτου, λέγοντος, Φωνὴ ἐν
Ῥαμᾶ ἠκούσθη, κλαυθμὸς καὶ ὀδυρμὸς πολύς, Ῥαχὴλ κλαίουσα τὰ τέκνα
19 αὐτῆς· καὶ οὐκ ἤθελε παρακληθῆναι, ὅτι οὐκ εἰσί. τελευτήσαντος δὲ τοῦ
Ἡρώδου, ἰδού, ἄγγελος Κυρίου φαίνεται κατ' ὄναρ τῷ Ἰωσὴφ ἐν
20 Αἰγύπτῳ, λέγων, Ἐγερθεὶς παράλαβε τὸ παιδίον καὶ τὴν μητέρα αὐτοῦ,
καὶ πορεύου εἰς γῆν Ἰσραήλ· τεθνήκασι γὰρ οἱ ζητοῦντες τὴν ψυχὴν τοῦ
21 παιδίου. ὁ δὲ ἐγερθεὶς παρέλαβε τὸ παιδίον καὶ τὴν μητέρα αὐτοῦ, καὶ
22 ἦλθεν εἰς γῆν Ἰσραήλ. ἀκούσας δὲ ὅτι Ἀρχέλαος βασιλεύει τῆς Ἰουδαίας
ἀντὶ Ἡρώδου τοῦ πατρὸς αὐτοῦ, ἐφοβήθη ἐκεῖ ἀπελθεῖν· χρηματισθεὶς δὲ
23 κατ' ὄναρ ἀνεχώρησεν εἰς τὰ μέρη τῆς Γαλιλαίας. καὶ ἐλθὼν κατῴκησεν
εἰς πόλιν λεγομένην Ναζαράθ· ὅπως πληρωθῇ τὸ ῥηθὲν διὰ τῶν προφητῶν,
Ὅτι Ναζωραῖος κληθήσεται.

III. Ἐν δὲ ταῖς ἡμέραις ἐκείναις παραγίνεται Ἰωάννης ὁ βαπτιστὴς Γ' ζ
2 κηρύσσων ἐν τῇ ἐρήμῳ τῆς Ἰουδαίας, καὶ λέγων, Μετανοεῖτε· ἤγγικε γὰρ γ
3 ἡ βασιλεία τῶν οὐρανῶν. οὗτος ἐστιν ὁ ῥηθεὶς διὰ Ἡσαΐου τοῦ η
προφήτου, λέγοντος, Φωνὴ βοῶντος ἐν τῇ ἐρήμῳ, Ἑτοιμάσατε τὴν ὁδὸν α

8 ακριβως εξετασατε ς 9 εστη ς 11 ευρον ς 12 χωραν 209
αυτων 209 ς 15 του Κυριου 209 ς 18 θρηνος και κλαυθμος 209 ς ς
19 κατ οναρ φαινεται ς 22 επι της ς 23 Ναζαρετ 209 ς
3 ουτος γαρ ς δια] υπο ς

θ̄ Κυρίου, εὐθείας ποιεῖτε τὰς τρίβους αὐτοῦ. αὐτὸς δὲ ὁ Ἰωάννης εἶχε 4
ς τὸ ἔνδυμα αὐτοῦ ἀπὸ τριχῶν καμήλου, καὶ ζώνην δερματίνην περὶ τὴν
ὀσφὺν αὐτοῦ· ἡ δὲ τροφὴ ἦν αὐτοῦ ἀκρίδες καὶ μέλι ἄγριον.
Τότε ἐξεπορεύετο πρὸς αὐτὸν πᾶσα ἡ Ἱεροσόλυμα καὶ πᾶσα ἡ Ἰουδαία 5
καὶ πᾶσα ἡ περίχωρος τοῦ Ἰορδάνου· καὶ ἐβαπτίζοντο ἐν τῷ Ἰορδάνῃ 6
ῑ ποταμῷ ὑπ' αὐτοῦ, ἐξομολογούμενοι τὰς ἁμαρτίας αὐτῶν. ἰδὼν δὲ 7
ε πολλοὺς τῶν Φαρισαίων καὶ Σαδδουκαίων ἐρχομένους ἐπὶ τὸ βάπτισμα
αὐτοῦ, εἶπεν αὐτοῖς, Γεννήματα ἐχιδνῶν, τίς ὑπέδειξεν ὑμῖν φυγεῖν ἀπὸ
τῆς μελλούσης ὀργῆς; ποιήσατε οὖν καρπὸν ἄξιον τῆς μετανοίας· 8
καὶ μὴ δόξητε λέγειν ἐν ἑαυτοῖς, ὅτι Πατέρα ἔχομεν τὸν Ἀβραάμ· λέγω 9
γὰρ ὑμῖν ὅτι δύναται ὁ Θεὸς ἐκ τῶν λίθων τούτων ἐγεῖραι τέκνα τῷ
Ἀβραάμ. ἤδη δὲ ἡ ἀξίνη πρὸς τὴν ῥίζαν τῶν δένδρων κεῖται· πᾶν οὖν 10
ῑα δένδρον μὴ ποιοῦν καρπὸν καλὸν ἐκκόπτεται καὶ εἰς πῦρ βάλλεται. ἐγὼ 11
α μὲν ὑμᾶς βαπτίζω ἐν ὕδατι εἰς μετάνοιαν· ὁ δὲ ὀπίσω μου ἐρχόμενος
ἰσχυρότερός μου ἐστίν, οὗ οὐκ εἰμὶ ἱκανὸς τὰ ὑποδήματα βαστάσαι. αὐτὸς
ῑβ ὑμᾶς βαπτίσει ἐν Πνεύματι Ἁγίῳ καὶ πυρί· οὗ τὸ πτύον ἐν τῇ χειρὶ αὐτοῦ, 12
ε καὶ διακαθαριεῖ τὴν ἅλωνα αὐτοῦ, καὶ συνάξει τὸν σῖτον αὐτοῦ εἰς τὴν
ἀποθήκην, τὸ δὲ ἄχυρον κατακαύσει πυρὶ ἀσβέστῳ.
ῑγ Τότε παραγίνεται ὁ Ἰησοῦς ἀπὸ τῆς Γαλιλαίας ἐπὶ τὸν Ἰορδάνην πρὸς 13
ι τὸν Ἰωάννην, τοῦ βαπτισθῆναι ὑπ' αὐτοῦ. ὁ δὲ Ἰωάννης διεκώλυεν αὐτόν, 14
λέγων, Ἐγὼ χρείαν ἔχω ὑπὸ σοῦ βαπτισθῆναι, καὶ σὺ ἔρχῃ πρός με;
ἀποκριθεὶς δὲ ὁ Ἰησοῦς εἶπε πρὸς αὐτόν, Ἄφες ἄρτι· οὕτω γὰρ πρέπον 15
ῑδ ἐστὶν ἡμῖν πληρῶσαι πᾶσαν δικαιοσύνην. τότε ἀφίησιν αὐτόν. καὶ 16
α βαπτισθεὶς ὁ Ἰησοῦς εὐθὺς ἀνέβη ἀπὸ τοῦ ὕδατος· καὶ ἰδού, ἀνεῴχθησαν
αὐτῷ οἱ οὐρανοί, καὶ εἶδε τὸ Πνεῦμα τοῦ Θεοῦ καταβαῖνον ὡσεὶ περιστεράν,
καὶ ἐρχόμενον ἐπ' αὐτόν. καὶ ἰδού, φωνὴ ἐκ τῶν οὐρανῶν λέγουσα, Οὗτός 17
ἐστιν ὁ υἱός μου ὁ ἀγαπητός, ἐν ᾧ εὐδόκησα.
ῑε IV. Τότε ὁ Ἰησοῦς ἀνήχθη εἰς τὴν ἔρημον ὑπὸ τοῦ Πνεύματος,
β πειρασθῆναι ὑπὸ τοῦ διαβόλου. καὶ νηστεύσας ἡμέρας τεσσαράκοντα 2
ῑς ε ὕστερον ἐπείνασε. καὶ προσελθὼν ὁ πειράζων εἶπεν αὐτῷ, Εἰ υἱὸς εἶ τοῦ 3
Θεοῦ, εἰπὲ ἵνα οἱ λίθοι οὗτοι ἄρτοι γένωνται. ὁ δὲ ἀποκριθεὶς εἶπε, 4
Γέγραπται, Οὐκ ἐπ' ἄρτῳ μόνῳ ζήσεται ὁ ἄνθρωπος, ἀλλ' ἐπὶ παντὶ
ῥήματι ἐκπορευομένῳ διὰ στόματος Θεοῦ. τότε παραλαμβάνει αὐτὸν ὁ 5
διάβολος εἰς τὴν ἁγίαν πόλιν, καὶ ἔστησεν αὐτὸν ἐπὶ τὸ πτερύγιον τοῦ

IV. **4** ο ante *ανθρωπος* nunc erasum est

209 **4** *αυτου ην* ς **5** om *πασα η* ς **6** om *ποταμω* ς **8** *καρπους*
ς *αξιους* ς **9** om *οτι* ς *'Αβρααμ* bis ς **10** *δε*] + *και* 209 ς
11 *βαπτιζω υμας* ς **16** *ανεβη ευθυς* ς

2 *τεσσαρακοντα*] + *και νυκτας τεσσαρακοντα* ς **3** *αυτω*] ante *ο πειρ.* ς
4 ο 2°] om ς **5** *ιστησιν* ς

6 ἱεροῦ, καὶ λέγει αὐτῷ, Εἰ υἱὸς εἶ τοῦ Θεοῦ, βάλε σεαυτὸν κάτω· γέγραπται
γάρ, Ὅτι τοῖς ἀγγέλοις αὐτοῦ ἐντελεῖται περὶ σοῦ, καὶ ἐπὶ χειρῶν ἀροῦσί
7 σε, μήποτε προσκόψῃς πρὸς λίθον τὸν πόδα σου. ἔφη αὐτῷ ὁ Ἰησοῦς,
8 Πάλιν γέγραπται, Οὐκ ἐκπειράσεις Κύριον τὸν Θεόν σου. πάλιν παρα-
λαμβάνει αὐτὸν ὁ διάβολος εἰς ὄρος ὑψηλὸν λίαν, καὶ δείκνυσιν αὐτῷ πάσας
9 τὰς βασιλείας τοῦ κόσμου καὶ τὴν δόξαν αὐτῶν, καὶ λέγει αὐτῷ, Ταῦτά
10 σοι πάντα δώσω, ἐὰν πεσὼν προσκυνήσῃς μοι. τότε λέγει αὐτῷ ὁ
Ἰησοῦς, Ὕπαγε Σατανᾶ· γέγραπται γάρ, Κύριον τὸν Θεόν σου προσκυ-
11 νήσεις, καὶ αὐτῷ μόνῳ λατρεύσεις. τότε ἀφίησιν αὐτὸν ὁ διάβολος· καὶ ιζ/ϛ
ἰδού, ἄγγελοι προσῆλθον καὶ διηκόνουν αὐτῷ.
12 Ἀκούσας δὲ ὁ Ἰησοῦς ὅτι Ἰωάννης παρεδόθη, ἀνεχώρησεν εἰς τὴν ιη/δ
13 Γαλιλαίαν· καὶ καταλιπὼν τὴν Ναζαρέθ, ἐλθὼν κατῴκησεν εἰς Καπερ- ιθ/ζ
14 ναοὺμ τὴν παραθαλασσίαν, ἐν ὁρίοις Ζαβουλὼν καὶ Νεφθαλείμ· ἵνα
15 πληρωθῇ τὸ ῥηθὲν διὰ Ἡσαΐου τοῦ προφήτου, λέγοντος· Γῆ Ζαβουλὼν καὶ
γῆ Νεφθαλείμ, ὁδὸν θαλάσσης πέραν τοῦ Ἰορδάνου, Γαλιλαία τῶν ἐθνῶν,
16 ὁ λαὸς ὁ καθήμενος ἐν σκότει φῶς εἶδε μέγα, καὶ τοῖς καθημένοις ἐν
χώρᾳ καὶ σκιᾷ θανάτου, φῶς ἀνέτειλεν αὐτοῖς.
17 Ἀπὸ τότε ἤρξατο ὁ Ἰησοῦς κηρύσσειν καὶ λέγειν, Μετανοεῖτε· ἤγγικε Δ′
18 γὰρ ἡ βασιλεία τῶν οὐρανῶν. περιπατῶν δὲ παρὰ τὴν θάλασσαν τῆς κ/ϛ
Γαλιλαίας εἶδε δύο ἀδελφούς, Σίμωνα τὸν λεγόμενον Πέτρον καὶ Ἀνδρέαν
τὸν ἀδελφὸν αὐτοῦ, βάλλοντας ἀμφίβληστρον εἰς τὴν θάλασσαν· ἦσαν
19 γὰρ ἁλιεῖς· καὶ λέγει αὐτοῖς, Δεῦτε ὀπίσω μου, καὶ ποιήσω ὑμᾶς ἁλιεῖς κα/β
20 21 ἀνθρώπων. οἱ δὲ εὐθέως ἀφέντες τὰ δίκτυα ἠκολούθησαν αὐτῷ. καὶ κβ/ϛ
προβὰς ἐκεῖθεν εἶδεν ἄλλους δύο ἀδελφούς, Ἰάκωβον τὸν τοῦ Ζεβεδαίου
καὶ Ἰωάννην τὸν ἀδελφὸν αὐτοῦ, ἐν τῷ πλοίῳ μετὰ Ζεβεδαίου τοῦ πατρὸς
22 αὐτῶν καταρτίζοντας τὰ δίκτυα αὐτῶν· καὶ ἐκάλεσεν αὐτούς. οἱ δὲ εὐθέως
ἀφέντες τὸ πλοῖον καὶ τὸν πατέρα αὐτῶν ἠκολούθησαν αὐτῷ.
23 Καὶ περιῆγεν ὁ Ἰησοῦς ὅλην τὴν Γαλιλαίαν, διδάσκων ἐν ταῖς κγ/α
συναγωγαῖς αὐτῶν καὶ κηρύσσων τὸ εὐαγγέλιον τῆς βασιλείας, καὶ
24 θεραπεύων πᾶσαν νόσον καὶ πᾶσαν μαλακίαν ἐν τῷ λαῷ. καὶ ἐξῆλθεν
ἡ ἀκοὴ αὐτοῦ εἰς ὅλην τὴν Συρίαν· καὶ προσήνεγκαν αὐτῷ πάντας τοὺς
κακῶς ἔχοντας, ποικίλαις νόσοις καὶ βασάνοις συνεχομένους καὶ δαιμονιζο-
μένους καὶ σεληνιαζομένους καὶ παραλυτικούς, καὶ ἐθεράπευσεν αὐτούς.
25 καὶ ἠκολούθησαν αὐτῷ ὄχλοι πολλοὶ ἀπὸ τῆς Γαλιλαίας καὶ Δεκαπόλεως
καὶ Ἱεροσολύμων καὶ Ἰουδαίας καὶ πέραν τοῦ Ἰορδάνου.
V. Ἰδὼν δὲ τοὺς ὄχλους ἀνέβη εἰς τὸ ὄρος· καὶ καθίσαντος αὐτοῦ, Ε′/κδ
2 προσῆλθον αὐτῷ οἱ μαθηταὶ αὐτοῦ· καὶ ἀνοίξας τὸ στόμα αὐτοῦ ἐδίδασκεν ι/κε/ε

9 παντα σοι ς **10** υπαγε] + οπισω μου 209 **13** Ναζαρετ 209 ς 209/ς
16 ειδε φως ς **18** δε] + ο Ιησους ς **23** ο Ιησους] post Γαλ. ς
24 απηλθεν ς

αὐτούς, λέγων, Μακάριοι οἱ πτωχοὶ τῷ πνεύματι· ὅτι αὐτῶν ἐστιν ἡ 3
κϛ βασιλεία τῶν οὐρανῶν. μακάριοι οἱ πενθοῦντες· ὅτι αὐτοὶ παρακλη- 4
ε κζ θήσονται. μακάριοι οἱ πραεῖς· ὅτι αὐτοὶ κληρονομήσουσι τὴν γῆν. 5
ι κη μακάριοι οἱ πεινῶντες καὶ διψῶντες τὴν δικαιοσύνην· ὅτι αὐτοὶ χορτασθή- 6
ε κθ σονται. μακάριοι οἱ ἐλεήμονες· ὅτι αὐτοὶ ἐλεηθήσονται. μακάριοι οἱ 7 8
ι καθαροὶ τῇ καρδίᾳ· ὅτι αὐτοὶ τὸν Θεὸν ὄψονται. μακάριοι οἱ εἰρηνοποιοί· 9
ὅτι αὐτοὶ υἱοὶ Θεοῦ κληθήσονται. μακάριοι οἱ δεδιωγμένοι ἕνεκεν δικαιο- 10
λ σύνης· ὅτι αὐτῶν ἐστιν ἡ βασιλεία τῶν οὐρανῶν. μακάριοί ἐστε, ὅταν 11
ε ὀνειδίσωσιν ὑμᾶς καὶ διώξωσι καὶ εἴπωσι πᾶν πονηρὸν ῥῆμα καθ' ὑμῶν
ψευδόμενοι, ἕνεκεν ἐμοῦ. χαίρετε καὶ ἀγαλλιᾶσθε, ὅτι ὁ μισθὸς ὑμῶν 12
πολὺς ἐν τοῖς οὐρανοῖς. οὕτως γὰρ ἐδίωξαν τοὺς προφήτας τοὺς πρὸ ὑμῶν.
λα Ὑμεῖς ἐστε τὸ ἅλας τῆς γῆς· ἐὰν δὲ τὸ ἅλας μωρανθῇ, ἐν τίνι 13
β ἁλισθήσεται; εἰς οὐδὲν ἰσχύει ἔτι, εἰ μὴ βληθὲν ἔξω καταπατεῖσθαι ὑπὸ
λβ τῶν ἀνθρώπων. ὑμεῖς ἐστε τὸ φῶς τοῦ κόσμου· οὐ δύναται πόλις κρυβῆναι 14
β ἐπάνω ὄρους κειμένη. οὐδὲ καίουσι λύχνον καὶ τιθέασιν αὐτὸν ὑπὸ τὸν 15
μόδιον, ἀλλ' ἐπὶ τὴν λυχνίαν, καὶ λάμπει πᾶσι τοῖς ἐν τῇ οἰκίᾳ. οὕτω 16
λαμψάτω τὸ φῶς ὑμῶν ἔμπροσθεν τῶν ἀνθρώπων, ὅπως ἴδωσιν ὑμῶν τὰ
καλὰ ἔργα, καὶ δοξάσωσι τὸν πατέρα ὑμῶν τὸν ἐν τοῖς οὐρανοῖς.
λγ Μὴ νομίσητε ὅτι ἦλθον καταλῦσαι τὸν νόμον ἢ τοὺς προφήτας· οὐκ 17
ι λδ ἦλθον καταλῦσαι, ἀλλὰ πληρῶσαι. ἀμὴν γὰρ λέγω ὑμῖν, ἕως ἂν παρέλθῃ 18
ε ὁ οὐρανὸς καὶ ἡ γῆ, ἰῶτα ἓν ἢ μία κεραία οὐ μὴ παρέλθῃ ἀπὸ τοῦ νόμου
λε ἕως ἂν πάντα γένηται. ὃς ἐὰν οὖν λύσῃ μίαν τῶν ἐντολῶν τούτων τῶν 19
ι ἐλαχίστων, καὶ διδάξῃ οὕτως τοὺς ἀνθρώπους, ἐλάχιστος κληθήσεται ἐν τῇ
βασιλείᾳ τῶν οὐρανῶν· ὃς δ' ἂν ποιήσῃ καὶ διδάξῃ, οὗτος μέγας κληθήσεται
ἐν τῇ βασιλείᾳ τῶν οὐρανῶν. λέγω γὰρ ὑμῖν ὅτι ἐὰν μὴ περισσεύσῃ ἡ 20
δικαιοσύνη ὑμῶν πλεῖον τῶν γραμματέων καὶ Φαρισαίων, οὐ μὴ εἰσέλθητε
εἰς τὴν βασιλείαν τῶν οὐρανῶν. ἠκούσατε ὅτι ἐρρέθη τοῖς ἀρχαίοις, Οὐ 21
φονεύσεις· ὃς δ' ἂν φονεύσῃ, ἔνοχος ἔσται τῇ κρίσει· ἐγὼ δὲ λέγω ὑμῖν ὅτι 22
πᾶς ὁ ὀργιζόμενος τῷ ἀδελφῷ αὐτοῦ εἰκῇ ἔνοχος ἔσται τῇ κρίσει· ὃς δ' ἂν
εἴπῃ τῷ ἀδελφῷ αὐτοῦ, Ῥακά, ἔνοχος ἔσται τῷ συνεδρίῳ· ὃς δ' ἂν εἴπῃ τῷ
ἀδελφῷ αὐτοῦ, Μωρέ, ἔνοχος ἔσται εἰς τὴν γέεναν τοῦ πυρός. ἐὰν 23
οὖν προσφέρῃς τὸ δῶρόν σου ἐπὶ τὸ θυσιαστήριον, καὶ ἐκεῖ μνησθῇς ὅτι ὁ
ἀδελφός σου ἔχει τι κατὰ σοῦ, ἄφες ἐκεῖ τὸ δῶρόν σου ἔμπροσθεν τοῦ 24
θυσιαστηρίου, καὶ ὕπαγε, πρῶτον διαλλάγηθι τῷ ἀδελφῷ σου, καὶ τότε
λϛ ἐλθὼν πρόσφερε τὸ δῶρόν σου. ἴσθι εὐνοῶν τῷ ἀντιδίκῳ σου ταχύ, ἕως 25
ε ὅτου εἶ μετ' αὐτοῦ ἐν τῇ ὁδῷ· μήποτέ σε παραδῷ ὁ ἀντίδικος τῷ κριτῇ,

209 ς 12 ουτω ς 13 βληθεν] βληθηναι et ins. και ante καταπ. ς 15 τη λυχνιαν 209* primum scripsit sed ipse, errore detecto, ν post τη addidit et accentum mutavit 19 ουτω ς 22 om τω αδελφω αυτου 3° ς γεενναν 209 ς 23 κακει ς 25 εν τη οδω μετ αυτου ς

26 καὶ ὁ κριτὴς τῷ ὑπηρέτῃ, καὶ εἰς φυλακὴν βληθήσῃ. ἀμὴν λέγω σοι, οὐ
27 μὴ ἐξέλθῃς ἐκεῖθεν, ἕως ἂν ἀποδῷς τὸν ἔσχατον κοδράντην. ἠκούσατε ὅτι λς
28 ἐρρέθη Οὐ μοιχεύσεις· ἐγὼ δὲ λέγω ὑμῖν ὅτι πᾶς ὁ βλέπων γυναῖκα πρὸς ι
29 τὸ ἐπιθυμῆσαι αὐτῆς ἤδη ἐμοίχευσεν αὐτὴν ἐν τῇ καρδίᾳ αὐτοῦ. εἰ δὲ ὁ
ὀφθαλμός σου ὁ δεξιὸς σκανδαλίζει σε, ἔξελε αὐτὸν καὶ βάλε ἀπὸ σοῦ·
συμφέρει γάρ σοι ἵνα ἀπόληται ἓν τῶν μελῶν σου, καὶ μὴ ὅλον τὸ σῶμά
30 σου βληθῇ εἰς γέενναν. καὶ εἰ ἡ δεξιά σου χεὶρ σκανδαλίζει σε, ἔκκοψον
αὐτὴν καὶ βάλε ἀπὸ σοῦ· συμφέρει γάρ σοι ἵνα ἀπόληται ἓν τῶν μελῶν
31 σου, καὶ μὴ ὅλον τὸ σῶμά σου εἰς γέενναν ἀπέλθῃ. ἐρρήθη δὲ Ὃς ἂν
32 ἀπολύσῃ τὴν γυναῖκα αὐτοῦ, δότω αὐτῇ ἀποστάσιον· ἐγὼ δὲ λέγω ὑμῖν ὅτι
πᾶς ὁ ἀπολύων τὴν γυναῖκα αὐτοῦ, παρεκτὸς λόγου πορνείας, ποιεῖ
33 αὐτὴν μοιχευθῆναι· καὶ ὃς ἐὰν ἀπολελυμένην γαμήσῃ, μοιχᾶται. πάλιν
ἠκούσατε ὅτι ἐρρέθη τοῖς ἀρχαίοις, Οὐκ ἐπιορκήσεις, ἀποδώσεις δὲ Κυρίῳ
34 τοὺς ὅρκους σου· ἐγὼ δὲ λέγω ὑμῖν μὴ ὀμόσαι ὅλως, μήτε ἐν τῷ οὐρανῷ,
35 ὅτι θρόνος ἐστὶ τοῦ Θεοῦ· μήτε ἐν τῇ γῇ, ὅτι ὑποπόδιόν ἐστι τῶν ποδῶν
36 αὐτοῦ· μήτε εἰς Ἱεροσόλυμα, ὅτι πόλις ἐστὶ τοῦ μεγάλου βασιλέως· μήτε
ἐν τῇ κεφαλῇ σου ὀμόσῃς, ὅτι οὐ δύνασαι ποιῆσαι μίαν τρίχα λευκὴν ἢ
37 μέλαιναν. ἔστω δὲ ὁ λόγος ὑμῶν, ναὶ ναί, οὒ οὔ· τὸ δὲ περισσὸν τούτου
38 ἐκ τοῦ πονηροῦ ἐστιν. ἠκούσατε ὅτι ἐρρέθη, Ὀφθαλμὸν ἀντὶ ὀφθαλμοῦ,
39 καὶ ὀδόντα ἀντὶ ὀδόντος· ἐγὼ δὲ λέγω ὑμῖν μὴ ἀντιστῆναι τῷ πονηρῷ· λη
ἀλλ' ὅστις σε ῥαπίσει ἐπὶ τὴν δεξιὰν σιαγόνα, στρέψον αὐτῷ καὶ τὴν ε
40 ἄλλην· καὶ τῷ θέλοντί σοι κριθῆναι καὶ τὸν χιτῶνά σου λαβεῖν, ἄφες
41 αὐτῷ καὶ τὸ ἱμάτιον· καὶ ὅστις σε ἀγγαρεύσει μίλιον ἕν, ὕπαγε μετ' αὐτοῦ λθ
42 δύο. τῷ αἰτοῦντί σε δίδου· καὶ τὸν θέλοντα ἀπὸ σοῦ δανείσασθαι μὴ ι
43 ἀποστραφῇς. ἠκούσατε ὅτι ἐρρέθη, Ἀγαπήσεις τὸν πλησίον σου, καὶ
44 μισήσεις τὸν ἐχθρόν σου· ἐγὼ δὲ λέγω ὑμῖν, ἀγαπᾶτε τοὺς ἐχθροὺς ὑμῶν, μ
45 καὶ προσεύχεσθε ὑπὲρ τῶν διωκόντων ὑμᾶς· ὅπως γένησθε υἱοὶ τοῦ ε
πατρὸς ὑμῶν τοῦ ἐν οὐρανοῖς, ὅτι τὸν ἥλιον αὐτοῦ ἀνατέλλει ἐπὶ
46 πονηροὺς καὶ ἀγαθούς, καὶ βρέχει ἐπὶ δικαίους καὶ ἀδίκους. ἐὰν γὰρ μα
ἀγαπήσητε τοὺς ἀγαπῶντας ὑμᾶς, τίνα μισθὸν ἔχετε; οὐχὶ καὶ οἱ τελῶναι ε
47 τοῦτο ποιοῦσι; καὶ ἐὰν ἀσπάσησθε τοὺς ἀδελφοὺς ὑμῶν μόνον, τί
48 περισσὸν ποιεῖτε; οὐχὶ καὶ οἱ ἐθνικοὶ τὸ αὐτὸ ποιοῦσιν; ἔσεσθε οὖν
ὑμεῖς τέλειοι, ὡς ὁ πατὴρ ὑμῶν ὁ οὐράνιος τέλειός ἐστι.

25 κριτης] + σε παραδω ς **27** ερρεθη] + τοις αρχαιοις ς **29** κανδαλιζει 209 209 ς **30** βληθη εις γεενναν ς **31** ερρεθη ς ος] pr οτι ς **32** ος αν απολυση ς μοιχασθαι ς **33** τω Κυριω ς **36** ποιησαι post μελαιν. ς **37** ναί, ναί· οὔ, οὔ· 209 τουτων ς **39** δεξιαν] + σου ς **44** υμων] ημων 209, + ευλογειτε τους καταρωμενους υμας, καλως ποιειτε τους μισουντας υμας, ς διωκοντων] pr επηρεαζοντων υμας, και ς **45** υμων] ημων 209 ουρανοις] pr τοις 209 και 2°] bis 209 **46** το αυτο ς **47** τελωναι ουτω ς **48** ωσπερ ς ο εν τοις ουρανοις ς

μβ VI. Προσέχετε δὲ τὴν δικαιοσύνην ὑμῶν μὴ ποιεῖν ἔμπροσθεν τῶν
ι ἀνθρώπων, πρὸς τὸ θεαθῆναι αὐτοῖς· εἰ δὲ μήγε, μισθὸν οὐκ ἔχετε παρὰ
τῷ πατρὶ ὑμῶν τῷ ἐν οὐρανοῖς. ὅταν οὖν ποιῇς ἐλεημοσύνην, μὴ 2
σαλπίσῃς ἔμπροσθέν σου, ὥσπερ οἱ ὑποκριταὶ ποιοῦσιν ἐν ταῖς συναγωγαῖς
καὶ ἐν ταῖς ῥύμαις, ὅπως δοξασθῶσιν ὑπὸ τῶν ἀνθρώπων· ἀμὴν λέγω ὑμῖν,
ἀπέχουσι τὸν μισθὸν αὐτῶν. σοῦ δὲ ποιοῦντος ἐλεημοσύνην, μὴ γνώτω 3
ἡ ἀριστερά σου τί ποιεῖ ἡ δεξιά σου, ὅπως ᾖ σου ἡ ἐλεημοσύνη ἐν τῷ 4
κρυπτῷ· καὶ ὁ πατήρ σου ὁ βλέπων ἐν τῷ κρυπτῷ αὐτὸς ἀποδώσει σοι.
καὶ ὅταν προσεύχησθε, οὐκ ἔσεσθε ὥσπερ οἱ ὑποκριταί, ὅτι φιλοῦσιν 5
ἐν ταῖς συναγωγαῖς καὶ ἐν ταῖς γωνίαις τῶν πλατειῶν ἑστῶτες προσεύχεσθαι,
ὅπως φανῶσι τοῖς ἀνθρώποις· ἀμὴν λέγω ὑμῖν ἀπέχουσι τὸν μισθὸν
αὐτῶν. σὺ δὲ ὅταν προσεύχῃ, εἴσελθε εἰς τὸ ταμιεῖόν σου, καὶ κλείσας 6
τὴν θύραν σου πρόσευξαι τῷ πατρί σου ἐν τῷ κρυπτῷ· καὶ ὁ πατήρ σου ὁ
μγ βλέπων ἐν τῷ κρυπτῷ ἀποδώσει σοι. προσευχόμενοι δὲ μὴ βαττολο- 7
ε γήσητε, ὥσπερ οἱ ἐθνικοί· δοκοῦσι γὰρ ὅτι ἐν τῇ πολυλογίᾳ αὐτῶν
εἰσακουσθήσονται. μὴ οὖν ὁμοιωθῆτε αὐτοῖς· οἶδε γὰρ ὁ πατὴρ ἡμῶν ὧν 8
χρείαν ἔχετε, πρὸ τοῦ ὑμᾶς αἰτῆσαι αὐτόν. οὕτως οὖν προσεύχεσθε ὑμεῖς· 9
Πάτερ ἡμῶν ὁ ἐν τοῖς οὐρανοῖς, ἁγιασθήτω τὸ ὄνομά σου· ἐλθέτω ἡ 10
βασιλεία σου· γενηθήτω τὸ θέλημά σου, ὡς ἐν οὐρανῷ καὶ ἐπὶ γῆς· τὸν 11
ἄρτον ἡμῶν τὸν ἐπιούσιον δὸς ἡμῖν σήμερον· καὶ ἄφες ἡμῖν τὰ ὀφειλή- 12
ματα ἡμῶν, ὡς καὶ ἡμεῖς ἀφήκαμεν τοῖς ὀφειλέταις ἡμῶν· καὶ μὴ 13
μδ εἰσενέγκῃς ἡμᾶς εἰς πειρασμόν, ἀλλὰ ῥῦσαι ἡμᾶς ἀπὸ τοῦ πονηροῦ. ἐὰν 14
ϛ γὰρ ἀφῆτε τοῖς ἀνθρώποις τὰ παραπτώματα αὐτῶν, ἀφήσει καὶ ὑμῖν ὁ
πατὴρ ὑμῶν ὁ οὐράνιος· ἐὰν δὲ μὴ ἀφῆτε τοῖς ἀνθρώποις, οὐδὲ ὁ πατὴρ 15
με ὑμῶν ἀφήσει τὰ παραπτώματα ὑμῶν. ὅταν δὲ νηστεύητε, μὴ γίνεσθε ὡς οἱ 16
ι ὑποκριταὶ σκυθρωποί· ἀφανίζουσι γὰρ τὰ πρόσωπα αὐτῶν, ὅπως φανῶσι τοῖς
ἀνθρώποις νηστεύοντες· ἀμὴν λέγω ὑμῖν ἀπέχουσι τὸν μισθὸν αὐτῶν. σὺ 17
δὲ νηστεύων ἄλειψαί σου τὴν κεφαλὴν καὶ τὸ πρόσωπόν σου νίψαι, ὅπως 18
μὴ φανῇς τοῖς ἀνθρώποις νηστεύων, ἀλλὰ τῷ πατρί σου τῷ ἐν τῷ κρυφαίῳ·
καὶ ὁ πατήρ σου ὁ βλέπων ἐν τῷ κρυφαίῳ ἀποδώσει σοι.

μϛ Μὴ θησαυρίζετε ὑμῖν θησαυροὺς ἐπὶ τῆς γῆς, ὅπου σὴς καὶ βρῶσις 19
ε ἀφανίζει, καὶ ὅπου κλέπται διορύσσουσι καὶ κλέπτουσι· θησαυρίζετε 20

118 209 ϛ 1 om δε ϛ ελεημοσυνην ϛ τοις ουρανοις 209 ϛ 3 σου] hoc verbo inc. 118 4 σοι]+εν τω φανερω ϛ 5 προσευχη ϛ εση ϛ οπως] +αν ϛ απεχουσι] pr οτι ϛ 6 θυρα 118 σου]+τω 118 209 ϛ σοι] +εν τω φανερω 118[2] ϛ 8 υμων ϛ 10 γης] pr της 118 209 ϛ 12 αφιεμεν 118 209 ϛ 13 ad fin. vers. add. οτι σου εστιν η βασιλεια και η δυναμις και η δοξα εις τους αιωνας 118[2] ϛ, et add. αμην ϛ 14 γαρ punctis rubris delet. 118 υμων] ημων 118 15 ανθρωποις]+τα παραπτωματα αυτων ϛ 16 ωσπερ ϛ υμιν]+οτι ϛ 17 σου 2°] om 118 209 18 κρυπτω bis 118 209 ϛ σοι]+εν τω φανερω 118 209 ϛ 19 θησαυριζητε 209 κλαιπτουσι 118

δὲ ὑμῖν θησαυροὺς ἐν οὐρανῷ, ὅπου οὔτε σὴς οὔτε βρῶσις ἀφανίζει, καὶ
21 ὅπου κλέπται οὐ διορύσσουσιν καὶ κλέπτουσιν. ὅπου γάρ ἐστιν ὁ
22 θησαυρὸς ὑμῶν, ἐκεῖ ἔσται καὶ ἡ καρδία ὑμῶν. ὁ λύχνος τοῦ σώματός μς ε
ἐστιν ὁ ὀφθαλμός· ἐὰν οὖν ὁ ὀφθαλμός σου ἁπλοῦς ᾖ, ὅλον τὸ σῶμά σου
23 φωτεινὸν ἔσται· ἐὰν δὲ ὁ ὀφθαλμός σου πονηρὸς ᾖ, ὅλον τὸ σῶμά σου
σκοτεινὸν ἔσται. εἰ οὖν τὸ φῶς τὸ ἐν σοὶ σκότος ἐστὶ, τὸ σκότος πόσον;
24 οὐδεὶς δύναται δυσὶ κυρίοις δουλεύειν· ἢ γὰρ τὸν ἕνα μισήσει καὶ τὸν μη ε
ἕτερον ἀγαπήσει, ἢ ἑνὸς ἀνθέξεται καὶ τοῦ ἑτέρου καταφρονήσει· οὐ
25 δύνασθε Θεῷ δουλεύειν καὶ μαμωνᾶ. διὰ τοῦτο λέγω ὑμῖν, μὴ μθ ε
μεριμνᾶτε τῇ ψυχῇ ὑμῶν, τί φάγητε, μηδὲ τῷ σώματι ὑμῶν, τί
ἐνδύσησθε. οὐχὶ ἡ ψυχὴ πλεῖόν ἐστι τῆς τροφῆς, καὶ τὸ σῶμα τοῦ
26 ἐνδύματος; ἐμβλέψατε εἰς τὰ πετεινὰ τοῦ οὐρανοῦ, ὅτι οὐ σπείρουσιν
οὐδὲ θερίζουσιν οὐδὲ συνάγουσιν εἰς ἀποθήκας, καὶ ὁ πατὴρ ὑμῶν ὁ
27 οὐράνιος τρέφει αὐτά· οὐχ ὑμεῖς μᾶλλον διαφέρετε αὐτῶν; τίς δὲ ἐξ
28 ὑμῶν μεριμνῶν δύναται προσθεῖναι ἐπὶ τὴν ἡλικίαν αὐτοῦ πῆχυν ἕνα; καὶ
περὶ ἐνδύματος τί μεριμνᾶτε; καταμάθετε τὰ κρίνα τοῦ ἀγροῦ, πῶς
29 αὐξάνουσι· οὐ κοπιῶσι οὐδὲ νήθουσι· λέγω δὲ ὑμῖν ὅτι οὐδὲ Σολομὼν
30 ἐν πάσῃ τῇ δόξῃ αὐτοῦ περιεβάλετο ὡς ἓν τούτων. εἰ δὲ τὸν χόρτον τοῦ
ἀγροῦ, σήμερον ὄντα, καὶ αὔριον εἰς κλίβανον βαλλόμενον, ὁ Θεὸς οὕτως
31 ἀμφιέννυσιν, οὐ πολλῷ μᾶλλον ὑμᾶς, ὀλιγόπιστοι; μὴ οὖν μεριμνήσητε,
32 λέγοντες, Τί φάγωμεν, ἢ τί πίωμεν, ἢ τί περιβαλώμεθα; πάντα γὰρ
ταῦτα τὰ ἔθνη ἐπιζητοῦσι· οἶδε γὰρ ὁ πατὴρ ὑμῶν ὁ οὐράνιος ὅτι
33 χρῄζετε τούτων ἁπάντων· ζητεῖτε δὲ πρῶτον τὴν βασιλείαν τοῦ Θεοῦ καὶ
34 τὴν δικαιοσύνην αὐτοῦ, καὶ ταῦτα πάντα προστεθήσεται ὑμῖν· μὴ οὖν
μεριμνήσητε εἰς τὴν αὔριον· ἡ γὰρ αὔριον μεριμνήσει τὰ ἑαυτῆς. ἀρκετὸν
τῇ ἡμέρᾳ ἡ κακία αὐτῆς.
2 VII. Μὴ κρίνετε, ἵνα μὴ κριθῆτε· ἐν ᾧ γὰρ κρίματι κρίνετε, κρι- ν β
3 θήσεσθε· καὶ ἐν ᾧ μέτρῳ μετρεῖτε, μετρηθήσεται ὑμῖν. τί δὲ βλέπεις να
τὸ κάρφος τὸ ἐν τῷ ὀφθαλμῷ τοῦ ἀδελφοῦ σου, τὴν δὲ ἐν τῷ σῷ ὀφθαλμῷ ε
4 δοκὸν οὐ κατανοεῖς; ἢ πῶς ἐρεῖς τῷ ἀδελφῷ σου, Ἄφες ἐκβάλω τὸ
κάρφος ἐκ τοῦ ὀφθαλμοῦ σου· καὶ ἰδού, ἡ δοκὸς ἐν τῷ ὀφθαλμῷ σου;
5 ὑποκριτά, ἔκβαλε πρῶτον τὴν δοκὸν ἐκ τοῦ ὀφθαλμοῦ σου, καὶ
τότε διαβλέψεις ἐκβαλεῖν τὸ κάρφος ἐκ τοῦ ὀφθαλμοῦ τοῦ ἀδελφοῦ σου.
6 μὴ δότε τὸ ἅγιον τοῖς κυσί· μηδὲ βάλητε τοὺς μαργαρίτας ὑμῶν νβ ι

20 και] ουδε ϛ **24** μαμμωνα ϛ **25** φαγητε]+η τι πιητε 118 209, +και τι πιητε ϛ **28** αυξανει ϛ κοπια ϛ νηθει ϛ **30** ἴδε 118 209* sed εἰ δὲ (hoc accentu) 209[2] **31** μεριμνησετε 118 209 περιβαλλωμεθα 118 209 **32** επιζητει ϛ 118 209 ϛ

2 αντιμετρηθησεται ϛ **4** εκ] απο ϛ **4...5**] και...σου om 118* sed ins. 118[2] in mg. **6** δωτε ϛ τα αγια 118 209 μαργαριτ 118 sp. rel. in quo m. s. litt. rubr. ας scripsit

ἔμπροσθεν τῶν χοίρων, μήποτε καταπατήσωσιν αὐτοὺς τοῖς ποσὶν αὐτῶν,
νγ ε καὶ στραφέντες ῥήξωσιν ὑμᾶς. αἰτεῖτε, καὶ δοθήσεται ὑμῖν· ζητεῖτε, καὶ 7
εὑρήσετε· κρούετε, καὶ ἀνοιγήσεται ὑμῖν. πᾶς γὰρ ὁ αἰτῶν λαμβάνει, 8
καὶ ὁ ζητῶν εὑρίσκει, καὶ τῷ κρούοντι ἀνοιγήσεται. ἢ τίς ἐστιν ἐξ ὑμῶν 9
ἄνθρωπος, ὃν ἐὰν αἰτήσῃ ὁ υἱὸς αὐτοῦ ἄρτον, μὴ λίθον ἐπιδώσει αὐτῷ; ἢ 10
καὶ ἰχθὺν αἰτήσῃ, μὴ ὄφιν ἐπιδώσει αὐτῷ; εἰ οὖν ὑμεῖς, πονηροὶ ὄντες, 11
οἴδατε ἀγαθὰ δόματα διδόναι τοῖς τέκνοις ὑμῶν, πόσῳ μᾶλλον ὁ πατὴρ
νδ ε ὑμῶν ὁ ἐν τοῖς οὐρανοῖς δώσει ἀγαθὰ τοῖς αἰτοῦσιν αὐτόν; πάντα οὖν 12
ὅσ' ἂν θέλητε ἵνα ποιῶσιν ὑμῖν οἱ ἄνθρωποι, οὕτως καὶ ὑμεῖς ποιεῖτε
αὐτοῖς· οὗτος γάρ ἐστιν ὁ νόμος καὶ οἱ προφῆται.

νε ε Εἰσέλθετε διὰ τῆς στενῆς πύλης· ὅτι πλατεῖα ἡ πύλη καὶ εὐρύχωρος ἡ 13
ὁδὸς ἡ ἀπάγουσα εἰς τὴν ἀπώλειαν, καὶ πολλοί εἰσιν οἱ εἰσπορευόμενοι
δι' αὐτῆς· τί στενὴ ἡ πύλη καὶ τεθλιμμένη ἡ ὁδὸς ἡ ἀπάγουσα εἰς τὴν 14
νϛ ι ζωήν, καὶ ὀλίγοι εἰσὶν οἱ εὑρίσκοντες αὐτήν. προσέχετε δὲ ἀπὸ τῶν 15
ψευδοπροφητῶν, οἵτινες ἔρχονται πρὸς ὑμᾶς ἐν ἐνδύμασι προβάτων, ἔσωθεν
νζ ε δέ εἰσι λύκοι ἅρπαγες. ἀπὸ τῶν καρπῶν αὐτῶν ἐπιγνώσεσθε αὐτούς· 16
νη ε μήτι συλλέγουσιν ἀπὸ ἀκανθῶν σταφυλὰς ἢ ἀπὸ τριβόλων σῦκα; οὕτως 17
πᾶν δένδρον ἀγαθὸν καρποὺς καλοὺς ποιεῖ, τὸ δὲ σαπρὸν δένδρον καρποὺς
πονηροὺς ποιεῖ· οὐ δύναται δένδρον ἀγαθὸν καρποὺς πονηροὺς ποιεῖν, οὐδὲ 18
δένδρον σαπρὸν καρποὺς καλοὺς ποιεῖν. πᾶν δένδρον μὴ ποιοῦν καρπὸν 19
καλὸν ἐκκόπτεται καὶ εἰς πῦρ βάλλεται. ἄραγε ἀπὸ τῶν καρπῶν αὐτῶν 20
ἐπιγνώσεσθε αὐτούς.

νθ γ Οὐ πᾶς ὁ λέγων μοι, Κύριε, κύριε, εἰσελεύσεται εἰς τὴν βασιλείαν τῶν 21
οὐρανῶν· ἀλλ' ὁ ποιῶν τὸ θέλημα τοῦ πατρός μου τοῦ ἐν τοῖς οὐρανοῖς.
ξ ε πολλοὶ ἐροῦσί μοι ἐν ἐκείνῃ τῇ ἡμέρᾳ, κύριε, κύριε, οὐ τῷ σῷ ὀνόματι 22
προεφητεύσαμεν, καὶ τῷ σῷ ὀνόματι δαιμόνια ἐξεβάλομεν, καὶ τῷ σῷ
ὀνόματι δυνάμεις πολλὰς ἐποιήσαμεν; καὶ τότε ὁμολογήσω αὐτοῖς ὅτι 23
Οὐδέποτε ἔγνων ὑμᾶς· ἀποχωρεῖτε ἀπ' ἐμοῦ οἱ ἐργαζόμενοι τὴν ἀνομίαν.
ξα ε πᾶς οὖν ὅστις ἀκούει μου τοὺς λόγους τούτους καὶ ποιεῖ αὐτούς, ὁμοιω- 24
θήσεται αὐτὸν ἀνδρὶ φρονίμῳ, ὅστις ᾠκοδόμησε αὐτοῦ τὴν οἰκίαν ἐπὶ
τὴν πέτραν· καὶ κατέβη ἡ βροχὴ καὶ ἦλθον οἱ ποταμοὶ καὶ ἔπνευσαν οἱ 25
ἄνεμοι, καὶ προσέπεσαν τῇ οἰκίᾳ ἐκείνῃ, καὶ οὐκ ἔπεσεν· τεθεμελίωτο
γὰρ ἐπὶ τὴν πέτραν. καὶ πᾶς ὁ ἀκούων μου τοὺς λόγους τούτους καὶ μὴ 26

14 *τι*] corr. pr *ο* ita ut *οτι* scriberet **24** *τουτους*] *τοτους* cod.

118 209 ϛ **6** *εν τοις* ϛ **7** *ζητητε* 118 **9** *εστιν*] om 118 **10** *η και*] *και εαν* ϛ **11** *δοματα αγαθα* ϛ **12** *οσα* 209 ϛ *ουτω* ϛ **13** *οτι*] *και τι* 118* sed *οτι* 118[2] *εισερχομενοι* ϛ **14** *τι*] *και* 209, *οτι* ϛ, spat. rel. 118* in quo 118[2] *οτι* scripsit **15** *εσοθεν* 118 209 **16** *σταφυλην* ϛ **17** *ουτω* ϛ **21** om *τοις* ϛ **24** *ομοιωσω αυτον* ϛ *την οικιαν αυτου* 118 209 ϛ **25** *προσεπεσον* ϛ

ποιῶν αὐτοὺς ὁμοιωθήσεται ἀνδρὶ μωρῷ, ὅστις ᾠκοδόμησε αὐτοῦ τὴν
27 οἰκίαν ἐπὶ τὴν ἄμμον· καὶ κατέβη ἡ βροχὴ καὶ ἦλθον οἱ ποταμοὶ καὶ
ἔπνευσαν οἱ ἄνεμοι, καὶ προσέρρηξαν τῇ οἰκίᾳ ἐκείνῃ, καὶ ἔπεσεν· καὶ
28 ἦν ἡ πτῶσις αὐτῆς μεγάλη. καὶ ἐγένετο ὅτε ἐτέλεσεν ὁ Ἰησοῦς τοὺς ξβ
29 λόγους τούτους, ἐξεπλήσοντο πάντες οἱ ὄχλοι ἐπὶ τῇ διδαχῇ αὐτοῦ· ἦν β
γὰρ διδάσκων αὐτοὺς ὡς ἐξουσίαν ἔχων, καὶ οὐχ ὡς οἱ γραμματεῖς αὐτῶν.
VIII. Καταβάντος δὲ αὐτοῦ ἀπὸ τοῦ ὄρους, ἠκολούθησαν αὐτῷ ϛ'
2 ὄχλοι πολλοί· καὶ ἰδού, λεπρὸς προσελθὼν προσεκύνει αὐτῷ, λέγων, ξγ β
3 Κύριε, ἐὰν θέλῃς, δύνασαί με καθαρίσαι. καὶ ἐκτείνας τὴν χεῖρα ἥψατο
αὐτοῦ λέγων, Θέλω, καθαρίσθητι. καὶ εὐθέως ἐκαθαρίσθη αὐτοῦ ἡ
4 λέπρα. καὶ λέγει αὐτῷ ὁ Ἰησοῦς, Μηδενὶ εἴπῃς· ἀλλ' ὕπαγε, σεαυτὸν
δεῖξον τῷ ἱερεῖ, καὶ προσένεγκε τὸ δῶρον ὃ προσέταξε Μωσῆς, εἰς
μαρτύριον αὐτοῖς.
5 Εἰσελθόντος δὲ αὐτοῦ εἰς Καπερναοὺμ προσῆλθεν αὐτῷ ἑκατόν- Ζ' ξδ
6 ταρχος παρακαλῶν αὐτόν, καὶ λέγων, Κύριε, ὁ παῖς μου βέβληται ἐν τῇ γ
7 οἰκίᾳ παραλυτικός, δεινῶς βασανιζόμενος. καὶ λέγει αὐτῷ ὁ Ἰησοῦς, Ἐγὼ
8 ἐλθὼν θεραπεύσω αὐτόν. καὶ ἀποκριθεὶς ὁ ἑκατόνταρχος ἔφη, Κύριε, οὐκ
εἰμὶ ἱκανὸς ἵνα μου ὑπὸ τὴν στέγην εἰσέλθῃς· ἀλλὰ μόνον εἰπὲ λόγῳ, καὶ
9 ἰαθήσεται· καὶ γὰρ ἐγὼ ἄνθρωπός εἰμι ὑπὸ ἐξουσίαν, ἔχων ὑπ' ἐμαυτὸν
στρατιώτας· καὶ λέγω τούτῳ, Πορεύθητι, καὶ πορεύεται· καὶ ἄλλῳ, Ἔρχου,
10 καὶ ἔρχεται· καὶ τῷ δούλῳ μου, Ποίησον τοῦτο, καὶ ποιεῖ. ἀκούσας δὲ ὁ
Ἰησοῦς ἐθαύμασε, καὶ εἶπε τοῖς ἀκολουθοῦσιν, Ἀμὴν λέγω ὑμῖν, παρ'
11 οὐδενὶ τοσαύτην πίστιν εὗρον. λέγω δὲ ὑμῖν πολλοὶ ἀπὸ ἀνατολῶν ξε
καὶ δυσμῶν ἥξουσι καὶ ἀνακλιθήσονται μετὰ Ἀβραὰμ καὶ Ἰσαὰκ καὶ ε
12 Ἰακὼβ ἐν τῇ βασιλείᾳ τῶν οὐρανῶν· οἱ δὲ υἱοὶ τῆς βασιλείας ἐκβλη-
θήσονται εἰς τὸ σκότος τὸ ἐξώτερον· ἐκεῖ ἔσται ὁ κλαυθμὸς καὶ ὁ
13 βρυγμὸς τῶν ὀδόντων. καὶ εἶπεν ὁ Ἰησοῦς τῷ ἑκατοντάρχῳ, Ὕπαγε, καὶ ξϛ
ὡς ἐπίστευσας γενηθήτω σοι. καὶ ἰάθη ὁ παῖς ἐν τῇ ὥρᾳ ἐκείνῃ. καὶ ε
ὑποστρέψας ὁ ἑκατόνταρχος εἰς τὸν οἶκον αὐτοῦ ἐν αὐτῇ τῇ
ὥρᾳ εὗρεν τὸν παῖδα ὑγιαίνοντα.

4 μηδενι] pr ορ 1* sed eras.

26 την οικιαν αυτου 118 209 ϛ 27 ο ποταμοι 118 προσεκοψαν ϛ 118 209 ϛ
28 συνετελεσεν ϛ τους] ους 118*, τους 118[2] εξεπλησσοντο 118 209 ϛ
om παντες ϛ 29 om αυτων ϛ, delevit rubricator 118
1 καταβαντι ϛ αυτω ϛ 2 ελθων ϛ 3 λεγων] pr ο Ιησους ϛ
4 μηδενι] pr ορα 118 209 ϛ αλλα ϛ 5 εισελθοντι δε τω Ιησου ϛ
8 λογον ϛ ιαθησεται]+ο παις μου ϛ 10 παρ ουδενι] παρ om 118* sed
spat. rel., add. in mg. εν τω ιηλ 118[2], ουδε εν τω Ισραηλ ϛ 11 υμιν]+οτι ϛ
'Αβρααμ ϛ 12 εμβληθησονται 118 209 13 παις]+αυτου ϛ
και υποστρ....υγιαινοντα] om ϛ

Η' Καὶ ἐλθὼν ὁ Ἰησοῦς εἰς τὴν οἰκίαν Πέτρου εἶδε τὴν πενθερὰν αὐτοῦ 14
ξζ β βεβλημένην καὶ πυρέσσουσαν· καὶ ἥψατο τῆς χειρὸς αὐτῆς, καὶ ἀφῆκεν 15
Θ' αὐτὴν ὁ πυρετός, καὶ ἠγέρθη καὶ διηκόνει αὐτοῖς. ὀψίας δὲ γενομένης 16
προσήνεγκαν αὐτῷ δαιμονιζομένους πολλούς· καὶ ἐξέβαλε τὰ πνεύματα
λόγῳ, καὶ πάντας τοὺς κακῶς ἔχοντας ἐθεράπευσεν· ὅπως πληρωθῇ τὸ 17
ῥηθὲν διὰ Ἡσαΐου τοῦ προφήτου, λέγοντος, Αὐτὸς τὰς ἀσθενείας ἡμῶν
ἔλαβε καὶ τὰς νόσους ἐβάστασεν.

Ἰδὼν δὲ ὁ Ἰησοῦς ὄχλους περὶ αὐτόν, ἐκέλευσεν ἀπελθεῖν εἰς τὸ 18
Ι' ξη πέραν. καὶ προσελθὼν εἷς γραμματεὺς εἶπεν αὐτῷ, Διδάσκαλε, ἀκολουθήσω 19
ε σοι ὅπου ἐὰν ἀπέρχῃ. καὶ λέγει αὐτῷ ὁ Ἰησοῦς, Αἱ ἀλώπεκες φωλεοὺς 20
ἔχουσι, καὶ τὰ πετεινὰ τοῦ οὐρανοῦ κατασκηνώσεις, ὁ δὲ υἱὸς τοῦ ἀνθρώπου
οὐκ ἔχει ποῦ τὴν κεφαλὴν κλίνῃ. ἕτερος δὲ τῶν μαθητῶν αὐτοῦ εἶπεν 21
αὐτῷ, Κύριε, ἐπίτρεψόν μοι πρῶτον ἀπελθεῖν καὶ θάψαι τὸν πατέρα μου.
ὁ δὲ Ἰησοῦς λέγει αὐτῷ, Ἀκολούθει μοι, καὶ ἄφες τοὺς νεκροὺς θάψαι 22
ΙΑ' τοὺς ἑαυτῶν νεκρούς. καὶ ἐμβάντι αὐτῷ εἰς πλοῖον, ἠκολούθησαν αὐτῷ 23
ξθ β οἱ μαθηταὶ αὐτοῦ· καὶ ἰδού, σεισμὸς μέγας ἐγένετο ἐν τῇ θαλάσσῃ, ὥστε 24
τὸ πλοῖον καλύπτεσθαι ὑπὸ τῶν κυμάτων· αὐτὸς δὲ ἐκάθευδεν. καὶ 25
προσελθόντες οἱ μαθηταὶ αὐτοῦ ἤγειραν αὐτόν, λέγοντες, Κύριε, σῶσον,
ἀπολλύμεθα. καὶ λέγει αὐτοῖς, Τί δειλοί ἐστε, ὀλιγόπιστοι; τότε ἐγερθεὶς 26
ἐπετίμησε τῷ ἀνέμῳ καὶ τῇ θαλάσσῃ, καὶ ἐγένετο γαλήνη μεγάλη· οἱ δὲ 27
ἄνθρωποι ἐθαύμασαν, λέγοντες, Ποταπός ἐστιν οὗτος, ὅτι καὶ οἱ ἄνεμοι καὶ
ἡ θάλασσα αὐτῷ ὑπακούουσιν;

ΙΒ' Καὶ ἐλθόντος αὐτοῦ εἰς τὸ πέραν εἰς τὴν χώραν τῶν Γεργεσινῶν, 28
ὑπήντησαν αὐτῷ δύο δαιμονιζόμενοι ἐκ τῶν μνημείων ἐξερχόμενοι, χαλεποὶ
λίαν, ὥστε μὴ ἰσχύειν τινὰ παρελθεῖν διὰ τῆς ὁδοῦ ἐκείνης· καὶ ἰδού, 29
ἔκραξαν, λέγοντες, Τί ἡμῖν καὶ σοί, υἱὲ τοῦ Θεοῦ; ἦλθες ὧδε πρὸ καιροῦ
βασανίσαι ἡμᾶς; ἦν δὲ μακρὰν ἀπ' αὐτῶν ἀγέλη χοίρων πολλῶν βοσκο- 30
μένη. οἱ δὲ δαίμονες παρεκάλουν αὐτόν, λέγοντες, Εἰ ἐκβάλλεις ἡμᾶς, 31
ἀπόστειλον ἡμᾶς εἰς τὴν ἀγέλην τῶν χοίρων· καὶ εἶπεν αὐτοῖς, Ὑπάγετε. 32
οἱ δὲ ἐξελθόντες ἀπῆλθον εἰς τοὺς χοίρους· καὶ ἰδού, ὥρμησεν πᾶσα
ἡ ἀγέλη κατὰ τοῦ κρημνοῦ εἰς τὴν θάλασσαν, καὶ ἀπέθανον ἐν τοῖς
ὕδασιν. οἱ δὲ βόσκοντες ἔφυγον, καὶ ἀπελθόντες εἰς τὴν πόλιν ἀπήγγειλαν 33
πάντα, καὶ τὰ τῶν δαιμονιζομένων. καὶ ἰδού, πᾶσα ἡ πόλις ἐξῆλθεν εἰς 34

118 209 ς **14** Πετρου] suprascr. σιμ 118² **18** οχλους] χλους 209* οχλους 209corr, pr πολλους 118 209corr in mg. ς **20** απεκριθη ῷ (sic) 118 κλῖναι 118 209 **22** ειπεν ς **23** πλοιον] pr το ς **25** σωσον] + ημας ς **26** τοις ανεμοις ς **27** υπακουουσιν αυτω 118 209 ς **28** ελθοντι αυτω ς, ελθοντι αυτου 118² Γεργεσηνων 118 209 ς **29** υιε] pr Ιησου ς **31** αποστειλον ημας] επιτρεψον ημιν απελθειν ς, om ημας 118 209 **32** την αγελην των χοιρων ς αγελη] + των χοιρων ς **33** και τα] τα κατα 118 209

ὑπάντησιν τῷ Ἰησοῦ· καὶ ἰδόντες αὐτὸν παρεκάλεσαν μεταβῆναι ἀπὸ
τῶν ὁρίων αὐτῶν.

IX. Καὶ ἐμβὰς εἰς πλοῖον διεπέρασε καὶ ἦλθεν εἰς τὴν ἰδίαν πόλιν. ο α
2 καὶ ἰδού, προσέφερον αὐτῷ παραλυτικὸν ἐπὶ κλίνης βεβλημένον· καὶ ἰδὼν ΙΓ'
ὁ Ἰησοῦς τὴν πίστιν αὐτῶν εἶπε τῷ παραλυτικῷ, Θάρσει, τέκνον, ἀφέωνταί
3 σου αἱ ἁμαρτίαι. καὶ ἰδού, τινὲς τῶν γραμματέων εἶπον ἐν ἑαυτοῖς,
4 Οὗτος βλασφημεῖ. καὶ εἰδὼς ὁ Ἰησοῦς τοὺς διαλογισμοὺς αὐτῶν
5 εἶπεν, Ἵνα τί ἐνθυμεῖσθε πονηρὰ ἐν ταῖς καρδίαις ὑμῶν; τί γάρ ἐστιν
εὐκοπώτερον, εἰπεῖν Ἀφέωνταί σοι αἱ ἁμαρτ αι, ἢ εἰπεῖν Ἔγειρε καὶ
6 περιπάτει; ἵνα δὲ εἰδῆτε ὅτι ἐξουσίαν ἔχει ὁ υἱὸς τοῦ ἀνθρώπου ἐπὶ τῆς
γῆς ἀφιέναι ἁμαρτίας, τότε λέγει τῷ παραλυτικῷ, Ἐγερθεὶς ἆρόν σου τὴν
7 κλίνην καὶ ὕπαγε εἰς τὸν οἶκόν σου. καὶ ἐγερθεὶς ἀπῆλθεν εἰς τὸν οἶκον
8 αὐτοῦ. ἰδόντες δὲ οἱ ὄχλοι ἐφοβήθησαν, καὶ ἐδόξασαν τὸν Θεὸν τὸν
δόντα ἐξουσίαν τοιαύτην τοῖς ἀνθρώποις.

9 Καὶ παράγων ὁ Ἰησοῦς ἐκεῖθεν εἶδεν ἄνθρωπον καθήμενον ἐπὶ τὸ ΙΔ'
τελώνιον, Ματθαῖον λεγόμενον, καὶ λέγει αὐτῷ, Ἀκολούθει μοι. καὶ οα β
10 ἀναστὰς ἠκολούθει αὐτῷ. καὶ ἐγένετο αὐτοῦ ἀνακειμένου ἐν τῇ οἰκίᾳ, οβ β
καὶ ἰδού, πολλοὶ τελῶναι καὶ ἁμαρτωλοὶ ἐλθόντες συνανέκειντο τῷ Ἰησοῦ
11 καὶ τοῖς μαθηταῖς αὐτοῦ. καὶ ἰδόντες οἱ Φαρισαῖοι ἔλεγον τοῖς μαθηταῖς
αὐτοῦ, Διατί μετὰ τῶν τελωνῶν καὶ ἁμαρτωλῶν ὁ διδάσκαλος ὑμῶν ἐσθίει;
12 ὁ δὲ Ἰησοῦς ἀκούσας εἶπεν αὐτοῖς, Οὐ χρείαν ἔχουσιν οἱ ἰσχύοντες ἰατροῦ, ογ β
13 ἀλλ' οἱ κακῶς ἔχοντες. πορευθέντες δὲ μάθετε τί ἐστιν, Ἔλεος θέλω καὶ
οὐ θυσίαν· οὐ γὰρ ἦλθον καλέσαι δικαίους, ἀλλὰ ἁμαρτωλούς.

14 Τότε προσέρχονται αὐτῷ οἱ μαθηταὶ Ἰωάννου, λέγοντες, Διατί ἡμεῖς
καὶ οἱ Φαρισαῖοι νηστεύομεν πολλά, οἱ δὲ μαθηταί σου οὐ νηστεύουσι;
15 καὶ εἶπεν αὐτοῖς ὁ Ἰησοῦς, Μὴ δύνανται οἱ υἱοὶ τοῦ νυμφῶνος πενθεῖν, ἐφ'
ὅσον μετ' αὐτῶν ἐστιν ὁ νυμφίος; ἐλεύσονται δὲ ἡμέραι ὅταν ἀρθῇ ἀπ'
16 αὐτῶν ὁ νυμφίος, καὶ τότε νηστεύσουσιν. οὐδεὶς δὲ ἐπιβάλλει ἐπίβλημα
ῥάκους ἀγνάφου ἐπὶ ἱματίῳ παλαιῷ· αἴρει γὰρ τὸ πλήρωμα αὐτοῦ ἀπὸ τοῦ
17 ἱματίου, καὶ χεῖρον σχίσμα γίνεται. οὐδὲ βάλλουσιν οἶνον νέον εἰς ἀσκοὺς
παλαιούς· εἰ δὲ μήγε, ῥήγνυνται οἱ ἀσκοί, καὶ ὁ οἶνος ἐκχεῖται καὶ οἱ ἀσκοὶ
ἀπόλλυνται· ἀλλὰ βάλλουσιν οἶνον νέον εἰς ἀσκοὺς καινούς, καὶ ἀμφό-
τεροι συντηροῦνται.

13 αμαρτωλους] rubr.[2] add. εις μετανοιαν

34 συναντησιν ς του Ιησου 118 209 οπως μεταβη ς 118 209 ς
1 το πλοιον ς 2 σοι αι αμαρτιαι σου ς 4 ιδων ς τας ενθυμησεις ς ενθυμεισθε] pr υμεις ς 5 om γαρ 118 209 εγειραι 118 209 ς 8 εθαυμασαν ς 9 ηκολουθησεν ς 11 ειπον ς εσθιει] ante ο διδασκ. ς 13 ελεον 118 209 ς αλλ ς αμαρτωλους]+εις μετανοιαν 118[2] ς 15 απαρθη ς 17 απολουνται ς αμφοτερα ς

ΙΕ' Ταῦτα αὐτοῦ λαλοῦντος ἰδού, ἄρχων εἰσελθὼν προσεκύνει αὐτῷ, 18
οδ/β λέγων, Ἡ θυγάτηρ μου ἄρτι ἐτελεύτησεν· ἀλλὰ ἐλθὼν ἐπίθες τὴν χεῖρά
Ις' σου ἐπ' αὐτήν, καὶ ζήσεται. καὶ ἐγερθεὶς ὁ Ἰησοῦς ἠκολούθησεν αὐτῷ 19
καὶ οἱ μαθηταὶ αὐτοῦ.
Καὶ ἰδού, γυνὴ αἱμορροοῦσα δώδεκα ἔτη προσελθοῦσα ὄπισθεν ἥψατο 20
τοῦ κρασπέδου τοῦ ἱματίου αὐτοῦ· ἔλεγε γὰρ ἐν ἑαυτῇ, Ἐὰν μόνον ἅψωμαι 21
τοῦ ἱματίου αὐτοῦ, σωθήσομαι. ὁ δὲ Ἰησοῦς ἐπιστραφεὶς καὶ ἰδὼν αὐτὴν 22
εἶπε, Θάρσει, θύγατερ, ἡ πίστις σου σέσωκέ σε. καὶ ἐσώθη ἡ γυνὴ ἀπὸ
τῆς ὥρας ἐκείνης. καὶ ἐλθὼν ὁ Ἰησοῦς εἰς τὴν οἰκίαν τοῦ ἄρχοντος, καὶ 23
ἰδὼν τοὺς αὐλητὰς καὶ τὸν ὄχλον θορυβούμενον, ἔλεγεν, Ἀναχωρεῖτε· οὐ 24
γὰρ ἀπέθανεν τὸ κοράσιον, ἀλλὰ καθεύδει. καὶ κατεγέλων αὐτοῦ. ὅτε δὲ 25
ἐξεβλήθη ὁ ὄχλος, εἰσελθὼν ἐκράτησε τῆς χειρὸς αὐτῆς; καὶ ἠγέρθη τὸ
κοράσιον. καὶ ἐξῆλθεν ἡ φήμη αὐτῆς εἰς ὅλην τὴν γῆν ἐκείνην. 26
ΙΖ' Καὶ παράγοντι ἐκεῖθεν τῷ Ἰησοῦ, ἠκολούθησαν αὐτῷ δύο τυφλοὶ 27
οε/ι κράζοντες καὶ λέγοντες, Ἐλέησον ἡμᾶς, υἱὲ Δαβίδ. ἐλθόντι δὲ εἰς τὴν 28
οἰκίαν προσῆλθον αὐτῷ οἱ τυφλοί, καὶ λέγει αὐτοῖς ὁ Ἰησοῦς, Πιστεύετε
ὅτι δύναμαι τοῦτο ποιῆσαι; λέγουσιν αὐτῷ, Ναί, Κύριε. τότε ἥψατο τῶν 29
ὀφθαλμῶν αὐτῶν, καὶ εἶπεν, Κατὰ τὴν πίστιν ὑμῶν γενηθήτω ὑμῖν· καὶ 30
ἀνεῴχθησαν αὐτῶν οἱ ὀφθαλμοί· καὶ ἐνεβριμήθη αὐτοῖς ὁ Ἰησοῦς, λέγων,
Ὁρᾶτε, μηδεὶς γινωσκέτω. οἱ δὲ ἐξελθόντες διεφήμισαν αὐτὸν ἐν ὅλῃ τῇ 31
γῇ ἐκείνῃ.
ΙΗ' Αὐτῶν δὲ ἐξερχομένων, ἰδού, προσήνεγκαν αὐτῷ ἄνθρωπον κωφὸν δαι- 32
μονιζόμενον. καὶ ἐκβληθέντος τοῦ δαιμονίου ἐλάλησεν ὁ κωφός· καὶ 33
ἐθαύμασαν οἱ ὄχλοι, λέγοντες, Οὐδέποτε ἐφάνη οὕτως ἐν τῷ Ἰσραήλ.
οἱ δὲ Φαρισαῖοι ἔλεγον, Ἐν τῷ ἄρχοντι τῶν δαιμονίων ἐκβάλλει τὰ 34
δαιμόνια.
ος/β Καὶ περιῆγεν ὁ Ἰησοῦς τὰς πόλεις πάσας καὶ τὰς κώμας, διδάσκων ἐν 35
ταῖς συναγωγαῖς αὐτῶν καὶ κηρύσσων τὸ εὐαγγέλιον τῆς βασιλείας καὶ
οζ/ϛ θεραπεύων πᾶσαν νόσον καὶ πᾶσαν μαλακίαν. ἰδὼν δὲ τοὺς ὄχλους 36
ἐσπλαγχνίσθη περὶ αὐτῶν, ὅτι ἦσαν ἐσκυλμένοι καὶ ἐρριμμένοι ὡς
οη/ε πρόβατα μὴ ἔχοντα ποιμένα. τότε λέγει τοῖς μαθηταῖς αὐτοῦ, Ὁ μὲν 37
θερισμὸς πολύς, οἱ δὲ ἐργάται ὀλίγοι· δεήθητε οὖν τοῦ κυρίου τοῦ θερισμοῦ, 38

35 μαλακιαν] rubr.[2] addidit in marg. εν τω λαω

118 209 ϛ 18 λαλουντος]+αυτοις ϛ ελθων ϛ λεγων]+οτι ϛ 19 αυτου] αυτ. spat. rel. 118 23 λεγει αυτοις ϛ 26 αυτης] αύτη ϛ 29 και ειπεν] λεγων ϛ 30 ενεβριμησατο ϛ 33 και] αι 118* κ add. 118[2] λεγοντες]+οτι ϛ ουτως] οὗτος 118, οὗτος 209 35 post βασιλειας spat. rel. 118* in quo 118[2] εν τω λαω scripsit quae ad lineae prox. finem pertinent μαλακιαν]+εν τω λαω 118[2] ϛ 36 ησαν] om 118 εκλελυμενοι ϛ ερριμενοι 209 ωσει ϛ

1 ὅπως ἐκβάλῃ ἐργάτας εἰς τὸν θερισμὸν αὐτοῦ. X. καὶ προσκαλεσά- ΙΘ'
μενος τοὺς δώδεκα μαθητὰς αὐτοῦ, ἔδωκεν αὐτοῖς ἐξουσίαν πνευμάτων οθ β
ἀκαθάρτων, ὥστε ἐκβάλλειν αὐτά, καὶ θεραπεύειν πᾶσαν νόσον καὶ πᾶσαν
2 μαλακίαν. τῶν δὲ δώδεκα ἀποστόλων τὰ ὀνόματά ἐστι ταῦτα· πρῶτος π
Σίμων ὁ λεγόμενος Πέτρος, καὶ Ἀνδρέας ὁ ἀδελφὸς αὐτοῦ, Ἰάκωβος ὁ τοῦ β
3 Ζεβεδαίου καὶ Ἰωάννης ὁ ἀδελφὸς αὐτοῦ, Φίλιππος καὶ Βαρθολομαῖος,
Θωμᾶς καὶ Ματθαῖος ὁ τελώνης, Ἰάκωβος ὁ τοῦ Ἀλφαίου καὶ Λεββαῖος ὁ
4 ἐπικληθεὶς Θαδδαῖος, Σίμων ὁ καναναῖος, καὶ Ἰούδας ὁ Ἰσκαριώτης ὁ
καὶ παραδοὺς αὐτόν.

5 Τούτους τοὺς δώδεκα ἀπέστειλεν ὁ Ἰησοῦς παραγγείλας αὐτοῖς, λέγων, πα ι
Εἰς ὁδὸν ἐθνῶν μὴ ἀπέλθητε, καὶ εἰς πόλιν Σαμαρειτῶν μὴ εἰσέλθητε·
6 πορεύεσθε δὲ μᾶλλον πρὸς τὰ πρόβατα τὰ ἀπολωλότα οἴκου Ἰσραήλ.
7 πορευόμενοι δὲ κηρύσσετε, λέγοντες ὅτι Ἤγγικεν ἡ βασιλεία τῶν οὐρανῶν.
8 ἀσθενοῦντας θεραπεύετε, νεκροὺς ἐγείρετε, λεπροὺς καθαρίζετε,
9 δαιμόνια ἐκβάλλετε. δωρεὰν ἐλάβετε, δωρεὰν δότε. μὴ κτήσησθε πβ
10 χρυσὸν μηδὲ ἄργυρον μηδὲ χαλκὸν εἰς τὰς ζώνας ὑμῶν, μὴ πήραν εἰς β
ὁδόν, μηδὲ δύο χιτῶνας μηδὲ ὑποδήματα μηδὲ ῥάβδον· ἄξιος γὰρ ὁ ἐργάτης
11 τῆς τροφῆς αὐτοῦ. εἰς ἣν δ' ἂν πόλιν εἰσέλθητε, ἐξετάσατε τίς ἐν αὐτῇ πγ β
12 ἄξιός ἐστι· κἀκεῖ μείνατε ἕως ἂν ἐξέλθητε. εἰσερχόμενοι δὲ εἰς τὴν οἰκίαν πδ
13 ἀσπάσασθε αὐτήν, λέγοντες Εἰρήνη τῷ οἴκῳ τούτῳ. καὶ ἐὰν μὲν ᾖ ἡ ε
οἰκία ἀξία, ἐλθέτω ἡ εἰρήνη ὑμῶν ἐπ' αὐτήν· ἐὰν δὲ μὴ ᾖ ἀξία, ἡ εἰρήνη
14 ὑμῶν πρὸς ὑμᾶς ἐπιστραφήτω. καὶ ὃς ἐὰν μὴ δέξηται ὑμᾶς μηδὲ ἀκούσῃ πε
τοὺς λόγους ὑμῶν, ἐξερχόμενοι τῆς οἰκίας ἢ τῆς πόλεως ἐκείνης ἐκτινάξατε β
15 τὸν κονιορτὸν τῶν ποδῶν ὑμῶν. ἀμὴν ἀμὴν λέγω ὑμῖν, ἀνεκτότερον
ἔσται γῇ Σοδόμων καὶ Γομόρρας ἐν ἡμέρᾳ κρίσεως ἢ τῇ πόλει ἐκείνῃ.

16 Ἰδού, ἐγὼ ἀποστέλλω ὑμᾶς ὡς πρόβατα ἐν μέσῳ λύκων· γίνεσθε οὖν πς ε
17 φρόνιμοι ὡς οἱ ὄφεις, καὶ ἀκέραιοι ὡς αἱ περιστεραί. προσέχετε δὲ ἀπὸ πζ
τῶν ἀνθρώπων· παραδώσουσι γὰρ ὑμᾶς εἰς συνέδρια, καὶ ἐν ταῖς συναγωγαῖς α
18 αὐτῶν μαστιγώσουσιν ὑμᾶς· καὶ ἐπὶ ἡγεμόνας δὲ καὶ βασιλεῖς ἀχθήσεσθε
19 ἕνεκεν ἐμοῦ, εἰς μαρτύριον αὐτοῖς καὶ τοῖς ἔθνεσιν. ὅταν δὲ παραδῶσι πη
ὑμᾶς, μὴ μεριμνήσητε πῶς ἢ τί λαλήσητε· δοθήσεται γὰρ ὑμῖν ἐν ἐκείνῃ β
20 τῇ ὥρᾳ τί λαλήσητε· οὐ γὰρ ὑμεῖς ἐστε οἱ λαλοῦντες, ἀλλὰ τὸ Πνεῦμα
21 τοῦ πατρὸς ὑμῶν τὸ λαλοῦν ἐν ὑμῖν. παραδώσει δὲ ἀδελφὸς ἀδελφὸν εἰς
θάνατον, καὶ πατὴρ τέκνον· καὶ ἐπαναστήσονται τέκνα ἐπὶ γονεῖς καὶ θανατώ-

4 Κανανιτης ϛ Ισκαριωτης sine ο ϛ 8 νεκρους εγειρετε] post 118 209 λεπ. καθαρ. ϛ, om 118 209 ϛ 9 χρυσον suprascr. in litur. 118 μηδε om sed spat. rel. 118 10 αυτου]+εστιν ϛ 11 πολιν] +η κωμην 209[2] ϛ μηνατε 118 12 om λεγ. ειρ. τω οικ. τουτω ϛ 14 δεξεται 118 15 om αμην 2° ϛ Γομορρων ϛ 19 παραδω spat. rel. 118 παραδιδωσιν ϛ λαλησητε 2°] λαλησετε ϛ

σουσιν αὐτούς. καὶ ἔσεσθε μισούμενοι ὑπὸ πάντων διὰ τὸ ὄνομά μου· ὁ δὲ ὑπο- 22
πθ ι μείνας εἰς τέλος, οὗτος σωθήσεται. ὅταν δὲ διώκωσιν ὑμᾶς ἐν τῇ πόλει 23
ταύτῃ, φεύγετε εἰς τὴν ἑτέραν, κἂν ἐκ ταύτης διώκωσιν ὑμᾶς φεύγετε
εἰς τὴν ἄλλην. ἀμὴν γὰρ λέγω ὑμῖν, οὐ μὴ τελέσητε τὰς πόλεις τοῦ
ϟ γ Ἰσραὴλ ἕως ἂν ἔλθῃ ὁ υἱὸς τοῦ ἀνθρώπου. οὐκ ἔστι μαθητὴς ὑπὲρ τὸν 24
διδάσκαλον, οὐδὲ δοῦλος ὑπὲρ τὸν κύριον αὐτοῦ. ἀρκετὸν τῷ μαθητῇ 25
ϟα ι ἵνα γένηται ὡς ὁ διδάσκαλος αὐτοῦ, καὶ ὁ δοῦλος ὡς ὁ κύριος αὐτοῦ. εἰ
τὸν οἰκοδεσπότην Βεελζεβοὺλ ἐκάλεσαν, πόσῳ μᾶλλον τοὺς οἰκειακοὺς
ϟβ β αὐτοῦ; μὴ οὖν φοβηθῆτε αὐτούς· οὐδὲν γάρ ἐστι κεκαλυμμένον ὃ οὐκ 26
ϟγ ε ἀποκαλυφθήσεται, καὶ κρυπτὸν ὃ οὐ γνωσθήσεται. ὃ λέγω ὑμῖν ἐν τῇ 27
σκοτίᾳ, εἴπατε ἐν τῷ φωτί· καὶ ὃ εἰς τὸ οὖς ἠκούσατε, κηρύξατε ἐπὶ τῶν
δωμάτων ὑμῶν. καὶ μὴ φοβηθῆτε ἀπὸ τῶν ἀποκτεννόντων τὸ σῶμα 28
τὴν δὲ ψυχὴν μὴ δυναμένων ἀποκτεῖναι· φοβήθητε μᾶλλον τὸν δυνά-
μενον καὶ ψυχὴν καὶ σῶμα ἀπολέσαι ἐν γεέννῃ. οὐχὶ δύο στρουθία 29
ἀσσαρίου πωλεῖται; καὶ ἓν ἐξ αὐτῶν οὐ πεσεῖται ἐπὶ τὴν γῆν ἄνευ τοῦ
πατρὸς ὑμῶν· ὑμῶν δὲ καὶ αἱ τρίχες τῆς κεφαλῆς πᾶσαι ἠριθμημέναι εἰσί. 30
ϟδ β μὴ οὖν φοβεῖσθε· πολλῶν στρουθίων διαφέρετε ὑμεῖς. πᾶς οὖν ὅστις 31 32
ὁμολογήσει ἐν ἐμοὶ ἔμπροσθεν τῶν ἀνθρώπων, ὁμολογήσω κἀγὼ ἐν αὐτῷ
ἔμπροσθεν τοῦ πατρός μου τοῦ ἐν οὐρανοῖς. ὅστις δ' ἂν ἀπαρνήσηταί 33
με ἔμπροσθεν τῶν ἀνθρώπων, ἀπαρνήσομαι κἀγὼ αὐτὸν ἔμπροσθεν
ϟε ε τοῦ πατρός μου τοῦ ἐν οὐρανοῖς. μὴ νομίσητε ὅτι ἦλθον βαλεῖν εἰρήνην 34
ἐπὶ τὴν γῆν· οὐκ ἦλθον βαλεῖν εἰρήνην, ἀλλὰ μάχαιραν· ἦλθον γὰρ 35
διχάσαι ἄνθρωπον κατὰ τοῦ πατρὸς αὐτοῦ, καὶ θυγατέρα κατὰ τῆς μητρὸς
αὐτῆς, καὶ νύμφην κατὰ τῆς πενθερᾶς αὐτῆς· καὶ ἐχθροὶ τοῦ ἀνθρώπου οἱ 36
ϟϛ ε οἰκειακοὶ αὐτοῦ. ὁ φιλῶν πατέρα ἢ μητέρα ὑπὲρ ἐμὲ οὐκ ἔστι μου 37
ἄξιος· καὶ ὁ φιλῶν υἱὸν ἢ θυγατέρα ὑπὲρ ἐμὲ οὐκ ἔστι μου ἄξιος· καὶ ὃς 38
οὐ λαμβάνει τὸν σταυρὸν αὐτοῦ καὶ ἀκολουθεῖ ὀπίσω μου, οὐκ ἔστι μου
ϟζ γ ἄξιος. ὁ εὑρὼν τὴν ψυχὴν αὐτοῦ ἀπολέσει αὐτήν· καὶ ὁ ἀπολέσας τὴν 39
ϟη α ψυχὴν αὐτοῦ ἕνεκεν ἐμοῦ εὑρήσει αὐτήν. ὁ δεχόμενος ὑμᾶς ἐμὲ δέχεται· 40
ϟθ ι καὶ ὁ ἐμὲ δεχόμενος δέχεται τὸν ἀποστείλαντά με. ὁ δεχόμενος προφήτην 41
εἰς ὄνομα προφήτου μισθὸν προφήτου λήψεται· καὶ ὁ δεχόμενος δίκαιον
ρ ϛ εἰς ὄνομα δικαίου μισθὸν δικαίου λήψεται· καὶ ὃς ἐὰν ποτίσῃ ἕνα τῶν 42
μικρῶν τούτων ποτήριον ψυχροῦ μόνον εἰς ὄνομα μαθητοῦ, ἀμὴν λέγω
ὑμῖν, οὐ μὴ ἀπολέσει τὸν μισθὸν αὐτοῦ.

118 209 ϛ **23** ετεραν] αλλην ϛ om καν...αλλην ϛ **25** οικιακους ϛ **27** ακουετε ϛ om υμων ϛ **28** αποκτενοντων 118 209, αποκτεινοντων ϛ φοβηθητε]+δε 118 209 ϛ **30** φοβηθητε ϛ **32** εμοι εμπροσθεν] αυτω μπροσθεν 118* sed αυτω eras. **33** αρνησηται ϛ αρνησομαι ϛ αυτον καγω ϛ **34** επι την γην...ειρηνην] om 118 209 **36** οικιακοι ϛ **39** ευρησει] ουτος σωσει 118 209 **40** εμε 2°] μη 118* εμε corr. forsan ipse * **42** απολεση 118 209 ϛ

XI. Καὶ ἐγένετο ὅτε ἐτέλεσεν ὁ Ἰησοῦς διατάσσων τοῖς μαθηταῖς ρα
αὐτοῦ, μετέβη ἐκεῖθεν τοῦ διδάσκειν καὶ κηρύσσειν ἐν ταῖς πόλεσιν αὐτῶν. ι
2 Ὁ δὲ Ἰωάννης ἀκούσας ἐν τῷ δεσμωτηρίῳ τὰ ἔργα τοῦ Χριστοῦ, Κ′
3 πέμψας δύο τῶν μαθητῶν αὐτοῦ εἶπεν αὐτῷ, Σὺ εἶ ὁ ἐρχόμενος, ἢ ἕτερον ρβ ε
4 προσδοκῶμεν; καὶ ἀποκριθεὶς ὁ Ἰησοῦς εἶπεν αὐτοῖς, Πορευθέντες ἀπαγ-
5 γείλατε Ἰωάννῃ ἃ ἀκούετε καὶ βλέπετε· τυφλοὶ ἀναβλέπουσι καὶ χωλοὶ
περιπατοῦσι, λεπροὶ καθαρίζονται καὶ κωφοὶ ἀκούουσι, καὶ νεκροὶ
6 ἐγείρονται καὶ πτωχοὶ εὐαγγελίζονται· καὶ μακάριός ἐστιν, ὃς ἂν μὴ
7 σκανδαλισθῇ ἐν ἐμοί. τούτων δὲ πορευομένων ἤρξατο ὁ Ἰησοῦς λέγειν
τοῖς ὄχλοις περὶ Ἰωάννου, Τί ἐξήλθετε εἰς τὴν ἔρημον θεάσασθαι; κάλαμον
8 ὑπὸ ἀνέμου σαλευόμενον; ἀλλὰ τί ἐξήλθετε ἰδεῖν; ἄνθρωπον ἐν μαλακίοις
ἱματίοις ἠμφιεσμένον; ἰδού, οἱ τὰ μαλακὰ φοροῦντες ἐν τοῖς οἴκοις τῶν
9 βασιλέων εἰσίν· ἀλλὰ τί ἐξήλθετε ἰδεῖν; προφήτην; ναί, λέγω ὑμῖν, καὶ
10 περισσότερον προφήτου· οὗτος γάρ ἐστι περὶ οὗ γέγραπται, Ἰδού, ἐγὼ ργ
ἀποστέλλω τὸν ἄγγελόν μου πρὸ προσώπου σου, ὃς κατασκευάσει τὴν β
11 ὁδόν σου ἔμπροσθέν σου. ἀμὴν λέγω ὑμῖν, οὐκ ἐγήγερται ἐν γεννητοῖς ρδ
γυναικῶν μείζων Ἰωάννου τοῦ βαπτιστοῦ· ὁ δὲ μικρότερος ἐν τῇ βασιλείᾳ ε
12 τῶν οὐρανῶν μείζων αὐτοῦ ἐστιν· ἀπὸ δὲ τῶν ἡμερῶν Ἰωάννου τοῦ ρε
βαπτιστοῦ ἕως ἄρτι ἡ βασιλεία τῶν οὐρανῶν βιάζεται, καὶ βιασταὶ ε
13 ἁρπάζουσιν αὐτήν. πάντες γὰρ οἱ προφῆται καὶ ὁ νόμος ἕως Ἰωάννου
14 ἐπροφήτευσαν· καὶ εἰ θέλετε δέξασθαι, αὐτός ἐστιν Ἡλίας ὁ μέλλων ρς
15 16 ἔρχεσθαι. ὁ ἔχων ὦτα ἀκούειν ἀκουέτω. τίνι δὲ ὁμοιώσω τὴν γενεὰν ι ρζ
ταύτην; ὁμοία ἐστὶ παιδίοις ἐν ἀγορᾷ, καθημένοις ἐν ταῖς ε
17 ἀγοραῖς, ἃ προσφωνοῦντα τοῖς ἑτέροις λέγουσιν, Ηὐλήσαμεν ὑμῖν,
18 καὶ οὐκ ὠρχήσασθε· ἐθρηνήσαμεν καὶ οὐκ ἐκόψασθε. ἦλθε γὰρ
19 Ἰωάννης μήτε ἐσθίων μήτε πίνων, καὶ λέγουσι, Δαιμόνιον ἔχει. ἦλθεν
ὁ υἱὸς τοῦ ἀνθρώπου ἐσθίων καὶ πίνων, ἰδού, ἄνθρωπος φάγος καὶ
οἰνοπότης, τελωνῶν φίλος καὶ ἁμαρτωλῶν. καὶ ἐδικαιώθη ἡ σοφία ἀπὸ
τῶν τέκνων αὐτῆς. ρη
20 Τότε ἤρξατο ὁ Ἰησοῦς ὀνειδίζειν τὰς πόλεις ἐν αἷς ἐγένοντο αἱ ε
21 πλεῖσται δυνάμεις αὐτοῦ, ὅτι οὐ μετενόησαν. Οὐαί σοι, Χοραζίν, οὐαί
σοι, Βηθσαϊδά, ὅτι εἰ ἐν Τύρῳ καὶ Σιδῶνι ἐγένοντο αἱ δυνάμεις
αἱ γενόμεναι ἐν ὑμῖν, πάλαι ἂν ἐν σάκκῳ καὶ σποδῷ καθήμεναι
22 μετενόησαν. πλὴν λέγω ὑμῖν, Τύρῳ καὶ Σιδῶνι ἀνεκτότερον ἔσται ἐν

19 οινοπωτης cod.

1 τοις μαθηταις] τους δωδεκα μαθητας 118, τοις δωδεκα μαθηταις 209 ς 118 209 ς
5 και νεκροι] νεκροι 118 209 ς **6** αν] εαν 118 209 ς **8** μαλακοις 118 209 ς βασιλειων 118 209 **13** προεφητευσαν 118 209 ς **16** παιδαριοις ς εν αγοραις καθημενοις και προσφωνουσι τοις εταιροις και λεγουσιν 118 209 ς **17** εθρηνησαμεν]+υμιν 118 209 ς **19** πινων]+και λεγουσιν 118 209 ς **20** om ο Ιησους 118 209 ς **21** Βηθσαιδαν ς om καθημεναι 118 209 ς

ἡμέρᾳ κρίσεως ἢ ὑμῖν. καὶ σύ, Καπερναούμ, μὴ ἕως τοῦ οὐρανοῦ 23
ρθ ι ὑψωθήσῃ, ἕως ᾅδου καταβιβασθήσῃ· ὅτι εἰ ἐν Σοδόμοις ἐγενήθησαν
αἱ δυνάμεις αἱ γενόμεναι ἐν σοί, ἔμεινεν ἂν μέχρι τῆς σήμερον. πλὴν 24
λέγω ὑμῖν ὅτι γῇ Σοδόμων ἀνεκτότερον ἔσται ἐν ἡμέρᾳ κρίσεως ἢ σοί.
ρι ε ἐν ἐκείνῳ τῷ καιρῷ ἀποκριθεὶς ὁ Ἰησοῦς εἶπεν, Ἐξομολογοῦμαί σοι, 25
πάτερ, κύριε τοῦ οὐρανοῦ καὶ τῆς γῆς, ὅτι ἀπέκρυψας ταῦτα ἀπὸ σοφῶν
καὶ δυνάτων καὶ ἀπεκάλυψας αὐτὰ νηπίοις. ναί, ὁ πατήρ, ὅτι οὕτως 26
ρια γ εὐδοκία ἐγένετο ἔμπροσθέν σου. πάντα μοι παρεδόθη ὑπὸ τοῦ πατρός 27
ριβ γ μου· καὶ οὐδεὶς ἐπιγινώσκει τὸν υἱόν, εἰ μὴ ὁ πατήρ· οὐδὲ τὸν πατέρα
τις ἐπιγινώσκει, εἰ μὴ ὁ υἱός, καὶ ᾧ ἐὰν βούληται ὁ υἱὸς ἀποκα-
ριγ ι λύψαι. δεῦτε πρός με πάντες οἱ κοπιῶντες καὶ πεφορτισμένοι, κἀγὼ 28
ἀναπαύσω ὑμᾶς. ἄρατε τὸν ζυγόν μου ἐφ' ὑμᾶς καὶ μάθετε ἀπ' ἐμοῦ, 29
ὅτι πρᾶός εἰμι καὶ ταπεινὸς τῇ καρδίᾳ· καὶ εὑρήσετε ἀνάπαυσιν ταῖς
ψυχαῖς ὑμῶν. ὁ γὰρ ζυγός μου χρηστὸς καὶ τὸ φορτίον μου ἐλαφρόν 30
ἐστιν.

ριδ β XII. Ἐν ἐκείνῳ τῷ καιρῷ ἐπορεύθη ὁ Ἰησοῦς τοῖς σάββασι διὰ
τῶν σπορίμων· οἱ δὲ μαθηταὶ αὐτοῦ ἐπείνασαν, καὶ ἤρξαντο τίλλειν
στάχυας καὶ ἐσθίειν. οἱ δὲ Φαρισαῖοι ἰδόντες εἶπον αὐτῷ, Ἰδού, οἱ 2
μαθηταί σου ποιοῦσιν ὃ οὐκ ἔξεστι ποιεῖν ἐν σαββάτῳ. ὁ δὲ εἶπεν 3
αὐτοῖς, Οὐκ ἀνέγνωτε τί ἐποίησε Δαβίδ, ὅτε ἐπείνασεν καὶ οἱ μετ'
αὐτοῦ; πῶς εἰσῆλθεν εἰς τὸν οἶκον τοῦ Θεοῦ καὶ τοὺς ἄρτους τῆς 4
προθέσεως ἔφαγεν, οὓς οὐκ ἐξὸν ἦν αὐτῷ φαγεῖν οὐδὲ τοῖς μετ'
ριε ι αὐτοῦ, ἀλλ' ἢ τοῖς ἱερεῦσιν; ἢ οὐκ ἀνέγνωτε ἐν τῷ νόμῳ ὅτι τοῖς 5
σάββασιν οἱ ἱερεῖς ἐν τῷ ἱερῷ τὸ σάββατον βεβηλοῦσι, καὶ ἀναίτιοί
εἰσι; λέγω δὲ ὑμῖν ὅτι τοῦ ἱεροῦ μεῖζόν ἐστιν ὧδε. εἰ δὲ ἐγνώκειτε 6 7
τί ἐστιν, Ἔλεος θέλω καὶ οὐ θυσίαν, οὐκ ἂν κατεδικάσατε τοὺς ἀναιτίους.
κύριος γάρ ἐστι ὁ υἱὸς τοῦ ἀνθρώπου καὶ τοῦ σαββάτου. 8
ΚΑ΄ Καὶ μεταβὰς ἐκεῖθεν ἦλθεν εἰς τὴν συναγωγὴν αὐτῶν. καὶ ἰδού, 9 10
ρις β ἄνθρωπος ἦν ἐκεῖ τὴν χεῖρα ἔχων ξαράν· καὶ ἐπηρώτησαν αὐτόν, λέ-
γοντες, Εἰ ἔξεστι τοῖς σάββασι θεραπεύειν; ἵνα κατηγορήσωσιν αὐτοῦ.
ὁ δὲ εἶπεν αὐτοῖς, Τίς ἔσται ἐξ ὑμῶν ἄνθρωπος, ὃς ἕξει πρόβατον ἕν, 11

118 209 ς 23 μη] ἡ 118 209, ἡ ς υψωθης 118 209, υψωθεισα ς καταβιβασθεισῃ 118 209 εγενηθησαν] εγενοντο 118 209 ς εμειναν 118 209 ς 25 δυνατων] συνετων 118 209 ς 26 εγενετο ευδοκια 118 209 ς 28 προς με] om 118 209

1 τους σταχυας 118 3 επεινασεν] + αυτος ς 4 εξον ην αυτω] post ξ eras. 118* et in rasura 118[2] εστιν scrips. quod autem scrips. 118* legi non potest αλλ η] ει μη 118 209 ς ιερευσι μονοις 118 209 ς 6 μειζων 118 209 ς 7 ελεον 118 209 ς 8 του σαββατου ο υιος του ανθρωπου 118 209, και του σαβ. ο υ. τ. α. ς 10 om εκει 118 209 ς χειραν 118 209 ξηραν 118 209 ς

καὶ ἐὰν ἐμπέσῃ τοῦτο τοῖς σάββασιν εἰς βόθυνον, οὐχὶ κρατήσει αὐτὸ
12 καὶ ἐγερεῖ; πόσῳ οὖν διαφέρει ἄνθρωπος προβάτου; ὥστε ἔξεστι τοῖς
13 σάββασι καλῶς ποιεῖν. τότε λέγει τῷ ἀνθρώπῳ, Ἔκτεινόν σου τὴν
14 χεῖρα. καὶ ἐξέτεινε· καὶ ἀποκατέστη ὑγιὴς ὡς ἡ ἄλλη. ἐξελθόντες δὲ ρις δ
οἱ Φαρισαῖοι συμβούλιον ἔλαβον κατ' αὐτοῦ, ὅπως αὐτὸν ἀπολέσωσιν.
15 ὁ δὲ Ἰησοῦς γνοὺς ἀνεχώρησεν ἐκεῖθεν· καὶ ἠκολούθησαν αὐτῷ ὄχλοι ρ̄ιη ι
16 πολλοί, καὶ ἐθεράπευσεν αὐτούς, πάντας δὲ οὓς ἐθεράπευσεν ἐπέ-
17 πλησσεν αὐτοῖς, ἵνα μὴ φανερὸν αὐτὸν ποιήσωσιν· ἵνα πληρωθῇ
18 τὸ ῥηθὲν διὰ Ἡσαΐου τοῦ προφήτου, λέγοντος, Ἰδού, ὁ παῖς μου
ὃν ᾑρέτισα, ὁ ἀγαπητός μου ἐν ᾧ εὐδόκησεν ἡ ψυχή μου· θήσω
19 τὸ πνεῦμά μου ἐπ' αὐτόν, καὶ κρίσιν τοῖς ἔθνεσιν ἀπαγγελεῖ· οὐκ ἐρίσει
οὐδὲ κραυγάσει, οὐδὲ ἀκούσει τις ἐν ταῖς πλατείαις τὴν φωνὴν αὐτοῦ·
20 κάλαμον συντετριμμένον οὐ κατεάξει, καὶ λίνον τυφόμενον οὐ σβέσει,
21 ἕως ἂν ἐκβάλῃ εἰς νῖκος τὴν κρίσιν. καὶ τῷ ὀνόματι αὐτοῦ ἔθνη
ἐλπιοῦσι.
22 Τότε προσηνέχθη αὐτῷ δαιμονιζόμενος τυφλὸς καὶ κωφός· καὶ ἐθερά- ΚΒ'
23 πευσεν αὐτόν, ὥστε τὸν κωφὸν καὶ τυφλὸν λαλεῖν καὶ βλέπειν. καὶ ρ̄ιθ ε
ἐξίσταντο πάντες οἱ ὄχλοι καὶ ἔλεγον, Μήτι οὗτός ἐστιν ὁ υἱὸς Δαβίδ; ρ̄κ ϛ
24 οἱ δὲ Φαρισαῖοι ἀκούσαντες εἶπον, Οὗτος οὐκ ἐκβάλλει τὰ δαιμόνια, εἰ ρ̄κα β
25 μὴ ἐν τῷ Βεελζεβοὺλ ἄρχοντι τῶν δαιμονίων. εἰδὼς δὲ ὁ Ἰησοῦς τὰς ρ̄κβ β
ἐνθυμήσεις αὐτῶν εἶπεν αὐτοῖς, Πᾶσα βασιλεία μερισθεῖσα καθ'
ἑαυτῆς ἐρημοῦται· καὶ πᾶσα πόλις ἢ οἰκία μερισθεῖσα καθ' ἑαυτῆς
26 οὐ σταθήσεται. καὶ εἰ ὁ Σατανᾶς τὸν Σατανᾶν ἐκβάλλει, ἐφ' ἑαυτὸν
27 ἐμερίσθη· πῶς οὖν σταθήσεται ἡ βασιλεία αὐτοῦ; εἰ δὲ ἐγὼ ἐν Βεελζε-
βοὺλ ἐκβάλλω τὰ δαιμόνια, οἱ υἱοὶ ὑμῶν ἐν τίνι ἐκβάλλουσι; διὰ τοῦτο
28 αὐτοὶ κριταὶ ὑμῶν ἔσονται. εἰ δὲ ἐγὼ ἐν Πνεύματι Θεοῦ ἐγὼ
29 ἐκβάλλω τὰ δαιμόνια, ἄρα ἔφθασεν ἐφ' ὑμᾶς ἡ βασιλεία τοῦ Θεοῦ. ἢ
πῶς δύναταί τις εἰσελθεῖν εἰς τὴν οἰκίαν τοῦ ἰσχυροῦ καὶ τὰ σκεύη
αὐτοῦ ἁρπάσαι, ἐὰν μὴ πρῶτον δήσῃ τὸν ἰσχυρόν, καὶ τότε τὴν
30 οἰκίαν αὐτοῦ διαρπάσει; ὁ μὴ ὢν μετ' ἐμοῦ κατ' ἐμοῦ ἐστι· καὶ ὁ μὴ
31 συνάγων μετ' ἐμοῦ σκορπίζει. διὰ τοῦτο λέγω ὑμῖν, Πᾶσα ἁμαρτία καὶ ρ̄κγ β

25 πολις η οικια] πολις οικια cod. sed m. recent. add. η in marg.

13 την χειρα σου 118 209 ς αποκατεστη] αποκατεσταθη ς, απεκατεσταθη 118 209 ς
η χειρ αυτου 118 209 **14** εξελθοντες post αυτου et δε post οι ς **15** om
δε ους εθεραπευσεν 118 209 ς επεπλησσεν] και επετιμησεν 118 209 ς
17 ινα] οπως 118 209 ς **18** εν ω] εις ον 118 209 ς **20** τυφωμενον 209
εκβαλλ spat. rel. 118 **21** εν τω ονομ. ς **22** τυφλον και κωφον και
118 209 ς **25** καθ εαυτην bis 118 209 **27** ει δε] και ει 118 209 ς
υμων εσονται κριται ς, κριται και υμων εσονται 118 **28** εγω 1°] om 118 209
εγω 2°] om ς **29** διαρπασαι 118 209 ς

βλασφημία ἀφεθήσεται ὑμῖν τοῖς ἀνθρώποις· ἡ δὲ τοῦ Πνεύματος
βλασφημία οὐκ ἀφεθήσεται. καὶ ὃς ἂν εἴπῃ λόγον κατὰ τοῦ υἱοῦ 32
τοῦ ἀνθρώπου, ἀφεθήσεται αὐτῷ· ὃς δ' ἂν εἴπῃ κατὰ τοῦ Πνεύματος
τοῦ Ἁγίου, οὐκ ἀφεθήσεται αὐτῷ οὔτε ἐν τούτῳ τῷ αἰῶνι οὔτε ἐν τῷ
ρκδ μέλλοντι. ἢ ποιήσατε τὸ δένδρον καλὸν καὶ τὸν καρπὸν αὐτοῦ καλόν, 33
ι ἢ ποιήσατε τὸ δένδρον σαπρὸν καὶ τὸν καρπὸν αὐτοῦ σαπρόν· ἐκ γὰρ
τοῦ καρποῦ τὸ δένδρον γινώσκεται. γεννήματα ἐχιδνῶν, πῶς δύνασθε 34
ρκε ἀγαθὰ λαλεῖν πονηροὶ ὄντες; ἐκ γὰρ τοῦ περισσεύματος τῆς καρδίας τὸ
ε στόμα λαλεῖ. ὁ ἀγαθὸς ἄνθρωπος ἐκ τοῦ ἀγαθοῦ θησαυροῦ τῆς καρ- 35
δίας αὐτοῦ ἐκβάλλει τὰ ἀγαθά· καὶ ὁ πονηρὸς ἄνθρωπος ἐκ τοῦ
ρκϛ πονηροῦ θησαυροῦ ἐκβάλλει πονηρά. λέγω ὑμῖν ὅτι πᾶν ῥῆμα ἀργὸν 36
ι ὃ ἐὰν λαλήσωσιν οἱ ἄνθρωποι, ἀποδώσουσι περὶ αὐτοῦ λόγον ἐν ἡμέρᾳ
κρίσεως. ἐκ γὰρ τῶν λόγων σου δικαιωθήσῃ, καὶ ἐκ τῶν λόγων σου κατα- 37
δικασθήσῃ.

κγ' Τότε ἀπεκρίθησάν τινες τῶν γραμματέων καὶ Φαρισαίων, λέγοντες, 38
ρκζ ε Διδάσκαλε, θέλομεν ἀπὸ σοῦ σημεῖον ἰδεῖν. ὁ δὲ ἀποκριθεὶς εἶπεν αὐ- 39
ρκη τοῖς, Γενεὰ πονηρὰ καὶ μοιχαλὶς σημεῖον ἐπιζητεῖ· καὶ σημεῖον οὐ
ε δοθήσεται αὐτῇ, εἰ μὴ τὸ σημεῖον Ἰωνᾶ τοῦ προφήτου. ὥσπερ γὰρ ἦν 40
Ἰωνᾶς ἐν τῇ κοιλίᾳ τοῦ κήτους τρεῖς ἡμέρας καὶ τρεῖς νύκτας, οὕτως
ἔσται ὁ υἱὸς τοῦ ἀνθρώπου ἐν τῇ καρδίᾳ τῆς γῆς τρεῖς ἡμέρας καὶ
τρεῖς νύκτας. ἄνδρες Νινευῖται ἀναστήσονται ἐν τῇ κρίσει μετὰ τῆς 41
γενεᾶς ταύτης καὶ κατακρινοῦσιν αὐτήν· ὅτι μετενόησαν εἰς τὸ κήρυγμα
Ἰωνᾶ· καὶ ἰδού, πλεῖον Ἰωνᾶ ὧδε. βασίλισσα νότου ἐγερθήσεται ἐν τῇ 42
κρίσει μετὰ τῆς γενεᾶς ταύτης καὶ κατακρινεῖ αὐτήν· ὅτι ἦλθεν ἐκ
τῶν περάτων τῆς γῆς ἀκοῦσαι τὴν σοφίαν Σολομῶνος· καὶ ἰδού, πλεῖον
ρκθ Σολομῶνος ὧδε. ὅταν δὲ τὸ ἀκάθαρτον πνεῦμα ἐξέλθῃ ἀπὸ τοῦ ἀν- 43
ε θρώπου, διέρχεται δι' ἀνύδρων τόπων ζητοῦν ἀνάπαυσιν, καὶ οὐχ εὑρίσκει.
τότε λέγει, Ὑποστρέψω εἰς τὸν οἶκόν μου ὅθεν ἐξῆλθον· καὶ ἐλθὸν εὑρί- 44
σκει σχολάζοντα, σεσαρωμένον καὶ κεκοσμημένον. τότε πορεύεται καὶ 45
παραλαμβάνει μεθ' ἑαυτοῦ ἑπτὰ ἕτερα πνεύματα πονηρότερα ἑαυτοῦ, καὶ
εἰσελθόντα κατοικεῖ ἐκεῖ· καὶ γίνεται τὰ ἔσχατα τοῦ ἀνθρώπου ἐκείνου
χείρονα τῶν πρώτων. οὕτως ἔσται καὶ τῇ γενεᾷ ταύτῃ τῇ πονηρᾷ.

ρλ Ἔτι δὲ αὐτοῦ λαλοῦντος τοῖς ὄχλοις, ἰδοὺ ἡ μήτηρ καὶ οἱ ἀδελφοὶ 46
β

38 λεγωντες cod.

118 209 ϛ **31** *υμιν* 2°] om 118 209 ϛ *αφεθησεται*] + *τοις ανθρωποις* ϛ **32** *αν* 1°] *εαν* 118 *τουτω τω*] *τω νυν* 118 209 **34** *το στομα*] om 118* spat. rel. in quo scrips. *λαλει* 118² **35** om *της καρδιας αυτου* 118 209, om *αυτου* ϛ *τα πονηρα* 118 209 **36** *λεγω δε* 118 209 ϛ **37** *κατακριθηση* 118 209 **40** *καρδια*] *κοιλια* 118 209 **42** *Σολομωντος* bis 118 209 ϛ **44** *επιστρεψω* 118 209 ϛ *και σεσαρωμενον* 118 209

47 αὐτοῦ εἱστήκεισαν ἔξω, ζητοῦντες αὐτῷ λαλῆσαι. εἶπε δέ τις αὐτῷ,
Ἰδοὺ ἡ μήτηρ σου καὶ οἱ ἀδελφοί σου ἑστήκασι, ζητοῦντές σοι λαλῆσαι.
48 ὁ δὲ ἀποκριθεὶς εἶπε τῷ εἰπόντι αὐτῷ, Τίς ἐστιν ἡ μήτηρ μου, καὶ τίνες
49 εἰσὶν οἱ ἀδελφοί μου; καὶ ἐκτείνας τὴν χεῖρα αὐτοῦ ἐπὶ τοὺς μαθητὰς
50 αὐτοῦ εἶπεν, Ἰδοὺ ἡ μήτηρ μου καὶ οἱ ἀδελφοί μου. ὅστις γὰρ ἂν ποιήσῃ
τὸ θέλημα τοῦ πατρός μου τοῦ ἐν οὐρανοῖς, αὐτός μου ἀδελφὸς καὶ
ἀδελφὴ καὶ μήτηρ ἐστίν.

XIII. Ἐν δὲ τῇ ἡμέρᾳ ἐκείνῃ ἐξελθὼν ὁ Ἰησοῦς τῆς οἰκίας ρλα
2 ἐκάθητο παρὰ τὴν θάλασσαν· καὶ συνήχθησαν πρὸς αὐτὸν ὄχλοι πολλοί, β
ὥστε αὐτὸν εἰς πλοῖον ἐμβάντα καθῆσθαι· καὶ πᾶς ὁ ὄχλος ἐπὶ
3 τὸν αἰγιαλὸν εἱστήκει. καὶ ἐλάλησεν αὐτοῖς πολλὰ ἐν παραβολαῖς, ΚΔ'
4 λέγων, Ἰδοὺ ἐξῆλθεν ὁ σπείρων τοῦ σπεῖραι. καὶ ἐν τῷ σπείρειν
αὐτὸν ἃ μὲν ἔπεσε παρὰ τὴν ὁδόν, καὶ ἦλθε τὰ πετεινὰ καὶ κατέφαγεν
5 αὐτά· ἄλλα δὲ ἔπεσεν ἐπὶ τὰ πετρώδη, ὅπου οὐκ εἶχε γῆν πολλήν, καὶ
6 εὐθέως ἐξανέτειλε διὰ τὸ μὴ ἔχειν βάθος γῆς, ἡλίου δὲ ἀνατείλαντος
7 ἐκαυματίσθη, καὶ διὰ τὸ μὴ ἔχειν ῥίζαν ἐξηράνθη· ἄλλα δὲ ἔπεσεν ἐπὶ
8 τὰς ἀκάνθας, καὶ ἀνέβησαν αἱ ἄκανθαι καὶ ἀπέπνιξαν αὐτά· ἄλλα δὲ
ἔπεσεν ἐπὶ τὴν γῆν τὴν καλήν, καὶ ἐδίδου καρπόν, ὃ μὲν ἑκατόν, ὃ δὲ
9 10 ἑξήκοντα, ὃ δὲ τριάκοντα. ὁ ἔχων ὦτα ἀκούειν ἀκουέτω. καὶ προσελ-
11 θόντες οἱ μαθηταὶ εἶπον αὐτῷ, Διατί ἐν παραβολαῖς λαλεῖς αὐτοῖς; ὁ
δὲ ἀποκριθεὶς εἶπεν αὐτοῖς ὅτι Ὑμῖν δέδοται γνῶναι τὰ μυστήρια τῆς
12 βασιλείας τῶν οὐρανῶν, ἐκείνοις δὲ οὐ δέδοται. ὅστις γὰρ ἔχει, δοθή- ρλβ
σεται αὐτῷ καὶ περισσευθήσεται· ὅστις δὲ οὐκ ἔχει, καὶ ὃ ἔχει ἀρθήσεται ε
13 ἀπ' αὐτοῦ. διὰ τοῦτο ἐν παραβολαῖς λαλῶ αὐτοῖς, ἵνα βλέποντες ρλγ
μὴ βλέπωσι, καὶ ἀκούοντες μὴ ἀκούωσι καὶ μὴ συνίωσι μή- α
14 ποτε ἐπιστρέψωσι· καὶ τότε πληροῦται αὐτοῖς ἡ προφητεία
Ἠσαΐου ἡ λέγουσα, Ἀκοῇ ἀκούσετε καὶ οὐ μὴ συνῆτε· καὶ βλέποντες
15 βλέψετε καὶ οὐ μὴ ἴδητε. ἐπαχύνθη γὰρ ἡ καρδία τοῦ λαοῦ τούτου,
καὶ τοῖς ὠσὶ βαρέως ἤκουσαν, καὶ τοὺς ὀφθαλμοὺς αὐτῶν ἐκάμμυσαν·
μήποτε ἴδωσι τοῖς ὀφθαλμοῖς καὶ τοῖς ὠσὶν ἀκούσωσι καὶ τῇ καρδίᾳ
16 συνῶσι καὶ ἐπιστρέψωσι, καὶ ἰάσωμαι αὐτούς. ὑμῶν δὲ μακάριοι ρλδ
ε

50 *αδελφος*] *δελφος* cod. *α* eras. **11** *ουρανων*] cod. om

47 *εστηκασι*] pr *εξω* 118 209 ϛ 118 209 ϛ
1 *της οικιας*] pr *απο* 118 209 ϛ *εκαθισε* 118 209 **2** *αυτον εμβαντα εις το πλοιον* 209, *πολλον εμβαντα εις το πλοιον* 118* sed ipse* ut vdr. *πολλ* del. et corr. *αυτον* in marg. scripsit, *αυτον εις το πλ. εμβαντα* ϛ **3** *σπειρειν* ϛ **7** *ταις ακανθαις* 118 209 **11** om *ου δεδοται* 118* sed spat. rel. in quo corr. txt. rescrips. **13** *αυτοις λαλω* 118 209 ϛ *οτι βλεποντες ου βλεπουσι και ακουοντες ουκ ακουουσιν ουδε συνιουσι* 118 209 ϛ **14** *αναπληρουται* et om *τοτε* 118 209 ϛ *επ αυτοις* ϛ *ακουσητε* 118 209 *βλεψητε* 118 209 **15** *μηπο* 209* *μηποτε* 209corr *επιστρεψουσι* 118 209 *ιασομαι* 118 209

οἱ ὀφθαλμοί, ὅτι βλέπουσι· καὶ τὰ ὦτα ὑμῶν, ὅτι ἀκούουσιν. ἀμὴν 17
γὰρ λέγω ὑμῖν ὅτι πολλοὶ προφῆται καὶ δίκαιοι ἐπεθύμησαν ἰδεῖν ἃ
ρλε β βλέπετε, καὶ οὐκ εἶδον, καὶ ἀκοῦσαι ἃ ἀκούετε, καὶ οὐκ ἤκουσαν. ὑμεῖς 18
οὖν ἀκούσατε τὴν παραβολὴν τοῦ σπείροντος. παντὸς ἀκούοντος τὸν 19
λόγον τῆς βασιλείας καὶ μὴ συνιέντος, ἔρχεται ὁ πονηρὸς καὶ ἁρπάζει τὸ
ἐσπαρμένον ἐν τῇ καρδίᾳ αὐτοῦ· οὗτός ἐστιν ὁ παρὰ τὴν ὁδὸν σπαρείς. ὁ 20
δὲ ἐπὶ τὰ πετρώδη σπαρείς, οὗτός ἐστιν ὁ τὸν λόγον ἀκούων καὶ εὐθὺς μετὰ
χαρᾶς λαμβάνων αὐτόν, οὐκ ἔχει δὲ ῥίζαν ἐν ἑαυτῷ, ἀλλὰ πρόσκαιρός 21
ἐστι, γενομένης δὲ θλίψεως ἢ διωγμοῦ διὰ τὸν λόγον εὐθὺς σκανδαλίζεται.
ὁ δὲ εἰς τὰς ἀκάνθας σπαρείς, οὗτός ἐστιν ὁ τὸν λόγον ἀκούων, καὶ ἡ 22
μέριμνα τοῦ αἰῶνος τούτου καὶ ἡ ἀπάτη τοῦ πλούτου συμπνίγει τὸν λόγον,
καὶ ἄκαρπος γίνεται. ὁ δὲ ἐπὶ τὴν καλὴν γῆν σπαρείς, οὗτός ἐστιν 23
ὁ τὸν λόγον ἀκούων καὶ συνιῶν, ὃς δὴ καρποφορεῖ καὶ ποιεῖ ὁ μὲν ἑκατόν,
ὁ δὲ ἑξήκοντα, ὁ δὲ τριάκοντα.

ρλϛ ι Ἄλλην παραβολὴν παρέθηκεν αὐτοῖς λέγων, Ὡμοιώθη ἡ βασιλεία 24
τῶν οὐρανῶν ἀνθρώπῳ σπείροντι καλὸν σπέρμα ἐν τῷ ἀγρῷ αὐτοῦ· ἐν δὲ 25
τῷ καθεύδειν τοὺς ἀνθρώπους ἦλθεν αὐτοῦ ὁ ἐχθρὸς καὶ ἐπέσπειρεν ζιζάνια
ἀνὰ μέσον τοῦ σίτου, καὶ ἀπῆλθεν. ὅτε δὲ ἐβλάστησεν ὁ χόρτος καὶ 26
καρπὸν ἐποίησε, τότε ἐφάνη καὶ τὰ ζιζάνια. προσελθόντες δὲ οἱ δοῦλοι 27
τοῦ οἰκοδεσπότου εἶπον αὐτῷ, Κύριε, οὐχὶ καλὸν σπέρμα ἔσπειρας ἐν τῷ
σῷ ἀγρῷ; πόθεν οὖν ἔχει ζιζάνια; ὁ δὲ ἔφη αὐτοῖς, Ἐχθρὸς ἄνθρωπος 28
τοῦτο ἐποίησεν. οἱ δὲ δοῦλοι εἶπον αὐτῷ, Θέλεις οὖν ἀπελθόντες συλ-
λέξομεν αὐτά; ὁ δὲ ἔφη, Οὔ, μήποτε συλλέγοντες τὰ ζιζάνια ἐκριζώσητε 29
ἅμα αὐτοῖς τὸν σῖτον. ἄφετε οὖν αὐξάνεσθαι ἀμφότερα μέχρι τοῦ 30
θερισμοῦ· καὶ ἐν καιρῷ τοῦ θερισμοῦ ἐρῶ τοῖς θερισταῖς, Συλλέξατε πρῶτον
τὰ ζιζάνια, καὶ δήσατε αὐτὰ δέσμας πρὸς τὸ κατακαῦσαι αὐτά· τὸν δὲ σῖτον
συνάγετε εἰς τὴν ἀποθήκην μου.

ρλζ β Ἄλλην παραβολὴν παρέθηκεν αὐτοῖς λέγων, Ὁμοία ἐστὶν ἡ βασιλεία 31
τῶν οὐρανῶν κόκκῳ σινάπεως, ὃν λαβὼν ἄνθρωπος ἔσπειρεν ἐν τῷ ἀγρῷ
αὐτοῦ· ὃ μικρότερον μέν ἐστι πάντων τῶν σπερμάτων· ὅταν δὲ αὐξηθῇ, 32
μεῖζον τῶν λαχάνων ἐστὶ καὶ γίνεται δένδρον, ὥστε τὰ πετεινὰ τοῦ
οὐρανοῦ ἐλθεῖν καὶ κατασκηνοῦν ἐν τοῖς κλάδοις αὐτοῦ.

ρλη ε Ἄλλην παραβολὴν ἐλάλησεν αὐτοῖς, Ὁμοία ἐστὶν ἡ βασιλεία τῶν 33
οὐρανῶν ζύμῃ, ἣν λαβοῦσα γυνὴ ἔκρυψεν εἰς ἀλεύρου σάτα τρία, ἕως
οὗ ἐζυμώθη ὅλον.

23 τριακοντα] λ̄ cod.

118 209 ϛ **16** ακουει ϛ **20** λαμβανει 118 209 **23** την γην την καλην 118 209 ϛ **25** εσπειρε 118 209 ϛ **27** om σω 118 209 om ουν 118 209 τα ζιζανια ϛ **28** συλλεξωμεν ϛ **30** ουν αυξανεσθαι] συναυξανεσθαι 118 209 ϛ et + αυτους 118 209 τω καιρω ϛ εις δεσμας 118 209 ϛ συναγαγετε 118 209 ϛ om μεν 118 209 **32** ελθειν τα π. του ουρ. 118 209 ϛ **33** ενεκρυψεν ϛ

34 Ταῦτα πάντα ἐλάλησεν ὁ Ἰησοῦς ἐν παραβολαῖς τοῖς ὄχλοις, καὶ ρλθ
35 χωρὶς παραβολῆς οὐκ ἐλάλει αὐτοῖς, ὅπως πληρωθῇ τὸ ῥηθὲν διὰ Ἡσαίου ς/ρμ
τοῦ προφήτου λέγοντος, Ἀνοίξω ἐν παραβολαῖς τὸ στόμα μου· ἐρεύξομαι ι
κεκρυμμένα ἀπὸ καταβολῆς.

36 Τότε ἀφεὶς τοὺς ὄχλους ἦλθεν εἰς τὴν οἰκίαν αὐτοῦ καὶ προσῆλθον
αὐτῷ οἱ μαθηταὶ λέγοντες, Φράσον ἡμῖν τὴν παραβολὴν τῶν ζιζανίων
37 τοῦ ἀγροῦ. ὁ δὲ ἀποκριθεὶς εἶπεν αὐτοῖς, Ὁ σπείρων τὸ καλὸν σπέρμα
38 ἐστὶν ὁ υἱὸς τοῦ ἀνθρώπου· ὁ δὲ ἀγρός ἐστιν ὁ κόσμος· τὸ δὲ καλὸν
σπέρμα, οὗτοί εἰσιν οἱ υἱοὶ τῆς βασιλείας· τὰ δὲ ζιζάνιά εἰσιν οἱ υἱοὶ τοῦ
39 πονηροῦ· ὁ δὲ ἐχθρὸς ὁ σπείρας αὐτά ἐστιν ὁ διάβολος· ὁ δὲ θερισμὸς
40 συντέλεια τοῦ αἰῶνός ἐστιν· οἱ δὲ θερισταὶ ἄγγελοί εἰσιν. ὥσπερ οὖν
συλλέγεται τὰ ζιζάνια καὶ πυρὶ κατακαίεται, οὕτως ἔσται ἐν τῇ συν-
41 τελείᾳ τοῦ αἰῶνος τούτου· ἀποστελεῖ ὁ υἱὸς τοῦ ἀνθρώπου τοὺς ἀγγέλους
αὐτοῦ, καὶ συλλέξουσιν ἐκ τῆς βασιλείας αὐτοῦ πάντα τὰ σκάνδαλα
42 καὶ τοὺς ποιοῦντας τὴν ἀνομίαν, καὶ βαλοῦσιν αὐτοὺς εἰς τὴν κάμινον
43 τοῦ πυρός· ἐκεῖ ἔσται ὁ κλαυθμὸς καὶ ὁ βρυγμὸς τῶν ὀδόντων. τότε οἱ
δίκαιοι ἐκλάμψουσιν ὡς ὁ ἥλιος ἐν τῇ βασιλείᾳ τοῦ πατρὸς αὐτῶν. ὁ ἔχων
ὦτα ἀκούειν ἀκουέτω.

44 Πάλιν ὁμοία ἐστὶν ἡ βασιλεία τῶν οὐρανῶν θησαυρῷ κεκρυμμένῳ
ἐν τῷ ἀγρῷ, ὃν εὑρὼν ἄνθρωπος ἔκρυψε, καὶ ἀπὸ τῆς χαρᾶς αὐτοῦ
ὑπάγει καὶ πωλεῖ πάντα ὅσα ἔχει, καὶ ἀγοράζει τὸν ἀγρὸν ἐκεῖνον.

45 Πάλιν ὁμοία ἐστὶν ἡ βασιλεία τῶν οὐρανῶν ἀνθρώπῳ ἐμπόρῳ
46 ζητοῦντι καλοὺς μαργαρίτας· εὑρὼν δὲ ἕνα πολύτιμον μαργαρίτην, ἀπελ-
θὼν πέπρακε πάντα ὅσα εἶχε, καὶ ἠγόρασεν αὐτόν.

47 Πάλιν ὁμοία ἐστὶν ἡ βασιλεία τῶν οὐρανῶν σαγήνῃ βληθείσῃ εἰς
48 τὴν θάλασσαν καὶ ἐκ παντὸς γένους συναγαγούσῃ· ἥν, ὅτε ἐπληρώθη,
ἀναβιβάσαντες καὶ ἐπὶ τὸν αἰγιαλὸν καθίσαντες συνέλεξαν τὰ καλὰ
49 εἰς ἀγγῆ, τὰ δὲ σαθρὰ ἔξω ἔβαλον. οὕτως ἔσται ἐν τῇ συντελείᾳ
τοῦ αἰῶνος· ἐξελεύσονται οἱ ἄγγελοι καὶ ἀφοριοῦσι τοὺς πονηροὺς ἐκ
50 μέσου τῶν δικαίων, καὶ βαλοῦσιν αὐτοὺς εἰς τὴν κάμινον τοῦ πυρός·
51 ἐκεῖ ἔσται ὁ κλαυθμὸς καὶ ὁ βρυγμὸς τῶν ὀδόντων. λέγει αὐτοῖς ὁ Ἰησοῦς,
52 Συνήκατε ταῦτα πάντα; λέγουσιν αὐτῷ, Ναί. ὁ δὲ εἶπεν αὐτοῖς, Διὰ
τοῦτο πᾶς γραμματεὺς μαθητευθεὶς τῇ βασιλείᾳ τῶν οὐρανῶν ὅμοιός

44 πωλει] πολει cod. **49** ξελευσονται cod.

35 om Ησαιου 118 209 ς καταβολης κοσμου 118 209 ς **36** αυτου] 118 209 ς ο Ιησους ς μαθηται αυτου 118 209 ς **40** καιεται 118 209 **44** παντα οσα εχ. πωλ. ς **45** αλιν 118* rubric. neglig. παλιν 118[2] **46** ευρων δε] ος ευρων 118 209 ς **48** αναβασαντες 118 209 και post αιγιαλον 118 209 ς αγγεια 118 209 ς σαπρα 118 209 ς **51** ναι]+κυριε 118 209 ς **52** εις την βασιλειαν 118 209 ς

ἐστιν ἀνθρώπῳ οἰκοδεσπότῃ, ὅστις προφέρει ἐκ τοῦ θησαυροῦ αὐτοῦ
καινὰ καὶ παλαιά.
ρμα Καὶ ἐγένετο ὅτε ἐτέλεσεν ὁ Ἰησοῦς τὰς παραβολὰς ταύτας, μετῆρεν 53
α ἐκεῖθεν, καὶ ἐλθὼν εἰς τὴν πατρίδα αὐτοῦ ἐδίδασκεν αὐτοὺς ἐν τῇ συνα- 54
γωγῇ αὐτῶν, ὥστε ἐκπλήσσεσθαι αὐτοὺς καὶ λέγειν, Πόθεν τούτῳ ἡ
σοφία αὕτη; οὐχ οὗτός ἐστιν ὁ τοῦ τέκτονος υἱός; οὐχὶ ἡ μήτηρ 55
αὐτοῦ λέγεται Μαριάμ, καὶ οἱ ἀδελφοὶ αὐτοῦ Ἰάκωβος καὶ Ἰωσὴφ καὶ
Σίμων καὶ Ἰούδας; καὶ αἱ ἀδελφαὶ αὐτοῦ οὐχὶ πᾶσαι πρὸς ἡμᾶς εἰσι; 56
ρμβ πόθεν οὖν τούτῳ ταῦτα πάντα; καὶ ἐσκανδαλίζοντο ἐν αὐτῷ. ὁ δὲ 57
α Ἰησοῦς εἶπεν αὐτοῖς, Οὐκ ἔστι προφήτης ἄτιμος, εἰ μὴ ἐν τῇ πατρίδι
αὐτοῦ καὶ ἐν τῇ οἰκίᾳ αὐτοῦ. καὶ οὐκ ἐποίησεν ἐκεῖ δυνάμεις πολλὰς 58
διὰ τὴν ἀπιστίαν αὐτῶν.
ΚΕ' XIV. Ἐν ἐκείνῳ τῷ καιρῷ ἤκουσεν Ἡρώδης ὁ τετράρχης τὴν ἀκοὴν
ρμγ β Ἰησοῦ, καὶ εἶπε τοῖς παισὶν αὐτοῦ, Οὗτός ἐστιν Ἰωάννης ὁ Βαπτιστής· 2
οὗτος ἠγέρθη ἀπὸ τῶν νεκρῶν, καὶ διὰ τοῦτο αἱ δυνάμεις ἐνεργοῦσιν ἐν
ρμδ αὐτῷ. ὁ γὰρ Ἡρώδης κρατήσας τὸν Ἰωάννην ἔδησεν αὐτὸν καὶ ἀπέθετο 3
β ἐν τῇ φυλακῇ διὰ Ἡρωδιάδα τὴν γυναῖκα Φιλίππου τοῦ ἀδελφοῦ
αὐτοῦ· ἔλεγε γὰρ αὐτῷ ὁ Ἰωάννης, Οὐκ ἔξεστί σοι ἔχειν αὐτήν. 4
καὶ θέλων αὐτὸν ἀποκτεῖναι ἐφοβήθη τὸν ὄχλον, ὅτι ὡς προφήτην αὐτὸν 5
ρμε εἶχον. γενεσίοις δὲ ἀγομένοις τοῦ Ἡρώδου ὠρχήσατο ἡ θυγάτηρ 6
ϛ τῆς Ἡρωδιάδος ἐν τῷ μέσῳ καὶ ἤρεσε τῷ Ἡρώδῃ· ὅθεν μεθ' ὅρκου 7
ὡμολόγησε δοῦναι αὐτῇ ὃ ἐὰν αἰτήσηται. ἡ δὲ προβιβασθεῖσα ὑπὸ 8
τῆς μητρὸς αὐτῆς, Δός μοι, φησίν, ὧδε ἐπὶ πίνακι τὴν κεφαλὴν
Ἰωάννου τοῦ Βαπτιστοῦ. καὶ λυπηθεὶς ὁ βασιλεύς, διὰ τοὺς ὅρκους 9
καὶ τοὺς συνανακειμένους ἐκέλευσε δοθῆναι αὐτῇ· καὶ πέμψας ἀπεκεφά- 10
λισε Ἰωάννην ἐν τῇ φυλακῇ. καὶ ἠνέχθη ἡ κεφαλὴ αὐτοῦ ἐν τῷ πίνακι 11
καὶ ἐδόθη τῷ κορασίῳ· καὶ ἤνεγκε τῇ μητρὶ αὐτῆς. καὶ προσελθόντες οἱ 12
μαθηταὶ αὐτοῦ ἦραν τὸ πτῶμα καὶ ἔθαψαν αὐτό· καὶ ἐλθόντες ἀπήγγειλαν
ρμϛ τῷ Ἰησοῦ. ἀκούσας δὲ ὁ Ἰησοῦς ἀνεχώρησεν ἐκεῖθεν ἐν πλοίῳ εἰς 13
γ ἔρημον τόπον κατ' ἰδίαν. καὶ ἀκούσαντες οἱ ὄχλοι ἠκολούθησαν αὐτῷ πεζῇ
ἀπὸ τῶν πόλεων.

7 ωμολογησεν sic m. p. sed nunc eras. est ν εφελκυστ.

118 209 ϛ 52 προφερει] εκβαλλει 118 209 ϛ 54 εκπληττεσθαι ϛ αυτη] + και αι δυναμεις 118 209 ϛ 55 Ιωσηφ] Ιωσης ϛ, Ιωση 118 209 57 om και εν τη οικ. αυτ. 118 209

2 ουτος] αυτος 118 209 ϛ 3 απεθετο] εθετο 209 ϛ, εθ spat. rel. 118 om τη 118 209 ϛ om την 118 om την γυναικα 209 6 γενεσιων δε αγομενων 118 209 ϛ 7 αυτη δουναι 118 209 ϛ 9 ελυπηθη 118 209 ϛ δια] + δε 118 209 ϛ om αυτη 118 209 ϛ 10 τον Ιω. 118 209 ϛ 11 επι πινακι 118 209 ϛ 12 πτωμα] σωμα 118 209 ϛ 13 ακουσας δε] κουσας δε 118 per incuriam rubricatoris, και ακουσας ϛ

14 Καὶ ἐξελθὼν εἶδε πολὺν ὄχλον, καὶ ἐσπλαγχνίσθη ἐπ' αὐτοῖς καὶ
15 ἐθεράπευσε τοὺς ἀρρώστους αὐτῶν. ὀψίας δὲ γενομένης προσῆλθον αὐτῷ κϛ'
οἱ μαθηταὶ αὐτοῦ λέγοντες, Ἔρημός ἐστιν ὁ τόπος, καὶ ἡ ὥρα παρῆλθεν ρμϛ α
ἤδη· ἀπόλυσον οὖν τοὺς ὄχλους, ἵνα ἀπελθόντες εἰς τὰς κώμας ἀγορά-
16 σωσιν ἑαυτοῖς βρώματα. ὁ δὲ Ἰησοῦς φησιν, Οὐ χρείαν ἔχουσιν ἀπελ-
17 θεῖν· δότε αὐτοῖς ὑμεῖς φαγεῖν. οἱ δὲ λέγουσιν αὐτῷ, Οὐκ ἔχομεν ὧδε
18 19 εἰ μὴ πέντε ἄρτους καὶ δύο ἰχθύας. ὁ δὲ εἶπε, Φέρετέ μοι αὐτούς. καὶ
κελεύσας τοὺς ὄχλους ἀνακλιθῆναι ἐπὶ τοῦ χόρτου, λαβὼν τοὺς πέντε
ἄρτους καὶ τοὺς δύο ἰχθύας, ἀναβλέψας εἰς τὸν οὐρανὸν εὐλόγησε, καὶ
20 κλάσας ἔδωκε τοῖς μαθηταῖς τοὺς ἄρτους, οἱ δὲ μαθηταὶ τοῖς ὄχλοις. καὶ
ἔφαγον πάντες καὶ ἐχορτάσθησαν· καὶ ἦραν τὸ περισσεῦον τῶν κλασμάτων,
21 δώδεκα κοφίνους πλήρεις. οἱ δὲ ἐσθίοντες ἦσαν ἄνδρες ὡς πεντακισχίλιοι,
22 χωρὶς παίδων καὶ γυναικῶν. καὶ εὐθέως ἠνάγκασεν τοὺς μαθητὰς κζ'
ἐμβῆναι εἰς πλοῖον καὶ προάγειν αὐτὸν εἰς τὸ πέραν, ἕως οὗ ἀπολύσῃ ρμη ϛ
23 τοὺς ὄχλους. καὶ ἀπολύσας τοὺς ὄχλους ἀνέβη εἰς τὸ ὄρος κατ' ἰδίαν ρμθ β
24 προσεύξασθαι. ὀψίας δὲ γενομένης μόνος ἦν ἐκεῖ· τὸ δὲ πλοῖον ἤδη ρν δ
μέσον τῆς θαλάσσης ἦν βασανιζόμενον ὑπὸ τῶν κυμάτων· ἦν γὰρ ἐναντίος
25 ὁ ἄνεμος. τετάρτῃ δὲ φυλακῇ τῆς νυκτὸς ἦλθε πρὸς αὐτοὺς περιπατῶν
26 ἐπὶ τὴν θαλάσσαν. καὶ ἰδόντες αὐτὸν ἐπὶ τῆς θαλάσσης περιπα-
τοῦντα ἐταράχθησαν, λέγοντες ὅτι Φάντασμά ἐστι· καὶ ἀπὸ τοῦ φόβου
27 ἔκραξαν. εὐθέως δὲ ἐλάλησεν αὐτοῖς ὁ Ἰησοῦς λέγων, Θαρσεῖτε· ἐγώ εἰμι,
28 μὴ φοβεῖσθε. ἀποκριθεὶς δὲ αὐτῷ ὁ Πέτρος εἶπε, Κύριε, εἰ σὺ εἶ, κέλευσόν ρνα ι
29 με ἐλθεῖν πρός σε ἐπὶ τὰ ὕδατα. ὁ δὲ εἶπεν, Ἐλθέ. καὶ καταβὰς ἀπὸ
τοῦ πλοίου ὁ Πέτρος περιεπάτησεν ἐπὶ τὰ ὕδατα, ἐλθεῖν πρὸς τὸν Ἰησοῦν.
30 βλέπων δὲ τὸν ἄνεμον ἰσχυρὸν ἐφοβήθη, καὶ ἀρξάμενος καταποντίζεσθαι
31 ἔκραξε λέγων, Κύριε, σῶσον. εὐθέως δὲ ὁ Ἰησοῦς ἐκτείνας τὴν χεῖρα
32 ἐπελάβετο αὐτοῦ καὶ λέγει αὐτῷ, Ὀλιγόπιστε, εἰς τί ἐδίστασας; καὶ ρνβ ϛ
33 ἐμβάντων αὐτῶν εἰς τὸ πλοῖον ἐκόπασεν ὁ ἄνεμος· οἱ δὲ ἐν τῷ πλοίῳ
προσεκύνησαν αὐτῷ, λέγοντες, Ἀληθῶς Θεοῦ υἱὸς εἶ.
34 35 Καὶ διαπεράσαντες ἦλθον εἰς τὴν γῆν Γεννησαρέτ. καὶ ἐπιγνόντες ρνγ β

14 εξελθων]+ο Ιησους ϛ αυτους ϛ **15** ηδη παρηλθεν 118 209 ϛ om ουν 118 209 ϛ **16** φησιν] ειπεν αυτοις 118 209 ϛ **18** αυτους] +ωδε 118 209 ϛ **19** τους χορτους 209 ϛ, τους οχλους 118* sed ipse* ut vdr. οχλους delevit et ους perrexit spat. rel. in quo scribere χορτ casu neglexit λαβων] pr και ϛ **21** ωσει 118 209 ϛ γυναικων και παιδιων 118 209 ϛ **22** τους μαθητας] ο Ιησους τους μαθ. αυτου ϛ το πλοιον ϛ προσαγειν 118 209 **25** απηλθε 118 209 ϛ αυτους]+ο Ιησους 118 209 ϛ της θαλασσης 118 209 ϛ **26** αυτον]+οι μαθηται 118 209 ϛ την θαλασσαν 118 209 ϛ **28** om αυτω 118 209 προς σε ελθειν 118 209 ϛ **30** σωσον]+με 118 209 ϛ **33** πλοιω]+οντες 118 209, +ελθοντες ϛ **34** Γενησαρετ 118 209 118 209 ϛ

αὐτὸν οἱ ἄνδρες τοῦ τόπου ἐκείνου ἀπέστειλαν εἰς ὅλην τὴν περίχωρον
ἐκείνην, καὶ προσήνεγκαν αὐτῷ πάντας τοὺς κακῶς ἔχοντας, καὶ παρεκάλουν 36
αὐτὸν ἵνα κἂν μόνον ἅψονται τοῦ κρασπέδου τοῦ ἱματίου αὐτοῦ· καὶ ὅσοι
ἥψαντο, διεσώθησαν.
κη' XV. Τότε προσέρχονται αὐτῷ Φαρισαῖοι καὶ γραμματεῖς ἀπὸ
ρνδ/ϛ Ἱεροσολύμων λέγοντες, Διατί οἱ μαθηταί σου παραβαίνουσι τὴν παρά- 2
δοσιν τῶν πρεσβυτέρων; οὐ γὰρ νίπτονται τὰς χεῖρας ὅταν ἄρτον
ἐσθίωσιν. ὁ δὲ ἀποκριθεὶς εἶπεν αὐτοῖς, Διατί καὶ ὑμεῖς παραβαίνετε 3
τὴν ἐντολὴν τοῦ Θεοῦ διὰ τὴν παράδοσιν ὑμῶν; ὁ γὰρ Θεὸς εἶπε, Τίμα 4
τὸν πατέρα καὶ τὴν μητέρα· καί, Ὁ κακολογῶν πατέρα ἢ μητέρα θανάτῳ
τελευτάτω· ὑμεῖς δὲ λέγετε, Ὃς ἂν εἴπῃ τῷ πατρὶ ἢ τῇ μητρί, Δῶρον, ὃ ἂν 5
ἐξ ἐμοῦ ὠφεληθῇς, οὐ μὴ τιμήσει τὸν πατέρα ἢ τὴν μητέρα αὐτοῦ· 6
καὶ ἠκυρώσατε τὴν ἐντολὴν τοῦ Θεοῦ διὰ τὴν παράδοσιν ὑμῶν. ὑποκριταί, 7
καλῶς προεφήτευσε περὶ ὑμῶν Ἡσαΐας λέγων, Ὁ λαὸς οὗτος ἐγγίζει 8
μοι, τοῖς χείλεσί με τιμᾷ· ἡ δὲ καρδία αὐτῶν πόρρω ἀπέχει ἀπ' ἐμοῦ.
μάτην δὲ σέβονταί με, διδάσκοντες διδασκαλίας ἐντάλματα ἀνθρώπων. καὶ 9 10
προσκαλεσάμενος τὸν ὄχλον εἶπεν αὐτοῖς, Ἀκούετε καὶ συνίετε· οὐ τὸ 11
εἰσερχόμενον εἰς τὸ στόμα κοινοῖ τὸν ἄνθρωπον· ἀλλὰ τὸ ἐκπορευόμενον
ρνε/ι ἐκ τοῦ στόματος. τότε προσελθόντες οἱ μαθηταὶ αὐτοῦ λέγουσιν 12
αὐτῷ, Οἶδας ὅτι οἱ Φαρισαῖοι ἀκούσαντες τὸν λόγον ἐσκανδαλίσθησαν;
ὁ δὲ ἀποκριθεὶς εἶπε, Πᾶσα φυτεία, ἣν οὐκ ἐφύτευσεν ὁ πατήρ μου ὁ 13
ρνϛ/ε οὐράνιος, ἐκριζωθήσεται. ἄφετε αὐτούς· τυφλοί εἰσι ὁδηγοὶ τυφλῶν· 14
ρνζ/ϛ τυφλὸς δὲ τυφλὸν ἐὰν ὁδηγῇ, ἀμφότεροι πεσοῦνται εἰς βόθρον. ἀποκρι- 15
θεὶς δὲ ὁ Πέτρος εἶπεν αὐτῷ, Φράσον ἡμῖν τὴν παραβολήν. ὁ δὲ 16
Ἰησοῦς εἶπεν, Ἀκμὴν καὶ ὑμεῖς ἀσύνετοί ἐστε; οὔπω νοεῖτε ὅτι πᾶν τὸ 17
εἰσπορευόμενον εἰς τὸ στόμα εἰς τὴν κοιλίαν χωρεῖ καὶ εἰς ἀφεδρῶνα
ἐκβάλλεται; τὰ δὲ ἐκπορευόμενα ἐκ τοῦ στόματος ἐκ τῆς καρδίας 18
ἐξέρχεται, κἀκεῖνα κοινοῖ τὸν ἄνθρωπον. ἐκ γὰρ τῆς καρδίας ἐξέρχονται 19
διαλογισμοὶ πονηροί, φθόνοι, μοιχεῖαι, πορνεῖαι, κλοπαί, ψευδομαρτυρίαι,
βλασφημίαι· ταῦτά ἐστι τὰ κοινοῦντα τὸν ἄνθρωπον· τὸ δὲ ἀνίπτοις χερσὶ 20
φαγεῖν οὐ κοινοῖ τὸν ἄνθρωπον.
κθ' Καὶ ἐξελθὼν ἐκεῖθεν ὁ Ἰησοῦς ἀνεχώρησεν εἰς τὰ μέρη Τύρου καὶ 21

118 209 ϛ **36** om καν 118 209 ϛ αψωνται 118 209 ϛ
1 τω Ιησου οι απο Ιεροσολυμων γραμματεις και Φαρισαιοι 118 209 ϛ
2 χειρας]+αυτων 118 209 ϛ **4** ειπε] ενετειλατο λεγων 118 209 ϛ
πατερα σου ϛ **5** ο εαν 118 209 ϛ ου] pr και ϛ τιμηση 118 209 ϛ
πατερα αυτου ϛ **8** εγγιζει μοι ο λαος ουτος τω στοματι αυτων, και 118 209 ϛ
11 στοματος]+τουτο κοινοι τον ανθρωπον 118 209 ϛ **12** ειπον 118 209 ϛ
14 οδηγοι εισι τυφλοι ϛ εις βοθυνον πεσουνται 118 209 ϛ **15** παραβολην ταυτην 118 209 ϛ **19** φθονοι] φονοι 118 209 ϛ **20** φαγειν] εσθιειν 118 209

22 Σιδῶνος. καὶ ἰδοὺ γυνὴ Χαναναία ἀπὸ τῶν ὁρίων ἐκείνων ἐξελθοῦσα
ἔκραζεν αὐτῷ, Ἐλέησόν με, κύριε, υἱὲ Δαβίδ· ἡ θυγάτηρ μου δεινῶς
23 δαιμονίζεται. ὁ δὲ οὐκ ἀπεκρίθη αὐτῇ λόγον. καὶ προσελθόντες οἱ
μαθηταὶ αὐτοῦ ἠρώτων αὐτὸν λέγοντες, Ἀπόλυσον αὐτήν, ὅτι κράζει
24 ὄπισθεν ἡμῶν. ὁ δὲ ἀποκριθεὶς εἶπεν, Οὐκ ἀπεστάλην εἰ μὴ εἰς τὰ ρνη
25 πρόβατα τὰ ἀπολωλότα οἴκου Ἰσραήλ. ἡ δὲ ἐλθοῦσα προσεκύνει ε ρνθ
26 αὐτῷ λέγουσα, Κύριε, βοήθει μοι. ὁ δὲ ἀποκριθεὶς εἶπεν, Οὐκ ἔστι ς
27 καλὸν λαβεῖν τὸν ἄρτον τῶν τέκνων καὶ βαλεῖν τοῖς κυναρίοις. ἡ δὲ εἶπε,
Ναί, κύριε· καὶ γὰρ τὰ κυνάρια ἐσθίει ἀπὸ τῶν ψιχίων τῶν πιπτόντων ἀπὸ
28 τῆς τραπέζης τῶν κυρίων αὐτῶν. τότε ἀποκριθεὶς ὁ Ἰησοῦς εἶπεν αὐτῇ,
Ὦ γύναι, μεγάλη σου ἡ πίστις· γενηθήτω σοι ὡς θέλεις. καὶ ἰάθη ἡ
θυγάτηρ αὐτῆς ἀπὸ τῆς ὥρας ἐκείνης.

29 Καὶ μεταβὰς ἐκεῖθεν ὁ Ἰησοῦς ἦλθε παρὰ τὴν θάλασσαν τῆς Γαλιλαίας, Λ'
30 καὶ ἀναβὰς εἰς τὸ ὄρος ἐκάθητο ἐκεῖ. καὶ προσῆλθον αὐτῷ ὄχλοι πολλοὶ
ἔχοντες μεθ' ἑαυτῶν χωλούς, τυφλούς, κωφούς, κυλλούς, καὶ ἑτέρους πολλούς,
καὶ ἔρριψαν αὐτοὺς παρὰ τοὺς πόδας τοῦ Ἰησοῦ· καὶ ἐθεράπευσεν αὐτούς·
31 ὥστε τὸν ὄχλον θαυμάσαι βλέποντας κωφοὺς λαλοῦντας, καὶ χωλοὺς
περιπατοῦντας, καὶ τυφλοὺς βλέποντας· καὶ ἐδόξαζον τὸν Θεὸν Ἰσραήλ.
32 ὁ δὲ Ἰησοῦς προσκαλεσάμενος τοὺς μαθητὰς αὐτοῦ εἶπε, Σπλαγχνίζομαι ΛΑ'
ἐπὶ τὸν ὄχλον, ὅτι ἤδη ἡμέραι τρεῖς προσμένουσί μοι καὶ οὐκ ἔχουσι ρξ ς
τί φάγωσι. καὶ ἀπολῦσαι αὐτοὺς νήστεις οὐ θέλω, μὴ ἐκλυθῶσιν ἐν
33 τῇ ὁδῷ. καὶ λέγουσιν αὐτῷ οἱ μαθηταὶ αὐτοῦ, Πόθεν οὖν ἡμῖν ἐν
34 ἐρημίᾳ ἄρτοι τοσοῦτοι ὥστε χορτάσαι ὄχλον τοσοῦτον; καὶ λέγει αὐτοῖς ὁ
Ἰησοῦς, Πόσους ἄρτους ἔχετε; οἱ δὲ εἶπαν, Ἑπτά, καὶ ὀλίγα ἰχθύδια.
35 36 καὶ παραγγείλας τῷ ὄχλῳ ἀναπεσεῖν ἐπὶ τὴν γῆν, ἔλαβε τοὺς ἑπτὰ
ἄρτους καὶ τοὺς ἰχθύας, καὶ εὐχαριστήσας ἔκλασε καὶ ἔδωκε τοῖς μαθηταῖς,
37 οἱ δὲ μαθηταὶ τοῖς ὄχλοις. καὶ ἔφαγον πάντες καὶ ἐχορτάσθησαν. καὶ
38 τὸ περισσεῦον τῶν κλασμάτων ἦραν, ἑπτὰ σπυρίδας πλήρεις. οἱ δὲ
ἐσθίοντες ἦσαν τετρακισχίλιοι ἄνδρες, χωρὶς παίδων καὶ γυναικῶν.

22 εκραυγασεν 118 209 ς   αυτω] + λεγουσα 118 209 ς   δεινως] κακως 118 209 ς   **25** απελθουσα 118 209   **27** η] οι 118   **30** αυτους 1° om 118   **31** τους οχλους 118 209 ς   ante βλεποντας 1° spat. rel. 209 in quo nihil certius distingui potest sed forsitan 209* τυφλους (βλεπ. 1° cum βλεπ. 2° confuso) scripserit   λαλουντας] + κυλλους υγιεις 209 ς   om και 1° 209 ς, om και χωλους περιπατουντας και 118*, 118corr aliquid omissum esse signo Λ notavit sed verba ipsa non rescripsit   εδοξασαν ς   **32** ημεραι] ημερας ς, ημερ spat. rel. 118   νηστις αυτους 118 209   μη] μηποτε 118 209 ς   **34** ειπον 118 209 ς   **35** εκελευσε τω οχλω 118 209 ς   **36** ελαβε] και λαβων 118 209 ς   om και ante ευχαρ. 118 209 ς   μαθηταις] + αυτου 118 209 ς   τω οχλω 118 209 ς   **37** ηραν ante το περισσ. 118 209 ς   **38** γυναικων και παιδιων 118 209 ς   118 209 ς

Καὶ ἀπολύσας τοὺς ὄχλους ἐνέβη εἰς πλοῖον, καὶ ἦλθεν εἰς τὰ ὅρια 39
ρξα δ Μαγδαλά. XVI. καὶ προσελθόντες Φαρισαῖοι καὶ Σαδδουκαῖοι πειρά-
ρξβ ε ζοντες ἐπηρώτων αὐτὸν σημεῖον ἐκ τοῦ οὐρανοῦ ἐπιδεῖξαι αὐτοῖς. ὁ δὲ 2
ἀποκριθεὶς εἶπεν αὐτοῖς, Ὀψίας γενομένης λέγετε, Εὐδία· πυρράζει γὰρ
ὁ οὐρανός. καὶ πρωΐ, Σήμερον χειμών· πυρράζει γὰρ στυγνάζων ὁ 3
οὐρανός. τὸ μὲν πρόσωπον τοῦ οὐρανοῦ γινώσκετε διακρίνειν, τὰ δὲ
ρξγ ϛ σημεῖα τῶν καιρῶν οὐ δύνασθε; γενεὰ πονηρὰ καὶ μοιχαλὶς σημεῖον 4
ἐπιζητεῖ· καὶ σημεῖον οὐ δοθήσεται αὐτῇ, εἰ μὴ τὸ σημεῖον Ἰωνᾶ τοῦ
προφήτου. καὶ καταλιπὼν αὐτοὺς ἀπῆλθεν.
ΛΒ Καὶ ἐλθόντες οἱ μαθηταὶ αὐτοῦ εἰς τὸ πέραν ἐπελάθοντο ἄρτους λαβεῖν. 5
ρξδ β ὁ δὲ Ἰησοῦς εἶπεν αὐτοῖς, Ὁρᾶτε καὶ προσέχετε ἀπὸ τῆς ζύμης τῶν 6
ρξε ϛ Φαρισαίων καὶ Σαδδουκαίων. οἱ δὲ διελογίζοντο ἐν ἑαυτοῖς λέγοντες ὅτι 7
Ἄρτους οὐκ ἐλάβομεν. γνοὺς δὲ ὁ Ἰησοῦς εἶπε, Τί διαλογίζεσθε ἐν ἑαυ- 8
τοῖς, ὀλιγόπιστοι, ὅτι ἄρτους οὐκ ἐλάβετε; οὔπω νοεῖτε οὐδὲ μνημονεύετε 9
τοὺς πέντε ἄρτους τῶν πεντακισχιλίων, καὶ πόσους κοφίνους ἐλάβετε, οὐδὲ 10
τοὺς ἑπτὰ ἄρτους τῶν τετρακισχιλίων, καὶ πόσας σπυρίδας ἐλάβετε; πῶς οὐ 11
νοεῖτε ὅτι οὐ περὶ ἄρτων εἶπον ὑμῖν; προσέχετε δὲ ἀπὸ τῆς ζύμης
τῶν Φαρισαίων καὶ Σαδδουκαίων. τότε συνῆκαν ὅτι οὐκ εἶπεν προσέχειν 12
ἀπὸ τῶν ἄρτων, ἀλλὰ ἀπὸ τῆς διδαχῆς τῶν Φαρισαίων καὶ Σαδδουκαίων.
ΛΓ' Ἐλθὼν δὲ ὁ Ἰησοῦς εἰς τὰ μέρη Καισαρείας τῆς Φιλίππου ἠρώτα τοὺς 13
ρξϛ α μαθητὰς αὐτοῦ λέγων, Τίνα με λέγουσιν εἶναι οἱ ἄνθρωποι, τὸν υἱὸν τοῦ
ἀνθρώπου; οἱ δὲ εἶπον, Οἱ μὲν Ἰωάννην τὸν Βαπτιστήν, ἄλλοι δὲ Ἡλίαν, 14
ἕτεροι δὲ Ἱερεμίαν, ἢ ἕνα τῶν προφητῶν. λέγει αὐτοῖς, Ὑμεῖς δὲ τίνα με 15
λέγετε εἶναι; ἀποκριθεὶς δὲ Σίμων Πέτρος εἶπε, Σὺ εἶ ὁ Χριστός, ὁ υἱὸς 16
ρξζ ι τοῦ Θεοῦ τοῦ ζῶντος. ἀποκριθεὶς δὲ ὁ Ἰησοῦς εἶπεν αὐτῷ, Μακάριος 17
εἶ, Σίμων Βὰρ Ἰωνᾶ, ὅτι σὰρξ καὶ αἷμα οὐκ ἀπεκάλυψέν σοι, ἀλλ' ὁ πατήρ
μου ὁ ἐν τοῖς οὐρανοῖς. κἀγὼ δὲ σοὶ λέγω Σὺ εἶ Πέτρος, καὶ ἐπὶ ταύτῃ 18
τῇ πέτρᾳ οἰκοδομήσω μου τὴν ἐκκλησίαν, καὶ πύλαι ᾅδου οὐ κατισχύ-
σουσιν αὐτῆς. δώσω σοὶ τὰς κλεῖς τῆς βασιλείας τῶν οὐρανῶν· καὶ 19
ὅσα ἂν δήσῃς ἐπὶ τῆς γῆς, ἔσται δεδεμένα ἐν τοῖς οὐρανοῖς, καὶ ὅσα ἂν
ρξη β λύσῃς ἐπὶ τῆς γῆς, ἔσται λελυμένα ἐν τοῖς οὐρανοῖς. τότε διεστείλατο 20
τοῖς μαθηταῖς αὐτοῦ ἵνα μηδενὶ εἴπωσιν ὅτι αὐτός ἐστιν ὁ Χριστός.

118 209 ϛ **39** *το πλοιον* 118 209 ϛ *ηλθον* 118 209 **1** *οι Φαρισ.* 118 209 ϛ *επηρωτησαν* 118 209 ϛ **3** *το*] pr *υποκριται* 118 209 ϛ *ου συνιετε* 118 209 **5** om *αυτου* 118 209 **8** *ειπεν αυτοις* ϛ **11** *αρτου* ϛ *ειπον υμιν προσεχειν* ϛ, *υμιν ειπον προσεχειν* 118 209 om *προσεχετε δε* ϛ **12** *της ζυμης του αρτου* 118 209 ϛ *αλλ* ϛ **13** om *εις* 118 209 *οι ανθ. ειναι* 118 209 ϛ **17** *και αποκριθεις* 118 209 ϛ **18** *συ*] pr *οτι* 118 209 ϛ **19** *και δωσω* 118 209 ϛ *οσα αν*] *ο εαν* 118 209 ϛ *δεδεμενον* 118 209 ϛ *οσα αν*] *ο εαν* 118 209 ϛ *λελυμενον* 118 209 ϛ **20** *ο Χριστος*] pr *Ιησους* 209 ϛ, pr spat. 118* in quo corr. scripsit *ο χσ*

21 Ἀπὸ τότε ἤρξατο ὁ Ἰησοῦς δεικνύειν τοῖς μαθηταῖς αὐτοῦ ὅτι δεῖ
αὐτὸν εἰς Ἱεροσόλυμα ἀπελθεῖν, καὶ πολλὰ παθεῖν ἀπὸ τῶν πρεσβυτέρων
καὶ ἀρχιερέων καὶ γραμματέων τοῦ λαοῦ, καὶ ἀποκτανθῆναι, καὶ τῇ τρίτῃ
22 ἡμέρᾳ ἐγερθῆναι. καὶ προσλαβόμενος αὐτὸν ὁ Πέτρος ἤρξατο αὐτῷ ρξθ ς
23 ἐπιτιμᾶν λέγων, Ἵλεώς σοι, κύριε· οὐ μὴ ἔσται σοι τοῦτο. ὁ δὲ στραφεὶς
εἶπε τῷ Πέτρῳ, Ὕπαγε ὀπίσω μου, Σατανᾶ, σκάνδαλόν μου εἶ· ὅτι οὐ
24 φρονεῖς τὰ τοῦ Θεοῦ ἀλλὰ τὰ τῶν ἀνθρώπων. τότε ὁ Ἰησοῦς εἶπε τοῖς ρο β
μαθηταῖς αὐτοῦ, Εἴ τις θέλει ὀπίσω μου ἐλθεῖν, ἀπαρνησάσθω ἑαυτὸν καὶ
25 ἀρὰς τὸν σταυρὸν αὐτοῦ ἀκολουθείτω μοι. ὃς γὰρ ἂν θέλῃ τὴν ψυχὴν
αὐτοῦ σῶσαι, ἀπολέσει αὐτήν· ὃς δ' ἂν ἀπολέσῃ τὴν ψυχὴν αὐτοῦ ἕνεκεν
26 ἐμοῦ, οὗτος σώσει αὐτήν· τί γὰρ ὠφεληθήσεται ἄνθρωπος, ἐὰν τὸν
κόσμον ὅλον κερδήσῃ, τὴν δὲ ψυχὴν αὐτοῦ ζημιωθῇ; ἢ τί δώσει ἄνθρωπος
27 ἀντάλλαγμα τῆς ψυχῆς αὐτοῦ; μέλλει γὰρ ὁ υἱὸς τοῦ ἀνθρώπου ἔρχεσθαι ροα ι
ἐν τῇ δόξῃ τοῦ πατρὸς αὐτοῦ μετὰ τῶν ἀγγέλων αὐτοῦ· καὶ τότε ἀποδώσει
28 ἑκάστῳ κατὰ τὰ ἔργα αὐτοῦ. ἀμὴν δὲ λέγω ὑμῖν, εἰσί τινες τῶν ὧδε ροβ β
ἑστώτων, οἵτινες οὐ μὴ γεύσονται θανάτου ἕως ἂν ἴδωσι τὸν υἱὸν τοῦ
ἀνθρώπου ἐρχόμενον ἐν τῇ βασιλείᾳ αὐτοῦ.

XVII. Καὶ μεθ' ἡμέρας ἓξ παραλαμβάνει ὁ Ἰησοῦς τὸν Πέτρον καὶ ΛΔ'
Ἰάκωβον καὶ Ἰωάννην τὸν ἀδελφὸν αὐτοῦ, καὶ ἀνάγει αὐτοὺς εἰς ὄρος
2 ὑψηλὸν κατ' ἰδίαν. καὶ μετεμορφώθη ἔμπροσθεν αὐτῶν, καὶ ἔλαμψε τὸ
πρόσωπον αὐτοῦ ὡς ὁ ἥλιος, τὰ δὲ ἱμάτια αὐτοῦ ἐγένετο λευκὰ ὡς τὸ
3 φῶς. καὶ ἰδοὺ ὤφθησαν αὐτοῖς Μωσῆς καὶ Ἡλίας συλλαλοῦντες
4 μετ' αὐτοῦ. ἀποκριθεὶς δὲ ὁ Πέτρος εἶπε τῷ Ἰησοῦ, Κύριε, καλόν ἐστιν
ἡμᾶς ὧδε εἶναι· θέλεις ποιήσομεν ὧδε τρεῖς σκηνάς, σοὶ μίαν, καὶ
5 Μωσεῖ μίαν, καὶ Ἡλίᾳ μίαν; ἔτι αὐτοῦ λαλοῦντος ἰδοὺ νεφέλη φωτεινὴ
ἐπεσκίασεν αὐτούς· καὶ ἰδοὺ φωνὴ ἐκ τῆς νεφέλης λέγουσα, Οὗτός ἐστιν ὁ
6 υἱός μου ὁ ἀγαπητός, ἐν ᾧ εὐδόκησα· ἀκούετε αὐτοῦ. καὶ ἀκούσαντες
7 οἱ μαθηταὶ ἔπεσον ἐπὶ πρόσωπον αὐτῶν, καὶ ἐφοβήθησαν σφόδρα. καὶ
προσελθὼν ὁ Ἰησοῦς ἥψατο αὐτῶν καὶ εἶπεν, Ἐγέρθητε καὶ μὴ φοβεῖσθε.
8 ἐπάραντες δὲ τοὺς ὀφθαλμοὺς αὐτῶν οὐδένα εἶδον εἰ μὴ τὸν Ἰησοῦν
μόνον.

21 απελθειν ante Ιεροσ. 118 209 ς του λαου] om 118 209 ς **22** επιτιμαν αυτω 118 209 ς **24** om ο Ιησους 118 209 αρας] αρατω 118 209 ς ακολουθ.] pr και 118 209 ς **25** ευρησει αυτην ς **26** ωφελειται 118 209 ς **27** τα εργα] την πραξιν 209 ς, τα πραξιν 118* sed ipse* τα ad την correxit **28** om δε 118 209 ς εστηκοτων 118 ς γευσωνται 118 209 ς (118 209 ς)

1 αναγει] αναφερει 118 209 ς **2** εγενοντο 118 209 **3** Μωυσης 118 209 μετ αυτου συλλ. 118 209 ς **4** ει θελεις 118 209 ς ποιησωμεν 118 209 ς Μωση ς μιαν Ηλια 118 209 ς **5** φωτεινη] φωτος 209, φωτ spat. rel. 118 αυτου ακουετε 118 209 ς

Καὶ καταβαινόντων αὐτῶν ἐκ τοῦ ὄρους, ἐνετείλατο αὐτοῖς ὁ υἱὸς 9
λέγων, Μηδενὶ εἴπητε τὸ ὅραμα, ἕως οὗ ὁ υἱὸς τοῦ ἀνθρώπου ἐκ νεκρῶν
ρογ ἀναστῇ. καὶ ἐπηρώτησαν αὐτὸν οἱ μαθηταὶ λέγοντες, Τί οὖν οἱ γραμ- 10
ς ματεῖς λέγουσιν ὅτι Ἠλίαν δεῖ ἐλθεῖν πρῶτον; ὁ δὲ ἀποκριθεὶς αὐτοῖς 11
εἶπεν, Ἠλίας μὲν ἔρχεται καὶ ἀποκαταστήσει πάντα· λέγω δὲ ὑμῖν ὅτι 12
Ἠλίας ἤδη ἦλθε, καὶ οὐκ ἐπέγνωσαν αὐτόν, ἀλλ' ἐποίησαν ἐν αὐτῷ ὅσα
ἠθέλησαν· οὕτω καὶ ὁ υἱὸς τοῦ ἀνθρώπου μέλλει πάσχειν ὑπ' αὐτῶν.
τότε συνῆκαν οἱ μαθηταὶ ὅτι περὶ Ἰωάννου τοῦ Βαπτιστοῦ εἶπεν αὐτοῖς. 13
ΛΕ' Καὶ ἐλθόντων πρὸς τὸν ὄχλον προσῆλθεν αὐτῷ ἄνθρωπος γονυπετῶν 14
ροδ β αὐτὸν καὶ λέγων, Κύριε, ἐλέησόν μου τὸν υἱόν, ὅτι σεληνιάζεται καὶ 15
κακῶς πάσχει· πολλάκις γὰρ πίπτει εἰς τὸ πῦρ καὶ ἐνίοτε εἰς τὸ ὕδωρ.
καὶ προσήνεγκα αὐτὸν τοῖς μαθηταῖς σου, καὶ οὐκ ἠδυνήθησαν αὐτὸν 16
θεραπεῦσαι. ἀποκριθεὶς δὲ ὁ Ἰησοῦς εἶπεν, Ὦ γενεὰ ἄπιστος καὶ διεστραμ- 17
μένη, ἕως πότε μεθ' ὑμῶν ἔσομαι; ἕως πότε ἀνέξομαι ὑμῶν; φέρετέ μοι
αὐτὸν ὧδε. καὶ ἐπετίμησεν αὐτῷ ὁ Ἰησοῦς, καὶ ἐξῆλθεν ἀπ' αὐτοῦ τὸ 18
ροε δαιμόνιον, καὶ ἐθεραπεύθη ὁ παῖς ἀπὸ τῆς ὥρας ἐκείνης. τότε προσελ- 19
ε θόντες οἱ μαθηταὶ τῷ Ἰησοῦ κατ' ἰδίαν εἶπον, Διατί ἡμεῖς οὐκ ἠδυνήθημεν
ἐκβαλεῖν αὐτό; ὁ δὲ Ἰησοῦς λέγει αὐτοῖς, Διὰ τὴν ὀλιγοπιστίαν 20
ὑμῶν. ἀμὴν γὰρ λέγω ὑμῖν, ἐὰν ἔχητε πίστιν ὡς κόκκον σινάπεως, ἐρεῖτε
τῷ ὄρει τούτῳ, Μετάβα ἔνθεν ἐκεῖ, καὶ μεταβήσεται· καὶ οὐδὲν ἀδυνα-
τήσει ὑμῖν. τοῦτο δὲ τὸ γένος οὐκ ἐκπορεύεται εἰ μὴ ἐν προσευχῇ καὶ 21
νηστείᾳ.
ρος Συστρεφομένων δὲ αὐτῶν ἐν τῇ Γαλιλαίᾳ, εἶπεν αὐτοῖς ὁ Ἰησοῦς, 22
β Μέλλει ὁ υἱὸς τοῦ ἀνθρώπου παραδίδοσθαι εἰς χεῖρας ἀνθρώπων, καὶ 23
ἀποκτενοῦσιν αὐτόν, καὶ τῇ τρίτῃ ἡμέρᾳ ἐγερθήσεται. καὶ ἐλυπήθησαν
σφόδρα.
ΛϚ' Ἐλθόντων δὲ αὐτῶν εἰς Καπερναοὺμ προσῆλθον οἱ τὰ δίδραγμα 24
ροζ ι λαμβάνοντες τῷ Πέτρῳ καὶ εἶπον, Ὁ διδάσκαλος ὑμῶν οὐ τελεῖ τὰ
δίδραχμα; λέγει, Ναί. καὶ ἐλθόντα εἰς τὴν οἰκίαν, προέφθασεν αὐτὸν 25
ὁ Ἰησοῦς, λέγων, Τί σοὶ δοκεῖ, Σίμων; οἱ βασιλεῖς τῆς γῆς ἀπὸ τίνων
λαμβάνουσι τέλη ἢ κῆνσον; ἀπὸ τῶν υἱῶν αὐτῶν, ἢ ἀπὸ τῶν ἀλλοτρίων;

9 *υιος*] *υ̅ς̅* cod. sed ut vdr. in rasura

118 209 ς **9** *εκ*] *απο* ς *υιος*] *Ιησους* ς, om *ο υιος* 118 209 **10** *μαθηται αυτου* 118 209 ς **11** *ο δε*]+*Ιησους* 118 209 ς *ειπεν αυτοις* 118 209 ς *ερχεται πρωτον* 118 209 ς **12** *αλλα* 118 209 *ουτως* 118 209 **14** *ελθοντων*] +*αυτων* 118 209 ς *αυτον*] *αυτω* 118 209 ς *ενιοτε*] *πολλακις* 118 209 ς **17** *εσομαι μεθ υμων* 118 209 ς **20** *λεγει*] *ειπεν* 118 209 ς *ολιγοπ.*] *απιστιαν* 118 209 ς *μεταβηθι εντευθεν* 118 209 ς **21** *εξερχεται* 118 209 **22** *αναστρεφ.* 118 209 ς **23** *αναστησηται* 118 209 **24** *διδραγμα*] *διδραχμα* 209 ς *διδραχμα*] *διδραγμα* 118 **25** *ελθοντα*] *οτε εισηλθεν* 118 209 ς

26 εἰπόντος δέ, Ἀπὸ τῶν ἀλλοτρίων, ἔφη αὐτῷ ὁ Ἰησοῦς, Ἄραγε ἐλεύ-
27 θεροί εἰσιν οἱ υἱοί. ἵνα δὲ μὴ σκανδαλίσωμεν αὐτούς, πορευθεὶς εἰς
θάλασσαν βάλε ἄγκιστρον, καὶ τὸν ἀναβάντα πρῶτον ἰχθὺν ἆρον· καὶ
ἀνοίξας τὸ στόμα αὐτοῦ εὑρήσεις στατῆρα· ἐκεῖνον λαβὼν δὸς αὐτοῖς ἀντὶ
ἐμοῦ καὶ σοῦ.
XVIII. Ἐν ἐκείνῃ τῇ ἡμέρᾳ προσῆλθον οἱ μαθηταὶ τῷ Ἰησοῦ ΛΖ'
2 λέγοντες, Τίς ἄρα μείζων ἐστὶν ἐν τῇ βασιλείᾳ τῶν οὐρανῶν; καὶ ροη β
3 προσκαλεσάμενος παιδίον ἔστησεν αὐτὸ ἐν μέσῳ αὐτῶν, καὶ εἶπεν,
Ἀμὴν λέγω ὑμῖν, ἐὰν μὴ στραφῆτε καὶ γένησθε ὡς τὰ παιδία, οὐ μὴ
4 εἰσέλθητε εἰς τὴν βασιλείαν τῶν οὐρανῶν. ὅστις οὖν ταπεινώσει ἑαυτὸν
ὡς τὸ παιδίον τοῦτο, οὗτός ἐστιν ὁ μείζων ἐν τῇ βασιλείᾳ τῶν οὐρανῶν.
5 καὶ ὃς ἐὰν δέξηται ἓν παιδίον τοιοῦτον ἐπὶ τῷ ὀνόματί μου, ἐμὲ δέχεται·
6 ὃς δ' ἂν σκανδαλίσῃ ἕνα τῶν μικρῶν τούτων τῶν πιστευόντων εἰς ἐμέ, ροθ β
συμφέρει αὐτῷ ἵνα κρεμασθῇ μύλος ὀνικὸς εἰς τὸν τράχηλον αὐτοῦ, καὶ
7 καταποντισθῇ ἐν τῷ πελάγει τῆς θαλάσσης. οὐαὶ τῷ κόσμῳ ἀπὸ τῶν
σκανδάλων· ἀνάγκη γὰρ ἐλθεῖν τὰ σκάνδαλα· πλὴν οὐαὶ τῷ ἀνθρώπῳ
8 δι' οὗ τὸ σκάνδαλον ἔρχεται. εἰ δὲ ἡ χείρ σου ἢ ὁ πούς σου σκανδαλίζει ρπ ς
σε, ἔκκοψον αὐτὸν καὶ βάλε ἀπὸ σοῦ· καλόν σοί ἐστιν εἰσελθεῖν εἰς τὴν
ζωὴν χωλὸν ἢ κυλλόν, ἢ δύο χεῖρας ἢ δύο πόδας ἔχοντα βληθῆναι εἰς
9 τὴν γέενναν τοῦ πυρός. καὶ εἰ ὁ ὀφθαλμός σου σκανδαλίζει σε,
ἔξελε αὐτὸν καὶ βάλε ἀπὸ σοῦ· καλόν σοί ἐστι μονόφθαλμον εἰς τὴν
ζωὴν εἰσελθεῖν, ἢ δύο ὀφθαλμοὺς ἔχοντα βληθῆναι εἰς τὴν γέενναν τοῦ
10 πυρός. ὁρᾶτε μὴ καταφρονήσητε ἑνὸς τῶν μικρῶν τούτων· λέγω γὰρ ὑμῖν ρπα ι
ὅτι οἱ ἄγγελοι αὐτῶν διὰ παντὸς βλέπουσι τὸ πρόσωπον τοῦ πατρός μου
12 τοῦ ἐν οὐρανοῖς. τί ὑμῖν δοκεῖ; ἐὰν γένηταί τινι ἀνθρώπῳ ἑκατὸν ΛΗ'
πρόβατα, καὶ πλανηθῇ ἓν ἐξ αὐτῶν, οὐχὶ ἀφεὶς τὰ ἐνενηκονταεννέα ρπβ ε
13 ἐπὶ τὰ ὄρη πορευθεὶς ζητεῖ τὸ πλανώμενον; καὶ ἐὰν γένηται εὑρεῖν αὐτό,
ἀμὴν λέγω ὑμῖν ὅτι χαίρει ἐπ' αὐτῷ μᾶλλον ἢ ἐπὶ τοῖς ἐνενηκονταεννέα
14 τοῖς μὴ πεπλανημένοις. οὕτως οὐκ ἔστι θέλημα ἔμπροσθεν τοῦ πατρὸς
15 ὑμῶν τοῦ ἐν οὐρανοῖς ἵνα ἀπόληται εἷς τῶν μικρῶν τούτων. ἐὰν δὲ ρπγ ε
ἁμαρτήσῃ ὁ ἀδελφός σου, ὕπαγε καὶ ἔλεγξον αὐτὸν μεταξὺ σοῦ καὶ

5 τοιουτον] cod. nunc habet τοιουτο

11 rubr.[2] add. in marg. ηλθε γαρ ο υιος του ανθρωπου σωσε το απολολος

26 ειπ. δε] λεγει αυτω ο Πετρος 118 209 ς **27** την θαλασσαν 118 209 ς 118 20 ς
1 ημερ.] ωρα 118 209 ς **2** προσκαλεσαμενος]+ο Ιησους 118 209 ς
4 ταπεινωση ς **5** παιδιον τοιουτον εν 118 209 ς **6** εις] επι ς
7 ελθειν] pr εστιν 118 209 ς ανθρωπω εκεινω 118 209 ς **8** αυτον]
αυτα 118 209 ς την γ. του π.] το πυρ το αιωνιον 118 209 ς **10** αυτων]
+εν ουρανοις 118 209 ς **11** ηλθε γαρ ο υιος του ανθρωπου σωσαι το
απολωλος 118 209 ς **12** εννενηκονταεννεα ς **13** εννενηκ. ς **15** αμαρ-
τηση εις σε 118 209 ς, αμαρτησει εις σε 209[2]

ρπδ αὐτοῦ μόνου. ἐάν σου ἀκούσῃ, ἐκέρδησας τὸν ἀδελφόν σου. ἐὰν δὲ μὴ 16
ι ἀκούσῃ, παράλαβε μετὰ σεαυτοῦ ἔτι ἕνα ἢ δύο, ἵνα ἐπὶ στόματος δύο
μαρτύρων ἢ τριῶν σταθῇ πᾶν ῥῆμα. ἐὰν δὲ παρακούσῃ αὐτῶν, εἰπὲ τῇ 17
ἐκκλησίᾳ· ἐὰν δὲ καὶ τῆς ἐκκλησίας παρακούσῃ, ἔστω σοι λοιπὸν ὥσπερ
ρπε ὁ ἐθνικὸς καὶ ὁ τελώνης. ἀμὴν λέγω ὑμῖν, ὅσα ἐὰν δήσητε ἐπὶ τῆς γῆς 18
ζ ἔσται δεδεμένα ἐν τῷ οὐρανῷ, καὶ ὅσα ἐὰν λύσητε ἐπὶ τῆς γῆς ἔσται
ρπς λελυμένα ἐν τῷ οὐρανῷ. πάλιν λέγω ὑμῖν ὅτι ἐὰν δύο ὑμῶν συμφωνή- 19
ι σωσιν ἐπὶ τῆς γῆς περὶ παντὸς πράγματος οὗ ἐὰν αἰτήσωνται, γενήσεται
αὐτοῖς παρὰ τοῦ πατρός μου τοῦ ἐν οὐρανοῖς. οὗ γάρ εἰσι δύο ἢ τρεῖς 20
συνηγμένοι εἰς τὸ ἐμὸν ὄνομα, ἐκεῖ εἰμὶ ἐν μέσῳ αὐτῶν.
ρπζ Τότε προσελθὼν αὐτῷ ὁ Πέτρος εἶπε, Κύριε, ποσάκις ἁμαρτήσει εἰς 21
ε ἐμὲ ὁ ἀδελφός μου, καὶ ἀφήσω αὐτῷ; ἕως ἑπτάκις; λέγει αὐτῷ ὁ Ἰησοῦς, 22
ΛΘ' Οὐ λέγω σοι, ἕως ἑπτάκις, ἀλλ' ἕως ἑβδομηκοντάκις ἑπτά. διὰ τοῦτο 23
ρπη ι ὡμοιώθη ἡ βασιλεία τῶν οὐρανῶν ἀνθρώπῳ βασιλεῖ, ὃς ἠθέλησε συνᾶραι
λόγον μετὰ τῶν δούλων αὐτοῦ. ἀρξαμένου δὲ αὐτοῦ συναίρειν, προση- 24
νέχθη αὐτῷ εἷς ὀφειλέτης μυρίων ταλάντων. μὴ ἔχοντος δὲ αὐτοῦ 25
ἀποδοῦναι, ἐκέλευσεν αὐτὸν πραθῆναι καὶ τὴν γυναῖκα καὶ τὰ τέκνα
καὶ πάντα ὅσα ἔχει, καὶ ἀποδοθῆναι. πεσὼν οὖν ὁ δοῦλος προσεκύνει 26
αὐτῷ λέγων, Κύριε, μακροθύμησον ἐπ' ἐμοί, καὶ πάντα σοι ἀποδώσω.
σπλαγχνισθεὶς δὲ ὁ κύριος τοῦ δούλου ἀπέλυσεν αὐτὸν καὶ πᾶσαν τὴν 27
ὀφειλὴν ἀφῆκεν αὐτῷ. ἐξελθὼν δὲ ὁ δοῦλος ἐκεῖνος εὗρεν ἕνα τῶν 28
συνδούλων αὐτοῦ, ὃς ὤφειλεν αὐτῷ ἑκατὸν δηνάρια, καὶ κρατήσας αὐτὸν
ἔπνιγε λέγων, Ἀπόδος εἴ τι ὀφείλεις. πεσὼν οὖν ὁ σύνδουλος αὐτοῦ 29
παρεκάλει αὐτὸν λέγων, Μακροθύμησον ἐπ' ἐμοί, καὶ πάντα ἀποδώσω
σοι. ὁ δὲ οὐκ ἤθελεν, ἀλλὰ ἀπελθὼν ἔβαλεν αὐτὸν εἰς φυλακὴν ἕως οὗ 30
ἀποδῷ τὸ ὀφειλόμενον. ἰδόντες δὲ οἱ σύνδουλοι αὐτοῦ τὰ γενόμενα 31
ἐλυπήθησαν σφόδρα, καὶ ἐλθόντες διεσάφησαν τῷ κυρίῳ αὐτῶν ἅπαντα
τὰ γενόμενα. τότε προσκαλεσάμενος αὐτὸν ὁ κύριος αὐτοῦ λέγει αὐτῷ, 32
Δοῦλε πονηρέ, πᾶσαν τὴν ὀφειλὴν ἐκείνην ἀφῆκά σοι, ἐπεὶ παρεκάλεσάς
με· οὐκ ἔδει καὶ σὲ ἐλεῆσαι τὸν σύνδουλόν σου, ὡς καὶ ἐγὼ σὲ ἠλέησα; 33
καὶ ὀργισθεὶς ὁ κύριος αὐτοῦ παρέδωκεν αὐτὸν τοῖς βασανισταῖς ἕως οὗ 34
ἀποδῷ πᾶν τὸ ὀφειλόμενον αὐτῷ. οὕτως οὖν καὶ ὑμῖν ποιήσει ὁ 35

28 *ωφειλεν*] *ωφολεν* cod.

118 209 ς **16** *σεαυτου*] *σου* 118 209 ς **17** om *λοιπον* 118 209 ς **18** *αμην δε* 118 209 **19** *παλιν αμην λεγω* 118 209 *υμων*] *ημων* 209, *μων* 118* pr spat. in quo 118[2] *υ* scripsit **25** *αυτον*] + *ο κυριος αυτου* 118 209 ς *γυναικα αυτου* 118 209 ς *εχει* 118 209 ς **27** *δουλου*] + *εκεινου* 118 209 ς *πασαν την οφ.*] *το δανειον* 118 209 ς **28** *αποδος μοι* 118 209 ς *ει τι*] *ο τι* ς **29** *παρεκαλει*] pr *εις τους ποδας αυτου* 118 209 ς om *παντα* 118 209 **31** *απαντα*] *παντα* 118 209 ς **35** *ουτως και ο πατηρ υμων ο ουρανιος ποιησει υμιν* 118 209, *ουτω και ο πατηρ μου ο επουρανιος ποιησει υμιν* ς

πατήρ μου ὁ ἐπουράνιος ἐὰν μὴ ἀφῆτε ἕκαστος τῷ ἀδελφῷ αὐτοῦ ἀπὸ
τῶν καρδιῶν ὑμῶν.

XIX. Καὶ ἐγένετο ὅτε ἐτέλεσεν ὁ Ἰησοῦς τοὺς λόγους τούτους, ρπθ ς
μετῆρεν ἀπὸ τῆς Γαλιλαίας καὶ ἦλθεν εἰς τὰ ὅρια τῆς Ἰουδαίας πέραν τοῦ
2 Ἰορδάνου. καὶ ἠκολούθησαν αὐτῷ ὄχλοι πολλοί, καὶ ἐθεράπευσεν αὐτοὺς
3 ἐκεῖ. καὶ προσῆλθον αὐτῷ Φαρισαῖοι πειράζοντες αὐτὸν καὶ λέγοντες, Μ'
Εἰ ἔξεστιν ἀνθρώπῳ ἀπολῦσαι τὴν γυναῖκα αὐτοῦ κατὰ πᾶσαν αἰτίαν;
4 ὁ δὲ ἀποκριθεὶς εἶπεν αὐτοῖς, Οὐκ ἀνέγνωτε ὅτι ὁ κτίσας ἀπ' ἀρχῆς
5 ἄρσεν καὶ θῆλυ ἐποίησεν αὐτούς, καὶ εἶπεν, Ἕνεκεν τούτου καταλείψει
ἄνθρωπος τὸν πατέρα αὐτοῦ καὶ τὴν μητέρα καὶ προσκολληθήσεται τῇ
6 γυναικὶ αὐτοῦ, καὶ ἔσονται οἱ δύο εἰς σάρκα μίαν; ὥστε οὐκέτι εἰσὶ
δύο, ἀλλὰ σὰρξ μία· ὃ οὖν ὁ Θεὸς συνέζευξεν, ἄνθρωπος μὴ χωριζέτω.
7 λέγουσιν αὐτῷ, Τί οὖν Μωσῆς ἐνετείλατο δοῦναι βιβλίον ἀποστασίου
8 καὶ ἀπολῦσαι; λέγει αὐτοῖς ὅτι Μωσῆς πρὸς τὴν σκληροκαρδίαν ὑμῶν
ἐπέτρεψεν ὑμῖν ἀπολῦσαι τὰς γυναῖκας ὑμῶν· ἀπ' ἀρχῆς δὲ οὐ γέγονεν
9 οὕτω. λέγω δὲ ὑμῖν ὅτι ὃς ἂν ἀπολύσῃ τὴν γυναῖκα αὐτοῦ, παρεκτὸς ρϛ β
λόγου πορνείας, ποίει αὐτὴν μοιχευθῆναι· καὶ ὁ ἀπολελυμένην
10 γαμῶν μοιχᾶται. λέγουσιν αὐτῷ οἱ μαθηταὶ αὐτοῦ, Εἰ οὕτως ἐστὶν ἡ ρϛα ι
11 αἰτία τοῦ ἀνθρώπου μετὰ τῆς γυναικός, οὐ συμφέρει γαμῆσαι. ὁ δὲ
12 εἶπεν αὐτοῖς, Οὐ πάντες χωροῦσι τὸν λόγον, ἀλλ' οἷς δέδοται. εἰσὶ γὰρ
εὐνοῦχοι, οἵτινες ἐκ κοιλίας μητρὸς ἐγεννήθησαν οὕτω· καί εἰσιν εὐνοῦχοι,
οἵτινες εὐνουχίσθησαν ὑπὸ τῶν ἀνθρώπων· καί εἰσιν εὐνοῦχοι, οἵτινες
εὐνούχισαν ἑαυτοὺς διὰ τὴν βασιλείαν τῶν οὐρανῶν. ὁ δυνάμενος χωρεῖν
χωρείτω.

13 Τότε προσηνέχθη αὐτῷ παιδία, ἵνα τὰς χεῖρας ἐπιθῇ αὐτοῖς καὶ ρϛβ β
14 προσεύξηται· οἱ δὲ μαθηταὶ ἐπετίμησαν αὐτοῖς· ὁ δὲ Ἰησοῦς εἶπεν, Ἄφετε
τὰ παιδία, μὴ κωλύετε αὐτὰ ἐλθεῖν πρός με· τῶν γὰρ τοιούτων ἐστὶν ἡ
15 βασιλεία τῶν οὐρανῶν. καὶ ἐπιθεὶς αὐτοῖς τὰς χεῖρας ἐπορεύθη ἐκεῖθεν.
16 Καὶ ἰδοὺ εἷς προσελθὼν εἶπεν αὐτῷ, Διδάσκαλε, τί ἀγαθὸν ποιήσω ΜΑ'
17 ἵνα ἔχω ζωὴν αἰώνιον; ὁ δὲ εἶπεν αὐτῷ, Τί με ἐρωτᾷς περὶ τοῦ ἀγαθοῦ; ρϛγ β
εἷς ἐστιν ἀγαθός. εἰ δὲ θέλεις εἰσελθεῖν εἰς τὴν ζωήν, τήρησον τὰς

35 υμων]+τα παραπτωματα αυτων 118 209 ϛ — 118 209 ϛ
3 οι Φαρ. 118 209 ϛ λεγοντες αυτω 118 209 ϛ **4** κτισας] ποιησας 118 209 ϛ **5** om αυτου post πατερα 118 209 ϛ **7** αυτω] ουν 118 209 Μωυσης 118 209 απολυσαι]+αυτην 118 209 ϛ **8** οτι] om 118 209 ο Μωυσης 118 209 **9** ει μη επι πορνεια και γαμηση αλλην μοιχαται 118 209 ϛ om και...μοιχαται 209* sed add. in mg. 209² γαμων] γαμησας 118 209² ϛ **11** λογον τουτον 118 209 ϛ **12** ουτως 118 209 **13** επ αυτοις 118 209 **14** και μη ϛ **15** om αυτοις 118 209 χειρας]+αυτου 118 209 **16** εις] τις 118 209 διδασκαλε αγαθε 118 209 ϛ **17** τι με λεγεις αγαθον; ουδεις αγαθος ει μη εις ο Θεος 118 209 ϛ

ἐντολάς. ὁ δὲ λέγει αὐτῷ, Ποίας; ὁ δὲ Ἰησοῦς εἶπε, Τὸ οὐ φονεύσεις· 18
οὐ μοιχεύσεις· οὐ κλέψεις· οὐ ψευδομαρτυρήσεις· τίμα τὸν πατέρα καὶ τὴν 19
μητέρα· καί, ἀγαπήσεις τὸν πλησίον σου ὡς σεαυτόν. λέγει αὐτῷ ὁ νεανί- 20
ρλδ σκος, Ταῦτα πάντα ἐφύλαξα· τί ἔτι ὑστερῶ; ἔφη αὐτῷ ὁ Ἰησοῦς, Εἰ 21
β θέλεις τέλειος εἶναι, ὕπαγε πώλησόν σου τὰ ὑπάρχοντα καὶ δὸς πτωχοῖς·
ρλε καὶ ἕξεις θησαυρὸν ἐν οὐρανῷ· καὶ δεῦρο ἀκολούθει μοι. ἀκούσας δὲ 22
β ὁ νεανίσκος τὸν λόγον ἀπῆλθε λυπούμενος· ἦν γὰρ ἔχων κτήματα
πολλά.

Ὁ δὲ Ἰησοῦς εἶπε τοῖς μαθηταῖς αὐτοῦ, Ἀμὴν λέγω ὑμῖν ὅτι πλούσιος 23
δυσκόλως εἰσελεύσεται εἰς τὴν βασιλείαν τῶν οὐρανῶν. πάλιν λέγω ὑμῖν, 24
εὐκοπώτερόν ἐστι κάμηλον διὰ τρυπήματος ῥαφίδος εἰσελθεῖν, ἢ πλούσιον
εἰς τὴν βασιλείαν τῶν οὐρανῶν. ἀκούσαντες δὲ οἱ μαθηταὶ αὐτοῦ ἐξεπλήσ- 25
σοντο σφόδρα, λέγοντες, Τίς ἄρα δύναται σωθῆναι; ἐμβλέψας δὲ ὁ Ἰησοῦς 26
εἶπεν αὐτοῖς, Παρὰ ἀνθρώποις τοῦτο ἀδύνατόν ἐστι, παρὰ δὲ Θεῷ πάντα
δυνατά.

Τότε ἀποκριθεὶς ὁ Πέτρος εἶπεν αὐτῷ, Ἰδοὺ ἡμεῖς ἀφήκαμεν πάντα καὶ 27
ρλς ἠκολουθήσαμέν σοι· τί ἄρα ἔσται ἡμῖν; ὁ δὲ Ἰησοῦς εἶπεν αὐτοῖς, Ἀμὴν 28
ι λέγω ὑμῖν ὅτι ὑμεῖς οἱ ἀκολουθήσαντές μοι, ἐν τῇ παλιγγενεσίᾳ, ὅταν καθίσῃ
ρλζ ὁ υἱὸς τοῦ ἀνθρώπου ἐπὶ θρόνου δόξης αὐτοῦ, καθεσθήσεσθε καὶ αὐτοὶ
ε ρλη ἐπὶ δώδεκα θρόνους κρίνοντες τὰς δώδεκα φυλὰς τοῦ Ἰσραήλ. καὶ πᾶς 29
β ὅστις ἀφῆκεν ἀδελφοὺς ἢ ἀδελφὰς ἢ γονεῖς ἢ τέκνα ἢ ἀγροὺς ἢ οἰκίας
ρλθ ἕνεκεν τοῦ ὀνόματός μου, ἑκατονταπλασίονα λήψεται, καὶ ζωὴν αἰώνιον
β ΜΒʹ κληρονομήσει. πολλοὶ δὲ ἔσονται πρῶτοι ἔσχατοι, καὶ ἔσχατοι πρῶτοι. 30
σ XX. ὁμοία γάρ ἐστιν ἡ βασιλεία τῶν οὐρανῶν ἀνθρώπῳ οἰκοδεσπότῃ,
ι ὅστις ἐξῆλθεν ἅμα πρωῒ μισθώσασθαι ἐργάτας εἰς τὸν ἀμπελῶνα αὐτοῦ.
συμφωνήσας δὲ μετὰ τῶν ἐργατῶν ἐκ δηναρίου τὴν ἡμέραν ἀπέστειλεν 2
αὐτοὺς εἰς τὸν ἀμπελῶνα. καὶ ἐξελθὼν περὶ τρίτην ὥραν εἶδεν ἄλλους 3
ἑστῶτας ἐν τῇ ἀγορᾷ ἀργούς· κἀκείνοις εἶπεν, Ὑπάγετε καὶ ὑμεῖς εἰς 4
τὸν ἀμπελῶνα, καὶ ὃ ἂν ᾖ δίκαιον δώσω ὑμῖν. οἱ δὲ ἀπῆλθον. πάλιν 5
ἐξελθὼν περὶ ἕκτην καὶ ἐνάτην ὥραν ἐποίησεν ὡσαύτως. περὶ δὲ τὴν 6
ἑνδεκάτην ὥραν ἐξελθὼν εὗρεν ἄλλους ἑστῶτας ἀργούς, καὶ λέγει αὐτοῖς, Τί

118 209 **18** ο δε 1°] om 118 209 ς **19** πατερα]+σου ς εαυτον 118 209
ς **20** παντα ταυτα εφυλαξαμην εκ νεοτητος μου 118 209 ς **23** δυσκολως πλουσιος 118 209 ς **24** παλιν δε 118 209 ς διελθειν ς του Θεου εισελθειν ς **26** δυνατα εστι ς **27** ημιν] υμιν 209 **28** καθεσθησεσθε] καθηση 118, καθισεσθε 209 ς αυτοι] υμεις 118 209 ς **29** οστις] ος 118 209 ς αδελφους] pr οικιας η 118 209 ς γονεις] πατερα η μητερα η γυναικα 118 209 ς om η οικιας 118 209 ς

2 και συμφωνησας 118 209 αμπελωνα αυτου 118 209 ς **3** την τριτην ς **4** κακεινοις ς αν] εαν 118 209 ς **5** εννατην 118 209 ς

7 ὧδε ἑστήκατε ὅλην τὴν ἡμέραν ἀργοί; λέγουσιν αὐτῷ, Ὅτι οὐδεὶς ἡμᾶς
8 ἐμισθώσατο. λέγει αὐτοῖς, Ὑπάγετε καὶ ὑμεῖς εἰς τὸν ἀμπελῶνα. ὀψίας
δὲ γενομένης λέγει ὁ κύριος τοῦ ἀμπελῶνος τῷ ἐπιτρόπῳ αὐτοῦ, Κάλεσον
τοὺς ἐργάτας καὶ ἀπόδος αὐτοῖς τὸν μισθόν, ἀρξάμενος ἀπὸ τῶν ἐσχάτων
9 ἕως τῶν πρώτων. καὶ ἐλθόντες οἱ περὶ τὴν ἑνδεκάτην ὥραν ἔλαβον ἀνὰ
10 δηνάριον. ἐλθόντες δὲ οἱ πρῶτοι ἐνόμισαν ὅτι πλεῖον λήψονται· καὶ
11 ἔλαβον καὶ αὐτοὶ ἀνὰ δηνάριον. λαβόντες δὲ ἐγόγγυζον κατὰ τοῦ οἰκοδεσ-
12 πότου, λέγοντες, Οὗτοι οἱ ἔσχατοι μίαν ὥραν ἐποίησαν, καὶ ἴσους ἡμῖν
αὐτοὺς ἐποίησας τοῖς βαστάσασι τὸ βάρος τῆς ἡμέρας καὶ τὸν καύσωνα.
13 ὁ δὲ ἀποκριθεὶς εἶπεν ἑνὶ αὐτῶν, Ἑταῖρε, οὐκ ἀδικῶ σε· οὐχὶ δηναρίου συνε-
14 φώνησάς μοι; ἆρον τὸ σὸν καὶ ὕπαγε· θέλω δὲ τούτῳ τῷ ἐσχάτῳ δοῦναι
15 ὡς καὶ σοί. ἢ οὐκ ἔξεστί μοι ποιῆσαι ὃ θέλω ἐν τοῖς ἐμοῖς; ἢ ὁ ὀφθαλμός
16 σου πονηρός ἐστιν, ὅτι ἐγὼ ἀγαθός εἰμι; οὕτως ἔσονται οἱ ἔσχατοι πρῶτοι
καὶ οἱ πρῶτοι ἔσχατοι· πολλοὶ γάρ εἰσι κλητοί, ὀλίγοι δὲ ἐκλεκτοί.

17 Μέλλων δὲ ὁ Ἰησοῦς ἀναβαίνειν εἰς Ἱεροσόλυμα παρέλαβε τοὺς σα
18 δώδεκα κατ' ἰδίαν, καὶ ἐν τῇ ὁδῷ εἶπεν αὐτοῖς, Ἰδοὺ ἀναβαίνομεν εἰς β
Ἱεροσόλυμα· καὶ ὁ υἱὸς τοῦ ἀνθρώπου παραδοθήσεται τοῖς ἀρχιερεῦσι καὶ
19 γραμματεῦσι, καὶ κατακρινοῦσιν αὐτὸν θανάτῳ, καὶ παραδώσουσιν αὐτὸν
τοῖς ἔθνεσιν εἰς τὸ ἐμπαῖξαι καὶ μαστιγῶσαι καὶ σταυρῶσαι· καὶ τῇ τρίτῃ
ἡμέρᾳ ἀναστήσεται.

20 Τότε προσῆλθεν αὐτῷ ἡ μήτηρ τῶν υἱῶν Ζεβεδαίου μετὰ τῶν υἱῶν ΜΓ
21 αὐτῆς προσκυνοῦσα καὶ αἰτοῦσά τι παρ' αὐτοῦ. ὁ δὲ εἶπεν αὐτῇ, Τί θέλεις; σβ ϛ
λέγει αὐτῷ, Εἰπὲ ἵνα καθίσωσιν οὗτοι οἱ δύο υἱοί μου εἷς ἐκ δεξιῶν σου
22 καὶ εἷς ἐξ εὐωνύμων ἐν τῇ βασιλείᾳ σου. ἀποκριθεὶς δὲ ὁ Ἰησοῦς εἶπεν,
Οὐκ οἴδατε τί αἰτεῖσθε. δύνασθε πιεῖν τὸ ποτήριον ὃ ἐγὼ μέλλω πίνειν;
23 λέγουσιν αὐτῷ, Δυνάμεθα. λέγει αὐτοῖς, Τὸ μὲν ποτήριόν μου πίεσθε,
τὸ δὲ καθίσαι ἐκ δεξιῶν μου ἢ ἐξ εὐωνύμων οὐκ ἔστιν ἐμὸν δοῦναι, ἀλλ'
24 οἷς ἡτοίμασται ὑπὸ τοῦ πατρός μου. καὶ ἀκούσαντες οἱ δέκα ἠγανά- σγ
25 κτησαν περὶ τῶν δύο ἀδελφῶν. ὁ δὲ Ἰησοῦς προσκαλεσάμενος αὐτοὺς εἶπεν, β
Οἴδατε ὅτι οἱ ἄρχοντες τῶν ἐθνῶν κατακυριεύουσιν αὐτῶν, καὶ οἱ μεγάλοι
26 κατεξουσιάζουσιν αὐτῶν. οὐχ οὕτως ἔσται ἐν ὑμῖν· ἀλλ' ὃς ἐὰν θέλῃ ἐν

22 *αιτεισθε*] *αιτίσθε* hoc accentu cod.

6 *ωδε* 118 209 **7** *αμπελωνα*] + *και ο εαν η δικαιον ληψεσθε* 118 209 ϛ 118 209 ϛ
10 *πλειονα* ϛ **12** *ουτοι*] pr *οτι* 118 209 ϛ **14** *και τουτῳ* 118 209
17 *και αναβαινων ο Ιησους* 118 209 ϛ *δωδεκα μαθητας* 118 209 ϛ *και*] ante *ειπεν* 118 209 ϛ **21** *λεγει*] *η δε ειπεν* 118 209 *ευωνυμων σου* 118 209 om *ειπε* 118 209 **22** *μελλω πινειν*] *πινω* 118 209, + *και το βαπτισμα ο εγω βαπτιζομαι βαπτισθηναι* 118 209 ϛ **23** *και λεγει* ϛ *πιεσθε*] + *και το βαπτισμα ο εγω βαπτιζομαι βαπτισθησεσθε* 118 209 ϛ *και εξ ευωνυμων μου* 118 209 ϛ *ητοιμασθαι* 118 209 **26** *ουτως δε* ϛ

ὑμῖν μέγας γενέσθαι, ἔσται ὑμῶν διάκονος· καὶ ὃς ἐὰν θέλῃ ἐν ὑμῖν εἶναι 27
σδ πρῶτος, ἔσται ὑμῶν δοῦλος· ὥσπερ ὁ υἱὸς τοῦ ἀνθρώπου οὐκ ἦλθε διακονη- 28
δ θῆναι, ἀλλὰ διακονῆσαι, καὶ δοῦναι τὴν ψυχὴν αὐτοῦ λύτρον ἀντὶ πολλῶν.

ΜΔ' Καὶ ἐκπορευομένων αὐτῶν ἀπὸ Ἱεριχὼ ἠκολούθησεν αὐτῷ ὄχλος πολύς. 29
σε καὶ ἰδοὺ δύο τυφλοὶ καθήμενοι παρὰ τὴν ὁδόν, ἀκούσαντες ὅτι Ἰησοῦς 30
β παράγει, ἔκραξαν λέγοντες, Ἐλέησον ἡμᾶς, κύριε, υἱὲ Δαβίδ. ὁ δὲ ὄχλος 31
ἐπετίμησεν αὐτοῖς ἵνα σιωπήσωσιν· οἱ δὲ μεῖζον ἔκραζον λέγοντες, Ἐλέησον
ἡμᾶς, κύριε, υἱὸς Δαβίδ. καὶ στὰς ὁ Ἰησοῦς ἐφώνησεν αὐτοὺς καὶ εἶπε, 32
Τί θέλετε ποιήσω ὑμῖν; λέγουσιν αὐτῷ, Κύριε, ἵνα ἀνοιχθῶσιν ἡμῶν οἱ 33
ὀφθαλμοί. σπλαγχνισθεὶς δὲ ὁ Ἰησοῦς ἥψατο τῶν ὀφθαλμῶν αὐτῶν· καὶ 34
εὐθέως ἀνέβλεψαν καὶ ἠκολούθησαν αὐτῷ.

ΜΕ' XXI. Καὶ ὅτε ἤγγισαν εἰς Ἱεροσόλυμα καὶ ἦλθον εἰς Βηθφαγῆ πρὸς
σϛ τὸ ὄρος τῶν ἐλαιῶν, τότε ὁ Ἰησοῦς ἀπέστειλε δύο μαθητάς, λέγων αὐτοῖς, 2
β Πορεύθητε εἰς τὴν κώμην τὴν ἀπέναντι ὑμῶν, καὶ εὐθέως εὑρήσετε ὄνον
δεδεμένην, καὶ πῶλον μετ' αὐτῆς· λύσαντες ἀγάγετέ μοι. καὶ ἐάν τις ὑμῖν εἴπῃ 3
τι, ἐρεῖτε ὅτι Ὁ Κύριος αὐτῶν χρείαν ἔχει· εὐθέως δὲ ἀποστέλλει αὐτούς.
σζ τοῦτο δὲ ὅλον γέγονεν ἵνα πληρωθῇ τὸ ῥηθὲν διὰ τοῦ προφήτου λέγοντος, 4
ζ Εἴπατε τῇ θυγατρὶ Σιών, Ἰδοὺ ὁ βασιλεύς σου ἔρχεταί σοι πραῢς καὶ ἐπι- 5
ση βεβηκὼς ἐπὶ ὄνον καὶ ἐπὶ πῶλον νέον. πορευθέντες δὲ οἱ μαθηταὶ καὶ 6
β ποιήσαντες καθὼς προσέταξεν αὐτοῖς ὁ Ἰησοῦς ἤγαγον τὴν ὄνον καὶ τὸν 7
πῶλον, καὶ ἐπέθηκαν ἐπάνω αὐτῶν τὰ ἱμάτια αὐτῶν. ὁ δὲ πλεῖστος ὄχλος 8
ἔστρωσαν ἑαυτῶν τὰ ἱμάτια ἐν τῇ ὁδῷ, ἄλλοι δὲ ἔκοπτον κλάδους ἀπὸ τῶν
σθ δένδρων καὶ ἐστρώννυον ἐν τῇ ὁδῷ. οἱ δὲ ὄχλοι οἱ προάγοντες αὐτὸν καὶ 9
α οἱ ἀκολουθοῦντες ἔκραζον λέγοντες, Ὡσαννὰ τῷ υἱῷ Δαβίδ· εὐλογημένος ὁ
ἐρχόμενος ἐν ὀνόματι Κυρίου· ὡσαννὰ ἐν τοῖς ὑψίστοις.

Καὶ εἰσελθόντος αὐτοῦ εἰς Ἱεροσόλυμα, ἐσείσθη πᾶσα ἡ πόλις λέγουσα, 10
σι ι Τίς ἐστιν οὗτος; πολλοὶ δὲ ἔλεγον, Οὗτός ἐστιν Ἰησοῦς ὁ προφήτης ὁ 11
ἀπὸ Ναζαρὲθ τῆς Γαλιλαίας.

Καὶ εἰσῆλθεν ὁ Ἰησοῦς εἰς τὸ ἱερὸν τοῦ Θεοῦ, καὶ ἐξέβαλε πάντας τοὺς 12
σια α πωλοῦντας καὶ ἀγοράζοντας ἐν τῷ ἱερῷ, καὶ τὰς τραπέζας τῶν κολλυβιστῶν
κατέστρεψε καὶ τὰς καθέδρας τῶν πωλούντων τὰς περιστεράς. καὶ λέγει 13
αὐτοῖς, Γέγραπται, Ὁ οἶκός μου οἶκος προσευχῆς κληθήσεται· ὑμεῖς δὲ αὐτὸν
ΜϚ' σιβ ι πεποιήκατε σπήλαιον λῃστῶν. καὶ προσῆλθον αὐτῷ τυφλοὶ καὶ χωλοὶ 14

118 209 ϛ **26** εστω ϛ **27** εστω ϛ **30** εκραζον 118 209 om κυριε 118 209 υιος 118 209 ϛ **31** om κυριε 118 209 **33** ημων] υμων 118 209 **34** ανεβλεψαν]+αυτων οι οφθαλμοι 118 209 ϛ

4 αποστελει ϛ **5** om επι 2° 118 209 ϛ νεον] υιον υποζυγιου 118 209 ϛ **7** αυτων]+και επεκαθισεν επανω αυτων (118) 209 ϛ, επεκαθήσεν 118 **8** εαυτων] αυτων 118 209 **9** om αυτον 118 209 ϛ **11** οι δε οχλοι 118 209 ϛ Ναζαρετ 118 209 ϛ **13** κληθησεται] γενησεται 118 209 εποιησατε 118 209 ϛ **14** χωλοι και τυφλοι 118 209

15 ἐν τῷ ἱερῷ, καὶ ἐθεράπευσεν αὐτούς. ἰδόντες δὲ οἱ ἀρχιερεῖς καὶ οἱ γραμ- σιγ
ματεῖς τὰ θαυμάσια ἃ ἐποίησε, καὶ τοὺς παῖδας κράζοντας ἐν τῷ ἱερῷ καὶ ε
16 λέγοντας, Ὡσαννὰ τῷ υἱῷ Δαβίδ, ἠγανάκτησαν, καὶ εἶπον αὐτῷ, Ἀκούεις τί
οὗτοι λέγουσιν; ὁ δὲ Ἰησοῦς λέγει αὐτοῖς, Ναί· οὐδέποτε ἀνέγνωτε ὅτι Ἐκ
17 στόματος νηπίων καὶ θηλαζόντων κατηρτίσω αἶνον; καὶ καταλιπὼν αὐτοὺς σιδ
ἐξῆλθεν ἔξω τῆς πόλεως εἰς Βηθανίαν καὶ ηὐλίσθη ἐκεῖ. ς
18 Πρωΐας δὲ ἐπανάγων εἰς τὴν πόλιν ἐπείνασε· καὶ ἰδὼν συκῆν μίαν ἐπὶ ΜΖ'
19 τῆς ὁδοῦ ἦλθεν ἐπ' αὐτήν, καὶ οὐδὲν εὗρεν ἐν αὐτῇ εἰ μὴ φύλλα μόνον· καὶ
λέγει αὐτῇ, Μηκέτι ἐκ σοῦ καρπὸς γένηται εἰς τὸν αἰῶνα. καὶ ἐξηράνθη
20 παραχρῆμα ἡ συκῆ. καὶ ἰδόντες οἱ μαθηταὶ ἐθαύμασαν λέγοντες, Πῶς
21 παραχρῆμα ἐξηράνθη ἡ συκῆ; ἀποκριθεὶς δὲ ὁ Ἰησοῦς εἶπεν αὐτοῖς, Ἀμὴν σιε
λέγω ὑμῖν, ἐὰν ἔχητε πίστιν καὶ μὴ διακριθῆτε, οὐ μόνον τὸ τῆς συκῆς ς
ποιήσετε, ἀλλὰ κἂν τῷ ὄρει τούτῳ εἴπητε, Ἄρθητι καὶ βλήθητι εἰς τὴν
22 θάλασσαν, γενήσεται· καὶ πάντα ὅσα ἂν αἰτήσητε ἐν τῇ προσευχῇ πιστεύ- σις
οντες, λήψεσθε. δ
23 Καὶ ἐλθόντος αὐτοῦ εἰς τὸ ἱερόν, προσῆλθον αὐτῷ διδάσκοντι οἱ ΜΗ'
ἀρχιερεῖς καὶ οἱ πρεσβύτεροι τοῦ λαοῦ λέγοντες, Ἐν ποίᾳ ἐξουσίᾳ ταῦτα σιζ β
24 ποιεῖς; καὶ τίς σοι ἔδωκε τὴν ἐξουσίαν ταύτην; ἀποκριθεὶς δὲ ὁ Ἰησοῦς
εἶπεν αὐτοῖς, Ἐρωτήσω ὑμᾶς κἀγὼ λόγον ἕνα, ὃν ἐὰν εἴπητέ μοι, κἀγὼ ὑμῖν
25 ἐρῶ ἐν ποίᾳ ἐξουσίᾳ ταῦτα ποιῶ. τὸ βάπτισμα τοῦ Ἰωάννου πόθεν ἦν; ἐξ
οὐρανοῦ ἢ ἐξ ἀνθρώπων; οἱ δὲ διελογίζοντο παρ' ἑαυτοῖς λέγοντες, Ἐὰν
26 εἴπωμεν, Ἐξ οὐρανοῦ, ἐρεῖ ἡμῖν, Διατί οὖν οὐκ ἐπιστεύσατε αὐτῷ; ἐὰν δὲ
εἴπωμεν, Ἐξ ἀνθρώπων, φοβούμεθα τὸν ὄχλον· πάντες γὰρ εἶχον τὸν
27 Ἰωάννην ὡς προφήτην. καὶ ἀποκριθέντες τῷ Ἰησοῦ εἶπον, Οὐκ οἴδαμεν·
ἔφη αὐτοῖς καὶ αὐτός, Οὐδὲ ἐγὼ λέγω ὑμῖν ἐν ποίᾳ ἐξουσίᾳ ταῦτα ποιῶ.
28 τί δὲ ὑμῖν δοκεῖ; ἄνθρωπός τις εἶχε τέκνα δύο· καὶ προσελθὼν τῷ πρώτῳ ΜΘ'
29 εἶπε, Τέκνον, ὕπαγε σήμερον ἐργάζου ἐν τῷ ἀμπελῶνι· ὁ δὲ ἀποκριθεὶς σιη ι
30 εἶπεν, Οὐ θέλω· ὕστερον δὲ μεταμεληθεὶς ἀπῆλθε. προσελθὼν δὲ τῷ
δευτέρῳ εἶπεν ὡσαύτως· ὁ δὲ ἀποκριθεὶς εἶπεν, Ἐγώ, κύριε· καὶ οὐκ ἀπῆλθε.
31 τίς ἐκ τῶν δύο ἐποίησε τὸ θέλημα τοῦ πατρός; λέγουσιν αὐτῷ, Ὁ πρῶτος.
λέγει αὐτοῖς ὁ Ἰησοῦς, Ἀμὴν λέγω ὑμῖν ὅτι οἱ τελῶναι καὶ αἱ πόρναι προά-
32 γουσιν ὑμᾶς εἰς τὴν βασιλείαν τοῦ Θεοῦ. ἦλθε γὰρ πρὸς ὑμᾶς Ἰωάννης
ἐν ὁδῷ δικαιοσύνης, καὶ οὐκ ἐπιστεύσατε αὐτῷ, οἱ δὲ τελῶναι καὶ αἱ πόρναι

16 *αινον*] *αινων* cod. **28** *δε*] *δαι* cod.

22 *αν*] *εαν* 118 209 **23** *ελθοντι αυτω* 118 209 ς *διδασκοντες* 118 118 209 ς
24 *ενα λογον* 118 209 **25** om *του* 118 209 **26** *εχουσι* 118 209 ς
27 *και* 2°] om 118 sed erasum habet aliquid quod quamvis legere non possim non esse *και* pro certo habeo **28** om *τις* 118 209 ς *αμπελωνι*]+*μου* 118 209 ς **30** *και προσελθων* 118 209 ς **32** *Ιωαννης προς υμας* 118 209

ἐπίστευσαν αὐτῷ· ὑμεῖς δὲ ἰδόντες οὐδὲ μετεμελήθητε ὕστερον τοῦ πιστεῦσαι
αὐτῷ.
N′ Ἄλλην παραβολὴν ἀκούσατε. ἄνθρωπος ἦν οἰκοδεσπότης, ὅστις 33
σιθ β ἐφύτευσεν ἀμπελῶνα, καὶ φραγμὸν αὐτῷ περιέθηκε καὶ ὤρυξεν ἐν αὐτῷ
ληνὸν καὶ ᾠκοδόμησε πύργον, καὶ ἐξέδοτο αὐτὸν γεωργοῖς, καὶ ἀπεδήμησεν.
ὅτε δὲ ἤγγισεν ὁ καιρὸς τῶν καρπῶν, ἀπέστειλε τοὺς δούλους αὐτοῦ πρὸς 34
τοὺς γεωργοὺς λαβεῖν τοὺς καρποὺς αὐτοῦ· καὶ λαβόντες οἱ γεωργοὶ τοὺς 35
δούλους αὐτοῦ ὃν μὲν ἔδειραν ὃν δὲ ἀπέκτειναν ὃν δὲ ἐλιθοβόλησαν. πάλιν 36
ἀπέστειλεν ἄλλους δούλους πλείονας τῶν πρώτων· καὶ ἐποίησαν αὐτοῖς
ὡσαύτως. ὕστερον δὲ ἀπέστειλε πρὸς αὐτοὺς τὸν υἱὸν αὐτοῦ, λέγων, 37
Ἐντραπήσονται τὸν υἱόν μου. οἱ δὲ γεωργοὶ ἰδόντες τὸν υἱὸν εἶπον ἐν 38
ἑαυτοῖς, Οὗτός ἐστιν ὁ κληρονόμος· δεῦτε ἀποκτείνωμεν αὐτὸν καὶ σχῶμεν
αὐτοῦ τὴν κληρονομίαν. καὶ λαβόντες αὐτὸν ἐξέβαλον ἔξω τοῦ ἀμπε- 39
λῶνος καὶ ἀπέκτειναν. ὅταν οὖν ἔλθῃ ὁ κύριος τοῦ ἀμπελῶνος, τί ποιήσει 40
τοῖς γεωργοῖς ἐκείνοις; λέγουσιν αὐτῷ, Κακοὺς κακῶς ἀπολέσει αὐτούς· 41
καὶ τὸν ἀμπελῶνα ἐκδώσεται ἄλλοις γεωργοῖς, οἵτινες ἀποδώσουσιν αὐτῷ
τοὺς καρποὺς ἐν τοῖς καιροῖς αὐτῶν. λέγει αὐτοῖς ὁ Ἰησοῦς, Οὐδέποτε 42
ἀνέγνωτε ἐν ταῖς γραφαῖς, Λίθον ὃν ἀπεδοκίμασαν οἱ οἰκοδομοῦντες, οὗτος
ἐγενήθη εἰς κεφαλὴν γωνίας· παρὰ Κυρίου ἐγένετο αὕτη, καὶ ἔστι θαυμαστὴ
ἐν ὀφθαλμοῖς ὑμῶν; διὰ τοῦτο λέγω ὑμῖν ὅτι ἀρθήσεται ἀφ᾽ ὑμῶν ἡ 43
βασιλεία τοῦ Θεοῦ καὶ δοθήσεται ἔθνει ποιοῦντι τοὺς καρποὺς αὐτῆς. καὶ 44
ὁ πεσὼν ἐπὶ τὸν λίθον τοῦτον συνθλασθήσεται· ἐφ᾽ ὃν δ᾽ ἂν πέσῃ, λικμήσει
σκ α αὐτόν. καὶ ἀκούσαντες οἱ ἀρχιερεῖς καὶ οἱ Φαρισαῖοι τὰς παραβολὰς αὐτοῦ 45
ἔγνωσαν ὅτι περὶ αὐτῶν λέγει· καὶ ζητοῦντες αὐτὸν κρατῆσαι ἐφοβήθησαν 46
τοὺς ὄχλους, ἐπεὶ εἰς προφήτην αὐτὸν εἶχον.
NA′ XXII. Καὶ ἀποκριθεὶς ὁ Ἰησοῦς πάλιν εἶπεν ἐν παραβολαῖς
σκα ε αὐτοῖς, λέγων, Ὡμοιώθη ἡ βασιλεία τῶν οὐρανῶν ἀνθρώπῳ βασιλεῖ, ὅστις 2
ποιῶν γάμους τῷ υἱῷ αὐτοῦ· ἀπέστειλε τοὺς δούλους αὐτοῦ καλέσαι τοὺς 3
κεκλημένους εἰς τοὺς γάμους, καὶ οὐκ ἤθελον ἐλθεῖν. πάλιν ἀπέστειλεν 4
ἄλλους δούλους λέγων, Εἴπατε τοῖς κεκλημένοις, Ἰδοὺ τὸ ἄριστον ἡτοίμακα,
οἱ ταῦροί μου καὶ τὰ σιτιστὰ τεθυμένα, καὶ πάντα ἕτοιμα· δεῦτε εἰς τοὺς
γάμους. οἱ δὲ ἀμελήσαντες ἀπῆλθον, ὃς μὲν εἰς τὸν ἴδιον ἀγρόν, ὃς δὲ 5
εἰς τὴν ἐμπορίαν αὐτοῦ· οἱ δὲ λοιποὶ κρατήσαντες τοὺς δούλους αὐτοῦ 6

2 ομοιωθη cod.

118 209 ς **32** ουδε] ου 118 209 ς **33** ανθρωπος] + τις ς **38** σχωμεν] κατασχωμεν 118 209 ς αυτου post κληρονομιαν 118 209 ς **41** εκδοσεται 118 209 ς **42** υμων] ημων ς **43** om οτι 118 209 **45** αυτου] αυ eras. 118 **46** επειδη ς εις] ως 118 209 ς

1 αυτοις εν παραβολαις ς **2** ποιων] εποιησε et add. και ante απεστειλε ς **4** αριστον μου ητοιμασα ς **5** ο μεν ς ο δε ς

7 ὕβρισαν καὶ ἀπέκτειναν. ὁ δὲ βασιλεὺς ὠργίσθη, καὶ πέμψας τὸ στρά-
τευμα αὐτοῦ ἀνεῖλε τοὺς φονεῖς ἐκείνους καὶ τὴν πόλιν αὐτῶν ἐνέπρησε.
8 τότε λέγει τοῖς δούλοις αὐτοῦ, Ὁ μὲν γάμος ἕτοιμός ἐστιν, οἱ δὲ κεκλημένοι
9 οὐκ ἦσαν ἄξιοι. πορεύεσθε οὖν ἐπὶ τὰς διεξόδους τῶν ὁδῶν, καὶ ὅσους ἐὰν
10 εὕρητε καλέσατε εἰς τοὺς γάμους. καὶ ἐξελθόντες οἱ δοῦλοι ἐκεῖνοι εἰς τὰς
ὁδοὺς συνήγαγον πάντας ὅσους εὗρον, πονηρούς τε καὶ ἀγαθούς· καὶ ἐπλήσθη
11 ὁ γάμος ἀνακειμένων. εἰσελθὼν δὲ ὁ βασιλεὺς θεάσασθαι τοὺς ἀνακειμένους σκβ
12 εἶδεν ἐκεῖ ἄνθρωπον οὐκ ἐνδεδυμένον ἔνδυμα γάμου, καὶ λέγει αὐτῷ, Ἑταῖρε, ι
13 πῶς εἰσῆλθες ὧδε μὴ ἔχων ἔνδυμα γάμου; ὁ δὲ ἐφιμώθη· τότε εἶπεν ὁ
βασιλεὺς τοῖς διακόνοις, Δήσαντες αὐτοῦ πόδας καὶ χεῖρας ἐκβάλετε
αὐτὸν εἰς τὸ σκότος τὸ ἐξώτερον· ἐκεῖ ἔσται ὁ κλαυθμὸς καὶ ὁ βρυγμὸς
14 τῶν ὀδόντων. πολλοὶ γάρ εἰσι οἱ κλητοί, ὀλίγοι δὲ οἱ ἐκλεκτοί.
15 Τότε πορευθέντες οἱ Φαρισαῖοι συμβούλιον ἔλαβον κατ' αὐτοῦ ὅπως ΝΒ'
16 αὐτὸν παγιδεύσωσιν ἐν λόγῳ· καὶ ἀποστέλλουσιν αὐτῷ τοὺς μαθητὰς σκγ β
αὐτῶν μετὰ τῶν Ἡρωδιανῶν λέγοντες, Διδάσκαλε, οἴδαμεν ὅτι ἀληθὴς εἶ
καὶ τὴν ὁδὸν τοῦ Θεοῦ ἐν ἀληθείᾳ διδάσκεις, καὶ μέλλει σοι περὶ οὐδενός,
17 οὐ γὰρ βλέπεις εἰς πρόσωπον ἀνθρώπου. εἰπὲ οὖν ἡμῖν, τί σοι δοκεῖ;
18 ἔξεστιν ἡμῖν δοῦναι κῆνσον Καίσαρι, ἢ οὔ; γνοὺς δὲ ὁ Ἰησοῦς τὴν πονη-
19 ρίαν αὐτῶν εἶπε, Τί με πειράζετε, ὑποκριταί; ἐπιδείξατέ μοι τὸ νόμισμα
20 τοῦ κήνσου· οἱ δὲ προσήνεγκαν αὐτῷ δηνάριον. καὶ λέγει αὐτοῖς, Τίνος ἡ
21 εἰκὼν αὕτη καὶ ἡ ἐπιγραφή; λέγουσιν αὐτῷ, Καίσαρος. τότε λέγει αὐτοῖς,
22 Ἀπόδοτε οὖν τὰ Καίσαρος Καίσαρι, καὶ τὰ τοῦ Θεοῦ τῷ Θεῷ. καὶ ἀκού-
σαντες ἐθαύμασαν, καὶ ἀφέντες αὐτὸν ἀπῆλθον.
23 Ἐν ἐκείνῃ τῇ ἡμέρᾳ προσῆλθον αὐτῷ Σαδδουκαῖοι, λέγοντες μὴ εἶναι ΝΓ'
24 ἀνάστασιν, καὶ ἐπηρώτησαν αὐτὸν λέγοντες, Διδάσκαλε, Μωσῆς εἶπεν,
Ἐάν τις ἀποθάνῃ μὴ ἔχων τέκνα, ἐπιγαμβρεύσει ὁ ἀδελφὸς αὐτοῦ τὴν
25 γυναῖκα αὐτοῦ καὶ ἀναστήσει σπέρμα τῷ ἀδελφῷ αὐτοῦ. ἦσαν δὲ παρ'
ἡμῖν ἑπτὰ ἀδελφοί· καὶ ὁ πρῶτος γήμας ἐτελεύτησε· καὶ μὴ ἔχων σπέρμα
26 ἀφῆκε τὴν γυναῖκα αὐτοῦ τῷ ἀδελφῷ αὐτοῦ. ὁμοίως καὶ ὁ δεύτερος καὶ ὁ
27 28 τρίτος, ἕως τῶν ἑπτά. ὕστερον δὲ πάντων ἀπέθανε ἡ γυνή. ἐν τῇ
ἀναστάσει οὖν τίνος τῶν ἑπτὰ ἔσται ἡ γυνή; πάντες γὰρ ἔσχον αὐτήν.
29 ἀποκριθεὶς δὲ ὁ Ἰησοῦς εἶπεν αὐτοῖς, Πλανᾶσθε, μὴ εἰδότες τὰς γραφὰς

23 επηρωτισαν cod.

7 ακουσας δε ο ϛ τα στρατευματα ϛ ανειλε] ανηλε 118, απωλεσε ϛ 118 209 ϛ
9 εαν] αν ϛ **13** ποδας] πο tum spat. rel. et perg. εκβαλετε κ.τ.λ. 118
χειρας]+αρατε αυτον και ϛ αυτον] om ϛ **14** εισι] om 118^* sed spat. rel. in quo 118^2 εισι scrips., εστι 209^*, εισι 209^2 sup. lin. om οι bis 118 209 ϛ
15 om κατ αυτου ϛ **16** ου μελει ϛ ανθρωπου ϛ **17** om ημιν ϛ
23 οι λεγοντες ϛ **25** γαμησας ϛ **27** και η γυνη ϛ **28** ουν ante αναστ. ϛ om η ante γυνη 118 209 ϛ

μηδὲ τὴν δύναμιν τοῦ Θεοῦ. ἐν γὰρ τῇ ἀναστάσει οὔτε γαμοῦσιν οὔτε 30
γαμίζονται, ἀλλ' εἰσὶν ὡς οἱ ἄγγελοι ἐν τῷ οὐρανῷ. περὶ δὲ τῆς 31
ἀναστάσεως τῶν νεκρῶν, οὐκ ἀνέγνωτε τὸ ῥηθὲν ὑμῖν ὑπὸ τοῦ Θεοῦ λέγοντος,
Ἐγώ εἰμι ὁ Θεὸς Ἀβραὰμ καὶ ὁ Θεὸς Ἰσαὰκ καὶ ὁ Θεὸς Ἰακώβ; οὐκ ἔστιν 32
ὁ Θεὸς νεκρῶν, ἀλλὰ ζώντων. καὶ ἀκούσαντες οἱ ὄχλοι ἐξεπλήσσοντο ἐπὶ 33
τῇ διδαχῇ αὐτοῦ.

ΝΔ′ Οἱ δὲ Φαρισαῖοι ἀκούσαντες ὅτι ἐφίμωσε τοὺς Σαδδουκαίους, συνή- 34
σκδ ς χθησαν ἐπὶ τὸ αὐτό· καὶ ἐπηρώτησεν εἷς ἐξ αὐτῶν πειράζων αὐτὸν καὶ 35
λέγων, Διδάσκαλε, ποία ἐντολὴ μεγάλη ἐν τῷ νόμῳ; ὁ δὲ Ἰησοῦς ἔφη 36 37
αὐτῷ, Ἀγαπήσεις Κύριον τὸν Θεόν σου ἐν ὅλῃ τῇ καρδίᾳ σου καὶ ὅλῃ τῇ
ψυχῇ σου καὶ ἐν ὅλῃ τῇ διανοίᾳ σου. αὕτη ἐστὶν ἡ μεγάλη καὶ πρώτη 38
ἐντολή. δευτέρα δὲ ὁμοία αὐτῇ, Ἀγαπήσεις τὸν πλησίον σου ὡς ἑαυτόν 39
σου. ἐν ταύταις ταῖς δυσὶν ἐντολαῖς ὅλος ὁ νόμος καὶ οἱ προφῆται 40
κρέμανται.

ΝΕ′ Συνηγμένων δὲ τῶν Φαρισαίων, ἐπηρώτησεν αὐτοὺς ὁ Ἰησοῦς λέγων, 41 42
σκε β Τί ὑμῖν δοκεῖ περὶ τοῦ Χριστοῦ; τίνος υἱός ἐστι; λέγουσιν αὐτῷ, Τοῦ
Δαβίδ. λέγει αὐτοῖς ὁ Ἰησοῦς, Πῶς οὖν Δαβὶδ ἐν πνεύματι κύριον 43
αὐτὸν καλεῖ, λέγων, Εἶπεν ὁ Κύριος τῷ κυρίῳ μου, Κάθου ἐκ δεξιῶν μου, 44
ἕως ἂν θῶ τοὺς ἐχθρούς σου ὑποπόδιον τῶν ποδῶν σου; εἰ οὖν Δαβὶδ 45
σκς β καλεῖ αὐτὸν κύριον, πῶς υἱὸς αὐτοῦ ἐστι; καὶ οὐδεὶς ἠδύνατο αὐτῷ ἀπο- 46
κριθῆναι λόγον· οὐδὲ ἐτόλμησέ τις ἀπ' ἐκείνης τῆς ὥρας ἐπερωτῆσαι
αὐτὸν οὐκέτι.

ΝϚ′ XXIII. Τότε ὁ Ἰησοῦς ἐλάλησε τοῖς ὄχλοις καὶ τοῖς μαθηταῖς αὐτοῦ
σκζ ι λέγων, Ἐπὶ τῆς Μωσέως καθέδρας ἐκάθισαν οἱ γραμματεῖς καὶ οἱ Φαρισαῖοι· 2
πάντα οὖν ὅσα ἐὰν εἴπωσιν ὑμῖν, ποιεῖτε καὶ τηρεῖτε· κατὰ δὲ τὰ ἔργα 3
σκη ε αὐτῶν μὴ ποιεῖτε· λέγουσι γὰρ καὶ οὐ ποιοῦσι. δεσμεύουσι δὲ φορτία 4
βαρέα, καὶ ἐπιτιθέασιν ἐπὶ τοὺς ὤμους τῶν ἀνθρώπων, τῷ δὲ δακτύλῳ αὐτῶν
σκθ β οὐ θέλουσι κινῆσαι αὐτά. πάντα δὲ τὰ ἔργα αὐτῶν ποιοῦσι πρὸς τὸ 5
θεαθῆναι τοῖς ἀνθρώποις. πλατύνουσι γὰρ τὰ φυλακτήρια ἑαυτῶν καὶ
μεγαλύνουσι τὰ κράσπεδα, φιλοῦσι δὲ τὰς πρωτοκλισίας ἐν τοῖς 6
δείπνοις καὶ τὰς πρωτοκαθεδρίας ἐν ταῖς συναγωγαῖς καὶ τοὺς ἀσπασμοὺς 7
ἐν ταῖς ἀγοραῖς, καὶ καλεῖσθαι ὑπὸ τῶν ἀνθρώπων ῥαββί. ὑμεῖς δὲ μὴ 8

118 209 ς **30** εκγαμιζονται ς αλλ ως αγγελοι του Θεου εν ουρανω εισι ς **32** νεκρων] pr Θεος ς **35** αυτων]+νομικος ς **37** εφη] ειπεν ς ολη 2°] pr εν 118 209 ς **38** εστι πρωτη και μεγαλη ς **39** εαυτον σου] σεαυτον ς, om σου 118 sed spat. rel. **43** om ο Ιησους ς **46** εδυνατο ς αποκριθηναι αυτω 118 209 ωρας] ημερας ς αυτον] αυτων 118* sed ω delet.

3 οσα] om 118 εαν] αν ς υμιν]+τηρειν ς τηρειτε και ποιειτε ς **4** δε] γαρ ς βαρεα και δυσβαστακτα ς **5** κρασπεδα]+των ιματιων αυτων ς **6** τε την πρωτοκλισιαν ς **7** ραββι ραββι ς

κληθῆτε ῥαββί· εἷς γάρ ἐστιν ὑμῶν ὁ καθηγητής, πάντες δὲ ὑμεῖς σλ ι
9 ἀδελφοί ἐστε. καὶ πατέρα μὴ καλέσητε ὑμῶν ἐπὶ τῆς γῆς· εἷς γάρ ἐστιν ὁ
10 πατὴρ ὑμῶν ὁ ἐν οὐρανοῖς. μηδὲ κληθῆτε καθηγηταί· ὅτι καθηγητὴς
11 12 ὑμῶν ὁ Χριστός. ὁ δὲ μείζων ὑμῶν ἔσται ὑμῶν διάκονος. ὅστις οὖν σλα ε
ὑψώσει ἑαυτὸν ταπεινωθήσεται, καὶ ὅστις ταπεινώσει ἑαυτὸν ὑψωθήσεται.
14 Οὐαὶ δὲ ὑμῖν, γραμματεῖς καὶ Φαρισαῖοι, ὑποκριταί, ὅτι κλείετε τὴν σλβ ε
βασιλείαν τῶν οὐρανῶν ἔμπροσθεν τῶν ἀνθρώπων· ὑμεῖς γὰρ οὐκ εἰσέρ-
15 χεσθε, οὐδὲ τοὺς εἰσερχομένους ἀφίετε εἰσελθεῖν. οὐαὶ ὑμῖν, γραμματεῖς σλγ ι
καὶ Φαρισαῖοι, ὑποκριταί, ὅτι περιάγετε τὴν θάλασσαν καὶ τὴν ξηρὰν
ποιῆσαι ἕνα προσήλυτον, καὶ ὅταν γένηται, ποιεῖτε αὐτὸν υἱὸν γεέννης
16 διπλότερον ὑμῶν. οὐαὶ ὑμῖν, ὁδηγοὶ τυφλοί, οἱ λέγοντες, Ὃς ἂν ὀμόσῃ ἐν
17 τῷ ναῷ, οὐδέν ἐστιν, ὃς δ' ἂν ὀμόσῃ ἐν τῷ χρυσῷ τοῦ ναοῦ ὀφείλει. μωροὶ
καὶ τυφλοί· τίς γὰρ μείζων ἐστίν, ὁ χρυσός, ἢ ὁ ναὸς ὁ ἁγιάζων τὸν
18 χρυσόν; καί, Ὃς δ' ἂν ὀμόσῃ ἐν τῷ θυσιαστηρίῳ, οὐδέν ἐστιν, ὃς δ' ἂν
19 ὀμόσῃ ἐν τῷ δώρῳ τῷ ἐπάνω αὐτοῦ ὀφείλει. τυφλοί· τί γὰρ μεῖζον,
20 τὸ δῶρον, ἢ τὸ θυσιαστήριον τὸ ἁγιάζον τὸ δῶρον; ὁ οὖν ὀμόσας ἐν τῷ
21 θυσιαστηρίῳ ὀμνύει ἐν αὐτῷ καὶ ἐν πᾶσι τοῖς ἐπάνω αὐτοῦ· καὶ ὁ ὀμόσας
22 ἐν τῷ ναῷ ὀμνύει ἐν αὐτῷ καὶ ἐν τῷ κατοικοῦντι αὐτόν· καὶ ὁ ὀμόσας ἐν
τῷ οὐρανῷ ὀμνύει ἐν τῷ θρόνῳ τοῦ Θεοῦ καὶ ἐν τῷ καθημένῳ ἐπάνω αὐτοῦ.
23 Οὐαὶ ὑμῖν, γραμματεῖς καὶ Φαρισαῖοι, ὑποκριταί, ὅτι ἀποδεκατοῦτε τὸ σλδ ε
ἡδύοσμον καὶ τὸ ἄνηθον καὶ τὸ κύμινον, καὶ ἀφήκατε τὰ βάρεα τοῦ
νόμου, τὴν κρίσιν καὶ τὸν ἔλεον καὶ τὴν πίστιν· ταῦτα ἔδει ποιῆσαι,
24 κἀκεῖνα μὴ ἀφιέναι. ὁδηγοὶ τυφλοί, οἱ διϋλίζοντες τὸν κώνωπα τὴν δὲ σλε ι
25 κάμηλον καταπίνοντες. οὐαὶ ὑμῖν, γραμματεῖς καὶ Φαρισαῖοι, ὑποκριταί, σλς ε
ὅτι καθαρίζετε τὸ ἔξωθεν τοῦ ποτηρίου καὶ τῆς παροψίδος, ἔσωθεν δὲ
26 γέμουσιν ἐξ ἁρπαγῆς καὶ ἀκρασίας. Φαρισαῖε τυφλέ, καθάρισον πρῶτον
τὸ ἐντὸς τοῦ ποτηρίου, ἵνα γένηται καὶ τὸ ἐκτὸς αὐτοῦ καθαρόν.
27 Οὐαὶ ὑμῖν, γραμματεῖς καὶ Φαρισαῖοι, ὑποκριταί, ὅτι ὁμοιάζετε σλζ ε
τάφοις κεκονιαμένοις, οἵτινες ἔξωθεν μὲν φαίνονται ὡραῖοι, ἔσωθεν δὲ
28 γέμουσιν ὀστέων νεκρῶν καὶ πάσης ἀκαθαρσίας. οὕτω καὶ ὑμεῖς ἔξωθεν
μὲν φαίνεσθε τοῖς ἀνθρώποις δίκαιοι, ἔσωθεν δὲ μεστοί ἐστε ὑποκρίσεως
29 καὶ ἀνομίας. οὐαὶ ὑμῖν, γραμματεῖς καὶ Φαρισαῖοι, ὑποκριταί, ὅτι οἰκο- σλη ε

18 τω επανω] του επανω cod.

8 καθηγητης] + ο Χριστος ς **9** τοις ουρανοις ς **10** εις γαρ υμων εστιν ο καθηγητης ο Χριστος ς **12** ουν] δε ς **13** ουαι υμιν γραμματεις και Φαρισαιοι υποκριται οτι κατεσθιετε τας οικιας των χηρων και προφασει μακρα προσευχομενοι· δια τουτο ληψεσθε περισσοτερον κριμα ς **14** om δε ς **15** ποιειται 118 **18** ος δ αν 1°] ος εαν ς **19** μωροι και τυφλοι ς **23** βαρυτερα ς **26** ποτηριου] + και της παροψιδος ς αυτων ς **27** παρομοιαζετε 118 209 ς 118 209 ς

δομεῖτε τοὺς τάφους τῶν προφητῶν καὶ κοσμεῖτε τὰ μνημεῖα τῶν δικαίων,
καὶ λέγετε, Εἰ ἦμεν ἐν ταῖς ἡμέραις τῶν πατέρων ἡμῶν, οὐκ ἂν ἦμεν αὐτῶν 30
κοινωνοὶ ἐν τῷ αἵματι τῶν προφητῶν· ὥστε μαρτυρεῖτε αὐτοῖς ὅτι υἱοί 31
σλθ ἐστε τῶν φονευσάντων τοὺς προφήτας· καὶ ὑμεῖς πληρώσατε τὸ μέτρον 32
ι τῶν πατέρων ὑμῶν. ὄφεις, γεννήματα ἐχιδνῶν, πῶς φύγητε ἀπὸ τῆς 33
σμ κρίσεως τῆς γεέννης; διὰ τοῦτο ἰδοὺ ἐγὼ ἀποστέλλω πρὸς ὑμᾶς προφήτας 34
ε καὶ σοφοὺς καὶ γραμματεῖς· ἐξ αὐτῶν ἀποκτενεῖτε καὶ σταυρώσετε, καὶ
ἐξ αὐτῶν μαστιγώσετε ἐν ταῖς συναγωγαῖς ὑμῶν καὶ διώξετε ἀπὸ πόλεως
εἰς πόλιν, ὅπως ἔλθῃ ἐφ' ὑμᾶς πᾶν αἷμα δίκαιον ἐκχυννόμενον ἐπὶ τῆς 35
γῆς, ἀπὸ τοῦ αἵματος Ἄβελ τοῦ δικαίου ἕως τοῦ αἵματος Ζαχαρίου υἱοῦ
Βαραχίου, ὃν ἐφονεύσατε μεταξὺ τοῦ ναοῦ καὶ τοῦ θυσιαστηρίου. ἀμὴν 36
σμα λέγω ὑμῖν, ἥξει πάντα ταῦτα ἐπὶ τὴν γενεὰν ταύτην. Ἱερουσαλήμ, 37
ε Ἱερουσαλήμ, ἡ ἀποκτείνουσα τοὺς προφήτας καὶ λιθοβολοῦσα τοὺς
ἀπεσταλμένους πρὸς αὐτήν, ποσάκις ἠθέλησα ἐπισυναγαγεῖν τὰ τέκνα σου,
ὃν τρόπον ὄρνις ἐπισυνάγει τὰ νοσσία ἑαυτῆς ὑπὸ τὰς πτέρυγας, καὶ οὐκ
ἠθελήσατε; ἰδοὺ ἀφίεται ὑμῖν ὁ οἶκος ὑμῶν ἔρημος. λέγω γὰρ ὑμῖν ὅτι 38 39
Οὐ μή με ἴδητε ἀπ' ἄρτι, ἕως ἂν εἴπητε, Εὐλογημένος ὁ ἐρχόμενος ἐν ὀνόματι
Κυρίου.

σμβ β XXIV. Καὶ ἐξελθὼν ὁ Ἰησοῦς ἀπὸ τοῦ ἱεροῦ ἐπορεύετο· καὶ
προσῆλθον οἱ μαθηταὶ αὐτοῦ ἐπιδεῖξαι αὐτῷ τὰς οἰκοδομὰς τοῦ ἱεροῦ. ὁ 2
δὲ ἀποκριθεὶς εἶπεν αὐτοῖς, Οὐ βλέπετε ταῦτα πάντα; ἀμὴν λέγω ὑμῖν,
ΝΖ' οὐ μὴ ἀφεθῇ ὧδε λίθος ἐπὶ λίθον ὃς οὐ μὴ καταλυθήσεται. καθημένου δὲ 3
σμγ β αὐτοῦ ἐπὶ τοῦ ὄρους τῶν ἐλαιῶν, προσῆλθον αὐτῷ οἱ μαθηταὶ κατ' ἰδίαν
λέγοντες, Εἶπον ἡμῖν, πότε ταῦτα ἔσται; καὶ τί τὸ σημεῖον τῆς σῆς
παρουσίας καὶ συντελείας τοῦ αἰῶνος; ἀποκριθεὶς δὲ ὁ Ἰησοῦς εἶπεν 4
αὐτοῖς, Βλέπετε μή τις ὑμᾶς πλανήσῃ. πολλοὶ γὰρ ἐλεύσονται ἐπὶ τῷ 5
ὀνόματί μου, λέγοντες, Ἐγώ εἰμι ὁ Χριστός, καὶ πολλοὺς πλανήσουσι.
μελλήσετε δὲ ἀκούειν πολέμους καὶ ἀκοὰς πολέμων. ὁρᾶτε, μὴ θροεῖσθε· 6
δεῖ γὰρ γενέσθαι· ἀλλ' οὔπω ἐστὶ τὸ τέλος. ἐγερθήσεται γὰρ ἔθνος ἐπ' 7
ἔθνος καὶ βασιλεία ἐπὶ βασιλείαν· καὶ ἔσονται λιμοὶ καὶ λοιμοὶ καὶ
σμδ α σεισμοὶ κατὰ τόπους. ταῦτα δὲ πάντα ἀρχὴ ὠδίνων. τότε παραδώ- 8 9

3 ειπον] ν deletum est

118 209 ς 30 κοινωνοι αυτων ς 31 εαυτοις ς 34 εξ αυτων] pr και ς 35 εκχυνομενον 118 209 ς om του 3° 118 209 36 ταυτα παντα ς 37 αποκτ νουσα 118 επισυναγει ορνις ς 39 om οτι ς

1 επορευετο ante απο του ιερου ς 2 ο δε Ιησους ς om αποκριθεις ς παντα ταυτα ς 3 ειπε 118 209corr ς, 209* legere non potui sed rasura quae etiam accentum mutavisse videatur ειπον scriptum esse confirmat της συντελειας ς 4 και αποκριθεις ς 6 θροηθητε 118 209 παντα γενεσθαι ς 7 επ] επι 118 209 ς 8 παντα δε ταυτα ς

σουσιν ὑμᾶς εἰς θλίψεις, καὶ ἀποκτενοῦσιν ὑμᾶς, καὶ ἔσεσθε μισούμενοι
10 ὑπὸ πάντων διὰ τὸ ὄνομά μου. καὶ τότε σκανδαλισθήσονται πολλοί, καὶ σμε
11 ἀλλήλους παραδώσουσι καὶ μισήσουσιν ἀλλήλους· καὶ πολλοὶ ψευδο- ι
12 προφῆται ἐγερθήσονται καὶ πλανήσουσι πολλούς· καὶ διὰ τὸ πληθυν-
13 θῆναι τὴν ἀνομίαν ψυγήσεται ἡ ἀγάπη τῶν πολλῶν· ὁ δὲ ὑπομείνας εἰς
14 τέλος, οὗτος σωθήσεται. καὶ κηρυχθήσεται τοῦτο τὸ εὐαγγέλιον τῆς σμϛ
βασιλείας ὅλῃ τῇ οἰκουμένῃ εἰς μαρτύριον πᾶσι τοῖς ἔθνεσι. καὶ τότε ϛ
15 ἥξει τὸ τέλος. ὅταν οὖν ἴδητε τὸ βδέλυγμα τῆς ἐρημώσεως, τὸ ῥηθὲν σμζ
διὰ Δανιὴλ τοῦ προφήτου, ἑστὼς ἐν τόπῳ ἁγίῳ (ὁ ἀναγινώσκων νοείτω), ϛ
16 17 τότε οἱ ἐν τῇ Ἰουδαίᾳ φευγέτωσαν εἰς τὰ ὄρη· ὁ ἐπὶ τοῦ δώματος μὴ σμη
18 καταβαινέτω ἆραί τι ἐκ τῆς οἰκίας αὐτοῦ· καὶ ὁ ἐν τῷ ἀγρῷ μὴ ἐπιστρε- β
19 ψάτω ὀπίσω ἆραι τὸ ἱμάτιον αὐτοῦ. οὐαὶ δὲ ταῖς ἐν γαστρὶ ἐχούσαις σμθ β
20 καὶ ταῖς θηλαζούσαις ἐν ἐκείναις ταῖς ἡμέραις. προσεύχεσθε δὲ ἵνα μὴ σν
21 γένηται ἡ φυγὴ ὑμῶν χειμῶνος, μηδὲ σαββάτῳ. ἔσται γὰρ τότε θλῖψις ϛ σνα
μεγάλη, οἵα οὐ γέγονεν ἀπ' ἀρχῆς τοῦ κόσμου ἕως τοῦ νῦν, οὐδ' οὐ μὴ β
22 γένηται. καὶ εἰ μὴ ἐκολοβώθησαν αἱ ἡμέραι ἐκεῖναι, οὐκ ἂν ἐσώθη πᾶσα σνβ
23 σάρξ· διὰ δὲ τοὺς ἐκλεκτοὺς κολοβωθήσονται αἱ ἡμέραι ἐκεῖναι. τότε ϛ σνγ
24 ἐάν τις ὑμῖν εἴπῃ, Ἰδοὺ ὧδε ὁ Χριστός, ἢ ὧδε, μὴ πιστεύσητε. ἐγερθή- β σνδ
σονται γὰρ ψευδόχριστοι καὶ ψευδοπροφῆται καὶ δώσουσι σημεῖα μεγάλα ϛ
25 καὶ τέρατα, ὥστε πλανᾶσθαι, εἰ δυνατόν, καὶ τοὺς ἐκλεκτούς. ἰδοὺ σνε
26 προείρηκα ὑμῖν. ἐὰν οὖν εἴπωσιν ὑμῖν, Ἰδοὺ ἐν τῇ ἐρήμῳ ἐστί, μὴ ε
27 ἐξέλθητε, Ἰδοὺ ἐν τοῖς ταμιείοις, μὴ πιστεύσητε. ὥσπερ γὰρ ἡ ἀστραπὴ σνϛ
ἐξέρχεται ἀπὸ ἀνατολῶν καὶ φαίνει ἕως δυσμῶν, οὕτως ἔσται ἡ παρουσία ε
28 τοῦ υἱοῦ τοῦ ἀνθρώπου. ὅπου ἐὰν ᾖ τὸ πτῶμα, ἐκεῖ συναχθήσονται οἱ σνζ
29 ἀετοί. εὐθέως δὲ μετὰ τὴν θλῖψιν τῶν ἡμερῶν ἐκείνων ὁ ἥλιος σκοτισ- ε σνη
θήσεται καὶ ἡ σελήνη οὐ δώσει τὸ φέγγος αὐτῆς, καὶ οἱ ἀστέρες πεσοῦνται β
30 ἀπὸ τοῦ οὐρανοῦ, καὶ αἱ δυνάμεις τῶν οὐρανῶν σαλευθήσονται. καὶ τότε σνθ
φανήσεται τὸ σημεῖον τοῦ υἱοῦ τοῦ ἀνθρώπου ἐν τῷ οὐρανῷ· καὶ κόψονται β
τότε αἱ φυλαὶ τῆς γῆς, καὶ ὄψονται τὸν υἱὸν τοῦ ἀνθρώπου ἐρχόμενον ἐπὶ
31 τῶν νεφελῶν τοῦ οὐρανοῦ μετὰ δυνάμεως καὶ δόξης πολλῆς· καὶ ἀπο-
στελεῖ τοὺς ἀγγέλους αὐτοῦ μετὰ σάλπιγγος μεγάλης, καὶ ἐπισυνάξουσι
τοὺς ἐκλεκτοὺς αὐτοῦ ἐκ τῶν τεσσάρων ἀνέμων, ἀπ' ἄκρων οὐρανῶν ἕως
τῶν ἄκρων αὐτῶν.

31 αγγελλους cod. σαλπηγγος cod.

9 θλιψιν ϛ παντων των εθνων ϛ **11** εγερθησονται bis scrips. 209 118 209 ϛ **14** ολη] pr εν ϛ **15** εστος ϛ αναγινωσκον 118 **16** εις] επι ϛ **18** τα ιματια ϛ **20** εν σαββατω ϛ **21** om του ϛ **24** πλανησαι ϛ **26** ταμειοις 118 209 ϛ **27** φαινεται ϛ εσται] + και 118 209 ϛ **28** οπου γαρ ϛ **29** σκοτασθησεται 209 **30** τοτε κοψονται πασαι 118 ϛ των] τον 118 **31** μεγαλης] pr φωνης 118² ϛ, om 118* spat. rel. των 2°] om ϛ ακρων αυτων] om 118* spat. rel. in quo 118² ακρων γης scripsit

Ἀπὸ δὲ τῆς συκῆς μάθετε τὴν παραβολήν· ὅταν ἤδη ὁ κλάδος αὐτῆς 32
γένηται ἁπαλὸς καὶ τὰ φύλλα ἐκφύῃ, γινώσκετε ὅτι ἐγγὺς τὸ θέρος· οὕτω 33
καὶ ὑμεῖς, ὅταν ἴδητε ταῦτα πάντα, γινώσκετε ὅτι ἐγγύς ἐστιν ἐπὶ θύραις.
ἀμὴν λέγω ὑμῖν, ὅτι οὐ μὴ παρέλθῃ ἡ γενεὰ αὕτη ἕως ἂν πάντα ταῦτα 34
ΝΗ' γένηται· ὁ οὐρανὸς καὶ ἡ γῆ παρελεύσονται, οἱ δὲ λόγοι μου οὐ μὴ 35
σξ παρέλθωσι. περὶ δὲ τῆς ἡμέρας ἐκείνης καὶ τῆς ὥρας οὐδεὶς οἶδεν, 36
ς σξα οὐδὲ οἱ ἄγγελοι τῶν οὐρανῶν, εἰ μὴ ὁ πατὴρ μόνος. ὥσπερ δὲ αἱ ἡμέραι 37
ε τοῦ Νῶε, οὕτως ἔσται καὶ ἡ παρουσία τοῦ υἱοῦ τοῦ ἀνθρώπου· ὥσπερ γὰρ 38
ἦσαν ἐν ταῖς ἡμέραις ταῖς πρὸ τοῦ κατακλυσμοῦ τρώγοντες καὶ πίνοντες,
γαμοῦντες καὶ ἐκγαμίζοντες, ἄχρι ἧς ἡμέρας εἰσῆλθε Νῶε εἰς τὴν κιβωτόν,
καὶ οὐκ ἔγνωσαν ἕως ἦλθεν ὁ κατακλυσμὸς καὶ ἦρεν ἅπαντας, οὕτως ἔσται 39
καὶ ἡ παρουσία τοῦ υἱοῦ τοῦ ἀνθρώπου.
σξβ Τότε δύο ἔσονται ἐν τῷ ἀγρῷ· εἷς παραλαμβάνεται καὶ εἷς ἀφίεται· 40
ε δύο ἀλήθουσαι ἐν τῷ μύλωνι· μία παραλαμβάνεται καὶ μία ἀφίεται. 41
σξγ Γρηγορεῖτε οὖν, ὅτι οὐκ οἴδατε ποίᾳ ἡμέρᾳ ὁ κύριος ὑμῶν ἔρχεται. 42
ς σξδ ἐκεῖνο δὲ γινώσκετε, ὅτι εἰ ᾔδει ὁ οἰκοδεσπότης ποίᾳ φυλακῇ ὁ κλέπτης 43
β ἔρχεται, ἐγρηγόρησεν ἂν καὶ οὐκ ἂν εἴασε διορυγῆναι τὴν οἰκίαν αὐτοῦ.
διὰ τοῦτο καὶ ὑμεῖς γίνεσθε ἕτοιμοι· ὅτι ᾗ ὥρᾳ οὐ γινώσκετε ὁ υἱὸς τοῦ 44
σξε ἀνθρώπου ἔρχεται. τίς ἄρα ἐστὶν ὁ πιστὸς δοῦλος καὶ φρόνιμος, ὃν 45
ε κατέστησεν ὁ κύριος ἐπὶ τῆς θεραπείας αὐτοῦ, τοῦ δοῦναι αὐτοῖς τὴν
σξς τροφὴν ἐν καιρῷ; μακάριος ὁ δοῦλος ἐκεῖνος ὃν ἐλθὼν ὁ κύριος αὐτοῦ 46
ε εὑρήσει οὕτως ποιοῦντα· ἀμὴν λέγω ὑμῖν ὅτι ἐπὶ πᾶσι τοῖς ὑπάρχουσιν 47
σξζ αὐτοῦ καταστήσει αὐτόν. ἐὰν δὲ εἴπῃ ὁ κακὸς δοῦλος ἐκεῖνος ἐν τῇ 48
ε καρδίᾳ αὐτοῦ, Χρονίζει ὁ κύριός μου ἔρχεσθαι, καὶ ἄρξηται τύπτειν τοὺς 49
συνδούλους αὐτοῦ, ἐσθίῃ τε καὶ πίνῃ μετὰ τῶν μεθυόντων, ἥξει ὁ κύριος 50
τοῦ δούλου ἐκείνου ἐν ἡμέρᾳ ᾗ οὐ προσδοκᾷ καὶ ἐν ὥρᾳ ᾗ οὐ γινώσκει,
καὶ διχοτομήσει αὐτόν, καὶ τὸ μέρος αὐτοῦ μετὰ τῶν ὑποκριτῶν θήσει· 51
ἐκεῖ ἔσται ὁ κλαυθμὸς καὶ ὁ βρυγμὸς τῶν ὀδόντων.
ΝΘ' XXV. Τότε ὁμοιωθήσεται ἡ βασιλεία τῶν οὐρανῶν δέκα παρθένοις,
σξη ι αἵτινες λαβοῦσαι τὰς λαμπάδας αὐτῶν ἐξῆλθον εἰς ὑπάντησιν τοῦ
νυμφίου καὶ τῆς νύμφης· πέντε δὲ ἐξ αὐτῶν ἦσαν μωραὶ καὶ πέντε 2
φρόνιμοι. λαβοῦσαι δὲ αἱ μωραὶ τὰς λαμπάδας ἑαυτῶν οὐκ ἔλαβον 3

1 in margine latine notatur *hic habet et sponsae* et in textu και της νυμφης partim erasum esse videtur

118 209 ς **33** παντα ταυτα ς **34** om οτι 118 ς **36** πατηρ μου ς **40** ο εις bis ς **42** ημερα] ωρα 118 209 ς **44** γινωσκετε] δοκειτε 118 ς **45** κυριος αυτου 118 ς διδοναι ς **46** ποιουντα ουτως 118 ς **48** om κακος 118 ελθειν ς **49** om αυτου ς εσθιειν δε και πινειν ς

1 απαντησιν 118 209 ς και της νυμφης] om 118 ς, nunc eras. 209 **2** ησαν εξ αυτων 118 209 ς φρονιμοι και αι πεντε μωραι. αιτινες μωραι λαβουσαι 118 ς

4 μεθ' ἑαυτῶν ἔλαιον· αἱ δὲ φρόνιμοι ἔλαβον ἔλαιον ἐν τοῖς ἀγγείοις μετὰ
5 τῶν λαμπάδων αὐτῶν. χρονίζοντος δὲ τοῦ νυμφίου ἐνύσταξαν πᾶσαι καὶ
6 ἐκάθευδον. μέσης δὲ νυκτὸς κραυγὴ γέγονεν, Ἰδοὺ ὁ νυμφίος ἔρχεται,
7 ἐγείρεσθε εἰς ἀπάντησιν αὐτοῦ. τότε ἠγέρθησαν πᾶσαι αἱ παρθένοι
8 ἐκεῖναι καὶ ἐκόσμησαν τὰς λαμπάδας αὐτῶν. αἱ δὲ μωραὶ ταῖς φρονίμοις
εἶπον, Δότε ἡμῖν ἐκ τοῦ ἐλαίου ὑμῶν, ὅτι αἱ λαμπάδες ἡμῶν σβέννυνται.
9 ἀπεκρίθησαν δὲ αἱ φρόνιμοι λέγουσαι, Μήποτε οὐ μὴ ἀρκέσῃ ἡμῖν καὶ
ὑμῖν· πορεύεσθε δὲ μᾶλλον πρὸς τοὺς πωλοῦντας καὶ ἀγοράσετε ἑαυταῖς.
10 ἀπερχομένων δὲ αὐτῶν ἀγοράσαι, ἦλθεν ὁ νυμφίος· καὶ αἱ ἕτοιμοι
11 εἰσῆλθον μετ' αὐτοῦ εἰς τοὺς γάμους, καὶ ἐκλείσθη ἡ θύρα. ὕστερον δὲ
ἔρχονται καὶ αἱ λοιπαὶ παρθένοι λέγουσαι, Κύριε κύριε, ἄνοιξον ἡμῖν.
12 13 ὁ δὲ ἀποκριθεὶς εἶπεν, Οὐκ οἶδα ὑμᾶς. γρηγορεῖτε οὖν, ὅτι οὐκ οἴδατε
τὴν ἡμέραν οὐδὲ τὴν ὥραν.
14 Ὥσπερ γὰρ ἄνθρωπος ἀποδημῶν ἐκάλεσε τοὺς ἰδίους δούλους καὶ Ξ' σξθ
15 παρέδωκεν αὐτοῖς τὰ ὑπάρχοντα αὐτοῦ, καὶ ᾧ μὲν ἔδωκε πέντε τάλαντα, β
16 ᾧ δὲ δύο, ᾧ δὲ ἕν, ἑκάστῳ κατὰ τὴν ἰδίαν δύναμιν, καὶ ἀπεδήμησεν. εὐθέως σο ε
δὲ πορευθεὶς ὁ τὰ πέντε τάλαντα λαβὼν εἰργάσατο ἐπ' αὐτοῖς καὶ
17 ἐκέρδησεν ἄλλα πέντε τάλαντα. ὡσαύτως καὶ ὁ τὰ δύο ἐκέρδησε καὶ
18 αὐτὸς ἄλλα δύο. ὁ δὲ τὸ ἓν λαβὼν ἀπελθὼν ὤρυξεν ἐν τῇ γῇ καὶ ἀπέκρυψε
19 τὸ ἀργύριον τοῦ κυρίου αὐτοῦ. μετὰ δὲ πολὺν χρόνον ἔρχεται ὁ κύριος
20 τῶν δούλων ἐκείνων, καὶ συναίρει λόγον μετ' αὐτῶν. καὶ προσελθὼν ὁ
τὰ πέντε τάλαντα λαβὼν προσήνεγκεν ἄλλα πέντε τάλαντα, λέγων, Κύριε,
πέντε τάλαντά μοι δέδωκας· ἴδε ἄλλα πέντε τάλαντα ἐκέρδησα ἐπ' αὐτοῖς.
21 ἔφη δὲ αὐτῷ ὁ κύριος αὐτοῦ, Εὖ, δοῦλε ἀγαθὲ καὶ πιστέ, ἐπὶ ὀλίγα ἦς πιστός,
22 ἐπὶ πολλῶν σε καταστήσω· εἴσελθε εἰς τὴν χαρὰν τοῦ κυρίου σου. παρελ-
θὼν δὲ καὶ ὁ τὰ δύο τάλαντα εἶπε, Κύριε, δύο τάλαντά μοι παρέδωκας· ἴδε
23 ἄλλα δύο τάλαντα ἐκέρδησα ἐπ' αὐτοῖς. ἔφη αὐτῷ ὁ κύριος αὐτοῦ, Εὖ, δοῦλε
ἀγαθὲ καὶ πιστέ, ἐπὶ ὀλίγα ἦς πιστός, ἐπὶ πολλῶν σε καταστήσω· εἴσελθε εἰς
24 τὴν χαρὰν τοῦ κυρίου σου. προσελθὼν δὲ καὶ ὁ τὸ ἓν τάλαντον εἰληφὼς
εἶπε, Κύριε, ἔγνων σε ὅτι αὔστηρος εἶ ἄνθρωπος, θερίζων ὅθεν οὐκ

13 scriba idem ni fallor qui supra latine scripsit ad finem vers. add. in marg. *εν η ο υιος του ανθρωπου ερχεται*

4 *αγγειοις*]+*αυτων* ς **6** *εγειρεσθε*] *εξερχεσθε* 118 ς **9** *ου μη*] *ουκ* 118 209 ς 118 209 ς *αγορασετε*] 118 209 habent ε 1° ambigue scriptum ita ut scribae dubitavisse videantur utrum *αγορασετε* an *αγορασατε* scribendum sit **12** *ουκ*] pr *αμην λεγω υμιν* ς **13** *ωραν*]+*εν η ο υιος του ανθρωπου ερχεται* 118 ς **15 16** *απεδημησεν ευθεως. πορευθεις δε* ς **16** *επ*] *εν* 118* ς sed 118 nunc eras. *εκερδησεν*] *εποιησεν* ς **19** *χρονον πολυν* ς *μετ αυτων λογον* ς **20** *παρεδωκας* 118 ς **22** *προσελθων* 118 209 ς *ειπε*] pr *λαβων* ς, pr spat. 118* in quo 118[2] *λαβων* scrips. **24** *αυστηρος*] *σκληρος* 118 209 *οθεν*] *οπου* 118 ς

ἔσπειρας καὶ συνάγων ὅθεν οὐ διεσκόρπισας· καὶ φοβηθείς, ἀπελθὼν 25
ἔκρυψα τὸ τάλαντόν σου ἐν τῇ γῇ· ἴδε ἔχεις τὸ σόν. ἀποκριθεὶς δὲ ὁ 26
κύριος αὐτοῦ εἶπεν αὐτῷ, Πονηρὲ δοῦλε καὶ ὀκνηρέ, ᾔδεις ὅτι θερίζω ὅπου
οὐκ ἔσπειρα καὶ συνάγω ὅθεν οὐ διεσκόρπισα; ἔδει οὖν σε βαλεῖν τὸ 27
ἀργύριόν μου τοῖς τραπεζίταις, καὶ ἐλθὼν ἐγὼ ἐκομισάμην ἂν τὸ ἐμὸν σὺν
τόκῳ. ἄρατε οὖν ἀπ' αὐτοῦ τὸ τάλαντον, καὶ δότε τῷ ἔχοντι τὰ δέκα 28
σοα β τάλαντα. τῷ γὰρ ἔχοντι παντὶ δοθήσεται καὶ περισσευθήσεται· τοῦ δὲ 29
σοβ ε μὴ ἔχοντος καὶ ὃ ἔχει ἀρθήσεται ἀπ' αὐτοῦ. καὶ τὸν ἀχρεῖον δοῦλον 30
ἐκβάλετε εἰς τὸ σκότος τὸ ἐξώτερον· ἐκεῖ ἔσται ὁ κλαυθμὸς καὶ ὁ βρυγμὸς
τῶν ὀδόντων.

ΞΑ' Ὅταν δὲ ἔλθῃ ὁ υἱὸς τοῦ ἀνθρώπου ἐν τῇ δόξῃ αὐτοῦ, καὶ πάντες οἱ 31
σογ ι ἄγγελοι μετ' αὐτοῦ, τότε καθίσει ἐπὶ θρόνου δόξης αὐτοῦ, καὶ συναχ- 32
θήσεται ἔμπροσθεν αὐτοῦ πάντα τὰ ἔθνη, καὶ ἀφορίσει αὐτοὺς ἀπ'
ἀλλήλων, ὥσπερ ὁ ποιμὴν ἀφορίζει τὰ πρόβατα ἀπὸ τῶν ἐρίφων, καὶ 33
στήσει τὰ μὲν πρόβατα ἐκ δεξιῶν αὐτοῦ, τὰ δὲ ἐρίφια ἐξ εὐωνύμων.

Τότε ἐρεῖ ὁ βασιλεὺς τοῖς ἐκ δεξιῶν αὐτοῦ, Δεῦτε οἱ εὐλογημένοι τοῦ 34
πατρός μου, κληρονομήσατε τὴν ἡτοιμασμένην ὑμῖν βασιλείαν ἀπὸ κατα-
βολῆς κόσμου. ἐπείνασα γάρ, καὶ ἐδώκατέ μοι φαγεῖν· ἐδίψησα, καὶ 35
ἐποτίσατέ με· ξένος ἤμην, καὶ συνηγάγετέ με· γυμνός, καὶ περι- 36
εβάλετέ με· ἠσθένησα, καὶ ἐπεσκέψασθέ με· ἐν φυλακῇ ἤμην, καὶ ἤλθετε
πρός με.. τότε ἀποκριθήσονται αὐτῷ οἱ δίκαιοι λέγοντες, Κύριε, πότε σὲ 37
εἴδομεν πεινῶντα καὶ ἐθρέψαμεν, ἢ διψῶντα καὶ ἐποτίσαμεν; πότε δέ σε 38
εἴδομεν ξένον καὶ συνηγάγομεν, ἢ γυμνὸν καὶ περιεβάλομεν; πότε δέ σε 39
εἴδομεν ἀσθενῆ, ἢ ἐν φυλακῇ, καὶ ἤλθομεν πρός σε; καὶ ἀποκριθεὶς ὁ 40
βασιλεὺς ἐρεῖ αὐτοῖς, Ἀμὴν λέγω ὑμῖν, ἐφ' ὅσον ἐποιήσατε ἑνὶ τούτων τῶν
ἀδελφῶν μοῦ τῶν ἐλαχίστων, ἐμοὶ ἐποιήσατε.

Τότε ἐρεῖ καὶ τοῖς ἐξ εὐωνύμων, Πορεύεσθε ἀπ' ἐμοῦ οἱ κατηραμένοι 41
εἰς τὸ πῦρ τὸ αἰώνιον ὁ ἡτοίμασεν ὁ πατήρ μου τῷ διαβόλῳ καὶ τοῖς
ἀγγέλοις αὐτοῦ. ἐπείνασα γάρ, καὶ οὐκ ἐδώκατέ μοι φαγεῖν· ἐδίψησα, 42
καὶ οὐκ ἐποτίσατέ με· ξένος ἤμην, καὶ οὐ συνηγάγετέ με· γυμνός, καὶ οὐ 43
περιεβάλετέ με· ἀσθενής, καὶ ἐν φυλακῇ, καὶ οὐκ ἐπεσκέψασθέ με. τότε 44
ἀποκριθήσονται καὶ αὐτοὶ αὐτῷ λέγοντες, Κύριε, πότε σὲ εἴδομεν πει-
νῶντα, ἢ διψῶντα, ἢ ξένον, ἢ γυμνόν, ἢ ἀσθενῆ, ἢ ἐν φυλακῇ, καὶ οὐ
διηκονήσαμέν σοι; τότε ἀποκριθήσεται αὐτοῖς λέγων, Ἀμὴν λέγω ὑμῖν, 45
ἐφ' ὅσον οὐκ ἐποιήσατε ἑνὶ τούτων τῶν ἐλαχίστων, οὐδὲ ἐμοὶ ἐποιήσατε.

118 209 ς **25** σου 118 **26** ου bis scrips. 118 **29** απο δε του 118 ς **30** εκβαλετε] εκβαλλετε ς, βαλετε 118 sed pr spat. **31** αγιοι αγγελοι ς **32** αφοριει ς, αφορ 118 spat. rel. **33** ερριφων 209 **35** ξενος...συνηγ. με] om 118 **40** ελαχιστων] 118* ελαχ scrips. omisso των αδ. μου tum errore detecto των αδελφων μου scripsit supra ελαχ **41** το ητοιμασμενον 118 ς **44** αυτω και αυτοι ς

46 καὶ ἀπελεύσονται οὗτοι εἰς κόλασιν αἰώνιον· οἱ δὲ δίκαιοι εἰς ζωὴν
αἰώνιον.

XXVI. Καὶ ἐγένετο ὅτε ἐτέλεσεν ὁ Ἰησοῦς πάντας τοὺς λόγους σοδ
2 τούτους, εἶπε τοῖς μαθηταῖς αὐτοῦ, Οἴδατε ὅτι μετὰ δύο ἡμέρας τὸ πάσχα α
3 γίνεται, καὶ ὁ υἱὸς τοῦ ἀνθρώπου παραδίδοται εἰς τὸ σταυρωθῆναι. τότε σοε
συνήχθησαν οἱ ἀρχιερεῖς καὶ οἱ πρεσβύτεροι τοῦ λαοῦ εἰς τὴν αὐλὴν τοῦ ς
4 ἀρχιερέως τοῦ λεγομένου Καϊάφα, καὶ συνεβουλεύσαντο ἵνα τὸν Ἰησοῦν
5 δόλῳ κρατήσωσι καὶ ἀποκτείνωσιν. ἔλεγον δέ, Μὴ ἐν τῇ ἑορτῇ, ἵνα μὴ
θόρυβος γένηται ἐν τῷ λαῷ.

6 Τοῦ δὲ Ἰησοῦ γενομένου ἐν Βηθανίᾳ ἐν οἰκίᾳ Σίμωνος τοῦ λεπροῦ, ΞΒʹ
7 προσῆλθεν αὐτῷ γυνὴ ἀλάβαστρον μύρου ἔχουσα βαρυτίμου, καὶ κατέχεεν σος α
8 ἐπὶ τῆς κεφαλῆς αὐτοῦ ἀνακειμένου. ἰδόντες δὲ οἱ μαθηταὶ αὐτοῦ
9 ἠγανάκτησαν λέγοντες, Εἰς τί ἡ ἀπώλεια αὕτη; ἠδύνατο γὰρ τοῦτο
10 πραθῆναι πολλοῦ καὶ δοθῆναι πτωχοῖς. γνοὺς δὲ ὁ Ἰησοῦς εἶπεν αὐτοῖς,
11 Τί κόπους παρέχετε τῇ γυναικί; ἔργον καλὸν εἰργάσατο εἰς ἐμέ· πάντοτε
12 γὰρ τοὺς πτωχοὺς ἔχετε μεθ' ἑαυτῶν, ἐμὲ δὲ οὐ πάντοτε ἔχετε. βαλοῦσα σοζ
γὰρ αὕτη τὸ μύρον τοῦτο ἐπὶ τοῦ σώματός μου, πρὸς τὸ ἐνταφιάσαι με δ
13 ἐποίησεν. ἀμὴν λέγω ὑμῖν, ὅπου ἐὰν κηρυχθῇ τὸ εὐαγγέλιον τοῦτο ἐν ὅλῳ
τῷ κόσμῳ, λαληθήσεται καὶ ὃ ἐποίησεν αὕτη, εἰς μνημόσυνον αὐτῆς.

14 Τότε πορευθεὶς εἷς τῶν δώδεκα, ὁ λεγόμενος Ἰούδας Ἰσκαριώτης, πρὸς σοη
15 τοὺς ἀρχιερεῖς εἶπε, Τί θέλετέ μοι δοῦναι, κἀγὼ ὑμῖν παραδώσω αὐτόν; β
16 οἱ δὲ ἔστησαν αὐτῷ τριάκοντα στατῆρας ἀργυρίου· καὶ ἀπὸ τότε ἐζήτει
εὐκαιρίαν ἵνα αὐτὸν παραδῷ.

17 Τῇ δὲ πρώτῃ τῶν ἀζύμων προσῆλθον οἱ μαθηταὶ λέγοντες τῷ Ἰησοῦ, ΞΓʹ
18 Ποῦ θέλεις ἑτοιμάσομέν σοι φαγεῖν τὸ πάσχα; ὁ δὲ εἶπεν, Ὑπάγετε εἰς
τὴν πόλιν πρὸς τὸν δεῖνα, καὶ εἴπατε αὐτῷ, Ὁ διδάσκαλος λέγει, Ὁ καιρός
19 μου ἐγγύς ἐστι· πρὸς σὲ ποιῶ τὸ πάσχα μετὰ τῶν μαθητῶν μου. καὶ
ἐποίησαν οἱ μαθηταὶ ὡς συνέταξεν αὐτοῖς ὁ Ἰησοῦς, καὶ ἡτοίμασαν τὸ
πάσχα.

20 21 Ὀψίας δὲ γενομένης ἀνέκειτο μετὰ τῶν δώδεκα. καὶ ἐσθιόντων αὐτῶν σοθ δ
22 εἶπεν, Ἀμὴν λέγω ὑμῖν ὅτι εἷς ἐξ ὑμῶν παραδώσει με. καὶ λυπούμενοι σπ
23 σφόδρα ἤρξαντο λέγειν αὐτῷ ἕκαστος αὐτῶν, Μήτι ἐγώ εἰμι, κύριε; ὁ δὲ α σπα
ἀποκριθεὶς εἶπεν, Ὁ ἐμβάψας μετ' ἐμοῦ ἐν τῷ τρυβλίῳ τὴν χεῖρα, οὗτός με β
24 παραδώσει. ὁ μὲν υἱὸς τοῦ ἀνθρώπου ὑπάγει, καθὼς γέγραπται περὶ αὐτοῦ· σπβ ς

3 αρχιερεις] + και οι γραμματεις ς **5** κρατησωσι δολω ς **7** την κεφαλην ς, τ κεφαλ 118 spat. rel. **9** τουτο] + το μυρον ς τοις πτωχοις ς εργον γαρ 118 209 ς **11** τους πτωχους γαρ παντοτε 118 τους πτωχους παντοτε 209 **15** καγω 118 209 ς αργυρια 118 ς **17** τω Ιησου λεγοντες αυτω 118 ς ετοιμασωμεν ς **20** γενομενοις 118 **24** και ο μεν 118 209 118 209 ς

οὐαὶ δὲ τῷ ἀνθρώπῳ ἐκείνῳ δι' οὗ ὁ υἱὸς τοῦ ἀνθρώπου παραδίδοται· καλὸν
σπγ ἦν αὐτῷ εἰ οὐκ ἐγεννήθη ὁ ἄνθρωπος ἐκεῖνος. ἀποκριθεὶς δὲ Ἰούδας ὁ 25
ι παραδιδοὺς αὐτὸν εἶπε, Μήτι ἐγώ εἰμι, ῥαββί; λέγει αὐτῷ, Σὺ εἶπας.
ΞΔ' Ἐσθιόντων δὲ αὐτῶν λαβὼν ὁ Ἰησοῦς ἄρτον καὶ εὐχαριστήσας 26
σπδ α ἔκλασε καὶ δοὺς τοῖς μαθηταῖς εἶπε, Λάβετε, φάγετε· τοῦτό ἐστι τὸ
σπε σῶμά μου. καὶ λαβὼν ποτήριον εὐχαριστήσας ἔδωκεν αὐτοῖς λέγων, 27
β Πίετε ἐξ αὐτοῦ πάντες· τοῦτό ἐστι τὸ αἷμά μου τὸ τῆς καινῆς διαθήκης, 28
τὸ περὶ πολλῶν ἐκχυννόμενον εἰς ἄφεσιν ἁμαρτιῶν. λέγω δὲ ὑμῖν, οὐ 29
μὴ πίω ἀπ' ἄρτι ἐκ τούτου τοῦ γενήματος τῆς ἀμπέλου, ἕως τῆς ἡμέρας
ἐκείνης ὅταν αὐτὸ πίνω καινὸν μεθ' ὑμῶν ἐν τῇ βασιλείᾳ τοῦ πατρός
μου.
σπϛ ϛ Καὶ ὑμνήσαντες ἐξῆλθον εἰς τὸ ὄρος τῶν ἐλαιῶν. τότε λέγει αὐτοῖς ὁ 30 31
σπζ Ἰησοῦς, Πάντες ὑμεῖς σκανδαλισθήσεσθε ἐν ἐμοὶ ἐν τῇ νυκτὶ ταύτῃ.
δ σπη γέγραπται γάρ, Πατάξω τὸν ποιμένα, καὶ διασκορπισθήσεται τὰ πρόβατα
ϛ τῆς ποίμνης. μετὰ δὲ τὸ ἐγερθῆναί με προάξω ὑμᾶς εἰς τὴν Γαλιλαίαν. 32
σπθ ἀποκριθεὶς δὲ ὁ Πέτρος εἶπεν αὐτῷ, Εἰ πάντες σκανδαλισθήσονται ἐν σοί, 33
α ἐγὼ οὐδέποτε σκανδαλισθήσομαι. ἔφη αὐτῷ ὁ Ἰησοῦς, Ἀμὴν λέγω σοὶ 34
σϟ ὅτι ἐν ταύτῃ τῇ νυκτὶ πρὶν ἀλεκτοροφωνίας τρὶς ἀπαρνήσῃ με. λέγει 35
ϛ αὐτῷ ὁ Πέτρος, Κἂν δέῃ με σὺν σοὶ ἀποθανεῖν, οὐ μή σε ἀπαρνήσομαι.
ὁμοίως δὲ καὶ πάντες οἱ μαθηταὶ εἶπον.
σϟα Τότε ἔρχεται μετ' αὐτῶν ὁ Ἰησοῦς εἰς χωρίον λεγόμενον Γεθσημανεῖ, 36
α σϟβ καὶ λέγει τοῖς μαθηταῖς αὐτοῦ, Καθίσατε αὐτοῦ ἕως ἂν ἀπελθὼν προσεύ-
ϛ ξωμαι ἐκεῖ· καὶ παραλαβὼν τὸν Πέτρον καὶ τοὺς δύο υἱοὺς Ζεβεδαίου 37
σϟγ ἤρξατο λυπεῖσθαι καὶ ἀδημονεῖν. τότε λέγει αὐτοῖς, Περίλυπός ἐστιν ἡ 38
δ σϟδ ψυχή μου ἕως θανάτου· μείνατε ὧδε καὶ γρηγορεῖτε μετ' ἐμοῦ. καὶ 39
α προσελθὼν μικρὸν ἔπεσεν ἐπὶ πρόσωπον αὐτοῦ προσευχόμενος καὶ λέγων,
σϟε Πάτερ, εἰ δυνατόν ἐστι, παρελθέτω ἀπ' ἐμοῦ τὸ ποτήριον τοῦτο· πλὴν οὐχ
α σϟϛ ὡς ἐγὼ θέλω, ἀλλ' ὡς σύ. καὶ ἔρχεται πρὸς τοὺς μαθητὰς καὶ εὑρίσκει 40
β αὐτοὺς καθεύδοντας, καὶ λέγει τῷ Πέτρῳ, Οὐκ ἰσχύσατε μίαν ὥραν
σϟζ γρηγορῆσαι μετ' ἐμοῦ; γρηγορεῖτε καὶ προσεύχεσθε, ἵνα μὴ εἰσέλθητε εἰς 41
δ σϟη πειρασμόν. τὸ μὲν πνεῦμα πρόθυμον, ἡ δὲ σὰρξ ἀσθενής. πάλιν ἐκ 42
ϛ δευτέρου ἀπελθὼν προσηύξατο ὁ Ἰησοῦς λέγων, Πάτερ μου, εἰ οὐ δύναται
τοῦτο παρελθεῖν ἐὰν μὴ αὐτὸ πίω, γενηθήτω τὸ θέλημά σου. καὶ ἐλθὼν 43

118 209 ϛ **26** τον αρτον ϛ ευχαριστησας] ευλογησας ϛ δους] εδιδου et pr και ante ειπε ϛ **27** το ποτηρ. και ϛ **28** τουτο γαρ ϛ εκχυνομενον 118 209 ϛ **29** υμιν]+οτι ϛ γεννηματος 118 209 ϛ καινον post υμων ϛ **31** διασκορπισθησονται 118 **33** και παντ. ϛ **34** αλεκτορα φωνησαι 118 ϛ **35** απαρνησωμαι 118 209 om δε ϛ **36** Γεθσημαινη 118 209 ϛ om αυτου ϛ αν] ου ϛ **39** προελθων ϛ πατερ μου ϛ **40** ουκ] pr ουτως 118 ϛ **42** om ο Ιησους ϛ τουτο το ποτηριον 118 ϛ παρελθειν απ εμου 118 ϛ

πάλιν εὗρεν αὐτοὺς καθεύδοντας· ἦσαν γὰρ αὐτῶν οἱ ὀφθαλμοὶ βεβαρη-
44 μένοι. καὶ ἀφεὶς αὐτοὺς ἀπελθὼν προσηύξατο τὸν αὐτὸν λόγον
45 εἰπών. τότε ἔρχεται πρὸς τοὺς μαθητὰς καὶ λέγει αὐτοῖς, Καθεύδετε τὸ σϟθ
λοιπὸν καὶ ἀναπαύεσθε· ἤγγικε γὰρ ἡ ὥρα μου, καὶ ὁ υἱὸς τοῦ ἀνθρώπου δ
46 παραδίδοται εἰς χεῖρας ἁμαρτωλῶν. ἐγείρεσθε, ἄγωμεν· ἰδοὺ ἤγγικεν ὁ
παραδιδούς με.
47 Καὶ ἔτι αὐτοῦ λαλοῦντος, ἰδοὺ Ἰούδας εἷς τῶν δώδεκα ἦλθε, καὶ μετ' ΞΕ'
αὐτοῦ ὄχλος πολὺς μετὰ μαχαιρῶν καὶ ξύλων ἀπὸ τῶν ἀρχιερέων καὶ τ α
48 πρεσβυτέρων τοῦ λαοῦ. ὁ δὲ παραδιδοὺς αὐτὸν ἔδωκεν αὐτοῖς σημεῖον τα
49 λέγων, Ὃν ἂν φιλήσω, αὐτός ἐστι· κρατήσατε αὐτόν. καὶ εὐθέως προσ- β
50 ελθὼν τῷ Ἰησοῦ εἶπε, Χαῖρε, ῥαββί, καὶ κατεφίλησεν αὐτόν. ὁ δὲ
Ἰησοῦς εἶπεν αὐτῷ, Ἑταῖρε, ἐφ' ᾧ πάρει; τότε προσελθόντες ἐπέβαλον
51 τὰς χεῖρας ἐπὶ τὸν Ἰησοῦν καὶ ἐκράτησαν αὐτόν. καὶ ἰδοὺ εἷς τῶν μετὰ τβ
Ἰησοῦ ἐκτείνας τὴν χεῖρα ἀπέσπασε τὴν μάχαιραν αὐτοῦ, καὶ πατάξας τὸν α
52 δοῦλον τοῦ ἀρχιερέως ἀφεῖλεν αὐτοῦ τὸ ὠτίον. τότε λέγει αὐτῷ ὁ Ἰησοῦς, τγ
Ἀπόστρεψον τὴν μάχαιράν σου εἰς τὸν τόπον αὐτῆς· πάντες γὰρ οἱ ι
53 λαμβάνοντες μάχαιραν ἐν μαχαίρᾳ ἀπολοῦνται. ἢ δοκεῖ σοι ὅτι οὐ
δύναμαι ἄρτι παρακαλέσαι τὸν πατέρα μου, καὶ παραστήσει μοι ὧδε
54 πλείους ἢ δώδεκα λεγεῶνας ἀγγέλων; πῶς οὖν πληρωθῶσιν αἱ γραφαὶ
ὅτι οὕτως ἔδει γενέσθαι;
55 Ἐν ἐκείνῃ τῇ ὥρᾳ εἶπεν ὁ Ἰησοῦς τοῖς ὄχλοις, Ὡς ἐπὶ λῃστὴν ἐξήλθετε τδ
μετὰ μαχαιρῶν καὶ ξύλων συλλαβεῖν με; καθ' ἡμέραν πρὸς ὑμᾶς ἐν τῷ α
56 ἱερῷ ἐκαθεζόμην, καὶ οὐκ ἐκρατήσατέ με· τοῦτο δὲ ὅλον γέγονεν ἵνα τε
πληρωθῶσιν αἱ γραφαὶ τῶν προφητῶν. τότε οἱ μαθηταὶ πάντες ἀφέντες ς
αὐτὸν ἔφυγον.
57 Οἱ δὲ κρατήσαντες τὸν Ἰησοῦν ἀπήγαγον πρὸς Καϊάφαν τὸν ἀρχιερέα, τς α
58 ὅπου οἱ γραμματεῖς καὶ οἱ πρεσβύτεροι συνήχθησαν. ὁ δὲ Πέτρος τζ
ἠκολούθει αὐτῷ μακρόθεν ἕως τῆς αὐλῆς τοῦ ἀρχιερέως· καὶ εἰσελθὼν δ
59 ἔσω ἐκάθητο μετὰ τῶν ὑπηρετῶν ἰδεῖν τὸ τέλος. οἱ δὲ ἀρχιερεῖς καὶ τη
οἱ πρεσβύτεροι καὶ τὸ συνέδριον ὅλον ἐζήτουν ψευδομαρτυρίαν κατὰ τοῦ β
60 Ἰησοῦ, ὅπως αὐτὸν θανατώσωσι· καὶ οὐχ εὗρον. προσελθόντων
πολλῶν ψευδομαρτύρων οὐχ εὗρον. ὕστερον δὲ προσελθόντες δύο τθ
61 εἶπον, Οὗτος ἔφη, Δύναμαι καταλῦσαι τὸν ναὸν τοῦ Θεοῦ καὶ διὰ τριῶν ς
62 ἡμερῶν οἰκοδομῆσαι. καὶ ἀναστὰς ὁ ἀρχιερεὺς εἶπεν αὐτῷ, Οὐδὲν

43 ευρισκει αυτους παλιν ϛ **44** απελθων παλιν ϛ προσηυξατο] + εκ τριτου 118 ϛ **45** μαθητας αυτου 118 ϛ ιδου ηγγικεν η ωρα omisso μου ϛ **52** σου την μαχαιραν ϛ λαβοντες 118 ϛ **53** δοκει σοι] δοκεις ϛ **54** ουτω δει ϛ **55** εκαθεζομην διδασκων εν τω ιερω ϛ **58** απο μακροθεν ϛ **60** και πολλων ψευδομαρτυρων προσελθοντων ϛ δυο] + ψευδομαρτυρες ϛ **61** οικοδομησαι αυτον 118 ϛ

118 209 ϛ

ἀποκρίνῃ; τί οὗτοί σου καταμαρτυροῦσιν; ὁ δὲ Ἰησοῦς ἐσιώπα. καὶ 63
ὁ ἀρχιερεὺς εἶπεν αὐτῷ, Ἐξορκίζω σε κατὰ τοῦ Θεοῦ τοῦ ζῶντος, ἵνα ἡμῖν
εἴπῃς εἰ σὺ εἶ ὁ Χριστός, ὁ υἱὸς τοῦ Θεοῦ. λέγει αὐτῷ ὁ Ἰησοῦς, Σὺ 64
τι α εἶπας. πλὴν λέγω ὑμῖν, ἀπ᾽ ἄρτι ὄψεσθε τὸν υἱὸν τοῦ ἀνθρώπου καθήμενον
τια ς ἐκ δεξιῶν τῆς δυνάμεως καὶ ἐρχόμενον ἐπὶ τῶν νεφελῶν τοῦ οὐρανοῦ. τότε 65
τιβ ὁ ἀρχιερεὺς διέρρηξε τὰ ἱμάτια αὐτοῦ λέγων ὅτι Ἐβλασφήμησε· τί ἔτι
β χρείαν ἔχομεν μαρτύρων; ἴδε νῦν ἠκούσατε τὴν βλασφημίαν αὐτοῦ· τί 66
τιγ α ὑμῖν δοκεῖ; οἱ δὲ ἀποκριθέντες εἶπον, Ἔνοχος θανάτου ἐστί. τότε ἐνέ- 67
πτυσαν εἰς τὸ πρόσωπον αὐτοῦ καὶ ἐκολάφισαν αὐτόν· οἱ δὲ ἐρράπισαν
αὐτόν, λέγοντες, Προφήτευσον ἡμῖν, Χριστέ, τίς ἐστιν ὁ παίσας σε; 68
ΞϚʹ Ὁ δὲ Πέτρος ἐκάθητο ἔξω ἐν τῇ αὐλῇ, καὶ προσῆλθεν αὐτῷ μία 69
τιδ α παιδίσκη λέγουσα, Καὶ σὺ ἦσθα μετὰ Ἰησοῦ τοῦ Γαλιλαίου. ὁ δὲ 70
ἠρνήσατο ἔμπροσθεν αὐτῶν πάντων, λέγων, Οὐκ οἶδα ὃ λέγεις οὐδὲ
τιε α ἐπίσταμαι. ἐξελθόντα δὲ αὐτὸν εἰς τὸν πυλῶνα εἶδεν ἄλλη, καὶ λέγει 71
αὐτοῖς· Ἐκεῖ καὶ οὗτος ἦν μετὰ Ἰησοῦ τοῦ Ναζαρήνου. καὶ πάλιν 72
ἠρνήσατο μεθ᾽ ὅρκου ὅτι Οὐκ οἶδα τὸν ἄνθρωπον. μετὰ μικρὸν δὲ πάλιν 73
προσελθόντες οἱ ἑστῶτες εἶπον τῷ Πέτρῳ, Ἀληθῶς ἐξ αὐτῶν εἶ· καὶ γὰρ
ἡ λαλιά σου δῆλόν σε ποιεῖ. τότε ἤρξατο καταθεματίζειν καὶ ὀμνύειν 74
τιϛ β ὅτι Οὐκ οἶδα τὸν ἄνθρωπον. καὶ εὐθέως ἀλέκτωρ ἐφώνησε. καὶ ἐμνήσθη 75
ὁ Πέτρος τοῦ ῥήματος τοῦ Ἰησοῦ εἰρηκότος αὐτῷ ὅτι Πρὶν ἀλεκτορο-
φωνίας τρὶς ἀπαρνήσῃ με· καὶ ἐξελθὼν ἔξω ἔκλαυσε πικρῶς.
τιζ β XXVII. Πρωΐας δὲ γενομένης συμβούλιον ἔλαβον πάντες οἱ
ἀρχιερεῖς καὶ οἱ πρεσβύτεροι τοῦ λαοῦ κατὰ τοῦ Ἰησοῦ, ὥστε θανατῶσαι
τιη α αὐτόν· καὶ δήσαντες αὐτὸν ἀπήγαγον καὶ παρέδωκαν αὐτὸν Ποντίῳ 2
Πιλάτῳ τῷ ἡγεμόνι.
ΞΖʹ Τότε ἰδὼν ὁ Ἰούδας ὁ παραδιδοὺς αὐτὸν ὅτι κατεκρίθη, μεταμεληθεὶς 3
τιθ ι ἀπέστρεψε τὰ τριάκοντα ἀργύρια τοῖς ἀρχιερεῦσι καὶ τοῖς πρεσβυτέροις
λέγων, Ἥμαρτον παραδοὺς αἷμα ἀθῷον. οἱ δὲ εἶπον, Τί πρὸς ἡμᾶς; σὺ 4
ὄψει. καὶ ῥίψας τὰ ἀργύρια ἐν τῷ ναῷ ἀνεχώρησε, καὶ ἀπελθὼν ἀπήγξατο. 5
οἱ δὲ ἀρχιερεῖς λαβόντες τὰ ἀργύρια εἶπον, Οὐκ ἔξεστι βαλεῖν αὐτὰ εἰς τὸν 6
κορβανᾶν, ἐπεὶ τιμὴ αἵματός ἐστι. συμβούλιον δὲ λαβόντες ἠγόρασαν ἐξ 7
αὐτῶν τὸν ἀγρὸν τοῦ κεραμέως εἰς ταφὴν τοῖς ξένοις. διὸ ἐκλήθη ὁ ἀγρὸς 8
ἐκεῖνος ἀγρὸς αἵματος ἕως τῆς σήμερον. τότε ἐπληρώθη τὸ ῥηθὲν διὰ 9

5 ανεχωρισεν cod.

118 209 ς **63** και]+αποκριθεις ς **67** εραπισαν] εραπησαν 118 om αυτον 118 209 ς **69** εξω εκαθητο ς **70** om αυτων ς ο] τι ς om ουδε επισταμαι ς **71** ειδεν αυτον 118 ς αυτοις· εκει] τοις εκει, ς Ναζαρηνου] Ναζ spat. rel. 118, Ναζωραιου ς **73** om παλιν ς αληθως]+και συ 118 209 ς **74** katαναθεματιζειν ς **75** αλεκτορα φωνησαι 118 ς
2 αυτον 2°] om 118 209 **3** ο 1°] om ς μεταμεληθης 118

ʽΙερεμίου τοῦ προφήτου λέγοντος, Καὶ ἔλαβον τὰ τριάκοντα ἀργύρια, τὴν
10 τιμὴν τοῦ τετιμημένου, ὃν ἐτιμήσαντο ἀπὸ υἱῶν Ἰσραήλ, καὶ ἔδωκαν αὐτὰ εἰς
τὸν ἀγρὸν τοῦ κεραμέως, καθὼς συνέταξέ μοι ὁ Κύριος.
11 ʽΟ δὲ Ἰησοῦς ἐστάθη ἔμπροσθεν τοῦ ἡγεμόνος· καὶ ἐπηρώτησεν αὐτὸν τκ
ὁ ἡγεμὼν λέγων, Σὺ εἶ ὁ βασιλεὺς τῶν Ἰουδαίων; ὁ δὲ Ἰησοῦς ἔφη α
12 αὐτῷ, Σὺ λέγεις. καὶ ἐν τῷ κατηγορεῖσθαι αὐτὸν ὑπὸ τῶν ἀρχιερέων τκα
13 καὶ πρεσβυτέρων οὐδὲν ἀπεκρίνατο. τότε λέγει αὐτῷ ὁ Πιλάτος, δ
14 Οὐκ ἀκούεις πόσα σοῦ κατηγοροῦσιν; καὶ οὐκ ἀπεκρίθη αὐτῷ πρὸς
οὐδὲ ἓν ῥῆμα, ὥστε θαυμάζειν τὸν ἡγεμόνα λίαν.
15 Κατὰ δὲ ἑορτὴν εἰώθει ὁ ἡγεμὼν ἀπολύειν ἕνα τῷ ὄχλῳ δέσμιον, ὃν τκβ
16 ἤθελον. εἶχον δὲ τότε δέσμιον ἐπίσημον λεγόμενον Ἰησοῦν Βαραββᾶν. β τκγ
17 συνηγμένων οὖν αὐτῶν εἶπεν αὐτοῖς ὁ Πιλάτος, Τίνα θέλετε ἀπολύσω δ
ὑμῖν τῶν δύο; Ἰησοῦν τὸν Βαραββᾶν, ἢ Ἰησοῦν τὸν λεγόμενον
18 19 Χριστόν; ᾔδει γὰρ ὅτι διὰ φθόνον παρέδωκαν αὐτόν. καθημένου δὲ τκδ
αὐτοῦ ἐπὶ τοῦ βήματος, ἀπέστειλε πρὸς αὐτὸν ἡ γυνὴ αὐτοῦ λέγουσα, ι
Μηδὲν σοὶ καὶ τῷ δικαίῳ ἐκείνῳ· πολλὰ γὰρ ἔπαθον σήμερον κατ᾽ ὄναρ
20 δι᾽ αὐτόν. οἱ δὲ ἀρχιερεῖς καὶ οἱ πρεσβύτεροι ἔπεισαν τοὺς ὄχλους, ἵνα τκε
21 αἰτήσωνται τὸν Βαραββᾶν, τὸν δὲ Ἰησοῦν ἀπολέσωσιν. ἀποκριθεὶς δὲ α
ὁ ἡγεμὼν εἶπεν αὐτοῖς, Τίνα θέλετε ἀπὸ τῶν δύο ἀπολύσω ὑμῖν; οἱ δὲ
22 εἶπον, Τὸν Βαραββᾶν. λέγει αὐτοῖς ὁ Πιλάτος, Τί οὖν ποιήσω Ἰησοῦν τκϛ
23 τὸν λεγόμενον Χριστόν; λέγουσι πάντες, Σταυρωθήτω. λέγει αὐτοῖς α
ὁ ἡγεμών, Τί γὰρ κακὸν ἐποίησεν; οἱ δὲ περισσότερον ἔκραζον,
24 Σταυρωθήτω. ἰδὼν δὲ ὁ Πιλάτος ὅτι οὐδὲν ὠφελεῖ, ἀλλὰ μᾶλλον τκζ
θόρυβος γίνεται, λαβὼν ὕδωρ ἀπενίψατο τὰς χεῖρας ἀπέναντι τοῦ ὄχλου ι
λέγων, Ἀθῷός εἰμι ἀπὸ τοῦ αἵματος τοῦ δικαίου τούτου· ὑμεῖς ὄψεσθε.
25 καὶ ἀποκριθεὶς πᾶς ὁ λαὸς εἶπε, Τὸ αἷμα αὐτοῦ ἐφ᾽ ἡμᾶς καὶ ἐπὶ τὰ
26 τέκνα ἡμῶν. τότε ἀπέλυσεν αὐτοῖς τὸν Βαραββᾶν, τὸν δὲ Ἰησοῦν τκη
φραγελλώσας παρέδωκεν αὐτοῖς ἵνα σταυρωθῇ. α
27 Τότε οἱ στρατιῶται τοῦ ἡγεμόνος παραλαβόντες τὸν Ἰησοῦν εἰς τὸ τκθ
28 πραιτώριον συνήγαγον ἐπ᾽ αὐτὸν ὅλην τὴν σπεῖραν· καὶ ἐκδύσαντες αὐτὸν δ

16 Ιησουν quod praeter consuetudinem codicis plene scriptum est nunc erasum **17** Ιησουν τον 1°] plene script. et nunc erasum est **22** τι] ι cod. linea ineunte cui, ni fallor, τ addere neglexit deaurator **24** οτι] τι cod. per incuriam deauratoris

9 Ηερεμιου 118 **10** καθως] καθα ϛ Κυριος sine ο ϛ **11** εσταθη] εστη 118 209² ϛ, quid autem scripserit 209* legere non possum **12** των πρεσβυτερων ϛ **13** καταμαρτυρουσι ϛ **16** Ιησουν] plene script. 118 209*, nunc eras. 209, om ϛ **17** των δυο; Ιησουν τον] om ϛ Ιησουν τον nunc eras. 209, Ιησουν plene script. 118 209* **21** om τον ϛ **22** λεγουσιν αυτω ϛ **23** ο δε ηγεμων εφη ϛ περισσως ϛ εκραζον]+λεγοντες 118² ϛ **26** om αυτοις ϛ 118 209 ϛ

περιέθηκαν αὐτῷ χλαμύδα κοκκίνην, καὶ πλέξαντες στέφανον ἐξ ἀκανθῶν 29
ἔθηκαν ἐπὶ τὴν κεφαλὴν αὐτοῦ, καὶ κάλαμον ἐν τῇ δεξιᾷ αὐτοῦ· καὶ
γονυπετήσαντες ἔμπροσθεν αὐτοῦ ἐνέπαιζον αὐτῷ λέγοντες, Χαῖρε βασι-
λεῦ τῶν Ἰουδαίων· καὶ ἐμπτύσαντες εἰς αὐτὸν ἔλαβον τὸν κάλαμον καὶ 30
τλ ἔτυπτον εἰς τὴν κεφαλὴν αὐτοῦ. καὶ ὅτε ἐνέπαιξαν αὐτῷ, ἐξέδυσαν αὐτὸν 31
ς τὴν χλαμύδα, καὶ ἐνέδυσαν αὐτὸν τὰ ἱμάτια αὐτοῦ· καὶ ἀπήγαγον αὐτὸν
τλα εἰς τὸ σταυρῶσαι. ἐξερχόμενοι δὲ εὗρον ἄνθρωπον Κυρηναῖον ὀνόματι 32
α Σίμωνα· τοῦτον ἠγγάρευσαν ἵνα ἄρῃ τὸν σταυρὸν αὐτοῦ.
τλβ Καὶ ἐλθόντες εἰς τόπον λεγόμενον Γολγοθά, ὅ ἐστι κρανίου τόπος 33
α τλγ λεγόμενος, ἔδωκαν αὐτῷ πιεῖν οἶνον μετὰ χολῆς μεμιγμένον· καὶ γευσά- 34
δ τλδ μενος οὐκ ἠθέλησε πιεῖν. σταυρώσαντες δὲ αὐτὸν διεμερίσαντο τὰ 35
α ἱμάτια αὐτοῦ, βαλόντες κλῆρον· ἵνα πληρωθῇ τὸ ῥηθὲν ὑπὸ τοῦ προ-
φήτου, Διεμερίσαντο τὰ ἱμάτιά μου ἑαυτοῖς, καὶ ἐπὶ τὸν ἱματισμόν
τλε μου ἔβαλον κλῆρον. καὶ καθήμενοι ἐτήρουν αὐτὸν ἐκεῖ. καὶ ἐπέθηκαν 36 37
α ἐπάνω τῆς κεφαλῆς αὐτοῦ τὴν αἰτίαν αὐτοῦ γεγραμμένην, Οὗτός ἐστιν
τλς Ἰησοῦς ὁ βασιλεὺς τῶν Ἰουδαίων. τότε σταυροῦνται σὺν αὐτῷ δύο 38
α λῃσταί, εἷς ἐκ δεξιῶν καὶ εἷς ἐξ εὐωνύμων.
τλζ Οἱ δὲ παραπορευόμενοι ἐβλασφήμουν αὐτὸν κινοῦντες τὰς κεφαλὰς 39
ς αὐτῶν καὶ λέγοντες, Ὁ καταλύων τὸν ναὸν καὶ ἐν τρισὶν ἡμέραις οἰκοδο- 40
μῶν, σῶσον σεαυτόν· εἰ υἱὸς εἶ τοῦ Θεοῦ, κατάβηθι ἀπὸ τοῦ σταυροῦ.
τλη ὁμοίως καὶ οἱ ἀρχιερεῖς ἐμπαίζοντες μετὰ τῶν γραμματέων καὶ πρεσ- 41
β βυτέρων ἔλεγον, Ἄλλους ἔσωσεν, ἑαυτὸν οὐ δύναται σῶσαι. εἰ βασιλεὺς 42
Ἰσραήλ ἐστι, καταβάτω νῦν ἀπὸ τοῦ σταυροῦ, καὶ πιστεύσομεν αὐτῷ.
εἰ πέποιθεν ἐπὶ τὸν Θεὸν ῥυσάσθω νῦν αὐτόν, εἰ θέλει αὐτόν· εἶπε γὰρ 43
τλθ ὅτι Θεοῦ εἰμι υἱός. τὸ δ' αὐτὸ καὶ οἱ λῃσταὶ οἱ συσταυρωθέντες αὐτῷ 44
β ὠνείδιζον αὐτόν.
τμ Ἀπὸ δὲ ἕκτης ὥρας σκότος ἐγένετο ἐπὶ πᾶσαν τὴν γῆν ἕως ὥρας 45
β τμα ἐνάτης· περὶ δὲ τὴν ἐνάτην ὥραν ἀνεβόησεν ὁ Ἰησοῦς φωνῇ μεγάλῃ 46
ς λέγων, Ἠλεὶ Ἠλεὶ λαμὰ σαβαχθανεῖ; τοῦτ' ἔστι, Θεέ μου, Θεέ μου,
ἱνατί με ἐγκατέλιπες; τινὲς δὲ τῶν ἐκεῖ ἑστώτων ἀκούσαντες ἔλεγον 47
τμβ ὅτι Ἠλίαν φωνεῖ οὗτος. καὶ εὐθέως δραμὼν εἷς ἐξ αὐτῶν καὶ λαβὼν 48
β σπόγγον, πλήσας τε ὄξους καὶ περιθεὶς καλάμῳ, ἐπότιζεν αὐτόν. οἱ δὲ 49
λοιποὶ ἔλεγον, Ἄφες ἴδωμεν εἰ ἔρχεται Ἠλίας καὶ σώσει αὐτόν.

118 209 ς **29** επεθηκαν ς   επι την δεξιαν 118 ς, sed ipse 118* εν τη δεξια sub lin. scrips.   ο βασιλευς ς   **33** ο] ος ς   λεγομενος κρανιου τοπος 118 ς   **34** οινον] οξος 118 ς   ηθελε 118 ς   **35** βαλλοντες ς   **37** om Ιησους 118   **41** ομοιως δε 118 ς   **42** πιστευσωμεν 118   αυτω] om 118 sp. rel.   **43** om ει 1° ς   **44** ονειδιζον 118   αυτω ς   **45** γενετο 209   εννατης 118 209 ς   **46** εννατην 118 209 ς   Ηλι Ηλι λαμα σαβαχθανι ς, Ηλι Ηλι λιμας αβαχθανη 118 209   **49** και σωσει] σωσων ς, σωσον 118

50 Ὁ δὲ Ἰησοῦς πάλιν κράξας φωνῇ μεγάλῃ ἀφῆκε τὸ πνεῦμα. τμγ α
51 Καὶ ἰδοὺ τὸ καταπέτασμα τοῦ ναοῦ ἐσχίσθη εἰς δύο ἀπὸ ἄνωθεν ἕως τμδ β
52 κάτω· καὶ ἡ γῆ ἐσείσθη, καὶ αἱ πέτραι ἐσχίσθησαν, καὶ τὰ μνημεῖα τμε ι
ἠνεῴχθησαν, καὶ πολλὰ σώματα τῶν κεκοιμημένων ἁγίων ἠγέρθησαν,
53 καὶ ἐξελθόντες ἐκ τῶν μνημείων μετὰ τὴν ἔγερσιν αὐτοῦ εἰσῆλθον εἰς τὴν
ἁγίαν πόλιν καὶ ἐνεφανίσθησαν πολλοῖς.
54 Ὁ δὲ ἑκατόνταρχος καὶ οἱ μετ᾽ αὐτοῦ τηροῦντες τὸν Ἰησοῦν ἰδόντες τμς β
τὸν σεισμὸν καὶ τὰ γενόμενα ἐφοβήθησαν σφόδρα, λέγοντες, Ἀληθῶς
Θεοῦ υἱὸς ἦν οὗτος.
55 Ἦσαν δὲ ἐκεῖ γυναῖκες πολλαὶ ἀπὸ μακρόθεν θεωροῦσαι, αἵτινες τμζ ς
56 ἠκολούθησαν τῷ Ἰησοῦ ἀπὸ τῆς Γαλιλαίας διακονοῦσαι αὐτῷ· ἐν αἷς ἦν
Μαριὰμ ἡ Μαγδαληνή, καὶ Μαρία ἡ τοῦ Ἰακώβου καὶ Ἰωσῆ μήτηρ,
καὶ ἡ μήτηρ τῶν υἱῶν Ζεβεδαίου.
57 Ὀψίας δὲ γενομένης ἦλθεν ἄνθρωπος πλούσιος ἀπὸ Ἀριμαθαίας, ΞΗ′
58 τοὔνομα Ἰωσήφ, ὃς καὶ αὐτὸς ἐμαθητεύθη τῷ Ἰησοῦ· οὗτος προσελ- τμη α
θὼν τῷ Πιλάτῳ ᾐτήσατο τὸ σῶμα τοῦ Ἰησοῦ. τότε οὖν ὁ Πιλάτος
59 ἐκέλευσεν ἀποδοθῆναι. καὶ λαβὼν τὸ σῶμα ὁ Ἰωσὴφ ἐνετύλιξεν αὐτὸ τμθ α
60 σινδόνι καθαρᾷ, καὶ ἔθηκεν αὐτὸ ἐν τῷ κενῷ αὐτοῦ μνημείῳ ὃ ἐλατό-
μησεν ἐν τῇ πέτρᾳ· καὶ προσκυλίσας λίθον μέγαν τῇ θύρᾳ τοῦ μνημείου
61 ἀπῆλθεν. ἦν δὲ ἐκεῖ Μαριὰμ ἡ Μαγδαληνὴ καὶ ἡ ἄλλη Μαρία καθή- τν ς
μεναι ἀπέναντι τοῦ τάφου.
62 Τῇ δὲ ἐπαύριον, ἥτις ἐστὶ μετὰ τὴν παρασκευήν, συνήχθησαν οἱ τνα ι
63 ἀρχιερεῖς καὶ οἱ Φαρισαῖοι πρὸς Πιλάτον λέγοντες, Κύριε, ἐμνήσθημεν
ὅτι ἐκεῖνος ὁ πλάνος εἶπεν ἔτι ζῶν, Μετὰ τρεῖς ἡμέρας ἐγείρομαι.
64 κέλευσον οὖν ἀσφαλισθῆναι τὸν τάφον ἕως τῆς τρίτης ἡμέρας, μήποτε
ἐλθόντες οἱ μαθηταὶ αὐτοῦ κλέψωσιν αὐτὸν καὶ εἴπωσι τῷ λαῷ, Ἠγέρθη
65 ἀπὸ τῶν νεκρῶν· καὶ ἔσται ἡ ἐσχάτη πλάνη χείρων τῆς πρώτης. ἔφη
δὲ αὐτοῖς ὁ Πιλάτος, Ἔχετε κουστωδίαν· ὑπάγετε, ἀσφαλίσασθε ὡς
66 οἴδατε. οἱ δὲ πορευθέντες ἠσφαλίσαντο τὸν τάφον, σφραγίσαντες τὸν
λίθον μετὰ τῆς κουστωδίας.
XXVIII. Ὀψὲ δὲ σαββάτων, τῇ ἐπιφωσκούσῃ εἰς μίαν σαββάτων, τνβ α
2 ἦλθε Μαρία ἡ Μαγδαληνὴ καὶ ἡ ἄλλη Μαρία θεωρῆσαι τὸν τάφον. καὶ
ἰδοὺ σεισμὸς ἐγένετο μέγας· ἄγγελος γὰρ Κυρίου καταβὰς ἐξ οὐρανοῦ,
προσελθὼν ἀπεκύλισε τὸν λίθον ἀπὸ τῆς θύρας τοῦ μνημείου, καὶ

52 *ανεωχθησαν* ς *ηγερθη* ς **56** *Μαριαμ*] *Μαρια* 118 209 ς 118 209 ς
57 *εμαθητευσε* ς **58** om *ουν* ς *αποδοθηναι*] + *το σωμα* ς, + *το σωμα* Xῡ (ni fallor, sed Xῡ pro certo non habeo) 118[2] **60** *εθετο* 118 209 *κενω*] *καινω* 118 ς **61** *Μαριαμ*] *Μαρια* 118 ς **63** *ο πλανος εκεινος* 118 209
64 *κλεψωσιν*] pr *νυκτος* ς
2 om *του μνημειου* ς

ἐκάθητο ἐπάνω αὐτοῦ. ἦν δὲ ἡ ἰδέα αὐτοῦ ὡς ἀστραπή, καὶ τὸ ἔνδυμα 3
αὐτοῦ λευκὸν ὡς χιών. ἀπὸ δὲ τοῦ φόβου αὐτοῦ ἐσείσθησαν οἱ τηροῦντες 4
τνγ καὶ ἐγένοντο ὡς νεκροί. ἀποκριθεὶς δὲ ὁ ἄγγελος εἶπε ταῖς γυναιξί, Μὴ 5
β φοβεῖσθε ὑμεῖς· οἶδα γὰρ ὅτι Ἰησοῦν τὸν ἐσταυρωμένον ζητεῖτε. οὐκ 6
ἔστιν ὧδε· ἠγέρθη γάρ, καθὼς εἶπε. δεῦτε ἴδετε τὸν τόπον ὅπου ἔκειτο
ὁ Κύριος. καὶ ταχὺ πορευθεῖσαι εἴπατε τοῖς μαθηταῖς αὐτοῦ ὅτι ἠγέρθη 7
ἀπὸ τῶν νεκρῶν, καὶ ἰδοὺ προάγει ὑμᾶς εἰς τὴν Γαλιλαίαν· ἐκεῖ αὐτὸν
τνδ ὄψεσθε. ἰδοὺ εἶπον ὑμῖν. καὶ ἐξελθοῦσαι ταχὺ ἀπὸ τοῦ μνημείου μετὰ 8
β τνε φόβου καὶ χαρᾶς μεγάλης ἔδραμον ἀπαγγεῖλαι τοῖς μαθηταῖς αὐτοῦ. ὡς 9
ι δὲ ἐπορεύοντο ἀπαγγεῖλαι τοῖς μαθηταῖς αὐτοῦ, καὶ ἰδοὺ ὁ Ἰησοῦς ὑπήν-
τησεν αὐταῖς λέγων, Χαίρετε. αἱ δὲ προσελθοῦσαι ἐκράτησαν αὐτοῦ
τοὺς πόδας καὶ προσεκύνησαν αὐτῷ. τότε λέγει αὐταῖς ὁ Ἰησοῦς, Μὴ 10
φοβεῖσθε· ὑπάγετε, ἀπαγγείλατε τοῖς ἀδελφοῖς μου ἵνα ἀπέλθωσιν εἰς
τὴν Γαλιλαίαν, κἀκεῖ με ὄψονται.

Πορευομένων δὲ αὐτῶν ἰδού τινες τῆς κουστωδίας ἐλθόντες εἰς τὴν 11
πόλιν ἀπήγγειλαν τοῖς ἀρχιερεῦσιν ἅπαντα τὰ γενόμενα. καὶ συναχ- 12
θέντες μετὰ τῶν πρεσβυτέρων συμβούλιόν τε λαβόντες ἀργύρια ἱκανὰ
ἔδωκαν τοῖς στρατιώταις λέγοντες, Εἴπατε ὅτι Οἱ μαθηταὶ αὐτοῦ νυκτὸς 13
ἐλθόντες ἔκλεψαν αὐτὸν ἡμῶν κοιμωμένων. καὶ ἐὰν ἀκουσθῇ τοῦτο ἐπὶ 14
τοῦ ἡγεμόνος, ἡμεῖς πείσομεν αὐτὸν καὶ ὑμᾶς ἀμερίμνους ποιήσομεν.
οἱ δὲ λαβόντες τὰ ἀργύρια ἐποίησαν ὡς ἐδιδάχθησαν. καὶ διεφημίσθη 15
ὁ λόγος οὗτος παρὰ Ἰουδαίοις μέχρι τῆς σήμερον.

Οἱ δὲ ἕνδεκα μαθηταὶ ἐπορεύθησαν εἰς τὴν Γαλιλαίαν, εἰς τὸ ὄρος 16
οὗ ἐτάξατο αὐτοῖς ὁ Ἰησοῦς. καὶ ἰδόντες αὐτὸν προσεκύνησαν αὐτῷ· οἱ 17
δὲ ἐδίστασαν. καὶ προσελθὼν ὁ Ἰησοῦς ἐλάλησεν αὐτοῖς λέγων, Ἐδόθη 18
μοι πᾶσα ἐξουσία ἐν οὐρανῷ καὶ ἐπὶ γῆς. πορευθέντες οὖν μαθητεύσατε 19
πάντα τὰ ἔθνη, βαπτίζοντες αὐτοὺς εἰς τὸ ὄνομα τοῦ Πατρὸς καὶ τοῦ
Υἱοῦ καὶ τοῦ Ἁγίου Πνεύματος, διδάσκοντες αὐτοὺς τηρεῖν πάντα ὅσα 20
ἐνετειλάμην ὑμῖν· καὶ ἰδοὺ ἐγὼ μεθ' ὑμῶν εἰμι πάσας τὰς ἡμέρας ἕως
τῆς συντελείας τοῦ αἰῶνος.

118 209 ς

3 ως 2°] ωσει ς, ωσ spat. rel. 118 **4** ως] ωσει ς, ω spat. rel. 118 **5** om τον 118 **9** υπηντισεν 118, απηντησεν ς **10** οψωνται 118 209 **20** αιωνος] + αμην 118 209 ς ad fin. evan. 209 scriba eiusdem fere temporis addidit ιστεον οτι μετα χρονους οκτω της του κυ ημων και θυ Ιυ Χυ εκ νεκρων αναστασεως και εις ουνους αναληψεως εγραφη το κατα Ματθαιον αγιον ευαγγελιον

ΕΥΑΓΓΕΛΙΟΝ ΚΑΤΑ ΜΑΡΚΟΝ

2 I. Ἀρχὴ τοῦ εὐαγγελίυυ Ἰησοῦ Χριστοῦ υἱοῦ τοῦ Θεοῦ· καθὼς α
γέγραπται ἐν Ἡσαΐᾳ τῷ προφήτῃ, Ἰδοὺ ἐγὼ ἀποστέλλω τὸν ἄγγελόν β
μου πρὸ προσώπου σου, ὃς κατασκευάσει τὴν ὁδόν σου ἔμπροσθέν σου·
3 φωνὴ βοῶντος ἐν τῇ ἐρήμῳ, Ἑτοιμάσατε τὴν ὁδὸν Κυρίου, εὐθείας ποιεῖτε β
4 τὰς τρίβους αὐτοῦ, ἐγένετο Ἰωάννης βαπτίζων ἐν τῇ ἐρήμῳ καὶ κηρύσ- α γ
5 σων βάπτισμα μετανοίας εἰς ἄφεσιν ἁμαρτιῶν. καὶ ἐξεπορεύετο πρὸς ϛ
αὐτὸν πᾶσα ἡ Ἰουδαία χώρα, καὶ οἱ Ἱεροσολυμῖται, καὶ ἐβαπτίζοντο
πάντες ἐν τῷ Ἰορδάνῃ ποταμῷ ὑπ᾽ αὐτοῦ, ἐξομολογούμενοι τὰς ἁμαρτίας
6 αὐτῶν. ἦν δὲ ὁ Ἰωάννης ἐνδεδυμένος τρίχας καμήλου καὶ ζώνην δερμα-
7 τίνην περὶ τὴκ ὀσφὺν αὐτοῦ, καὶ ἐσθίων ἀκρίδας καὶ μέλι ἄγριον. καὶ δ
ἐκήρυσσε λέγων, Ἔρχεται ὁ ἰσχυρότερός μου ὀπίσω μου, οὗ οὐκ εἰμὶ α
8 ἱκανὸς κύψας λῦσαι τὸν ἱμάντα τῶν ὑποδημάτων αὐτοῦ. ἐγὼ μὲν ἐβάπ-
9 τισα ὑμᾶς ἐν ὕδατι· αὐτὸς δὲ βαπτίσει ὑμᾶς ἐν Πνεύματι Ἁγίῳ. καὶ ε
ἐγένετο ἐν ἐκείναις ταῖς ἡμέραις, ἦλθεν Ἰησοῦς ἀπὸ Ναζαρὲθ τῆς α
10 Γαλιλαίας, καὶ ἐβαπτίσθη ἐν τῷ Ἰορδάνῃ ὑπὸ Ἰωάννου. καὶ εὐ-
θέως ἀναβαίνων ἀπὸ τοῦ ὕδατος εἶδε σχιζομένους τοὺς οὐρανοὺς καὶ
11 τὸ Πνεῦμα ὡσεὶ περιστερὰν καταβαῖνον ἐπ᾽ αὐτόν· καὶ φωνὴ ἐγένετο
ἐκ τῶν οὐρανῶν, Σὺ εἶ ὁ υἱὸς μου ὁ ἀγαπητός, ἐν σοὶ εὐδόκησα.
12 13 καὶ εὐθέως τὸ Πνεῦμα αὐτὸν ἐκβάλλει εἰς τὴν ἔρημον. καὶ ἦν ἐκεῖ ϛ β
ἐπὶ ἡμέρας τεσσαράκοντα πειραζόμενος ὑπὸ τοῦ Σατανᾶ, καὶ ἦν μετὰ ζ
τῶν θηρίων· καὶ οἱ ἄγγελοι διηκόνουν αὐτῷ. ϛ
14 Μετὰ δὲ τὸ παραδοθῆναι τὸν Ἰωάννην ἦλθεν ὁ Ἰησοῦς εἰς τὴν η δ
15 Γαλιλαίαν κηρύσσων τὸ εὐαγγέλιον τοῦ Θεοῦ, καὶ λέγων, Πεπλή- θ ϛ

Titul. Το κατα Μαρκον αγιον ευαγγελιον 209 ϛ, om 118 118 131 209 ϛ
1 hic inc. collatio 131 **2** ως 118 131 ϛ εν τοις προφηταις 118 ϛ **6** ο] om ϛ οφυν 209 μελλι 209 **9** Ναζαρετ 118 209 ϛ υπο Ιωαννου εις τον Ιορδανην 118 ϛ **10** αναβαινον 118 και ειδε 131 **11** εν ω ϛ ηυδοκησα 118 209 **12** ευθυς ϛ **13** εκει]+εν τη ερημω 118 ϛ om επι 118 ϛ **14** κηρυσσον 131 ευαγγελιον]+της βασιλειας 118 131 ϛ **15** λεγων]+οτι 118 ϛ

ρωται ὁ καιρὸς καὶ ἤγγικεν ἡ βασιλεία τοῦ Θεοῦ· μετανοεῖτε καὶ
πιστεύετε ἐν τῷ εὐαγγελίῳ.
Περιπατῶν δὲ παρὰ τὴν θάλασσαν τῆς Γαλιλαίας εἶδε Σίμωνα καὶ 16
Ἀνδρέαν τὸν ἀδελφὸν τοῦ Σίμωνος ἀμφίβληστρα βάλλοντας
ι ἐν τῇ θαλάσσῃ· ἦσαν γὰρ ἁλιεῖς· καὶ εἶπεν αὐτοῖς ὁ Ἰησοῦς, Δεῦτε 17
β ὀπίσω μου, καὶ ποιήσω ὑμᾶς ἁλιεῖς ἀνθρώπων. καὶ εὐθέως ἀφέντες τὰ 18
ια δίκτυα αὐτῶν ἠκολούθησαν αὐτῷ. καὶ προβὰς ὀλίγον εἶδεν Ἰάκωβον 19
ϛ τὸν τοῦ Ζεβεδαίου καὶ Ἰωάννην τὸν ἀδελφὸν αὐτοῦ, καὶ αὐτοὺς ἐν τῷ
πλοίῳ καταρτίζοντας τὰ δίκτυα. καὶ εὐθέως ἐκάλεσεν αὐτούς· καὶ 20
ἀφέντες τὸν πατέρα αὐτῶν Ζεβεδαῖον ἐν τῷ πλοίῳ μετὰ τῶν μισθίων
ἀπῆλθον ὀπίσω αὐτοῦ.
ιβ Καὶ εἰσπορεύεται εἰς Καπερναούμ· καὶ εὐθὺς τοῖς σάββασιν εἰσελ- 21
η ιγ θὼν εἰς τὴν συναγωγὴν ἐδίδασκε· καὶ ἐξεπλήσσοντο ἐπὶ τῇ διδαχῇ αὐτοῦ· 22
β Λ' ἦν γὰρ διδάσκων αὐτοὺς ὡς ἐξουσίαν ἔχων, καὶ οὐχ ὡς οἱ γραμματεῖς. καὶ 23
ιδ εὐθὺς ἦν ἐν τῇ συναγωγῇ αὐτῶν ἄνθρωπος ἐν πνεύματι ἀκαθάρτῳ, καὶ
η ἀνέκραξε λέγων, Ἔα, τί ἡμῖν καὶ σοί, Ἰησοῦ Ναζαρηνέ; ἦλθες ἀπολέσαι 24
ἡμᾶς; οἶδά σε τίς εἶ, ὁ ἅγιος τοῦ Θεοῦ. καὶ ἐπετίμησεν αὐτῷ ὁ Ἰησοῦς 25
λέγων, Φιμώθητι καὶ ἔξελθε ἐξ αὐτοῦ. καὶ σπαράξαν αὐτὸν τὸ πνεῦμα τὸ 26
ἀκάθαρτον καὶ κράξαν φωνῇ μεγάλῃ ἐξῆλθεν ἐξ αὐτοῦ. καὶ ἐθαμβήθησαν 27
πάντες, ὥστε συζητεῖν πρὸς ἑαυτοὺς λέγοντας, Τί ἐστι τοῦτο; διδαχὴ
καινὴ αὕτη, κατ' ἐξουσίαν καὶ τοῖς πνεύμασι τοῖς ἀκαθάρτοις ἐπιτάσσει,
καὶ ὑπακούουσιν αὐτῷ. ἐξῆλθε δὲ ἡ ἀκοὴ αὐτοῦ εἰς ὅλην τὴν περίχωρον 28
τῆς Γαλιλαίας.
Β' Καὶ εὐθὺς ἐκ τῆς συναγωγῆς ἐξελθὼν ἦλθεν εἰς τὴν οἰκίαν Σίμωνος 29
ιε β καὶ Ἀνδρέου, μετὰ Ἰακώβου καὶ Ἰωάννου. ἡ δὲ πενθερὰ τοῦ Σίμωνος 30
κατέκειτο πυρέσσουσα· καὶ εὐθέως λέγουσιν αὐτῷ περὶ αὐτῆς. καὶ προσ- 31
ελθὼν ἤγειρεν αὐτὴν κρατήσας τῆς χειρὸς αὐτῆς· καὶ ἀφῆκεν αὐτὴν ὁ
Γ' πυρετός, καὶ διηκόνει αὐτοῖς. ὀψίας δὲ γενομένης, ὅτε ἔδυ ὁ ἥλιος, 32
ἔφερον πρὸς αὐτὸν πάντας τοὺς κακῶς ἔχοντας καὶ τοὺς δαιμονιζομένους·
καὶ ἡ πόλις ὅλη ἐπισυνηγμένη ἦν πρὸς τὴν θύραν· καὶ ἐθεράπευσε πολλοὺς 33
ιϛ κακῶς ἔχοντας ποικίλαις νόσοις, καὶ δαιμόνια πολλὰ ἐξέβαλε, καὶ οὐκ 34
η ἤφιε λαλεῖν τὰ δαιμόνια, ὅτι ᾔδεισαν αὐτὸν Χριστὸν εἶναι.

118 131 209 ϛ

16 του Σιμωνος] αυτου ϛ, αδελφον αυτου Σιμωνος 131 βαλλοντας αμφιβληστρον ϛ **17** υμας]+γενεσθαι ϛ **19** προβας εκειθεν ϛ **20** μισθιων] μισθωτων 131 ϛ μισθ spat. rel. 118 **21** εισπορευονται ϛ ευθεως ϛ ευθ spat. rel. 118 **23** om ευθυς 118 ϛ **27** αυτους ϛ τις η διδαχη η[νς] καινη ϛ κατ] pr οτι ϛ **28** αυτου]+ευθυς ϛ **29** ευθεως ϛ, ευθεως 118 εξελθοντες ηλθον[ων] ϛ, εξελθοντες ηλθον[εν] 118 Ιωαννου και Ιακωβου 131 **30** om του ϛ **31** πυρετος] + ευθεως ϛ **34** om χριστον ειναι ϛ

35 Καὶ πρωῒ ἔννυχα λίαν ἀναστὰς ἐξῆλθε καὶ ἀπῆλθεν εἰς ἔρημον τόπον, ιζ η
36 κἀκεῖ προσηύχετο. καὶ κατεδίωξαν αὐτὸν ὅ τε Σίμων καὶ οἱ μετ' αὐτοῦ,
37 38 καὶ εὑρόντες αὐτὸν λέγουσιν αὐτῷ ὅτι Πάντες ζητοῦσί σε. καὶ λέγει
αὐτοῖς, Ἄγωμεν εἰς τὰς ἐχομένας κωμοπόλεις, ἵνα καὶ ἐκεῖ κηρύξω· εἰς
39 τοῦτο γὰρ ἐξελήλυθα. καὶ ἦν κηρύσσων εἰς τὰς συναγωγὰς αὐτῶν εἰς
ὅλην τὴν Γαλιλαίαν, καὶ τὰ δαιμόνια ἐκβάλλων.
40 Καὶ ἔρχεται πρὸς αὐτὸν λεπρὸς παρακαλῶν αὐτὸν καὶ γονυπετῶν καὶ Δ'
41 λέγων αὐτῷ ὅτι Ἐὰν θέλῃς, δύνασαί με καθαρίσαι. ὁ δὲ Ἰησοῦς σπλαγ- ιη β
χνισθεὶς ἐκτείνας τὴν χεῖρα ἥψατο αὐτοῦ, καὶ λέγει, Θέλω, καθαρίσθητι.
42 καὶ εἰπόντος αὐτοῦ εὐθέως ἀπῆλθεν ἀπ' αὐτοῦ ἡ λέπρα, καὶ ἐκαθερίσθη.
43 44 καὶ ἐμβριμησάμενος αὐτῷ εὐθέως ἐξέβαλεν αὐτόν, καὶ λέγει αὐτῷ, Ὅρα
μηδενὶ μηδὲν εἴπῃς· ἀλλ' ὕπαγε, σεαυτὸν δεῖξον τῷ ἱερεῖ καὶ προσένεγκε
45 περὶ τοῦ καθαρισμοῦ σου ἃ προσέταξε Μωσῆς, εἰς μαρτύριον αὐτοῖς. ὁ ιθ ι
δὲ ἐξελθὼν ἤρξατο κηρύσσειν πολλὰ καὶ διαφημίζειν τὸν λόγον, ὥστε
μηκέτι αὐτὸν δύνασθαι φανερῶς εἰς πόλιν εἰσελθεῖν· ἀλλ' ἔξω ἐν ἐρήμοις
τόποις ἦν, καὶ ἤρχοντο πρὸς αὐτὸν παντόθεν.

II. Καὶ εἰσῆλθε πάλιν εἰς Καπερναοὺμ δι' ἡμερῶν· καὶ ἠκούσθη κ α
2 ὅτι εἰς οἶκόν ἐστι, καὶ εὐθέως συνήχθησαν ὄχλοι πολλοί, ὥστε μηκέτι
3 χωρεῖν μηδὲ τὰ πρὸς τὴν θύραν· καὶ ἐλάλει αὐτοῖς τὸν λόγον. καὶ E'
ἔρχονται πρὸς αὐτὸν φέροντες παραλυτικὸν αἰρόμενον ὑπὸ τεσσάρων.
4 καὶ μὴ δυνάμενοι προσεγγίσαι αὐτῷ διὰ τὸν ὄχλον ἀπεστέγασαν τὴν
στέγην ὅπου ἦν, καὶ ἐξορύξαντες χαλῶσι τὸν κράβαττον ἐφ' ᾧ ὁ παραλυ-
5 τικὸς κατέκειτο. ἰδὼν δὲ ὁ Ἰησοῦς τὴν πίστιν αὐτῶν λέγει τῷ παραλυτικῷ,
6 Τέκνον, ἀφέωνταί σου αἱ ἁμαρτίαι. ἦσαν δέ τινες τῶν γραμματέων ἐκεῖ
7 καθήμενοι καὶ διαλογιζόμενοι ἐν ταῖς καρδίαις αὐτῶν, Τί οὗτος οὕτω λαλεῖ
8 βλασφημίας; τίς δύναται ἀφιέναι ἁμαρτίας εἰ μὴ εἷς ὁ Θεός; καὶ εὐθέως
ἐπιγνοὺς ὁ Ἰησοῦς τῷ πνεύματι αὐτοῦ ὅτι οὕτως διαλογίζονται ἐν
9 ἑαυτοῖς, εἶπεν αὐτοῖς, Τί ταῦτα διαλογίζεσθε ἐν ταῖς καρδίαις ὑμῶν; τί
ἐστιν εὐκοπώτερον, εἰπεῖν τῷ παραλυτικῷ, Ἀφέωνταί σου αἱ ἁμαρτίαι, ἢ
10 εἰπεῖν, Ἔγειρε ἆρον τὸν κράβαττόν σου καὶ περιπάτει; ἵνα δὲ εἰδῆτε ὅτι

5 ιδον cod.

35 εννυχον ϛ, εννυχον[a] 118 **36** om τε ϛ **37** σε ζητουσι 131 118 131 209 ϛ **38** κακει ϛ **39** εν ταις συναγωγαις ϛ **40** γονυπετων αυτον 131 ϛ θελεις 131 **41** λεγει αυτω 118 ϛ **42** εκαθαρισθη 118 131 ϛ **44** Μωυσης 131 αυτοις] αυτης 209, αυτ spat. rel. 118 **45** πανταχοθεν ϛ

1 παλιν εισηλθεν ϛ **2** om οχλοι ϛ **3** παραλυτικον φεροντες ϛ **4** κραββατον 118 209 ϛ et sic passim κατεκειτο] 118* primum scripsit εκει tum κε deleto et ι ad σ mutato στοειτο perrexit, quid autem voluerit minime intelligo **5** σοι αι αμαρτιαι σου ϛ **7** ουτως 131 **8** λογιζονται 118 209 **9** σου 1°] σοι 131 ϛ εγειραι 118 131 209, εγειραι και ϛ σου ante τον κραβ. ϛ

ἐξουσίαν ἔχει ὁ υἱὸς τοῦ ἀνθρώπου ἀφιέναι ἐπὶ τῆς γῆς ἁμαρτίας, (λέγει
τῷ παραλυτικῷ) Σοὶ λέγω, ἔγειρε καὶ ἆρον τὸν κράβαττόν σου, καὶ ὕπαγε 11
εἰς τὸν οἶκόν σου. καὶ ἠγέρθη εὐθέως, καὶ ἄρας τὸν κράβαττον ἐξῆλθεν 12
ἐναντίον πάντων· ὥστε ἐξίστασθαι πάντας καὶ δοξάζειν τὸν Θεὸν λέγοντας
ὅτι Οὐδέποτε οὕτως εἴδομεν.
ς' Καὶ ἐξῆλθε πάλιν παρὰ τὴν θάλασσαν· καὶ πᾶς ὁ ὄχλος ἤρχετο πρὸς 13
κα β αὐτόν, καὶ ἐδίδασκεν αὐτούς. καὶ παράγων εἶδε Λευὶν τὸν τοῦ Ἀλφαίου 14
καθήμενον ἐπὶ τὸ τελώνιον, καὶ λέγει αὐτῷ, Ἀκολούθει μοι. καὶ ἀναστὰς
κβ β ἠκολούθει αὐτῷ. καὶ ἐγένετο ἐν τῷ κατακεῖσθαι αὐτὸν ἐν τῇ οἰκίᾳ 15
αὐτοῦ, πολλοὶ τελῶναι καὶ ἁμαρτωλοὶ συνανέκειντο τῷ Ἰησοῦ καὶ τοῖς
μαθηταῖς αὐτοῦ· ἦσαν γὰρ πολλοί, καὶ ἠκολούθησαν αὐτῷ. καὶ οἱ γραμ- 16
ματεῖς καὶ οἱ Φαρισαῖοι ἰδόντες αὐτὸν ἐσθίοντα μετὰ τῶν τελωνῶν καὶ
ἁμαρτωλῶν ἔλεγον τοῖς μαθηταῖς αὐτοῦ, Τί ὅτι μετὰ τῶν τελωνῶν καὶ
κγ β ἁμαρτωλῶν ἐσθίει καὶ πίνει; καὶ ἀκούσας ὁ Ἰησοῦς λέγει, Οὐ χρείαν 17
ἔχουσιν οἱ ἰσχύοντες ἰατροῦ, ἀλλ' οἱ κακῶς ἔχοντες. οὐκ ἦλθον καλέσαι
δικαίους, ἀλλ' ἁμαρτωλούς. καὶ ἦσαν οἱ μαθηταὶ Ἰωάννου καὶ οἱ τῶν 18
Φαρισαίων νηστεύοντες· καὶ ἔρχονται καὶ λέγουσιν αὐτῷ, Διατί οἱ μαθηταὶ
Ἰωάννου καὶ οἱ τῶν Φαρισαίων νηστεύουσιν, οἱ δὲ σοὶ μαθηταὶ οὐ νηστεύ-
ουσι; καὶ εἶπεν αὐτοῖς ὁ Ἰησοῦς, Μὴ δύνανται οἱ υἱοὶ τοῦ νυμφῶνος 19
ἐν ᾧ ὁ νυμφίος μετ' αὐτῶν ἐστι νηστεύειν; ἐλεύσονται δὲ ἡμέραι ὅταν 20
ἀπαρθῇ ἀπ' αὐτῶν ὁ νυμφίος, καὶ τότε νηστεύουσιν ἐν ἐκείνῃ τῇ ἡμέρᾳ.
οὐδεὶς ἐπίβλημα ῥάκους ἀγνάφου ἐπιράπτει ἐπὶ ἱματίῳ παλαιῷ· εἰ δὲ 21
μή, αἴρει τὸ πλήρωμα ἀπ' αὐτοῦ τὸ καινὸν τοῦ παλαιοῦ, καὶ χεῖρον σχίσμα
γίνεται. καὶ οὐδεὶς βάλλει οἶνον νέον εἰς ἀσκοὺς παλαιούς· εἰ δὲ μή, 22
ῥήσσει ὁ οἶνος ὁ νέος τοὺς ἀσκούς, καὶ ὁ οἶνος ἐκχεῖται καὶ οἱ ἀσκοὶ
ἀπολοῦνται· ἀλλ' οἶνον νέον εἰς ἀσκοὺς καινοὺς βλητέον.
κδ β Καὶ ἐγένετο παραπορεύεσθαι αὐτὸν τοῖς σάββασι διὰ τῶν σπορίμων, 23
καὶ ἤρξαντο οἱ μαθηταὶ αὐτοῦ ὁδοποιεῖν τίλλοντες τοὺς στάχυας. καὶ 24
οἱ Φαρισαῖοι ἔλεγον αὐτῷ, Ἴδε τί ποιοῦσιν οἱ μαθηταί σου τοῖς
σάββασιν ὃ οὐκ ἔξεστι; καὶ αὐτὸς ἔλεγεν αὐτοῖς, Οὐδέποτε ἀνέγνωτε τί 25

15 και εγενετο in rasura, sed, ni fallor, prima manu
17 αμαρτωλους] m. recent. add. in marg. εις μετανοιαν

118 131 209 ς **10** επι της γης αφιεναι 118 209 **11** εγειραι 118 131 209 ς **14** Λευι 118 209 ηκολουθησεν ς **15** και πολλοι ς **17** λεγει αυτοις ς αλλα 118 131 209 ς αμαρτωλους]+εις μετανοιαν 118[2] in mg. 131 ς **19** νηστευειν] +οσον χρονον εχουσι μεθ εαυτων τον νυμφιον ου δυνανται νηστευειν 131 ς sed μεθ εαυτων εχουσι ς **20** νηστευσουσιν 118 209 ς εκειναις ταις ημεραις 118 131 ς **21** και ουδεις ς επιρραπτει 118 209 ς om απ 118 ς om αυτου 118 spat. rel. **22** ο νεος οινος 118 209 αλλα ς **23** εν τοις ς οδον ποιειν 118 131 ς **24** om οι μαθηται σου ς εν τοις ς

ἐποίησε Δαβίδ, ὅτε χρείαν ἔσχε καὶ ἐπείνασεν αὐτὸς καὶ οἱ μετ' αὐτοῦ;
26 πῶς εἰσῆλθεν εἰς τὸν οἶκον τοῦ Θεοῦ ἐπὶ Ἀβιάθαρ τοῦ ἀρχιερέως, καὶ τοὺς
ἄρτους τῆς προθέσεως ἔφαγεν, οὓς οὐκ ἔξεστι φαγεῖν εἰ μὴ τοῖς ἱερεῦσι,
27 καὶ ἔδωκε καὶ τοῖς σὺν αὐτῷ οὖσι; καὶ ἔλεγεν αὐτοῖς, Τὸ σάββατον διὰ κε
28 τὸν ἄνθρωπον ἐκτίσθη, οὐχ ὁ ἄνθρωπος διὰ τὸ σάββατον. ὥστε κύριός β
ἐστιν ὁ υἱὸς τοῦ ἀνθρώπου καὶ τοῦ σαββάτου.

III. Καὶ εἰσῆλθε πάλιν εἰς τὴν συναγωγήν· καὶ ἦν ἐκεῖ ἄνθρωπος Ζ'
2 ἐξηραμμένην ἔχων τὴν χεῖρα· καὶ παρετηροῦντο αὐτὸν εἰ τοῖς σάββασι
3 θεραπεύσει αὐτόν, ἵνα κατηγορήσωσιν αὐτοῦ. καὶ λέγει τῷ ἀνθρώπῳ
4 ὁ Ἰησοῦς τῷ ἐξηραμμένην ἔχοντι τὴν χεῖρα, Ἔγειρε εἰς τὸ μέσον. καὶ
λέγει αὐτοῖς, Τί ἔξεστι τοῖς σάββασιν, ἀγαθοποιῆσαι ἢ κακοποιῆσαι,
5 ψυχὴν σῶσαι ἢ ἀπολέσαι; οἱ δὲ ἐσιώπων. καὶ περιβλεψάμενος αὐτοὺς
μετ' ὀργῆς, συλλυπούμενος ἐπὶ τῇ πωρώσει τῆς καρδίας αὐτῶν, λέγει τῷ
ἀνθρώπῳ, Ἔκτεινον τὴν χεῖρά σου· καὶ ἐξέτεινε, καὶ ἀποκατεστάθη ἡ
6 χεὶρ αὐτοῦ. καὶ ἐξελθόντες οἱ Φαρισαῖοι εὐθέως μετὰ τῶν Ἡρωδιανῶν κς
συμβούλιον ἐποίουν κατ' αὐτοῦ, ὅπως αὐτὸν ἀπολέσωσι. δ
7 Καὶ ὁ Ἰησοῦς μετὰ τῶν μαθητῶν αὐτοῦ ἀνεχώρησε πρὸς τὴν κζ
θάλασσαν· καὶ πολὺ πλῆθος ἀπὸ τῆς Γαλιλαίας ἠκολούθησεν αὐτῷ· α
8 καὶ ἀπὸ Ἱεροσολύμων, καὶ ἀπὸ τῆς Ἰουδαίας, καὶ πέραν τοῦ
Ἰορδάνου, καὶ οἱ περὶ Τύρον καὶ Σιδῶνα, καὶ πλῆθος πολύ, ἀκούοντες
9 ὅσα ἐποίει, ἦλθον πρὸς αὐτόν. καὶ εἶπε τοῖς μαθηταῖς αὐτοῦ ἵνα πλοιάριον
10 προσκαρτερῇ αὐτῷ διὰ τὸν ὄχλον, ἵνα μὴ θλίβωσιν αὐτόν. πολλοὺς γὰρ
ἐθεράπευσεν· ὥστε ἐπιπίπτειν αὐτῷ ἵνα αὐτοῦ ἅψωνται ὅσοι εἶχον μάστιγας·
11 καὶ τὰ πνεύματα τὰ ἀκάθαρτα, ὅταν αὐτὸν ἐθεώρει, προσέπιπτεν αὐτῷ κη
12 καὶ ἔκραζον λέγοντα ὅτι Σὺ εἶ ὁ υἱὸς τοῦ Θεοῦ· καὶ πολλὰ ἐπετίμα η
13 αὐτοῖς ἵνα μὴ αὐτὸν φανερὸν ποιήσωσι. καὶ ἀνέβη εἰς τὸ ὄρος καὶ Η'
14 προσκαλεῖται οὓς ἤθελεν αὐτός, καὶ ἀπῆλθον πρὸς αὐτόν. καὶ ἐποίησε κθ
15 δώδεκα, ἵνα ὦσι μετ' αὐτοῦ, καὶ ἵνα ἀποστέλλῃ αὐτοὺς κηρύσσειν καὶ β

26 *του* 2°] om 118, in rasura 209 *μετ αυτου* 131 **27** *εκτισθη*] *εγενετο* 118 131 209 ϛ. 118* videtur primum scripsisse *εγενετο* tum erasisse denique rescripsisse in rasura

2 *παρετηρουν* ϛ *κατηγορησουσι* 118 **3** om *ο Ιησους* ϛ *εγειραι* 118 131 (209) ϛ. dubium est utrum 209* *εγειρε* primum scripserit, nunc enim habet *εγειραι* sed *αι* nimium compressum et in rasura esse scriptum videtur **4** om *τι* ϛ *απολεσαι*] *αποκτειναι* ϛ **5** *αποκατεσταθη*] + *αυτου* 209* sed punctis rubr. damnavit *αυτου*] + *ως η αλλη* 131, + *υγιης ως η αλλη* 118[2] ϛ **6** *ελθοντες* 131 **7** *ανεχωρησε μετα των μαθητων αυτου* 118 131 ϛ *προς*] *εις* 131 209, *προς* (*εις* supra) 118 *ηκουλουθησαν* ϛ **7 8** *και απο της Ιουδαιας και απο Ιεροσολυμων και απο της Ιδουμαιας* ϛ **8** *Σιδονα* 118 131 om *και* ult. ϛ *ακουσαντες* ϛ **11** *προσεπιπεν* 118 *εκραζε* 131 ϛ **13** *αναβαινει* ϛ **15** *αποστελει* 131

λ̄ ἔχειν ἐξουσίαν θεραπεύειν τὰς νόσους καὶ ἐκβάλλειν τὰ δαιμόνια· καὶ 16
β ἐπέθηκε τῷ Σίμωνι ὄνομα Πέτρον· καὶ Ἰάκωβον τὸν τοῦ Ζεβεδαίου, 17
καὶ Ἰωάννην τὸν ἀδελφὸν Ἰακώβου, καὶ ἐπέθηκεν αὐτοῖς ὀνόματα Βοαν-
ηργές, ὅ ἐστιν Υἱοὶ βροντῆς· καὶ Ἀνδρέαν, καὶ Φίλιππον, καὶ Βαρθο- 18
λομαῖον, καὶ Ματθαῖον, καὶ Θωμᾶν, καὶ Ἰάκωβον τὸν τοῦ Ἀλφαίου, καὶ
Θαδδαῖον, καὶ Σίμωνα τὸν Κανανίτην, καὶ Ἰούδαν Ἰσκαριώτην ὃς καὶ παρ- 19
έδωκεν αὐτόν.

λᾱ Καὶ ἔρχονται εἰς οἶκον· καὶ συνέρχεται πάλιν ὄχλος πολύς, ὥστε 20
ι μὴ δύνασθαι αὐτοὺς μήτε ἄρτον φαγεῖν. καὶ ἀκούσαντες οἱ παρ' αὐτοῦ 21
λβ̄ ἐξῆλθον κρατῆσαι αὐτόν· ἔλεγον γὰρ ὅτι Ἐξέστη. καὶ οἱ γραμματεῖς οἱ 22
β ἀπὸ Ἱεροσολύμων καταβάντες ἔλεγον ὅτι Βεελζεβοὺλ ἔχει, καὶ ὅτι Ἐν τῷ
λγ̄ ἄρχοντι τῶν δαιμονίων ἐκβάλλει τὰ δαιμόνια. καὶ προσκαλεσάμενος 23
β αὐτοὺς ἐν παραβολαῖς ἔλεγεν αὐτοῖς, Πῶς δύναται Σατανᾶς Σατανᾶν
ἐκβάλλειν; καὶ ἐὰν βασιλεία ἐφ' ἑαυτὴν μερισθῇ, οὐ δύναται σταθῆναι ἡ 24
βασιλεία ἐκείνη· καὶ ἐὰν οἰκία ἐφ' ἑαυτὴν μερισθῇ, οὐ δύναται σταθῆναι 25
ἡ οἰκία ἐκείνη· καὶ εἰ ὁ Σατανᾶς ἀνέστη ἐφ' ἑαυτὸν καὶ μεμέρισται, οὐ 26
δύναται σταθῆναι, ἀλλὰ τέλος ἔχει. ἀλλ' οὐδεὶς δύναται τὰ σκεύη τοῦ 27
ἰσχυροῦ εἰσελθὼν εἰς τὴν οἰκίαν αὐτοῦ διαρπάσαι, ἐὰν μὴ πρῶτον τὸν
λδ̄ ἰσχυρὸν δήσῃ, καὶ τότε τὴν οἰκίαν αὐτοῦ διαρπάσει. ἀμὴν λέγω ὑμῖν 28
β ὅτι πάντα ἀφεθήσεται τοῖς υἱοῖς τῶν ἀνθρώπων τὰ ἁμαρτήματα, καὶ
αἱ βλασφημίαι ὅσας ἂν βλασφημήσωσιν· ὃς δ' ἂν βλασφημήσῃ εἰς τὸ 29
Πνεῦμα τὸ Ἅγιον, οὐκ ἔχει ἄφεσιν, ἀλλ' ἔνοχός ἐστιν αἰωνίου κρίσεως·
λε̄ ὅτι ἔλεγον, Πνεῦμα ἀκάθαρτον ἔχει. καὶ ἔρχεται ἡ μήτηρ καὶ οἱ 30 31
β ἀδελφοὶ αὐτοῦ, καὶ ἔξω ἑστηκότες ἀπέστειλαν πρὸς αὐτὸν καλοῦντες
αὐτόν. καὶ ἐκάθητο περὶ αὐτὸν ὄχλος· εἶπον δὲ αὐτῷ, Ἰδοὺ ἡ μήτηρ 32
σου καὶ οἱ ἀδελφοί σου ἔξω ζητοῦσί σε. ἀπεκρίθη αὐτοῖς καὶ λέγει, 33
Τίς ἐστιν ἡ μήτηρ μου καὶ οἱ ἀδελφοί μου; καὶ περιβλεψάμενος τοὺς 34
κύκλῳ περὶ αὐτὸν καθημένους λέγει, Ἰδοὺ ἡ μήτηρ μου καὶ οἱ ἀδελφοί
μου· ὃς γὰρ ἂν ποιήσῃ τὸ θέλημα τοῦ Θεοῦ, οὗτος ἀδελφός μου καὶ 35
ἀδελφὴ καὶ μήτηρ ἐστί.

λς̄ IV. Καὶ πάλιν ἤρξατο διδάσκειν παρὰ τὴν θάλασσαν· καὶ
β συνέρχεται πρὸς αὐτὸν ὄχλος πολύς, ὥστε αὐτὸν ἐμβάντα εἰς πλοῖον

118 131 209 ς

17 του Ιακωβου ς Βοανεργες 131 ς **20** συνερχονται 131 om πολυς ς **21** οι] υ 118 εξεστη] εξεσται 131 **27** αλλ] om 118 ς sed spat. rel. 118 ου δυναται ουδεις ς **28** τοις ανθρωποις τα αμαρτηματα 118 209, τα αμαρτηματα τοις υιοις των ανθρωπων ς αι] om 131 ς **29** αφεσιν]+εις τον αιωνα 118 131 ς **31** ερχονται ουν ς μητηρ αυτου 131 οι αδελφοι και η μητηρ αυτου ς εστωτες ς φωνουντες ς **32** οχλος περι αυτον ς **33** και απεκριθη 118 ς και λεγει] λεγων 118 ς και 2°] η ς **34** κυκλω τους ς, om τους 131 ιδε ς **35** αδελφη μου ς

1 ηρξατο παλιν (om και) 209 συνερχονται 131, συνηχθη 118 ς το πλοιον ς

καθῆσθαι ἐν τῇ θαλάσσῃ· καὶ πᾶς ὁ ὄχλος παρὰ τὴν θάλασσαν ἐπὶ τῆς
2 γῆς ἦν· καὶ ἐδίδασκεν αὐτοὺς ἐν παραβολαῖς πολλά, καὶ ἔλεγεν αὐτοῖς ἐν θ'
3 τῇ διδαχῇ αὐτοῦ, Ἀκούετε. ἰδοὺ ἐξῆλθεν ὁ σπείρων τοῦ σπεῖραι· καὶ
4 ἐγένετο ἐν τῷ σπείρειν, ὃ μὲν ἔπεσε παρὰ τὴν ὁδόν, καὶ ἦλθε τὰ πετεινὰ
5 καὶ κατέφαγεν αὐτό· ἄλλο δὲ ἔπεσεν ἐπὶ τὰ πετρώδη ὅπου οὐκ εἶχε γῆν
6 πολλήν, καὶ εὐθέως ἐξεβλάστησε διὰ τὸ μὴ ἔχειν βάθος γῆς, ἡλίου δὲ
7 ἀνατείλαντος ἐκαυματίσθη, καὶ διὰ τὸ μὴ ἔχειν ῥίζαν ἐξηράνθη· καὶ ἄλλο
ἔπεσεν εἰς τὰς ἀκάνθας, καὶ ἀνέβησαν αἱ ἄκανθαι καὶ συνέπνιξαν αὐτό,
8 καὶ καρπὸν οὐκ ἔδωκε· καὶ ἄλλο ἔπεσεν ἐπὶ τὴν γῆν τὴν καλήν, καὶ
ἐδίδου καρπὸν ἀναβαίνοντα καὶ αὐξάνοντα, καὶ ἔφερεν ἐν τριάκοντα καὶ ἐν
9 ἑξήκοντα καὶ ἐν ἑκατόν. καὶ ἔλεγεν, Ὁ ἔχων ὦτα ἀκούειν ἀκουέτω. ὅτε
10 δὲ ἐγένετο καταμόνας, ἠρώτησαν αὐτὸν οἱ περὶ αὐτὸν σὺν τοῖς δώδεκα τὴν
11 παραβολήν. καὶ ἔλεγεν αὐτοῖς, Ὑμῖν δέδοται γνῶναι τὰ μυστήρια τῆς
βασιλείας τοῦ Θεοῦ· ἐκείνοις δὲ τοῖς ἔξω ἐν παραβολαῖς τὰ πάντα γίνεται, λς α
12 ἵνα βλέποντες βλέπωσι καὶ μὴ ἴδωσι, καὶ ἀκούοντες ἀκούωσι καὶ μὴ συνῶσι·
13 μήποτε ἐπιστρέψωσι, καὶ ἀφεθῇ αὐτοῖς. καὶ λέγει αὐτοῖς, Οὐκ οἴδατε τὴν
14 παραβολὴν ταύτην; καὶ πῶς πάσας τὰς παραβολὰς γνώσεσθε; ὁ σπείρων
15 τὸν λόγον σπείρει. οὗτοι δέ εἰσιν οἱ παρὰ τὴν ὁδόν, ὅπου σπείρεται ὁ λη β
λόγος, καὶ ὅταν ἀκούσωσιν, ἔρχεται ὁ Σατανᾶς καὶ αἴρει τὸν λόγον τὸν
16 ἐσπαρμένον εἰς αὐτούς· καὶ οὗτοί εἰσιν οἱ ἐπὶ τὰ πετρώδη σπειρόμενοι,
17 οἳ ὅταν ἀκούσωσι τὸν λόγον, εὐθέως μετὰ χαρᾶς δέχονται, καὶ οὐκ ἔχουσι
ῥίζαν ἐν ἑαυτοῖς, ἀλλὰ πρόσκαιροί εἰσιν, εἶτα γενομένης θλίψεως σκαν-
18 δαλίζονται· καὶ οἱ εἰς τὰς ἀκάνθας σπειρόμενοι, οὗτοί εἰσιν οἱ τὸν
19 λόγον μου ἀκούοντες, καὶ αἱ μέριμναι τοῦ αἰῶνος καὶ ἡ ἀπάτη τοῦ
πλούτου εἰσπορευόμεναι συμπνίγουσι τὸν λόγον, καὶ ἄκαρπος γίνε-
20 ται· καὶ οὗτοί εἰσιν οἱ ἐπὶ τὴν γῆν τὴν καλήν, οἵτινες ἀκούουσι τὸν
λόγον καὶ παραδέχονται καὶ καρποφοροῦσιν, ἐν τριάκοντα καὶ ἐν ἑξή-
21 κοντα καὶ ἐν ἑκατόν. καὶ λέγει αὐτοῖς, Μήτι ἔρχεται ὁ λύχνος ἵνα λθ β
ὑπὸ τὸν μόδιον τεθῇ ἢ ἵνα ὑπὸ τὴν κλίνην; οὐχ ἵνα ἐπὶ τὴν λυχνίαν

15 ακουσωσην cod.

1 παρα] προς ς 4 πετεινα του ουρανου ς 5 το πετρωδες ς 118 131 209 ς εβλαστησε 131, εξανετειλε ς 8 επι] εις ς ἐν ter] ἓν ter ς, om ante εξηκ. 118 9 ελεγεν αυτοις 118 ς 11 το μυστηριον ς 12 συνιωσι 131 ς αυτοις] + τα αμαρτηματα 131 ς 14 σπερει 118 15 ευθεως ερχεται 131 ς εις αυτους] εν ταις καρδιαις αυτων 131 ς 16 εισιν ομοιως ς δεχονται] λαμβανουσιν αυτον ς 17 θλιψεως] + η διωγμου δια τον λογον ευθεως 131 ς 18 και] + ουτοι εισιν 131 ς εισιν οι] om 131 om μου 131 ς 19 αιωνος τουτου 131 ς πλουτου] + και αι περι τα λοιπα επιθυμιαι ς εισπορευομενα 131 20 καλην] + σπαρεντες 131 ς ἐν ter] ἓν ter ς 21 ελεγεν ς om ο ante λυχνος 118 209 ο λυχνος ερχεται ς ινα 2°] om ς

μ/β ἐπιτεθῇ; οὐ γάρ ἐστί κρυπτόν, εἰ μὴ ἵνα φανερωθῇ· οὐδὲ ἐγένετο 22
ἀπόκρυφον, εἰ μὴ ἵνα εἰς φανερὸν ἔλθῃ. εἴτις ἔχει ὦτα ἀκούειν, ἀκουέτω. 23
μα/β καὶ λέγει αὐτοῖς, Βλέπετε τί ἀκούετε. ἐν ᾧ μέτρῳ μετρεῖτε μετρηθή- 24
μβ/β σεται ὑμῖν, καὶ προστεθήσεται ὑμῖν τοῖς ἀκούουσιν. ὃς γὰρ ἂν ἔχῃ, 25
δοθήσεται αὐτῷ· καὶ ὃς οὐκ ἔχει, καὶ ὃ ἔχει ἀρθήσεται ἀπ' αὐτοῦ.
μγ/ι Καὶ ἔλεγεν, Οὕτως ἐστὶν ἡ βασιλεία τοῦ Θεοῦ, ὡς ἄνθρωπος ὅταν 26
βάλῃ τὸν σπόρον ἐπὶ τὴν γῆν, καὶ καθεύδῃ καὶ ἐγείρηται νύκτα καὶ 27
ἡμέραν, καὶ ὁ σπόρος βλαστάνῃ καὶ μηκύνηται ὡς οὐκ οἶδεν αὐτός.
αὐτομάτη γὰρ ἡ γῆ καρποφορεῖ πρῶτον χόρτον, εἶτα στάχυν, εἶτα πλήρη 28
σῖτον ἐν τῷ στάχυϊ. ὅταν δὲ παραδῷ ὁ καρπός, τότε ἀποστέλλει τὸ 29
δρέπανον, ὅτι παρέστηκεν ὁ θερισμός.
μδ/β Καὶ ἔλεγε, Τίνι ὁμοιώσομεν τὴν βασιλείαν τοῦ Θεοῦ; ἢ ἐν τίνι 30
ὁμοιώματι παραβάλωμεν αὐτήν; ὡς κόκκον σινάπεως, ὃς ὅταν σπαρῇ 31
ἐπὶ τῆς γῆς, μικρότερος πάντων τῶν σπερμάτων ἐστὶ τῶν ἐπὶ τῆς γῆς·
καὶ ὅταν σπαρῇ, ἀναβαίνει καὶ γίνεται μείζων πάντων τῶν λαχάνων, 32
καὶ ποιεῖ κλάδους μεγάλους ὥστε δύνασθαι ὑπὸ τὴν σκιὰν αὐτοῦ τὰ
με/ς πετεινὰ τοῦ οὐρανοῦ κατασκηνοῦν. καὶ τοιαύταις παραβολαῖς ἐλάλει 33
αὐτοῖς τὸν λόγον, καθὼς ἠδύναντο ἀκούειν· χωρὶς δὲ παραβολῆς οὐκ 34
μς/ι ἐλάλει αὐτοῖς· κατ' ἰδίαν δὲ τοῖς μαθηταῖς αὐτοῦ ἐπέλυε πάντα.
Ι' Καὶ λέγει αὐτοῖς ἐν ἐκείνῃ τῇ ἡμέρᾳ ὀψίας γενομένης, Διέλθωμεν 35
μζ/β εἰς τὸ πέραν. καὶ ἀφέντες τὸν ὄχλον παραλαμβάνουσιν αὐτὸν ὡς ἦν 36
ἐν τῷ πλοίῳ· καὶ τὰ ἄλλα τὰ ὄντα μετ' αὐτοῦ πλοῖα. καὶ γίνεται 37
λαῖλαψ μεγάλη ἀνέμου, καὶ τὰ κύματα ἐπέβαλλεν εἰς τὸ πλοῖον, ὥστε
αὐτὸ ἤδη βυθίζεσθαι. καὶ ἦν αὐτὸς ἐν τῇ πρύμνῃ ἐπὶ προσκεφάλαιον 38
καθεύδων· καὶ διεγείρουσιν αὐτόν, καὶ λέγουσιν αὐτῷ, Διδάσκαλε, οὐ
μέλει σοι ὅτι ἀπολλύμεθα; καὶ διεγερθεὶς ἐπετίμησε τῷ ἀνέμῳ καὶ 39
τῇ θαλάσσῃ, καὶ εἶπε, Σιώπα, πεφίμωσο. καὶ ἐκόπασεν ὁ ἄνεμος,
καὶ ἐγένετο γαλήνη μεγάλη. καὶ εἶπεν αὐτοῖς, Τί οὕτως δειλοί ἐστε; 40
οὔπω ἔχετε πίστιν; καὶ ἐφοβήθησαν φόβον μέγαν, καὶ ἔλεγον πρὸς 41

36 πλοιω] πλιω cod.

118 131 209 ς

22 τι κρυπτον ς ει μη ινα 1°] ο εαν μη 118 ς ει μη ινα 2°] αλλ ινα ς 24 λεγει] ελεγεν 131 ς 26 ως εαν ς om οταν ς βαλλει 131 της γης ς εγειρεται 131, εγειρ(η)εται 118 29 τοτε] ευθεως ς 30 om τινι 1°...η εν 118 ομοιωσωμεν 131 ς τινι ομοιωματι] ποια παραβολη ς 31 κοκκω ς 32 μειζων post λαχανων ς 33 παραβολαις πολλαις ς, αραβολαις 118 per incuriam rubricatoris 36 τα αλλα...πλοια] αλλα δε πλοιαρια ην μετ αυτου ς 37 ανεμου μεγαλη ς τα δε κυματα ς βυθιζεσθαι] γεμιζεσθαι ς 38 εν] επι ς το προσκεφ. ς μελλει 118 131 209 και ειπε τη θαλασση ς 40 ουτως post εστε 118 ς et ουτω ς ουπω] πως ουκ 118 ς

ἀλλήλους, Τίς ἄρα οὗτός ἐστιν, ὅτι καὶ οἱ ἄνεμοι καὶ ἡ θάλασσα
αὐτῷ ὑπακούει;
V. Καὶ ἦλθον εἰς τὸ πέραν τῆς θαλάσσης εἰς τὴν χώραν τῶν ΙΑ'
2 Γεργεσηνῶν. καὶ ἐξελθόντος αὐτοῦ ἐκ τοῦ πλοίου, εὐθέως ὑπήν-
3 τησεν αὐτῷ ἐκ τῶν μνημείων ἄνθρωπος ἐν πνεύματι ἀκαθάρτῳ, ὃς τὴν
κατοίκησιν εἶχεν ἐν τοῖς μνημείοις· καὶ οὔτε ἁλύσεσιν οὐδεὶς ἔτι ἠδύ-
4 νατο αὐτὸν δῆσαι, διὰ τὸ αὐτὸν πολλὰς πέδας καὶ ἁλύσεις αἷς
ἔδησαν αὐτὸν διεσπακέναι καὶ συντετριφέναι, καὶ οὐδεὶς ἴσχυ-
5 σεν αὐτὸν δαμάσαι· καὶ διαπαντὸς νυκτὸς καὶ ἡμέρας ἐν τοῖς μνη-
μείοις καὶ ἐν τοῖς ὄρεσιν ἦν κράζων καὶ κατακόπτων ἑαυτὸν λίθοις.
6 7 καὶ ἰδὼν τὸν Ἰησοῦν ἀπὸ μακρόθεν ἔδραμε καὶ προσεκύνησεν αὐτῷ, καὶ
κράξας φωνῇ μεγάλῃ λέγει, Τί ἐμοὶ καὶ σοί, υἱὲ τοῦ Θεοῦ τοῦ ὑψίστου;
8 ὁρκίζω σε τὸν Θεόν, μή με βασανίσῃς· ἔλεγε γὰρ αὐτῷ, Ἔξελθε τὸ
9 πνεῦμα τὸ ἀκάθαρτον ἐκ τοῦ ἀνθρώπου. καὶ ἐπηρώτα αὐτόν, Τί ὄνομά
10 σοι; καὶ λέγει αὐτῷ, Λεγεὼν ὄνομα, ὅτι πολλοί ἐσμεν. καὶ παρεκα-
11 λοῦν αὐτὸν πολλά, ἵνα μὴ ἔξω τῆς χώρας αὐτοὺς ἀποστείλῃ. ἦν
12 δὲ ἐκεῖ ἀγέλη χοίρων μεγάλη βοσκομένη· καὶ παρεκάλεσαν αὐτὸν
λέγοντες, Πέμψον ἡμᾶς εἰς τοὺς χοίρους, ἵνα εἰς αὐτοὺς εἰσέλθωμεν.
13 καὶ ἐπέτρεψεν αὐτοῖς. καὶ ἐξελθόντα τὰ πνεύματα τὰ ἀκάθαρτα εἰσῆλ-
θον εἰς τοὺς χοίρους· καὶ ὥρμησεν ἡ ἀγέλη κατὰ τοῦ κρημνοῦ εἰς τὴν
14 θάλασσαν ὡς δισχίλιοι· καὶ ἐπνίγοντο ἐν τῇ θαλάσσῃ. καὶ οἱ βόσκοντες
τοὺς χοίρους ἔφυγον καὶ ἀπήγγειλαν εἰς τὴν πόλιν καὶ εἰς τοὺς ἀγρούς.
15 καὶ ἐξῆλθον ἰδεῖν τί ἐστι τὸ γεγονός· καὶ ἔρχονται πρὸς τὸν Ἰησοῦν,
καὶ θεωροῦσι τὸν δαιμονιζόμενον καθήμενον ἱματισμένον καὶ σωφρο-
16 νοῦντα, τὸν ἐσχηκότα τὸν λεγεῶνα· καὶ ἐφοβήθησαν. καὶ διηγήσαντο

10 *παρακαλουν* cod.

118 131 209 ς

41 *ο ανεμος* ς *υπακουουσιν αυτω* ς **1** *Γαδαρηνων* 118[mg] ς **2** *εξελθοντι αυτω* ς *απηντησεν* ς **3** *μνημασι* 131 om *ετι* ς **4** *πολλας...συντετριφεναι*] *πολλακις πεδαις και αλυσεσι δεδεσθαι και διεσπασθαι υπ αυτου τας αλυσεις και τας πεδας συντετριφθαι* ς, om *και συντετριφεναι* 209*, ins. in marg. 209[2] *αυτον ισχυε* ς **5** *ορεσι και εν τοις μνημασι* ς *κραζων και*] *ραζων και* litteris contractis 209* scripsit in rasura quia primum ni fallor scripsisset *κραζων κατακοπτ.* omisso *και* **6** *ιδων δε* 118 209 ς **7** *λεγει*] *ειπε* ς *σοι*] + *Ιησου* 131 ς **8** *εκ*] *απο* 118 **9** *σοι ονομα* ς *λεγει αυτω*] *απεκριθη λεγων* ς *ονομα μοι* 118 131 209 ς **10** *παρεκαλει* ς *αυτους αποστειλη εξω της χωρας* ς **11** *εκει*] + *προς τω ορει* 118 131 209, + *προς τα ορη* ς om *μεγαλη* 131 **12** *λεγοντες* pr *παντες οι δαιμονες* ς **13** *αυτοις*] + *ευθεως ο Ιησους* ς *ως*] pr *ησαν δε* 118 131 209 ς *επνιγνοντον* 118 **14** *και οι*] *οι δε* 118 209 ς *ανηγγειλαν* ς *εξηλθον*] *ηλθον* 118 209 **15** *και ιματισμενον* ς **16** *διηγησατο* 209

αὐτοῖς οἱ ἰδόντες πῶς ἐσώθη ὁ δαιμονισθείς, καὶ περὶ τῶν χοίρων.
μη η καὶ ἤρξαντο παρακαλεῖν αὐτὸν ἀπελθεῖν ἀπὸ τῶν ὁρίων αὐτῶν. καὶ 17 18
ἐμβαίνοντος αὐτοῦ εἰς τὸ πλοῖον, παρεκάλει αὐτὸν ὁ δαιμονισθεὶς ἵνα
μετ' αὐτοῦ ᾖ. καὶ οὐκ ἀφῆκεν αὐτόν, ἀλλὰ λέγει αὐτῷ, Ὕπαγε εἰς 19
τὸν οἶκόν σου πρὸς τοὺς σούς, καὶ διάγγειλον αὐτοῖς ὅσα σοι ὁ
Κύριος ἐποίησε καὶ ἠλέησέ σε. καὶ ἀπῆλθε καὶ ἤρξατο κηρύσσειν ἐν 20
τῇ Δεκαπόλει ὅσα ἐποίησεν αὐτῷ ὁ Ἰησοῦς· καὶ πάντες ἐθαύμαζον.
μθ β Καὶ διαπεράσαντος τοῦ Ἰησοῦ πάλιν εἰς τὸ πέραν, συνήχθη ὄχλος 21
ΙΒ′ πολὺς ἐπ' αὐτόν· καὶ ἦν παρὰ τὴν θάλασσαν. καὶ ἰδοὺ ἔρχεται εἷς τῶν 22
ἀρχισυναγώγων, ὀνόματι Ἰάειρος, καὶ ἰδὼν αὐτὸν πίπτει αὐτοῦ πρὸς
τοὺς πόδας, καὶ παρεκάλει αὐτὸν πολλά, λέγων ὅτι Τὸ θυγάτριόν 23
μου ἐσχάτως ἔχει· ἵνα ἐλθὼν ἐπιθῇς τὰς χεῖρας αὐτῇ, ὅπως σωθῇ
καὶ ζήσεται. καὶ ἀπῆλθε μετ' αὐτοῦ· καὶ ἠκολούθει αὐτῷ ὄχλος πολύς, 24
καὶ συνέθλιβον αὐτόν.
ΙΓ′ Καὶ γυνὴ οὖσα ἐν ῥύσει αἵματος δώδεκα ἔτη, καὶ πολλὰ παθοῦσα 25 26
ὑπὸ πολλῶν ἰατρῶν καὶ δαπανήσασα τὰ ἑαυτῆς πάντα, καὶ μηδὲν
ὠφεληθεῖσα ἀλλὰ μᾶλλον εἰς τὸ χεῖρον ἐλθοῦσα, ἀκούσασα περὶ τοῦ 27
Ἰησοῦ, ἐλθοῦσα ὄπισθεν ἥψατο τοῦ κρασπέδου τοῦ ἱματίου αὐτοῦ·
ἔλεγε γὰρ ἐν ἑαυτῇ ὅτι Κἂν τῶν ἱματίων αὐτοῦ ἅψωμαι, σωθήσομαι. 28
καὶ εὐθέως ἐξηράνθη ἡ πηγὴ τοῦ αἵματος αὐτῆς, καὶ ἔγνω τῷ σώματι 29
ὅτι ἴαται ἀπὸ τῆς μάστιγος. καὶ εὐθέως ὁ Ἰησοῦς, ἐπιγνοὺς ἐν ἑαυτῷ 30
τὴν ἐξ αὐτοῦ δύναμιν ἐξελθοῦσαν, ἐπιστραφεὶς ἐν τῷ ὄχλῳ ἔλεγε, Τίς
μου ἥψατο τῶν ἱματίων; καὶ ἔλεγον αὐτῷ οἱ μαθηταὶ αὐτοῦ, Βλέπεις 31
τὸν ὄχλον συνθλίβοντά σε, καὶ λέγεις, Τίς μου ἥψατο; καὶ περιεβλέ- 32
πετο ἰδεῖν τὴν τοῦτο πεποιηκυῖαν. ἡ δὲ γυνὴ φοβηθεῖσα καὶ τρέ- 33
μουσα, εἰδυῖα ὃ γέγονεν ἐπ' αὐτῇ, ἦλθε καὶ προσέπεσεν αὐτῷ καὶ εἶπεν
αὐτῷ πᾶσαν τὴν αἰτίαν. ὁ δὲ Ἰησοῦς εἶπε, Θύγατερ, ἡ πίστις σου 34
σέσωκέ σε· ὕπαγε εἰς εἰρήνην καὶ ἴσθι ὑγιὴς ἀπὸ τῆς μάστιγός σου.
ἔτι αὐτοῦ λαλοῦντος ἔρχονται ἀπὸ τοῦ ἀρχισυναγώγου λέγοντες ὅτι 35
Ἡ θυγάτηρ σου ἀπέθανε· τί ἔτι σκύλλεις τὸν διδάσκαλον; ὁ δὲ Ἰησοῦς 36
ἀκούσας τὸν λόγον λαλούμενον λέγει τῷ ἀρχισυναγώγῳ, Μὴ φόβου,

18 131 209 ς **16** ιδοτες 118 πως εγενετο τω δαιμονιζομενω ς **18** εμβαντος 118 209 ς η μετ αυτου ς **19** και 1ο] ο δε Ιησους ς αναγγειλον ς **21** Ιησου]+εν τω πλοιω ς **22** προς τους ποδας αυτου 118 209 ς **23** αυτη τας χειρας ς αυτη] αυτω 118 **25** γυνη τις 118 131 ς ετη δωδεκα 118 ς **26** τα παρ εαυτης ς **27** ελθουσα]+εν τω οχλω 131 ς om του κρασπεδου 131 ς om εν εαυτη 131 ς **32** ποιησασαν 118 131 ς **33** αιτιαν] αληθειαν 118 131 209 ς **34** om Ιησους 131 ς ειπεν αυτη 118 131 ς **35** απο] πο 118 per incuriam rubricatoris **36** ακουσας] pr ευθεως ς, +ευθεως 131

37 μόνον πίστευε. καὶ οὐκ ἀφῆκεν οὐδένα αὐτῷ παρακολουθῆσαι εἰ μὴ
38 Πέτρον καὶ Ἰάκωβον καὶ Ἰωάννην τὸν ἀδελφὸν αὐτοῦ. καὶ ἔρχονται
εἰς τὸν οἶκον τοῦ ἀρχισυναγώγου, καὶ θεωρεῖ θόρυβον καὶ κλαίοντας καὶ
39 ἀλαλάζοντας πολλά· καὶ λέγει αὐτοῖς, Τί θορυβεῖσθε καὶ κλαίετε; τὸ
40 παιδίον οὐκ ἀπέθανεν, ἀλλὰ καθεύδει. καὶ κατεγέλων αὐτοῦ. ὁ δὲ
Ἰησοῦς ἐκβαλὼν πάντας παραλαμβάνει τὸν πατέρα τοῦ παιδίου καὶ
τὴν μητέρα καὶ τοὺς μετ' αὐτοῦ, καὶ εἰσπορεύεται ὅπου ἦν τὸ παιδίον
41 κατακείμενον· καὶ κρατήσας τῆς χειρὸς τοῦ παιδίου λέγει αὐτῇ, Ταλιθὰ
42 κοῦμ· ὅ ἐστι μεθερμηνευόμενον, Τὸ κοράσιον, σοὶ λέγω, ἔγειρε. καὶ
εὐθέως ἀνέστη τὸ κοράσιον καὶ περιεπάτει, ἦν γὰρ ὡς ἐτῶν δεκαδύο·
43 καὶ ἐξέστησαν ἐκστάσει μεγάλῃ. καὶ διεστείλατο αὐτοῖς πολλά, ἵνα
μηδεὶς γνῷ τοῦτο· καὶ εἶπε δοθῆναι αὐτῇ φαγεῖν.

VI. Καὶ ἐξῆλθεν ἐκεῖθεν καὶ ἦλθεν εἰς τὴν πατρίδα αὐτοῦ· καὶ ν̄ α
2 ἀκολουθοῦσιν αὐτῷ οἱ μαθηταὶ αὐτοῦ. καὶ γενομένου σαββάτου ἤρξατο
ἐν τῇ συναγωγῇ διδάσκειν· καὶ πολλοὶ ἀκούοντες ἐξεπλήσσοντο, λέγοντες,
Πόθεν τούτῳ ταῦτα; καὶ τίς ἡ σοφία ἡ δοθεῖσα αὐτῷ, καὶ δυνάμεις
3 τοιαῦται διὰ τῶν χειρῶν αὐτοῦ γίνονται; οὐχ οὗτός ἐστιν ὁ τέκτων, ὁ
υἱὸς Μαρίας ἀδελφὸς δὲ Ἰακώβου καὶ Ἰωσῆ καὶ Ἰούδα καὶ Σίμωνος;
καὶ οὐκ εἰσὶν αἱ ἀδελφαὶ αὐτοῦ ὧδε πρὸς ἡμᾶς; καὶ ἐσκανδαλίζοντο ἐν
4 αὐτῷ. ἔλεγε δὲ ὁ Ἰησοῦς ὅτι Οὐκ ἔστι προφήτης ἄτιμος, εἰ μὴ ἐν να̅ α
5 τῇ πατρίδι αὐτοῦ καὶ ἐν τοῖς συγγενεῦσι καὶ ἐν τῇ οἰκίᾳ αὐτοῦ. καὶ
οὐκ ἠδύνατο ἐκεῖ ποιῆσαι οὐδεμίαν δύναμιν, εἰ μὴ ὀλίγοις ἀρρώστοις
6 ἐπιθεὶς τὰς χεῖρας ἐθεράπευσε· καὶ ἐθαύμαζε διὰ τὴν ἀπιστίαν αὐτῶν.
καὶ περιῆγε τὰς κώμας κύκλῳ διδάσκων. νβ̅ β

7 Καὶ προσκαλεσάμενος τοὺς δώδεκα, ἤρξατο ἀποστέλλειν αὐ- ΙΔ'
τοὺς δύο δύο, καὶ ἐδίδου αὐτοῖς ἐξουσίαν τῶν πνευμάτων τῶν ἀκαθάρτων· νγ̅ β
8 καὶ παρήγγειλεν αὐτοῖς ἵνα μηδὲν αἴρωσιν εἰς ὁδὸν εἰ μὴ ῥάβδον μόνον·
9 μὴ πήραν, μὴ ἄρτον, μὴ εἰς τὴν ζώνην χαλκόν, ἀλλ' ὑποδεδεμένους
10 σανδάλια· καὶ μὴ ἐνδύσησθε δύο χιτῶνας. καὶ ἔλεγεν αὐτοῖς, Ὅπου νδ̅ β
11 ἐὰν εἰσέλθητε εἰς οἰκίαν, ἐκεῖ μένετε ἕως ἂν ἐξέλθητε ἐκεῖθεν. καὶ νε̅ β

37 ει μη] ει μι cod.

37 συνακολουθησαι 131 ς αυτου] Ιακωβου 131 ς **38** ερχεται 131 ς 118 131 209 ς
και 3°] om 118 131 ς **39** εισελθων λεγει 118 131 209 ς **40** om Ιησους
131 ς απαντας ς ανακειμενον 131 ς **41** κουμι ς εγειρε] εγειραι
131 209 ς, 118* primum εγειρε postea εγειραι scripsisse videtur **42** om
ως 131 ς δωδεκα 131 ς

1 hic desinit collatio 131 **2** αυτω] + οτι ς **4** ο Ιησους] pr αυτοις
118 209 ς συγγενεσι ς, συγγεν σι spat. sic relict. 118 **5** ποιησαι post
δυναμιν 118 ς ουδε μιαν 118 209 **7** προσκαλειται et pr και ante ηρξατο ς
αυτους αποστελλειν ς **9** ενδυσησθαι 118, ενδυσησθε (αι superscr.) 209

ὃς ἂν μὴ δέξηται ὑμᾶς μηδὲ ἀκούσῃ τοὺς λόγους ὑμῶν, ἐκπορευό-
μενοι ἐκεῖθεν τὸν κονιορτὸν ἐκτινάξατε τὸν ὑποκάτω τῶν ποδῶν ὑμῶν,
εἰς μαρτύριον αὐτοῖς. ἀμὴν λέγω ὑμῖν, ἀνεκτότερον ἔσται Σοδόμοις ἢ
νς Γομόρροις ἐν ἡμέρᾳ κρίσεως ἢ τῇ πόλει ἐκείνῃ. καὶ ἐξελθόντες ἐκή- 12
η ρυσσον ἵνα μετανοήσωσι, καὶ δαιμόνια πολλὰ ἐξέβαλλον, καὶ ἤλειφον 13
ἐλαίῳ πολλοὺς ἀρρώστους καὶ ἐθεράπευον.
ΙΕʹ Καὶ ἤκουσεν ὁ βασιλεὺς Ἡρώδης (φανερὸν γὰρ ἐγένετο τὸ ὄνομα 14
νζ β αὐτοῦ), καὶ ἔλεγεν ὅτι Ἰωάννης ὁ βαπτίζων ἐκ νεκρῶν ἠγέρθη, καὶ διὰ
τοῦτο ἐνεργοῦσιν αἱ δυνάμεις ἐν αὐτῷ. ἄλλοι δὲ ἔλεγον ὅτι Ἡλίας 15
νη ἐστίν· ἄλλοι δὲ ὅτι Προφήτης, ἢ ὡς εἷς τῶν προφητῶν. ἀκούσας δὲ 16
ι ὁ Ἡρώδης εἶπεν, Ὃν ἐγὼ ἀπεκεφάλισα, οὗτός ἐστιν Ἰωάννης· αὐτὸς
νθ ἠγέρθη ἐκ νεκρῶν. αὐτὸς γὰρ ὁ Ἡρώδης ἀποστείλας ἐκράτησε τὸν 17
β Ἰωάννην καὶ ἔδησεν αὐτὸν ἐν τῇ φυλακῇ διὰ Ἡρωδιάδα τὴν γυναῖκα
Φιλίππου τοῦ ἀδελφοῦ αὐτοῦ, ὅτι αὐτὴν ἐγάμησεν. ἔλεγε γὰρ ὁ Ἰωάννης 18
τῷ Ἡρώδῃ ὅτι Οὐκ ἔξεστί σοι τὴν γυναῖκα ἔχειν τοῦ ἀδελφοῦ σου.
ἡ δὲ Ἡρωδιὰς ἐνεῖχεν αὐτῷ καὶ ἤθελεν αὐτὸν ἀποκτεῖναι· καὶ οὐκ ἠδύ- 19
νατο· ὁ γὰρ Ἡρώδης ἐφοβεῖτο τὸν Ἰωάννην, εἰδὼς αὐτὸν ἄνδρα δίκαιον, 20
καὶ συνετήρει αὐτόν, καὶ ἀκούσας αὐτοῦ πολλὰ ἐποίει, καὶ ἡδέως αὐτοῦ
ξ ἤκουε. καὶ γενομένης ἡμέρας εὐκαίρου, ὅτε Ἡρώδης τοῖς γενεσίοις αὐτοῦ 21
ϛ δεῖπνον ἐποίει τοῖς μεγιστᾶσιν καὶ τοῖς χιλιάρχοις καὶ τοῖς πρώτοις
τῆς Γαλιλαίας, καὶ εἰσελθούσης τῆς θυγατρὸς τῆς Ἡρωδιάδος καὶ 22
ὀρχησαμένης, καὶ ἀρεσάσης τῷ Ἡρώδῃ καὶ τοῖς συνανακειμένοις, εἶπεν
ὁ βασιλεὺς τῷ κορασίῳ, Αἴτησόν με ὃ θέλεις, καὶ δώσω σοι ἕως 23
ἡμίσους τῆς βασιλείας μου. καὶ ὤμοσεν αὐτῇ. ἡ δὲ ἐξελθοῦσα εἶπε 24
τῇ μητρὶ αὐτῆς, Τί αἰτήσομαι; ἡ δὲ εἶπε, Τὴν κεφαλὴν Ἰωάννου τοῦ
Βαπτιστοῦ. καὶ εἰσελθοῦσα μετὰ σπουδῆς πρὸς τὸν βασιλέα εἶπε, 25
Θέλω ἵνα μοι δῷς ἐξ αὐτῆς ἐπὶ πίνακι τὴν κεφαλὴν Ἰωάννου τοῦ Βαπ-
τιστοῦ. καὶ περίλυπος γενόμενος ὁ βασιλεὺς διὰ τοὺς ὅρκους καὶ τοὺς 26

14 ιωαννης] Ιω̅ per compendium cod. **21** πρωτοις] προτοις cod. **24** Βαπτισστου cod. **26** ὁρκους cod.

118 209 ϛ **11** οσοι ϛ δεξωνται ϛ ακουση ϛ om τους λογους ϛ totum comma 118 sic habet οσοι αν μη δεξονται μηδε ακουσωσιν υμων (superscr. ος, η, υμας, μηδε ακου) εκτιναξατε τον χουν ϛ ημερα] καιρω 209 **13** εξεβαλον 118 209 **15** om δε 1° ϛ δε 2°]+ελεγον ϛ προφητης εστιν ϛ ειπεν οτι ϛ **16** Ιωαννην, ουτος εστιν 118 209 ϛ **18** εχειν την γυναικα ϛ **20** δικαιον]+και αγιον 118 ϛ **21** μεγιστασιν αυτου 118 209 ϛ **22** θυγατρος αυτης ϛ ο]+εαν 118 ϛ **23** εως] pr και ωμοσεν αυτη οτι ο εαν με αιτησης δωσω σοι 118 ϛ, sed 118 om ο om και ωμοσεν αυτη 118 ϛ **25** εισελθουσα ευθεως 118 ϛ ειπε] ητησατο λεγουσα ϛ, ειπε θελωεγουσα literis ω et ε confuse scriptis

27 συνανακειμένους οὐκ ἤθελεν αὐτὴν ἀθετῆσαι. καὶ εὐθέως ἀπολύσας
σπεκουλάτορα ἐπέταξεν ἐνεχθῆναι τὴν κεφαλὴν αὐτοῦ. καὶ ἀπελ-
28 θὼν ἀπεκεφάλισεν αὐτὸν ἐν τῇ φυλακῇ, καὶ ἤνεγκε τὴν κεφαλὴν αὐτοῦ
ἐπὶ πίνακι, καὶ ἔδωκε τῷ κορασίῳ· καὶ τὸ κοράσιον ἔδωκεν αὐτὴν τῇ
29 μητρὶ αὐτῆς. καὶ ἀκούσαντες οἱ μαθηταὶ αὐτοῦ ἦλθον καὶ ἦραν τὸ
πτῶμα αὐτοῦ καὶ ἔθηκαν αὐτὸ ἐν τῷ μνημείῳ.
30 Καὶ συνάγονται οἱ ἀπόστολοι πρὸς τὸν Ἰησοῦν, καὶ ἀπήγγειλαν αὐτῷ ξα/η
31 πάντα ὅσα ἐποίησαν καὶ ἐδίδαξαν. καὶ εἶπεν αὐτοῖς, Δεῦτε ὑμεῖς ξβ/ι
κατ' ἰδίαν εἰς ἔρημον τόπον καὶ ἀναπαύεσθε ὀλίγον. ἦσαν γὰρ οἱ ἐρχό-
32 μενοι καὶ οἱ ὑπάγοντες πολλοί, καὶ οὐδὲ φαγεῖν ηὐκαίρουν. καὶ ἀπῆλθον
33 εἰς ἔρημον τόπον τῷ πλοιαρίῳ κατ' ἰδίαν. καὶ ἰδόντες αὐτοὺς ὑπά-
γοντας ἔγνωσαν πολλοί· καὶ πεζῇ ἀπὸ πασῶν τῶν πόλεων συνέδραμον,
34 καὶ ἦλθον ἐκεῖ. καὶ ἐξελθὼν εἶδε πολὺν ὄχλον, καὶ ἐσπλαγχνίσθη ις´
ἐπ' αὐτοῖς, ὅτι ἦσαν ὡς πρόβατα μὴ ἔχοντα ποιμένα· καὶ ἤρξατο δι- ξγ/ϛ
35 δάσκειν αὐτοὺς πολλά. καὶ ἤδη ὥρας πολλῆς γενομένης προσελθόντες ξδ/α
αὐτῷ οἱ μαθηταὶ λέγουσιν ὅτι Ἔρημός ἐστιν ὁ τόπος, καὶ ἡ ὥρα ἤδη
36 πολλή· ἀπόλυσον αὐτούς, ἵνα ἀπελθόντες εἰς τοὺς κύκλῳ κώμας καὶ
37 ἀγροὺς καταλύσωσι· τί γὰρ φάγωσιν οὐκ ἔχουσιν. ὁ δὲ ἀποκριθεὶς
εἶπε, Δότε αὐτοῖς ὑμεῖς φαγεῖν. καὶ λέγουσιν, Ἀπελθόντες ἀγο-
38 ράσομεν δηναρίων διακοσίων ἄρτους, καὶ δῶμεν αὐτοῖς φαγεῖν; ὁ
δὲ λέγει αὐτοῖς, Πόσους ἄρτους ἔχετε; ὑπάγετε ἴδετε. καὶ γνόντες
39 λέγουσι, Πέντε, καὶ δύο ἰχθύας. καὶ ἐπέταξεν αὐτοῖς ἀνακλιθῆναι
40 πάντας συμπόσια συμπόσια ἐπὶ τῷ χλωρῷ χόρτῳ. καὶ ἀνέπεσαν πρα-
41 σιαὶ πρασιαί, ἀνὰ ἑκατὸν καὶ ἀνὰ πεντήκοντα. καὶ λαβὼν τοὺς πέντε
ἄρτους καὶ τοὺς δύο ἰχθύας, ἀναβλέψας εἰς τὸν οὐρανόν, εὐλόγησε· καὶ
κατέκλασε τοὺς ἄρτους καὶ ἐδίδου τοῖς μαθηταῖς αὐτοῦ, ἵνα παραθῶσιν
42 αὐτοῖς· καὶ τοὺς δύο ἰχθύας ἐμέρισε πᾶσι. καὶ ἔφαγον καὶ ἐχορτά-
43 σθησαν πάντες· καὶ ἦραν δώδεκα κοφίνων πληρώματα, καὶ ἀπὸ
44 45 τῶν ἰχθύων. καὶ ἦσαν οἱ φαγόντες ὡσεὶ πεντακισχίλιοι ἄνδρες. καὶ ξε/ϛ

26 ηθελησεν 118 ϛ **27** απολυσας] αποστειλας 118 ϛ, et + ο βασιλευς ϛ 118 209 ϛ
σπεκουλατωρα 118 209 ϛ ο δε απελθων 118 ϛ **28** εδωκε] εδωκεν αυτην ϛ,
εδωκ spat. rel. 118 **29** om τω 118 209 **30** και οσα εποιησαν και οσα 118 ϛ
31 υμεις αυτοι 118 ϛ **32** πλοιω ϛ **33** ιδοντες] ειδον ϛ εγνωσαν] οι οχλοι
και επεγνωσαν αυτον ϛ και ηλθον εκει] om και ηλθον 209, εκει και προηλθον
αυτους και συνηλθον προς αυτον 118 ϛ **34** ειδεν ο Ιησους 118 ϛ
35 μαθηται αυτου 118 ϛ ηδη ωρα πολλη ϛ **36** αγρους και κωμας 118 ϛ
καταλυσωσι] αγορασωσιν εαυτοις αρτους 118 209 ϛ **37** ειπεν αυτοις 118 ϛ
λεγουσιν αυτω 118 ϛ αγορασωμεν 118 ϛ διακοσιων δηναριων ϛ
38 και ιδετε ϛ **39** ανακλιναι ϛ **40** ανεπεσον ϛ **42** εφαγον παντες
118 ϛ om παντες 118 ϛ **43** κλασματων δωδεκα κοφινους πληρεις 118 ϛ
44 φαγοντες τους αρτους ϛ

εὐθέως ἠνάγκασε τοὺς μαθητὰς αὐτοῦ ἐμβῆναι εἰς πλοῖον καὶ προάγειν
ξϛ β αὐτὸν εἰς Βηθσαιδά, ἕως αὐτὸς ἀπολύει τοὺς ὄχλους. καὶ ἀπο- 46
ΙΖ' ταξάμενος αὐτοῖς ἀνῆλθεν εἰς τὸ ὄρος προσεύξασθαι. καὶ ὀψίας 47
ξζ δ γενομένης ἦν πάλαι τὸ πλοῖον ἐν μέσῳ τῆς θαλάσσης, καὶ αὐτὸς μόνος
ἐπὶ τῆς γῆς. καὶ εἶδεν αὐτοὺς βασανιζομένους ἐν τῷ ἐλαύνειν· ἦν γὰρ 48
ἐναντίος ὁ ἄνεμος· καὶ περὶ τετάρτην φυλακὴν τῆς νυκτὸς ἔρχεται
πρὸς αὐτοὺς ἐπὶ τῆς θαλάσσης περιπατῶν· καὶ ἤθελε παρελθεῖν
αὐτούς· οἱ δὲ ἰδόντες αὐτὸν περιπατοῦντα ἐπὶ τῆς θαλάσσης φάντασμα 49
ἔδοξαν εἶναι, καὶ ἀνέκραξαν· πάντες γὰρ αὐτὸν εἶδον, καὶ ἐταράχθησαν. 50
καὶ εὐθέως ἐλάλησε μετ' αὐτῶν, καὶ λέγει αὐτοῖς, Θαρσεῖτε· ἐγώ εἰμι,
ξη ϛ μὴ φοβεῖσθε. καὶ ἀνέβη πρὸς αὐτοὺς εἰς τὸ πλοῖον, καὶ ἐκόπασεν ὁ 51
ἄνεμος· καὶ ἐκπερισσῶς ἐν ἑαυτοῖς ἐξεπλήσσοντο. οὐ γὰρ συνῆκαν 52
ἐπὶ τοῖς ἄρτοις· ἦν γὰρ ἡ καρδία αὐτῶν πεπωρωμένη.
ξθ β Καὶ διαπεράσαντες ἦλθον ἐπὶ τὴν γῆν Γεννησαρέθ. καὶ ἐξελ- 53 54
θόντων αὐτῶν ἐκ τοῦ πλοίου εὐθέως ἐπιγνόντες αὐτὸν οἱ ἄνδρες τοῦ
τόπου ἐκείνου, καὶ ἐκπεριδραμόντες ὅλην τὴν περίχωρον ἐκείνην 55
ἤρξαντο ἐπὶ κραβάττοις τοὺς κακῶς ἔχοντας φέρειν ὅπου ἤκουον ὅτι
ἐστὶ ἐκεῖ. καὶ ὁπότ' ἂν εἰσεπορεύετο εἰς κώμας ἢ πόλεις, ἐν ταῖς 56
ἀγοραῖς ἐτίθουν τοὺς ἀσθενεῖς, καὶ παρεκάλουν αὐτὸν ἵνα κἂν τοῦ
κρασπέδου τοῦ ἱματίου αὐτοῦ ἅψωνται· καὶ ὅσοι ἥψαντο αὐτοῦ διε-
σώζοντο.

ΙΗ' VII. Καὶ συνάγονται πρὸς αὐτὸν Φαρισαῖοι καί τινες τῶν γραμ-
ο ι ματέων ἐλθόντες ἀπὸ Ἱεροσολύμων· καὶ ἰδόντες τινὰς τῶν μαθητῶν αὐτοῦ 2
κοιναῖς χερσί, τοῦτ' ἔστιν ἀνίπτοις, ἐσθίοντας ἄρτους ἐμέμψαντο· οἱ γὰρ 3
Φαρισαῖοι καὶ πάντες οἱ Ἰουδαῖοι, ἐὰν μὴ πυγμῇ νίψωνται τὰς χεῖρας,
οὐκ ἐσθίουσι, κρατοῦντες τὴν παράδοσιν τῶν πρεσβυτέρων· καὶ ἀπὸ 4
ἀγορᾶς, ἐὰν μὴ βαπτίσωνται, οὐκ ἐσθίουσι· καὶ ἄλλα πολλά ἐστιν ἃ
παρέλαβον κρατεῖν, βαπτισμοὺς ποτηρίων καὶ ξεστῶν καὶ χαλκίων καὶ

56 κωμας] κομας cod.

118 209 ς **45** το πλοιον 118 209 ς αυτον] 118 nunc habet partim deletum, om ς εις] προς 118 Βηθσαιδα] Βηθσαιδαν 118 209, το περαν προς Βηθσαιδαν ς εως ου 118 209 απολυση τον οχλον 118 209 ς **46** απηλθεν 118² ς **47** om παλαι ς **48** ο ανεμος εναντιος αυτοις 118 ς περιπατων επι της θαλασσης 118 ς **49** εδοξαν φαντασμα 118 ς **51** εν τω πλοιον (sic) 118 λιαν εκ περισσου 118 209 ς εξεπλησσοντο] εξισταντο και εθαυμαζον ς **52** πεπωρομενη 209 **53** Γεννησαρετ 118, Γεννησαρετ και προσωρμισθησαν ς **54** om οι ανδρες...και ς **55** περιδραμοντες 118 209 ς κραββατοις 118 209, τοις κραββατοις ς φερειν] περιφερειν ς εκει εστι 118 ς **56** οποτ] οπου 118² ς πολεις]+η αγρους ς ασθενεις] ασθενουντας 118 ς αν ηπτοντο 118 ς εσωζοντο 118 ς

1 οι Φαρισαιοι ς

5 κλινῶν. καὶ ἐπερωτῶσιν αὐτὸν οἱ Φαρισαῖοι καὶ οἱ γραμματεῖς, Διατί οα ς
οἱ μαθηταί σου οὐ περιπατοῦσι κατὰ τὴν παράδοσιν τῶν πρεσβυτέρων,
6 ἀλλὰ κοιναῖς χερσὶν ἐσθίουσι τὸν ἄρτον; ὁ δὲ ἀποκριθεὶς εἶπεν αὐτοῖς
ὅτι Καλῶς ἐπροφήτευσεν Ἡσαΐας περὶ ὑμῶν τῶν ὑποκριτῶν, ὡς εἶπεν,
Οὗτος ὁ λαὸς τοῖς χείλεσί με τιμᾷ, ἡ δὲ καρδία αὐτῶν πόρρω ἀπέχει
7 ἀπ᾽ ἐμοῦ. μάτην δὲ σέβονταί με, διδάσκοντες διδασκαλίας ἐντάλματα
8 ἀνθρώπων. ἀφέντες γὰρ τὴν ἐντολὴν τοῦ Θεοῦ κρατεῖτε τὴν παράδοσιν
9 τῶν ἀνθρώπων. καὶ ἔλεγεν αὐτοῖς, Καλῶς ἀθετεῖτε τὴν ἐντολὴν τοῦ
10 Θεοῦ, ἵνα τὴν παράδοσιν ὑμῶν στήσητε. Μωσῆς γὰρ εἶπε, Τίμα τὸν
πατέρα σου καὶ τὴν μητέρα σου· καί, Ὁ κακολογῶν πατέρα ἢ μητέρα
11 θανάτῳ τελευτάτω· ὑμεῖς δὲ λέγετε, Ἐὰν εἴπῃ ἄνθρωπος τῷ πατρὶ ἢ
12 τῇ μητρί, Κορβᾶν (ὅ ἐστι Δῶρον) ὃ ἐὰν ἐξ ἐμοῦ ὠφεληθῇς, οὐκέτι
13 ἀφίετε αὐτὸν οὐδὲν ποιῆσαι τῷ πατρὶ αὐτοῦ ἢ τῇ μητρί, ἀκυροῦντες
τὴν ἐντολὴν τοῦ Θεοῦ τῇ παραδόσει ὑμῶν ᾗ παρεδώκατε· καὶ παρό-
14 μοια πολλὰ τοιαῦτα ποιεῖτε. καὶ προσκαλεσάμενος πάντα τὸν ὄχλον
15 ἔλεγεν αὐτοῖς, Ἀκούετέ μου πάντες, καὶ συνίετε. οὐδέν ἐστιν ἔξωθεν
τοῦ ἀνθρώπου εἰσπορευόμενον εἰς αὐτόν, ὃ δύναται αὐτὸν κοινῶσαι· ἀλλὰ
16 τὰ ἐκπορευόμενα ἀπ᾽ αὐτοῦ, ἐκεῖνά ἐστι τὰ κοινοῦντα τὸν ἄνθρωπον. εἴ τις
17 ἔχει ὦτα ἀκούειν ἀκουέτω. καὶ ὅτε εἰσῆλθεν εἰς οἶκον ἀπὸ τοῦ ὄχλου, οβ ς
18 ἐπηρώτησαν αὐτὸν οἱ μαθηταὶ αὐτοῦ περὶ τῆς παραβολῆς. καὶ ἔλεγεν
αὐτοῖς, Οὕτω καὶ ὑμεῖς ἀσύνετοί ἐστε; οὔπω νοεῖτε ὅτι πᾶν τὸ ἔξωθεν
19 εἰσπορευόμενον εἰς τὸν ἄνθρωπον οὐ δύναται αὐτὸν κοινῶσαι, ὅτι οὐκ
εἰσπορεύεται αὐτοῦ εἰς τὴν καρδίαν, ἀλλ᾽ εἰς τὴν κοιλίαν, καὶ εἰς ἀφε-
20 δρῶνα ἐκπορεύεται;—καθαρίζων πάντα τὰ βρώματα. ἔλεγε δὲ ὅτι Τὸ
21 ἐκ τοῦ ἀνθρώπου ἐκπορευόμενον, ἐκεῖνο κοινοῖ τὸν ἄνθρωπον. ἔσωθεν
γάρ, ἐκ τῆς καρδίας, οἱ διαλογισμοὶ οἱ κακοὶ ἐκπορεύονται, μοιχεῖαι,
22 πορνεῖαι, κλοπαί, φόνοι, πλεονεξίαι, πονηρίαι, δόλος, ἀσέλγεια, ὀφ-
23 θαλμὸς πονηρός, βλασφημία, ὑπερηφανία, ἀφροσύνη· πάντα ταῦτα
ἔσωθεν ἐκπορεύεται, καὶ κοινοῖ τὸν ἄνθρωπον.
24 Καὶ ἐκεῖθεν ἀναστὰς ἀπῆλθεν εἰς τὰ ὅρια Τύρου καὶ Σιδῶνος. καὶ

9 στησηται cod.

5 και] επειτα ς κοιναις] ανιπτοις ς 6 προεφητευσεν 118 209 ς 118 209 ς
ειπεν] γεγραπται 118² ς, om 118* spat. rel. 8 ανθρωπων] + βαπτισμους
ξεστων και ποτηριων και αλλα παρομοια τοιαυτα πολλα ποιειτε 118 ς sed 118*
καπτισμους primum scripsit postea autem κ ad β mutavit 9 στησητε]
τηρησητε 118 ς 12 και ουκετι 118 ς μητρι αυτου 118 209 ς 13 την
εντολην] τον λογον ς τοιαυτα πολλα 118 ς 17 επηρωτων 118 ς
18 λεγει ς ουπω] ου ς 19 αφεδρωνα] pr τον ς καθαριζον ς
20 κοινει 118 21 καρδιας] + των ανθρωπων ς φονοι κλοπαι ς
23 ταυτα] + εσω τα πονηρα 118, + τα πονηρα ς 24 μεθορια 118 ς

ιθ' εἰσελθὼν εἰς οἰκίαν, οὐδένα ἤθελε γνῶναι, καὶ οὐκ ἠδυνήθη λαθεῖν. ἀκού- 25
σασα γὰρ γυνὴ περὶ αὐτοῦ, ἧς εἶχε τὸ θυγάτριον πνεῦμα ἀκάθαρτον,
ἐλθοῦσα ἔπεσεν αὐτῷ· ἡ δὲ γυνὴ ἦν Ἑλληνίς, Συροφοινίκισσα 26
ογ/ς τῷ γένει· καὶ ἠρώτα αὐτὸν ἵνα τὸ δαιμόνιον ἐκβάλῃ τῆς θυγατρὸς
αὐτῆς. ὁ δὲ Ἰησοῦς εἶπεν, Ἄφες πρῶτον χορτασθῆναι τὰ τέκνα· οὐ 27
γάρ ἐστι καλὸν λαβεῖν τὸν ἄρτον τῶν τέκνων καὶ τοῖς κυναρίοις
βαλεῖν. ἡ δὲ ἀπεκρίθη λέγουσα αὐτῷ, Ναί, Κύριε· καὶ γὰρ τὰ 28
κυνάρια ὑποκάτω τῆς τραπέζης ἐσθίουσιν ἀπὸ τῶν ψιχίων τῶν παιδίων.
καὶ εἶπεν αὐτῇ, Ὕπαγε διὰ τοῦτον τὸν λόγον· ἐξελήλυθεν ἐκ τῆς 29
θυγατρός σου τὸ δαιμόνιον. καὶ ἀπελθοῦσα εἰς τὸν οἶκον, εὗρε 30
τὴν θυγατέρα βεβλημένην ἐπὶ τῆς κλίνης, καὶ τὸ δαιμόνιον
ἐξεληλυθός.

κ' Καὶ πάλιν ἐξελθὼν ἐκ τῶν ὁρίων Τύρου καὶ Σιδῶνος, ἦλθεν εἰς 31
οδ/ι τὴν θάλασσαν τῆς Γαλιλαίας, ἀνὰ μέσον τῶν ὁρίων Δεκαπόλεως. καὶ 32
φέρουσιν αὐτῷ κωφὸν μογιλάλον, καὶ παρακαλοῦσιν αὐτὸν ἵνα ἐπιθῇ αὐτῷ
τὴν χεῖρα. καὶ ἀπολαβόμενος αὐτὸν ἀπὸ τοῦ ὄχλου κατ' ἰδίαν, ἔβαλε 33
τοὺς δακτύλους αὐτοῦ εἰς τὰ ὦτα αὐτοῦ, καὶ πτύσας ἥψατο τῆς γλώσσης
αὐτοῦ, καὶ ἀναβλέψας εἰς τὸν οὐρανὸν ἐστέναξε, καὶ λέγει αὐτῷ, Ἐφφαθά, 34
ὅ ἐστι Διανοίχθητι. καὶ εὐθέως ἠνοίγησαν αὐτοῦ αἱ ἀκοαί, καὶ ἐλύθη ὁ 35
οε/η δεσμὸς τῆς γλώσσης αὐτοῦ, καὶ ἐλάλει ὀρθῶς. καὶ διεστείλατο αὐτοῖς 36
ἵνα μηδενὶ εἴπωσιν· ὅσον δὲ αὐτοῖς διεστέλλετο, μᾶλλον περισσότερον
ἐκήρυσσον· καὶ ὑπερεκπερισσῶς ἐξεπλήσσοντο λέγοντες, Καλῶς πάντα 37
πεποίηκε· καὶ τοὺς κωφοὺς ποιεῖ ἀκούειν, καὶ τοὺς ἀλάλους λαλεῖν.

κα' VIII. Ἐν ἐκείναις ταῖς ἡμέραις, πάλιν πολλοῦ ὄχλου ὄντος, καὶ
ος/ς μὴ ἐχόντων τί φάγωσι, προσκαλεσάμενος τοὺς μαθητὰς λέγει αὐ-
τοῖς, Σπλαγχνίζομαι ἐπὶ τὸν ὄχλον, ὅτι ἡμέρας ἤδη τρεῖς προσμένουσί 2
μοι, καὶ οὐκ ἔχουσι τί φάγωσι. καὶ ἐὰν ἀπολύσω αὐτοὺς νήστεις εἰς 3
οἶκον αὐτῶν, ἐκλυθήσονται ἐν τῇ ὁδῷ· καί τινες αὐτῶν ἀπὸ μακρόθεν
ἥκασι. καὶ ἀπεκρίθησαν αὐτῷ οἱ μαθηταὶ αὐτοῦ, Πόθεν ὧδε δυνή- 4

118 209 / ς **24** οικιαν] pr την ς **25** θυγατριον]+αυτης ς επεσεν αυτω] προσεπεσε προς τους ποδας αυτου 118 ς **26** ην δε η γυνη ς Συροφοινισσα ς εκβαλλη 118 209, εκβαλλη εκ ς **27** ειπεν αυτη 118 ς καλον εστι 118 ς βαλειν τ. κυναρ. 118 ς **28** λεγουσα] και λεγει ς εσθιει ς **29** υπαγε] post δια τ. τ. λογον ς το δαιμονιον] ante εκ τ. θ. σ. 118 209 ς (sed απο non εκ 118) **30** οικον]+αυτης 118 ς το δ. εξελ. και την θυγ. βεβλ. επι τ. κλ. ς **31** εις] προς 118 ς **33** επιλαβομενος 118 209 εβαλλε 118 209 **34** εφαθα 209* **35** διηνοιχθησαν 118 ς **36** αυτοις] pr αυτος ς **37** υπερπερισσως ς

1 παλιν πολλου] παμπολλου ς, πα οχ οχλου spat. rel. et οχ 1° del. 118 προσκαλ.]+ο Ιησους 118 ς μαθητας αυτου 118 ς **2** ηδη ημερας ς **3** τινες γαρ 118 ς om απο ς **4** ποθεν τουτους 118 ς ωδε post τις 118 ς

5 σεταί τις χορτάσαι αὐτοὺς ἄρτον ἐπ' ἐρημίας; καὶ ἐπηρώτα αὐτούς,
6 Πόσους ἔχετε ἄρτους; οἱ δὲ εἶπον, Ἑπτά. καὶ παρήγγειλε τῷ ὄχλῳ
ἀναπεσεῖν ἐπὶ τὴν γῆν· καὶ λαβὼν τοὺς ἑπτὰ ἄρτους εὐχαριστήσας
ἔκλασε καὶ ἐδίδου τοῖς μαθηταῖς αὐτοῦ, ἵνα παραθῶσι· καὶ παρέθηκαν
7 τῷ ὄχλῳ. καὶ εἶχον ἰχθύδια ὀλίγα· καὶ αὐτὰ εὐλογήσας εἶπε παρα-
8 θεῖναι. καὶ ἔφαγον καὶ ἐχορτάσθησαν· καὶ ἦραν περισσεύματα κλασ-
9 μάτων ἑπτὰ σπυρίδας. ἦσαν δὲ οἱ φαγόντες ὡς τετρακισχίλιοι. καὶ
ἀπέλυσεν αὐτούς.
10 Καὶ ἐμβὰς εὐθὺς εἰς πλοῖον μετὰ τῶν μαθητῶν αὐτοῦ ἦλθεν εἰς
11 τὰ μέρη Μαγδαλά. καὶ ἐξῆλθον οἱ Φαρισαῖοι καὶ ἤρξαντο συζητεῖν οϛ δ
αὐτῷ, ζητοῦντες παρ' αὐτοῦ σημεῖον ἀπὸ τοῦ οὐρανοῦ, πειράζοντες αὐτόν.
12 καὶ ἀναστενάξας τῷ πνεύματι λέγει, Τί ἡ γενεὰ αὕτη ζητεῖ σημεῖον; οη ς
13 ἀμὴν λέγω ὑμῖν, εἰ δοθήσεται τῇ γενεᾷ ταύτῃ σημεῖον. καὶ ἀφεὶς
αὐτούς, ἐμβὰς πάλιν εἰς τὸ πλοῖον ἀπῆλθεν εἰς τὸ πέραν.
14 Καὶ ἐπελάθοντο λαβεῖν ἄρτους, ἕνα μόνον ἄρτον ἔχοντες μεθ'
15 ἑαυτῶν ἐν τῷ πλοίῳ. καὶ διεστέλλετο αὐτοῖς λέγων, Βλέπετε ἀπὸ ΚΒ'
16 τῆς ζύμης τῶν Φαρισαίων καὶ ἀπὸ τῆς ζύμης τῶν Ἡρωδιανῶν. καὶ οθ β
17 διελογίζοντο πρὸς ἀλλήλους ὅτι ἄρτους οὐκ ἔχουσιν. καὶ γνοὺς ὁ π ς
Ἰησοῦς λέγει αὐτοῖς, Τί διαλογίζεσθε, ὅτι ἄρτους οὐκ ἔχετε; οὔπω
18 νοεῖτε; πεπωρωμένην ἔχετε τὴν καρδίαν ὑμῶν; ὀφθαλμοὺς ἔχοντες οὐ
19 βλέπετε, καὶ ὦτα ἔχοντες οὐκ ἀκούετε, καὶ οὐ μνημονεύετε ὅτε τοὺς
πέντε ἄρτους ἔκλασα εἰς τοὺς πεντακισχιλίους, καὶ πόσους κοφίνους
20 κλασμάτων πλήρεις ἤρατε; λέγουσιν αὐτῷ, Δώδεκα. Ὅτε δὲ τοὺς
ἑπτὰ εἰς τοὺς τετρακισχιλίους, πόσων σπυρίδων πληρώματα κλασμάτων
21 ἤρατε; οἱ δὲ εἶπον, Ἑπτά. καὶ εἶπεν αὐτοῖς, Οὔπω συνίετε;
22 Καὶ ἔρχεται εἰς Βηθσαιδά· καὶ φέρουσιν αὐτῷ τυφλόν, καὶ παρα- ΚΓ'
23 καλοῦσιν αὐτὸν ἵνα αὐτοῦ ἅψηται. καὶ ἐπιλαβόμενος τῆς χειρὸς αὐτοῦ πα ι
ἐξήγαγεν αὐτὸν ἔξω τῆς κώμης· καὶ πτύσας εἰς τὰ ὄμματα αὐτοῦ, καὶ
24 ἐπιθεὶς τὰς χεῖρας αὐτῷ, ἐπηρώτα αὐτὸν εἴ τι βλέπει. καὶ ἀναβλέψας

22 ἀψηται cod.

4 om *αυτους* 118 ς *αρτων* ς 6 *της γης* ς *και ευχαριστησας* 118 118 209 ς
7 om *αυτα* 118 ς *παραθειναι*] + *και αυτα* 118 ς 8 *εφαγον δε* ς
9 *ωσει* 118 209 10 *ευθεως εμβας* ς *το πλοιον* ς Μαγδαλα] om 118 spat. rel., *Δαλμανουθα* ς 12 *πνευματι αυτου* ς *σημειον επιζητει* ς *ταυτη*] *αυτη* 118 14 *ενα...εχοντες*] *και ει μη ενα αρτον ουκ ειχον* ς
15 *ορατε βλεπετε* ς *απο* 2°] om ς *των Ηρωδ.*] *Ηρωδου* ς 16 *οτι*] pr *λεγοντες* 118 ς *εχουσιν*] *εχομεν* 118 ς 17 *ουπω νοειτε*] + *ουδε συνιετε; ετι* 118 ς 19 *οτι* 209 om *και* 118 ς *πληρεις κλασματων* 118 ς
21 *ειπεν*] *ελεγεν* ς *ουπω*] *πως ου* ς 22 *Βηθσαιδαν* ς 23 *αυτου*] *του τυφλου* ς, 118* primum *αυτ* scripsit postea autem hoc eraso *του τυφλου* rescripsit om *και* 3° ς

ἔλεγε, Βλέπω τοὺς ἀνθρώπους ὡς δένδρα περιπατοῦντας. εἶτα πάλιν 25
ἐπέθηκε τὰς χεῖρας ἐπὶ τοὺς ὀφθαλμοὺς αὐτοῦ καὶ διέβλεψε· καὶ ἀπο-
κατεστάθη, καὶ ἐνέβλεψε τηλαυγῶς ἅπαντα· καὶ ἀπέστειλεν αὐτὸν εἰς 26
τὸν οἶκον αὐτοῦ λέγων, Μηδὲ εἰς τὴν κώμην εἰσέλθῃς.

ΚΔ' Καὶ ἐξῆλθεν ὁ Ἰησοῦς καὶ οἱ μαθηταὶ αὐτοῦ εἰς τὰς κώμας Καισαρείας 27
πβ α τῆς Φιλίππου· καὶ ἐν τῇ ὁδῷ ἐπηρώτα τοὺς μαθητὰς αὐτοῦ λέγων αὐτοῖς,
Τίνα με λέγουσιν οἱ ἄνθρωποι εἶναι; οἱ δὲ ἀπεκρίθησαν, Ἰωάννην τὸν 28
Βαπτιστήν, καὶ ἄλλοι Ἡλίαν, ἄλλοι δὲ ἕνα τῶν προφητῶν. λέγει 29
αὐτοῖς, Ὑμεῖς δὲ τίνα με λέγετε εἶναι; ἀποκριθεὶς δὲ ὁ Πέτρος λέγει
πγ β αὐτῷ, Σὺ εἶ ὁ Χριστός. καὶ ἐπετίμησεν αὐτοῖς ἵνα μηδενὶ λέγωσι 30
περὶ αὐτοῦ.

Καὶ ἤρξατο διδάσκειν αὐτοὺς ὅτι δεῖ τὸν υἱὸν τοῦ ἀνθρώπου πολλὰ 31
παθεῖν καὶ ἀποδοκιμασθῆναι ἀπὸ τῶν πρεσβυτέρων καὶ ἀρχιερέων καὶ
γραμματέων, καὶ ἀποκτανθῆναι, καὶ τῇ τρίτῃ ἡμέρᾳ ἀναστῆναι· καὶ 32
πδ ς παρρησίᾳ τὸν λόγον ἐλάλει. Καὶ προσλαβόμενος αὐτὸν ὁ Πέτρος ἤρξατο
ἐπιτιμᾶν αὐτῷ. ὁ δὲ ἐπιστραφεὶς καὶ ἰδὼν τοὺς μαθητὰς αὐτοῦ ἐπετί- 33
μησε τῷ Πέτρῳ λέγων, Ὕπαγε ὀπίσω μου, Σατανᾶ· ὅτι οὐ φρονεῖς τὰ
τοῦ Θεοῦ, ἀλλὰ τὰ τῶν ἀνθρώπων.

πε β Καὶ προσκαλεσάμενος τὸν ὄχλον σὺν τοῖς μαθηταῖς αὐτοῦ εἶπεν 34
αὐτοῖς, Εἴ τις θέλει ὀπίσω μου ἀκολουθεῖν, ἀπαρνησάσθω ἑαυτὸν καὶ
ἀράτω τὸν σταυρὸν αὐτοῦ, καὶ ἀκολουθείτω μοι. ὃς γὰρ ἐὰν θέλῃ τὴν 35
ψυχὴν αὐτοῦ σῶσαι, ἀπολέσει αὐτήν· ὃς δ' ἂν ἀπολέσῃ τὴν ψυχὴν
αὐτοῦ ἕνεκεν ἐμοῦ καὶ τοῦ εὐαγγελίου, σώσει αὐτήν. τί γὰρ ὠφελήσει 36
ἄνθρωπος, ἐὰν κερδήσῃ τὸν κόσμον ὅλον καὶ ζημιωθῇ τὴν ψυχὴν
πς β αὐτοῦ; ἢ τί δώσει ἄνθρωπος ἀντάλλαγμα τῆς ψυχῆς αὐτοῦ; ὃς γὰρ 37 38
ἂν ἐπαισχυνθῇ με καὶ τοὺς ἐμοὺς λόγους ἐν τῇ γενεᾷ ταύτῃ τῇ μοι-
χαλίδι καὶ ἁμαρτωλῷ, καὶ ὁ υἱὸς τοῦ ἀνθρώπου ἐπαισχυνθήσεται αὐτόν,
πζ β ὅταν ἔλθῃ ἐν τῇ δόξῃ τοῦ πατρὸς αὐτοῦ μετὰ τῶν ἀγγέλων. IX. Καὶ
ἔλεγεν αὐτοῖς, Ἀμὴν λέγω ὑμῖν ὅτι εἰσί τινες τῶν ἑστηκότων ὧδε,
οἵτινες οὐ μὴ γεύσωνται θανάτου ἕως ἂν ἴδωσι τὴν βασιλείαν τοῦ Θεοῦ
ἐληλυθυῖαν ἐν δυνάμει.

26 εισελθης] m. recent. add. in marg. μηδε ειπης τινι εν τη κωμη
34 μοι] μου cod. **1** ωδε] οδε cod.

118 209 ς **24** οτι ως δενδρα ορω ς **25** διεβλεψε] και εποιησεν αυτον αναβλεψαι
118 ς απαντας 118 ς **26** εισελθης]+μηδε ειπης τινι εν τη κωμη 118 ς
29 λεγει] pr και αυτος ς **31** πολα 118 μετα τρεις ημερας ς **34** οστις
118 ς ακολουθειν] ελθειν ς **35** εαν] αν 118 ς, αν εαν 209 την εαυτου
ψυχην 118 209 ουτος σωσει 118 ς **36** ανθρωπον ς **38** αγγελων]
+των αγιων 118 ς
1 ωδε ante εστηκοτων 118 209 ς

2 Καὶ μεθ' ἡμέρας ἓξ παραλαμβάνει ὁ Ἰησοῦς τὸν Πέτρον καὶ τὸν ΚΕ'
Ἰάκωβον καὶ τὸν Ἰωάννην, καὶ ἀναφέρει αὐτοὺς εἰς ὄρος ὑψηλὸν κατ'
3 ἰδίαν μόνους· καὶ μετεμορφώθη ἔμπροσθεν αὐτῶν· καὶ τὰ ἱμάτια αὐτοῦ
ἐγένοντο λευκὰ λίαν, οἷα γναφεὺς ἐπὶ τῆς γῆς οὐ δύναται λευκᾶναι.
4 καὶ ὤφθη αὐτοῖς Ἡλίας σὺν Μωυσεῖ, καὶ συνελάλουν τῷ Ἰησοῦ.
5 καὶ ἀποκριθεὶς ὁ Πέτρος ἔλεγε τῷ Ἰησοῦ, Ῥαββί, καλόν ἐστιν ἡμᾶς
ὧδε εἶναι· καὶ ποιήσωμεν σκηνὰς τρεῖς, σοὶ μίαν, καὶ Μωυσεῖ μίαν,
6 7 καὶ Ἡλίᾳ μίαν. οὐ γὰρ ᾔδει τί ἀποκρίθῃ· ἦσαν γὰρ ἔκφοβοι. καὶ
ἐγένετο νεφέλη ἐπισκιάζουσα αὐτοῖς· καὶ φωνὴ ἐκ τῆς νεφέλης λέγουσα,
8 Οὗτός ἐστιν ὁ υἱός μου ὁ ἀγαπητός· ἀκούετε αὐτοῦ. καὶ ἐξάπινα
περιβλεψάμενοι οὐκέτι οὐδένα εἶδον ἀλλὰ τὸν Ἰησοῦν μόνον μεθ'
9 ἑαυτῶν. καταβαινόντων δὲ αὐτῶν ἀπὸ τοῦ ὄρους, διεστέλλετο αὐτοῖς
ἵνα μηδενὶ ἃ εἶδον διηγήσωνται, εἰ μὴ ὅταν ὁ υἱὸς τοῦ ἀνθρώπου ἐκ
10 νεκρῶν ἀναστῇ. καὶ τὸν λόγον ἐκράτησαν πρὸς ἑαυτούς, συζητοῦντες τί πη
11 ἐστι ὅταν ἐκ νεκρῶν ἀναστῇ. καὶ ἐπηρώτησαν αὐτὸν λέγοντες, ι πθ
12 Ὅτι λέγουσιν οἱ γραμματεῖς Ἡλίαν δεῖ ἐλθεῖν πρῶτον; ὁ δὲ ἀποκρι- ϛ
θεὶς εἶπεν αὐτοῖς, Ἡλίας ἐλθὼν πρῶτον ἀποκαθιστάνει πάντα· καὶ
πῶς γέγραπται ἐπὶ τὸν υἱὸν τοῦ ἀνθρώπου ἵνα πολλὰ πάθῃ καὶ ἐξου-
13 θενηθῇ. ἀλλὰ λέγω ὑμῖν ὅτι Ἡλίας ἤδη ἦλθε, καὶ ἐποίησαν αὐτῷ
ὅσα ἠθέλησαν, καθὼς γέγραπται ἐπ' αὐτόν.
14 Καὶ ἐλθὼν πρὸς τοὺς μαθητὰς εἶδεν ὄχλον περὶ αὐτούς, καὶ γραμ- ϟ ι
15 ματεῖς συζητοῦντας πρὸς αὐτούς. καὶ εὐθὺς πᾶς ὁ ὄχλος ἰδόντες
16 ἐξεθαμβήθησαν, καὶ προστρέχοντες ἠσπάζοντο αὐτόν. καὶ ἐπηρώ-
17 τησεν αὐτούς, Τί συζητεῖτε πρὸς αὐτούς; καὶ ἀποκριθεὶς ἐκ τοῦ ΚϚ'
ὄχλου εἷς εἶπεν αὐτῷ, Διδάσκαλε, ἤνεγκα τὸν υἱόν μου πρός σε, ϟα β
18 ἔχοντα πνεῦμα ἄλαλον· καὶ ὅπου αὐτὸν καταλάβῃ, ῥήσσει αὐτόν, καὶ

2 *τον* 2° et 3°] om 118 **3** *εγενετο* ϛ *λευκα*] pr *στιλβοντα* 118 ϛ 118 209 ϛ *λιαν*]+*ως χιων* 118 ϛ **4** *Μωσει* 118 209 ϛ, sed ni fallor 209* primum *Μωυσει* scripsit et ipse * correxit *συνελαλουν*] *ησαν συλλαλουντες* 118 ϛ **5** *ελεγε*] *λεγει* 118 ϛ *Μωσει* 118 209 ϛ **6** *αποκριθη*] *λαλησει* 118 *λαληση* ϛ **7** *φωνη*] pr *ηλθε* ϛ 118 nunc habet *φω* (delet.) *θε φωνη* i.e. m. prim. omisit *ηλθε* et *φωνη* scribere coepit tum autem *φω* delevit eo ut *ηλθε* scriberet sed *ηλ* in litura addere neglexit *αυτου ακουετε* 118 ϛ **8** *αλλα τον αλλα ονον* 118* sed *τον αλλα* delet **9** *διεστειλατο* 118 ϛ *διηγησωνται α ειδον* 118 ϛ **10** *οταν εκ νεκρων αναστη*] *το εκ νεκρων αναστηναι* ϛ **11** *επηρωτων* 118* ϛ sed in lectionis ecclesiasticae titulo 118[rubr] *επηρωτησαν* scripsit *οτι Ηλιαν* ϛ **12** *Ηλιας μεν* 118 ϛ *αποκαθιστα* ϛ *εξουδενωθη* ϛ **13** *και Ηλιας* ϛ *ηδη ηλθε*] *εληλυθε* 118* ϛ, sed in 118[marg] m. vel prima vel eiusdem fere temporis *ηδη ηλθε* scripsit **14** *οχλον πολυν* 118 ϛ *προς αυτους*] *αυτοις* ϛ **15** *ευθεως* ϛ *ιδων αυτον εξεθαμβηθη* 118 ϛ **16** *αυτους*] *τους γραμματεις* 118 ϛ **17** *εις εκ του οχλου* 118 ϛ om *αυτω* ϛ **18** *οπου αν* 118 ϛ

ἀφρίζει καὶ τρίζει τοὺς ὀδόντας καὶ ξηραίνεται· καὶ εἶπα τοῖς μαθη-
ταῖς σου ἵνα αὐτὸ ἐκβάλλωσι, καὶ οὐκ ἴσχυσαν. καὶ ἀποκριθεὶς 19
αὐτοῖς λέγει, Ὦ γενεὰ ἄπιστος, ἕως πότε πρὸς ὑμᾶς ἔσομαι; ἕως
πότε ἀνέξομαι ὑμῶν; φέρετε αὐτὸν πρός με. καὶ ἤνεγκαν αὐτὸν πρὸς 20
αὐτόν· καὶ ἰδὼν αὐτὸν εὐθέως τὸ πνεῦμα ἐσπάραξεν αὐτόν, καὶ πεσὼν
ἐπὶ τῆς γῆς ἐκυλίετο ἀφρίζων. καὶ ἐπηρώτησεν ὁ Ἰησοῦς τὸν πατέρα 21
αὐτοῦ, Πόσος χρόνος ἐστὶν ὡς τοῦτο γέγονεν αὐτῷ; ὁ δὲ εἶπε, Ἐκ
παιδόθεν· καὶ πολλάκις αὐτὸν εἰς πῦρ ἔβαλλε καὶ εἰς ὕδατα, ἵνα 22
αὐτὸν ἀπολέσῃ· ἀλλ' εἴ τι δύνῃ, βοήθησον ἡμῖν σπλαγχνισθεὶς ἐφ'
ἡμᾶς. ὁ δὲ Ἰησοῦς εἶπεν αὐτῷ, Τὸ εἰ δύνῃ· πάντα δυνατὰ τῷ πιστεύ- 23
οντι. καὶ εὐθέως κράξας ὁ πατὴρ τοῦ παιδὸς μετὰ δακρύων ἔλεγε, 24
Πιστεύω, κύριε, βοήθει μου τῇ ἀπιστίᾳ. ἰδὼν δὲ ὁ Ἰησοῦς ὅτι ἐπι- 25
συντρέχει ὄχλος πολύς, ἐπετίμησε τῷ πνεύματι, λέγων αὐτῷ, Τὸ
ἄλαλον καὶ κωφὸν πνεῦμα, ἐγώ σοι ἐπιτάσσω, ἔξελθε ἐξ αὐτοῦ, καὶ
μηκέτι εἰσέλθῃς εἰς αὐτόν. καὶ κράξαν πολλὰ καὶ σπαράξαν αὐτὸν 26
ἐξῆλθε· καὶ ἐγένετο ὡσεὶ νεκρός, ὥστε πολλοὺς λέγειν ὅτι ἀπέθανεν· ὁ 27
δὲ Ἰησοῦς κρατήσας τῆς χειρὸς αὐτοῦ ἤγειρεν αὐτόν, καὶ ἀνέστη.

λβ Καὶ εἰσελθόντος αὐτοῦ εἰς οἶκον, οἱ μαθηταὶ αὐτοῦ κατ' ἰδίαν 28
ι ἠρώτων αὐτόν, Ὅτι ἡμεῖς οὐκ ἠδυνήθημεν ἐκβαλεῖν αὐτό; καὶ εἶπεν 29
αὐτοῖς, Τοῦτο τὸ γένος ἐν οὐδενὶ δύναται ἐξελθεῖν εἰ μὴ ἐν προσευχῇ
καὶ νηστείᾳ.

λγ Καὶ ἐκεῖθεν ἐξελθόντες παρεπορεύοντο διὰ τῆς Γαλιλαίας, καὶ οὐκ 30
β ἤθελεν ἵνα τις γνῷ· ἐδίδασκε γὰρ τοὺς μαθητὰς αὐτοῦ καὶ ἔλεγεν αὐτοῖς 31
ὅτι Ὁ υἱὸς τοῦ ἀνθρώπου παραδίδοται εἰς χεῖρας ἀνθρώπων, καὶ ἀποκτε-
νοῦσιν αὐτόν, καὶ ἀποκτανθεὶς τῇ τρίτῃ ἡμέρᾳ ἐγερθήσεται. οἱ δὲ 32
ἠγνόουν τὸ ῥῆμα, καὶ ἐφοβοῦντο αὐτὸν ἐρωτῆσαι.

κζ' Καὶ ἦλθον εἰς Καπερναούμ· καὶ ἐν τῇ οἰκίᾳ γενόμενος ἐπηρώτα 33
λδ ι αὐτούς, Τί ἐν τῇ ὁδῷ διελεχθῆτε πρὸς ἑαυτούς; οἱ δὲ ἐσιώπων· 34
λε β πρὸς ἀλλήλους γὰρ διηνέχθησαν ἐν τῇ ὁδῷ, τίς μείζων. καὶ καθί- 35
σας ἐφώνησε τοὺς δώδεκα καὶ λέγει αὐτοῖς, Εἴ τις θέλει πρῶτος εἶναι,

28 οἶκον cod.

118 209 ς 18 οδοντας αυτου 118 ς ξηρενεται 118 ειπον ς εκβαλωσι ς 19 και] ο δε ς αυτοις] αυτω ς 21 om ο Ιησους ς εκ παιδοθεν] παιδιοθεν ς 22 εις] pr και ς το πυρ 118 εβαλε ς απολεση αυτον ς δυνη] δυνασαι ς 23 δυνη] δυνασαι πιστευσαι ς 24 παιδος] παιδιου ς 25 om πολυς ς πνευματι τω ακαθαρτω ς το πνευμα το αλαλον και κωφον ς 26 και πολλα ς 27 αυτον της χειρος ς 28 εισελθοντα αυτον ς επηρωτων αυτον κατ ιδιαν 118 ς 29 εν 1°] επ 118 31 εγερθησεται] αναστησεται 118 209 ς 32 επερωτησαι 118 ς 33 ηλθεν ς προς εαυτους διελογιζεσθε 118 ς sed 118 διαλ. 34 διελεχθησαν 118 209 ς 35 καθησας 118

36 ἔσται πάντων διάκονος. καὶ λαβὼν παιδίον ἔστησεν ἐν μέσῳ αὐτῶν,
37 καὶ ἐναγκαλισάμενος αὐτὸ λέγει αὐτοῖς, Ὃς ἂν ἓν τῶν τοιούτων παιδίων ϟϛ
δέξηται ἐπὶ τῷ ὀνόματί μου, ἐμὲ δέχεται· καὶ ὃς ἐὰν ἐμὲ δέξηται, α
οὐκ ἐμὲ δέχεται, ἀλλὰ τὸν ἀποστείλαντά με.
38 Ἀπεκρίθη δὲ αὐτῷ Ἰωάννης καὶ λέγει, Εἴδομέν τινα ἐν τῷ ὀνό- ϟζ
ματί σου ἐκβάλλοντα δαιμόνια, ὃς οὐκ ἀκολουθεῖ ἡμῖν, καὶ ἐκωλύομεν η
39 αὐτόν. ὁ δὲ εἶπε, Μὴ κωλύετε αὐτόν. οὐδεὶς γάρ ἐστιν ὃς ποιήσει
40 δύναμιν ἐν τῷ ὀνόματί μου, καὶ δυνήσεταί με κακολογῆσαι. ὃς γὰρ
41 οὐκ ἔστι καθ' ἡμῶν, ὑπὲρ ἡμῶν ἐστιν. ὃς γὰρ ἂν ποτίσῃ ὑμᾶς ποτή- ϟη
ριον ὕδατος ἐν ὀνόματι ὅτι Χριστοῦ ἐστε, ἀμὴν λέγω ὑμῖν, οὐ μὴ ϛ
42 ἀπολέσῃ τὸν μισθὸν αὐτοῦ. καὶ ὃς ἂν σκανδαλίσῃ ἕνα τῶν μικρῶν ϟθ
τούτων τῶν πιστευόντων εἰς ἐμέ, καλόν ἐστιν αὐτῷ μᾶλλον εἰ περί- β
κειται μύλος ὀνικὸς περὶ τὸν τράχηλον αὐτοῦ, καὶ βέβληται εἰς τὴν
43 θάλασσαν. καὶ ἐὰν σκανδαλίζῃ σε ἡ χείρ σου, ἀπόκοψον αὐτήν· καλόν ρ
σοί ἐστι κυλλὸν εἰς τὴν ζωὴν εἰσελθεῖν, ἢ τὰς δύο χεῖρας ἔχοντα ἀπελ- ϛ
45 θεῖν εἰς τὸ πῦρ τὸ ἄσβεστον. καὶ ἐὰν ὁ πούς σου σκανδαλίζῃ σε, ρα
ἀπόκοψον αὐτόν· καλόν ἐστί σε εἰσελθεῖν εἰς τὴν ζωὴν χωλόν, ἢ τοὺς ι
47 δύο πόδας ἔχοντα ἀπελθεῖν εἰς τὴν γέενναν. καὶ ἐὰν ὁ ὀφθαλμός
σου σκανδαλίζῃ σε, ἔκβαλε αὐτόν· καλόν σοί ἐστι μονόφθαλμον εἰσελ-
θεῖν εἰς τὴν βασιλείαν τοῦ Θεοῦ, ἢ δύο ὀφθαλμοὺς ἔχοντα ἀπελθεῖν
48 εἰς τὴν γέενναν, ὅπου ὁ σκώληξ αὐτῶν οὐ τελευτήσει καὶ τὸ πῦρ
49 50 οὐ σβέννυται. πᾶς γὰρ πυρὶ ἁλισθήσεται. καλὸν τὸ ἅλας· ἐὰν δὲ ρβ
τὸ ἅλας ἄναλον γένηται, ἐν τίνι ἀρτυθήσεται; ἔχετε ἐν ἑαυτοῖς ἅλα, β
καὶ εἰρηνεύετε ἐν ἀλλήλοις.

X. Καὶ ἐκεῖθεν ἀναστὰς ἔρχεται εἰς τὰ ὅρια τῆς Ἰουδαίας πέραν ργ
τοῦ Ἰορδάνου. καὶ συμπορεύεται πάλιν ὄχλος πολὺς πρὸς αὐτόν· ϛ

35 διακονος] pr εσχατος και παντων 118[2] ϛ haec verba 118* omisisse constat sed spatium relictum esse videtur in quo vel nihil vel saltem nihil quod nunc legi possit prima manus scripsit 118 209 ϛ **36** εστησεν αυτο ϛ λεγει] ειπεν ϛ **37** ος εαν 118 ϛ εμε...δεξηται] om 209* sed add. in mg. 209[2] **38** εκωλυσαμεν 118 ϛ αυτον] + οτι ουκ ακολουθει ημιν 118 ϛ **39** ο δε Ιησους ϛ εν] επι ϛ ταχυ κακολογησαι με 118 ϛ **40** ημων 1°] υμων 118 ϛ ημων 2°] υμων ϛ (non 118) **41** εν τω ϛ ονοματι μου 118 209 ϛ **42** om τουτων ϛ λιθος μυλικος ϛ **43** εις το πυρ] pr εις την γεενναν ϛ **44** οπου ο σκωληξ αυτων ου τελευτα και το πυρ ου σβεννυται ϛ **45** σε 2°] σοι ϛ βληθηναι ϛ γεενναν] + εις το πυρ το ασβεστον ϛ **46** οπου ο σκωληξ αυτων ου τελευτα και το πυρ ου σβεννυται ϛ **47** απελθειν] βληθηναι ϛ γεενναν του πυρος ϛ **48** τελευτα 118 ϛ **49** αλισθησεται] + και πασα θυσια αλι αλισθησεται ϛ **50** αυτο αρτυσετε ϛ, αυτω αρτυθησεται 118 αλας 118 ϛ

1 κακειθεν 118 ϛ δια του περαν ϛ συμπορευονται ϛ οχλοι ϛ om πολυς ϛ

ΚΗ′ καὶ ὡς εἰώθει πάλιν ἐδίδασκεν αὐτούς. καὶ προσελθόντες ἐπηρώτησαν 2
αὐτὸν οἱ Φαρισαῖοι εἰ ἔξεστιν ἀνδρὶ γυναῖκα ἀπολῦσαι, πειράζοντες
αὐτόν. ὁ δὲ ἀποκριθεὶς εἶπεν αὐτοῖς, Τί ὑμῖν ἐνετείλατο Μωσῆς; οἱ 3 4
δὲ εἶπον, Μωυσῆς ἐνετείλατο βιβλίον ἀποστασίου γράψαι καὶ ἀπο-
λῦσαι. καὶ ἀποκριθεὶς ὁ Ἰησοῦς εἶπεν αὐτοῖς, Πρὸς τὴν σκληροκαρδίαν 5
ὑμῶν ἔγραψεν ὑμῖν τὴν ἐντολὴν ταύτην· ἀπὸ δὲ ἀρχῆς κτίσεως ἄρσεν 6
καὶ θῆλυ ἐποίησεν αὐτοὺς ὁ Θεός· Ἕνεκεν τούτου καταλείψει ἄνθρωπος 7
τὸν πατέρα αὐτοῦ καὶ τὴν μητέρα, καὶ προσκολληθήσεται τῇ γυναικὶ
αὐτοῦ, καὶ ἔσονται οἱ δύο εἰς σάρκα μίαν. ὥστε οὐκέτι εἰσὶ δύο, ἀλλὰ 8
ρδ σὰρξ μία. ὃ οὖν ὁ Θεὸς συνέζευξεν, ἄνθρωπος μὴ χωριζέτω. καὶ ἐν 9 10
ι τῇ οἰκίᾳ πάλιν οἱ μαθηταὶ αὐτοῦ περὶ τούτου ἐπηρώτησαν αὐτόν. καὶ 12
λέγει αὐτοῖς, Ἐὰν ἀπολύσῃ γυνὴ τὸν ἄνδρα αὐτῆς καὶ γαμήσῃ
ρε/β ἄλλον μοιχᾶται· καὶ ἐὰν ἀνὴρ ἀπολύσῃ τὴν γυναῖκα αὐτοῦ καὶ 11
γαμήσῃ ἄλλην μοιχᾶται.

ρϛ/β Καὶ προσέφερον αὐτῷ παιδία, ἵνα ἅψηται αὐτῶν· οἱ δὲ μαθηταὶ 13
ἐπετίμων τοῖς φέρουσιν. ἰδὼν δὲ ὁ Ἰησοῦς ἠγανάκτησε, καὶ ἐπιτι- 14
μήσας εἶπεν αὐτοῖς, Ἄφετε τὰ παιδία ἔρχεσθαι πρός με, καὶ μὴ κω-
λύετε αὐτά· τῶν γὰρ τοιούτων ἐστὶν ἡ βασιλεία τοῦ Θεοῦ· ἀμὴν λέγω 15
ὑμῖν, ὃς ἂν μὴ δέξηται τὴν βασιλείαν τοῦ Θεοῦ ὡς παιδίον, οὐ μὴ
εἰσέλθῃ εἰς αὐτήν. καὶ ἐναγκαλισάμενος αὐτά, καὶ τίθων τὰς χεῖρας 16
ἐπ' αὐτά, ηὐλόγει αὐτά.

ΚΘ′ Καὶ ἐκπορευομένου αὐτοῦ εἰς ὁδόν, προσδραμὼν εἷς καὶ γονυπετήσας 17
ρζ/β αὐτὸν ἐπηρώτα αὐτόν, Διδάσκαλε ἀγαθέ, τί ποιήσω ἵνα ζωὴν αἰώνιον
κληρονομήσω; ὁ δὲ Ἰησοῦς εἶπεν αὐτῷ, Τί με λέγεις ἀγαθόν; οὐδεὶς 18
ἀγαθὸς εἰ μὴ εἷς ὁ Θεός. τὰς ἐντολὰς οἶδας, Μὴ μοιχεύσῃς· μὴ 19
κλέψῃς· μὴ ψευδομαρτυρήσῃς· τίμα τὸν πατέρα σου καὶ τὴν μη-
τέρα. ὁ δὲ ἀποκριθεὶς εἶπεν αὐτῷ, Ταῦτα πάντα ἐποίησα ἐκ νεότητός 20
ρη/β μου. ὁ δὲ Ἰησοῦς ἐμβλέψας αὐτῷ ἠγάπησεν αὐτόν, καὶ εἶπεν αὐτῷ, 21
Ἕν σοι ὑστερεῖ· ὕπαγε, ὅσα ἔχεις πώλησον καὶ δὸς τοῖς πτωχοῖς, καὶ
ἕξεις θησαυρὸν ἐν οὐρανῷ· καὶ ἄρας τὸν σταυρὸν δεῦρο ἀκολούθει
ρθ/β μοι. ὁ δὲ στυγνάσας ἐπὶ τῷ λόγῳ ἀπῆλθε λυπούμενος· ἦν γὰρ ἔχων 22
κτήματα πολλά. καὶ περιβλεψάμενος ὁ Ἰησοῦς λέγει τοῖς μαθηταῖς 23

118 209 ϛ **2** οι Φαρισαιοι επηρωτησαν αυτον 118 ϛ sed om οι 118 **4** Μωσης επετρεψε ϛ **7** προς την γυναικα ϛ **8** μια σαρξ ϛ **10** τουτου] του αυτου ϛ **11 12** και λεγει αυτοις, ος εαν απολυση την γυναικα αυτου και γαμηση αλλην μοιχαται επ αυτην· και εαν γυνη απολυση τον ανδρα αυτης και γαμηθη αλλω μοιχαται 118 ϛ, om και εαν ανηρ...μοιχαται 209 **13** φερουσιν] προσφερουσιν ϛ **14** om επιτιμησας 118 ϛ **15** αν] εαν 118 ϛ **16** om και 2° ϛ τιθεις 118 209 ϛ **19** μοιχευσης] + μη φονευσης ϛ ψευδομαρτυρησης] + μη αποστερησης ϛ **20** ταυτα] pr διδασκαλε ϛ εποιησα] εφυλαξαμην ϛ **21** αρας τον σταυρον post μοι ϛ

αὐτοῦ, Πῶς δυσκόλως οἱ τὰ χρήματα ἔχοντες εἰς τὴν βασιλείαν τοῦ
24 Θεοῦ εἰσελεύσονται. οἱ δὲ μαθηταὶ αὐτοῦ ἐθαμβοῦντο ἐπὶ τοῖς λόγοις
αὐτοῦ. ὁ δὲ Ἰησοῦς πάλιν ἀποκριθεὶς λέγει αὐτοῖς, Τέκνια, πῶς δύσ-
κολόν ἐστι τοὺς πεποιθότας ἐπὶ τοῖς χρήμασιν εἰς τὴν βασιλείαν τοῦ
25 Θεοῦ εἰσελθεῖν. εὐκοπώτερόν ἐστι κάμηλον διὰ τρυμαλιᾶς ῥαφίδος
26 διελθεῖν, ἢ εἰς τὴν βασιλείαν τοῦ Θεοῦ πλούσιον εἰσελθεῖν. οἱ δὲ
περισσῶς ἐξεπλήσσοντο, λέγοντες πρὸς ἑαυτούς, Καὶ τίς δύναται σω-
27 θῆναι; ἐμβλέψας αὐτοῖς ὁ Ἰησοῦς λέγει, Παρὰ ἀνθρώποις ἀδύνατον,
28 ἀλλ' οὐ παρὰ Θεῷ. ἤρξατο αὐτῷ λέγειν ὁ Πέτρος, Ἰδοὺ ἡμεῖς
29 ἀφήκαμεν πάντα καὶ ἠκολουθήσαμέν σοι. καὶ ἀποκριθεὶς ὁ Ἰησοῦς ρι/β
εἶπεν, Ἀμὴν λέγω ὑμῖν, οὐδείς ἐστιν ὃς ἀφῆκεν οἰκίαν, ἢ ἀδελφούς, ἢ
ἀδελφάς, ἢ πατέρα, ἢ μητέρα, ἢ τέκνα, ἢ ἀγρούς, ἕνεκεν ἐμοῦ ἢ
30 ἕνεκεν τοῦ εὐαγγελίου, ἐὰν μὴ ἀπολάβῃ ἑκατονταπλασίονα νῦν ἐν
τῷ καιρῷ τούτῳ, οἰκίας καὶ ἀδελφοὺς καὶ ἀδελφὰς καὶ πατέρα καὶ
μητέρα καὶ τέκνα καὶ ἀγρούς, μετὰ διωγμῶν, καὶ ἐν τῷ αἰῶνι τῷ ἐρχο-
31 μένῳ ζωὴν αἰώνιον. πολλοὶ δὲ ἔσονται πρῶτοι ἔσχατοι, καὶ ἔσχατοι ρια/β
πρῶτοι.
32 Ἦσαν δὲ ἐν τῇ ὁδῷ ἀναβαίνοντες εἰς Ἱεροσόλυμα· καὶ ἦν προάγων ριβ/β
αὐτοὺς ὁ Ἰησοῦς· καὶ ἐθαμβοῦντο, οἱ δὲ ἀκολουθοῦντες ἐφοβοῦντο. καὶ
παραλαβὼν πάλιν τοὺς δώδεκα ἤρξατο αὐτοῖς λέγειν τὰ μέλλοντα αὐτῷ
33 συμβαίνειν ὅτι Ἰδοὺ ἀναβαίνομεν εἰς Ἱεροσόλυμα, καὶ ὁ υἱὸς τοῦ
ἀνθρώπου παραδοθήσεται τοῖς ἀρχιερεῦσι καὶ τοῖς γραμματεῦσι, καὶ
34 κατακρινοῦσιν αὐτὸν θανάτῳ, καὶ παραδώσουσιν αὐτὸν τοῖς ἔθνεσι, καὶ
ἐμπαίξουσιν αὐτῷ καὶ μαστιγώσουσιν αὐτὸν καὶ ἐμπτύσουσιν αὐτῷ, καὶ
ἀποκτενοῦσι· καὶ τῇ τρίτῃ ἡμέρᾳ ἀναστήσεται.
35 Καὶ προσπορεύονται αὐτῷ Ἰάκωβος καὶ Ἰωάννης οἱ υἱοὶ Ζεβεδαίου Λ'
λέγοντες, Διδάσκαλε, θέλομεν ἵνα ὃ ἐάν σε ἐρωτήσωμεν ποιήσῃς ἡμῖν. ριγ/ϛ
36 37 ὁ δὲ εἶπεν αὐτοῖς, Τί θέλετε ποιήσω ὑμῖν; οἱ δὲ εἶπον αὐτῷ, Δὸς
ἡμῖν ἵνα ἐκ δεξιῶν σου καὶ ἐξ εὐωνύμων καθίσωμεν ἐν τῇ δόξῃ σου.
38 ὁ δὲ Ἰησοῦς ἀποκριθεὶς εἶπεν αὐτοῖς, Οὐκ οἴδατε τί αἰτεῖσθε. δύ-

23 om τα 209 **24** om αυτου 1° ϛ τεκνα ϛ om τοις 2° 118 **25** της τρυμαλιας της ϛ διελθειν] εισελθειν ϛ πλουσιον ante εις 118 209 ϛ **27** εμβλεψας δε 118 209 ϛ Θεω] τω Θεω· παντα γαρ δυνατα εστι παρα τω Θεω 118 ϛ sed 118 απτα quod forsitan απαντα negligenter scriptum significet **28** και ηρξατο ο Πετρος λεγειν αυτω 118 209 ϛ **29** αποκριθεις δε ϛ μητερα] + η γυναικα 118 ϛ η ενεκεν] και ϛ **30** λαβη 118 ϛ om και πατερα ϛ μητερας ϛ **31** οι εσχατοι 118 ϛ **32** οι δε] και 118 ϛ **34** αποκτενουσιν αυτον 118 ϛ **35** om σε ϛ αιτησωμεν 118 209 ϛ **36** ποιησαι με ϛ **37** αυτον 118 εκ] pr εις 118 ϛ εξ] pr εις 118 ϛ ευωνυμων σου 118 209 ϛ **38** om αποκριθεις 118 ϛ 118 209 ϛ

νασθε πιεῖν τὸ ποτήριον ὃ ἐγὼ πίνω, ἢ τὸ βάπτισμα ὃ ἐγὼ βαπτί-
ζομαι βαπτισθῆναι; οἱ δὲ εἶπον, Δυνάμεθα. ὁ δὲ Ἰησοῦς εἶπεν 39
αὐτοῖς, Τὸ μὲν ποτήριον ὃ ἐγὼ πίνω πίεσθε, καὶ τὸ βάπτισμα ὃ ἐγὼ
βαπτίζομαι βαπτισθήσεσθε· τὸ δὲ καθίσαι ἐκ δεξιῶν μου καὶ ἐξ εὐω- 40
νύμων οὐκ ἔστιν ἐμὸν δοῦναι, ἀλλ' οἷς ἡτοίμασται ὑπὸ τοῦ πατρός
ριδ μου. καὶ ἀκούσαντες οἱ δέκα ἠγανάκτησαν περὶ Ἰακώβου καὶ Ἰωάννου. 41
β ὁ δὲ Ἰησοῦς προσκαλεσάμενος λέγει αὐτοῖς, Οἴδατε ὅτι οἱ δοκοῦντες 42
ἄρχειν τῶν ἐθνῶν κατακυριεύουσιν αὐτῶν· καὶ οἱ μεγάλοι κατεξουσιά-
ζουσιν αὐτῶν. οὐχ οὕτως δὲ ἔσται ἐν ὑμῖν· ἀλλ' ὃς ἐὰν θέλῃ μέγας 43
γενέσθαι ἐν ὑμῖν, ἔσται ὑμῶν διάκονος· καὶ ὃς ἐὰν θέλῃ ὑμῶν 44
ριε εἶναι πρῶτος, ἔσται πάντων δοῦλος· καὶ γὰρ ὁ υἱὸς τοῦ ἀνθρώπου οὐκ 45
δ ἦλθε διακονηθῆναι, ἀλλὰ διακονῆσαι, καὶ δοῦναι τὴν ψυχὴν αὐτοῦ λύτρον
ἀντὶ πολλῶν.

ΛΑ' Καὶ ἔρχονται εἰς Ἱεριχώ· καὶ ἐκπορευομένου αὐτοῦ ἀπὸ Ἱεριχὼ καὶ 46
ρις β τῶν μαθητῶν αὐτοῦ καὶ ὄχλου ἱκανοῦ, ὁ υἱὸς Τιμαίου Βαρτίμαιος ὁ
τυφλὸς ἐκάθητο παρὰ τὴν ὁδὸν προσαιτῶν. καὶ ἀκούσας ὅτι Ἰησοῦς 47
ὁ Ναζαρηνός ἐστιν, ἤρξατο κράζειν καὶ λέγειν, Ὁ υἱὸς Δαβὶδ Ἰησοῦ,
ἐλέησόν με. καὶ ἐπετίμων αὐτῷ πολλοί, ἵνα σιωπήσῃ· ὁ δὲ πολλῷ 48
μᾶλλον ἔκραζεν, Ὁ υἱὸς Δαβίδ, ἐλέησόν με. καὶ στὰς ὁ Ἰησοῦς εἶπε 49
φωνηθῆναι αὐτόν· καὶ φωνοῦσι τὸν τυφλόν, λέγοντες αὐτῷ, Θάρσων
ἐγείρου, φωνεῖ σε. ὁ δὲ ἀποβαλὼν τὸ ἱμάτιον αὐτοῦ ἀναστὰς ἦλθε 50
πρὸς τὸν Ἰησοῦν· καὶ ἀποκριθεὶς λέγει αὐτῷ ὁ Ἰησοῦς, Τί θέλεις ποιήσω 51
σοι; ὁ δὲ τυφλὸς εἶπεν αὐτῷ, Ῥαββουνί, ἵνα ἀναβλέψω. ὁ δὲ Ἰησοῦς 52
εἶπεν αὐτῷ, Ὕπαγε, ἡ πίστις σου σέσωκέ σε. καὶ εὐθέως ἀνέβλεψε, καὶ
ἠκολούθει αὐτῷ ἐν τῇ ὁδῷ.

ΛΒ' XI. Καὶ ὅτε ἐγγίζουσιν εἰς Ἱεροσόλυμα, εἰς Βηθσφαγῆ καὶ
ριζ β Βηθανίαν πρὸς τὸ ὄρος τῶν Ἐλαιῶν, ἀπέστειλε δύο τῶν μαθητῶν
αὐτοῦ λέγων, Ὑπάγετε εἰς τὴν κώμην τὴν κατέναντι ὑμῶν· καὶ εὐθέως 2

1 Βηθσφαγη] σ nunc erasum est nec satis certum

118 209 ς **38** η] και 118 ς βαπιζω 209*, βαπιζωμαι 209[2] **39** ειπον αυτω 118 ς **40** ευωνυμων μου 118 209 ς om υπο του πατρος μου ς **41** ηρξαντο αγανακτειν ς **42** προσκαλεσαμενος αυτους 118 ς μεγαλοι αυτων ς **43** ουτω ς γενεσθαι μεγας 118 ς διακονος υμων ς **44** εαν] αν ς ειναι] γενεσθαι ς **46** om ο 1° ς **47** om Ιησους 118* sed inter ο et Ναζαρηνος spatium est in quo aliquid erasum equidem certius legere non possum sed ni fallor scriba οτι bis scripsit et τι erasit **48** υιε ς **49** αυτον φωνηθηναι ς θαρσει ς εγειραι ς **51** ραββονι ς **52** αυτω] τω Ιησου 118 ς

1 Ιερουσαλημ 118 ς Βηθφαγη ς αποστελλει 118 ς **2** λεγων] και λεγει αυτοις 118 ς

εἰσπορευόμενοι εἰς αὐτὴν εὑρήσητε πῶλον δεδεμένον, ἐφ' ὃν οὐδεὶς
3 ἀνθρώπων κεκάθικε· λύσαντες αὐτὸν ἀγάγετε· καὶ ἐάν τις ὑμῖν εἴπῃ
τι εἴπατε ὅτι Ὁ κύριος αὐτοῦ χρείαν ἔχει· καὶ εὐθέως αὐτὸν ἀποστελεῖ
4 ὧδε. ἀπῆλθον οὖν καὶ εὗρον πῶλον δεδεμένον πρὸς τὴν θύραν ἔξω ριη β
5 ἐπὶ τοῦ ἀμφόδου, καὶ λύουσιν αὐτόν. τινὲς δὲ τῶν ἐκεῖ ἑστηκότων
6 ἔλεγον αὐτοῖς, Τί ποιεῖτε λύοντες τὸν πῶλον; οἱ δὲ εἶπον αὐτοῖς καθὼς
7 εἶπεν αὐτοῖς ὁ Ἰησοῦς· καὶ ἀφῆκαν αὐτούς. καὶ ἄγουσι τὸν πῶλον
πρὸς τὸν Ἰησοῦν, καὶ ἐπιβάλλουσιν αὐτῷ ἱμάτια, καὶ καθίζει ἐπ'
8 αὐτῷ. πολλοὶ δὲ τὰ ἱμάτια αὐτῶν ἐστρώννυον εἰς τὴν ὁδόν· ἄλλοι
9 στοιβάδας ἔκοπτον ἐκ τῶν δένδρων καὶ ἐστρώννυον εἰς τὴν ὁδόν· καὶ οἱ ριθ α
προάγοντες καὶ οἱ ἀκολουθοῦντες ἔκραζον λέγοντες, Ὡσαννά, εὐλογη-
10 μένος ὁ ἐρχόμενος ἐν ὀνόματι Κυρίου· εὐλογημένη ἡ βασιλεία τοῦ
πατρὸς ἡμῶν Δαβίδ· Ὡσαννὰ ἐν τοῖς ὑψίστοις· εἰρήνη ἐν οὐράνῳ
11 καὶ δόξα ἐν ὑψίστοις. καὶ εἰσῆλθεν εἰς Ἱεροσόλυμα καὶ εἰς τὸ ρκ ϛ
ἱερόν· καὶ περιβλεψάμενος πάντα, ὀψίας οὔσης ἤδη τῆς ὥρας, ἐξῆλθεν
εἰς Βηθανίαν μετὰ τῶν δώδεκα.

12 13 Καὶ τῇ ἐπαύριον ἐξελθόντων αὐτῶν ἐπείνασε, καὶ ἰδὼν συκῆν ΛΓ
ἀπὸ μακρόθεν ἔχουσαν φύλλα ἦλθεν εἰ ἄρα τι εὑρήσει ἐν αὐτῇ·
καὶ ἐλθὼν ἐπ' αὐτὴν οὐδὲν εὗρεν εἰ μὴ φύλλα· οὔπω γὰρ ἦν καιρὸς
14 σύκων. καὶ ἀποκριθεὶς εἶπεν αὐτῇ, Μηκέτι εἰς τὸν αἰῶνα ἐκ σοῦ
15 καρπὸν μηδεὶς φάγῃ. καὶ ἤκουον οἱ μαθηταὶ αὐτοῦ. καὶ ἔρχονται ρκα α
εἰς Ἱεροσόλυμα· καὶ εἰσελθὼν εἰς τὸ ἱερὸν ἤρξατο ἐκβάλλειν τοὺς
πωλοῦντας καὶ ἀγοράζοντας ἐν τῷ ἱερῷ, καὶ τὰς τραπέζας τῶν κολλυ-
βιστῶν καὶ τὰς καθέδρας τῶν πωλούντων τὰς περιστερὰς κατέστρεψε·
16 17 καὶ οὐκ ἤφιεν ἵνα τις διενέγκῃ σκεῦος διὰ τοῦ ἱεροῦ· καὶ ἐδίδασκε λέγων
αὐτοῖς, Γέγραπται ὅτι Ὁ οἶκός μου οἶκος προσευχῆς κληθήσεται
18 πᾶσι τοῖς ἔθνεσιν, ὑμεῖς δὲ αὐτὸν ἐποιήσατε σπήλαιον λῃστῶν. καὶ ρκβ α
ἤκουσαν οἱ ἀρχιερεῖς καὶ οἱ γραμματεῖς, καὶ ἐζήτουν πῶς αὐτὸν

3 ειπη] ειπε cod.

2 ευρησητε] ευρησετε ϛ, 118* primum ευρησετε scripsit, postea ε 2° del. et spat. rel. 3 ειπη τί 118 209, ειπη τι ποιειτε τουτο; ϛ αποστελλει 118 4 ουν] δε ϛ τον πωλον ϛ 5 και τινες 118* ϛ, τινες δε 118[2] in marg. 6 ειπεν] ενετειλατο 118 ϛ om αυτοις ϛ 7 αγουσι] ηγαγον 118 ϛ επεβαλον 118 ϛ τα ιματια αυτων 118 ϛ εκαθισεν 118[2] ϛ quae scripserit 118* incertum est, nam εκαθισεν επ αυτω manu recenti in rasura rescriptum est 8 αυτων] εαυτων 118* εστρωσαν 118 ϛ αλλοι δε 118 ϛ 10 η ερχομενη βασιλεια εν ονοματι κυριου 118 ϛ om ειρηνη...υψιστοις ϛ 11 Ιεροσολυμα]+ο Ιησους ϛ ηδη ουσης 118 ϛ 12 αυτων]+απο Βηθανιας 118 ϛ 13 om απο 118 ϛ ευρησει τι ϛ ουπω] ου 118 ϛ 14 αποκριθεις ο Ιησους 118 ϛ εκ σου εις τον αιωνα μηδεις καρπον φαγοι ϛ 15 Ιεροσολυμα] pr ισ 118* nec correctum est εισελθων]+ο Ιησους 118 ϛ 17 ου γεγραπται ϛ εποιησατε αυτον 118 ϛ 18 οι γραμματεις και οι αρχιερεις ϛ

118 209 ϛ

ἀπολέσωσιν· ἐφοβοῦντο γὰρ αὐτόν, πᾶς γὰρ ὁ ὄχλος ἐξεπλήσσετο
ἐπὶ τῇ διδαχῇ αὐτοῦ.
ρκγ ι Καὶ ὅτε ὀψὲ ἐγένετο, ἔξω τῆς πόλεως ἐξεπορεύετο. καὶ παρα- 19 20
πορευόμενοι πρωῒ εἶδον τὴν συκῆν ἐξηραμμένην ἐκ ῥιζῶν· καὶ ἀνα- 21
μνησθεὶς ὁ Πέτρος λέγει αὐτῷ, Ῥαββί, ἴδε ἡ συκῆ ἣν κατηράσω
ρκδ ς ἐξηράνθη. καὶ ἀποκριθεὶς ὁ Ἰησοῦς λέγει αὐτοῖς, Ἔχετε πίστιν Θεοῦ· 22
ἀμὴν λέγω ὑμῖν, ὅτι ὃς ἐὰν εἴπῃ τῷ ὄρει τούτῳ ἀρθῆναι καὶ βλη- 23
θῆναι εἰς τὴν θάλασσαν, καὶ μὴ διακριθῇ ἐν τῇ καρδίᾳ αὐτοῦ, ἀλλὰ
ρκε δ πιστεύσῃ ὅτι ἃ λέγει γίνεται, ἔσται αὐτῷ. διὰ τοῦτο λέγω ὑμῖν, Πάντα 24
ὅσα ἂν προσευχόμενοι αἰτῆσθε, πιστεύετε ὅτι λήψεσθε, καὶ ἔσται
ΑΔ' ὑμῖν. καὶ ὅταν στήκετε προσευχόμενοι, ἀφίετε εἴ τι ἔχετε κατά τινος, 25
ρκς ς ἵνα καὶ ὁ πατὴρ ὑμῶν ὁ ἐν τοῖς οὐρανοῖς ἀνῇ ὑμῖν τὰ παραπτώματα
ὑμῶν· εἰ δὲ ὑμεῖς οὐκ ἀφίετε, οὐδὲ ὁ πατὴρ ὑμῶν ὁ ἐν οὐρανοῖς ἀφήσει 26
τὰ παραπτώματα ὑμῶν.
ΑΕ' Καὶ ἔρχονται πάλιν εἰς Ἱεροσόλυμα. καὶ ἐν τῷ ἱερῷ περιπατοῦντος 27
ρκζ β αὐτοῦ, ἔρχονται πρὸς αὐτὸν οἱ ἀρχιερεῖς καὶ οἱ γραμματεῖς, καὶ ἔλεγον 28
αὐτῷ, Ἐν ποίᾳ ἐξουσίᾳ ταῦτα ποιεῖς; καὶ τίς σοι ἔδωκε ταύτην
τὴν ἐξουσίαν ἵνα ταῦτα ποιῇς; ὁ δὲ Ἰησοῦς ἀποκριθεὶς εἶπεν αὐτοῖς, 29
Ἐπερωτήσω ὑμᾶς κἀγὼ λόγον ἕνα, καὶ ἀποκρίθητέ μοι, καὶ ἐρῶ
ὑμῖν ἐν ποίᾳ ἐξουσίᾳ ταῦτα ποιῶ. τὸ βάπτισμα Ἰωάννου ἀπ' οὐρανοῦ 30
ἦν ἢ ἐξ ἀνθρώπων; ἀποκρίθητέ μοι. καὶ διελογίζοντο πρὸς ἑαυτοὺς 31
λέγοντες, Ἐὰν εἴπωμεν, Ἐξ οὐρανοῦ, ἐρεῖ ἡμῖν, Διατί οὖν οὐκ ἐπιστεύ-
σατε αὐτῷ; ἀλλ' εἴπωμεν, Ἐξ ἀνθρώπων;—ἐφοβοῦντο τὸν λαόν· πάντες 32
γὰρ εἶχον τὸν Ἰωάννην ὅτι προφήτης ἦν. καὶ ἀποκριθέντες λέγουσι 33
τῷ Ἰησοῦ, Οὐκ οἴδαμεν. καὶ ἀποκριθεὶς ὁ Ἰησοῦς λέγει αὐτοῖς,
Οὐδὲ ἐγὼ λέγω ὑμῖν ἐν ποίᾳ ἐξουσίᾳ ταῦτα ποιῶ.
Αϛ' XII. Καὶ ἤρξατο αὐτοῖς ἐν παραβολαῖς λαλεῖν, Ἀμπελῶνα ἐφύ-
ρκη β τευσεν ἄνθρωπος, καὶ περιέθηκε φραγμὸν καὶ ὤρυξεν ὑπολήνιον καὶ

23 αυτω] m. recent. add. in marg. ο εαν ειπη   24 ληψεσθαι cod.

118 209 ϛ 18 απολεσουσιν ϛ   πας γαρ] οτι πας 118 209 ϛ   19 εξεπορευετο εξω της πολεως ϛ   20 πρωι παραπορευομενοι ϛ   21 εξηρανται ϛ   22 om ο ϛ   23 αμην γαρ ϛ   εαν] αν ϛ   αρθητι 118^{2} ϛ, αρθη spat. rel. 118*   βληθητι 118^{2} ϛ, βληθη spat. rel. 118*   αυτω] + ο εαν ειπη 118 ϛ   24 αιτεισθε 118 ϛ   λαμβανετε ϛ   25 στηκητε ϛ   ανη] αφη 118 ϛ   26 τοις ουρανοις 118 ϛ   27 γραμματεις] + και οι πρεσβυτεροι 118 ϛ   28 ελεγον] λεγουσιν 118 ϛ   τις] τι 209   την εξουσιαν ταυτην εδωκεν 118 ϛ   29 επερωτησω] επερω 118   ενα λογον 118 ϛ   30 απ] εξ 118 ϛ   31 ελογιζοντο ϛ   om ημιν ϛ   32 αλλ] αν 118* 209, εαν 118^{2}, αλλ εαν ϛ et ante αν spat. rel. 118*   απαντες ϛ   οντως προφητης ϛ   33 ο Ιησους αποκριθεις 118 ϛ

1 λεγειν ϛ

2 ᾠκοδόμησε πύργον, καὶ ἐξέδοτο αὐτὸν γεωργοῖς, καὶ ἀπεδήμησε. καὶ
ἀπέστειλε πρὸς τοὺς γεωργοὺς τῷ καιρῷ δοῦλον, ἵνα παρὰ τῶν γεωργῶν
3 λάβῃ ἀπὸ τοῦ καρποῦ τοῦ ἀμπελῶνος· οἱ δὲ λαβόντες αὐτὸν ἔδειραν
4 καὶ ἀπέστειλαν κενόν. καὶ πάλιν ἀπέστειλε δοῦλον· κἀκεῖνον κεφα-
5 λαιώσαντες ἀπέστειλαν ἠτιμασμένον. καὶ πάλιν ἄλλον ἀπέστειλε·
κἀκεῖνον ἀπέκτειναν· καὶ πολλοὺς ἄλλους, οὓς μὲν δέροντες, οὓς δὲ
6 ἀποκτένοντες. ἔτι ἕνα υἱὸν ἔχων τὸν ἀγαπητὸν αὐτοῦ, ἀπέστειλε
7 πρὸς αὐτοὺς ἔσχατον, λέγων, Ἐντραπήσονται τὸν υἱόν μου. ἐκεῖνοι δὲ
οἱ γεωργοὶ πρὸς ἑαυτοὺς εἶπον, Οὗτός ἐστιν ὁ κληρονόμος· δεῦτε
8 ἀποκτείνωμεν αὐτόν, καὶ ἡμῶν ἔσται ἡ κληρονομία. καὶ λαβόντες
9 αὐτὸν ἀπέκτειναν καὶ ἐξέβαλον ἔξω τοῦ ἀμπελῶνος. τί οὖν ποιήσει ὁ
κύριος τοῦ ἀμπελῶνος; ἐλεύσεται καὶ ἀπολέσει τοὺς γεωργοὺς ἐκεί-
10 νους, καὶ δώσει τὸν ἀμπελῶνα ἄλλοις. οὐδὲ τὴν γραφὴν ταύτην ἀνέ-
γνωτε; Λίθον ὃν ἀπεδοκίμασαν οἱ οἰκοδομοῦντες, οὗτος ἐγενήθη εἰς
11 κεφαλὴν γωνίας· παρὰ Κυρίου ἐγένετο αὕτη, καὶ ἔστι θαυμαστὴ ἐν
12 ὀφθαλμοῖς ἡμῶν. καὶ ἐζήτουν αὐτὸν κρατῆσαι, καὶ ἐφοβήθησαν τὸν ρκθ
ὄχλον· ἔγνωσαν γὰρ ὅτι πρὸς αὐτοὺς τὴν παραβολὴν εἶπε· καὶ ἀφέντες α
αὐτὸν ἀπῆλθον.
13 Καὶ ἀποστέλλουσι πρὸς αὐτόν τινας τῶν Φαρισαίων καὶ τῶν Ἡρω- ΛΖ'
14 διανῶν, ἵνα αὐτὸν ἀγρεύσωσι λόγῳ. οἱ δὲ ἐλθόντες ἤρξαντο ἐρωτᾷν ρλ β
αὐτὸν ἐν δόλῳ λέγοντες, Διδάσκαλε, οἴδαμεν ὅτι ἀληθὴς εἶ, καὶ οὐ
μέλει σοι περὶ οὐδενός· οὐ γὰρ βλέπεις εἰς πρόσωπον ἀνθρώπου,
ἀλλ' ἐπ' ἀληθείας τὴν ὁδὸν τοῦ Θεοῦ διδάσκεις. ἔξεστι κῆνσον Καίσαρι
15 δοῦναι ἢ οὔ; δῶμεν, ἢ μὴ δῶμεν; ὁ δὲ Ἰησοῦς εἰδὼς αὐτῶν τὴν
ὑπόκρισιν εἶπεν αὐτοῖς, Τί με πειράζετε, ὑποκριταί; φέρετέ μοι δηνά-
16 ριον, ἵνα ἴδω. οἱ δὲ ἤνεγκαν. Τίνος ἡ εἰκὼν αὕτη καὶ ἡ ἐπιγραφή;
17 οἱ δὲ εἶπον, Καίσαρος. καὶ ἀποκριθεὶς ὁ Ἰησοῦς εἶπεν αὐτοῖς, Ἀπό-
δοτε τὰ Καίσαρος Καίσαρι, καὶ τὰ τοῦ Θεοῦ τῷ Θεῷ. καὶ ἐθαύμασαν
ἐπ' αὐτῷ.
18 Καὶ ἔρχονται Σαδδουκαῖοι πρὸς αὐτόν, οἵτινες λέγουσιν ἀνάστασις
19 οὐκ ἔστι· καὶ ἐπηρώτησαν αὐτόν, λέγοντες, Διδάσκαλε, Μωσῆς ἔγραψεν
ἡμῖν, ὅτι ἐάν τινος ἀποθάνῃ, καὶ καταλίπῃ γυναῖκα, καὶ τέκνον μὴ

4 δουλον] pr προς αυτους αλλον 118 ϛ λιθοβολησαντες εκεφαλαιωσαν 118 209 ϛ και ϛ ητιμωμενον ϛ **5** ους bis] τους bis 118 ϛ αποκτεινοντες ϛ **6** ετι ουν 118 ϛ εχων υιον 118 om τον 1° 118 ϛ προς] pr και αυτον 118 ϛ λεγων οτι 118 209 ϛ **7** εαυτους] αυτους 209 ειπον ante προς εαυτους 118 ϛ ουτος] pr οτι 118 ϛ **9** om εκεινους ϛ **13** λογω] 118* primum λογον scripsit postea autem ipse correxit **14** ηρξαντο...λεγοντες] λεγουσιν αυτω ϛ μελλει 118 209 ανθρωπων ϛ **15** om Ιησους ϛ om υποκριται ϛ **16** ηνεγκαν]+και λεγει αυτοις 118 209 ϛ ειπον]+αυτω ϛ **18** αναστασιν μη ειναι 118 ϛ **19** τινος]+αδελφος 118 209 ϛ τεκνα ϛ

ἀφῇ, ἵνα λάβῃ ὁ ἀδελφὸς αὐτοῦ τὴν γυναῖκα, καὶ ἐξαναστήσῃ
σπέρμα τῷ ἀδελφῷ αὐτοῦ· ἑπτὰ ἀδελφοὶ ἦσαν· καὶ ὁ πρῶτος ἔλαβε 20
γυναῖκα, καὶ ἀπέθανε καὶ οὐκ ἀφῆκε σπέρμα· καὶ ὁ δεύτερος ἔλαβεν 21
αὐτήν, καὶ ἀπέθανε, καὶ οὐδὲ αὐτὸς ἀφῆκε σπέρμα· καὶ ὁ τρίτος ἔλα-
βεν αὐτήν· ὡσαύτως οἱ ἑπτά, καὶ οὐκ ἀφῆκαν σπέρμα. ἔσχατον 22
δὲ πάντων καὶ ἡ γυνὴ ἀπέθανεν. ἐν τῇ ἀναστάσει οὖν, ὅταν 23
ἀναστῶσι, τίνος τῶν ἑπτὰ ἔσται γυνή; πάντες γὰρ ἔσχον αὐτὴν
γυναῖκα. ἀποκριθεὶς δὲ ὁ Ἰησοῦς εἶπεν αὐτοῖς, Οὐ διὰ τοῦτο πλα- 24
νᾶσθε, μὴ εἰδότες τὰς γραφάς, μηδὲ τὴν δύναμιν τοῦ Θεοῦ; ὅταν γὰρ 25
ἀναστῶσιν ἐκ νεκρῶν, οὔτε γαμοῦσιν, οὔτε γαμίζονται, ἀλλ' εἰσὶν
ὡς ἄγγελοι ἐν τοῖς οὐρανοῖς. περὶ δὲ τῶν νεκρῶν, ὅτι ἐγείρονται, 26
οὐκ ἀνέγνωτε ἐν τῇ βίβλῳ Μωυσέως, ἐπὶ τοῦ βάτου, ὡς εἶπεν ὁ
Θεός, λέγων, Ἐγὼ ὁ Θεὸς Ἀβραάμ, καὶ ὁ Θεὸς Ἰσαάκ, καὶ ὁ Θεὸς
Ἰακώβ; οὐκ ἔστιν ὁ Θεὸς νεκρῶν, ἀλλὰ ζώντων· ὑμεῖς δὲ πολὺ 27
πλανᾶσθε.

ΛΘ' Καὶ προσελθὼν εἷς τῶν γραμματέων, ἀκούων αὐτῶν συζητούν- 28
ρλα ς των, ἰδὼν ὅτι καλῶς ἀπεκρίθη αὐτοῖς, ἐπηρώτησεν αὐτόν, Ποία
ἐστὶ πρώτη ἐντολή; ὁ δὲ εἶπεν αὐτῷ, Πρῶτον πάντων, Ἄκουε, 29
Ἰσραήλ· Κύριος ὁ Θεὸς ἡμῶν Κύριος εἷς ἐστι. καὶ ἀγαπήσεις Κύριον 30
τὸν Θεόν σου ἐξ ὅλης τῆς καρδίας σου καὶ ἐξ ὅλης τῆς ψυχῆς σου
καὶ ἐξ ὅλης τῆς διανοίας σου καὶ ἐξ ὅλης τῆς ἰσχύος σου. αὕτη
πρώτη ἐντολή. καὶ δευτέρα ὁμοία αὕτη, Ἀγαπήσεις τὸν πλησίον σου 31
ρλβ ι ὡς σεαυτόν. μείζων τούτων ἄλλη ἐντολὴ οὐκ ἔστι. καὶ εἶπεν αὐτῷ ὁ 32
γραμματεύς, Καλῶς, διδάσκαλε, ἐπ' ἀληθείας εἶπας, ὅτι εἷς ἐστι, καὶ
οὐκ ἔστιν ἄλλος πλὴν αὐτοῦ. καὶ τὸ ἀγαπᾷν αὐτὸν ἐξ ὅλης τῆς καρ- 33
δίας καὶ ἐξ ὅλης τῆς ἰσχύος καὶ ἐξ ὅλης τῆς συνέσεως, καὶ
τὸ ἀγαπᾷν τὸν πλησίον ὡς ἑαυτόν, πλεῖόν ἐστι πάντων τῶν ὁλοκαυτω-

22 εσχατον] haud scio an m. prim. εσχατη scripserit et postea correxerit

118 209 ς **19** γυναικα αυτου 118 ς εξαναστησει 118 **20** απεθανε και] αποθνησκων ς **21 22** ωσαυτως· και ελαβον αυτην 118 ς εσχατον] 118 nunc habet ον delet., εσχατη ς om δε 118 ς απεθανε και η γυνη 118 ς **23** ουν ante αναστασει ς των επτα] αυτων 118 ς παντες γαρ] οι γαρ επτα 118 ς γυναικα αυτην 209 **24** και αποκριθεις 118 ς **25** εκ νεκρων αναστωσιν ς γαμισκονται 118 ς αγγελοι οι ς **26** Μωσεως ς, Μωυσεος 118 209 της βατου ς ειπεν αυτω 118 ς Ἀβρααμ ς **27** ζωντων] pr Θεος ς δε] ουν ς **28** ακουσας ς ειδως ς αυτοις απεκριθη ς εντολη] pr παντων 118, pr πασων ς **29** ο δε Ιησους απεκριθη αυτω οτι πρωτη πασων των εντολων 118 ς, sed 118 παντων non πασων **32** εστι] εστι Θεος ς **33** και εξ ολης της συνεσεως, και εξ ολης της ψυχης, και εξ ολης της ισχυος ς

34 μάτων καὶ τῶν θυσιῶν. καὶ ὁ Ἰησοῦς, ἰδὼν ὅτι νουνεχῶς ἀπεκρίθη,
εἶπεν αὐτῷ, Οὐ μακρὰν εἶ ἀπὸ τῆς βασιλείας τοῦ Θεοῦ. καὶ οὐδεὶς ρλγ β
οὐκέτι ἐτόλμα αὐτὸν ἐπερωτῆσαι.
35 Καὶ ἀποκριθεὶς ὁ Ἰησοῦς ἔλεγε διδάσκων ἐν τῷ ἱερῷ, Πῶς λέγουσιν Μ'
36 οἱ γραμματεῖς ὅτι ὁ Χριστὸς υἱὸς Δαβίδ ἐστιν; αὐτὸς γὰρ Δαβὶδ ρλδ β
εἶπεν ἐν Πνεύματι Ἁγίῳ, Εἶπεν ὁ Κύριος τῷ κυρίῳ μου, Κάθου
ἐκ δεξιῶν μου ἕως ἂν θῶ τοὺς ἐχθρούς σου ὑποπόδιον τῶν ποδῶν σου.
37 αὐτὸς οὖν Δαβὶδ λέγει αὐτὸν κύριον· καὶ πῶς υἱὸς αὐτοῦ ἐστι; καὶ
ὁ πολὺς ὄχλος ἤκουεν αὐτοῦ ἡδέως.
38 Καὶ ἔλεγεν ἐν τῇ διδαχῇ αὐτοῦ, Βλέπετε ἀπὸ τῶν γραμματέων τῶν ρλε β
39 θελόντων ἐν στολαῖς περιπατεῖν, καὶ ἀσπασμοὺς ἐν ταῖς ἀγοραῖς καὶ
πρωτοκαθεδρίας ἐν ταῖς συναγωγαῖς καὶ πρωτοκλισίας ἐν τοῖς δείπνοις·
40 οἱ κατεσθίουσιν τὰς οἰκίας τῶν χηρῶν, καὶ προφάσει μακρὰ προσευ- ρλϛ η
χόμενοι· οὗτοι λήψονται περισσότερον κρῖμα.
41 Καὶ ἑστὼς ὁ Ἰησοῦς κατέναντι τοῦ γαζοφυλακίου ἐθεώρει πῶς ὁ ΜΑ'
ὄχλος βάλλει τὸν χαλκὸν εἰς τὸ γαζοφυλάκιον. καὶ πολλοὶ πλούσιοι
42 ἔβαλλον πολλά· καὶ ἐλθοῦσα μία χήρα πτωχὴ ἔβαλε λεπτὰ δύο, ὅ
43 ἐστι κοδράντης. καὶ προσκαλεσάμενος τοὺς μαθητὰς αὐτοῦ λέγει αὐτοῖς,
Ἀμὴν λέγω ὑμῖν ὅτι ἡ χήρα αὕτη ἡ πτωχὴ πλεῖον πάντων βέβληκεν
44 εἰς τὸ γαζοφυλάκιον· πάντες γὰρ οὗτοι ἐκ τοῦ περισσεύοντος αὐτοῖς
ἔβαλον· αὕτη δὲ ἐκ τῆς ὑστερήσεως αὐτῆς πάντα ὅσα εἶχεν ἔβαλεν,
ὅλον τὸν βίον αὐτῆς.
XIII. Καὶ ἐκπορευομένου αὐτοῦ ἐκ τοῦ ἱεροῦ, λέγει αὐτῷ εἷς ἐκ ρλζ β
τῶν μαθητῶν αὐτοῦ, Διδάσκαλε, ἴδε ποταποὶ λίθοι καὶ ποταπαὶ οἰ-
2 κοδομαί. καὶ ἀποκριθεὶς ὁ Ἰησοῦς εἶπεν, Βλέπεις ταύτας τὰς
μεγάλας οἰκοδομάς; λέγω ὑμῖν οὐ μὴ ἀφεθῇ ὧδε λίθος ἐπὶ λίθον,
3 ὃς οὐ μὴ καταλυθῇ. καὶ καθημένου αὐτοῦ εἰς τὸ ὄρος τῶν Ἐλαιῶν ΜΒ'
κατέναντι τοῦ ἱεροῦ, ἐπηρώτων αὐτὸν κατ' ἰδίαν Πέτρος καὶ Ἰάκωβος ρλη β
4 καὶ Ἰωάννης καὶ Ἀνδρέας, Εἰπὸν ἡμῖν, πότε ταῦτα ἔσται, καὶ τί τὸ
5 σημεῖον ὅταν μέλλῃ ταῦτα πάντα συντελεῖσθαι; καὶ ἀποκριθεὶς
αὐτοῖς ὁ Ἰησοῦς ἤρξατο λέγειν, Βλέπετε μή τις ὑμᾶς πλανήσῃ.

34 ιδων αυτον ϛ **35** εστι Δαβιδ ϛ **36** ειπεν εν | ειπεν εν linea exeunte 209 τω πνευματι τω αγιω ϛ ειπεν] λεγει 118 **37** πως] ποθεν ϛ **38** ελεγεν αυτοις 118 ϛ **40** οι κατεσθιοντες ϛ **41** εστως] καθισας 118 ϛ om τον ϛ **43** βεβληκεν]+των βαλοντων ϛ **44** om ουτοι ϛ εβαλλεν 118 209 118 209 ϛ

1 om εκ 2° ϛ **2** ο Ιησους αποκριθεις ϛ ειπεν αυτω ϛ τας μεγαλας ταυτας 118 209 om λεγω υμιν ϛ om ωδε ϛ λιθω ϛ **4** ειπε 118 209 ϛ παντα ταυτα ϛ om παντα 118 209 **5** ο δε Ιησους αποκριθεις αυτοις ϛ αυτοις post λεγειν 118 209

πολλοὶ γὰρ ἐλεύσονται ἐπὶ τῷ ὀνόματί μου, λέγοντες ὅτι Ἐγώ εἰμι, 6
καὶ πολλοὺς πλανήσουσιν. ὅταν δὲ ἀκούσητε πολέμους καὶ ἀκοὰς 7
πολέμων, μὴ θροεῖσθε· δεῖ γὰρ γενέσθαι· ἀλλ' οὔπω τὸ τέλος. ἐγερ- 8
θήσεται γὰρ ἔθνος ἐπ' ἔθνος καὶ βασιλεία ἐπὶ βασιλείαν· καὶ ἔσονται
ρλθ α σεισμοὶ κατὰ τόπους, καὶ ἔσονται λιμοὶ καὶ ταραχαί· ἀρχαὶ ὠδίνων.
καὶ παραδώσουσιν ὑμᾶς εἰς συνέδρια, καὶ εἰς συναγωγὰς δαρήσεσθε, 9
καὶ ἐπὶ ἡγεμόνων καὶ βασιλέων ἀχθήσεσθε ἕνεκεν ἐμοῦ, εἰς μαρτύριον
ρμ ς αὐτοῖς· καὶ εἰς πάντα τὰ ἔθνη δεῖ πρῶτον κηρυχθῆναι τὸ εὐαγγέλιον. 10
ρμα β ὅταν δὲ ἄγωσιν ὑμᾶς παραδιδόντες, μὴ προμεριμνᾶτε τί λαλήσητε, 11
ἀλλ' ὃ ἐὰν δοθῇ ὑμῖν ἐν ἐκείνῃ τῇ ὥρᾳ, τοῦτο λαλήσετε· οὐ γάρ ἐστε
ὑμεῖς οἱ λαλοῦντες, ἀλλὰ τὸ Πνεῦμα τὸ Ἅγιον. παραδώσει δὲ ἀδελφὸς 12
ἀδελφὸν εἰς θάνατον, καὶ πατὴρ τέκνον· καὶ ἐπαναστήσονται τέκνα ἐπὶ
γονεῖς καὶ θανατώσουσιν αὐτούς· καὶ ἔσεσθε μισούμενοι ὑπὸ πάντων διὰ 13
τὸ ὄνομά μου· ὁ δὲ ὑπομείνας εἰς τέλος, οὗτος σωθήσεται.
ρμβ ς Ὅταν δὲ ἴδητε τὸ βδέλυγμα τῆς ἐρημώσεως, τὸ ῥηθὲν διὰ Δανιὴλ 14
τοῦ προφήτου, στῆκον ὅπου οὐ δεῖ (ὁ ἀναγινώσκων νοείτω), τότε οἱ ἐν
ρμγ β τῇ Ἰουδαίᾳ φευγέτωσαν εἰς τὰ ὄρη· ὁ δὲ ἐπὶ τοῦ δώματος μὴ καταβάτω 15
εἰς τὴν οἰκίαν, μηδὲ εἰσελθέτω ἆραί τι ἐκ τῆς οἰκίας αὐτοῦ· καὶ ὁ εἰς 16
ρμδ β τὸν ἀγρὸν μὴ ἐπιστρεψάτω εἰς τὰ ὀπίσω ἆραι τὸ ἱμάτιον αὐτοῦ. οὐαὶ 17
ρμε ς δὲ ταῖς ἐν γαστρὶ ἐχούσαις καὶ ταῖς θηλαζούσαις ἐν ἐκείναις ταῖς ἡμέ-
ραις. προσεύχεσθε δὲ ἵνα μὴ γένηται ἡ φυγὴ ὑμῶν χειμῶνος. ἔσονται 18 19
ρμς β γὰρ αἱ ἡμέραι ἐκεῖναι θλῖψις, οἵα οὐ γέγονε τοιαύτη ἀπ' ἀρχῆς κτίσεως
ρμζ ς ἧς ἔκτισεν ὁ Θεὸς ἕως τοῦ νῦν, οὐδ' οὐ μὴ γένηται. καὶ εἰ μὴ Κύριος 20
ἐκολόβωσε τὰς ἡμέρας ἐκείνας, οὐκ ἂν ἐσώθη πᾶσα σάρξ· διὰ δὲ
ρμη β τοὺς ἐκλεκτοὺς οὓς ἐξελέξατο ἐκολόβωσε τὰς ἡμέρας. τότε ἐάν τις 21
ρμθ ς ὑμῖν εἴπῃ, Ἰδοὺ ὧδε ὁ Χριστός, ἢ ἰδοὺ ἐκεῖ, μὴ πιστεύσητε· ἐγερθή- 22
σονται γὰρ ψευδόχριστοι καὶ ψευδοπροφῆται, καὶ δώσουσι σημεῖα καὶ
τέρατα πρὸς τὸ ἀποπλανᾷν, εἰ δυνατόν, καὶ τοὺς ἐκλεκτούς. ὑμεῖς δὲ 23
ρν β βλέπετε· ἰδοὺ προείρηκα ὑμῖν πάντα. ἀλλ' ἐν ἐκείναις ταῖς ἡμέραις 24
μετὰ τὴν θλῖψιν ἐκείνην ὁ ἥλιος σκοτισθήσεται, καὶ ἡ σελήνη οὐ δώσει
τὸ φέγγος αὐτῆς, καὶ οἱ ἀστέρες τοῦ οὐρανοῦ ἔσονται ἐκπίπτοντες, καὶ 25
ρνα β αἱ δυνάμεις αἱ ἐν τοῖς οὐρανοῖς σαλευθήσονται. καὶ τότε ὄψονται τὸν 26

8 ωδινων] corr. aliquis rubricatore secundo anterior *ταυτα* supr. lin. addidit
18 *εν χειμωνος* cod.

118 209 ς 7 *ακοας πολεμων*] *ακαταστασιας* 118 209 8 *επι εθνος* ς *ωδινων*] + *ταυτα* 118 209 ς 9 *βλεπετε δε υμεις εαυτους· παραδωσουσι γαρ* 118 209 ς *αχθησεσθε*] *σταθησεσθε* ς 11 *αγαγωσιν* ς *λαλησητε*] + *μηδε μελετατε* 118 ς *λαλησετε*] *λαλειτε* ς 14 *δια*] *υπο* ς *εστος* ς 16 *αγρον*] + *ων* 118 ς 19 *ουδ*] *και* ς 20 *εκολωβωσε* bis 118 209 om *εκεινας* ς *δια δε*] *αλλα δια* ς 21 *και τοτε* ς

υἱὸν τοῦ ἀνθρώπου ἐρχόμενον ἐν νεφέλῃ μετὰ δυνάμεως πολλῆς καὶ
27 δόξης. καὶ τότε ἀποστελεῖ τοὺς ἀγγέλους αὐτοῦ, καὶ ἐπισυνάξει τοὺς
ἐκλεκτοὺς ἐκ τῶν τεσσάρων ἀνέμων, ἀπ' ἄκρου τῆς γῆς ἕως ἄκρων
οὐρανῶν.

28 Ἀπὸ δὲ τῆς συκῆς μάθετε τὴν παραβολήν· ὅταν αὐτῆς ἤδη ὁ κλάδος
ἁπαλὸς γένηται καὶ τὰ φύλλα ἐκφυῇ, γινώσκετε ὅτι ἐγγὺς τὸ θέρος
29 ἐστίν· οὕτω καὶ ὑμεῖς, ὅταν ἴδητε ταῦτα γινόμενα, γινώσκετε ὅτι ἐγγύς
30 ἐστιν ἐπὶ θύραις. ἀμὴν λέγω ὑμῖν ὅτι οὐ μὴ παρέλθῃ ἡ γενεὰ αὕτη
31 ἕως ἂν πάντα ταῦτα γένηται. ὁ οὐρανὸς καὶ ἡ γῆ παρελεύσονται, οἱ
δὲ λόγοι μου οὐ μὴ παρέλθωσι.

32 Περὶ δὲ τῆς ἡμέρας ἐκείνης καὶ τῆς ὥρας οὐδεὶς οἶδεν, οὐδὲ οἱ ἄγγελοι ΜΓ'
οἱ ἐν οὐρανῷ, οὐδὲ ὁ υἱός, εἰ μὴ ὁ πατήρ. ρνβ ς

33 Βλέπετε, ἀγρυπνεῖτε καὶ προσεύχεσθε· οὐκ οἴδατε γὰρ πότε ὁ καιρός ρνγ ς
34 ἐστιν. ὥσπερ ἄνθρωπος ἀποδημῶν ἀφεὶς τὴν οἰκίαν αὐτοῦ, καὶ δοὺς
τοῖς δούλοις αὐτοῦ τὴν ἐξουσίαν, καὶ ἑκάστῳ τὸ ἔργον αὐτοῦ, καὶ τῷ ρνδ β
35 θυρωρῷ ἐνετείλατο ἵνα γρηγορῇ· γρηγορεῖτε οὖν· οὐκ οἴδατε γὰρ πότε ρνε β
ὁ κύριος τῆς οἰκίας ἔρχεται, ὀψέ, ἢ μεσονυκτίου, ἢ ἀλεκτοροφωνίας, ἢ
36 37 πρωΐ· μὴ ἐλθὼν ἐξαίφνης εὕρῃ ὑμᾶς καθεύδοντας. ἃ δὲ λέγω ὑμῖν,
πᾶσι λέγω, Γρηγορεῖτε.

XIV. Ἦν δὲ τὸ πάσχα καὶ τὰ ἄζυμα μετὰ δύο ἡμέρας· καὶ ἐζήτουν ρνς α
οἱ ἀρχιερεῖς καὶ οἱ γραμματεῖς πῶς αὐτὸν δόλῳ κρατήσαντες ἀποκτεί- ρνζ ς
2 νωσιν· ἔλεγον δέ, Μὴ ἐν τῇ ἑορτῇ, μήποτε θόρυβος ἔσται τοῦ λαοῦ.
3 καὶ ὄντος αὐτοῦ ἐν Βηθανίᾳ ἐν τῇ οἰκίᾳ Σίμωνος τοῦ λεπροῦ, κατα- ΜΔ'
κειμένου αὐτοῦ ἦλθε γυνὴ ἔχουσα ἀλάβαστρον μύρου νάρδου πιστικῆς ρνη α
πολυτίμου· καὶ συντρίψασα τὸ ἀλάβαστρον κατέχεεν αὐτοῦ τῆς κεφα-
4 λῆς. ἦσαν δέ τινες ἀγανακτοῦντες καὶ λέγοντες πρὸς ἑαυτούς, Εἰς
5 τί ἡ ἀπώλεια αὕτη γέγονεν; ἠδύνατο γὰρ τοῦτο τὸ μύρον πραθῆναι
ἐπάνω τριακοσίων δηναρίων καὶ δοθῆναι τοῖς πτωχοῖς· καὶ ἐνεβριμῶντο
6 αὐτῇ πολλά. ὁ δὲ Ἰησοῦς εἶπεν, Ἄφετε αὐτήν· τί αὐτῇ κόπους παρ-
7 έχετε; καλὸν ἔργον εἰργάσατο ἐν ἐμοί. πάντοτε γὰρ τοὺς πτωχοὺς
ἔχετε μεθ' ἑαυτῶν, καὶ ὅταν θέλητε δύνασθε αὐτοῖς εὖ ποιῆσαι· ἐμὲ
8 δὲ οὐ πάντοτε ἔχετε. ὃ εἶχεν ἐποίησε· προέλαβε μυρίσαι μου τὸ ρνθ δ

35 αλεκτοροφονιας cod.

26 νεφελαις ϛ και δοξης πολλης 118 **27** εκλεκτους αυτου 118 ϛ 118 209 ϛ
της γης ϛ ακρου ουρανου ϛ **28** εκφυη τα φυλλα 118 209 ϛ **29** ταυτα
ιδητε ϛ **30** εως αν] μεχρις ου ϛ **34** ωσπερ] ως ϛ αποδημος ϛ
36 ημας] υμας ϛ **37** υμιν λεγω ϛ

1 εν δολω ϛ **3** πολυτελους ϛ κατα της κεφ. 118 209 ϛ **4** προς
εαυτους και λεγοντες ϛ αυτη]+του μυρου ϛ **5** om το μυρον ϛ om
πολλα ϛ **6** εν εμοι] εις εμε ϛ **7** αυτοις] αυτους 118 209 ϛ **8** ειχεν]
+αυτη 118 209[2] ϛ

σῶμα πρὸς τὸν ἐνταφιασμόν. ἀμὴν λέγω ὑμῖν, ὅπου ἐὰν κηρυχθῇ τὸ 9
εὐαγγέλιον τοῦτο εἰς ὅλον τὸν κόσμον, καὶ ὃ ἐποίησεν αὕτη λαληθή-
ρξ/β σεται εἰς μνημόσυνον αὐτῆς. καὶ Ἰούδας ὁ Ἰσκαριώτης, εἷς τῶν 10
δώδεκα, ἀπῆλθε πρὸς τοὺς ἀρχιερεῖς, ἵνα παραδῷ αὐτὸν αὐτοῖς· οἱ δὲ 11
ἀκούσαντες ἐχάρησαν, καὶ συνέθεντο ἀργύριον αὐτῷ δοῦναι· καὶ
ἐζήτει πῶς εὐκαίρως αὐτὸν παραδῷ.
ΜΕ' Καὶ τῇ πρώτῃ ἡμέρᾳ τῶν ἀζύμων, ὅτε τὸ πάσχα ἔθυον, λέγουσιν 12
αὐτῷ οἱ μαθηταὶ αὐτοῦ, Ποῦ θέλεις ἀπελθόντες ἑτοιμάσομεν ἵνα
φάγῃς τὸ πάσχα; καὶ ἀποστέλλει δύο τῶν μαθητῶν αὐτοῦ καὶ λέγει 13
αὐτοῖς, Ὑπάγετε εἰς τὴν πόλιν· καὶ ἀπαντήσει ὑμῖν ἄνθρωπος κεράμιον
ὕδατος βαστάζων· ἀκολουθήσατε αὐτῷ, καὶ ὅπου ἐὰν εἰσέλθῃ εἴπατε τῷ 14
οἰκοδεσπότῃ ὅτι Ὁ διδάσκαλος λέγει, Ποῦ ἐστι τὸ κατάλυμά μου ὅπου
τὸ πάσχα μετὰ τῶν μαθητῶν μου φάγομαι; κἀκεῖνος ὑμῖν δείξει 15
ἀνώγεον μέγα ἐστρωμένον ἕτοιμον· ἐκεῖ ἑτοιμάσατε ἡμῖν. καὶ ἐξῆλθον 16
οἱ μαθηταὶ καὶ ἦλθον εἰς τὴν πόλιν, καὶ εὗρον καθὼς εἶπεν αὐτοῖς,
καὶ ἡτοίμασαν τὸ πάσχα.
Μϛ' Καὶ ὀψίας γενομένης ἔρχεται μετὰ τῶν δώδεκα· καὶ ἀνακειμένων 17 18
ρξα/δ αὐτῶν καὶ ἐσθιόντων εἶπεν ὁ Ἰησοῦς, Ἀμὴν λέγω ὑμῖν ὅτι εἷς ἐξ
ρξβ/α ὑμῶν παραδώσει με, ὁ ἐσθίων μετ' ἐμοῦ. οἱ δὲ ἤρξαντο λυπεῖσθαι, 19
καὶ λέγειν αὐτῷ εἷς καθ' εἷς, Μή τι ἐγώ; καὶ ἄλλος, Μή τι ἐγώ;
ρξγ/β ὁ δὲ ἀποκριθεὶς εἶπεν αὐτοῖς, Εἷς ἐκ τῶν δώδεκα, ὁ ἐμβαπτόμενος 20
μετ' ἐμοῦ εἰς τὸ τρυβλίον. ὁ μὲν υἱὸς τοῦ ἀνθρώπου ὑπάγει, καθὼς 21
γέγραπται περὶ αὐτοῦ· οὐαὶ δὲ τῷ ἀνθρώπῳ ἐκείνῳ δι' οὗ ὁ υἱὸς τοῦ
ρξδ/ϛ ἀνθρώπου παραδίδοται· καλὸν ἦν αὐτῷ, εἰ οὐκ ἐγεννήθη ὁ ἄνθρωπος
ἐκεῖνος.
ρξε/α Καὶ ἐσθιόντων αὐτῶν, λαβὼν ὁ Ἰησοῦς ἄρτον, εὐλογήσας ἔκλασε 22
ρξϛ/β καὶ ἐδίδου αὐτοῖς, καὶ εἶπε, Λάβετε, τοῦτό ἐστι τὸ σῶμά μου. καὶ 23
λαβὼν ποτήριον, εὐχαριστήσας ἔδωκεν αὐτοῖς· καὶ ἔπιον ἐξ αὐτοῦ
πάντες· καὶ εἶπεν αὐτοῖς, Τοῦτό ἐστι τὸ αἷμά μου τὸ τῆς καινῆς δια- 24
θήκης, τὸ περὶ πολλῶν ἐκχυνόμενον. ἀμὴν λέγω ὑμῖν ὅτι οὐκέτι οὐ μὴ 25
πίω ἐκ τοῦ γενήματος τῆς ἀμπέλου, ἕως τῆς ἡμέρας ἐκείνης ὅταν
αὐτὸ πίνω καινὸν ἐν τῇ βασιλείᾳ τοῦ Θεοῦ.
ρξζ/ϛ Καὶ ὑμνήσαντες ἐξῆλθον εἰς τὸ ὄρος τῶν Ἐλαιῶν. καὶ λέγει αὐτοῖς 26 27

18 εσθιωντων cod.

118 209 ϛ

8 προς] εις ϛ 9 εαν] αν ϛ λαληθησεται post αυτης 118 209 10 ο Ιουδας ϛ 11 επηγγειλατο αυτω αργυριον ϛ 12 ετοιμασωμεν ϛ 14 om μου 1° 118 209 ϛ φαγωμαι 118, φαγω ϛ 15 κακεινος] και αυτος ϛ αγωγεων 209, ανωγε spat. rel. 118* in quo ων add. 118[2] 16 μαθηται αυτου ϛ 22 εδιδου] εδωκεν ϛ λαβετε]+φαγετε 118 ϛ 23 το ποτηριον ϛ 25 αμην δε 118 γεννηματος ϛ

ὁ Ἰησοῦς ὅτι Πάντες σκανδαλισθήσεσθε ἐν ἐμοὶ ἐν τῇ νυκτὶ ταύτῃ· ρξη
ὅτι γέγραπται, Πατάξω τὸν ποιμένα, καὶ διασκορπισθήσονται τὰ πρό- δ
28 βατα. ἀλλὰ μετὰ τὸ ἐγερθῆναί με προάξω ὑμᾶς εἰς τὴν Γαλιλαίαν. ρξθ
29 ὁ δὲ Πέτρος ἀποκριθεὶς λέγει αὐτῷ, Εἰ καὶ πάντες σκανδαλισθή- ϛ ρο
30 σονται ἐν σοί, ἀλλ' οὐκ ἐγώ. καὶ λέγει αὐτῷ ὁ Ἰησοῦς, Ἀμὴν λέγω α
σοι, ὅτι σὺ σήμερον τῇ νυκτὶ ταύτῃ, πρὶν ἢ δὶς ἀλέκτορα φωνῆ-
31 σαι, τρίς ἀπαρνήσῃ με. ὁ δὲ Πέτρος μᾶλλον ἐκ περισσοῦ ἔλεγεν ροα
ὅτι Ἐὰν δέῃ με σύν σοι ἀποθανεῖν, οὐ μή σε ἀπαρνήσομαι· ὡσαύτως ϛ
καὶ πάντες ἔλεγον.

32 Καὶ ἔρχονται εἰς χωρίον οὗ τὸ ὄνομα Γηθσεμανεί· καὶ λέγει ροβ
33 τοῖς μαθηταῖς αὐτοῦ, Καθίσατε αὐτοῦ ἕως προσεύξωμαι. καὶ παρα- α ρογ
λαμβάνει τὸν Πέτρον καὶ τὸν Ἰάκωβον καὶ Ἰωάννην μεθ' ἑαυτοῦ· καὶ ϛ
34 ἤρξατο λυπεῖσθαι καὶ ἀδημονεῖν· καὶ λέγει αὐτοῖς, Περίλυπός ἐστιν ροδ
35 ἡ ψυχή μου ἕως θανάτου· μείνατε ὧδε καὶ γρηγορεῖτε μετ' ἐμοῦ. καὶ δ ροε
προσελθὼν μικρὸν ἔπεσεν ἐπὶ πρόσωπον ἐπὶ τῆς γῆς, καὶ προσ- α
36 ηύξατο, εἰ δυνατόν ἐστι, ἵνα παρέλθῃ ἀπ' αὐτοῦ ἡ ὥρα· καὶ ἔλεγεν,
Ἀββᾶ ὁ πατήρ, πάντα δυνατά σοί· παρένεγκε τοῦτο τὸ ποτήριον ἀπ' ροϛ
37 ἐμοῦ· ἀλλ' οὐ τί ἐγὼ θέλω, ἀλλ' ὅ τι σύ. καὶ ἔρχεται καὶ εὑρίσκει α ροζ
αὐτοὺς καθεύδοντας, καὶ λέγει τῷ Πέτρῳ, Σίμων, καθεύδεις; οὐκ ἰσχύ- β
38 σατε μίαν ὥραν γρηγορῆσαι; γρηγορεῖτε καὶ προσεύχεσθε ἵνα μὴ εἰσ-
έλθητε εἰς πειρασμόν· τὸ μὲν πνεῦμα πρόθυμον, ἡ δὲ σὰρξ ἀσθενής. ροη
39 40 καὶ πάλιν ἀπελθὼν προσηύξατο τὸν αὐτὸν λόγον εἰπών· καὶ ὑποστρέψας δ ροθ
εὗρεν αὐτοὺς πάλιν καθεύδοντας· ἦσαν γὰρ οἱ ὀφθαλμοὶ αὐτῶν κατα- ϛ
βαρυνόμενοι, καὶ οὐκ ᾔδεισαν τί αὐτῷ ἀποκριθῶσι.

41 Καὶ ἔρχεται τὸ τρίτον, καὶ λέγει αὐτοῖς, Καθεύδετε τὸ λοιπὸν καὶ ρπ
ἀναπαύεσθε. ἀπέχει, ἦλθεν ἡ ὥρα· ἰδοὺ παραδίδοται ὁ υἱὸς τοῦ ἀνθρώ- δ
42 που εἰς χεῖρας τῶν ἁμαρτωλῶν. ἐγείρεσθε, ἄγωμεν· ἰδοὺ ὁ παραδιδούς
με ἤγγικε.

43 Καὶ ἔτι αὐτοῦ λαλοῦντος παραγίνεται Ἰούδας, εἷς ὢν τῶν δώδεκα, ρπα α

27 διασκορπισθησωνται cod. **34** μετ' εμου] μετ' ου cod.

27 διασκορπισθησεται ϛ **29** om αποκριθεις ϛ λεγει] εφη ϛ και 118 209 ϛ
ει ϛ om εν σοι ϛ **30** om συ ϛ εν τη ϛ πριν αλεκτορα φωνησαι
δις τρις 209² in marg. **31** om Πετρος ϛ μαλλον post ελεγεν ϛ om
οτι ϛ με δεη συναποθανειν σοι ϛ και] δε και ϛ **32** ερχεται 209,
ερχονται 118 Γεθσημανη 118 ϛ, Γεθσημανι 209 αυτου] ωδε ϛ προσευ-
ξομαι 209, απελθων προσευξομαι 118 **33** λυπυσθαι 118, εκθαμβεισθαι ϛ
34 om μετ εμου ϛ **35** προελθων ϛ om επι προσωπον ϛ προσηυχετο
ινα ϛ om ινα ϛ **36** τουτο post εμου ϛ αλλα τι ϛ **37** ισχυσας ϛ
40 βεβαρημενοι 118 ϛ **41** τας χειρας ϛ **43** ετι] pr ευθεως ϛ

καὶ μετ' αὐτοῦ ὄχλος πολὺς μετὰ μαχαιρῶν καὶ ξύλων ἀπεσταλμένοι
ρπβ παρὰ τῶν ἀρχιερέων καὶ γραμματέων καὶ πρεσβυτέρων. δεδώκει 44
β δὲ ὁ παραδιδοὺς αὐτὸν σύσσημον αὐτοῖς, λέγων, Ὃν ἂν φιλήσω, αὐτός
ἐστι· κρατήσατε αὐτὸν καὶ ἀπαγάγετε ἀσφαλῶς. καὶ εὐθέως προσελ- 45
θὼν αὐτῷ λέγει, Χαῖρε Ῥαββί, καὶ κατεφίλησεν αὐτόν. οἱ δὲ ἐπέβαλον 46
τὰς χεῖρας αὐτῷ καὶ ἐκράτησαν αὐτόν.

ρπγ Καὶ εἷς τις τῶν παρεστηκότων σπασάμενος μάχαιραν ἔπαισε τὸν 47
α ρπδ δοῦλον τοῦ ἀρχιερέως καὶ ἀφεῖλεν αὐτοῦ τὸ ὠτάριον. καὶ ἀποκριθεὶς 48
α ὁ Ἰησοῦς εἶπεν αὐτοῖς, Ὡς ἐπὶ λῃστὴν ἐξήλθετε μετὰ μαχαιρῶν καὶ
ξύλων συλλαβεῖν με; καθ' ἡμέραν ἤμην πρὸς ὑμᾶς ἐν τῷ ἱερῷ δι- 49
ρπε δάσκων, καὶ οὐκ ἐκρατήσατέ με· ἀλλ' ἵνα πληρωθῶσιν αἱ γραφαί. καὶ 50
ϛ ρπϛ ἀφέντες αὐτὸν πάντες ἔφυγον. καὶ εἷς τις νεανίσκος ἠκολούθει αὐτῷ 51
ι περιβεβλημένος σινδόνα. οἱ δὲ νεανίσκοι κρατοῦσιν αὐτόν· ὁ δὲ 52
καταλιπὼν τὴν σινδόνα γυμνὸς ἔφυγεν ἀπ' αὐτῶν.

ρπζ Καὶ ἀπήγαγον τὸν Ἰησοῦν πρὸς τὸν ἀρχιερέα· καὶ συνέρχονται 53
α ρπη αὐτοῦ πάντες οἱ ἀρχιερεῖς καὶ οἱ πρεσβύτεροι καὶ οἱ γραμματεῖς. καὶ 54
δ ὁ Πέτρος ἀπὸ μακρόθεν ἠκολούθει αὐτῷ ἕως τῆς αὐλῆς τοῦ ἀρχιε-
ρέως· καὶ ἦν συγκαθήμενος μετὰ τῶν ὑπηρετῶν καὶ θερμαινόμενος.
ρπθ οἱ δὲ ἀρχιερεῖς καὶ ὅλον τὸ συνέδριον ἐζήτουν κατὰ τοῦ Ἰησοῦ μαρτυ- 55
β ρίαν εἰς τὸ θανατῶσαι αὐτόν· καὶ οὐχ ηὕρισκον· πολλοὶ γὰρ ἐψευδο- 56
ρϟ μαρτύρουν κατ' αὐτοῦ, καὶ ἴσαι αἱ μαρτυρίαι οὐκ ἦσαν. καί τινες 57
ϛ ἀναστάντες ἐψευδομαρτύρουν κατ' αὐτοῦ λέγοντες ὅτι Ἡμεῖς ἠκούσαμεν 58
αὐτοῦ λέγοντος ὅτι Ἐγὼ καταλύσω τὸν ναὸν τοῦτον τὸν χειροποίητον,
καὶ διὰ ἡμερῶν τριῶν ἄλλον ἀχειροποίητον οἰκοδομήσω. καὶ οὐδὲ 59
οὕτως ἦν ἴση ἡ μαρτυρία αὐτῶν. καὶ ἀναστὰς ὁ ἀρχιερεὺς εἰς τὸ 60
μέσον ἐπηρώτησε τὸν Ἰησοῦν λέγων, Οὐκ ἀποκρίνῃ οὐδέν; τί οὗτοί
σου καταμαρτυροῦσιν; ὁ δὲ ἐσιώπα καὶ οὐδὲν ἀπεκρίνατο. καὶ πάλιν 61
ὁ ἀρχιερεὺς ἐπηρώτα αὐτὸν λέγων αὐτῷ, Σὺ εἶ ὁ Χριστὸς ὁ υἱὸς τοῦ
εὐλογητοῦ; ὁ δὲ Ἰησοῦς ἀποκριθεὶς εἶπεν αὐτῷ, Ἐγώ εἰμι· καὶ 62
ρϟα ὄψεσθε τὸν υἱὸν τοῦ ἀνθρώπου καθήμενον ἐκ δεξιῶν τῆς δυνάμεως
α ρϟβ καὶ ἐρχόμενον ἐπὶ τῶν νεφελῶν τοῦ οὐρανοῦ. ὁ δὲ ἀρχιερεὺς διαρρήξας 63
ϛ

118 209 ϛ **43** om *απεσταλμενοι* ϛ *των γραμμ. και των πρεσβ.* ϛ **44** *εδεδωκει* 118 209 **45** *ευθεως*] pr *ελθων* ϛ *χαιρε*] *ραββι* ϛ *επ αυτον τας χειρας αυτων* 118 ϛ sed ni fallor 118* primum scripsit id quod habent 1 209 statim autem ipse correxit **47** *εις δε τις* 118 ϛ *την μαχαιραν* ϛ *ωτιον* ϛ **51** *σινδονα*]+*ετι γυμνου* ϛ *και κρατουσιν αυτον οι νεανισκοι* ϛ **53** *αρχιερεα*]+*Καιαφαν* 118 209 *αυτου*] *αυτω* 118 209 ϛ *οι*] *ι* 118 **54** *ηκολουθησεν* ϛ *εως εσω εις την αυλην* ϛ *θερμαινομενος*]+*προς το φως* 118[2] in mg. ϛ **55** *ευρισκον* 118[2] ϛ **56** *αυτου*]+*λεγοντες* 118 209 **58** *δια τριων ημερων* ϛ **59** *ιση ην* ϛ **61** om *και* ϛ *λεγων*] *και λεγει* ϛ **62** om *αποκριθεις* ϛ om *αυτω* ϛ *εκ δεξιων καθημενον* 118 209 *επι*] *μετα* ϛ

64 τοὺς χιτῶνας αὐτοῦ λέγει, Τί ἔτι χρείαν ἔχομεν μαρτύρων; ἠκούσατε ρϟγ β
πάντες τὴν βλασφημίαν αὐτοῦ· τί ὑμῖν φαίνεται; καὶ πάντες
65 κατέκριναν αὐτὸν εἶναι ἔνοχον θανάτου. καὶ ἤρξαντό τινες ἐμπτύειν ρϟδ α
αὐτῷ, καὶ περικαλύπτειν τὸ πρόσωπον αὐτοῦ καὶ κολαφίζειν αὐτὸν καὶ
λέγειν, Προφήτευσον νῦν· καὶ οἱ ὑπηρέται ῥαπίσμασιν αὐτὸν ἐλάμ-
βανον.
66 Καὶ ὄντος τοῦ Πέτρου ἐν τῇ αὐλῇ κάτω, ἔρχεται μία τῶν παιδισκῶν ΜΖ′
67 τοῦ ἀρχιερέως, καὶ ἰδοῦσα αὐτὸν θερμαινόμενον ἐμβλέψασα αὐτῷ λέγει, ρϟε α
68 Καὶ σὺ μετὰ τοῦ Ναζαρηνοῦ Ἰησοῦ ἦς. ὁ δὲ ἠρνήσατο λέγων, Οὐκ
οἶδα, οὔτε ἐπίσταμαι· σὺ τί λέγεις; καὶ ἐξῆλθεν εἰς τὴν ἔξω αὐλήν· ρϟϛ α
69 καὶ ἀλέκτωρ ἐφώνησε. καὶ ἡ παιδίσκη ἰδοῦσα αὐτὸν πάλιν ἤρξατο λέγειν
70 αὐτοῖς παρεστηκόσιν ὅτι Οὗτος ἐξ αὐτῶν ἐστιν. ὁ δὲ πάλιν ἠρνή-
σατο. καὶ μετὰ μικρὸν πάλιν οἱ περιεστῶτες ἔλεγον τῷ Πέτρῳ,
71 Ἀληθῶς ἐξ αὐτῶν εἶ· καὶ γὰρ Γαλιλαῖος εἶ. ὁ δὲ ἤρξατο ἀναθεματί-
72 ζειν καὶ ὀμνύειν ὅτι Οὐκ οἶδα τὸν ἄνθρωπον τοῦτον ὃν λέγετε· καὶ ἐκ ρϟζ β
δευτέρου ἀλέκτωρ ἐφώνησε. καὶ ἀναμνησθεὶς ὁ Πέτρος τοῦ ῥήματος
τοῦ Ἰησοῦ εἰπόντος ὅτι Πρὶν ἀλέκτορα φωνῆσαι δίς, ἀπαρνήσῃ με
τρίς, ἐπιβαλὼν ἔκλαιε.

XV. Καὶ εὐθέως ἐπὶ τὸ πρωῒ συμβούλιον ποιήσαντες οἱ ἀρχιερεῖς ρϟη β
μετὰ τῶν πρεσβυτέρων καὶ γραμματέων, καὶ ὅλον τὸ συνέδριον, δήσαντες ρϟθ
2 τὸν Ἰησοῦν ἀπήγαγον καὶ παρέδωκαν Πιλάτῳ. καὶ ἐπηρώτησεν αὐτὸν α
ὁ Πιλάτος, Σὺ εἶ ὁ βασιλεὺς τῶν Ἰουδαίων; ὁ δὲ ἀποκριθεὶς λέγει σ α
3 4 αὐτῷ, Σὺ λέγεις. καὶ κατηγόρουν αὐτοῦ οἱ ἀρχιερεῖς πολλά· ὁ δὲ σα
Πιλάτος πάλιν ἐπηρώτησεν αὐτὸν λέγων, Οὐκ ἀποκρίνῃ οὐδέν; ἴδε δ
5 πόσα σου κατηγοροῦσιν· ὁ δὲ Ἰησοῦς οὐκέτι οὐδὲν ἀπεκρίνατο,
ὥστε θαυμάζειν τὸν Πιλάτον.
6 7 Κατὰ δὲ ἑορτὴν ἀπέλυεν αὐτοῖς ἕνα δέσμιον, ὃν ᾐτοῦντο. ἦν δὲ ὁ σβ β
λεγόμενος Βαραββᾶς μετὰ τῶν στασιαστῶν δεδεμένος, οἵτινες ἐν τῇ σγ
8 στάσει φόνον πεποιήκεισαν. καὶ ἀναβοήσας ὁ ὄχλος ἤρξατο αἰτεῖσθαι, δ

64 om παντες ϛ της βλασφημιας 118 209 ϛ om αυτου ϛ οι δε 118 209
παντες ϛ **65** λεγειν αυτω 118 ϛ om νυν ϛ ελαμβανον] εβαλον 118 ϛ
209, εβαλλον ϛ **67** αυτον] τον Πετρον ϛ ης] ησθας, om 118* spat. rel.
in quo 118[2] ησθα scripsit **68** ουκ] ουτε 118 209 ουτε] ουδε ϛ τι συ ϛ
εξω εις το προαυλιον ϛ **69** αυτοις] τοις 118 209 ϛ **70** ηρνειτο ϛ
παρεστωτες 118 209 ϛ ει 2°] + και η λαλια σου ομοιαζει ϛ **71** τουτον]
om 118* 209 sed ins. 118[2] in mg. **72** ανεμνησθη ϛ ου ειπεν αυτω ο
Ιησους ϛ και επιβαλων ϛ

1 απηγαγον] απηνεγκαν ϛ τω Πιλατω ϛ **2** ειπεν αυτω ϛ **4** om
λεγων 209 αποκρινη (ει supra) 118 καταμαρτυρουσιν ϛ **5** απεκριθη ϛ
6 ουπερ ητουντο 118 209 ϛ **7** συστασιαστων 118 209 ϛ

καθὼς ἀεὶ ἐποίει αὐτοῖς. ὁ δὲ Πιλάτος ἀπεκρίθη αὐτοῖς λέγων, Θέλετε 9
ἀπολύσω ὑμῖν τὸν βασιλέα τῶν Ἰουδαίων; ᾔδει γὰρ ὅτι διὰ φθόνον 10
σδ/α παρέδωκαν αὐτόν. οἱ δὲ ἀρχιερεῖς ἀνέσεισαν τὸν ὄχλον, ἵνα μᾶλ- 11
σε/α λον τὸν Βαραββᾶν ἀπολύσῃ αὐτοῖς. ὁ δὲ Πιλάτος ἀποκριθεὶς πάλιν 12
εἶπεν αὐτοῖς, Τί οὖν ποιήσω τὸν βασιλέα τῶν Ἰουδαίων; οἱ δὲ 13
πάλιν ἔκραζον, Σταύρωσον αὐτόν. ὁ δὲ Πιλάτος ἔλεγεν αὐτοῖς, Τί 14
γὰρ κακὸν ἐποίησεν; οἱ δὲ περισσῶς ἔκραζον, Σταύρωσον αὐτόν.
σϛ/α ὁ δὲ Πιλάτος βουλόμενος τῷ ὄχλῳ τὸ ἱκανὸν ποιῆσαι ἀπέλυσεν αὐτοῖς 15
τὸν Βαραββᾶν, καὶ παρέδωκε τὸν Ἰησοῦν, φραγελλώσας, ἵνα σταυρωθῇ.
σζ/δ Οἱ δὲ στρατιῶται ὑπήγαγον αὐτὸν ἔσω εἰς τὴν αὐλήν, ὅ ἐστι 16
πραιτώριον, καὶ συγκαλοῦσιν ὅλην τὴν σπεῖραν, καὶ ἐνδιδύσκουσιν 17
αὐτὸν πορφύραν καὶ περιτιθέασιν αὐτῷ πλέξαντες στέφανον ἐξ ἀκάν-
θων, καὶ ἤρξαντο ἀσπάζεσθαι αὐτόν, Χαῖρε, βασιλεῦ τῶν Ἰουδαίων, καὶ 18 19
ἔτυπτον αὐτοῦ τὴν κεφαλὴν καλάμῳ, καὶ ἐνέπτυον αὐτῷ, καὶ τιθέντες
ση/ϛ τὰ γόνατα προσεκύνουν αὐτῷ. καὶ ὅτε ἐνέπαιξαν αὐτῷ, ἐξέδυσαν αὐτὸν 20
σθ/α τὴν χλαμύδα καὶ ἐνέδυσαν αὐτὸν τὰ ἱμάτια τὰ ἴδια· καὶ ἐξάγουσιν
αὐτὸν ὥστε σταυρῶσαι· καὶ ἀγγαρεύουσι παράγοντα Σίμωνά τινα 21
Κυρηναῖον, ἐρχόμενον ἀπὸ ἀγροῦ, τὸν πατέρα Ἀλεξάνδρου καὶ Ῥούφου,
ἵνα ἄρῃ τὸν σταυρὸν αὐτοῦ.
σι/α Καὶ φέρουσιν αὐτὸν ἐπὶ Γολγοθᾶ τόπον, ὅ ἐστι μεθερμηνευόμενον 22
σια/δ Κρανίου τόπος. καὶ ἐδίδουν αὐτῷ πιεῖν ἐσμυρνισμένον οἶνον· καὶ 23
σιβ/α γευσάμενος οὐκ ἔλαβε. καὶ σταυρώσαντες αὐτὸν διαμερίζονται 24
σιγ/ι τὰ ἱμάτια αὐτοῦ, βάλλοντες κλῆρον ἐπ' αὐτά, τίς τί ἄρῃ. ἦν δὲ ὥρα 25
τρίτη, καὶ ἐσταύρωσαν αὐτόν. καὶ ἦν ἡ ἐπιγραφὴ τῆς αἰτίας αὐτοῦ 26
σιδ/α ἐπιγεγραμμένη, Ὁ βασιλεὺς τῶν Ἰουδαίων. καὶ σὺν αὐτῷ σταυροῦσι 27
σιε/α δύο λῃστάς, ἕνα ἐκ δεξιῶν καὶ ἕνα ἐξ εὐωνύμων· καὶ ἐπληρώθη ἡ 28
σιϛ/η γραφὴ ἡ λέγουσα, Καὶ μετὰ ἀνόμων ἐλογίσθη. καὶ οἱ παραπορευόμενοι 29
σιζ/ϛ ἐβλασφήμουν αὐτὸν κινοῦντες τὰς κεφαλὰς αὐτῶν καὶ λέγοντες, Οὐὰ

20 ενεπαιξαν] ενεπεξαν cod.

118 209 ϛ

10 ηδει] εγινωσκε 118 209 ϛ   παρεδωκαν] παρεδεδωκεισαν 118 209, παραδεδωκεισαν ϛ   αυτον] + οι αρχιερεις 118 209 ϛ   **11** οι δε αρχιερεις] ουτοι δε 118 209   **12** θελετε ποιησω 118 209 ϛ   τον] ον λεγετε ϛ   **13** εκραξαν 118 209 ϛ   **14** περισσοτερως εκραξαν ϛ   **16** αυτον] αυτω 118* sed ipse correxit   εις την αυλην] της αυλης ϛ   **17** ενδυουσιν ϛ   ακανθινον στεφανον 118 209 ϛ   **18** αυτον] + και λεγειν 118 209   **20** χλαμυδα] πορφυραν 118 209 ϛ   τα ιδια] 118* omisisse videtur sed errore statim detecto και εξ delevit et δια perrexit spat. rel. in quo 118[2] τα ι scripsit   εξαγωσιν 118   ινα σταυρωσωσιν αυτον 118 209 ϛ   **21** τινα Σιμωνα 118 ϛ   απο] απ ϛ   **23** εδιδου 118 209*   και γευσαμενος] ο δε ϛ, και γευσαμεν spat. rel. 118* om ελαβε 118* spat. rel. in quo 118[2] ο δε ουκ ελαβεν scripsit et, litteris evanescentibus, 118[3] rescripsit   **24** διεμεριζον ϛ   **27** ευωνυμων αυτου ϛ

30 ὁ καταλύων τὸν ναὸν καὶ ἐν τρισὶν ἡμέραις οἰκοδομῶν, σῶσον σεαυτὸν
31 καὶ κατάβηθι ἀπὸ τοῦ σταυροῦ. ὁμοίως καὶ οἱ ἀρχιερεῖς ἐμπαίζοντες σιη
πρὸς ἀλλήλους μετὰ τῶν γραμματέων ἔλεγον, Ἄλλους ἔσωσεν, ἑαυτὸν β
32 οὐ δύναται σῶσαι. ὁ Χριστὸς ὁ βασιλεὺς Ἰσραὴλ καταβάτω νῦν ἀπὸ
τοῦ σταυροῦ, ἵνα ἴδωμεν καὶ πιστεύσωμεν αὐτῷ. καὶ οἱ συνεσταυ- σιθ
33 ρωμένοι αὐτῷ ὠνείδιζον αὐτῷ. καὶ γενομένης ὥρας ἕκτης σκότος β σκ
34 ἐγένετο ἐφ' ὅλην τὴν γῆν ἕως ὥρας ἐνάτης· καὶ τῇ ἐνάτῃ ὥρᾳ β
ἐβόησεν ὁ Ἰησοῦς φωνῇ μεγάλῃ, λέγων, Ἐλωΐ Ἐλωΐ, λαμᾶ σαβαχ- σκα ς
θανεί; ὅ ἐστι μεθερμηνευόμενον, Ὁ Θεός, ὁ Θεός μου, εἰς τί με
35 ἐγκατέλιπες; καί τινες τῶν παρεστηκότων ἀκούσαντες ἔλεγον, Ἴδε
36 Ἠλίαν φωνεῖ. καὶ δραμὼν εἷς, καὶ γεμίσας σπόγγον ὄξους καὶ περι- σκβ
θεὶς καλάμῳ, ἐπότιζεν αὐτόν, λέγων, Ἄφες ἴδωμεν εἰ ἔρχεται Ἠλίας β
καθελεῖν αὐτόν.
37 38 Ὁ δὲ Ἰησοῦς ἀφεὶς φωνὴν μεγάλην ἐξέπνευσε. καὶ τὸ καταπέ- σκγ α
39 τασμα τοῦ ναοῦ ἐσχίσθη εἰς δύο ἀπὸ ἄνωθεν ἕως κάτω. ἰδὼν δὲ ὁ σκδ
κεντυρίων ὁ παρεστηκὼς αὐτῷ ὅτι οὕτως κράξας ἐξέπνευσεν, εἶπεν, β
40 Ἀληθῶς ὁ ἄνθρωπος οὗτος υἱὸς ἦν Θεοῦ. ἦσαν δὲ καὶ γυναῖκες ἀπὸ σκε β
μακρόθεν θεωροῦσαι, ἐν αἷς ἦν Μαριὰμ ἡ Μαγδαληνὴ καὶ Μαριὰμ σκς
41 ἡ Ἰακώβου τοῦ μικροῦ καὶ Ἰωσῆπος μήτηρ καὶ Σαλώμη, αἳ καὶ ς
ὅτε ἦν ἐν τῇ Γαλιλαίᾳ ἠκολούθουν αὐτῷ καὶ διηκόνουν αὐτῷ, καὶ ἄλλαι
πολλαὶ αἱ συναναβᾶσαι αὐτῷ εἰς Ἱεροσόλυμα.
42 Καὶ ἤδη ὀψίας γενομένης, ἐπεὶ ἦν παρασκευή, ὅ ἐστι προσάββατον, ΜΗ'
43 ἐλθὼν Ἰωσὴφ ὁ ἀπὸ Ἀριμαθαίας, εὐσχήμων βουλευτής, ὃς καὶ αὐτὸς σκζ α
ἦν προσδεχόμενος τὴν βασιλείαν τοῦ Θεοῦ, τολμήσας εἰσῆλθε πρὸς
44 Πιλάτον, καὶ ᾐτήσατο τὸ σῶμα τοῦ Ἰησοῦ. ὁ δὲ Πιλάτος ἐθαύμασεν
εἰ ἤδη τέθνηκε· καὶ προσκαλεσάμενος τὸν κεντυρίωνα ἐπηρώτησεν εἰ
45 πάλαι ἀπέθανε· καὶ γνοὺς παρὰ τοῦ κεντυρίωνος ἐδωρήσατο τὸ σῶμα
46 τῷ Ἰωσήφ. καὶ ἀγοράσας σινδόνα καὶ καθελὼν αὐτὸν ἐνείλησεν ἐν σκη
τῇ σινδόνι, καὶ ἔθηκεν αὐτὸν ἐν μνημείῳ ὃ ἦν λελατομημένον ἐκ τῆς α
πέτρας· καὶ προσκυλίσας λίθον ἐπὶ τὴν θύραν τοῦ μνημείου ἀπῆλ-

30 καταβα ς **31** ομοιως δε ς **32** του Ισραηλ 118 ς om 118 209 ς αυτω 1° ς αυτω 2°] αυτον 118 209 ς **33** γενομενης δε 118 209 ς ενναт. 118 209 ς et sic infra **34** τη ωρα τη εννατη ς ανεβοησεν 118 209 λιμας αβαχθανη 118 209, λαμμα σαβαχθανι ς Θεος 1°]+μου ς **35** ιδου 118 209 ς **36** δραμων δε 118 209 ς om και 3° 118 209 ς περιθεις τε 118 209 ς αφετε 118 209 ς **39** αυτω] εξ εναντιας αυτου 118 209 ς ουτω ς **40** Μαριαμ 1°] και Μαρια ς om η Μαγδαληνη και Μαριαμ 118 Μαριαμ 2°] Μαρια ς του Ιακωβου ς Ιωσηπος] Ιωση 118 209 ς **41** συναναβαινουσαι 209 **43** ελθων] ηλθε ς **44** επηρωτησεν αυτον ς **45** παρα] απο 118 209 ς **46** ενειλισεν 209 om εν 1° ς κατεθηκεν ς om της 118 209 ς προσεκυλισε ς om απηλθεν ς

σκθ ς θεν. ἡ δὲ Μαριὰμ ἡ Μαγδαληνὴ καὶ Μαριὰμ Ἰωσῆτος ἐθεώρουν 47
ποῦ τίθεται.
σλ η XVI. Καὶ διαγενομένου τοῦ σαββάτου Μαριὰμ ἡ Μαγδαληνὴ
καὶ Μαριὰμ Ἰακώβου καὶ Σαλώμη ἠγόρασαν ἀρώματα, ἵνα ἐλθοῦ-
σλα α σαι ἀλείψωσιν αὐτόν. καὶ λίαν πρωῒ μιᾷ σαββάτων ἔρχονται ἐπὶ τὸ 2
μνημεῖον, ἔτι ἀνατείλαντος τοῦ ἡλίου. καὶ ἔλεγον πρὸς ἑαυτάς, Τίς 3
ἀποκυλίσει ἡμῖν τὸν λίθον ἐκ τῆς θύρας τοῦ μνημείου; καὶ ἀναβλέ- 4
ψασαι θεωροῦσιν ὅτι ἀποκεκύλισται ὁ λίθος· ἦν γὰρ μέγας σφόδρα.
καὶ εἰσελθοῦσαι εἰς τὸ μνημεῖον εἶδον νεανίσκον καθήμενον ἐν τοῖς 5
σλβ β δεξιοῖς περιβεβλημένον στολὴν λευκήν, καὶ ἐξεθαμβήθησαν. ὁ δὲ λέγει 6
αὐταῖς, Μὴ ἐκθαμβεῖσθε. Ἰησοῦν ζητεῖτε τὸν Ναζαρηνὸν τὸν ἐσταυρω-
μένον· ἠγέρθη, οὐκ ἔστιν ὧδε· ἴδε ὁ τόπος ὅπου ἔθηκαν αὐτόν. ἀλλ' 7
ὑπάγετε, εἴπατε τοῖς μαθηταῖς αὐτοῦ καὶ τῷ Πέτρῳ, ὅτι ἠγέρθη ἀπὸ
νεκρῶν καὶ ἰδοὺ προάγει ὑμᾶς εἰς τὴν Γαλιλαίαν· ἐκεῖ αὐτὸν ὄψεσθε,
σλγ β καθὼς εἶπεν ὑμῖν. καὶ ἐξελθοῦσαι ἔφυγον ἀπὸ τοῦ μνημείου· εἶχε δὲ 8
αὐτὰς τρόμος καὶ ἔκστασις· καὶ οὐδενὶ οὐδὲν εἶπον, ἐφοβοῦντο γάρ.

Ἔν τισι μὲν τῶν ἀντιγράφων ἕως ὧδε πληροῦται ὁ εὐαγγελιστὴς ἕως οὗ καὶ Εὐσέβιος ὁ Παμφίλου ἐκανόνισεν· ἐν πολλοῖς δὲ καὶ ταῦτα φέρεται·

Ἀναστὰς δὲ πρωῒ πρώτῃ σαββάτων ἐφάνη πρῶτον Μαρίᾳ τῇ 9
Μαγδαληνῇ, ἀφ' ἧς ἐκβεβλήκει ἑπτὰ δαιμόνια. ἐκείνη πορευθεῖσα 10
σλδ ι ἀπήγγειλε τοῖς μετ' αὐτοῦ γενομένοις, πενθοῦσι καὶ κλαίουσι. κἀκεῖνοι 11
σλε η ἀκούσαντες ὅτι ζῇ καὶ ἐθεάθη ὑπ' αὐτῆς ἠπίστησαν. μετὰ δὲ ταῦτα 12
δυσὶν ἐξ αὐτῶν ἐφανερώθη ἐν ἑτέρᾳ μορφῇ, πορευομένοις εἰς ἀγρόν.
κἀκεῖνοι ἀπελθόντες ἀπήγγειλαν τοῖς λοιποῖς· οὐδὲ ἐκείνοις ἐπίστευσαν. 13
σλς ι ὕστερον δὲ ἀνακειμένοις αὐτοῖς τοῖς ἕνδεκα ἐφανερώθη, καὶ ὠνείδισε τὴν 14
ἀπιστίαν αὐτῶν καὶ σκληροκαρδίαν, ὅτι τοῖς θεασαμένοις αὐτὸν ἐγηγερ-
μένον ἐκ νεκρῶν οὐκ ἐπίστευσαν. καὶ εἶπεν αὐτοῖς, Πορευθέντες εἰς 15
τὸν κόσμον ἅπαντα κηρύξατε τὸ εὐαγγέλιον πάσῃ τῇ κτίσει. ὁ πιστεύ- 16

5 ειδον] ιδον cod. 8 εν τισι...φερεται litt. rubr.

118 209 ς 47 Μαρια bis 118 ς Μαγδαλινη 118 Ιωση ς
1 Μαρια bis 118 209 ς Μαγδαλινη 118 η του Ιακωβου 118 209 ς
2 της μιας 118 209 ς om ετι 118 209 ς 7 om ηγερθη...ιδου ς
8 ταχυ εφυγον ς γαρ] in 209 linea in qua hoc verbum stat spatio lin. dimid. praeter codicis consuetudinem relicto abrupte hic desinit, tum linea nova Αναστας incipit et εν τισι...φερεται prima manus in margine litteris rubris addidit om εν τισι...φερεται 118 ς 9 δε]+ο Ιησους 118 209 σαββατου ς Μαγδαλινη 118 11 αυτοις 209 12 αυτων περιπατουσιν 118 209 ς 14 om δε 118 209 ς om εκ νεκρων 118 209 ς

17 σας καὶ βαπτισθεὶς σωθήσεται· ὁ δὲ ἀπιστήσας κατακριθήσεται. σημεῖα
δὲ τοῖς πιστεύσασι ταῦτα παρακολουθήσει· ἐν τῷ ὀνόματί μου δαιμόνια
18 ἐκβαλοῦσι, γλώσσαις λαλήσουσι καιναῖς, καὶ ἐν ταῖς χερσὶν ὄφεις
ἀροῦσι, κἂν θανάσιμόν τι πίωσιν, οὐ μὴ αὐτοὺς βλάψῃ· ἐπὶ ἀρρώστους
χεῖρας ἐπιθήσουσι, καὶ καλῶς ἕξουσιν.
19 Ὁ μὲν οὖν Κύριος Ἰησοῦς μετὰ τὸ λαλῆσαι αὐτοῖς ἀνελήφθη εἰς
20 τὸν οὐρανὸν καὶ ἐκάθισεν ἐκ δεξιῶν τοῦ πατρός· ἐκεῖνοι δὲ ἐξελθόντες
ἐκήρυξαν πανταχοῦ, τοῦ Κυρίου συνεργοῦντος καὶ τὸν λόγον βεβαιοῦντος
διὰ τῶν ἐπακολουθούντων σημείων.

19 πατρος] hoc verbum Tregellesio fretus edidi, sed incertum mihi videtur; cod. nunc habet θεου in rasura trium litterarum scriptum nec scio an prima manu sit

18 om και εν ταις χερσιν 118 209 ς βλαψει ς **19** om Ιησους 118 209 ς πατρος] Θεου 118 209 ς **20** σημειων] + αμην 118 209 ς ad fin. evan. 209^2 add. ιστεον οτι μετα χρονους δεκα της του κυ̅ ημων και θυ̅ Ιυ̅ Χυ̅ εκ νεκρων αναστασεως και εις ου̅ν̅ο̅υ̅ς̅ αναληψεως εγραφη το κατα Μαρκον αγιον ευαγγελιον 118 209 ς

ΕΥΑΓΓΕΛΙΟΝ ΚΑΤΑ ΛΟΥΚΑΝ

α ι I. Ἐπειδήπερ πολλοὶ ἐπεχείρησαν ἀνατάξασθαι διήγησιν περὶ τῶν
πεπληροφορημένων ἐν ἡμῖν πραγμάτων, καθὼς παρέδοσαν ἡμῖν οἱ ἀπ' 2
ἀρχῆς αὐτόπται καὶ ὑπηρέται γενόμενοι τοῦ λόγου, ἔδοξε κἀμοί, παρηκο- 3
λουθηκότι ἄνωθεν πᾶσιν ἀκριβῶς, καθεξῆς σοὶ γράψαι, κράτιστε Θεόφιλε,
ἵνα ἐπιγνῷς περὶ ὧν κατηχήθης λόγων τὴν ἀσφάλειαν. 4
Ἐγένετο ἐν ταῖς ἡμέραις Ἡρώδου τοῦ βασιλέως τῆς Ἰουδαίας ἱερεύς 5
τις ὀνόματι Ζαχαρίας ἐξ ἐφημερίας Ἀβιά· καὶ γυνὴ αὐτῷ ἐκ τῶν θυ-
γατέρων Ἀαρών, καὶ τὸ ὄνομα αὐτῆς Ἐλισάβετ. ἦσαν δὲ δίκαιοι 6
ἀμφότεροι ἐνώπιον τοῦ Θεοῦ, πορευόμενοι ἐν πάσαις ταῖς ἐντολαῖς καὶ
δικαιώμασι τοῦ Κυρίου ἄμεμπτοι. καὶ οὐκ ἦν αὐτοῖς τέκνον, καθότι ἡ 7
Ἐλισάβετ ἦν στεῖρα, καὶ ἀμφότεροι προβεβηκότες ἐν ἡμέραις αὐτῶν
ἦσαν. ἐγένετο δὲ ἐν τῷ ἱερατεύειν αὐτὸν ἐν τῇ τάξει τῆς ἐφημερίας 8
αὐτοῦ ἔναντι Θεοῦ, κατὰ τὸ ἔθος τῆς ἱερατείας ἔλαχε τοῦ θυμιᾶσαι 9
εἰσελθὼν εἰς τὸν ναὸν τοῦ Κυρίου· καὶ πᾶν τὸ πλῆθος τοῦ λαοῦ ἦν 10
προσευχόμενον ἔξω τῇ ὥρᾳ τοῦ θυμιάματος. ὤφθη δὲ αὐτῷ ἄγγελος 11
Κυρίου ἑστὼς ἐκ δεξιῶν τοῦ θυσιαστηρίου τοῦ θυμιάματος· καὶ ἐταράχθη 12
Ζαχαρίας ἰδών, καὶ φόβος ἐπέπεσεν ἐπ' αὐτόν. εἶπε δὲ πρὸς αὐτὸν 13
ὁ ἄγγελος, Μὴ φοβοῦ, Ζαχαρία· διότι εἰσηκούσθη ἡ δέησίς σου, καὶ
ἡ γυνή σου Ἐλισάβετ γεννήσει υἱόν, καὶ καλέσεις τὸ ὄνομα αὐτοῦ
Ἰωάννην· καὶ ἔσται χαρά σοι καὶ ἀγαλλίασις, καὶ πολλοὶ ἐπὶ τῇ γεν- 14
νήσει αὐτοῦ χαρήσονται. ἔσται γὰρ μέγας ἐνώπιον Κυρίου· καὶ 15
οἶνον καὶ σίκερα οὐ μὴ πίῃ· καὶ Πνεύματος Ἁγίου πλησθήσεται ἔτι
ἐκ κοιλίας μητρὸς αὐτοῦ. καὶ πολλοὺς τῶν υἱῶν Ἰσραὴλ ἐπιστρέψει 16

1 *επιχειρησαν* Tregellesius notat sed per errorem

118 131 209 ς **Titul.** hic inc. collatio 131. *το κατα Λουκαν αγιον ευαγγελιον* 209 ς, om 118 **5** *η γυνη αυτου* 118 131 209 ς **7** *ταις ημεραις* 118 131 209 ς **8** *του Θεου* 118 131 209 ς **10** *προσευχομενον*] *προσδεχομενον* 131 **12** *περι επεσεν* 131 **13** *υιον σοι* 118 131 209 ς **14** *χαρισονται* 118 **15** *του Κυριου* ς

17 πρὸς Κύριον τὸν Θεὸν αὐτῶν· καὶ αὐτὸς προελεύσεται ἐνώπιον αὐτοῦ
ἐν πνεύματι καὶ δυνάμει Ἠλίου, ἐπιστρέψαι καρδίας πατέρων ἐπὶ τέκνα,
καὶ ἀπειθεῖς ἐν φρονήσει δικαίων, ἑτοιμάσαι Κυρίῳ λαὸν κατεσκευασ-
18 μένον. καὶ εἶπε Ζαχαρίας πρὸς τὸν ἄγγελον, Κατὰ τί γνώσομαι τοῦτο;
ἐγὼ γάρ εἰμι πρεσβύτης, ἡ γυνή μου προβεβηκυῖα ἐν ταῖς ἡμέραις
19 αὐτῆς. καὶ ἀποκριθεὶς ὁ ἄγγελος εἶπεν αὐτῷ, Ἐγώ εἰμι Γαβριὴλ ὁ
παρεστηκὼς ἐνώπιον τοῦ Θεοῦ· καὶ ἀπεστάλην λαλῆσαι πρός σε καὶ
20 εὐαγγελίσασθαί σοι ταῦτα. καὶ ἰδοὺ ἔσῃ σιωπῶν καὶ μὴ δυνάμενος
λαλῆσαι ἄχρι ἧς ἡμέρας γένηται ταῦτα, ἀνθ' ὧν οὐκ ἐπίστευσας τοῖς
21 λόγοις μου, οἵτινες πληρωθήσονται εἰς τὸν καιρὸν αὐτῶν. καὶ ἦν ὁ
λαὸς προσδοκῶν τὸν Ζαχαρίαν· καὶ ἐθαύμαζον ἐν τῷ χρονίζειν αὐτὸν
22 ἐν τῷ ναῷ. ἐξελθὼν δὲ οὐκ ἠδύνατο λαλῆσαι αὐτοῖς· καὶ ἐπέγνωσαν
ὅτι ὀπτασίαν ἑώρακεν ἐν τῷ ναῷ· καὶ αὐτὸς ἦν διανεύων αὐτοῖς, καὶ
23 διέμενε κωφός. καὶ ἐγένετο ὡς ἐπληρώθησαν αἱ ἡμέραι τῆς λειτουρ-
24 γίας αὐτοῦ, ἀπῆλθεν εἰς τὸν οἶκον αὐτοῦ. μετὰ δὲ ταύτας τὰς ἡμέρας
συνέλαβεν Ἐλισάβετ ἡ γυνὴ αὐτοῦ, καὶ περιέκρυβεν ἑαυτὴν μῆνας
25 πέντε, λέγουσα ὅτι Οὕτως μοι πεποίηκεν ὁ Κύριος ἐν ἡμέραις αἷς
ἐπεῖδεν ἀφελεῖν ὄνειδός μου ἐν ἀνθρώποις.
26 Ἐν δὲ τῷ μηνὶ τῷ ἕκτῳ ἀπεστάλη ὁ ἄγγελος Γαβριὴλ ἀπὸ τοῦ
27 Θεοῦ εἰς πόλιν τῆς Γαλιλαίας, ᾗ ὄνομα Ναζαρέθ, πρὸς παρθένον
μεμνηστευμένην ἀνδρὶ ᾧ ὄνομα Ἰωσήφ, ἐξ οἴκου καὶ πατρίας Δαβίδ·
28 καὶ τὸ ὄνομα τῆς παρθένου Μαριάμ. καὶ εἰσελθὼν πρὸς αὐτὴν εἶπε,
29 Χαῖρε, κεχαριτωμένη· ὁ Κύριος μετὰ σοῦ. ἡ δὲ ἐπὶ τῷ λόγῳ διε-
30 ταράχθη, καὶ διελογίζετο ποταπὸς ὁ ἀσπασμὸς οὗτος. εἶπεν δὲ ὁ
31 ἄγγελος αὐτῇ, Μὴ φοβοῦ, Μαριάμ· εὗρες γὰρ χάριν παρὰ Θεοῦ. καὶ
ἰδοὺ συλλήψῃ ἐν γαστρί, καὶ τέξῃ υἱόν, καὶ καλέσεις τὸ ὄνομα αὐτοῦ
32 Ἰησοῦν. οὗτος ἔσται μέγας, καὶ υἱὸς ὑψίστου κληθήσεται· καὶ δώσει
33 αὐτῷ Κύριος ὁ Θεὸς τὸν θρόνον Δαβὶδ τοῦ πατρὸς αὐτοῦ, καὶ βασι-
λεύσει ἐπὶ τὸν οἶκον Ἰακὼβ εἰς τοὺς αἰῶνας, καὶ τῆς βασιλείας αὐτοῦ
34 οὐκ ἔσται τέλος. εἶπε δὲ Μαριὰμ πρὸς τὸν ἄγγελον, Πῶς ἔσται μοι
35 τοῦτο, ἐπεὶ ἄνδρα οὐ γινώσκω; καὶ ἀποκριθεὶς ὁ ἄγγελος εἶπεν αὐτῇ,
Πνεῦμα Ἅγιον ἐπελεύσεται ἐπί σε, καὶ δύναμις ὑψίστου ἐπισκιάσει σοι·

16 *προς*] *επι* 118 209 ϛ *αυτων*] *αυτου* 118 209 **18** *και η γυνη* 118 131 209 ϛ **20** *ἀχρι* 131 **22** *εδυνατο* 131 *διεμεινε* 118 **23** *επλησθησαν* 118 131 209 ϛ **25** *ουτω* ϛ *το ονειδος* 118 131 209 ϛ **26** *απεσταλει* 131 *απο*] *υπο* 118 209 ϛ *Ναζαρετ* 118 209 ϛ **27** om *και πατριας* 118 209 ϛ **28** *εισελθων*]+*ο αγγελος* 118 209 ϛ *σου*] + *ευλογημενη συ εν γυναιξιν* 118 209 ϛ **29** *η δε ιδουσα διεταραχθη επι τω λογω αυτου* 118 209 ϛ *ποταπος ειη* 118 131 209 ϛ **30** *και ειπεν* 118 209 ϛ *παρα τω Θεω* 118 131 209 ϛ **31** *συλληψει* 131 *τεξει* 131 **34** *και πως* 118 209 om *μοι* 118 209 ϛ

118 131 209 ϛ

διὸ καὶ τὸ γεννώμενον ἐκ σοῦ ἅγιον κληθήσεται Υἱὸς Θεοῦ. καὶ 36
ἰδοὺ Ἐλισάβετ ἡ συγγενής σου καὶ αὐτὴ συνειληφυῖα υἱὸν ἐν γήρει
αὐτῆς· καὶ οὗτος μὴν ἕκτος αὐτῇ τῇ καλουμένῃ στείρᾳ· ὅτι οὐκ ἀδυνα- 37
τήσει παρὰ Θεῷ πᾶν ῥῆμα. εἶπε δὲ Μαριάμ, Ἰδοὺ ἡ δούλη Κυρίου· 38
γένοιτό μοι κατὰ τὸ ῥῆμά σου. καὶ ἀπῆλθεν ἀπ' αὐτῆς ὁ ἄγγελος.

Ἀναστᾶσα δὲ Μαριὰμ ἐν ταῖς ἡμέραις ταύταις ἐπορεύθη εἰς τὴν 39
ὀρεινὴν μετὰ σπουδῆς εἰς πόλιν Ἰούδα, καὶ εἰσῆλθεν εἰς τὸν οἶκον 40
Ζαχαρίου, καὶ ἠσπάσατο τὴν Ἐλισάβετ. καὶ ἐγένετο ὡς ἤκουσεν τὸν 41
ἀσπασμὸν τῆς Μαρίας ἡ Ἐλισάβετ, ἐσκίρτησε τὸ βρέφος ἐν τῇ
κοιλίᾳ αὐτῆς· καὶ ἐπλήσθη Πνεύματος Ἁγίου ἡ Ἐλισάβετ, καὶ ἀνε- 42
φώνησε φωνῇ μεγάλῃ καὶ εἶπεν, Εὐλογημένη σὺ ἐν γυναιξί, καὶ εὐλο-
γημένος ὁ καρπὸς τῆς κοιλίας σου. καὶ πόθεν μοι τοῦτο, ἵνα ἔλθῃ ἡ 43
μήτηρ τοῦ Κυρίου μου πρός με; ἰδοὺ γάρ, ὡς ἐγένετο ἡ φωνὴ τοῦ 44
ἀσπασμοῦ σου εἰς τὰ ὦτά μου, ἐσκίρτησεν ἐν ἀγαλλιάσει τὸ βρέφος
ἐν τῇ κοιλίᾳ μου. καὶ μακαρία ἡ πιστεύσασα, ὅτι ἔσται τελείωσις τοῖς 45
λελαλημένοις αὐτῇ παρὰ Κυρίου.

Καὶ εἶπε Μαριάμ, Μεγαλύνει ἡ ψυχή μου τὸν Κύριον, καὶ ἠγαλ- 46 47
λίασε τὸ πνεῦμά μου ἐπὶ τῷ Θεῷ τῷ σωτῆρί μου, ὅτι ἐπέβλεψεν ἐπὶ 48
τὴν ταπείνωσιν τῆς δούλης αὐτοῦ. ἰδοὺ γὰρ ἀπὸ τοῦ νῦν μακαριοῦσί
με πᾶσαι αἱ γενεαί· ὅτι ἐποίησέ μοι μεγαλεῖα ὁ δυνατός· καὶ ἅγιον 49
τὸ ὄνομα αὐτοῦ, καὶ τὸ ἔλεος αὐτοῦ εἰς γενεὰν καὶ γενεὰν τοῖς 50
φοβουμένοις αὐτόν. ἐποίησε κράτος ἐν βραχίονι αὐτοῦ· διεσκόρπισεν 51
ὑπερηφάνους διανοίᾳ καρδίας αὐτῶν· καθεῖλε δυνάστας ἀπὸ θρόνων, 52
καὶ ὕψωσε ταπεινούς· πεινῶντας ἐνέπλησεν ἀγαθῶν, καὶ πλουτοῦντας 53
ἐξαπέστειλε κενούς. ἀντελάβετο Ἰσραὴλ παιδὸς αὐτοῦ, μνησθῆναι ἐλέους 54
(καθὼς ἐλάλησε πρὸς τοὺς πατέρας ἡμῶν) τῷ Ἀβραὰμ καὶ τῷ σπέρ- 55
ματι αὐτοῦ ἕως αἰῶνος. ἔμεινε δὲ Μαριὰμ σὺν αὐτῇ ὡς μῆνας τρεῖς, 56
καὶ ὑπέστρεψεν εἰς τὸν οἶκον αὐτῆς.

Τῇ δὲ Ἐλισάβετ ἐπλήσθη ὁ χρόνος τοῦ τεκεῖν αὐτήν, καὶ ἐγέν- 57
νησεν υἱόν. καὶ ἤκουσαν οἱ περίοικοι καὶ οἱ συγγενεῖς αὐτῆς ὅτι 58
ἐμεγάλυνε Κύριος τὸ ἔλεος αὐτοῦ μετ' αὐτῆς, καὶ συνέχαιρον

118 131 209 ς

35 *γενομενον* 131 om *εκ σου* 118 209 ς **36** *γηρα* ς *εκτος εστιν* 118 131 209 ς **37** *τω Θεω* 118 131 209 ς **41** om *της Μαριας* 131 *η Ελισαβετ* ante *τον ασπασμον* 118 209 ς **42** *ανεβωνησε* 118 **44** *το βρεφος εν αγαλλιασει* 118 131 209 *κοιλια*] 118* scripsisse videtur *κ* *α* spat. rel. in quo *αρδια* manu 118[2] scriptum nunc erasum est **47** *ηγαλλιασαι* 131 **50** *γενεας γενεων* ς **51** *διανοιας* 118 209 **55** *τω* 1°] *τον* 118 209 *Ἀβρααμ* 131 ς *το σπερμα το* 118 209, *το σπερματι* 131 *εις τον αιωνα* ς **56** *ως*] *ωσει* 118 131 209 ς **57** *επλησθη*] *επληρωθη* 118 209 **58** om *οτι...μετ αυτης* 118 209

59 αὐτῇ. καὶ ἐγενετο ἐν τῇ ὀγδόῃ ἡμέρᾳ, ἦλθον περιτεμεῖν τὸ παιδίον·
60 καὶ ἐκάλουν αὐτὸ ἐπὶ τῷ ὀνόματι τοῦ πατρὸς αὐτοῦ Ζαχαρίαν. καὶ
ἀποκριθεῖσα ἡ μήτηρ αὐτοῦ εἶπεν, Οὐχί, ἀλλὰ κληθήσεται Ἰωάννης.
61 καὶ εἶπαν πρὸς αὐτήν, Οὐδείς ἐστιν ἐν τῇ συγγενείᾳ σου, ὃς
62 καλεῖται τῷ ὀνόματι τούτῳ. ἐνένευον δὲ τῷ πατρὶ αὐτοῦ, τὸ τί ἂν
63 θέλοι καλεῖσθαι αὐτόν. καὶ αἰτήσας πινακίδιον ἔγραψε λέγων, Ἰωάννης
64 ἔσται τὸ ὄνομα αὐτοῦ· καὶ ἐθαύμασαν πάντες. ἀνεῴχθη δὲ τὸ στόμα
αὐτοῦ παραχρῆμα καὶ ἐλύθη ὁ δεσμὸς τῆς γλώσσης αὐτοῦ, καὶ
65 ἐλάλει εὐλογῶν τὸν Θεόν. καὶ ἐγένετο ἐπὶ πάντας φόβος τοὺς περιοι-
κοῦντας αὐτούς· καὶ ἐν ὅλῃ τῇ ὀρεινῇ τῆς Ἰουδαίας διελαλεῖτο πάντα
66 τὰ ῥήματα ταῦτα· καὶ ἔθεντο πάντες οἱ ἀκούσαντες ἐν τῇ καρδίᾳ
αὐτῶν, λέγοντες, Τί ἄρα τὸ παιδίον τοῦτο ἔσται; καὶ ἦν χεὶρ Κυρίου
67 μετ' αὐτοῦ. καὶ Ζαχαρίας ὁ πατὴρ αὐτοῦ ἐπλήσθη Πνεύματος Ἁγίου,
68 καὶ ἐπροφήτευσε λέγων, Εὐλογητὸς Κύριος ὁ Θεὸς τοῦ Ἰσραήλ,
69 ὅτι ἐπεσκέψατο καὶ ἐποίησε λύτρωσιν τῷ λαῷ αὐτοῦ, καὶ ἤγειρε κέρας
70 σωτηρίας ἡμῖν ἐν οἴκῳ Δαβὶδ τοῦ παιδὸς αὐτοῦ, καθὼς ἐλάλησε διὰ
71 στόματος τῶν ἁγίων τῶν ἀπ' αἰῶνος προφητῶν αὐτοῦ, σωτηρίαν ἐξ
72 ἐχθρῶν ἡμῶν καὶ ἐκ χειρὸς πάντων τῶν μισούντων ἡμᾶς· ποιῆσαι ἔλεος
73 μετὰ τῶν πατέρων ἡμῶν καὶ μνησθῆναι διαθήκης ἁγίας αὐτοῦ, ὅρκον ὃν
74 ὤμοσε πρὸς Ἁβραὰμ τὸν πατέρα ἡμῶν, τοῦ δοῦναι ἡμῖν ἀφόβως ἐκ
75 χειρὸς ἐχθρῶν ῥυσθέντας λατρεύειν αὐτῷ ἐν ὁσιότητι καὶ δικαιοσύνῃ
76 ἐνώπιον αὐτοῦ πάσας τὰς ἡμέρας τῆς ζωῆς ἡμῶν. καὶ σύ, παιδίον,
προφήτης ὑψίστου κληθήσῃ· προπορεύσῃ γὰρ πρὸ προσώπου Κυρίου
77 ἑτοιμάσαι ὁδοὺς αὐτοῦ, τοῦ δοῦναι γνῶσιν σωτηρίας τῷ λαῷ αὐτοῦ ἐν
78 ἀφέσει ἁμαρτιῶν ἡμῶν διὰ σπλάγχνα ἐλέους Θεοῦ ἡμῶν, ἐν οἷς ἐπ-
79 εσκέψατο ἡμᾶς ἀνατολὴ ἐξ ὕψους, ἐπιφᾶναι τοῖς ἐν σκότει καὶ σκιᾷ
θανάτου καθημένοις, τοῦ κατευθῦναι τοὺς πόδας ἡμῶν εἰς ὁδὸν εἰρήνης.
80 τὸ δὲ παιδίον ηὔξανε καὶ ἐκραταιοῦτο πνεύματι· καὶ ἦν ἐν ταῖς ἐρήμοις
ἕως ἡμέρας ἀναδείξεως αὐτοῦ πρὸς τὸν Ἰσραήλ.

II. Ἐγένετο δὲ ἐν ταῖς ἡμέραις ἐκείναις, ἐξῆλθε δόγμα παρὰ Καίσαρος Α'
2 Αὐγούστου, ἀπογράψασθαι πᾶσαν τὴν οἰκουμένην. αὕτη ἡ ἀπογραφὴ
3 πρώτη ἐγένετο ἡγεμονεύοντος τῆς Συρίας Κυρηνίου. καὶ ἐπορεύοντο
4 πάντες ἀπογράφεσθαι, ἕκαστος εἰς τὴν ἰδίαν πόλιν. ἀνέβη δὲ καὶ Ἰωσὴφ

59 εκαλουν] ελαλουν cod. **64** ελαλει] ελαλη cod.

61 ειπον 118 209 ς οὐδεις] pr οτι 118 131 ς εκ της συγγενειας 131 118 131 209 ς
63 εσται] εστι 131 ς **64** και ελυθη...αυτου] om 131, και η γλωσσα αυτου 118 209 ς **65** απαντα 118 209 **66** ακουοντες 118 209 χειρ Κυριου ην 118 209 ς **67** προεφητευσε 118 131 209 ς **69** τω οικω 118 131 209 ς **73** Ἀβρααμ 131 ς **74** των εχθρων ημων 118 131 209 ς **77** ημων] αυτων] 131 ς

1 απογραφεσθαι 118 209 ς **2** αυτη απογραφη πρωτη γεγονεν 131

ἀπὸ τῆς Γαλιλαίας ἐκ πόλεως Ναζαρὲθ εἰς τὴν Ἰουδαίαν, εἰς πόλιν
Δαβὶδ ἥτις καλεῖται Βηθλεέμ, διὰ τὸ εἶναι αὐτὸν ἐξ οἴκου καὶ πατριᾶς
Δαβίδ, ἀπογράψασθαι σὺν Μαριὰμ τῇ μεμνηστευμένῃ αὐτῷ, οὔσῃ ἐγκύῳ. 5
β ἐγένετο δὲ ἐν τῷ εἶναι αὐτοὺς ἐκεῖ, ἐπλήσθησαν αἱ ἡμέραι τοῦ τεκεῖν 6
ε αὐτήν, καὶ ἔτεκε τὸν υἱὸν αὐτῆς τὸν πρωτότοκον, καὶ ἐσπαργάνωσεν 7
αὐτὸν καὶ ἀνέκλινεν αὐτὸν ἐν τῇ φάτνῃ, διότι οὐκ ἦν αὐτοῖς τόπος
ἐν τῷ καταλύματι.

B′ Καὶ ποιμένες ἦσαν ἐν τῇ χώρᾳ τῇ αὐτῇ ἀγραυλοῦντες καὶ φυλάσ- 8
γ ι σοντες φυλακὰς τῆς νυκτὸς ἐπὶ τῆς ποίμνης αὐτῶν. καὶ ἰδοὺ ἄγγελος 9
Κυρίου ἐπέστη αὐτοῖς, καὶ δόξα Κυρίου περιέλαμψεν αὐτούς· καὶ ἐφοβή-
θησαν φόβον μέγαν. καὶ εἶπεν αὐτοῖς ὁ ἄγγελος, Μὴ φοβεῖσθε· ἰδοὺ 10
γὰρ εὐαγγελίζομαι ὑμῖν χαρὰν μεγάλην, ἥτις ἔσται παντὶ τῷ λαῷ, ὅτι 11
ἐτέχθη ὑμῖν σήμερον σωτήρ, ὅς ἐστι Χριστὸς Κύριος, ἐν πόλει Δαβίδ.
καὶ τοῦτο ὑμῖν τὸ σημεῖον· εὑρήσετε βρέφος ἐσπαργανωμένον καὶ 12
κείμενον ἐν φάτνῃ. καὶ ἐξαίφνης ἐγένετο σὺν τῷ ἀγγέλῳ πλῆθος 13
στρατιᾶς οὐρανίου, αἰνούντων τὸν Θεὸν καὶ λεγόντων, Δόξα ἐν ὑψίστοις 14
Θεῷ, καὶ ἐπὶ γῆς εἰρήνη, ἐν ἀνθρώποις εὐδοκία. καὶ ἐγένετο, ὡς ἀπῆλ- 15
θον ἀπ᾿ αὐτῶν εἰς τὸν οὐρανὸν οἱ ἄγγελοι, οἱ ποιμένες εἶπον πρὸς
ἀλλήλους, Διέλθωμεν δὴ ἕως Βηθλεὲμ καὶ ἴδωμεν τὸ ῥῆμα τοῦτο τὸ
γεγονός, ὃ ὁ Κύριος ἐγνώρισεν ἡμῖν. καὶ ἦλθον σπεύσαντες, καὶ εὗρον 16
τήν τε Μαριὰμ καὶ τὸν Ἰωσὴφ καὶ τὸ βρέφος κείμενον ἐν τῇ φάτνῃ·
ἰδόντες δὲ διεγνώρισαν περὶ τοῦ ῥήματος τοῦ λαληθέντος αὐτοῖς περὶ 17
τοῦ παιδίου. καὶ πάντες ἀκούσαντες ἐθαύμασαν περὶ τῶν λαλη- 18
θέντων ὑπὸ τῶν ποιμένων πρὸς αὐτούς· ἡ δὲ Μαριὰμ πάντα συνετήρει 19
τὰ ῥήματα ταῦτα συμβάλλουσα ἐν τῇ καρδίᾳ αὐτῆς. καὶ ὑπέστρεψαν 20
οἱ ποιμένες δοξάζοντες καὶ αἰνοῦντες τὸν Θεὸν ἐπὶ πᾶσιν οἷς ἤκουσαν
καὶ εἶδον, καθὼς ἐλαλήθη πρὸς αὐτούς.

Καὶ ὅτε ἐπλήσθησαν ἡμέραι ὀκτὼ τοῦ περιτεμεῖν αὐτόν, καὶ 21
ἐκλήθη τὸ ὄνομα αὐτοῦ Ἰησοῦς, τὸ κληθὲν ὑπὸ τοῦ ἀγγέλου πρὸ τοῦ
συλληφθῆναι αὐτὸν ἐν τῇ κοιλίᾳ.

Καὶ ὅτε ἐπλήσθησαν αἱ ἡμέραι τοῦ καθαρισμοῦ αὐτῶν κατὰ τὸν 22
νόμον Μωσέως, ἀνήγαγον αὐτὸν εἰς Ἱεροσόλυμα παραστῆσαι τῷ Κυρίῳ,
καθὼς γέγραπται ἐν νόμῳ Κυρίου, ὅτι Πᾶν ἄρσεν διανοῖγον μήτραν ἅγιον 23

11 ος] ὁ cod.

118 131 209 ς **4** Ναζαρετ 118 209 ς **5** αυτω] + γυναικι 118 209 ς **7** om και ανεκλινεν αυτον 131 **8** τας φυλακας 131 την ποιμνην 118 209 ς **9** om Κυριου 1° 118 209 **11** om ος εστι 118 209 **12** om και 2° 118 131 209 ς τη φατνη ς **15** αγγελοι] + και οι ανθρωποι 118 131 209 ς **16** ανευρον 118 209 ς **17** εγρωρισαν 118 209 παιδιου τουτου 118 209 ς **18** οι ακουσαντες 118 131 209 ς **20** επεστρεψαν ς **21** αι οκτω ημεραι 118 209 αυτον 1°] το παιδιον ς **22** Μωυσεος 118 209

24 τῷ Κυρίῳ κληθήσεται, καὶ τοῦ δοῦναι θυσίαν κατὰ τὸ εἰρημένον ἐν νόμῳ
Κυρίου, Ζεῦγος τρυγόνων ἢ δύο νεοσσοὺς περιστερῶν.
25 Καὶ ἰδοὺ ἦν ἄνθρωπος ἐν Ἱερουσαλὴμ ᾧ ὄνομα Συμεών, καὶ ὁ ἄνθρω- Γ'
πος οὗτος δίκαιος καὶ εὐλαβής, προσδεχόμενος παράκλησιν τῷ Ἰσραήλ·
26 καὶ Πνεῦμα Ἅγιον ἐπ' αὐτόν· καὶ ἦν αὐτῷ κεχρηματισμένον ὑπὸ τοῦ
Πνεύματος τοῦ Ἁγίου, μὴ ἰδεῖν θάνατον πρὶν ἢ ἴδῃ τὸν Χριστὸν Κυρίου.
27 καὶ ἦλθεν ἐν τῷ Πνεύματι εἰς τὸ ἱερόν· καὶ ἐν τῷ εἰσαγαγεῖν τοὺς
γονεῖς τὸ παιδίον Ἰησοῦν, τοῦ ποιῆσαι αὐτοὺς κατὰ τὸ εἰθισμένον τοῦ
28 νόμου περὶ αὐτοῦ, καὶ αὐτὸς ἐδέξατο αὐτὸ εἰς τὰς ἀγκάλας αὐτοῦ, καὶ
29 εὐλόγησε τὸν Θεὸν καὶ εἶπε, Νῦν ἀπολύεις τὸν δοῦλόν σου, δέσποτα,
30 κατὰ τὸ ῥῆμά σου ἐν εἰρήνῃ· ὅτι εἶδον οἱ ὀφθαλμοί μου τὸ σωτήριόν
31 32 σου, ὃ ἡτοίμασας κατὰ πρόσωπον πάντων λαῶν, φῶς εἰς ἀποκάλυψιν
33 ἐθνῶν, καὶ δόξαν λαοῦ σου Ἰσραήλ. καὶ ἦν ὁ πατὴρ αὐτοῦ καὶ ἡ
34 μήτηρ θαυμάζοντες ἐπὶ πᾶσι τοῖς λαλουμένοις περὶ αὐτοῦ. καὶ εὐλό-
γησεν αὐτοὺς Συμεών, καὶ εἶπε πρὸς Μαριὰμ τὴν μητέρα αὐτοῦ, Ἰδοὺ
οὗτος κεῖται εἰς πτῶσιν καὶ ἀνάστασιν πολλῶν ἐν τῷ Ἰσραήλ, καὶ εἰς
35 σημεῖον ἀντιλεγόμενον (καὶ σοῦ δὲ αὐτῆς τὴν ψυχὴν διελεύσεται ῥομφαία),
ὅπως ἂν ἀποκαλυφθῶσιν ἐκ πολλῶν καρδιῶν διαλογισμοί.
36 Καὶ ἦν Ἄννα προφήτης, θυγάτηρ Φανουήλ, ἐκ φυλῆς Ἀσήρ, αὕτη Δ'
προβεβηκυῖα ἐν ἡμέραις πολλαῖς, ζήσασα ἔτη μετὰ ἀνδρὸς ἑπτὰ ἀπὸ
37 τῆς παρθενίας αὐτῆς, καὶ αὕτη χήρα ὡς ἐτῶν ὀγδοηκοντατεσσάρων, ἣ
οὐκ ἀφίστατο ἀπὸ τοῦ ἱεροῦ, νηστείαις καὶ δεήσεσι λατρεύουσα νύκτα
38 καὶ ἡμέραν· καὶ αὕτη αὐτῇ τῇ ὥρᾳ ἐπιστᾶσα ἀνθωμολογεῖτο τῷ Κυρίῳ,
καὶ ἐλάλει περὶ αὐτοῦ πᾶσι τοῖς προσδεχομένοις λύτρωσιν Ἱερου-
39 σαλήμ. καὶ ὡς ἐτέλεσαν ἅπαντα κατὰ τὸν νόμον, ὑπέστρεψαν εἰς
40 τὴν Γαλιλαίαν εἰς πόλιν ἑαυτῶν Ναζαρά. τὸ δὲ παιδίον ηὔξανε, καὶ
ἐκραταιοῦτο πνεύματι, πληρούμενον σοφίας· καὶ χάρις Θεοῦ ἦν ἐπ' αὐτό.
41 Καὶ ἐπορεύοντο οἱ γονεῖς αὐτοῦ κατ' ἔτος εἰς Ἱερουσαλὴμ τῇ ἑορτῇ
42 τοῦ πάσχα. καὶ ὅτε ἐγένετο ἐτῶν δεκαδύο, ἀναβάντων αὐτῶν εἰς
43 Ἱεροσόλυμα κατὰ τὸ ἔθος τῆς ἑορτῆς, καὶ τελειωσάντων τὰς ἡμέρας,
ἐν τῷ ὑποστρέφειν αὐτοὺς ἀπέμεινεν Ἰησοῦς ὁ παῖς ἐν Ἱερουσαλήμ·
44 καὶ οὐκ ἔγνωσαν οἱ γονεῖς αὐτοῦ· νομίσαντες δὲ αὐτὸν εἶναι ἐν τῇ

39 Ναζαρα] Ναζαρετ rubr.[2]

25 του Ισρυηλ 118 209 ς ην επ αυτον 118 209 ς **26** om η 118 209 118 131 209 ς **28** Θεον Ισραηλ 131 **31** των λαων 118 131 209 ς **32** δοξα 209 **33** ο πατηρ αυτου] Ιωσηφ 118 209 ς μητηρ] + αυτου 118 209 ς om πασι 118 209 ς **36** προφητις ς, προφητ[ς] 118 209 **37** om απο 131 **38** εν Ιερουσαλημ 118 131 209 **39** παντα 118 209 τα κατα 118 131 209 ς νομον Κυριου 118 209 ς την πολιν αυτων 118 209 ς Ναζαρεθ 131, Ναζαρετ 118 209 ς **42** δωδεκα 118 209 ς **43** υπεμεινεν 118 209 ς εγνω Ιωση και η μητηρ ς . **44** εν τε συνοδια ειναι 131 ς

συνοδίᾳ ἦλθον ἡμέρας ὁδόν· καὶ ἀνεζήτουν αὐτὸν ἐν τοῖς συγγενεῦσι
καὶ ἐν τοῖς γνωστοῖς, καὶ μὴ εὑρόντες ὑπέστρεψαν εἰς Ἱερουσαλὴμ 45
ἀναζητοῦντες αὐτόν. καὶ ἐγένετο μετὰ ἡμέρας τρεῖς, εὗρον αὐτὸν ἐν 46
τῷ ἱερῷ καθήμενον ἐν μέσῳ τῶν διδασκάλων, καὶ ἀκούοντα αὐτῶν καὶ
δ/β ἐπερωτῶντα αὐτούς· ἐξίσταντο δὲ πάντες οἱ ἀκούοντες αὐτοῦ ἐπὶ τῇ 47
συνέσει καὶ ταῖς ἀποκρίσεσιν αὐτοῦ. καὶ ἰδόντες αὐτὸν ἐξεπλάγησαν· 48
ε/ι καὶ εἶπε πρὸς αὐτὸν ἡ μήτηρ αὐτοῦ, Τέκνον, τί ἐποίησας ἡμῖν οὕτως;
ἰδοὺ ὁ πατήρ σου καὶ ἐγὼ ὀδυνώμενοι ἐζητοῦμέν σε. καὶ εἶπε πρὸς 49
αὐτούς, Τί ὅτι ἐζητεῖτέ με; οὐκ ᾔδειτε ὅτι ἐν τοῖς τοῦ πατρός μου
δεῖ με εἶναι; καὶ αὐτοὶ οὐ συνῆκαν τὸ ῥῆμα ὃ εἶπεν αὐτοῖς. καὶ 50 51
κατέβη μετ' αὐτῶν καὶ ἦλθεν εἰς Ναζαρέθ, καὶ ἦν ὑποτασσόμενος
αὐτοῖς. καὶ ἡ μήτηρ αὐτοῦ διετήρει πάντα τὰ ῥήματα ταῦτα ἐν τῇ
καρδίᾳ αὐτῆς. καὶ Ἰησοῦς προέκοπτε σοφίᾳ καὶ ἡλικίᾳ καὶ χάριτι 52
παρὰ Θεῷ καὶ ἀνθρώποις.

E′ III. Ἐν ἔτει δὲ πεντεκαιδεκάτῳ τῆς ἡγεμονίας Τιβερίου Καίσαρος,
ς/γ ἡγεμονεύοντος Ποντίου Πιλάτου τῆς Ἰουδαίας, καὶ τετραρχοῦντος τῆς
Γαλιλαίας Ἡρώδου, Φιλίππου δὲ τοῦ ἀδελφοῦ αὐτοῦ τετραρχοῦντος τῆς
Ἰτουραίας καὶ Τραχωνίτιδος χώρας, καὶ Λυσανίου τῆς Ἀβιληνῆς τετραρ-
χοῦντος, ἐπὶ ἀρχιέρεως Ἄννα καὶ Καϊάφα, ἐγένετο ῥῆμα Θεοῦ ἐπὶ 2
ζ/α Ἰωάννην τὸν τοῦ Ζαχαρίου υἱὸν ἐν τῇ ἐρήμῳ· καὶ ἦλθεν εἰς πᾶσαν 3
τὴν περίχωρον τοῦ Ἰορδάνου, κηρύσσων βάπτισμα μετανοίας εἰς ἄφεσιν
ἁμαρτιῶν, ὡς γέγραπται ἐν βίβλῳ λόγων Ἡσαΐου τοῦ προφήτου, Φωνὴ 4
βοῶντος ἐν τῇ ἐρήμῳ, Ἑτοιμάσατε τὴν ὁδὸν Κυρίου, εὐθείας ποιεῖτε τὰς
τρίβους αὐτοῦ. πᾶσα φάραγξ πληρωθήσεται, καὶ πᾶν ὄρος καὶ βουνὸς 5
ταπεινωθήσεται, καὶ ἔσται τὰ σκολιὰ εἰς εὐθεῖαν, καὶ αἱ τραχεῖαι εἰς
η/ε ὁδοὺς λείας· καὶ ὄψεται πᾶσα σὰρξ τὸ σωτήριον τοῦ Θεοῦ. ἔλεγεν δὲ 6 7
τοῖς ἐκπορευομένοις βαπτισθῆναι ὑπ' αὐτοῦ, Γεννήματα ἐχιδνῶν, τίς
ὑπέδειξεν ὑμῖν φυγεῖν ἀπὸ τῆς μελλούσης ὀργῆς; ποιήσατε οὖν καρποὺς 8
ἀξίους τῆς μετανοίας· καὶ μὴ ἄρξησθε λέγειν ἐν ἑαυτοῖς, Πατέρα ἔχομεν
τὸν Ἀβραάμ· λέγω γὰρ ὑμῖν ὅτι δύναται ὁ Θεὸς ἐκ τῶν λίθων τούτων
ἐγεῖραι τέκνα τῷ Ἀβραάμ. ἤδη δὲ καὶ ἡ ἀξίνη πρὸς τὴν ῥίζαν τῶν 9
δένδρων κεῖται· πᾶν οὖν δένδρον μὴ ποιοῦν καρπὸν καλὸν ἐκκόπτεται καὶ
εἰς πῦρ βάλλεται.

118 131 209 ς

44 συγγενεσι 118[2] 131 ς, συγγεν σι spat. rel. 118* om εν 3° 131 **45** ευροντες αυτον ς ζητουντες ς **46** μεθ 118 ς καθεζομενον 118 ς **47** ακουσαντες 131 **48** ειπε post αυτου ς καγω 131 ς **49** ειναι με 131 ς **50** ειπεν] ελαλησεν ς **51** Ναζαρετ 118 209 ς **52** ο Ιησους 131

1 om δε 131 **2** επ αρχιερεων ς om του 131 **4** προφητου]+λεγοντος ς **7** δε] ουν ς εκπορευομενοις οχλοις 118 209 131 ς **8** Ἀβρααμ bis 131 ς

10 11 Καὶ ἐπηρώτων αὐτὸν οἱ ὄχλοι λέγοντες, Τί οὖν ποιήσομεν; ἀπο- ς̄
κριθεὶς δὲ ἔλεγεν αὐτοῖς, Ὁ ἔχων δύο χιτῶνας μεταδότω τῷ μὴ ἔχοντι· θ
12 καὶ ὁ ἔχων βρώματα ὁμοίως ποιείτω. ἦλθον δὲ καὶ τελῶναι βαπτι- ι
13 σθῆναι, καὶ εἶπον πρὸς αὐτόν, Διδάσκαλε, τί ποιήσομεν; ὁ δὲ εἶπε
πρὸς αὐτούς, Μηδὲν πλέον παρὰ τὸ διατεταγμένον ὑμῖν πράσσετε.
14 ἐπηρώτων δὲ αὐτὸν καὶ στρατευόμενοι λέγοντες, Τί ποιήσομεν καὶ
ἡμεῖς; καὶ εἶπεν αὐτοῖς, Μηδένα διασείσητε μηδὲ συκοφαντήσητε·
καὶ ἀρκεῖσθε τοῖς ὀψωνίοις ὑμῶν.
15 Προσδοκῶντος δὲ τοῦ λαοῦ, καὶ διαλογιζομένων πάντων ἐν ταῖς
16 καρδίαις αὐτῶν περὶ Ἰωάννου, μήτι αὐτὸς εἴη ὁ Χριστός, ἀπεκρί- ῑ
νατο πᾶσιν ὁ Ἰωάννης λέγων, Ἐγὼ μὲν ὑμᾶς βαπτίζω ἐν ὕδατι· α
ἔρχεται δὲ ὁ ἰσχυρότερός μου, οὗ οὐκ εἰμὶ ἱκανὸς λῦσαι τὸν ἱμάντα
τῶν ὑποδημάτων αὐτοῦ· αὐτὸς ὑμᾶς βαπτίσει ἐν Πνεύματι Ἁγίῳ καὶ
17 πυρί· οὗ τὸ πτύον ἐν τῇ χειρὶ αὐτοῦ, καὶ διακαθαριεῖ τὴν ἅλωνα αὐτοῦ, ῑα
καὶ συνάξει τὸν σῖτον εἰς τὴν ἀποθήκην αὐτοῦ, τὸ δὲ ἄχυρον κατακαύσει ε
18 πυρὶ ἀσβέστῳ. πολλὰ μὲν οὖν καὶ ἕτερα παρακαλῶν εὐηγγελίζετο τὸν
19 λαόν. ὁ δὲ Ἡρώδης ὁ τετράρχης, ἐλεγχόμενος ὑπ' αὐτοῦ περὶ Ἡρωδιάδος ῑβ
τῆς γυναικὸς τοῦ ἀδελφοῦ αὐτοῦ, καὶ περὶ πάντων ὧν ἐποίησε πονηρῶν β
20 ὁ Ἡρώδης, προσέθηκε καὶ τοῦτο ἐπὶ πᾶσι, καὶ κατέκλεισε τὸν Ἰωάννην
ἐν φυλακῇ.
21 Ἐγένετο δὲ ἐν τῷ βαπτισθῆναι ἅπαντα τὸν λαόν, καὶ Ἰησοῦ βαπ- ῑγ
22 τισθέντος καὶ προσευχομένου, ἀνεῳχθῆναι τὸν οὐρανόν, καὶ καταβῆναι α
τὸ Πνεῦμα τὸ Ἅγιον σωματικῷ εἴδει ὡσεὶ περιστερὰν ἐπ' αὐτόν, καὶ
φωνὴν ἐξ οὐρανοῦ γενέσθαι λέγουσαν, Σὺ εἶ ὁ υἱός μου ὁ ἀγαπητός,
23 ἐν σοὶ εὐδόκησα. καὶ αὐτὸς ἦν ὁ Ἰησοῦς ἀρχόμενος ὡσεὶ ἐτῶν ῑδ
24 τριάκοντα, ὢν υἱός, ὡς ἐνομίζετο, τοῦ Ἰωσήφ, τοῦ Ἡλεί, τοῦ γ
25 Ματθάν, τοῦ Λευεί, τοῦ Μελχεί, τοῦ Ἰωανναί, τοῦ Ἰωσήφ, τοῦ
26 Ματταθίου, τοῦ Ἀμώς, τοῦ Ναούμ, τοῦ Ἐσλεί, τοῦ Ναγγαί, τοῦ
27 Μαάθ, τοῦ Ματταθίου, τοῦ Σεμεεί, τοῦ Ἰωσήχ, τοῦ Ἰωαδά, τοῦ

10 ποιησωμεν 131 **11** λεγει 118 209 ς ποιητω 118 **14** και ημεις τι ποιησομεν 118 131 209 ς αυτοις] προς αυτους 118 209 ς **15** απαντων 131 om περι Ιωαννου 131, περι του Ιωαννου 118 209 ς μητι] μηποτε 118 209 ς **16** om πασιν 118 209 ς λεγων] pr απασι 118 209 ς υδατι βαπτιζω υμας 118 209 ς **18** τω λαω 131 **19** του αδελφου] pr Φιλιππου 118 209 ς **20** τη φυλακη 118 131 209 ς **22** ειδει ωσει] ειδεισει 118* sed ειδει delet. σοι] 131* primum ω scripsit, postea autem ipse punctis damnavit et σοι supra lineam scripsit ηυδοκησα 131 ς **23** ωσει ετων τριακοντα αρχομενος ς ως ενομιζετο υιος Ιωσηφ ς Ηλι ς **24** Ματθατ ς Λευι 118 131 209 ς Μελχι 118 131 209 ς Ιωανναν 131, Ιαννα 118 209 ς **25** Ματθιου 118 Εσλι 118 ς, Εσλιμ 131 **26** Σεμεϊ ς Ιωσηφ ς Ιωδα 131, Ιουδα 118 209 ς 118 131 209 ς

Ἰωαννάν, τοῦ Ῥησά, τοῦ Ζοροβάβελ, τοῦ Σαλαθιήλ, τοῦ Νηρεί,
τοῦ Μελχεί, τοῦ Ἀδδεί, τοῦ Κωσάμ, τοῦ Ἐλμωδάμ, τοῦ Ἤρ, τοῦ 28 29
Ἰησῶ, τοῦ Ἐλιέζερ, τοῦ Ἰωραίμ, τοῦ Ματθάν, τοῦ Λευεί, τοῦ 30
Συμεών, τοῦ Ἰούδα, τοῦ Ἰωσήφ, τοῦ Ἰωνάμ, τοῦ Ἐλιακείμ, τοῦ Μελεᾶ, 31
τοῦ Μενάν, τοῦ Ματταθάν, τοῦ Ναθάν, τοῦ Δαυείδ, τοῦ Ἰεσσαί, 32
τοῦ Ὠβήδ, τοῦ Βοόζ, τοῦ Σαλμᾶν, τοῦ Νaασσών, τοῦ Ἀμιναδάμ, 33
τοῦ Ἀράμ, τοῦ Ἀλμεί, τοῦ Ἀρνεί, τοῦ Ἐσρώμ, τοῦ Φαρές, τοῦ
Ἰούδα, τοῦ Ἰακώβ, τοῦ Ἰσαάκ, τοῦ Ἀβραάμ, τοῦ Θάρρα, τοῦ Ναχώρ, 34
τοῦ Σερούχ, τοῦ Ῥαγαῦ, τοῦ Φάλεγ, τοῦ Ἔβερ, τοῦ Σαλά, τοῦ 35 36
Καινάμ, τοῦ Ἀρφαξάδ, τοῦ Σήμ, τοῦ Νῶε, τοῦ Λάμεχ, τοῦ Μαθου- 37
σάλα, τοῦ Ἐνώχ, τοῦ Ἰαρέδ, τοῦ Μαλελεήλ, τοῦ Καϊνάν, τοῦ Ἐνώς, 38
τοῦ Σήθ, τοῦ Ἀδάμ, τοῦ Θεοῦ.

Ζ′ IV. Ἰησοῦς δὲ πλήρης Πνεύματος Ἁγίου ὑπέστρεψεν ἀπὸ τοῦ
ιε/β Ἰορδάνου· καὶ ἤγετο ἐν τῷ Πνεύματι εἰς τὴν ἔρημον ἡμέρας τεσσαρά- 2
ιϛ/ε κοντα πειραζόμενος ὑπὸ τοῦ διαβόλου· καὶ οὐκ ἔφαγεν οὐδὲν ἐν ταῖς
ἡμέραις ἐκείναις· καὶ συντελεσθεισῶν αὐτῶν ὕστερον ἐπείνασε. εἶπε δὲ 3
αὐτῷ ὁ διάβολος, Εἰ υἱὸς εἶ τοῦ Θεοῦ, εἰπὲ τῷ λίθῳ τούτῳ ἵνα γένηται
ἄρτος. καὶ ἀπεκρίθη ὁ Ἰησοῦς πρὸς αὐτὸν λέγων, Γέγραπται ὅτι Οὐκ 4
ἐπ' ἄρτῳ μόνῳ ζήσεται ὁ ἄνθρωπος, ἀλλ' ἐπὶ παντὶ ῥήματι Θεοῦ.
καὶ ἀναγαγὼν αὐτὸν εἰς ὄρος ὑψηλὸν ἔδειξεν αὐτῷ πάσας τὰς βασι- 5
λείας τῆς οἰκουμένης ἐν στίγματι χρόνου· καὶ εἶπεν αὐτῷ ὁ διάβολος, 6
Σοὶ δώσω τὴν ἐξουσίαν ταύτην ἅπασαν καὶ τὴν δόξαν αὐτῶν· ὅτι ἐμοὶ
παραδέδοται, καὶ ᾧ ἐὰν θέλω δίδωμι αὐτήν· σὺ οὖν ἐὰν πεσὼν προσ- 7
κυνήσῃς ἐνώπιόν ἐμοῦ, ἔσται σου πᾶσα. καὶ ἀποκριθεὶς ὁ Ἰησοῦς 8

31 Δαυειδ] hic praeter consuetudinem compendio Δᾱδ cod. non utitur
33 Αμιναδαμ] cod. nunc habet Αμιναδαβ parte inferiore μ secundi erasâ

118 131 209 ϛ **27** Ιωαννα ϛ Νηρι 118 131 209 ϛ **28** Μελχι 118 131 209 ϛ Αδδι 131 ϛ, Αδειμ 118 209 Ελμωδαμ] Εσλωδαν 131 **29** Ιωση 118 209 ϛ Ιωρειμ 118 209 ϛ, Ιωρλειμ 131 Μαθατ 118 209, Ματθατ ϛ Λευι 118 131 209 ϛ **30** Ιωναν 131 ϛ, Ιωνναν 118 209 **31** Μαϊναν 118 209 ϛ Ματταθα 118 209 ϛ, Ματθαν 131 Δαβιδ ϛ, compendio utuntur 118 131 **32** Ιωβηδ 118 209 Βοοσζ 118 209 Σαλμαναν 131, Σαλμων 118 209 ϛ **33** Αμιναδαβ 131 ϛ του Αλμει του Αρνει] om ϛ, του Αδμη του Αρνη 131, του Ιωραμ 118 209 **34** Ἀβρααμ 131 ϛ Θαρα 118 ϛ **35** Σαρουχ ϛ Ρεγαυ 131 Φαλε 118 209, Φαλεκ 131 ϛ **36** Καιναν 118 131 209 ϛ **37** Κιαναν 118

1 πληρης post αγιου ϛ **3** και ειπεν 118 209 ϛ **4** om ο 1° ϛ επ αρτω] 118 nunc habet literas επ αρ eras. et 118* επει scripsisse videtur sed incertum est om ο 2° 131 ρηματι]+εκπορευομενω δια στοματος 118 209 **5** αυτον ο διαβολος 118 209 ϛ στιγμη 118 131 209 ϛ **7** om πεσων 118 209 ϛ μου 118 209 ϛ παντα ϛ **8** αυτω ειπεν ο Ιησους υπαγε οπισω μου Σατανα ϛ

εἶπεν αὐτῷ, Γέγραπται, Κύριον τὸν Θεόν σου προσκυνήσεις, καὶ
9 αὐτῷ μόνῳ λατρεύσεις. καὶ ἤγαγεν αὐτὸν εἰς Ἱεροσόλυμα καὶ ἔστη-
σεν αὐτὸν ἐπὶ τὸ πτερύγιον τοῦ ἱεροῦ, καὶ εἶπεν αὐτῷ, Εἰ υἱὸς εἶ τοῦ
10 Θεοῦ, βάλε σεαυτὸν ἐντεῦθεν κάτω· γέγραπται γὰρ ὅτι Τοῖς ἀγγέ-
λοις αὐτοῦ ἐντελεῖται περὶ σοῦ, τοῦ διαφυλάξαι σε ἐν πάσαις ταῖς
11 ὁδοῖς σου· καὶ ὅτι Ἐπὶ χειρῶν ἀροῦσί σε μήποτε προσκόψῃς πρὸς
12 λίθον τὸν πόδα σου. καὶ ἀποκριθεὶς εἶπεν αὐτῷ ὁ Ἰησοῦς ὅτι Εἴρηται,
13 Οὐκ ἐκπειράσεις Κύριον τὸν Θεόν σου. καὶ συντελέσας πάντα πειρασμὸν
ὁ διάβολος ἀπέστη ἀπ' αὐτοῦ ἄχρι καιροῦ.
14 Καὶ ὑπέστρεψεν ὁ Ἰησοῦς ἐν τῇ δυνάμει τοῦ Πνεύματος εἰς τὴν ιζ
15 Γαλιλαίαν· καὶ φήμη ἐξῆλθε καθ' ὅλης τῆς περιχώρου περὶ αὐτοῦ. καὶ α
αὐτὸς ἐδίδασκεν ἐν ταῖς συναγωγαῖς αὐτῶν, δοξαζόμενος ὑπὸ πάντων.
16 καὶ ἦλθεν εἰς Ναζαρέθ, οὗ ἦν ἀνατεθραμμένος, καὶ εἰσῆλθε κατὰ ιη
17 τὸ εἰωθὸς αὐτῷ ἐν τῇ ἡμέρᾳ τῶν σαββάτων εἰς τὴν συναγωγήν. καὶ ι
ἐπεδόθη αὐτῷ βιβλίον Ἡσαΐου τοῦ προφήτου, καὶ ἀνέστη ἀναγνῶ-
ναι. καὶ ἀναπτύξας τὸ βιβλίον εὗρε τὸν τόπον οὗ ἦν γεγραμμένον,
18 Πνεῦμα Κυρίου ἐπ' ἐμέ, οὗ εἵνεκεν ἔχρισέ με εὐαγγελίσασθαι
πτωχοῖς, ἀπέσταλκέ με ἰάσασθαι τοὺς συντετριμμένους τὴν καρδίαν,
κηρῦξαι αἰχμαλώτοις ἄφεσιν καὶ τυφλοῖς ἀνάβλεψιν, ἀποστεῖλαι τε-
19 θραυσμένους ἐν ἀφέσει, κηρῦξαι ἐνιαυτὸν Κυρίου δεκτόν. καὶ πτύξας
20 τὸ βιβλίον, ἀποδοὺς τῷ ὑπηρέτῃ, ἐκάθισε· καὶ πάντων ἐν τῇ συναγωγῇ
21 οἱ ὀφθαλμοὶ ἦσαν ἀτενίζοντες αὐτῷ. ἤρξατο δὲ λέγειν πρὸς αὐτοὺς
22 ὅτι Σήμερον πεπλήρωται ἡ γραφὴ αὕτη ἐν τοῖς ὠσὶν ὑμῶν. καὶ πάντες ιθ
ἐμαρτύρουν αὐτῷ, καὶ ἐθαύμαζον ἐπὶ τοῖς λόγοις τῆς χάριτος τοῖς ἐκπο- α
ρευομένοις ἐκ τοῦ στόματος αὐτοῦ, καὶ ἔλεγον, Οὐχ οὗτός ἐστιν ὁ υἱὸς
23 Ἰωσήφ; καὶ εἶπε πρὸς αὐτούς, Πάντως ἐρεῖτέ μοι τὴν παραβολὴν κ
ταύτην, Ἰατρέ, θεράπευσον σεαυτόν· ὅσα ἠκούσαμεν γενόμενα ἐν τῇ ι
Καπερναοὺμ ποίησον καὶ ὧδε ἐν τῇ πατρίδι σου.
24 Εἶπε δέ, Ἀμὴν λέγω ὑμῖν ὅτι οὐδεὶς προφήτης δεκτός ἐστιν ἐν τῇ κα
25 πατρίδι αὐτοῦ. ἐπ' ἀληθείας δὲ λέγω ὑμῖν ὅτι πολλαὶ χῆραι ἦσαν α
ἐν ταῖς ἡμέραις Ἡλίου ἐν τῷ Ἰσραήλ, ὅτε ἐκλείσθη ὁ οὐρανὸς ἐπὶ κβ
ἔτη τρία καὶ μῆνας ἕξ, ὡς ἐγένετο λιμὸς μέγας ἐπὶ πᾶσαν τὴν γῆν· ι

25 χειραι cod.

8 γεγραπται γαρ ϛ προσκυνησεις ante Κυριον ϛ **9** Ιερουσαλημ 118 209 ϛ ο υιος ϛ κατω τευθεν κατω 118 **10** om εν πασαις ταις οδοις σου ϛ **11** om οτι 131 **14** om περι 131 **16** την Ναζαρετ 118 209 ϛ τεθραμμενος 118 209 ϛ **17** και ανεστη αναγνωναι ante και επεδοθη 118 209 ϛ **18** ενεκεν ϛ ευαγγελιζεσθαι ϛ τη καρδια 131 **19** Κυριω 118 **20** ησαν οι οφθαλμοι 118 209 **25** om οτι ϛ

118 131 209 ϛ

καὶ πρὸς οὐδεμίαν αὐτῶν ἐπέμφθη Ἠλίας, εἰ μὴ εἰς Σάρεφθα τῆς 26
Σιδωνίας πρὸς γυναῖκα χήραν. καὶ πολλοὶ λεπροὶ ἦσαν ἐν τῷ 27
Ἰσραὴλ ἐπὶ Ἐλισσαίου τοῦ προφήτου· καὶ οὐδεὶς αὐτῶν ἐκαθαρίσθη,
εἰ μὴ Ναιμὰν ὁ Σύρος. καὶ ἐπλήσθησαν πάντες θυμοῦ ἐν τῇ συνα- 28
γωγῇ ἀκούσαντες ταῦτα· καὶ ἀναστάντες ἐξέβαλον αὐτὸν ἔξω τῆς 29
πόλεως, καὶ ἤγαγον αὐτὸν ἕως ὀφρύος τοῦ ὄρους ἐφ᾽ οὗ ἡ πόλις αὐτῶν
ᾠκοδόμητο, ὥστε κατακρημνίσαι αὐτόν· αὐτὸς δὲ διελθὼν διὰ μέσου 30
αὐτῶν ἐπορεύετο.

κγ/η Καὶ κατῆλθεν εἰς Καπερναοὺμ πόλιν τῆς Γαλιλαίας· καὶ ἦν διδάσκων 31
κδ/β αὐτοῖς ἐν τοῖς σάββασι. καὶ ἐξεπλήσσοντο ἐπὶ τῇ διδαχῇ αὐτοῦ, ὅτι 32
ἐν ἐξουσίᾳ ἦν ὁ λόγος αὐτοῦ. καὶ ἐν τῇ συναγωγῇ ἦν ἄνθρωπος ἔχων 33
Η'/κε/η πνεῦμα δαιμονίου ἀκαθάρτου, καὶ ἀνέκραξε φωνῇ μεγάλῃ λέγων, Ἔα, 34
τί ἡμῖν καὶ σοί, Ἰησοῦ Ναζαρηνέ; ἦλθες ἀπολέσαι ἡμᾶς; οἶδά σε τίς
εἶ, ὁ ἅγιος τοῦ Θεοῦ. καὶ ἐπετίμησεν αὐτῷ ὁ Ἰησοῦς λέγων, Φιμώθητι, 35
καὶ ἔξελθε ἀπ᾽ αὐτοῦ. καὶ ῥίψαν αὐτὸν τὸ δαιμόνιον εἰς τὸ μέσον
ἐξῆλθεν ἀπ᾽ αὐτοῦ μηδὲν βλάψαν αὐτόν. καὶ ἐγένετο θάμβος ἐπὶ 36
πάντας, καὶ συνελάλουν πρὸς ἀλλήλους λέγοντες, Τίς ὁ λόγος οὗτος,
ὅτι ἐν ἐξουσίᾳ καὶ δυνάμει ἐπιτάσσει τοῖς ἀκαθάρτοις πνεύμασι, καὶ
ἐξέρχονται; καὶ ἐξεπορεύετο ἦχος περὶ αὐτοῦ εἰς πάντα τόπον τῆς 37
περιχώρου.

Θ'/κϛ/β Ἀναστὰς δὲ ἀπὸ τῆς συναγωγῆς εἰσῆλθεν εἰς τὴν οἰκίαν Σίμωνος· ἡ 38
πενθερὰ δὲ τοῦ Σίμωνος ἦν συνεχομένη πυρετῷ μεγάλῳ· καὶ ἠρώτησαν
αὐτὸν περὶ αὐτῆς. καὶ ἐπιστὰς ἐπάνω αὐτῆς ἐπετίμησε τῷ πυρετῷ, καὶ 39
ἀφῆκεν αὐτήν· παραχρῆμα δὲ ἀναστᾶσα διηκόνει αὐτοῖς.

Ι' Δύνοντος δὲ τοῦ ἡλίου ἅπαντες ὅσοι εἶχον ἀσθενοῦντας νόσοις ποι- 40
κίλαις ἤγαγον αὐτοὺς πρὸς αὐτόν· ὁ δὲ ἑνὶ ἑκάστῳ αὐτῶν τὰς χεῖρας
κζ/η ἐπιθεὶς ἐθεράπευσεν αὐτούς. ἐξήρχοντο δὲ καὶ δαιμόνια πολλῶν, 41
κράζοντα καὶ λέγοντα ὅτι Σὺ εἶ ὁ Χριστὸς ὁ υἱὸς τοῦ Θεοῦ. καὶ
ἐπιτιμῶν οὐκ εἴα αὐτὰ λαλεῖν, ὅτι ᾔδεισαν τὸν Χριστὸν αὐτὸν εἶναι.
κη/η γενομένης δὲ ἡμέρας ἐξελθὼν ἐπορεύθη εἰς ἔρημον τόπον, καὶ οἱ ὄχλοι 42
ἐπεζήτουν αὐτὸν καὶ ἦλθον ἕως αὐτοῦ, καὶ κατεῖχον αὐτὸν τοῦ μὴ
πορεύεσθαι ἀπ᾽ αὐτῶν. ὁ δὲ εἶπε πρὸς αὐτοὺς ὅτι Καὶ ταῖς ἑτέραις 43

27 εκαθαρσθη cod. **38** ηρωτισαν cod.

118 131 209 ϛ **26** Σαραφθα 131, Σαρεπτα ϛ Σιδωνος ϛ **27** εν τω Ισραηλ post προφητου ϛ Ναιεμαν 118 209, Νεεμαν 131 ϛ **28** ακουοντες 118 131 209 ϛ **29** εξεβαλλον 131 της οφρυος ϛ ωστε] εις το ϛ **31** αυτους 131 ϛ **34** ευα 118 **35** om εις το μεσον 131 απ] εξ ϛ **38** απο] εκ ϛ om η 118 209 δε ante πενθερα 131 **40** παντες ϛ **41** εξηρχετο ϛ απο πολλων 131 ϛ κραυγαζοντα 118 αυτω 131 **42** εζητουν ϛ

πόλεσιν εὐαγγελίσασθαί με δεῖ τὴν βασιλείαν τοῦ Θεοῦ· ὅτι εἰς τοῦτο
44 ἀπεστάλην. καὶ ἦν κηρύσσων ἐν ταῖς συναγωγαῖς τῆς Ἰουδαίας.
V. Ἐγένετο δὲ ἐν τῷ τὸν ὄχλον ἐπικεῖσθαι αὐτῷ καὶ ἀκούειν τὸν κθ
λόγον τοῦ Θεοῦ, καὶ αὐτὸς ἦν ἑστὼς παρὰ τὴν λίμνην Γεννησαρέτ· ι
2 καὶ εἶδε δύο πλοῖα ἑστῶτα παρὰ τὴν λίμνην· οἱ δὲ ἁλιεῖς ἀποβάντες
3 ἀπ' αὐτῶν ἀπέπλυναν τὰ δίκτυα. ἐμβὰς δὲ εἰς ἓν τῶν πλοίων, ὃ ἦν
τοῦ Σίμωνος, ἠρώτησεν αὐτὸν ἀπὸ τῆς γῆς ἐπανάγειν ὀλίγον, καὶ
4 καθίσας ἐδίδασκεν ἀπὸ τοῦ πλοίου τοὺς ὄχλους. ὡς δὲ ἐπαύσατο λαλῶν, ΙΑ'
εἶπε πρὸς τὸν Σίμωνα, Ἐπανάγαγε εἰς τὸ βάθος καὶ χαλάσατε τὰ δίκτυα λ θ
5 ὑμῶν. καὶ ἀποκριθεὶς ὁ Σίμων εἶπεν αὐτῷ, Ἐπιστάτα, δι' ὅλης τῆς
νυκτὸς κοπιάσαντες οὐδὲν ἐλάβομεν· ἐπὶ δὲ τῷ ῥήματί σου χαλάσω-
6 μεν τὰ δίκτυα. καὶ τοῦτο ποιήσαντες συνέκλεισαν πλῆθος ἰχθύων
7 πολύ· διερρήγνυτο δὲ τὰ δίκτυα αὐτῶν, καὶ κατένευσαν τοῖς μετόχοις
τοῖς ἐν τῷ ἑτέρῳ πλοίῳ, τοῦ ἐλθόντας συλλαβέσθαι αὐτοῖς· καὶ
8 ἦλθον, καὶ ἔπλησαν ἀμφότερα τὰ πλοῖα, ὥστε βυθίζεσθαι αὐτά. ἰδὼν λα
δὲ Σίμων Πέτρος προσέπεσε τοῖς ποσὶ τοῦ Ἰησοῦ λέγων, Ἔξελθε ἀπ' ι
9 ἐμοῦ, ὅτι ἀνὴρ ἁμαρτωλὸς ἐγώ εἰμι, κύριε. θάμβος γὰρ περιέσχεν
αὐτὸν καὶ πάντας τοὺς σὺν αὐτῷ ἐπὶ τῇ ἄγρᾳ τῶν ἰχθύων ᾗ συνέλαβον·
10 ὁμοίως δὲ καὶ Ἰάκωβον καὶ Ἰωάννην, υἱοὺς Ζεβεδαίου, οἳ ἦσαν κοινωνοὶ
τῷ Σίμωνι. καὶ εἶπε πρὸς τὸν Σίμωνα ὁ Ἰησοῦς, Μὴ φοβοῦ· ἀπὸ τοῦ λβ
11 νῦν ἀνθρώπους ἔσῃ ζωγρῶν. καὶ καταγαγόντες τὰ πλοῖα ἐπὶ τὴν γῆν, β
ἀφέντες ἅπαντα ἠκολούθησαν αὐτῷ.
12 Καὶ ἐγένετο ἐν τῷ εἶναι αὐτὸν ἐν μιᾷ τῶν πόλεων, καὶ ἰδοὺ ἀνὴρ ΙΒ'
πλήρης λέπρας· καὶ ἰδὼν τὸν Ἰησοῦν, πεσὼν ἐπὶ πρόσωπον ἐδεήθη αὐτοῦ λγ β
13 λέγων, Κύριε, ἐὰν θέλῃς, δύνασαί με καθαρίσαι. καὶ ἐκτείνας τὴν χεῖρα
ἥψατο αὐτοῦ εἰπών, Θέλω, καθαρίσθητι. καὶ εὐθέως ἡ λέπρα ἀπῆλθεν
14 ἀπ' αὐτοῦ. καὶ αὐτὸς παρήγγειλεν αὐτῷ μηδενὶ εἰπεῖν· Ἀλλ' ἀπελθὼν
δεῖξον σεαυτὸν τῷ ἱερεῖ, καὶ προσένεγκε περὶ τοῦ καθαρισμοῦ σου, καθὼς
15 προσέταξε Μωυσῆς, εἰς μαρτύριον αὐτοῖς. διήρχετο δὲ μᾶλλον ὁ λόγος λδ
περὶ αὐτοῦ· καὶ συνήρχοντο ὄχλοι πολλοὶ ἀκούειν, καὶ θεραπεύεσθαι α

2 *πλοῖα*] incertum est. spatium est inter *ι* et *α* satis idoneum ad *πλοιαρια* scribendum, nulla autem vestigia scripturae distingui possunt quamvis in spatio unius tantum literae rasura sit; equidem accentus testimonio fretus *πλοῖα* edidi, sed Tregellesius contra *πλοιάρια* maluit

43 *απεσταλ* spat. rel. 118, *απεσταλειν* 131, *απεσταλμαι* ς **44** *Γαλιλαιας* ς 118 131 209 ς

1 *και* 1°] *του* ς **3** *επαναγαγειν* 118 131 209 ς *απο*] *εκ* ς **4** *υμων*]+*εις αγραν* ς **5** om *της* 131 *χαλασω* 131 ς, *χαλασομεν* 209 *το δικτυον* ς **6** *ιχθυων πληθος* ς *το δικτυον* ς **7** *ελθοντος* 131 **8** *ποσι*] *γονασι* ς om *εγω* 118 ς *παντα* 131 **14** *αλλα* ς *Μωσης* ς **15** *θεραπευεσθαι υπ αυτου* ς

λε β ἀπὸ τῶν ἀσθενειῶν αὐτῶν· αὐτὸς δὲ ἦν ὑποχωρῶν ἐν ταῖς ἐρήμοις καὶ 16
προσευχόμενος.
λς β Καὶ ἐγένετο ἐν μιᾷ τῶν ἡμερῶν, καὶ αὐτὸς ἦν διδάσκων· καὶ ἦσαν 17
καθήμενοι Φαρισαῖοι καὶ νομοδιδάσκαλοι, οἳ ἦσαν συνεληλυθότες ἐκ
πάσης κώμης τῆς Γαλιλαίας καὶ Ἰουδαίας καὶ Ἱερουσαλήμ. καὶ δύναμις
ΙΓ' Κυρίου ἦν εἰς τὸ ἰᾶσθαι αὐτούς. καὶ ἰδοὺ ἄνδρες φέροντες ἐπὶ κλίνης 18
λζ α ἄνθρωπον ὃς ἦν παραλελυμένος, καὶ ἐζήτουν αὐτὸν εἰσενεγκεῖν καὶ θεῖναι
ἐνώπιον αὐτοῦ· καὶ μὴ εὑρόντες ποίας εἰσενέγκωσιν αὐτὸν διὰ τὸν 19
ὄχλον, ἀναβάντες ἐπὶ τὸ δῶμα διὰ τῶν κεράμων καθῆκαν αὐτὸν σὺν
τῷ κλινιδίῳ εἰς τὸ μέσον ἔμπροσθεν τοῦ Ἰησοῦ. καὶ ἰδὼν τὴν πίστιν 20
αὐτῶν εἶπε τῷ ἀνθρώπῳ, Ἀφέωνταί σοι αἱ ἁμαρτίαι σου. καὶ ἤρξαντο 21
διαλογίζεσθαι οἱ γραμματεῖς καὶ οἱ Φαρισαῖοι λέγοντες, Τίς ἐστιν οὗτος
ὃς λαλεῖ βλασφημίας; τίς δύναται ἁμαρτίας ἀφιέναι, εἰ μὴ μόνος
ὁ Θεός; ἐπιγνοὺς δὲ ὁ Ἰησοῦς τοὺς διαλογισμοὺς αὐτῶν ἀποκριθεὶς 22
εἶπε πρὸς αὐτούς, Τί διαλογίζεσθε ἐν ταῖς καρδίαις ὑμῶν; τί ἐστιν 23
εὐκοπώτερον, εἰπεῖν, Ἀφέωνταί σοι αἱ ἁμαρτίαι σου, ἢ εἰπεῖν, Ἔγειρε
καὶ περιπάτει; ἵνα δὲ εἰδῆτε ὅτι ἐξουσίαν ἔχει ὁ υἱὸς τοῦ ἀνθρώπου ἐπὶ 24
τῆς γῆς ἀφιέναι ἁμαρτίας, εἶπε τῷ παραλελυμένῳ, Σοὶ λέγω, ἔγειρε,
καὶ ἄρας τὸ κλινίδιόν σου πορεύου εἰς τὸν οἶκόν σου. καὶ παραχρῆμα 25
ἀναστὰς ἐνώπιον αὐτῶν, ἄρας ἐφ' ᾧ κατέκειτο, ἀπῆλθεν εἰς τὸν οἶκον
αὐτοῦ δοξάζων τὸν Θεόν. καὶ ἔκστασις ἔλαβεν ἅπαντας, καὶ ἐδόξαζον 26
τὸν Θεόν, καὶ ἐπλήσθησαν φόβου, λέγοντες ὅτι Εἴδομεν παράδοξα
σήμερον.
ΙΔ' Καὶ μετὰ ταῦτα ἐξῆλθε καὶ ἐθεάσατο τελώνην ὀνόματι Λευῒν καθή- 27
λη β μενον ἐπὶ τὸ τελώνιον, καὶ εἶπεν αὐτῷ, Ἀκολούθει μοι. καὶ καταλιπὼν 28
λθ β ἅπαντα ἀναστὰς ἠκολούθησεν αὐτῷ. καὶ ἐποίησε δοχὴν μεγάλην Λευῒς 29
αὐτῷ ἐν τῇ οἰκίᾳ αὐτοῦ· καὶ ἦν ὄχλος πολὺς τελωνῶν καὶ ἄλλων οἳ
ἦσαν μετ' αὐτοῦ κατακείμενοι. καὶ ἐγόγγυζον οἱ Φαρισαῖοι καὶ οἱ 30
γραμματεῖς αὐτῶν πρὸς τοὺς μαθητὰς αὐτοῦ λέγοντες, Διατί μετὰ
μ β τῶν τελωνῶν καὶ ἁμαρτωλῶν ἐσθίετε καὶ πίνετε; καὶ ἀποκριθεὶς ὁ 31
Ἰησοῦς εἶπε πρὸς αὐτούς, Οὐ χρείαν ἔχουσιν οἱ ὑγιαίνοντες ἰατροῦ,
ἀλλ' οἱ κακῶς ἔχοντες. οὐκ ἦλθον καλέσαι δικαίους, ἀλλ' ἁμαρτω- 32

118 131 209 ς **17** οι και 118 εληλυθοτες 118 ς **19** ποιας] πως 118 131 209, δια ποιας ς ενεγκωσιν 118 209 **20** τω ανθρωπω] αυτω, ανθρωπε 118 ς **21** αφιεναι αμαρτιας 131 ς **23** εγειραι 131 209 ς **24** εγειραι 131 209 ς, 118* primum εγειρε postea εγειραι scripsit **27** Λευι 131 **29** ο Λευις 131 ς τελωνων πολυς ς μετ αυτων ς **30** οι γραμματεις και οι Φαρισαιοι 118 209, οι γραμματεις και οι Φαρισαιοι αυτων 131, οι γραμματεις αυτων και οι Φαρισαιοι ς om των 118 ς **32** εληλυθα ς αλλα 118 131 209 ς

33 λοὺς εἰς μετάνοιαν. οἱ δὲ εἶπον πρὸς αὐτόν, Διατί οἱ μαθηταὶ Ἰωάννου
νηστεύουσι πυκνά, καὶ δεήσεις ποιοῦνται, ὁμοίως καὶ οἱ τῶν Φαρισαίων,
34 οἱ δὲ σοὶ ἐσθίουσι καὶ πίνουσιν; ὁ δὲ Ἰησοῦς εἶπε πρὸς αὐτούς, Μὴ
δύνασθε τοὺς υἱοὺς τοῦ νυμφῶνος, ἐν ᾧ ὁ νυμφίος μετ' αὐτῶν ἐστι,
35 ποιῆσαι νηστεύειν; ἐλεύσονται δὲ ἡμέραι, ὅταν ἄρθῃ ἀπ' αὐτῶν ὁ
36 νυμφίος, καὶ τότε νηστεύσουσιν ἐν ἐκείναις ταῖς ἡμέραις. ἔλεγε δὲ καὶ
παραβολὴν πρὸς αὐτούς, ὅτι Οὐδεὶς ἐπίβλημα ἀπὸ ἱματίου καινοῦ
σχίσας ἐπιβάλλει ἐπὶ ἱμάτιον παλαιόν· εἰ δὲ μήγε, καὶ τὸ καινὸν
σχίζει, καὶ τῷ παλαιῷ οὐ συμφωνεῖ τὸ ἐπίβλημα τὸ ἀπὸ τοῦ καινοῦ.
37 καὶ οὐδεὶς βάλλει οἶνον νέον εἰς ἀσκοὺς παλαιούς· εἰ δὲ μήγε, ῥήξει
ὁ οἶνος ὁ νέος τοὺς ἀσκούς, καὶ αὐτὸς ἐκχυθήσεται καὶ οἱ ἀσκοὶ ἀπο-
38 39 λοῦνται· ἀλλ' οἶνον νέον εἰς ἀσκοὺς καινοὺς βλητέον. καὶ οὐδεὶς πιὼν
παλαιὸν θέλει νέον· λέγει γάρ, Ὁ παλαιὸς χρηστότερός ἐστιν.

VI. Ἐγένετο δὲ ἐν σαββάτῳ διαπορεύεσθαι αὐτὸν διὰ σπορί- μα
μων· ἔτιλλον δὲ οἱ μαθηταὶ αὐτοῦ τοὺς στάχυας καὶ ἤσθιον, ψώχοντες β
2 ταῖς χερσί. τινὲς δὲ τῶν Φαρισαίων εἶπον, Τί ποιεῖτε ὃ οὐκ ἔξεστι
3 ποιεῖν τοῖς σάββασι; καὶ ἀποκριθεὶς ὁ Ἰησοῦς εἶπεν αὐτοῖς, Οὐδὲ
τοῦτο ἀνέγνωτε, ὃ ἐποίησε Δαβίδ, ὅτε ἐπείνασεν αὐτὸς καὶ οἱ μετ'
4 αὐτοῦ; πῶς εἰσῆλθεν εἰς τὸν οἶκον τοῦ Θεοῦ, καὶ τοὺς ἄρτους τῆς
προθέσεως ἔφαγε, καὶ ἔδωκε τοῖς μετ' αὐτοῦ, οὓς οὐκ ἔξεστι φαγεῖν
5 εἰ μὴ μόνους τοὺς ἱερεῖς; καὶ ἔλεγεν αὐτοῖς, Κύριός ἐστιν ὁ υἱὸς
τοῦ ἀνθρώπου καὶ τοῦ σαββάτου.

6 Ἐγένετο δὲ ἐν ἑτέρῳ σαββάτῳ εἰσελθεῖν αὐτὸν εἰς τὴν συναγωγὴν ΙΕ'
καὶ διδάσκειν· καὶ ἦν ἄνθρωπος ἐκεῖ, καὶ ἡ χεὶρ αὐτοῦ ἡ δεξιὰ ἦν μβ β
7 ξηρά. παρετηροῦντο δὲ οἱ γραμματεῖς καὶ οἱ Φαρισαῖοι, εἰ ἐν τῷ
8 σαββάτῳ θεραπεύσει, ἵνα εὕρωσι κατηγορεῖν αὐτοῦ. αὐτὸς δὲ ᾔδει
τοὺς διαλογισμοὺς αὐτῶν, εἶπε δὲ τῷ ἀνδρὶ τῷ ξηρὰν ἔχοντι τὴν
9 χεῖρα, Ἔγειρε καὶ στῆθι εἰς τὸ μέσον. καὶ ἀναστὰς ἔστη. εἶπεν

4 μη] μι cod.

34 om Ιησους ς **35** και οταν ς απαρθη 131 ς om και ς 118 131
36 om επιβλημα 1° 131 om απο ς om σχισας ς om το επιβλημα 118 209 ς
209, επιβλημα sine το ς **37** ο νεος οινος 118 209 ς **38** αλλα ς
βλητεον]+και αμφοτεροι συντηρουνται 118 ς **39** ευθεως θελει ς

1 σαββατω δευτεροπρωτω 131 ς των σποριμων 118 209 ς και ετιλ-
λον ς **2** ειπον αυτοις ς τοις] pr εν ς **3** ο Ιησους ειπε προς
αυτους 131, προς αυτους ειπεν ο Ιησους ς οτε] οποτε ς αυτου οντες ς
4 πως] ως ς ελαβε και εφαγε ς τοις] pr και 118 (sed suprascr.)
131 ς **5** αυτοις ο Ιησους 131 οτι κυριος 118 ς **6** δε]+και ς
εκει ανθρωπος ς **7** παρετηρουν 118 209 ς δε]+αυτον ς κατηγοριαν ς
8 και ειπε ς ανθρωπω ς εγειραι 131 209 ς **9** και] ο δε ς

οὖν ὁ Ἰησοῦς πρὸς αὐτούς, Ἐρωτήσω ὑμᾶς, τί ἔξεστι τοῖς σάββασιν,
ἀγαθοποιῆσαι ἢ κακοποιῆσαι, ψυχὴν σῶσαι ἢ ἀπολέσαι; καὶ περι- 10
βλεψάμενος πάντας αὐτοὺς ἐν ὀργῇ εἶπε τῷ ἀνθρώπῳ, Ἔκτεινον τὴν
χεῖρά σου. ὁ δὲ ἐξέτεινε. καὶ ἀποκατέστη ἡ χεὶρ αὐτοῦ ὡς καὶ
ἡ ἄλλη. αὐτοὶ δὲ ἐπλήσθησαν ἀνοίας, καὶ διελάλουν πρὸς ἀλλήλους 11
τί ἂν ποιήσαιεν τῷ Ἰησοῦ.
μγ β Ἐγένετο δὲ ἐν ταῖς ἡμέραις ταύταις, ἐξῆλθεν εἰς τὸ ὄρος προσ- 12
ΙϚ' εὔξασθαι, καὶ ἦν διανυκτερεύων ἐν τῇ προσευχῇ τοῦ Θεοῦ. καὶ ὅτε 13
μδ β ἐγένετο ἡμέρα, ἐφώνησε τοὺς μαθητὰς αὐτοῦ· καὶ ἐκλεξάμενος ἀπ'
αὐτῶν δώδεκα, οὓς καὶ ἀποστόλους ὠνόμασε, Σίμωνα ὃν καὶ ὠνό- 14
μασε Πέτρον καὶ Ἀνδρέαν τὸν ἀδελφὸν αὐτοῦ, Ἰάκωβον καὶ Ἰωάννην,
Φίλιππον καὶ Βαρθολομαῖον, Ματθαῖον καὶ Θωμᾶν, Ἰάκωβον Ἀλφαίου 15
καὶ Σίμωνα τὸν καλούμενον Ζηλωτήν, Ἰούδαν Ἰακώβου, καὶ Ἰούδαν 16
με α Ἰσκαριώτην ὃς καὶ ἐγένετο προδότης· καὶ καταβὰς μετ' αὐτῶν ἔστη 17
ἐπὶ τόπου πεδινοῦ, καὶ ὄχλος πολὺς μαθητῶν αὐτοῦ, καὶ πλῆθος πολὺ
ἀπὸ πάσης τῆς Ἰουδαίας καὶ Ἱερουσαλήμ, καὶ τῆς παραλίου Τύρου καὶ
Σιδῶνος, οἳ ἦλθον ἀκοῦσαι αὐτοῦ καὶ ἰαθῆναι ἀπὸ τῶν νόσων αὐτῶν,
καὶ οἱ ἐνοχλούμενοι ὑπὸ πνευμάτων ἀκαθάρτων, καὶ ἐθεραπεύοντο. 18
καὶ πᾶς ὁ ὄχλος ἐζήτει ἅπτεσθαι αὐτοῦ, ὅτι δύναμις παρ' αὐτοῦ 19
ἐξήρχετο καὶ ἰᾶτο πάντας.
ΙΖ' Καὶ αὐτὸς ἐπάρας τοὺς ὀφθαλμοὺς αὐτοῦ εἰς τοὺς μαθητὰς αὐτοῦ 20
μϛ ε ἔλεγε, Μακάριοι οἱ πτωχοὶ τῷ πνεύματι, ὅτι ὑμετέρα ἐστὶν ἡ βασι-
μζ ε λεία τοῦ Θεοῦ. μακάριοι οἱ πεινῶντες νῦν, ὅτι χορτασθήσεσθε. 21
μη ε μακάριοι οἱ κλαίοντες νῦν, ὅτι γελάσετε. μακάριοί ἐστε ὅταν μισή- 22
σωσιν ὑμᾶς οἱ ἄνθρωποι, καὶ ὅταν ἀφορίσωσιν ὑμᾶς καὶ ὀνειδίσωσι,
μθ ε καὶ ἐκβάλωσι τὸ ὄνομα ὑμῶν ὡς πονηρὸν ἕνεκα τοῦ υἱοῦ τοῦ ἀνθρώπου.
χάριτε ἐν ἐκείνῃ τῇ ἡμέρᾳ καὶ σκιρτήσατε· ἰδοὺ γὰρ ὁ μισθὸς ὑμῶν 23
πολὺς ἐν τῷ οὐρανῷ· κατὰ ταῦτα γὰρ ἐποίουν τοῖς προφήταις οἱ πατέρες
ν ι αὐτῶν. πλὴν οὐαὶ ὑμῖν τοῖς πλουσίοις, ὅτι ἀπέχετε τὴν παράκλησιν 24
ὑμῶν. οὐαὶ ὑμῖν, οἱ ἐμπεπλησμένοι, νῦν ὅτι πεινάσετε. οὐαί, οἱ 25
να ι γελῶντες νῦν, ὅτι πενθήσετε καὶ κλαύσετε. οὐαί, ὅταν καλῶς ὑμᾶς 26
εἴπωσι πάντες οἱ ἄνθρωποι· κατὰ ταῦτα γὰρ ἐποίουν τοῖς ψευδοπροφή-
ταις οἱ πατέρες αὐτῶν.

118 131 209 ς **9** επερωτησω 131 ς **10** om εν οργη ς εξετεινε] εποιησεν ουτω ς αποκατεστη 118 209, αποκατεσταθη ς ως και] υγιης ως ς **11** ποιησειαν ς **13** προσεφωνησε ς ονομασε 118 **15** τον του Αλφαιου ς **17** αυτων] αυτου 118 209 om πολυς ς πολυ του λαου ς **18** οχλουμενοι 118 209 ς **19** δυναμεις 131 **20** om τω πνευματι ς του Θεου] των ουρανων 118 209 **23** χαρητε 131, χαιρετε ς **24** οτι] τι 118 per rubricatoris incuriam **25** om νυν ς ουαι 2°]+υμιν ς **26** ουαι υμιν ς

27 Ἀλλ' ὑμῖν λέγω τοῖς ἀκούουσιν, Ἀγαπᾶτε τοὺς ἐχθροὺς ὑμῶν, καλῶς νβ
28 ποιεῖτε τοῖς μισοῦσιν ὑμᾶς, εὐλογεῖτε τοὺς καταρωμένους ὑμᾶς, προσ- ε
29 εύχεσθε ὑπὲρ τῶν ἐπηρεαζόντων ὑμᾶς. τῷ τύπτοντί σε ἐπὶ τὴν σιαγόνα νγ
πάρεχε καὶ τὴν ἄλλην· καὶ ἀπὸ τοῦ αἴροντός σου τὸ ἱμάτιον καὶ τὸν ε
30 χιτῶνα μὴ κωλύσῃς. παντὶ τῷ αἰτοῦντί σε δίδου· καὶ ἀπὸ τοῦ αἴροντος νδ ε
31 τὰ σὰ μὴ ἀπαίτει. καὶ καθὼς θέλετε ἵνα ποιῶσιν ὑμῖν οἱ ἄνθρωποι, νε
32 καὶ ὑμεῖς ποιεῖτε αὐτοῖς ὁμοίως. καὶ εἰ ἀγαπᾶτε τοὺς ἀγαπῶντας ε
33 ὑμᾶς, ποία ὑμῖν χάρις ἐστί; καὶ γὰρ οἱ ἁμαρτωλοὶ τὸ αὐτὸ ποιοῦσι.
34 καὶ ἐὰν δανείζητε παρ' ὧν ἐλπίζετε ἀπολαβεῖν, ποία ὑμῖν χάρις ἐστί;
καὶ γὰρ ἁμαρτωλοὶ ἁμαρτωλοῖς δανείζουσιν, ἵνα ἀπολάβωσι τὰ ἴσα.
35 πλὴν ἀγαπᾶτε τοὺς ἐχθροὺς ὑμῶν καὶ ἀγαθοποιεῖτε καὶ δανείζετε μηδὲν
ἀπελπίζοντες· καὶ ἔσται ὁ μισθὸς ὑμῶν πολύς, καὶ ἔσεσθε υἱοὶ τοῦ
ὑψίστου· ὅτι αὐτὸς χρηστός ἐστιν ἐπὶ τοὺς πονηροὺς καὶ ἀχαρί-
36 στους. γίνεσθε οἰκτίρμονες, καθὼς ὁ πατὴρ ὑμῶν οἰκτίρμων ἐστί.
37 μὴ κρίνετε, καὶ οὐ μὴ κριθῆτε. μὴ καταδικάζετε, καὶ οὐ μὴ καταδι- νϛ
38 κασθῆτε. ἀπολύετε, καὶ ἀπολυθήσεσθε· δίδοτε, καὶ δοθήσεται ὑμῖν· β
μέτρον καλόν, σεσαλευμένον, πεπιεσμένον, ὑπερεκχυνόμενον δώ-
σουσιν εἰς τὸν κόλπον ὑμῶν. ᾧ γὰρ μέτρῳ ᾧ μετρεῖτε, ἀντιμετρηθήσεται
ὑμῖν.
39 Εἶπε δὲ παραβολὴν αὐτοῖς, Μήτι δύναται τυφλὸς τυφλὸν ὁδηγεῖν; νζ
40 οὐχὶ ἀμφότεροι εἰς βόθυνον ἐμπεσοῦνται; οὐκ ἔστι μαθητὴς ὑπὲρ τὸν ε
41 διδάσκαλον· κατηρτισμένος δὲ πᾶς ἔσται ὡς ὁ διδάσκαλος αὐτοῦ. τί νη γ
δὲ βλέπεις τὸ κάρφος τὸ ἐν τῷ ὀφθαλμῷ τοῦ ἀδελφοῦ σου, τὴν δὲ νθ ε
42 δοκὸν τὴν ἐν τῷ ἰδίῳ ὀφθαλμῷ οὐ κατανοεῖς; ἢ πῶς δύνασαι λέγειν
τῷ ἀδελφῷ σου, Ἀδελφέ, ἄφες ἐκβάλω τὸ κάρφος τὸ ἐν τῷ ὀφθαλμῷ
σου, αὐτὸς τὴν ἐν τῷ ὀφθαλμῷ σου δοκὸν οὐ βλέπων; ὑποκριτά, ἔκ-
βαλε πρῶτον τὴν δοκὸν ἐκ τοῦ ὀφθαλμοῦ σου, καὶ τότε διαβλέψεις τὸ
43 κάρφος ἐκβαλεῖν τὸ ἐν τῷ ὀφθαλμῷ τοῦ ἀδελφοῦ σου. οὐ γάρ ξ
ἐστι δένδρον καλὸν ποιοῦν καρπὸν σαπρόν, οὐδὲ πάλιν δένδρον σαπρὸν ε

28 επηρεαζοτων cod. **41** δε 1°] δαι cod.

118 131 209 ϛ

28 υμας 1°] υμιν καί ϛ **30** παντι δε ϛ **32** αγαποντας 131 εστι]+και γαρ οι αμαρτωλοι τους αγαπωντας αυτους αγαπωσι. και εαν αγαθοποιητε τους αγαθοποιουντας υμας ποια υμιν χαρις εστι; 131 ϛ **34** οι αμαρτωλοι ϛ **35** χρηστος] χ̅ς̅ 131 αχαριστους και πονηρους ϛ γινεσθε ουν ϛ **36** καθως και ϛ **37** μη 1°] pr και ϛ **38** πεπιεσμενον και σεσαλευμενον και υπερεκχυνομενον ϛ ω γαρ] τω γαρ αυτω ϛ **39** πεσουνται ϛ **40** notandum est quod in cod. 118 duae paginae usque ad VII 26 ita sunt mutilae ut rem in praefatione tractare malim, sed hic quoque varias lectiones quae supersint indicavi διδασκαλον αυτου ϛ **42** εκβαλειν το καρφος 209 ϛ (118 deest) **43** om παλιν 209 ϛ (118 deest)

ξα ε ποιοῦν καρπὸν καλόν. ἕκαστον γὰρ δένδρον ἐκ τοῦ ἰδίου καρποῦ γινώ- 44
σκεται· οὐ γὰρ ἐξ ἀκανθῶν συλλέγουσι σῦκα, οὐδὲ ἐκ βάτου τρυγῶσι
ξβ ε σταφυλήν. ὁ ἀγαθὸς ἄνθρωπος ἐκ τοῦ ἀγαθοῦ θησαυροῦ τῆς καρδίας 45
αὐτοῦ προφέρει τὸ ἀγαθόν· καὶ ὁ πονηρὸς ἐκ τοῦ πονηροῦ προ-
φέρει τὸ πονηρόν· ἐκ γὰρ τοῦ περισσεύματος τῆς καρδίας λαλεῖ τὸ
στόμα αὐτοῦ.
ξγ γ Τί δέ με καλεῖτε, Κύριε, κύριε, καὶ οὐ ποιεῖτε ἃ λέγω; πᾶς ὁ ἐρχό- 46 47
ξδ ε μενος πρός με καὶ ἀκούων μου τῶν λόγων καὶ ποιῶν αὐτούς, ὑποδείξω
ὑμῖν τίνι ἐστὶν ὅμοιος. ὅμοιός ἐστιν ἀνθρώπῳ οἰκοδομοῦντι οἰκίαν, ὃς 48
ἔσκαψε καὶ ἐβάθυνε καὶ ἔθηκε θεμέλιον ἐπὶ τὴν πέτραν· πλημμύρας
δὲ γενομένης προσέρρηξεν ὁ ποταμὸς τῇ οἰκίᾳ ἐκείνῃ, καὶ οὐκ ἴσχυσε
σαλεῦσαι αὐτήν· τεθεμελίωτο γὰρ ἐπὶ τὴν πέτραν. ὁ δὲ ἀκούσας καὶ 49
μὴ ποιήσας ὅμοιός ἐστιν ἀνθρώπῳ οἰκοδομήσαντι οἰκίαν ἐπὶ τὴν γῆν
χωρὶς θεμελίου· ᾗ προσέρρηξεν ὁ ποταμός, καὶ εὐθέως συνέπεσε, καὶ
ἐγένετο τὸ ῥῆγμα τῆς οἰκίας ἐκείνης μέγα.
III′ VII. Ἐπεὶ δὲ ἐπλήρωσε πάντα τὰ ῥήματα αὐτοῦ εἰς τὰς ἀκοὰς
ξε γ τοῦ λαοῦ, εἰσῆλθεν εἰς Καπερναούμ. ἑκατοντάρχου δέ τινος δοῦλος 2
κακῶς ἔχων ἤμελλε τελευτᾶν, ὃς ἦν αὐτῷ ἔντιμος. ἀκούσας δὲ περὶ 3
τοῦ Ἰησοῦ ἀπέστειλε πρὸς αὐτὸν πρεσβυτέρους τῶν Ἰουδαίων, ἐρωτῶν
αὐτὸν ὅπως ἐλθὼν διασώσῃ τὸν δοῦλον αὐτοῦ. οἱ δὲ παραγενόμενοι 4
πρὸς τὸν Ἰησοῦν ἠρώτων αὐτὸν σπουδαίως, λέγοντες ὅτι Ἄξιός ἐστιν
ᾧ παρέξει τοῦτο· ἀγαπᾷ γὰρ τὸ ἔθνος ἡμῶν, καὶ τὴν συναγωγὴν αὐτὸς 5
ᾠκοδόμησεν ἡμῖν. ὁ δὲ Ἰησοῦς ἐπορεύετο σὺν αὐτοῖς. ἤδη δὲ αὐτοῦ οὐ 6
μακρὰν ἀπέχοντος τῆς οἰκίας, πέμψας πρὸς αὐτὸν ὁ ἑκατόνταρχος
φίλους ἔλεγεν αὐτῷ, Κύριε, μὴ σκύλλου· οὐ γάρ εἰμι ἱκανὸς ἵνα
μου ὑπὸ τὴν στέγην εἰσέλθῃς· διὸ οὐδὲ ἐμαυτὸν ἠξίωσα πρός σε ἐλθεῖν· 7
ἀλλ' εἰπὲ λόγῳ, καὶ ἰαθήσεται ὁ παῖς μου. καὶ γὰρ ἐγὼ ἄνθρωπός 8
εἰμι ὑπὸ ἐξουσίαν τασσόμενος, ἔχων ὑπ' ἐμαυτὸν στρατιώτας· καὶ λέγω
τούτῳ, Πορεύθητι, καὶ πορεύεται· καὶ ἄλλῳ, Ἔρχου, καὶ ἔρχεται· καὶ
τῷ δούλῳ μου, Ποίησον τοῦτο, καὶ ποιεῖ. ἀκούσας δὲ ταῦτα ὁ Ἰησοῦς 9
ἐθαύμασεν αὐτόν, καὶ στραφεὶς τῷ ἀκολουθοῦντι αὐτῷ ὄχλῳ εἶπε, Λέγω
ξϛ ε ὑμῖν, οὐδὲ ἐν τῷ Ἰσραὴλ τοσαύτην πίστιν εὗρον. καὶ ὑποστρέψαντες 10
οἱ πεμφθέντες εἰς τὸν οἶκον εὗρον τὸν δοῦλον ὑγιαίνοντα.

49 *ρηγμα*] *ρημα* cod. *τοις οικιας* cod. **4** *λεγωντες* cod.

118 131 209 ϛ **44** om *γαρ* 1° 209 (118 deest) **45** *προφερει* bis] *προσφερει* bis 131 *πονηρος ανθρωπος* 118 209 ϛ *πονηρου θησαυρου της καρδιας αυτου* 118 209 ϛ **49** *την οικιαν* 118 209 *επεσε* ϛ

1 om *παντα* 131 **4** *ηρωτων*] *παρεκαλουν* 118 209 ϛ **6** *απο της* 131 ϛ *επεμψε* ϛ *φιλους ο εκατονταρχος* 131 *λεγων* ϛ *μου* post *στεγην* ϛ **7** *αλλα* ϛ **8** *πορευου* 209 (118 deest) **10** *ασθενουντα δουλον* ϛ

11 Καὶ ἐγένετο ἐν τῷ, ἐπορεύετο εἰς πόλιν καλουμένην Ναείμ· καὶ ΙΘ'
12 συνεπορεύοντο αὐτῷ μαθηταὶ ἱκανοὶ καὶ ὄχλος πολύς. ὡς δὲ ἤγγισε ξζ ι
τῇ πύλῃ τῆς πόλεως, ἰδοὺ ἐξεκομίζετο τεθνηκὼς υἱὸς μονογενὴς τῇ
μητρὶ αὐτοῦ, καὶ αὕτη ἦν χήρα· καὶ ὄχλος ἱκανὸς τῆς πόλεως σὺν
13 αὐτῇ. καὶ ἰδὼν αὐτὴν ὁ Ἰησοῦς ἐσπλαγχνίσθη ἐπ' αὐτῇ, καὶ εἶπεν
14 αὐτῇ, Μὴ κλαῖε. καὶ προσελθὼν ἥψατο τῆς σοροῦ· οἱ δὲ βαστάζοντες
15 ἔστησαν· καὶ εἶπε, Νεανίσκε, σοὶ λέγω, ἐγέρθητι. καὶ ἀνεκάθισεν ὁ
16 νεκρός, καὶ ἤρξατο λαλεῖν· καὶ ἔδωκεν αὐτὸν τῇ μητρὶ αὐτοῦ· ἔλαβε δὲ
φόβος πάντας, καὶ ἐδόξαζον τὸν Θεόν, λέγοντες ὅτι Προφήτης μέγας
17 ἠγέρθη ἐν ἡμῖν, καὶ ὅτι Ἐπεσκέψατο ὁ Κύριος τὸν λαὸν αὐτοῦ. καὶ ξη ι
ἐξῆλθεν ὁ λόγος οὗτος ἐν ὅλῃ τῇ Ἰουδαίᾳ περὶ αὐτοῦ, καὶ πάσῃ τῇ
περιχώρῳ.

18 Καὶ ἀπήγγειλαν Ἰωάννῃ περὶ αὐτοῦ οἱ μαθηταὶ αὐτοῦ περὶ πάντων Κ'
19 τούτων. καὶ προσκαλεσάμενος δύο τινὰς τῶν μαθητῶν αὐτοῦ Ἰωάννης ξθ ε
ἔπεμψε πρὸς τὸν Ἰησοῦν, λέγων, Σὺ εἶ ὁ ἐρχόμενος, ἢ ἄλλον προσ-
20 δοκῶμεν; παραγενόμενοι δὲ πρὸς αὐτὸν οἱ ἄνδρες εἶπον, Ἰωάννης ὁ
Βαπτιστὴς ἀπέσταλκεν ἡμᾶς πρός σε, λέγων, Σὺ εἶ ὁ ἐρχόμενος, ἢ
21 ἕτερον προσδοκῶμεν; ἐν ἐκείνῃ τῇ ὥρᾳ ἐθεράπευσε πολλοὺς ἀπὸ
νόσων καὶ μαστίγων καὶ πνευμάτων πονηρῶν, καὶ τυφλοῖς πολλοῖς
22 ἐχαρίσατο τὸ βλέπειν. καὶ ἀποκριθεὶς ὁ Ἰησοῦς εἶπεν αὐτοῖς, Πορευ-
θέντες ἀπαγγείλατε Ἰωάννῃ ἃ εἴδετε καὶ ἠκούσατε· τυφλοὶ ἀναβλέ-
πουσι, χωλοὶ περιπατοῦσι, λεπροὶ καθαρίζονται, κωφοὶ ἀκούουσι, νεκροὶ
23 ἐγείρονται, καὶ πτωχοὶ εὐαγγελίζονται· καὶ μακάριός ἐστιν ὃς ἐὰν μὴ
24 σκανδαλισθῇ ἐν ἐμοί. ἀπελθόντων δὲ τῶν μαθητῶν Ἰωάννου ἤρξατο
λέγειν πρὸς τοὺς ὄχλους περὶ Ἰωάννου, Τί ἐξήλθετε εἰς τὴν ἔρημον
25 θεάσασθαι; κάλαμον ὑπὸ ἀνέμου σαλευόμενον; ἀλλὰ τί ἐξήλθετε
ἰδεῖν; ἄνθρωπον ἐν μαλακοῖς ἱματίοις ἠμφιεσμένον; ἰδοὺ οἱ ἐν ἱματισμῷ
26 ἐνδόξῳ καὶ τρυφῇ ὑπάρχοντες ἐν τοῖς βασιλείοις εἰσίν. ἀλλὰ τί ἐξήλ-
θετε ἰδεῖν; προφήτην; ναί, λέγω ὑμῖν, καὶ περισσότερον προφήτου.
27 οὗτος γάρ ἐστι περὶ οὗ γέγραπται, Ἰδοὺ ἀποστέλλω τὸν ἄγγελόν μου ο
πρὸ προσώπου σου, ὃς κατασκευάσει τὴν ὁδόν σου ἔμπροσθέν σου. β
28 λέγω γὰρ ὑμῖν, μείζων ἐν γεννητοῖς γυναικῶν Ἰωάννου οὐδείς ἐστιν. οα ε

11 τη εξης ϛ Ναιν 131 ϛ οι μαθηται αυτου ϛ **12** και ιδου 131 ϛ 118 131 209 ϛ
της πολεως ικανος ην ϛ **13** Ιησους] Κυριος ϛ **16** απαντας 131 ϛ
εγηγερται ϛ Κυριος] Θεος ϛ **17** εν παση 118 209 ϛ **18** om περι
αυτου 118 209 ϛ **19** ο Ιωαννης 118 209 ϛ **20** ετερον] αλλον ϛ
21 εκεινη] αυτη δε ϛ (118 deest) εχαρισατο] εδωρησατο 131 το] του 131
22 οτι τυφλοι ϛ (118 deest) και κωφοι 131 om και 3° 118 209 ϛ
24 μαθητων] αγγελων ϛ **24 25 26** εξηλθετε] εξεληλυθατε ter 118 209 ϛ
27 om γαρ ϛ ιδου εγω ϛ **28** προφητης Ιωαννου του Βαπτιστου 118
209 ϛ

οβ ι ὁ δὲ μικρότερος ἐν τῇ βασιλείᾳ τοῦ Θεοῦ μείζων αὐτοῦ ἐστι. καὶ πᾶς 29
ὁ λαὸς ἀκούσας καὶ οἱ τελῶναι ἐδικαίωσαν τὸν Θεόν, βαπτισθέντες εἰς
τὸ βάπτισμα Ἰωάννου· οἱ δὲ Φαρισαῖοι καὶ οἱ νομικοὶ τὴν βουλὴν 30
ογ ε τοῦ Θεοῦ ἠθέτησαν εἰς ἑαυτούς, μὴ βαπτισθέντες ὑπ' αὐτοῦ. τίνι οὖν 31
ὁμοιώσω τοὺς ἀνθρώπους τῆς γενεᾶς ταύτης, καὶ τίνι εἰσὶν ὅμοιοι;
ὅμοιοί εἰσι παιδίοις τοῖς ἐν ἀγορᾷ καθημένοις καὶ προσφωνοῦσιν ἀλλή- 32
λοις, ἃ λέγει, Ηὐλήσαμεν ὑμῖν, καὶ οὐκ ὠρχήσασθε· ἐθρηνήσαμεν ὑμῖν,
καὶ οὐκ ἐκλαύσατε. ἐλήλυθε γὰρ Ἰωάννης ὁ Βαπτιστὴς μήτε ἐσθίων 33
μήτε πίνων, καὶ λέγετε, Δαιμόνιον ἔχει. ἐλήλυθεν ὁ υἱὸς τοῦ ἀνθρώ- 34
που ἐσθίων καὶ πίνων, καὶ λέγετε, Ἰδοὺ ἄνθρωπος φάγος καὶ οἰνοπότης,
φίλος τελωνῶν καὶ ἁμαρτωλῶν. καὶ ἐδικαιώθη ἡ σοφία ἀπὸ τῶν 35
τέκνων αὐτῆς.

ΚΑ' Ἠρώτα δὲ αὐτόν τις τῶν Φαρισαίων ἵνα φάγῃ μετ' αὐτοῦ· καὶ 36
οδ α εἰσελθὼν εἰς τὸν οἶκον τοῦ Φαρισαίου κατεκλίθη. καὶ ἰδοὺ γυνὴ 37
ἥτις ἦν ἁμαρτωλὸς ἐν τῇ πόλει, ἐπιγνοῦσα ὅτι ἀνάκειται ἐν τῇ οἰκίᾳ
τοῦ Φαρισαίου, κομίσασα ἀλάβαστρον μύρου καὶ στᾶσα ὀπίσω παρὰ 38
τοὺς πόδας αὐτοῦ κλαίουσα, ἤρξατο βρέχειν τοὺς πόδας αὐτοῦ τοῖς
δάκρυσι, καὶ ταῖς θριξὶ τῆς κεφαλῆς αὐτῆς ἐξέμασσε, καὶ κατεφίλει
τοὺς πόδας αὐτοῦ καὶ ἤλειφε τῷ μύρῳ. ἰδὼν δὲ ὁ Φαρισαῖος ὁ καλέσας 39
αὐτὸν εἶπεν ἐν ἑαυτῷ, λέγων, Οὗτος, εἰ ἦν προφήτης, ἐγίνωσκεν ἂν τίς
καὶ ποταπὴ ἡ γυνὴ ἥτις ἅπτεται αὐτοῦ· ὅτι ἁμαρτωλός ἐστι.

Καὶ ἀποκριθεὶς ὁ Ἰησοῦς εἶπε πρὸς αὐτόν, Σίμων, ἔχω σοί τι εἰπεῖν. 40
ὁ δέ, Διδάσκαλε, εἰπέ, φησί. Δύο χρεωφειλέται ἦσαν δανειστῇ τινι· 41
ὁ εἷς ὤφειλε δηνάρια πεντακόσια, ὁ δὲ ἕτερος πεντήκοντα· μὴ ἐχόντων 42
δὲ αὐτῶν ἀποδοῦναι, ἀμφοτέροις ἐχαρίσατο. τίς οὖν αὐτῶν πλεῖον
αὐτὸν ἀγαπήσει; ὁ δὲ Σίμων εἶπεν, Ὑπολαμβάνω ὅτι ᾧ τὸ πλεῖον 43
ἐχαρίσατο. ὁ δὲ εἶπεν αὐτῷ, Ὀρθῶς ἔκρινας. καὶ στραφεὶς πρὸς τὴν 44
γυναῖκα τῷ Σίμωνι ἔφη, Βλέπεις ταύτην τὴν γυναῖκα; εἰσῆλθόν σου
εἰς τὴν οἰκίαν, ὕδωρ ἐπὶ τοὺς πόδας μου οὐκ ἔδωκας· αὕτη δὲ τοῖς
δάκρυσιν ἔβρεξέ μου τοὺς πόδας, καὶ ταῖς θριξὶ αὐτῆς ἐξέμαξε. φί- 45
λημά μοι οὐκ ἔδωκας· αὕτη δὲ ἀφ' ἧς εἰσῆλθον οὐ διέλιπε καταφι-
λοῦσά μου τοὺς πόδας. ἐλαίῳ τὴν κεφαλήν μου οὐκ ἤλειψας· αὕτη δὲ 46

34 οινοπωτης cod. **36** την οικον cod.

118 131 209 ς **29** om εις 131 ς τω βαπτισματι 131 **30** αυτου] + ειπε δε ο Κυριος ς **32** α λεγει] και λεγουσι 118 131 209 ς ου συνεκλαυσατε 118 209 **33** αρτον εσθιων 118 209 ς οινον πινων 118 209 ς **34** τελωνων φιλος ς **35** αυτης παντων ς **36** τις αυτον ς την οικιαν ς ανεκλιθη ς **37** ητις] τις 131 εν τη πολει ante ητις ς **38** οπισω post αυτου ς **40** διδασκαλε διδασκαλε 118 φησι ante διδασκαλε ς **42** αυτων 2°] + ειπε ς **43** ο δε] αποκριθεις δε ο ς **44** σου post οικιαν 131 θριξι της κεφαλης ς

47 μύρῳ ἤλειψέ μου τοὺς πόδας. οὗ χάριν, λέγω σοι, ἀφέωνται αἱ ἁμαρ-
τίαι αὐτῆς αἱ πολλαί, ὅτι ἠγάπησε πολύ· ᾧ δὲ ὀλίγον ἀφίεται, ὀλίγον
48 49 ἀγαπᾷ. εἶπε δὲ αὐτῇ, Ἀφέωνταί σου αἱ ἁμαρτίαι. καὶ ἤρξαντο οἱ
συνανακείμενοι λέγειν ἐν ἑαυτοῖς, Τίς ἐστιν οὗτος ὃς καὶ ἁμαρτίας
50 ἀφίησιν; εἶπε δὲ πρὸς τὴν γυναῖκα, Ἡ πίστις σου σέσωκέ σε· πορεύου
εἰς εἰρήνην.

VIII. Καὶ ἐγένετο ἐν τῷ καθεξῆς, καὶ αὐτὸς διώδευε κατὰ πόλιν οε ι
καὶ κώμην κηρύσσων καὶ εὐαγγελιζόμενος τὴν βασιλείαν τοῦ Θεοῦ, καὶ
2 οἱ δώδεκα σὺν αὐτῷ, καὶ γυναῖκές τινες ἦσαν ἀπὸ πνευμάτων πονηρῶν
τεθεραπευμέναι καὶ ἀσθενειῶν, Μαριὰμ ἡ καλουμένη Μαγδαληνή,
3 ἀφ' ἧς δαιμόνια ἑπτὰ ἐξεληλύθει, καὶ Ἰωάννα γυνὴ Χουζᾶ ἐπιτρόπου
Ἡρώδου, καὶ Σουσάννα, καὶ ἕτεραι πολλαί, αἵτινες διηκόνουν αὐτῷ
ἐκ τῶν ὑπαρχόντων αὐταῖς.

4 Συνιόντος δὲ ὄχλου πολλοῦ, καὶ τῶν κατὰ πόλιν ἐπιπορευομένων οϛ β
5 πρὸς αὐτόν, εἶπε διὰ παραβολῆς, Ἐξῆλθεν ὁ σπείρων τοῦ σπεῖραι τὸν
σπόρον αὐτοῦ· καὶ ἐν τῷ σπείρειν αὐτὸν ὃ μὲν ἔπεσε παρὰ τὴν ὁδόν,
6 καὶ κατεπατήθη, καὶ τὰ πετεινὰ τοῦ οὐρανοῦ κατέφαγεν αὐτό· καὶ ἕτερον
ἔπεσεν ἐπὶ τὴν πέτραν, καὶ φυὲν ἐξηράνθη διὰ τὸ μὴ ἔχειν ἰκμάδα·
7 καὶ ἕτερον ἔπεσεν ἐν μέσῳ τῶν ἀκανθῶν, καὶ συμφυεῖσαι αἱ ἄκανθαι
8 ἀπέπνιξαν αὐτό· καὶ ἕτερον ἔπεσεν εἰς τὴν γῆν τὴν ἀγαθήν, καὶ φυὲν
ἐποίησε καρπὸν ἑκατονταπλασίονα. ταῦτα λέγων ἐφώνει, Ὁ ἔχων ὦτα
9 ἀκούειν ἀκουέτω. ἐπηρώτων δὲ αὐτὸν οἱ μαθηταὶ αὐτοῦ, Τίς εἴη αὕτη
10 ἡ παραβολή; ὁ δὲ ἔφη αὐτοῖς, Ὑμῖν δέδοται γνῶναι τὰ μυστήρια
τῆς βασιλείας τοῦ Θεοῦ· τοῖς δὲ λοιποῖς ἐν παραβολαῖς, ἵνα βλέποντες οζ α
11 μὴ ἴδωσι καὶ ἀκούοντες μὴ συνῶσιν. ἔστι δὲ αὕτη ἡ παραβολή· ὁ οη β
12 σπόρος ἐστὶν ὁ λόγος τοῦ Θεοῦ· οἱ δὲ παρὰ τὴν ὁδόν εἰσιν οἱ ἀκού-
οντες, εἶτα ἔρχεται ὁ διάβολος καὶ αἴρει τὸν λόγον ἀπὸ τῆς καρδίας
13 αὐτῶν, ἵνα μὴ πιστεύσαντες σωθῶσιν. οἱ δὲ ἐπὶ τῆς πέτρας, οἳ ὅταν
ἀκούσωσι μετὰ χαρᾶς δέχονται τὸν λόγον, καὶ οὗτοι ῥίζαν οὐκ ἔχουσιν,
14 οἳ πρὸς καιρὸν πιστεύουσι καὶ ἐν καιρῷ πειρασμοῦ ἀφίστανται. τὸ δὲ
εἰς τὰς ἀκάνθας πεσόν, οὗτοί εἰσιν οἱ τὸν λόγον ἀκούσαντες, καὶ

4 *αυτον*] *αυτων* 1* sed ni fallor ipse correxit **7** *αυτό*] nunc habet *αυτῶ* sed 1* primum *αυτὸ* scripsisse, tum ipse ad *αυτῶ* correxisse videtur

49 *εστιν*] post *ουτος* ς, om 131 **118 131 209 ς**
2 *αι ησαν* 131 ς *ακαθαρτων πονηρων* 131 *τεθεραπευμεναι* ante *απο* ς *Μαρια* ς *Μαγδαλινη* 118 **3** *Σωσαννα* 118 209 *εκ*] *απο* ς **5** *αυτου*] *αυτων* 131 **8** *εις*] *επι* ς **9** *αυτου*]+*λεγοντες* 118 209 ς *αυτη* post *παραβολη* ς **10** *εφη αυτοις*] *ειπεν* ς *ιδωσι*] *βλεπωσι* 118 209 ς *συνιωσιν* 118 131 209 ς **12** *ακουοντες* 118 **14** *πεσων* 118 om *τον λογον* ς

ὑπὸ μεριμνῶν καὶ πλούτου καὶ ἡδονῶν τοῦ βίου πορευόμενοι συμπνί-
γονται καὶ οὐ τελεσφοροῦσι. τὸ δὲ ἐν τῇ καλῇ γῇ, οὗτοί εἰσιν οἵτινες 15
ἐν καρδίᾳ καλῇ καὶ ἀγαθῇ ἀκούσαντες τὸν λόγον κατέχουσι, καὶ καρπο-
φοροῦσιν ἐν ὑπομονῇ.
οθ β Οὐδεὶς δὲ λύχνον ἅψας καλύπτει εἰς σκεῦος, ἢ ὑποκάτω κλίνης 16
τίθησιν· ἀλλ' ἐπὶ λυχνίας τίθησιν, ἵνα οἱ εἰσπορευόμενοι τὸ φῶς
π β βλέπωσι. οὐ γάρ ἐστι κρυπτὸν ὃ οὐ φανερωθήσεται, οὐδὲ ἀπό- 17
πα κρυφον ὃ οὐ γνωσθήσεται καὶ εἰς φανερὸν ἔλθῃ. βλέπετε οὖν πῶς 18
ε ἀκούετε· ὃς γὰρ ἐὰν ἔχῃ, καὶ ὃ δοκεῖ ἔχειν ἀρθήσεται ἀπ' αὐτοῦ.
πβ β Παρεγένοντο δὲ πρὸς αὐτὸν ἡ μήτηρ καὶ οἱ ἀδελφοὶ αὐτοῦ, καὶ οὐκ 19
ἠδύναντο συντυχεῖν αὐτῷ διὰ τὸν ὄχλον. καὶ ἀπηγγέλη αὐτῷ ὅτι 20
Ἡ μήτηρ σου καὶ οἱ ἀδελφοί σου ἑστήκασιν ἔξω ἰδεῖν σε θέλοντες.
ὁ δὲ εἶπε πρὸς αὐτούς, Μήτηρ καὶ ἀδελφοί μου οὗτοί εἰσιν οἱ τὸν 21
λόγον τοῦ Θεοῦ ἀκούοντες καὶ ποιοῦντες.
ΚΓ' Ἐγένετο δὲ ἐν μιᾷ τῶν ἡμερῶν, καὶ αὐτὸς ἐνέβη εἰς πλοῖον καὶ 22
πγ β οἱ μαθηταὶ αὐτοῦ, καὶ εἶπε πρὸς αὐτούς, Διέλθωμεν εἰς τὸ πέραν τῆς
λίμνης· καὶ ἀνήχθησαν. πλεόντων δὲ αὐτῶν ἀφύπνωσε· καὶ κατέβη 23
λαῖλαψ ἀνέμου εἰς τὴν λίμνην, καὶ συνεπληροῦντο καὶ ἐκινδύνευον.
προσελθόντες δὲ διήγειραν αὐτόν, λέγοντες, Ἐπιστάτα, ἐπιστάτα, ἀπολ- 24
λύμεθα. ὁ δὲ ἐγερθεὶς ἐπετίμησε τῷ ἀνέμῳ καὶ τῷ κλύδωνι τοῦ ὕδατος·
καὶ ἐπαύσατο, καὶ ἐγένετο γαλήνη μεγάλη. εἶπε δὲ αὐτοῖς, Ποῦ ἡ 25
πίστις ὑμῶν; φοβηθέντες δὲ ἐθαύμαζον, λέγοντες πρὸς ἀλλήλους,
Τίς ἄρα οὗτός ἐστιν, ὅτι καὶ τοῖς ἀνέμοις ἐπιτάσσει καὶ τῷ ὕδατι, καὶ
ὑπακούουσιν αὐτῷ;
Καὶ κατέπλευσαν εἰς τὴν χώραν τῶν Γεργεσηνῶν, ἥτις ἐστὶν 26
ΚΔ' ἀντίπερα τῆς Γαλιλαίας. ἐξελθόντι δὲ αὐτῷ ἐπὶ τὴν γῆν, ὑπήντη- 27
σεν ἀνήρ τις ἐκ τῆς πόλεως, ὃς εἶχε δαιμόνια, καὶ χρόνῳ πολλῷ

15 υπομονη] rubr.[2] add. in mg. γρ (i.e. γραφε) ταυτα λεγων εφωνει ο εχων ωτα ακουην ακουετω **21** ποιουντες] rubr.[2] add. inter lineas αυτον

118 131 209 ς **15** υπομονη] 118[2] add. in marg. και λεγων ταυτα εφωνη ο εχων ωτα ακουειν ακουετω **16** καλυπτει]+αυτον 118 209 ς εις σκευος] σκευει 118 209 ς επιτιθησιν ς βλεπωσι το φως 118 209 ς **17** φανερωθησεται] φανερον γενησεται 118 209 ς **18** εαν] αν ς εχει 131 εχη]+δοθησεται αυτω· και ος αν μη εχη 118 131 209 ς **20** απηγγελει 131 οτι] λεγοντων ς εξω εστηκασιν 131 **21** ο δε αποκριθεις ς μητηρ μου 118 131 209 ς ποιουντες]+αυτον 118[2] (supra lin. ς) **22** εγενετο δε] και εγενετο ς, εγενετο 131 ενεβη] ανεβη 118 209, ανευη 131 **24** om και επαυσατο 131 επαυσαντο ς om μεγαλη ς **25** που] πως 131, που εστιν 118 209 ς εθαυμασαν ς **26** Γαδαρηνων ς αντιπεραν ς **27** υπηντησεν αυτω 131 ς και χρονω πολλω] εκ χρονων ικανων και 118 209 ς

οὐκ ἐνεδύσατο ἱμάτιον, καὶ ἐν οἰκίᾳ οὐκ ἔμεινεν ἀλλ' ἐν τοῖς μνή-
28 μασιν. ἰδὼν δὲ τὸν Ἰησοῦν καὶ ἀνακράξας προσέπεσεν αὐτῷ, καὶ φωνῇ
μεγάλῃ εἶπε, Τί ἐμοὶ καὶ σοί, υἱὲ τοῦ ὑψίστου; δέομαί σου, μή με
29 βασανίσῃς. παρήγγελλε γὰρ τῷ πνεύματι τῷ ἀκαθάρτῳ ἐξελθεῖν
ἀπὸ τοῦ ἀνθρώπου· πολλοῖς γὰρ χρόνοις συνηρπάκει αὐτόν, καὶ ἐδε-
σμεῖτο ἁλύσεσι καὶ πέδαις φυλασσόμενος, καὶ διαρήσσων τὰ δεσμὰ
30 ἠλαύνετο ὑπὸ τοῦ δαίμονος εἰς τὰς ἐρήμους. ἐπηρώτησε δὲ αὐτὸν ὁ
Ἰησοῦς, Τί σοι ὄνομά ἐστιν; ὁ δὲ εἶπε, Λεγεών· ὅτι δαιμόνια
31 πολλὰ εἰσῆλθεν εἰς αὐτόν· καὶ παρεκάλουν αὐτὸν ἵνα μὴ ἐπιτάξῃ
32 αὐτοῖς εἰς τὴν ἄβυσσον ἀπελθεῖν. ἦν δὲ ἐκεῖ ἀγέλη χοίρων ἱκανῶν
βοσκομένων ἐν τῷ ὄρει· καὶ παρεκάλεσαν αὐτὸν ἵνα ἐπιτρέψῃ αὐτοῖς
33 εἰς ἐκείνους εἰσελθεῖν· καὶ ἐπέτρεψεν αὐτοῖς. ἐξελθόντα δὲ τὰ δαι-
μόνια εἰσῆλθεν εἰς τοὺς χοίρους· καὶ ὥρμησεν ἡ ἀγέλη κατὰ τοῦ
34 κρημνοῦ εἰς τὴν λίμνην, καὶ ἀπεπνίγη. ἰδόντες δὲ οἱ βόσκοντες τὸ
γεγονὸς ἔφυγον, καὶ ἀπήγγειλαν εἰς τὴν πόλιν καὶ εἰς τοὺς ἀγρούς.
35 καὶ ἐξῆλθον ἰδεῖν τὸ γεγονός, καὶ ἔρχονται πρὸς τὸν Ἰησοῦν, καὶ
εὗρον τὸν ἄνθρωπον καθήμενον ἀφ' οὗ τὰ δαιμόνια ἐξεληλύθει,
ἱματισμένον καὶ σωφρονοῦντα, παρὰ τοὺς πόδας τοῦ Ἰησοῦ· καὶ ἐφοβή-
36 θησαν. ἀπήγγειλαν δὲ αὐτοῖς καὶ οἱ ἰδόντες πῶς ἐσώθη ὁ δαιμον-
37 ισθείς. καὶ ἠρώτησαν αὐτὸν ἅπαν τὸ πλῆθος τῆς περιχώρου τῶν
Γεργεσηνῶν ἀπελθεῖν ἀπ' αὐτῶν, ὅτι φόβῳ μεγάλῳ συνείχοντο· αὐτὸς πδ
38 δὲ ἐμβὰς εἰς πλοῖον ὑπέστρεψεν. ἐδέετο δὲ αὐτοῦ ὁ ἀνὴρ ἀφ' οὗ τὰ η
δαιμόνια ἐξεληλύθει, εἶναι σὺν αὐτῷ. ἀπέλυσε δὲ αὐτὸν λέγων,
39 Ὑπόστρεφε εἰς τὸν οἶκόν σου, καὶ διηγοῦ ὅσα σοι ἐποίησεν ὁ Θεὸς
καὶ ἠλέησέ σε. καὶ ἀπῆλθε, καθ' ὅλην τὴν πόλιν κηρύσσων ὅσα
ἐποίησεν αὐτῷ ὁ Θεός.
40 Ἐν δὲ τῷ ὑποστρέψαι τὸν Ἰησοῦν, ἀπεδέξατο αὐτὸν ὁ λαός· ἦσαν ΚΕ'
γὰρ ἅπαντες προσδοκῶντες αὐτόν. πε β

29 χρονοις] χρονος cod. 39 ελεησε cod.

27 ιματιον ουκ ενεδιδυσκετο 118 209 ς εμενε 118 209 ς 28 υιε] pr Ιησου 131 ς του Θεου του υψιστου 118 131 209 ς 29 παρηγγελλε γαρ] και παρηγγειλε 118 209, παρηγγειλε γαρ 131 διαρρησσων ς 30 Ιησους] +λεγων ς εστιν ονομα ς 31 παρεκαλει ς εισελθειν 131 32 παρεκαλουν 118 209 ς επιτρεψει 131 33 δαιμονια]+απο του ανθρωπου 118 209 ς 34 γεγενημενον ς απελθοντες απηγγειλαν ς 35 και εξηλθον] εξηλθον δε 118 209 ς ερχονται] ηλθον ς καθημενον τον ανθρωπον ς 36 om αυτοις 131 37 Γεργεσινων 118, Γαδαρηνων ς το πλοιον 118 209 ς 38 εξεληλυθει τα δαιμονια ς αυτον]+ο Ιησους ς 39 εποιησε σοι ς om και ηλεησε σε ς Θεος] Ιησους 131 ς 40 εν δε] εγενετο δε εν ς λαος] οχλος 131 ς παντες ς

118 131 209 ς

Καὶ ἰδοὺ ἦλθεν ἀνὴρ ᾧ ὄνομα Ἰάειρος, καὶ οὗτος ἄρχων τῆς 41
συναγωγῆς ὑπῆρχε, καὶ πεσὼν παρὰ τοὺς πόδας τοῦ Ἰησοῦ παρεκάλει
αὐτὸν εἰσελθεῖν εἰς τὸν οἶκον αὐτοῦ· ὅτι θυγάτηρ μονογενὴς ἦν αὐτῷ 42
ὡς ἐτῶν δεκαδύο, καὶ αὕτη ἀπέθνησκεν. ἐν δὲ τῷ ὑπάγειν αὐτὸν οἱ
κϛ′ ὄχλοι συνέπνιγον αὐτόν. καὶ γυνὴ οὖσα ἐν ῥύσει αἵματος ἀπὸ ἐτῶν 43
δεκαδύο, ἥτις ἰατροῖς προσαναλώσασα ὅλον τὸν βίον οὐκ ἴσχυσεν
ὑπ' οὐδενὸς θεραπευθῆναι, προσελθοῦσα ὄπισθεν ἥψατο τοῦ κρασπέδου 44
τοῦ ἱματίου αὐτοῦ· καὶ παραχρῆμα ἔστη ἡ ῥύσις τοῦ αἵματος αὐτῆς.
καὶ εἶπεν ὁ Ἰησοῦς, Τίς ὁ ἁψάμενός μου; ἀρνουμένων δὲ πάντων, εἶπεν 45
ὁ Πέτρος καὶ οἱ σὺν αὐτῷ, Ἐπιστάτα, οἱ ὄχλοι συνέχουσί σε καὶ
ἀποθλίβουσιν. ὁ δὲ Ἰησοῦς εἶπεν, Ἥψατό μού τις· ἐγὼ γὰρ ἔγνων 46
δύναμιν ἐξελθοῦσαν ἀπ' ἐμοῦ. ἰδοῦσα δὲ ἡ γυνὴ ὅτι οὐκ ἔλαθε, τρέ- 47
μουσα ἦλθε, καὶ προσπεσοῦσα αὐτῷ δι' ἣν αἰτίαν ἥψατο αὐτοῦ ἀπήγ-
γειλεν ἐνώπιον παντὸς τοῦ λαοῦ, καὶ ὡς ἰάθη παραχρῆμα. ὁ δὲ 48
εἶπεν αὐτῇ, Θύγατερ, ἡ πίστις σου σέσωκέ σε· πορεύου εἰς εἰρήνην.
ἔτι αὐτοῦ λαλοῦντος ἔρχεταί τις ἀπὸ τοῦ ἀρχισυναγώγου, λέγων ὅτι 49
Τέθνηκεν ἡ θυγάτηρ σου· μὴ σκύλλε αὐτόν. ὁ δὲ Ἰησοῦς ἀκούσας 50
ἀπεκρίθη αὐτῷ, Μὴ φοβοῦ· μόνον πίστευε, καὶ σωθήσεται. ἐλθὼν δὲ 51
εἰς τὴν οἰκίαν οὐκ ἀφῆκεν εἰσελθεῖν οὐδένα, εἰ μὴ Πέτρον καὶ Ἰωάννην
καὶ Ἰάκωβον καὶ τὸν πατέρα τῆς παιδὸς καὶ τὴν μητέρα. ἔκλαιον δὲ 52
πάντες καὶ ἐκόπτοντο αὐτήν. ὁ δὲ εἶπε, Μὴ κλαίετε· οὐ γὰρ ἀπέθα-
νε τὸ κοράσιον, ἀλλὰ καθεύδει. καὶ κατεγέλων αὐτοῦ, εἰδότες ὅτι 53
ἀπέθανεν. αὐτὸς δὲ κρατήσας τῆς χειρὸς αὐτῆς ἐφώνησεν, Ἡ παῖς, 54
ἔγειρε. καὶ ἐπέστρεψε τὸ πνεῦμα αὐτῆς, καὶ ἀνέστη παραχρῆμα· καὶ 55
διέταξε δοθῆναι αὐτῇ φαγεῖν. καὶ ἐξέστησαν οἱ γονεῖς αὐτῆς· ὁ δὲ 56
παρήγγειλεν αὐτοῖς μηδενὶ εἰπεῖν τὸ γεγονός.

κζ′ IX. Συγκαλεσάμενος δὲ τοὺς δώδεκα ἔδωκεν αὐτοῖς δύναμιν καὶ
πϛ/β ἐξουσίαν ἐπὶ πάντα τὰ δαιμόνια, καὶ νόσους θεραπεύειν· καὶ ἀπέστειλεν 2
αὐτοὺς κηρύσσειν τὴν βασιλείαν τοῦ Θεοῦ καὶ ἰᾶσθαι τοὺς ἀσθενεῖς.
πζ/β καὶ εἶπε πρὸς αὐτούς, Μηδὲν αἴρετε εἰς τὴν ὁδόν, μήτε ῥάβδον μήτε 3

118 131 209 ϛ

41 *ηλθεν*] *προσηλθεν τω Ιησου* 131 om *ανηρ* 131 *ουτος*] *αυτος* ϛ *υπηρχε*] *απηλθε* 118* 209, *υπηρχε* 118² **42** *δωδεκα* 118 ϛ *αυτων* 118 **43** *δωδεκα* ϛ *εις ιατρους* ϛ **45** *μετ αυτου* ϛ *αποθλιβουσιν*] + *και λεγεις, τις ο αψαμενος μου;* 118 ϛ (118* haec verba primum omisit et *ο* seq. scripsit, tum autem ipse *ο* erasit et *και λεγεις κ.τ.λ.* addidit) **47** *απηγγειλεν αυτω* ϛ **48** *θαρσει θυγατερ* ϛ **49** *απο*] *παρα* ϛ *λεγων αυτω* ϛ *αυτον*] *τον διδασκαλον* 118 209 ϛ **50** *αυτω λεγων* ϛ **51** *εισελθων* ϛ *και Ιακωβον και Ιωαννην* ϛ **52** *ου γαρ*] *ουκ* ϛ om *το κορασιον* ϛ **54** *κρατησας*] pr *εκβαλων εξω παντας και* ϛ *εφωνησε λεγων* ϛ *εγειραι* 131 209, *εγειρου* ϛ, *εγειρ* spat. rel. 118 **55** *αυτη δοθηναι* ϛ

1 *δωδεκα*] + *μαθητας αυτου* ϛ **2** *ασθενουντας* ϛ **3** *ραβδους* ϛ

4 πήραν μήτε ἄρτον μήτε ἀργύριον, μήτε ἀνὰ δύο χιτῶνας ἔχειν. καὶ εἰς
5 ἣν δ' ἂν οἰκίαν εἰσέλθητε, ἐκεῖ μένετε καὶ ἐκεῖθεν ἐξέρχεσθε. καὶ ὅσοι πη/β
ἂν μὴ δέχωνται, ἐξερχόμενοι ἀπὸ τῆς πόλεως ἐκείνης τὸν κονιορτὸν
6 ἀπὸ τῶν ποδῶν ὑμῶν ἀποτινάσσετε, εἰς μαρτύριον ἐπ' αὐτούς. ἐξερ- πθ/η
χόμενοι δὲ διήρχοντο κατὰ τὰς κώμας εὐαγγελιζόμενοι καὶ θεραπεύοντες
πανταχοῦ.

7 Ἤκουσε δὲ Ἡρώδης ὁ τετράρχης τὰ γενόμενα ὑπ' αὐτοῦ πάντα· ϟ/β
καὶ διηπόρει, διὰ τὸ λέγεσθαι ὑπό τινων ὅτι Ἰωάννης ἠγέρθη ἐκ
8 νεκρῶν, ὑπό τινων δὲ ὅτι Ἡλίας ἐφάνη, ἄλλων δὲ ὅτι Προφήτης τις
9 τῶν ἀρχαίων ἀνέστη. εἶπε δὲ ὁ Ἡρώδης, Ἰωάννην ἐγὼ ἀπεκεφά-
λισα· τίς δέ ἐστιν οὗτος, περὶ οὗ ἐγὼ ἀκούω τοιαῦτα; καὶ ἐζήτει
ἰδεῖν αὐτόν.

10 Καὶ ὑποστρέψαντες οἱ ἀπόστολοι διηγήσαντο αὐτῷ ὅσα ἐποίησαν. ϟα/η
καὶ παραλαβὼν αὐτοὺς ὑπεχώρησε κατ' ἰδίαν εἰς τόπον πόλεως καλου-
11 μένης Βηθσαϊδά. οἱ δὲ ὄχλοι γνόντες ἠκολούθησαν αὐτῷ· καὶ ἀποδεξά- ϟβ/γ
μενος αὐτοὺς ἐλάλει αὐτοῖς περὶ τῆς βασιλείας τοῦ Θεοῦ, καὶ τοὺς
12 χρείαν ἔχοντας θεραπείας ἰᾶτο. ἡ δὲ ἡμέρα ἤρξατο κλίνειν· προσελ- ΚΗ'
θόντες δὲ οἱ δώδεκα εἶπον αὐτῷ, Ἀπόλυσον τὸν ὄχλον, ἵνα ἀπελθόντες ϟγ/α
εἰς τὰς κύκλῳ κώμας καὶ ἀγροὺς καταλύσωσι, καὶ εὕρωσιν ἐπισιτισμόν·
13 ὅτι ὧδε ἐν ἐρήμῳ τόπῳ ἐσμέν. εἶπε δὲ πρὸς αὐτούς, Δότε αὐτοῖς ὑμεῖς
φαγεῖν. οἱ δὲ εἶπον, Οὐκ εἰσὶν ἡμῖν πλέον ἢ πέντε ἄρτοι καὶ ἰχθύες
δύο, εἰ μὴ πορευθέντες ἡμεῖς ἀγοράσομεν βρώματα εἰς πάντα τὸν
14 ὄχλον τοῦτον. ἦσαν γὰρ ἄνδρες ὡσεὶ πεντακισχίλιοι. εἶπε δὲ πρὸς
15 τοὺς μαθητὰς αὐτοῦ, Κατακλίνατε αὐτοὺς κλισίας ἀνὰ πεντήκοντα. καὶ
16 ἐποίησαν οὕτως καὶ κατέκλιναν αὐτούς. λαβὼν δὲ τοὺς πέντε ἄρ-
τους καὶ τοὺς δύο ἰχθύας, ἀναβλέψας εἰς τὸν οὐρανὸν εὐλόγησεν αὐτοὺς
17 καὶ κατέκλασε καὶ ἐδίδου τοῖς μαθηταῖς παραθεῖναι τῷ ὄχλῳ. καὶ
ἔφαγον καὶ ἐχορτάσθησαν πάντες· καὶ ἤρθη τὸ περισσεῦσαν αὐτοῖς
κλασμάτων κόφινοι δώδεκα.

18 Καὶ ἐγένετο ἐν τῷ εἶναι αὐτὸν προσευχόμενον καταμόνας, συνῆσαν ΚΘ'
αὐτῷ οἱ μαθηταὶ αὐτοῦ· καὶ ἐπηρώτησεν αὐτοὺς λέγων, Τίνα με οἱ ϟδ/α

9 εγω εγω cod.

ξ

4 δ αν] αν ϛ 5 δεξωνται υμας ϛ, δεχωνται υμας 118, δεξοντε υμας 118 131 209 ϛ
131 και τον ϛ αποτεινασετε 131, αποτιναξατε ϛ 7 γινομενα ϛ
εγηγερται ϛ 8 εφανει 118 209 τις] εις ϛ 9 ειπε δε] και ειπε ϛ
10 τοπον ερημον ϛ 11 δεξαμενος ϛ χρειαν] χρει 118 12 προελ-
θοντες 118 τους αγρους ϛ 13 πλειον 118 ϛ δυο ιχθυες ϛ μη] μητι ϛ
αγορασωμεν 118 131 209 ϛ βρωματα post τουτον 131 ϛ οχλον] λαον 118
209 ϛ 14 ωσει ανδρες ϛ 15 ουτω ϛ ανεκλιναν ϛ αυτους]
απαντας ϛ 16 παρατιθεναι ϛ 17 περισευσαν 131, περιττευσαν 118 209
18 om αυτου ϛ

ὄχλοι λέγουσιν εἶναι; οἱ δὲ ἀποκριθέντες εἶπον, Ἰωάννην τὸν 19
Βαπτιστήν, ἄλλοι δὲ Ἡλίαν, ἄλλοι δὲ Ἱερεμίαν, ἄλλοι δὲ ὅτι
προφήτης τις τῶν ἀρχαίων ἀνέστη. εἶπε δὲ αὐτοῖς, Ὑμεῖς δὲ τίνα με 20
λέγετε εἶναι; Πέτρος δὲ ἀποκριθεὶς εἶπε, Τὸν Χριστὸν τοῦ Θεοῦ.
ϛε ὁ δὲ ἐπιτιμήσας αὐτοῖς παρήγγειλε μηδενὶ λέγειν τοῦτο, εἰπὼν ὅτι 21 22
β Δεῖ τὸν υἱὸν τοῦ ἀνθρώπου πολλὰ παθεῖν, καὶ ἀποδοκιμασθῆναι ὑπὸ
τῶν πρεσβυτέρων καὶ ἀρχιερέων, καὶ ἀποκτανθῆναι, καὶ τῇ τρίτῃ
ἡμέρᾳ ἀναστῆναι.
ϛϛ β Ἔλεγε δὲ πρὸς πάντας, Εἴ τις θέλει ὀπίσω μου ἔρχεσθαι, ἀπαρνη- 23
σάσθω ἑαυτὸν καὶ ἀράτω τὸν σταυρὸν αὐτοῦ καθ' ἡμέραν, καὶ ἀκολου-
θείτω μοι. ὃς γὰρ ἐὰν θέλῃ τὴν ψυχὴν αὐτοῦ σῶσαι, ἀπολέσῃ 24
αὐτήν· ὃς δ' ἂν ἀπολέσῃ τὴν ψυχὴν αὐτοῦ ἕνεκεν ἐμοῦ, οὗτος σώσει
αὐτήν. τί γὰρ ὠφελεῖται ἄνθρωπος κερδήσας τὸν κόσμον ὅλον, ἑαυτὸν 25
ϛζ δὲ ἀπολέσας ἢ ζημιωθείς; ὃς γὰρ ἂν ἐπαισχυνθῇ με καὶ τοὺς ἐμοὺς 26
β λόγους, τοῦτον ὁ υἱὸς τοῦ ἀνθρώπου ἐπαισχυνθήσεται, ὅταν ἔλθῃ ἐν τῇ
δόξῃ αὐτοῦ καὶ τοῦ πατρὸς καὶ τῶν ἁγίων ἀγγέλων. λέγω δὲ ὑμῖν 27
ϛη ἀληθῶς, εἰσί τινες τῶν αὐτοῦ ἑστώτων, οἳ οὐ μὴ γεύσωνται θανάτου
β ἕως ἂν ἴδωσι τὴν βασιλείαν τοῦ Θεοῦ.
Λ' Ἐγένετο δὲ μετὰ τοὺς λόγους τούτους ὡσεὶ ἡμέραι ὀκτώ, καὶ 28
παραλαβὼν Πέτρον καὶ Ἰωάννην καὶ Ἰάκωβον ἀνέβη εἰς τὸ ὄρος
προσεύξασθαι. καὶ ἐγένετο ἐν τῷ προσεύξασθαι αὐτὸν τὸ εἶδος τοῦ 29
προσώπου αὐτοῦ ἕτερον, καὶ ὁ ἱματισμὸς αὐτοῦ λευκὸς ἐξαστράπτων.
καὶ ἰδοὺ ἄνδρες δύο συνελάλουν αὐτῷ, οἵτινες ἦσαν Μωσῆς καὶ Ἡλίας, 30
οἳ ὀφθέντες ἐν δόξῃ ἔλεγον τὴν ἔξοδον αὐτοῦ, ἣν ἔμελλε πληροῦν ἐν 31
Ἱερουσαλήμ. ὁ δὲ Πέτρος καὶ οἱ σὺν αὐτῷ ἦσαν βεβαρημένοι ὕπνῳ· 32
καὶ διαγρηγορήσαντες εἶδον τὴν δόξαν αὐτοῦ, καὶ τοὺς δύο ἄνδρας
συνεστῶτας αὐτῷ. καὶ ἐγένετο ἐν τῷ διαχωρίζεσθαι αὐτοὺς ἀπ' αὐτοῦ, 33
εἶπεν ὁ Πέτρος πρὸς τὸν Ἰησοῦν, Ἐπιστάτα, καλόν ἐστιν ἡμᾶς ὧδε
εἶναι· καὶ ποιήσωμεν σκηνὰς τρεῖς, σοὶ μίαν, καὶ μίαν Μωσῇ, καὶ
Ἡλίᾳ μίαν, μὴ εἰδὼς ὃ λέγει. ταῦτα δὲ αὐτοῦ λέγοντος ἐγένετο 34

21 επιτιμισας cod. **29** προσευξεσθαι cod.

118 131 209 ς **18** λεγουσιν οι οχλοι ς **19** om αλλοι δε Ιερεμιαν ς **20** αποκριθεις δε ο Πετρος 118 209 ς om αποκριθεις 131 **21** λεγειν] ειπειν ς **22** υπο] απο ς αρχιερεων]+και γραμματεων ς αναστηναι] εγερθηναι ς **23** ερχεσθαι] ελθειν 118 ς **24** εαν] αν ς θελει 131 απολεσει 118 131 209 ς **27** αυτου] ωδε 118 131 209 ς εστηκοτων ς (εστωτων in rasura 118*) γευσονται 131 ς **28** ωσει μεραι 118 τον Πετρον ς **29** προσευχεσθαι 118 131 209 ς **30** Μωυσης 131 **32** διαγρηγορησαντες δε ς τους συνεστωτας 131 ς **33** μιαν σοι ς Μωσει μιαν ς Μωυσει 131, Μωσει 118 209 ς μιαν Ηλια ς Ηλιαν 118 om μη ειδως ο λεγει 131

νεφέλη καὶ ἐπεσκίασεν αὐτούς· ἐφοβήθησαν δὲ ἐν τῷ ἐκείνους εἰσελθεῖν
35 εἰς τὴν νεφέλην. καὶ ἐγένετο φωνὴ ἐκ τῆς νεφέλης λέγουσα, Οὗτός
36 ἐστιν ὁ υἱός μου ὁ ἐκλεκτός· αὐτοῦ ἀκούετε. καὶ ἐν τῷ γενέσθαι
τὴν φωνὴν εὑρέθη ὁ Ἰησοῦς μόνος. καὶ αὐτοὶ ἐσίγησαν, καὶ οὐδενὶ
ἀπήγγειλαν ἐν ἐκείναις ταῖς ἡμέραις οὐδὲν ὧν ἑωράκασιν.
37 Ἐγένετο δὲ τῇ ἑξῆς ἡμέρᾳ, κατελθόντων αὐτῶν ἀπὸ τοῦ ὄρους λθ β
38 συνήντησεν αὐτῷ ὄχλος πολύς. καὶ ἰδοὺ ἀνὴρ ἀπὸ τοῦ ὄχλου ἀν- ΛΑ'
εβόησε λέγων, Διδάσκαλε, δέομαί σου, ἐπίβλεψον ἐπὶ τὸν υἱόν μου,
39 ὅτι μονογενής μοι ἐστί, καὶ ἰδοὺ πνεῦμα λαμβάνει αὐτόν, καὶ ἐξαίφνης
κράζει, καὶ ῥήσσει καὶ σπαράττει αὐτὸν μετὰ ἀφροῦ, καὶ μόλις
40 ἀποχωρεῖ ἀπ' αὐτοῦ συντρῖβον αὐτόν. καὶ ἐδεήθην τῶν μαθητῶν σου
41 ἵνα ἐκβάλλωσιν αὐτό, καὶ οὐκ ἠδυνήθησαν. ἀποκριθεὶς δὲ ὁ Ἰησοῦς
εἶπεν, Ὦ γενεὰ ἄπιστος καὶ διεστραμμένη, ἕως πότε ἔσομαι πρὸς
42 ὑμᾶς καὶ ἀνέξομαι ὑμῶν; προσάγαγε ὧδε τὸν υἱόν σου. ἔτι δὲ προσ-
ερχομένου αὐτοῦ, ἔρρηξεν αὐτὸν τὸ δαιμόνιον καὶ συνεσπάραξεν· ἐπετί-
μησε δὲ ὁ Ἰησοῦς τῷ πνεύματι τῷ ἀκαθάρτῳ, καὶ ἰάσατο τὸν παῖδα
43 καὶ ἀπέδωκεν αὐτὸν τῷ πατρὶ αὐτοῦ. ἐξεπλήσσοντο δὲ πάντες ἐπὶ τῇ ρ η
μεγαλειότητι τοῦ Θεοῦ. πάντων δὲ θαυμαζόντων ἐπὶ πᾶσιν οἷς ἐποίει,
44 εἶπε πρὸς τοὺς μαθητὰς αὐτοῦ, Θέσθε ὑμεῖς εἰς τὰ ὦτα ὑμῶν τοὺς ρα β
λόγους τούτους· ὁ γὰρ υἱὸς τοῦ ἀνθρώπου μέλλει παραδίδοσθαι εἰς
45 χεῖρας ἀνθρώπων. οἱ δὲ ἠγνόουν τὸ ῥῆμα τοῦτο, καὶ ἦν παρακεκαλυμ-
μένον ἀπ' αὐτῶν, ἵνα μὴ αἴσθωνται αὐτό· καὶ ἐφοβοῦντο ἐρωτῆσαι αὐτὸν
46 περὶ τοῦ ῥήματος τούτου. εἰσῆλθε δὲ διαλογισμὸς ἐν αὐτοῖς, τίς ἂν ΛΒ'
47 εἴη μείζων αὐτῶν. ὁ δὲ Ἰησοῦς γνοὺς τὸν διαλογισμὸν τῆς καρδίας ρβ β
48 αὐτῶν, ἐπιλαβόμενος παιδίου, ἔστησεν αὐτὸ παρ' ἑαυτῷ, καὶ εἶπεν αὐτοῖς,
Ὃς ἐὰν δέξηται τὸ παιδίον τοῦτο ἐπὶ τῷ ὀνόματί μου, ἐμὲ δέχεται·
καὶ ὃς ἐὰν ἐμὲ δέξηται, δέχεται τὸν ἀποστείλαντά με. ὁ γὰρ μικρότερος
ἐν πᾶσιν ὑμῖν ὑπάρχων οὗτός ἐστι μέγας.
49 Ἀποκριθεὶς δὲ ὁ Ἰωάννης εἶπεν, Ἐπιστάτα, εἴδομέν τινα ἐν τῷ ργ η
ὀνόματί σου ἐκβάλλοντα δαιμόνια· καὶ ἐκωλύσαμεν αὐτόν, ὅτι οὐκ
50 ἀκολουθεῖ μεθ' ἡμῶν. εἶπε δὲ πρὸς αὐτὸν ὁ Ἰησοῦς, Μὴ κωλύετε· ὃς
γὰρ οὐκ ἔστι καθ' ἡμῶν, ὑπὲρ ἡμῶν ἐστιν.

38 *μοι*] *ι* in rasura, haud scio an 1* *μου* scripserit
39 *μολις*] nunc habet *μογις*, *λ* in *γ* ab ipso 1* per rasuram mutato

35 *φωνη εγενετο* ς *αγαπητος* 118 131 209 ς **36** om *και* 1° 131 118 131 209 ς
37 *εν τη* ς **38** *ανενοησε* 131 *επιβλεψαι* 131 *εστι μοι* ς **39** om
και ρησσει ς *σπαρασσει* 131 ς *μογις* 131 ς **40** *εδυνηθησαν* 131
43 *επιει* 118, *εποιησεν* ς **44** om *ωτα* 131* *ειπε*] pr *ο Ιησους* 118 ς
46 *το τις* ς **47** *γνους*] *ιδων* ς *τους διαλογισμους* 131 **48** *τουτο το*
παιδιον ς *εστι*] *εσται* ς **49** *εν*] *επι* ς *τα δαιμονια* ς **50** *και ειπε* ς

ρδ/ι Ἐγένετο δὲ ἐν τῷ συμπληροῦσθαι τὰς ἡμέρας τῆς ἀναλήψεως αὐτοῦ, 51
καὶ αὐτὸς τὸ πρόσωπον ἐστήριξε τοῦ πορεύεσθαι εἰς Ἱερουσαλήμ. καὶ 52
ἀπέστειλεν ἀγγέλους πρὸ προσώπου αὐτοῦ· καὶ πορευθέντες εἰσῆλθον
εἰς κώμην Σαμαρειτῶν, ὥστε ἑτοιμάσαι αὐτῷ. καὶ οὐκ ἐδέξαντο αὐτόν, 53
ὅτι τὸ πρόσωπον αὐτοῦ ἦν πορευόμενον εἰς Ἱερουσαλήμ. ἰδόντες δὲ οἱ 54
μαθηταὶ Ἰάκωβος καὶ Ἰωάννης εἶπον, Κύριε, θέλεις εἴπωμεν πῦρ
καταβῆναι ἐκ τοῦ οὐρανοῦ καὶ ἀναλῶσαι αὐτούς, ὡς καὶ Ἡλίας ἐποίησε;
Στραφεὶς δὲ ἐπετίμησεν αὐτοῖς καὶ εἶπεν, Οὐκ οἴδατε ποίου πνεύματός 55
ἐστε ὑμεῖς; ὁ υἱὸς τοῦ ἀνθρώπου οὐκ ἦλθε ψυχὰς ἀνθρώπων ἀπολέσαι, 56
ἀλλὰ σῶσαι. καὶ ἐπορεύθησαν εἰς ἑτέραν κώμην.
ΛΓ' Ἐγένετο δὲ πορευομένων αὐτῶν ἐν τῇ ὁδῷ εἶπέ τις πρὸς αὐτόν, 57
ρε/ε Ἀκολουθήσω σοι ὅπου ἂν ἀπέρχῃ. καὶ εἶπεν αὐτῷ ὁ Ἰησοῦς, Αἱ 58
ἀλώπεκες φωλεοὺς ἔχουσι καὶ τὰ πετεινὰ τοῦ οὐρανοῦ κατασκηνώσεις,
ὁ δὲ υἱὸς τοῦ ἀνθρώπου οὐκ ἔχει ποῦ τὴν κεφαλὴν κλίνῃ. εἶπε δὲ 59
πρὸς ἕτερον, Ἀκολούθει μοι. ὁ δὲ εἶπε, Κύριε, ἐπίτρεψόν μοι πρῶτον
ἀπελθεῖν θάψαι τὸν πατέρα μου. εἶπε δὲ αὐτῷ ὁ Ἰησοῦς, Ἄφες τοὺς 60
νεκροὺς θάψαι τοὺς ἑαυτῶν νεκρούς· σὺ δὲ ἀπελθὼν διάγγελλε τὴν
ρϛ/ι βασιλείαν τοῦ Θεοῦ. εἶπε δὲ καὶ ἕτερος, Ἀκολουθήσω σοι, κύριε· 61
πρῶτον δὲ ἐπίτρεψόν μοι ἀποτάξασθαι τοῖς ἐν τῷ οἴκῳ. εἶπε δὲ πρὸς 62
αὐτὸν ὁ Ἰησοῦς, Οὐδεὶς ἐπιβαλὼν τὴν χεῖρα ἐπ' ἄροτρον, καὶ βλέπων
εἰς τὰ ὀπίσω, εὔθετός ἐστιν τῇ βασιλείᾳ τοῦ Θεοῦ.
ΛΔ' X. Μετὰ δὲ ταῦτα ἀνέδειξεν ὁ Κύριος καὶ ἑτέρους ἑβδομήκοντα,
ρζ/ι καὶ ἀπέστειλεν αὐτοὺς ἀνὰ δύο πρὸ προσώπου ἑαυτοῦ εἰς πᾶσαν πόλιν
ρη/ε καὶ τόπον οὗ ἔμελλεν αὐτὸς εἰσέρχεσθαι. εἶπε δὲ πρὸς αὐτούς, Ὁ 2
μὲν θερισμὸς πολύς, οἱ δὲ ἐργάται ὀλίγοι· δεήθητε οὖν τοῦ κυρίου τοῦ
ρθ/ε θερισμοῦ ὅπως ἐκβάλῃ ἐργάτας εἰς τὸν θερισμὸν αὐτοῦ. ὑπάγετε· 3
ρι/β ἰδοὺ ἐγὼ ἀποστέλλω ὑμᾶς ὡς ἄρνας ἐν μέσῳ λύκων. μὴ βαστάζετε 4
βαλλάντιον, μὴ πήραν, μὴ ὑποδήματα· καὶ μηδένα κατὰ τὴν ὁδὸν
ρια/ε ἀσπάσησθε. εἰς ἣν δ' ἂν οἰκίαν εἰσέλθητε, πρῶτον λέγετε, Εἰρήνη 5
τῷ οἴκῳ τούτῳ· καὶ ἐὰν ᾖ ἐκεῖ ὁ υἱὸς εἰρήνης, ἐπαναπαύσεται ἐπ' 6
ριβ/β αὐτὸν ἡ εἰρήνη ὑμῶν· εἰ δὲ μήγε, ἐφ' ὑμᾶς ἀνακάμψει. ἐν αὐτῇ δὲ 7
τῇ οἰκίᾳ μένετε, ἐσθίοντες καὶ πίνοντες τὰ παρ' αὐτῶν· ἄξιος γὰρ ὁ
ριγ/ι ἐργάτης τοῦ μισθοῦ αὐτοῦ ἐστι· μὴ μεταβαίνετε ἐξ οἰκίας εἰς οἰκίαν.

118 131 209 ς

51 προσωπον αυτου 131 ς **54** μαθηται αυτου ς και Ιακωβος 131 εκ] απο ς **55** οιου 131 ς **56** ο γαρ υιος ς **57** απερχη] + κυριε ς **58** κλινει 131, κλιναι 118 209 **59** απελθοντι πρωτον ς **60** διαγελλε 118 **61** εις τον οικον 131 ς **62** χειρα αυτου 118 ς εν τη βασιλεια 131, εις την βασιλειαν ς

1 αυτου ς ερχεσθαι ς **2** ειπε δε] ελεγεν ουν ς εκβαλλη 118 131 209 ς **4** βαλαντιον 118 209 ς μη 3°] μηδε ς **5** εισερχησθε ς **6** εαν μεν ς η υιος ειρηνης κει 131 **7** om γαρ 131

8 καὶ εἰς ἣν δ' ἂν πόλιν εἰσέρχησθε, καὶ δέχωνται ὑμᾶς, ἐσθίετε τὰ
9 παρατιθέμενα ὑμῖν, καὶ θεραπεύετε τοὺς ἐν αὐτῇ ἀσθενεῖς, καὶ λέγετε
10 αὐτοῖς, Ἤγγικεν ἐφ' ὑμᾶς ἡ βασιλεία τοῦ Θεοῦ. εἰς ἣν δ' ἂν πόλιν ριδ β
εἰσέλθητε, καὶ μὴ δέχωνται ὑμᾶς, ἐξελθόντες εἰς τὰς πλατείας αὐτῆς
11 εἴπατε, Καὶ τὸν κονιορτὸν τὸν κολληθέντα ἡμῖν ἐκ τῆς πόλεως ὑμῶν
εἰς τοὺς πόδας ἡμῶν ἀπομασσόμεθα ὑμῖν· πλὴν τοῦτο γινώσκετε,
12 ὅτι ἤγγικεν ἡ βασιλεία τοῦ Θεοῦ. λέγω ὑμῖν ὅτι Σοδόμοις ἐν τῇ
13 ἡμέρᾳ ἐκείνῃ ἀνεκτότερον ἔσται ἢ τῇ πόλει ἐκείνῃ. οὐαί σοι, Χοραζίν, ριε ε
οὐαί σοι, Βηθσαιδάν· ὅτι εἰ ἐν Τύρῳ καὶ Σιδῶνι ἐγένοντο αἱ δυνάμεις
αἱ γενόμεναι ἐν ὑμῖν, πάλαι ἂν ἐν σάκκῳ καὶ σποδῷ καθήμεναι μετ-
14 ενόησαν. πλὴν Τύρῳ καὶ Σιδῶνι ἐν τῇ κρίσει ἀνεκτότερον ἔσται
15 ἢ ὑμῖν. καὶ σύ, Καπερναούμ, ἡ ἕως τοῦ οὐρανοῦ ὑψωθήσῃ, ἢ ἕως
16 ᾅδου καταβιβασθήσῃ. ὁ ἀκούων ὑμῶν ἐμοῦ ἀκούει, καὶ ὁ ἀθετῶν ὑμᾶς ρις α
17 ἐμὲ ἀθετεῖ· ὁ δὲ ἐμὲ ἀθετῶν ἀθετεῖ τὸν ἀποστείλαντά με. ὑπέστρεψαν ριζ ι
δὲ οἱ ἑβδομήκοντα μετὰ χαρᾶς, λέγοντες, Κύριε, καὶ τὰ δαιμόνια ἡμῖν
18 ὑποτάσσεται ἐν τῷ ὀνόματί σου. εἶπε δὲ αὐτοῖς, Ἐθεώρουν τὸν
19 Σατανᾶν ὡς ἀστραπὴν ἐκ τοῦ οὐρανοῦ πεσόντα. ἰδοὺ δέδωκα ὑμῖν τὴν
ἐξουσίαν πατεῖν ἐπάνω ὄφεων καὶ σκορπίων, καὶ ἐπὶ πᾶσαν τὴν δύνα-
20 μιν τοῦ ἐχθροῦ· καὶ οὐδὲν ὑμᾶς οὐ μὴ ἀδικήσει. πλὴν ἐν τούτῳ μὴ
χαίρετε, ὅτι τὰ δαιμόνια ὑμῖν ὑποτάσσεται· χαίρετε δὲ ὅτι τὰ
21 ὀνόματα ὑμῶν ἐγγέγραπται ἐν τοῖς οὐρανοῖς. ἐν αὐτῇ τῇ ὥρᾳ ἠγαλ- ριη ε
λιάσατο τῷ πνεύματι τῷ ἁγίῳ ὁ Ἰησοῦς καὶ εἶπεν, Ἐξομολογοῦμαί
σοι, πάτερ, Κύριε τοῦ οὐρανοῦ καὶ τῆς γῆς, ὅτι ἀπέκρυψας ταῦτα ἀπὸ
σοφῶν καὶ συνετῶν, καὶ ἀπεκάλυψας αὐτὰ νηπίοις· ναί, ὁ πατήρ, ὅτι
22 οὕτως εὐδοκία ἐγένετο ἔμπροσθέν σου. Πάντα μοι παρεδόθη ὑπὸ ριθ γ
τοῦ πατρός μου· καὶ οὐδεὶς γινώσκει τίς ἐστιν ὁ υἱός, εἰ μὴ ὁ πατήρ,
καὶ τίς ἐστιν ὁ πατήρ, εἰ μὴ ὁ υἱός, καὶ ᾧ ἐὰν βούληται ὁ υἱὸς ἀπο-
23 καλύψαι. καὶ στραφεὶς πρὸς τοὺς μαθητὰς κατ' ἰδίαν εἶπεν αὐτοῖς, ρκ ε

13 om ει cod. **16** υμων] υμιν cod.

118 131 209 ϛ

8 δεχονται 131 **10** εισερχεσθε ϛ δεχονται 118 209 **11** om ημιν 131 om εις τους ποδας ημων ϛ απομασσωμεθα 118 209 η βασ. του Θεου] pr εφ υμας ϛ, + εφ υμας 118 209 **12** λεγω δε 118 209 ϛ **13** Χωραζειν 131, Χωραζιν ϛ Βηθσαιδα 118 131 209 ϛ καθημενοι 131 **14** ανεκτοτερον εσται εν τη κρισει ϛ **15** ἡ et υψωθεισα 118 131 209 ϛ om η 2° 118 131 209 ϛ **17** υποτασσεται ημιν ϛ **19** δεδωκα] διδωμι 118 131 ϛ του πατειν 118 ϛ αδικηση 118 131 209 ϛ **20** δαιμονια] πνευματα 118 ϛ υποτασσετε 131 δε] + μαλλον ϛ εγραφη 118 131 ϛ **21** om τω αγιω 118 131 209 ϛ εγενετο ευδοκια 118 131 209 ϛ **22** παντα] pr και στραφεις προς τους μαθητας ειπε ϛ παρεδοθη μοι ϛ επιγινωσκει 131 **23** om αυτοις ϛ

Μακάριοι οἱ ὀφθαλμοὶ οἱ βλέποντες ἃ βλέπετε. λέγω γὰρ ὑμῖν ὅτι 24
πολλοὶ προφῆται καὶ βασιλεῖς ἠθέλησαν ἰδεῖν ἃ ὑμεῖς βλέπετε, καὶ οὐκ
εἶδον, καὶ ἀκοῦσαι ἃ ἀκούετε, καὶ οὐκ ἤκουσαν.
ΛΕ' Καὶ ἰδοὺ νομικός τις ἀνέστη ἐκπειράζων αὐτὸν καὶ λέγων, Διδάσκαλε, 25
ρκα β τί ποιήσας ζωὴν αἰώνιον κληρονομήσω; ὁ δὲ εἶπε πρὸς αὐτόν, Ἐν 26
τῷ νόμῳ τί γέγραπται; πῶς ἀναγινώσκεις; ὁ δὲ ἀποκριθεὶς εἶπεν, Ἀγα- 27
πήσεις Κύριον τὸν Θεόν σου ἐν ὅλῃ καρδίᾳ σου καὶ ἐν ὅλῃ ψυχῇ
σου καὶ ἐν ὅλῃ ἰσχύϊ σου καὶ ἐν ὅλῃ τῇ διανοίᾳ σου· καὶ τὸν
πλησίον σου ὡς σεαυτόν. εἶπε δὲ αὐτῷ, Ὀρθῶς ἀπεκρίθης· τοῦτο ποίει, 28
ρκβ ι καὶ ζήσῃ. ὁ δὲ θέλων δικαιοῦν ἑαυτὸν εἶπε πρὸς τὸν Ἰησοῦν, Καὶ τίς 29
Λϛ' ἐστί μου πλησίον; ὑπολαβὼν δὲ ὁ Ἰησοῦς εἶπεν, Ἄνθρωπός τις κατ- 30
έβαινεν ἀπὸ Ἱερουσαλὴμ εἰς Ἱεριχώ, καὶ λησταῖς περιέπεσεν, οἳ καὶ
ἐξέδυσαν αὐτὸν καὶ πληγὰς ἐπιθέντες ἀπῆλθον, ἀφέντες ἡμιθανῆ.
κατὰ συγκυρίαν δὲ ἱερεύς τις κατέβαινεν τῇ ὁδῷ ἐκείνῃ, καὶ ἰδὼν 31
ἀντιπαρῆλθεν. ὁμοίως δὲ καὶ Λευΐτης κατὰ τὸν τόπον ἐλθὼν καὶ 32
ἰδὼν ἀντιπαρῆλθεν. Σαμαρείτης δέ τις ὁδεύων ἦλθε κατ' αὐτόν, καὶ 33
ἰδὼν ἐσπλαγχνίσθη· καὶ προσελθὼν κατέδησε τὰ τραύματα αὐτοῦ ἐπι- 34
χέων ἔλαιον καὶ οἶνον· ἐπιβιβάσας δὲ αὐτὸν ἐπὶ τὸ ἴδιον κτῆνος ἤγαγεν
εἰς πανδοχεῖον, καὶ ἐπεμελήθη αὐτοῦ. καὶ ἐπὶ τὴν αὔριον ἐκβαλὼν 35
δύο δηνάρια ἔδωκε τῷ πανδοχεῖ, καὶ εἶπεν, Ἐπιμελήθητι αὐτοῦ· καὶ
ὅ τι ἂν προσδαπανήσῃς ἐν τῷ ἐπανέρχεσθαί με ἀποδώσω σοι. τίς 36
τούτων τῶν τριῶν δοκεῖ σοι πλησίον γεγονέναι τοῦ ἐμπεσόντος εἰς
τοὺς λῃστάς; ὁ δὲ εἶπεν, Ὁ ποιήσας τὸ ἔλεος μετ' αὐτοῦ. εἶπεν δὲ 37
αὐτῷ ὁ Ἰησοῦς, Πορεύου καὶ σὺ ποίει ὁμοίως.
ΛΖ Ἐγένετο δὲ ἐν τῷ πορεύεσθαι αὐτόν, καὶ αὐτὸς εἰσῆλθεν εἰς κώμην· 38
γυνὴ δέ τις ὀνόματι Μάρθα ὑπεδέξατο αὐτὸν εἰς τὸν οἶκον αὐτῆς. καὶ 39
τῇδε ἦν ἀδελφὴ καλουμένη Μαρίαμ, ἣ καὶ παρακαθίσασα παρὰ τοὺς
πόδας τοῦ Ἰησοῦ ἤκουε τὸν λόγον αὐτοῦ. ἡ δὲ Μάρθα περιεσπᾶτο 40
περὶ πολλὴν διακονίαν· ἐπιστᾶσα δὲ εἶπε, Κύριε, οὐ μέλλει σοι ὅτι
ἡ ἀδελφή μου μόνην με κατέλιπε διακονεῖν; εἰπὲ οὖν αὐτῇ ἵνα μοι

35 προσδαπανησις 1* sed nunc προσδαπανησι
39 καλουμενῃ cod. 40 αυτη] αυτην cod.

118 131 209 ϛ 25 ποιησας ινα 131 26 om ο (sed non δε) 131 27 εξ ολης της καρδιας 118 ϛ εν ολη ψυχη] om 131, εξ ολης της ψυχης 118 ϛ εξ ολης της ισχυος 118 ϛ τη ισχυι 131 εξ ολης της διανοιας 118 ϛ 30 εκδυσαντες ϛ ημιθανη τυγχανοντα ϛ 31 εν τη 118 131 209 ϛ ιδων αυτον 131 ϛ Λευιτης γενομενος ϛ 33 ιδων αυτον ϛ 34 ηγαγεν αυτον ϛ 35 αυριον]+εξελθων ϛ εκβαλλων 131 ειπεν αυτω ϛ εν τω] pr εγω με] μοι 131 36 τις ουν 131 ϛ om τουτων 131 γεγονεναι πλησιον 118 209 37 δε 2°] ουν ϛ 38 εκπορευεσθαι 118 209 αυτον 1°] αυτους ϛ 39 Μαρια 118 131 209 ϛ των λογων 131 40 μελει 131 ϛ

41 συναντιλάβηται. ἀποκριθεὶς δὲ εἶπεν αὐτῇ ὁ Ἰησοῦς, Μάρθα, Μάρθα,
42 μεριμνᾷς καὶ θορυβάζῃ περὶ πολλά· ὀλίγων δέ ἐστι χρεία ἢ ἑνός·
Μαριὰμ γὰρ τὴν ἀγαθὴν μερίδα ἐξελέξατο, ἥτις οὐκ ἀφαιρεθήσεται
ἀπ' αὐτῆς.

XI. Καὶ ἐγένετο ἐν τῷ εἶναι αὐτὸν ἐν τόπῳ τινὶ προσευχόμενον, ΛΗ'
ὡς ἐπαύσατο, εἶπέ τις τῶν μαθητῶν αὐτοῦ πρὸς αὐτόν, Κύριε, δίδαξον ρκγ ε
2 ἡμᾶς προσεύχεσθαι, καθὼς Ἰωάννης ἐδίδαξε τοὺς μαθητὰς αὐτοῦ. εἶπε
δὲ αὐτοῖς, Ὅταν προσεύχεσθε, λέγετε, Πάτερ, ἁγιασθήτω τὸ ὄνομά
3 σου· ἐλθέτω ἡ βασιλεία σου· τὸν ἄρτον ἡμῶν τὸν ἐπιούσιον δίδου
4 ἡμῖν τὸ καθ' ἡμέραν· καὶ ἄφες ἡμῖν τὰ ἁμαρτήματα ἡμῶν, καὶ γὰρ
αὐτοὶ ἀφίομεν παντὶ ὀφείλοντι ἡμῖν· καὶ μὴ εἰσενέγκῃς ἡμᾶς εἰς πει-
5 ρασμόν. καὶ εἶπε πρὸς αὐτούς, Τίς ἐξ ὑμῶν ἕξει φίλον, καὶ πορεύσεται ρκδ ι
πρὸς αὐτὸν μεσονυκτίου καὶ εἴπῃ αὐτῷ, Φίλε, χρῆσόν μοι τρεῖς ἄρτους,
6 ἐπειδὴ φίλος μου παρεγένετο ἐξ ὁδοῦ πρός με, καὶ οὐκ ἔχω ὃ παρα-
7 θήσω αὐτῷ· κἀκεῖνος ἔσωθεν ἀποκριθεὶς εἴπῃ, Μή μοι κόπους πάρεχε·
ἤδη ἡ θύρα κέκλεισται, καὶ τὰ παιδία μετ' ἐμοῦ εἰς τὴν κοίτην
8 εἰσίν· οὐ δύναμαι ἀναστὰς δοῦναί σοι. λέγω ὑμῖν, εἰ καὶ οὐ δώσει
αὐτῷ ἀναστὰς διὰ τὸ εἶναι αὐτοῦ φίλον, διά γε τὴν ἀναίδειαν αὐτοῦ
9 ἐγερθεὶς δώσει αὐτῷ ὅσον χρῄζει. κἀγὼ ὑμῖν λέγω, Αἰτεῖτε, καὶ δο- ρκε ε
10 θήσεται ὑμῖν· ζητεῖτε, καὶ εὑρήσετε· κρούετε, καὶ ἀνοιγήσεται ὑμῖν. πᾶς
γὰρ ὁ αἰτῶν λαμβάνει, καὶ ὁ ζητῶν εὑρίσκει, καὶ τῷ κρούοντι ἀνοιγή-
11 σεται. τίνα δὲ ὑμῶν πατέρα αἰτήσει υἱὸς αὐτοῦ ἄρτον, μὴ λίθον
12 ἐπιδώσει αὐτῷ; ἢ καὶ ἰχθύν, μὴ ἀντὶ ἰχθύος ὄφιν ἐπιδώσει αὐτῷ; ἢ
13 καὶ αἰτήσει ᾠόν, μὴ ἐπιδώσει αὐτῷ σκορπίον; εἰ οὖν ὑμεῖς πονηροὶ
ὑπάρχοντες οἴδατε δόματα ἀγαθὰ διδόναι τοῖς τέκνοις ὑμῶν, πόσῳ
μᾶλλον ὁ πατὴρ ὁ ἐξ οὐρανοῦ δώσει Πνεῦμα Ἅγιον τοῖς αἰτοῦσιν
αὐτόν;

14 Καὶ ἦν ἐκβάλλων δαιμόνιον κωφόν· ἐγένετο δὲ τοῦ δαιμονίου ΛΘ'
15 ἐξελθόντος, ἐλάλησεν ὁ κωφός· καὶ ἐθαύμασαν οἱ ὄχλοι. τινὲς δὲ ἐξ ρκϛ ε ρκζ β

41 ο Ιησους ante ειπεν 131 θορυβαζη] τυρβαζη 118 131 209 ϛ **42** ενος δε εστι χρεια Μαρια δε 118 131 209 ϛ 118 131 209 ϛ

1 καθως] ως 131 και Ιωαννης 118 131 ϛ **2** προσευχησθε 118 131 209 ϛ Πατερ ημων ο εν τοις ουρανοις 118 131 209 ϛ σου 2°]+γενηθητω το θελημα σου ως εν ουρανω και επι της γης 118 131 209 ϛ **3** om ημων 131 **4** τα αμαρτηματα] τας αμαρτιας ϛ, τα οφειληματα 131 αφιεμεν 118 131 209 ϛ πειρασμον] + αλλα ρυσαι ημας απο του πονηρου 118 209 ϛ **5** om μου 118 209 **7** η θυρα ηδη 118 209 παιδια μου 118 209 ϛ επι της κοιτης 118 209 **8** οσων 118 209 ϛ **9** λεγω υμιν 118 209 **10** ανοιχθησεται 118 209 **11** τον πατερα 118 209 ϛ ο υιος 131 ϛ om αυτου ϛ η] ει ϛ **12** εαν αιτηση 118 ϛ **13** αγαθα δοματα ϛ **14** και αυτο ην κωφον ϛ

αὐτῶν εἶπον, Ἐν Βεελζεβοὺλ ἄρχοντι τῶν δαιμονίων ἐκβάλλει τὰ
ρκη ε δαιμόνια. ἕτεροι δὲ πειράζοντες σημεῖον ἐξ οὐρανοῦ ἐζήτουν παρ' 16
ρκθ β αὐτοῦ. αὐτὸς δὲ εἰδὼς αὐτῶν τὰ διανοήματα εἶπεν αὐτοῖς, Πᾶσα βασι- 17
λεία ἐφ' ἑαυτὴν διαμερισθεῖσα ἐρημοῦται· καὶ οἶκος ἐπὶ οἶκον πίπτει.
εἰ δὲ καὶ ὁ Σατανᾶς ἐφ' ἑαυτὸν διεμερίσθη, πῶς σταθήσεται ἡ βασιλεία 18
αὐτοῦ; ὅτι λέγετε ἐν Βεελζεβοὺλ ἐκβάλλειν με τὰ δαιμόνια. εἰ δὲ 19
ἐγὼ ἐν Βεελζεβοὺλ ἐκβάλλω τὰ δαιμόνια, οἱ υἱοὶ ὑμῶν ἐν τίνι ἐκβά-
λουσι; διὰ τοῦτο αὐτοὶ κριταὶ ὑμῶν ἔσονται. εἰ δὲ ἐν δακτύλῳ 20
Θεοῦ ἐκβάλλω τὰ δαιμόνια, ἄρα ἔφθασεν ἐφ' ὑμᾶς ἡ βασιλεία τοῦ
Θεοῦ. ὅταν ὁ ἰσχυρὸς καθωπλισμένος φυλάσσῃ τὴν ἑαυτοῦ αὐλήν, ἐν 21
εἰρήνῃ ἐστὶ τὰ ὑπάρχοντα αὐτοῦ· ἐπὰν δὲ ὁ ἰσχυρότερος αὐτοῦ ἐπελ- 22
θὼν νικήσῃ αὐτόν, τὴν πανοπλίαν αὐτοῦ αἴρει, ἐφ' ᾗ ἐπεποίθει, καὶ τὰ
σκῦλα αὐτοῦ διαδώσει. ὁ μὴ ὢν μετ' ἐμοῦ κατ' ἐμοῦ ἐστι· καὶ ὁ μὴ 23
ρλ ε συνάγων μετ' ἐμοῦ σκορπίζει. ὅταν τὸ ἀκάθαρτον πνεῦμα ἐξέλθῃ ἀπὸ 24
τοῦ ἀνθρώπου, διέρχεται δι' ἀνύδρων τόπων ζητοῦν ἀνάπαυσιν· καὶ μὴ
εὑρίσκον λέγει, Ὑποστρέψω εἰς τὸν οἶκόν μου ὅθεν ἐξῆλθον· καὶ ἐλθὸν 25
εὑρίσκει σχολάζοντα σεσαρωμένον καὶ κεκοσμημένον. τότε πορεύεται 26
καὶ παραλαμβάνει ἑπτὰ ἕτερα πνεύματα πονηρότερα ἑαυτοῦ, καὶ εἰσελ-
θόντα κατοικεῖ ἐκεῖ· καὶ γίνεται τὰ ἔσχατα τοῦ ἀνθρώπου ἐκείνου
χείρονα τῶν πρώτων.
Μ′ ρλα ι Ἐγένετο δὲ ἐν τῷ λέγειν αὐτὸν ταῦτα, ἐπάρασά τις γυνὴ ἐκ τοῦ 27
ὄχλου φωνὴν εἶπεν αὐτῷ, Μακαρία ἡ κοιλία ἡ βαστάσασά σε καὶ
μαστοὶ οὓς ἐθήλασας. αὐτὸς δὲ εἶπε, Μενοῦνγε μακάριοι οἱ ἀκούοντες 28
ΜΑ′ ρλβ ε τὸν λόγον τοῦ Θεοῦ καὶ φυλάσσοντες αὐτόν. τῶν δὲ ὄχλων ἐπαθροι- 29
ζομένων ἤρξατο λέγειν, Ἡ γενεὰ αὕτη γενεὰ πονηρά ἐστι· σημεῖον
ἐπιζητεῖ, καὶ σημεῖον οὐ δοθήσεται αὐτῇ, εἰ μὴ τὸ σημεῖον Ἰωάννου
τοῦ προφήτου. καθὼς γὰρ ἐγένετο Ἰωνᾶς σημεῖον τοῖς Νινευΐταις, οὕτως 30
ἔσται καὶ ὁ υἱὸς τοῦ ἀνθρώπου τῇ γενεᾷ ταύτῃ. βασίλισσα νότου ἐγερ- 31
θήσεται ἐν τῇ κρίσει μετὰ τῶν ἀνδρῶν τῆς γενεᾶς ταύτης καὶ κατα-
κρινεῖ αὐτούς· ὅτι ἦλθεν ἐκ τῶν περάτων τῆς γῆς ἀκοῦσαι τὴν σοφίαν
Σολομῶνος, καὶ ἰδοὺ πλεῖον Σολομῶνος ὧδε. ἄνδρες Νινευιταὶ 32

29 Ιωαννου] αν nunc eras.

118 131 209 ς 15 Βεεζεβουλ 209, Βεε βουλ 118* scripsisse videtur spat. rel. in quo 118[2] λζε scripsit 16 πειραζοντες αυτον 131 παρ αυτου εζητουν εξ ουρανου ς 18 λεγεται 209 19 εκβαλλουσι 118 209 ς κριται υμων αυτοι 118 209 ς 21 ισχυροτερος 131 22 επαν] εαν 131 διαδιδωσι 131 ς 25 om σχολαζοντα ς 26 εκει] αυτου 118* sed ipse partim correxit 27 φωνην ante εκ του οχλου 118 131 209 ς om αυτω 131 μασθοι 118 209 29 om γενεα 2° ς Ιωαννου] Ιωνα 118 131 209 ς 30 om και 131 31 om των ανδρων 131 Σολομωνος 1°] Σολομωντος 118 131 209 ς πλεον 209 Σολομωνος 2°] Σολομωντος 118 209 ς 32 Νινευιται] Νινευι ς

ἀναστήσονται ἐν τῇ κρίσει μετὰ τῆς γενεᾶς ταύτης καὶ κατακρινοῦσιν
αὐτήν· ὅτι μετενόησαν εἰς τὸ κήρυγμα Ἰωνᾶ, καὶ ἰδοὺ πλεῖον Ἰωνᾶ ὧδε.
33 Οὐδεὶς δὲ λύχνον ἅψας εἰς κρυπτὸν τίθησιν, ἀλλ' ἐπὶ τὴν λυχνίαν, ρλγ β
34 ἵνα οἱ εἰσπορευόμενοι τὸ φῶς βλέπωσιν. ὁ λύχνος τοῦ σώματός ρλδ
ἐστιν ὁ ὀφθαλμός· ὅταν οὖν ὁ ὀφθαλμός σου ἁπλοῦς ᾖ, καὶ ὅλον τὸ ε
σῶμα φωτεινόν ἔσται· ἐπὰν δὲ πονηρὸς ᾖ, καὶ ὅλον τὸ σῶμά σου
35 36 σκοτεινόν. σκόπει οὖν μὴ τὸ φῶς τὸ ἐν σοὶ σκότος ἐστίν. εἰ οὖν τὸ
σῶμά σου ὅλον φωτεινόν, μὴ ἔχον μέρος τι σκοτεινόν, ἔσται φωτεινὸν
ὅλον ὡς ὅταν ὁ λύχνος τῇ ἀστραπῇ φωτίζῃ σε.
37 Ἐν δὲ τῷ λαλῆσαι αὐτὸν ταῦτα ἠρώτα αὐτὸν Φαρισαῖος ὅπως ΜΒ′
38 ἀριστήσῃ παρ' αὐτῷ· εἰσελθὼν δὲ ἀνέπεσεν. ὁ δὲ Φαρισαῖος ἰδὼν ἐθαύ-
39 μασεν ὅτι οὐ πρῶτον ἐβαπτίσθη πρὸ τοῦ ἀρίστου. εἶπε δὲ ὁ Κύριος ρλε
πρὸς αὐτόν, Νῦν ὑμεῖς οἱ Φαρισαῖοι τὸ ἔξωθεν τοῦ ποτηρίου καὶ τοῦ ε
πίνακος καθαρίζετε· τὸ δὲ ἔσωθεν ὑμῶν γέμει ἁρπαγῆς καὶ πονηρίας.
40 41 ἄφρονες, οὐχ ὁ ποιήσας τὸ ἔξωθεν καὶ τὸ ἔσωθεν ἐποίησε; πλὴν τὰ
42 ἐνόντα δότε ἐλεημοσύνην, καὶ ἰδοὺ πάντα καθαρὰ ὑμῖν ἔσται. ἀλλ' ρλϛ
οὐαὶ ὑμῖν τοῖς Φαρισαίοις, ὅτι ἀποδεκατοῦτε τὸ ἡδύοσμον καὶ τὸ πήγα- ε
νον καὶ πᾶν λάχανον, καὶ παρέρχεσθε τὴν κρίσιν καὶ τὴν ἀγάπην
43 τοῦ Θεοῦ· ταῦτα ἔδει ποιῆσαι, κἀκεῖνα μὴ ἀφιέναι. οὐαὶ ὑμῖν τοῖς ρλζ
Φαρισαίοις, ὅτι ἀγαπᾶτε τὴν πρωτοκαθεδρίαν ἐν ταῖς συναγωγαῖς καὶ β
44 τοὺς ἀσπασμοὺς ἐν ταῖς ἀγοραῖς. οὐαὶ ὑμῖν, ὅτι ἐστὲ ὡς τὰ μνημεῖα ρλη
45 τὰ ἄδηλα, καὶ οἱ ἄνθρωποι περιπατοῦντες ἐπάνω οὐκ οἴδασιν. ἀπο- ε ρλθ
κριθεὶς δέ τις τῶν νομικῶν λέγει αὐτῷ, Διδάσκαλε, ταῦτα λέγων καὶ ε
46 ἡμᾶς ὑβρίζεις. ὁ δὲ εἶπε, Καὶ ὑμῖν τοῖς νομικοῖς οὐαί, ὅτι φορτίζετε ΜΓ′
τοὺς ἀνθρώπους φορτία δυσβάστακτα, καὶ αὐτοὶ ἐπὶ τῶν δακτύλων
47 ὑμῶν οὐ προσψαύετε τοῖς φορτίοις. οὐαὶ ὑμῖν, ὅτι οἰκοδομεῖτε τὰ ρμ
48 μνημεῖα τῶν προφητῶν, οἱ δὲ πατέρες ὑμῶν ἀπέκτειναν αὐτούς. ἄρα ε
μαρτυρεῖτε καὶ συνευδοκεῖτε τοῖς ἔργοις τῶν πατέρων ὑμῶν,
ὅτι αὐτοὶ μὲν ἀπέκτειναν αὐτούς, ὑμεῖς δὲ οἰκοδομεῖτε τοὺς

33 ἀψας cod. **45** ημας] 1* primum υμας scripsit sed ipse correxit

33 κρυπτην 131 τιθησιν] + ουδε υπο τον μοδιον ϛ το φως] post βλεπωσιν 118 209, το φεγγος ϛ βλεπουσιν 131 **34** σωμα 1°] + σου 118 131 209 ϛ φωτινον 118 εσται] εστιν ϛ om ολον 2° ϛ σκοτεινον εσται 131 **36** τι μερος ϛ φωτιζει 131 **37** om αυτον ταυτα ϛ Φαρισαιος τις 118 ϛ **38** εναπτισθη 131 **41** εσται] εστιν ϛ **44** υμιν] + γραμματεις και Φαραισαιοι υποκριται ϛ ανθρωποι] + οι ϛ περιπατουσιν 131 **46** φορτιζετε] φροντιζετε 131 δυσβαστακτα] pr βαρεα και 131 επι] ενι 131 ϛ **48** om αρα μαρτυρειτε...αυτους 118* 209 sed postquam 118* scripserat υμεις δε οικοδομειτε τους ταφους αυτων δια τουτο και η σοφια του Θεου haec verba delevit et verbis quae omiserat suprascriptis perrexit υμεις δε οικοδομειτε αυτων τα μνημεια δια τουτο κ.τ.λ. quae omnia habet ϛ 118 131 209 ϛ

ρμα τάφους αὐτῶν. διὰ τοῦτο καὶ ἡ σοφία τοῦ Θεοῦ εἶπεν, Ἀπο- 49
ε στελῶ εἰς αὐτοὺς προφήτας καὶ ἀποστόλους, ἐξ αὐτῶν ἀποκτενοῦσι καὶ
διώξουσιν· ἵνα ἐκζητηθῇ τὸ αἷμα πάντων τῶν προφητῶν τὸ ἐκχυνό- 50
μενον ἀπὸ καταβολῆς κόσμου ἀπὸ τῆς γενεᾶς ταύτης, ἀπὸ αἵματος 51
Ἄβελ ἕως αἵματος Ζαχαρίου τοῦ ἀπολομένου μεταξὺ τοῦ θυσιαστηρίου
καὶ τοῦ οἴκου· ναί, λέγω ὑμῖν, ἐκζητηθήσεται ἀπὸ τῆς γενεᾶς ταύτης.
ρμβ ε οὐαὶ ὑμῖν τοῖς νομικοῖς, ὅτι ἤρατε τὴν κλεῖδα τῆς γνώσεως· αὐτοὶ οὐκ 52
ρμγ ι εἰσήλθετε, καὶ τοὺς εἰσερχομένους ἐκωλύσατε. λέγοντος δὲ αὐτοῦ ταῦτα 53
πρὸς αὐτοὺς ἤρξαντο οἱ νομικοὶ καὶ οἱ Φαρισαῖοι δεινῶς ἐνέχειν αὐτῷ
καὶ ἀποστοματίζειν αὐτὸν περὶ πλειόνων, ἐνεδρεύοντες αὐτὸν θηρεῦσαί 54
τι ἐκ τοῦ στόματος αὐτοῦ, ἵνα κατηγορήσωσιν αὐτοῦ.

ΜΔ' XII. Ἐν οἷς ἐπισυναχθεισῶν τῶν μυριάδων τοῦ ὄχλου, ὥστε
ρμδ β καταπατεῖν ἀλλήλους, ἤρξατο λέγειν πρὸς τοὺς μαθητὰς αὐτοῦ πρῶτον,
Προσέχετε ἑαυτοῖς ἀπὸ τῆς ζύμης τῶν Φαρισαίων, ἥτις ἐστὶν ὑπόκρισις.
ρμε ε οὐδὲν δὲ συγκεκαλυμμένον ἐστίν, ὃ οὐκ ἀποκαλυφθήσεται, καὶ κρυπτόν, ὃ 2
οὐ γνωσθήσεται. ἀνθ' ὧν ὅσα ἐν τῇ σκοτίᾳ εἴπατε ἐν τῷ φωτὶ ἀκου- 3
σθήσεται· καὶ ὃ πρὸς τὸ οὖς ἐλαλήσατε ἐν τοῖς ταμίοις κηρυχθήσεται
ἐπὶ τῶν δωμάτων. λέγω δὲ ὑμῖν τοῖς φίλοις μου, Μὴ φοβηθῆτε ἀπὸ 4
τῶν ἀποκτενόντων τὸ σῶμα, καὶ μετὰ ταῦτα περισσότερον μὴ
ἐχόντων τι ποιῆσαι. ὑποδείξω δὲ ὑμῖν τίνα φοβηθῆτε· φοβήθητε τὸν 5
μετὰ τὸ ἀποκτεῖναι ἔχοντα ἐξουσίαν ἐμβαλεῖν εἰς τὴν γέενναν· ναί,
λέγω ὑμῖν, τοῦτο φοβήθητε. οὐχὶ πέντε στρουθία πωλεῖται ἀσσαρίων 6
δύο; καὶ ἓν ἐξ αὐτῶν οὐκ ἔστιν ἐπιλελησμένον ἐνώπιον τοῦ Θεοῦ· ἀλλὰ 7
καὶ αἱ τρίχες τῆς κεφαλῆς ὑμῶν πᾶσαι ἠρίθμηνται. μὴ οὖν φοβεῖσθε·
ρμϛ β πολλῶν στρουθίων διαφέρετε. λέγω δὲ ὑμῖν, Πᾶς ὃς ἂν ὁμολογήσῃ ἐν 8
ἐμοὶ ἔμπροσθεν τῶν ἀνθρώπων, καὶ ὁ υἱὸς τοῦ ἀνθρώπου ὁμολογήσει ἐν
αὐτῷ ἔμπροσθεν τῶν ἀγγέλων τοῦ Θεοῦ· ὁ δὲ ἀρνησάμενός με ἐνώπιον 9
ρμζ β τῶν ἀνθρώπων ἀπαρνηθήσεται ἐνώπιον τῶν ἀγγέλων τοῦ Θεοῦ. καὶ 10
πᾶς ὃς ἐρεῖ λόγον εἰς τὸν υἱὸν τοῦ ἀνθρώπου, ἀφεθήσεται αὐτῷ· τῷ
ρμη β δὲ εἰς τὸ Ἅγιον Πνεῦμα βλασφημήσαντι οὐκ ἀφεθήσεται. ὅταν δὲ 11

1 της] τοις cod. 3 ταμιοις] inter ι et ο est unius literae rasura in qua nihil legere possum, haud scio an 1* ταμιειοις primum scripserit, tum autem ipse correxerit 5 εκβαλην cod.

118 131 209 ϛ 49 και εξ 118 131 209 ϛ εκδιωξουσιν 118 209 ϛ 51 αιματος 1°] pr του 118 209 ϛ Αβελ του δικαιου 131 αιματος 2°] pr του ϛ ναι] και 131 53 om αυτου 118 131 νομικοι] γραμματεις ϛ om αυτω ϛ 54 θηρευσαι pr και ζητουντες ϛ

1 επισυναχθησοντων 131 3 ταμειοις 118 209, ταμειοις 131 ϛ 4 om μου 131 αποκτεινοντων ϛ μη εχοντων περισσοτερον ϛ 5 εξουσιαν εχοντα ϛ τουτον 131 ϛ 9 om με 131 απαρνηθησετε 118

εἰσφέρωσιν ὑμᾶς εἰς τὰς συναγωγὰς καὶ τὰς ἀρχὰς καὶ τὰς ἐξουσίας,
12 μὴ μεριμνήσετε πῶς ἢ τί ἀπολογήσησθε, ἢ τί εἴπητε· τὸ γὰρ Ἅγιον
Πνεῦμα διδάξει ὑμᾶς ἐν αὐτῇ τῇ ὥρᾳ ἃ δεῖ εἰπεῖν.
13 Εἶπε δέ τις αὐτῷ ἐκ τοῦ ὄχλου, Διδάσκαλε, εἰπὲ τῷ ἀδελφῷ μου ΜΕ'
14 μερίσασθαι μετ' ἐμοῦ τὴν κληρονομίαν. ὁ δὲ εἶπεν αὐτῷ, Ἄνθρωπε, ρμθ ι
15 τίς με κατέστησε κρίτην ἢ μεριστὴν ἐφ' ὑμᾶς; εἶπε δὲ πρὸς αὐτούς,
Ὁρᾶτε καὶ φυλάσσεσθε ἀπὸ πάσης πλεονεξίας· ὅτι οὐκ ἐν τῷ περισ-
16 σεύειν τινὶ ἡ ζωὴ αὐτῷ ἐστιν ἐκ τῶν ὑπαρχόντων αὐτοῦ. εἶπε δὲ ΜϚ'
καὶ παραβολὴν πρὸς αὐτοὺς λέγων, Ἀνθρώπου τινὸς πλουσίου εὐφό-
17 ρησεν ἡ χώρα· καὶ διελογίζετο ἐν ἑαυτῷ λέγων, Τί ποιήσω, ὅτι οὐκ
18 ἔχω ποῦ συνάξω τοὺς καρπούς μου; καὶ εἶπε, Τοῦτο ποιήσω· καθελῶ
μου τὰς ἀποθήκας καὶ μείζονας οἰκοδομήσω, καὶ συνάξω ἐκεῖ πάντα τὸν
19 σῖτον καὶ τὰ ἀγαθά μου, καὶ ἐρῶ τῇ ψυχῇ μου, Ψυχή, ἔχεις πολλὰ
20 ἀγαθὰ κείμενα εἰς ἔτη πολλά· ἀναπαύου, φάγε, πίε, εὐφραίνου. εἶπε
δὲ αὐτῷ ὁ Θεός, Ἄφρον, ταύτῃ τῇ νυκτὶ τὴν ψυχήν σου ἀπαιτοῦσιν
21 ἀπὸ σοῦ· ἃ δὲ ἡτοίμασας, τίνι ἔσται; οὕτως ὁ θησαυρίζων ἑαυτῷ καὶ
μὴ εἰς Θεὸν πλουτῶν.
22 Εἶπε δὲ πρὸς τοὺς μαθητὰς αὐτοῦ, Διὰ τοῦτο ὑμῖν λέγω, μὴ ρν
23 μεριμνᾶτε τῇ ψυχῇ τί φάγητε, μηδὲ τῷ σώματι τί ἐνδύσησθε. ἡ ε
24 γὰρ ψυχὴ πλεῖόν ἐστι τῆς τροφῆς, καὶ τὸ σῶμα τοῦ ἐνδύματος. κατα-
νοήσατε τοὺς κόρακας, ὅτι οὐ σπείρουσιν οὐδὲ θερίζουσιν· οἷς οὐκ ἔστι
ταμίειον οὐδὲ ἀποθήκη, καὶ ὁ Θεὸς τρέφει αὐτούς· πόσῳ μᾶλλον ὑμεῖς
25 διαφέρετε τῶν πετεινῶν; τίς δὲ ἐξ ὑμῶν μεριμνῶν δύναται προσθεῖναι
26 ἐπὶ τὴν ἡλικίαν αὐτοῦ πῆχυν ἕνα; εἰ οὖν οὐδὲ ἐλάχιστον δύνασθε, τί
27 περὶ τῶν λοιπῶν μεριμνᾶτε; κατανοήσατε τὰ κρίνα πῶς αὐξάνει· οὐ
κοπιᾷ οὐδὲ νήθει· λέγω δὲ ὑμῖν ὅτι Οὐδὲ Σολομὼν ἐν πάσῃ τῇ δόξῃ
28 αὐτοῦ περιεβάλετο ὡς ἓν τούτων. εἰ δὲ τὸν χόρτον σήμερον ἐν
τῷ ἀγρῷ ὄντα καὶ αὔριον εἰς κλίβανον βαλλόμενον ὁ Θεὸς οὕτως
29 ἀμφιέννυσι, πόσῳ μᾶλλον ὑμᾶς, ὀλιγόπιστοι; καὶ ὑμεῖς μὴ ζητεῖτε

25 προσθειναι] inter σ et θ spatium duarum literarum relictum est in quo nihil scriptum esse videtur

11 προσφερωσιν 118 209 ϛ εις] επι 118 209 ϛ μεριμνατε ϛ 118 131 209 ϛ **14** κριτην] δικαστην ϛ **15** πασης] της ϛ αυτω] αυτου ϛ αυτου] 209* primum scripsisse videtur vel αυτω vel potius αυτα sed ipse statim correxit, αυτ spat. rel. 118 **18** τον σιτον] τα γενηματα μου ϛ **20** αφρων ϛ **21** πλουτων] 118[2] add. in mg. και ταυτα λεγων εφωνει ο εχων ωτα ακουειν ακουετω **22** ψυχη υμων 118 131 209 ϛ **23** om γαρ ϛ **24** ταμειον 131 ϛ **26** ουτε ϛ **27** om οτι ϛ περιεβαλλετο 118 131 209 **28** ει δε] ιδε 118 209 χορτον]+του αγρου 118 209 εν τω αγρω σημερον ϛ **29** om μη 1° 131

τί φάγητε ἢ τί πίητε, καὶ μὴ μετεωρίζεσθε. πάντα γὰρ ταῦτα τὰ 30
ἔθνη τοῦ κοσμοῦ ἐπιζητεῖ· ὑμῶν δὲ ὁ πατὴρ οἶδεν ὅτι χρήζετε τούτων.
πλὴν ζητεῖτε τὴν βασιλείαν τοῦ Θεοῦ, καὶ ταῦτα πάντα προστεθήσεται 31
ρνα ὑμῖν. μὴ φοβοῦ, τὸ μικρὸν ποίμνιον· ὅτι εὐδόκησεν ὁ πατὴρ ὑμῶν 32
ι δοῦναι ὑμῖν τὴν βασιλείαν. πωλήσατε τὰ ὑπάρχοντα ὑμῶν καὶ δότε 33
ρνβ β ἐλεημοσύνην. ποιήσατε ἑαυτοῖς βαλλάντια μὴ παλαιούμενα, θησαυρὸν
ρνγ ε ἀνέκλειπτον ἐν τοῖς οὐρανοῖς, ὅπου κλέπτης οὐκ ἐγγίζει, οὐδὲ σὴς δια-
φθείρει. ὅπου γάρ ἐστιν ὁ θησαυρὸς ὑμῶν, ἐκεῖ καὶ ἡ καρδία ὑμῶν 34
ρνδ ἔσται. ἔστωσαν ὑμῶν αἱ ὀσφύες περιεζωσμέναι καὶ οἱ λύχνοι και- 35
ι όμενοι, καὶ ὑμεῖς ὅμοιοι ἀνθρώποις προσδεχομένοις τὸν κύριον αὐτῶν, 36
πότε ἀναλύσει ἐκ τῶν γάμων αὐτῶν, ἵνα ἐλθόντος καὶ κρούσαντος
ρνε εὐθέως ἀνοίξωσιν αὐτῷ. μακάριοι οἱ δοῦλοι ἐκεῖνοι οὓς ἐλθὼν ὁ 37
ε κύριος εὑρήσει γρηγοροῦντας. ἀμὴν λέγω ὑμῖν ὅτι περιζώ-
σεται καὶ ἀνακλινεῖ αὐτούς, καὶ παρελθὼν διακονήσει αὐτοῖς.
καὶ ἐὰν ἔλθῃ τῇ ἑσπερίνῃ φυλακῇ, καὶ εὕρῃ οὕτως ποιοῦντας, 38
μακάριοί εἰσιν, ὅτι ἀνακλινεῖ αὐτοὺς καὶ διακονήσει αὐτοῖς.
κἂν ἐν τῇ δευτέρᾳ κἂν ἐν τῇ τρίτῃ φυλακῇ ἔλθῃ καὶ εὕρῃ οὕτως,
ρνϛ μακάριοί εἰσι οἱ δοῦλοι ἐκεῖνοι. τοῦτο δὲ γινώσκετε, ὅτι εἰ ᾔδει 39
β ὁ οἰκοδεσπότης ποίᾳ ὥρᾳ ὁ κλέπτης ἔρχεται, ἐγρηγόρησεν ἂν καὶ οὐκ
ἀφῆκε διορυγῆναι τὸν οἶκον αὐτοῦ. εἶπε δὲ αὐτῷ ὁ Πέτρος, Κύριε, 41
ρνζ πρὸς ἡμᾶς τὴν παραβολὴν ταύτην λέγεις, ἢ καὶ πρὸς πάντας; καὶ 42
ε εἶπεν ὁ Κύριος, Τίς ἄρα ἐστὶν ὁ πιστὸς οἰκονόμος καὶ φρόνιμος, ὃν
καταστήσει ὁ κύριος ἐπὶ τῆς οἰκετίας αὐτοῦ, τοῦ διδόναι ἐν καιρῷ
τὸ σιτομέτριον; μακάριος ὁ δοῦλος ἐκεῖνος ὃν ἐλθὼν ὁ κύριος αὐτοῦ 43
εὑρήσει ποιοῦντα οὕτως. ἀληθῶς λέγω ὑμῖν ὅτι ἐπὶ πᾶσι τοῖς ὑπάρ- 44
ρνη χουσιν αὐτοῦ καταστήσει αὐτόν. ἐὰν δὲ εἴπῃ ὁ δοῦλος ἐκεῖνος ἐν τῇ 45
ε καρδίᾳ αὐτοῦ, Χρονίζει ὁ κύριός μου ἔρχεσθαι, καὶ ἄρξηται τύπτειν τοὺς
παῖδας καὶ τὰς παιδίσκας, ἐσθίειν τε καὶ πίνειν καὶ μεθύσκεσθαι, ἥξει 46
ὁ κύριος τοῦ δούλου ἐκείνου ἐν ἡμέρᾳ ᾗ οὐ προσδοκᾷ καὶ ἐν ὥρᾳ ᾗ
οὐ γινώσκει, καὶ διχοτομήσει αὐτόν, καὶ τὸ μέρος αὐτοῦ μετὰ τῶν

118 131 209 ϛ

30 ταυτα γαρ παντα ϛ τουτων] + απαντων 131 **31** om παντα 131 **33** βαλαντια 118 209 ϛ **35** αι οσφυες υμων 131 **36** αυτων 1°] εαυτων 118 ϛ αναλυση 131 om αυτων 2° 118 131 209 ϛ ελθοντες 118 κρουσαντες 118 **37** εκεινοι] + εισιν 131 **37 38** ους ελθων...εκεινοι] om 131 sed manus ut videtur prima literis minoribus in margine addidit iis autem usa lectionibus quas habet ϛ **38** om και εαν...διακονησει αυτοις ϛ καν εν 1°] και εαν ελθη εν ϛ καν εν 2°] φυλακη και εν ϛ ουτω ϛ **39** ουκ αν ϛ **40** και υμεις ουν γινεσθε ετοιμοι οτι η ωρα ου δοκειτε ο υιος του ανθρωπου ερχεται 131 ϛ (sed om ουν 131) **41** ταυτην] αυτην 118 209 **42** και ειπεν] ειπε δε ϛ οικετιας] οικιας 131, θεραπειας 118 209 ϛ διαδοναι 118

47 ὑποκριτῶν θήσει. ἐκεῖνος δὲ ὁ δοῦλος ὁ γνοὺς τὸ θέλημα τοῦ κυρίου ρνθ ι
αὐτοῦ καὶ μὴ ἑτοιμάσας μηδὲ ποιήσας πρὸς τὸ θέλημα αὐτοῦ, δαρή-
48 σεται πολλάς· ὁ δὲ μὴ γνούς, ποιήσας δὲ ἄξια πληγῶν, δαρήσεται
ὀλίγας. παντὶ δὲ ᾧ ἐδόθη πολύ, πολὺ ζητηθήσεται ἀπ' αὐτοῦ· καὶ ᾧ
49 παρέθεντο πολύ, περισσότερον αἰτήσουσιν αὐτόν. πῦρ ἦλθον βαλεῖν ρξ ε
50 ἐπὶ τὴν γῆν· καὶ τί θέλω, εἰ ἤδη ἀνήφθη; βάπτισμα δὲ ἔχω βαπτι-
51 σθῆναι, καὶ πῶς συνέχομαι ἕως οὗ τελεσθῇ; δοκεῖτε ὅτι εἰρήνην παρ-
εγενόμην δοῦναι ἐν τῇ γῇ; οὐχί, λέγω ὑμῖν, ἀλλ' ἢ διαμερισμόν.
52 ἔσονται γὰρ ἀπὸ τοῦ νῦν πέντε ἐν οἴκῳ ἑνὶ διαμεμερισμένοι, τρεῖς
53 ἐπὶ δυσὶ καὶ δύο ἐπὶ τρισί· διαμερισθήσεται πατὴρ ἐφ' υἱῷ καὶ υἱὸς
ἐπὶ πατρί, μήτηρ ἐπὶ τὴν θυγατέρα καὶ θυγάτηρ ἐπὶ τὴν μητέρα,
πενθερὰ ἐπὶ τὴν νύμφην αὐτῆς καὶ νύμφη ἐπὶ τὴν πενθερὰν αὐτῆς.
54 Ἔλεγε δὲ καὶ τοῖς ὄχλοις, Ὅταν ἴδητε νεφέλην ἀνατέλλουσαν ἀπὸ ρξα ε
55 δυσμῶν, εὐθέως λέγετε, Ὄμβρος ἔρχεται, καὶ γίνεται οὕτω· καὶ ὅταν
56 νότον πνέοντα, λέγετε ὅτι Καύσων ἔσται, καὶ γίνεται. ὑποκριταί, τὸ
πρόσωπον τῆς γῆς καὶ τοῦ οὐρανοῦ οἴδατε δοκιμάζειν· τὸν δὲ καιρὸν
57 τοῦτον πῶς οὐ δοκιμάζετε; τί δὲ καὶ ἀφ' ἑαυτῶν οὐ κρίνετε τὸ δίκαιον;
58 ὡς γὰρ ὑπάγεις μετὰ τοῦ ἀντιδίκου σου ἐπ' ἄρχοντα, ἐν τῇ ὁδῷ δὸς ρξβ ε
ἐργασίαν ἀπηλλάχθαι ἀπ' αὐτοῦ, μήποτε κατασύρῃ σε πρὸς τὸν κριτήν,
καὶ ὁ κριτής σε παραδῷ τῷ πράκτορι, καὶ ὁ πράκτωρ βάλῃ σε εἰς
59 φυλακήν. λέγω σοι, οὐ μὴ ἐξέλθῃς ἐκεῖθεν ἕως καὶ τὸ ἔσχατον λεπτὸν
ἀποδῷς.

XIII. Παρῆσαν δέ τινες ἐν αὐτῷ τῷ καιρῷ ἀπαγγέλλοντες αὐτῷ ΜΖ'
περὶ τῶν Γαλιλαίων, ὧν τὸ αἷμα Πιλάτος ἔμιξε μετὰ τῶν θυσιῶν αὐτῶν. ρξγ ι
2 καὶ ἀποκριθεὶς ὁ Ἰησοῦς εἶπεν αὐτοῖς, Δοκεῖτε ὅτι οἱ Γαλιλαῖοι οὗτοι
ἁμαρτωλοὶ παρὰ πάντας τοὺς Γαλιλαίους ἐγένοντο, ὅτι τοιαῦτα πεπόν-
3 θασιν; οὐχί, λέγω ὑμῖν· ἀλλ' ἐὰν μὴ μετανοήσητε, πάντες ὁμοίως
4 ἀπολεῖσθε. ἢ ἐκεῖνοι οἱ δέκα καὶ ὀκτὼ ἐφ' οὓς ἔπεσεν ὁ πύργος ἐν
τῷ Σιλωὰμ καὶ ἀπέκτεινεν αὐτούς, δοκεῖτε ὅτι οὗτοι ὀφειλέται ἐγένοντο
5 παρὰ πάντας τοὺς κατοικοῦντας Ἱερουσαλήμ; οὐχί, λέγω ὑμῖν· ἀλλ'
6 ἐὰν μὴ μετανοήσητε, πάντες ὡσαύτως ἀπολεῖσθε. ἔλεγε δὲ ταύτην ρξδ ι
τὴν παραβολήν, Συκῆν εἶχέ τις πεφυτευμένην ἐν τῷ ἀμπελῶνι

49 ηλθον] ηλθεν cod. 1* primum scripsit γης sed ipse correxit

46 υποκριτων] απιστων ϛ 47 αυτου 1°] εαυτου ϛ 48 απ] παρ ϛ 49 επι] εις ϛ και] αι 118 τι θελω; ει κ.τ.λ. ϛ 52 διαμεμερισμενοι 131 ϛ 53 θυγατρι ϛ μητρι ϛ 54 την νεφελην ϛ 58 βαλλη σε 118 209, σε βαλλη 131 ϛ 59 εως ου 118 209 ϛ 118 131 209 ϛ

2 om αυτοις 131 3 μετανοητε ϛ ομοιως] ωσαυτως ϛ 4 παντας ανθρωπους ϛ εν Ιερουσαλημ ϛ 5 μετανοητε ϛ ομοιως ϛ 6 εν τω αμπελωνι αυτου πεφυτευμενην ϛ

αὐτοῦ· καὶ ἦλθε ζητῶν καρπὸν ἐν αὐτῇ, καὶ οὐχ εὗρεν. εἶπε δὲ 7
πρὸς τὸν ἀμπελουργόν, Ἰδοὺ τρία ἔτη ἔρχομαι ζητῶν καρπὸν ἐν τῇ συκῇ
ταύτῃ καὶ οὐχ εὑρίσκω· ἔκκοψον αὐτήν· ἱνατί καὶ τὴν γῆν καταργεῖ;
ὁ δὲ ἀποκριθεὶς λέγει αὐτῷ, Κύριε, ἄφες αὐτὴν καὶ τοῦτο τὸ ἔτος, ἕως 8
ὅτου σκάψω περὶ αὐτὴν καὶ βάλω κόπρον· εἰ δὲ μήγε, εἰς τὸ μέλλον 9
ἐκκόψεις αὐτήν.

ΜΗ′ Ἦν δὲ διδάσκων ἐν μιᾷ τῶν συναγωγῶν τοῖς σάββασι· καὶ ἰδοὺ 10 11
ρξε β γυνὴ ἦν πνεῦμα ἔχουσα ἀσθενείας ἔτη δέκα ὀκτώ, καὶ ἦν συγκύπτουσα
καὶ μὴ δυναμένη ἀνακύψαι εἰς τὸ παντελές. ἰδὼν δὲ αὐτὴν ὁ Ἰησοῦς 12
προσεφώνησε καὶ εἶπεν αὐτῇ, Γύναι, ἀπολέλυσαι τῆς ἀσθενείας σου.
καὶ ἐπέθηκεν αὐτῇ τὰς χεῖρας· καὶ παραχρῆμα ἀνωρθώθη, καὶ ἐδόξαζε 13
τὸν Θεόν. ἀποκριθεὶς δὲ ὁ ἀρχισυνάγωγος, ἀγανακτῶν ὅτι τῷ σαββάτῳ 14
ἐθεράπευσεν ὁ Ἰησοῦς, ἔλεγε τῷ ὄχλῳ, Ἓξ ἡμέραι εἰσὶν ἐν αἷς δεῖ
ἐργάζεσθαι· ἐν αὐταῖς οὖν ἐρχόμενοι θεραπεύεσθε, καὶ μὴ τῇ ἡμέρᾳ
τοῦ σαββάτου. ἀπεκρίθη δὲ αὐτῷ ὁ Ἰησοῦς καὶ εἶπεν, Ὑποκριτά, 15
ἕκαστος ὑμῶν τῷ σαββάτῳ οὐ λύει τὸν βοῦν αὐτοῦ ἢ τὸν ὄνον ἀπὸ
τῆς φάτνης καὶ ἀπάγων ποτίζει; ταύτην δέ, θυγατέρα Ἀβραὰμ οὖσαν, 16
ἣν ἔδησεν ὁ Σατανᾶς, ἰδού, δέκα καὶ ὀκτὼ ἔτη, οὐκ ἔδει λυθῆναι ἀπὸ
ρξϛ ι τοῦ δεσμοῦ τούτου τῇ ἡμέρᾳ τοῦ σαββάτου; καὶ ταῦτα λέγοντος αὐτοῦ 17
κατῃσχύνοντο πάντες οἱ ἀντικείμενοι αὐτῷ, καὶ πᾶς ὁ ὄχλος ἔχαιρεν ἐπὶ
πᾶσι τοῖς ἐνδόξοις τοῖς γινομένοις ὑπ᾽ αὐτοῦ.

ΜΘ′ Ἔλεγε δὲ αὐτοῖς, Τίνι ὁμοία ἐστὶν ἡ βασιλεία τοῦ Θεοῦ, καὶ τίνι 18
ρξζ β ὁμοιώσω αὐτήν; Ὁμοία ἐστὶ κόκκῳ σινάπεως, ὃν λαβὼν ἄνθρωπος 19
ἔβαλεν εἰς κῆπον ἑαυτοῦ, καὶ ηὔξησε καὶ ἐγένετο δένδρον μέγα, καὶ
ρξη ε τὰ πετεινὰ τοῦ οὐρανοῦ κατεσκήνωσεν ἐν τοῖς κλάδοις αὐτοῦ. καὶ 20
πάλιν εἶπε, Τίνι ὁμοιώσω τὴν βασιλείαν τοῦ Θεοῦ; ὁμοία ἐστὶ ζύμῃ, 21
ἣν λαβοῦσα γυνὴ ἐνέκρυψεν εἰς ἀλεύρου σάτα τρία, ἕως οὗ ἐζυμώθη
ὅλον.

ρξθ β Καὶ διεπορεύετο κατὰ πόλιν καὶ κώμην διδάσκων, καὶ πορείαν 22
Ν′ ποιούμενος εἰς Ἱερουσαλήμ. εἶπε δέ τις αὐτῷ, Κύριε, εἰ ὀλίγοι οἱ σωζό- 23
ρο ε μενοι; ὁ δὲ εἶπε πρὸς αὐτούς, Ἀγωνίζεσθε εἰσελθεῖν διὰ τῆς στενῆς 24
θύρας· ὅτι πολλοί, λέγω ὑμῖν, ζητήσουσιν εἰσελθεῖν καὶ οὐκ ἰσχύ-
ροα ε σουσιν. ἀφ᾽ οὗ ἂν ἐγερθῇ ὁ οἰκοδεσπότης καὶ ἀποκλείσῃ τὴν θύραν, 25

24 εισελθειν 1°] δισελθειν cod.

118 131 209 ϛ 6 καρπον ζητων ϛ 8 κοπρια 131, κοπριαν 118 209 ϛ 9 ει] pr καν μεν ποιηση καρπον 118 131 ϛ 10 εν τοις 118 131 ϛ 11 και οκτω 118 131 ϛ 14 ταυταις ϛ 15 δε] ουν ϛ Ιησους] Κυριος ϛ απαγαγων 118 131 209 ϛ 16 Ἀβρααμ 131 ϛ 18 om αυτοις ϛ 19 εβαλλεν 131 εις δενδρον 118 209 ϛ 21 εκρυψεν 118 131 209 22 πολεις και κωμας ϛ 24 θυρας] πυλης 118 ϛ

καὶ ἄρξησθε ἔξω ἑστάναι καὶ κρούειν τὴν θύραν λέγοντες, Κύριε, Κύριε,
ἄνοιξον ἡμῖν, καὶ ἀποκριθεὶς ἐρεῖ ὑμῖν, Οὐκ οἶδα ὑμᾶς, πόθεν ἐστέ·
26 τότε ἄρξεσθε λέγειν, Ἐφάγομεν ἐνώπιόν σου καὶ ἐπίομεν, καὶ ἐν ταῖς
27 πλατείαις ἡμῶν ἐδίδαξας· καὶ ἐρεῖ, Λέγω ὑμῖν, οὐκ οἶδα ὑμᾶς, πόθεν
28 ἐστέ· ἀπόστητε ἀπ' ἐμοῦ πάντες οἱ ἐργάται τῆς ἀδικίας. ἐκεῖ ἔσται ὁ ροβ ε
κλαυθμὸς καὶ ὁ βρυγμὸς τῶν ὀδόντων, ὅταν ὄψησθε Ἀβραὰμ καὶ
Ἰσαὰκ καὶ Ἰακὼβ καὶ πάντας τοὺς προφήτας ἐν τῇ βασιλείᾳ τοῦ Θεοῦ,
29 ὑμᾶς δὲ ἐκβαλλομένους ἔξω· καὶ ἥξουσι πολλοὶ ἀπὸ ἀνατολῶν καὶ
δυσμῶν καὶ βορρᾶ καὶ νότου, καὶ ἀνακλιθήσονται ἐν τῇ βασιλείᾳ τοῦ
30 Θεοῦ. καὶ ἰδοὺ εἰσὶν ἔσχατοι οἳ ἔσονται πρῶτοι, καί εἰσι πρῶτοι οἳ ρογ β
ἔσονται ἔσχατοι.

31 Ἐν αὐτῇ τῇ ὥρᾳ προσῆλθόν τινες Φαρισαῖοι λέγοντες αὐτῷ, Ἔξελθε ΝΑ'
32 καὶ πορεύου ἐντεῦθεν, ὅτι Ἡρώδης θέλει σε ἀποκτεῖναι. καὶ εἶπεν ροδ ι
αὐτοῖς, Πορευθέντες εἴπατε τῇ ἀλώπεκι ταύτῃ, Ἰδοὺ ἐκβάλλω δαιμόνια
καὶ ἰάσεις ἐπιτελῶ σήμερον καὶ αὔριον, καὶ τῇ τρίτῃ τελειοῦμαι.
33 πλὴν δεῖ με σήμερον καὶ αὔριον καὶ τῇ ἐχομένῃ πορεύεσθαι, ὅτι
34 οὐκ ἐνδέχεται προφήτην ἀπολέσθαι ἔξω Ἱερουσαλήμ. Ἱερουσαλήμ, ροε ε
Ἱερουσαλήμ, ἡ ἀποκτένουσα τοὺς προφήτας καὶ λιθοβολοῦσα τοὺς
ἀπεσταλμένους πρὸς αὐτήν, ποσάκις ἠθέλησα ἐπισυνάξαι τὰ τέκνα
σου, ὃν τρόπον ὄρνις τὰ ἑαυτῆς νοσσία ὑπὸ τὰς πτέρυγας, καὶ οὐκ
35 ἠθελήσατε; ἰδού, ἀφίεται ὑμῖν ὁ οἶκος ὑμῶν· λέγω δέ, οὐ μή με
ἴδητε ἕως ἂν ἥξῃ ὅτε εἴπητε, Εὐλογημένος ὁ ἐρχόμενος ἐν ὀνόματι Κυρίου.

XIV. Καὶ ἐγένετο ἐν τῷ ἐλθεῖν αὐτὸν εἰς οἶκόν τινος τῶν ἀρχόντων ρος ι
τῶν Φαρισαίων σαββάτῳ φαγεῖν ἄρτον, καὶ αὐτοὶ ἦσαν παρατηρούμενοι
2 3 αὐτόν. καὶ ἰδοὺ ἄνθρωπος ἦν ὑδρωπικὸς ἔμπροσθεν αὐτοῦ· καὶ ἀπο- ΝΒ'
κριθεὶς εἶπε πρὸς τοὺς νομικοὺς καὶ Φαρισαίους λέγων, Εἰ ἔξεστι ἐν ροζ β
4 τοῖς σάββασι θεραπεῦσαι ἢ οὔ; οἱ δὲ ἡσύχασαν. καὶ ἐπιλα-
5 βόμενος αὐτοῦ ἰάσατο αὐτὸν καὶ ἀπέλυσε, καὶ πρὸς αὐτοὺς εἶπε,
Τίνος ὑμῶν ὄνος ἢ βοῦς εἰς φρέαρ πεσεῖται, καὶ οὐκ εὐθέως ἀνασπάσει
6 αὐτὸν ἐν τῇ ἡμέρᾳ τοῦ σαββάτου; καὶ οὐκ ἴσχυσαν ἀποκριθῆναι
πρὸς αὐτόν.

33 Ιερουσ.] Ιλη̄λ cod.

28 Ἀβρααμ 131 ϛ **29** om πολλοι ϛ απο βορρα ϛ **31** ωρα] ημερα ϛ 118 131 209 ϛ **34** αποκτεινουσα ϛ επισυναξαγαγειν 118 τα νοσσια εαυτης 131, την εαυτης νοσσιαν ϛ **35** υμιν] usque ad εγημα xiv 20 deest 118* sed 118[2] paginam amissam supplevit υμων]+ερημος 118[2] 131 ϛ αμην δε λεγω υμιν οτι ϛ

2 ανθρωπος τις 118[2] ϛ **3** αποκριθεις]+ο Ιησους 118[2] ϛ τω σαββατω θεραπευειν 118[2] ϛ om η ου 118[2] ϛ **4** επιλαβομενου 131 om αυτου ϛ **5** προς] pr αποκριθεις 118[2] ϛ εμπεσειται ϛ om τη 131 **6** ανταποκριθηναι αυτω ϛ αυτον] ταυτα ϛ

NΓ' Ἔλεγε δὲ πρὸς τοὺς κεκλημένους παραβολήν, ἐπέχων πῶς τὰς πρωτο- 7
ροη ι κλισίας ἐξελέγοντο, λέγων, Ὅταν κληθῇς ὑπό τινος εἰς γάμους, μὴ 8
κατακλιθῇς εἰς τὴν πρωτοκλισίαν, μήποτε ἐντιμότερός σου ᾖ κεκλημένος
ὑπ' αὐτοῦ, καὶ ἐλθὼν ὁ σὲ καὶ αὐτὸν καλέσας ἐρεῖ σοι, Δὸς τούτῳ 9
τόπον, καὶ τότε ἄρξῃ μετ' αἰσχύνης τὸν ἔσχατον τόπον κατέχειν. ἀλλ' 10
ὅταν κληθῇς, πορευθεὶς ἀνάπεσε εἰς τὸν ἔσχατον τόπον, ἵνα ὅταν ἔλθῃ
ὁ κεκληκώς σε, εἴπῃ σοι, Φίλε, προσανάβηθι ἀνώτερον· τότε ἔσται σοι
ροθ ε δόξα ἐνώπιον πάντων τῶν συνανακειμένων σοι. ὅτι πᾶς ὁ ὑψῶν ἑαυτὸν 11
ταπεινωθήσεται, καὶ ὁ ταπεινῶν ἑαυτὸν ὑψωθήσεται.

ρπ ι Ἔλεγε δὲ καὶ τῷ κεκληκότι αὐτόν, Ὅταν ποιῇς ἄριστον ἢ δεῖπνον, 12
μὴ φώνει τοὺς φίλους σου, μηδὲ τοὺς συγγενεῖς σου, μηδὲ γείτονας
πλουσίους· μήποτε καὶ αὐτοί ἀντικαλέσωσί σε καὶ γένηταί σοι ἀντ-
απόδομα. ἀλλ' ὅταν ποιῇς δοχήν, κάλει πτωχούς, ἀναπήρους, χωλούς, 13
τυφλούς· καὶ μακάριος ἔσῃ· ὅτι οὐκ ἔχουσιν ἀνταποδοῦναί σοι· ἀνταποδο- 14
θήσεται δέ σοι ἐν τῇ ἀναστάσει τῶν δικαίων.

Ἀκούσας δέ τις τῶν συνανακειμένων ταῦτα εἶπεν αὐτῷ, Μακάριος 15
NΔ' ὅστις φάγεται ἄρτον ἐν τῇ βασιλείᾳ τοῦ Θεοῦ. ὁ δὲ εἶπεν αὐτῷ, 16
ρπα ε ※Ἄνθρωπός τις ἐποίει δεῖπνον μέγα, καὶ ἐκάλεσε πολλούς· καὶ ἀπέστειλε 17
τὸν δοῦλον αὐτοῦ τῇ ὥρᾳ τοῦ δείπνου εἰπεῖν τοῖς κεκλημένοις, Ἔρχεσθε,
ὅτι ἤδη ἕτοιμά ἐστι πάντα. καὶ ἤρξαντο ἀπὸ μιᾶς πάντες παραι- 18
τεῖσθαι. ὁ πρῶτος εἶπεν, Ἀγρὸν ἠγόρασα, καὶ ἔχω ἀνάγκην ἐξελθεῖν
καὶ ἰδεῖν αὐτόν· ἐρωτῶ σε, ἔχε με παρῃτημένον. καὶ ἕτερος εἶπε, Ζεύγη 19
βοῶν ἠγόρασα πέντε, καὶ πορεύομαι δοκιμάσαι αὐτά· ἐρωτῶ σε, ἔχε με
παρῃτημένον. καὶ ἕτερος εἶπε, Γυναῖκα ἔγημα, καὶ διὰ τοῦτο οὐ δύνα- 20
μαι ἐλθεῖν. καὶ παραγενόμενος ὁ δοῦλος ἀπήγγειλε τῷ κυρίῳ 21
αὐτοῦ ταῦτα. τότε ὀργισθεὶς ὁ οἰκοδεσπότης εἶπε τῷ δούλῳ αὐτοῦ,
Ἔξελθε ταχέως εἰς τὰς πλατείας καὶ ῥύμας τῆς πόλεως, καὶ τοὺς
πτωχοὺς καὶ ἀναπήρους καὶ χωλοὺς καὶ τυφλοὺς εἰσάγαγε ὧδε. καὶ εἶπεν 22
ὁ δοῦλος, Κύριε, γέγονεν ὃ προσέταξας, καὶ ἔτι τόπος ἐστί. καὶ εἶπεν 23
ὁ κύριος πρὸς τὸν δοῦλον, Ἔξελθε εἰς τὰς ὁδοὺς καὶ φραγμούς, καὶ
ἀνάγκασον εἰσελθεῖν, ἵνα γεμισθῇ ὁ οἶκός μου. λέγω γὰρ ὑμῖν, ὅτι 24
οὐδεὶς τῶν ἀνδρῶν ἐκείνων τῶν κεκλημένων γεύσηταί μου τοῦ δείπνου.

24 δειπνου] m. recent. add. in mg. πολλοι κλητοι ολιγοι δε εκλεκτοι

118 131 209 ϛ

7 λεγων προς αυτους ϛ   κλιθης 118^{2} 10 αναπεσοι[illegible]   om παντων ϛ·
12 σου 1°] + μηδε τους αδελφους σου 118^{2} 131 ϛ   σε αντικαλεσωσι ϛ
14 δε] om 131, γαρ 118^{2} ϛ   15 ος ϛ   αρτον] αριστον 131   16 εποιησε
118^{2} 131 ϛ   18 παραιτεισθαι παντες 118^{2} 131 ϛ   ειπεν αυτω ϛ   20 και]
hic incipit 118*   21 om και παραγενομενος...ταυτα 131   δουλος εκεινος ϛ
22 ως επεταξας ϛ   24 γευσεται ϛ   δειπνου]+πολλοι γαρ εισι κλητοι ολιγοι
δε εκλεκτοι 118^{rubr} (et iterum in marg.) 131^{2} in marg.

25 Συνεπορεύοντο δὲ αὐτῷ ὄχλοι πολλοί· καὶ στραφεὶς εἶπε πρὸς αὐτούς, ρπβ
26 Εἴτις ἔρχεται πρός με, καὶ οὐ μισεῖ τὸν πατέρα αὐτοῦ καὶ τὴν μητέρα ε
καὶ τὴν γυναῖκα καὶ τὰ τέκνα καὶ τοὺς ἀδελφοὺς καὶ τὰς ἀδελφάς, ἔτι
27 δὲ καὶ τὴν ἑαυτοῦ ψυχήν, οὐ δύναταί μου μαθητὴς εἶναι. καὶ ὅστις οὐ
βαστάζει τὸν σταυρὸν αὐτοῦ καὶ ἔρχεται ὀπίσω μου, οὐ δύναταί μου
28 εἶναι μαθητής. τίς γὰρ ἐξ ὑμῶν, θέλων πύργον οἰκοδομῆσαι, οὐχὶ ΝΕ′
πρῶτον καθίσας ψηφίζει τὴν δαπάνην, εἰ ἔχει τὰ πρὸς ἀπαρτισμόν; ρπγ ι
29 ἵνα μήποτε, θέντος αὐτοῦ θεμέλιον καὶ μὴ ἰσχύσαντος ἐκτελέσαι,
30 πάντες οἱ θεωροῦντες ἄρξωνται αὐτῷ ἐμπαίζειν, λέγοντες ὅτι Οὗτος
31 ὁ ἄνθρωπος ἤρξατο οἰκοδομεῖν καὶ οὐκ ἴσχυσεν ἐκτελέσαι. ἢ τίς βασι-
λεὺς πορευόμενος συμβαλεῖν ἑτέρῳ βασιλεῖ εἰς πόλεμον οὐχὶ πρῶτον
καθίσας βουλεύεται εἰ δυνατός ἐστιν ἐν δέκα χιλιάσιν ὑπαντῆσαι
32 τῷ μετὰ εἴκοσι χιλιάδων ἐρχομένῳ ἐπ᾽ αὐτόν; εἰ δὲ μήγε, ἔτι αὐτοῦ
33 πόρρω ὄντος, πρεσβείαν ἀποστείλας ἐρωτᾷ τὰ πρὸς εἰρήνην. οὕτως ρπδ
οὖν πᾶς ἐξ ὑμῶν ὃς οὐκ ἀποτάσσεται πᾶσι τοῖς ἑαυτοῦ ὑπάρχουσιν, οὐ ε
34 δύναταί μου εἶναι μαθητής. καλὸν τὸ ἅλας· ἐὰν δὲ τὸ ἅλας μωρανθῇ, ρπε
35 ἐν τίνι ἁλισθήσεται; οὔτε εἰς γῆν, οὔτε εἰς κοπρίαν εὔθετόν ἐστιν· β
ἔξω βάλλουσιν αὐτό. ὁ ἔχων ὦτα ἀκούειν ἀκουέτω.

XV. Ἦσαν δὲ αὐτῷ ἐγγίζοντες πάντες οἱ τελῶναι καὶ οἱ ρπϛ
2 ἁμαρτωλοί, ἀκούειν αὐτοῦ. καὶ διεγόγγυζον οἱ Φαρισαῖοι καὶ οἱ γραμ- β
ματεῖς, λέγοντες ὅτι Οὗτος ἁμαρτωλοὺς προσδέχεται καὶ συνεσθίει
3/4 αὐτοῖς. εἶπε δὲ πρὸς αὐτοὺς τὴν παραβολὴν ταύτην λέγων, Τίς ἄν- ΝϚ′
θρωπος ἐξ ὑμῶν ἔχων ἑκατὸν πρόβατα καὶ ἀπολέσας ἐξ αὐτῶν ἓν ρπζ ε
οὐ καταλείπει τὰ ἐνενηκονταεννέα ἐν τῇ ἐρήμῳ, καὶ πορεύεται ἐπὶ
5 τὸ ἀπολωλὸς ἕως οὗ εὕρῃ αὐτό; καὶ εὑρὼν ἐπὶ τοὺς ὤμους αὐτοῦ
6 χαίρων, καὶ ἐλθὼν εἰς τὸν οἶκον συγκαλεῖται τοὺς φίλους καὶ τὰς
γείτονας, λέγων αὐτοῖς, Συγχάρητέ μοι, ὅτι εὗρον τὸ πρόβατόν μου
7 τὸ ἀπολωλός. λέγω ὑμῖν ὅτι οὕτω χαρὰ ἔσται ἐν τῷ οὐρανῷ ἐπὶ ἑνὶ
ἁμαρτωλῷ μετανοοῦντι, ἢ ἐπὶ ἐνενηκονταεννέα δικαίοις οἵτινες οὐ
8 χρείαν ἔχωσι μετανοίας. ἢ τίς γυνὴ δραχμὰς ἔχουσα, ἐὰν ἀπολέσῃ ρπη
δραχμὴν μίαν, οὐχὶ ἅπτει λύχνον καὶ σαροῖ τὴν οἰκίαν καὶ ζητεῖ ι

34 μορανθη cod. 35 ουτε 1°] ειστε cod.

26 αυτου] εαυτου ϛ 28 ο θελων 131 29 ισχυοντος ϛ αρξονται 118 131 209 ϛ 131 εμπαιζ[illegible] αυτω ϛ 31 καθισας πρωτον ϛ απαντησαι 131 ϛ 34 αρτυθησεται ϛ

1 εγγιζοντες αυτω ϛ om οι 2° 131 4 εν εξ αυτων ϛ εννενηκονταεννεα ϛ om ου ϛ 5 ευρων]+επιτιθησι 131 ϛ αυτου] εαυτου ϛ, +επιτιθησι 118 209 6 συγκαλει ϛ τας] τους 118 131 209 ϛ 7 εννενηκονταεννεα ϛ δικαιους 131 εχουσι 118 131 209 ϛ 8 εχουσα δεκα 118 131 209 ϛ

1 4 *

ἐπιμελῶς ἕως οὗ εὕρῃ; καὶ εὑροῦσα συγκαλεῖται τὰς φίλας καὶ τὰς 9
γείτονας λέγουσα, Συγχάρητέ μοι, ὅτι εὗρον τὴν δραχμὴν ἣν ἀπώλεσα.
ρπθ οὕτως, λέγω ὑμῖν, χαρὰ γίνεται ἐνώπιον τῶν ἀγγέλων τοῦ Θεοῦ ἐπὶ 10
ε ἑνὶ ἁμαρτωλῷ μετανοοῦντι.
NZ' Εἶπε δέ, Ἄνθρωπός τις εἶχε δύο υἱούς· καὶ εἶπεν ὁ νεώτερος αὐτῶν 11 12
ρλ ι τῷ πατρί, Πάτερ, δός μοι τὸ ἐπιβάλλον μέρος τῆς οὐσίας. καὶ διεῖλεν
αὐτοῖς τὸν βίον. καὶ μετ' οὐ πολλὰς ἡμέρας συναγαγὼν ἅπαντα ὁ 13
νεώτερος υἱὸς ἀπεδήμησεν εἰς χώραν μακράν, καὶ ἐκεῖ διεσκόρπισε τὴν
οὐσίαν αὐτοῦ ζῶν ἀσώτως. δαπανήσαντος δὲ αὐτοῦ πάντα ἐγένετο λιμὸς 14
ἰσχυρὰ κατὰ τὴν χώραν ἐκείνην, καὶ αὐτὸς ἤρξατο ὑστερεῖσθαι. καὶ 15
πορευθεὶς ἐκολλήθη ἑνὶ τῶν πολιτῶν τῆς χώρας ἐκείνης· καὶ ἔπεμψεν
αὐτὸν εἰς τοὺς ἀγροὺς αὐτοῦ βόσκειν χοίρους. καὶ ἐπεθύμει χορτα- 16
σθῆναι ἐκ τῶν κερατίων ὧν ἤσθιον οἱ χοῖροι· καὶ οὐδεὶς ἐδίδου αὐτῷ.
εἰς ἑαυτὸν δὲ ἐλθὼν εἶπε, Πόσοι μίσθιοι τοῦ πατρός μου περισσεύ- 17
ονται ἄρτων, ἐγὼ δὲ ὧδε λιμῷ ἀπόλλυμαι; ἀναστὰς πορεύσομαι πρὸς 18
τὸν πατέρα μου, καὶ ἐρῶ αὐτῷ, Πάτερ, ἥμαρτον εἰς τὸν οὐρανὸν καὶ
ἐνώπιόν σου, ποίησόν με ὡς ἕνα τῶν μισθίων σου. καὶ ἀναστὰς 19 20
ἦλθε πρὸς τὸν πατέρα ἑαυτοῦ. ἔτι δὲ αὐτοῦ μακρὰν ἀπέχοντος, εἶδεν
αὐτὸν ὁ πατὴρ αὐτοῦ καὶ ἐσπλαγχνίσθη, καὶ δραμὼν ἔπεσεν ἐπὶ τὸν
τράχηλον αὐτοῦ καὶ κατεφίλησεν αὐτόν. εἶπε δὲ ὁ υἱὸς αὐτῷ, Πάτερ, 21
ἥμαρτον εἰς τὸν οὐρανὸν καὶ ἐνώπιόν σου, οὐκέτι εἰμὶ ἄξιος κληθῆναι
υἱός σου. εἶπε δὲ ὁ πατὴρ πρὸς τοὺς παῖδας αὐτοῦ, Ἐξενέγκατε 22
τὴν στολὴν τὴν πρώτην καὶ ἐνδύσατε αὐτόν, καὶ δότε δακτύλιον εἰς
τὴν χεῖρα αὐτοῦ καὶ ὑποδήματα εἰς τοὺς πόδας, καὶ ἐνέγκαντες τὸν 23
μόσχον τὸν σιτευτὸν θύσατε, καὶ φαγόντες εὐφρανθῶμεν· ὅτι οὗτος 24
ὁ υἱός μου νεκρὸς ἦν καὶ ἀνέζησε, ἀπολωλὼς ἦν καὶ εὑρέθη. καὶ
ἤρξατο εὐφραίνεσθαι. ἦν δὲ ὁ υἱὸς αὐτοῦ ὁ πρεσβύτερος ἐν ἀγρῷ· 25
καὶ ὡς ἐρχόμενος ἤγγισε τῇ οἰκίᾳ, ἤκουσε συμφωνίας χορῶν· καὶ 26
προσκαλεσάμενος ἕνα τῶν παίδων ἐπυνθάνετο τί ἂν εἴη ταῦτα. ὁ δὲ 27
εἶπεν αὐτῷ ὅτι Ὁ ἀδελφός σου ἥκει, καὶ ἔθυσεν ὁ πατήρ σου τὸν

118 131 209 ς **8** ου] *οτου ς* **10** *ουτω ς* **11** *ειπε δε ο Κυριος* 118 **12** om *της ουσιας* 131 **14** *ισχυρος* 118 209 *ς* **15** *αυτου* om 118* 131 sed 118* postquam scripserat *βοσκ* erasit et *υ βοσκειν* perrexit spatio sic relicto quattuor litterarum in quo *αυτο* scribere casu neglexit **16** *χορτασθηναι*] *γεμισαι την κοιλιαν αυτου απο* 118 209 *ς* *κερατων* 131 **17** *ποσοι*] *πους οι* 131 *περισσευουσι* 131 *ς* om *ωδε ς* **19** *ποιησον*] pr *και ουκετι ειμι αξιος κληθηναι υιος σου* 131 *ς* (sed 131 *ειναι* non *κληθηναι*) **20** *εαυτου*] *αυτου* 118 131 209 *επεπεσεν* 131 *ς* **21** *αυτω ο υιος ς* *και ουκετι ς* **22** *πατηρ αυτου* 131 *παιδας*] *δουλους ς* om *αυτου* 131 **24** *και απολωλως ς* om *ην* 131 *ηρξαντο* 118 131 209 *ς* **25** *και χορων ς* **26** *παιδων αυτου ς* om *αν ς*

28 μόσχον τὸν σιτευτόν, ὅτι ὑγιαίνοντα αὐτὸν ἀπέλαβεν. ὠργίσθη δέ, καὶ
οὐκ ἤθελεν εἰσελθεῖν. ὁ δὲ πατὴρ αὐτοῦ ἐξελθὼν παρεκάλει αὐτόν.
29 ὁ δὲ ἀποκριθεὶς εἶπε τῷ πατρί, Ἰδοὺ τοσαῦτα ἔτη δουλεύω σοι, καὶ
οὐδέποτε ἐντολήν σου παρῆλθον, καὶ ἐμοὶ οὐδέποτε ἔδωκας ἔριφον, ἵνα
30 μετὰ τῶν φίλων μου εὐφρανθῶ· ὅτε δὲ ὁ υἱός σου οὗτος ὁ κατα-
φαγὼν τὸν βίον σου μετὰ πορνῶν ἦλθεν, ἔθυσας αὐτῷ τὸν μόσχον
31 τὸν σιτευτόν. ὁ δὲ εἶπεν αὐτῷ, Τέκνον, σὺ πάντοτε μετ' ἐμοῦ εἶ, καὶ
32 πάντα τὰ ἐμὰ σά ἐστιν· εὐφρανθῆναι δὲ καὶ χαρῆναι ἔδει, ὅτι ὁ ἀδελφός
σου οὗτος νεκρὸς ἦν καὶ ἀνέζησε, ἀπολωλὼς καὶ εὑρέθη.

XVI. Ἔλεγε δὲ καὶ πρὸς τοὺς μαθητὰς αὐτοῦ, Ἄνθρωπός τις ἦν ΝΗ'
πλούσιος ὃς εἶχεν οἰκονόμον, καὶ οὗτος διεβλήθη αὐτῷ ὡς διασκορ-
2 πίζων τὰ ὑπάρχοντα αὐτοῦ. καὶ φωνήσας αὐτὸν εἶπεν αὐτῷ, Τί τοῦτο
ἀκούω περὶ σοῦ; ἀπόδος τὸν λόγον τῆς οἰκονομίας σου· οὐ γὰρ δύνῃ
3 ἔτι οἰκονομεῖν. εἶπε δὲ ἐν ἑαυτῷ ὁ οἰκονόμος, Τί ποιήσω, ὅτι ὁ κύριός
μου ἀφαιρεῖται τὴν οἰκονομίαν ἀπ' ἐμοῦ; σκάπτειν οὐκ ἰσχύω, ἐπαιτεῖν
4 αἰσχύνομαι. ἔγνων τί ποιήσω, ἵνα ὅταν μετασταθῶ ἐκ τῆς οἰκονομίας,
5 δέξωνταί με εἰς τοὺς οἴκους αὐτῶν. καὶ προσκαλεσάμενος ἕνα ἕκαστον
τῶν χρεωφειλετῶν τοῦ κυρίου αὐτοῦ, ἔλεγε τῷ πρώτῳ, Πόσον ὀφείλεις
6 τῷ κυρίῳ μου; ὁ δὲ εἶπεν, Ἑκατὸν βάτους ἐλαίου· καὶ εἶπε, Δέξαι
7 σου τὸ γράμμα καὶ καθίσας ταχέως γράψον πεντήκοντα. ἔπειτα ἑτέρῳ
εἶπε, Σὺ δὲ πόσον ὀφείλεις; ὁ δὲ εἶπεν, Ἑκατὸν κόρους σίτου· καὶ
λέγει αὐτῷ, Δέξαι σου τὰ γράμματα καὶ καθίσας γράψον ὀγδοή-
8 κοντα. καὶ ἐπήνεσεν ὁ κύριος τὸν οἰκονόμον τῆς ἀδικίας, ὅτι φρονίμως
ἐποίησεν· ὅτι οἱ υἱοὶ τοῦ αἰῶνος τούτου φρονιμώτεροι ὑπὲρ τοὺς υἱοὺς
9 τοῦ φωτὸς εἰς τὴν γενεὰν τὴν ἑαυτῶν εἰσι. καὶ ἐγὼ ὑμῖν λέγω, Ποιή-
σατε ἑαυτοῖς φίλους ἐκ τοῦ μαμωνᾶ τῆς ἀδικίας, ἵνα ὅταν ἐκλίπῃ,
10 δέξωνται ὑμᾶς εἰς τὰς αἰωνίους σκηνάς. ὁ πιστὸς ἐν ἐλαχίστῳ καὶ
ἐν πολλῷ πιστός ἐστι, καὶ ὁ ἐν ὀλίγῳ ἄδικος καὶ ἐν πολλῷ ἄδικός
11 ἐστιν. εἰ οὖν ἐν τῷ ἀδίκῳ μαμωνᾷ πιστοὶ οὐκ ἐγένεσθε, τὸ ἀληθινὸν
12 τίς ὑμῖν πιστεύσει; καὶ εἰ ἐν τῷ ἀλλοτρίῳ πιστοὶ οὐκ ἐγένεσθε, τὸ
13 ὑμέτερον τίς ὑμῖν δώσει; οὐδεὶς οἰκέτης δύναται δυσὶ κυρίοις δουλεύειν· ρλα ε
ἢ γὰρ τὸν ἕνα μισήσει καὶ τὸν ἕτερον ἀγαπήσει, ἢ ἑνὸς ἀνθέξεται καὶ
τοῦ ἑτέρου καταφρονήσει. οὐ δύνασθε Θεῷ δουλεύειν καὶ μαμωνᾷ.

4 οτταν cod.

28 δε 2°] ουν ς **29** ειπεν αυτω πατερ 118 209 **30** σου τον βιον 118 131 209 ς
131 ς **32** και απολωλως ην ς

2 δυνηση 131 ς **4** om εκ ς **5** εαυτου ς **6** και ειπε] ο δε ειπε 118 131 209, +αυτω ς **7** το γραμμα 118 131 209 om καθισας ς **9** καγω ς εκλειπητε 131, εκλιπητε ς **10** ολιγω] ελαχιστω ς **11** om ουν 118 209

ρξβ ʼΗκουον δὲ ταῦτα πάντα καὶ οἱ Φαρισαῖοι, φιλάργυροι ὑπάρχοντες, 14
ι καὶ ἐξεμυκτήριζον αὐτόν. καὶ εἶπεν αὐτοῖς, Ὑμεῖς ἐστε οἱ δικαιοῦντες 15
ἑαυτοὺς ἐνώπιον τῶν ἀνθρώπων, ὁ δὲ Θεὸς γινώσκει τὰς καρδίας ὑμῶν·
ρξγ ὅτι τὸ ἐν ἀνθρώποις ὑψηλὸν βδέλυγμα ἐνώπιον τοῦ Θεοῦ. ὁ νόμος 16
ε ρξδ καὶ οἱ προφῆται μέχρις Ἰωάννου· ἀπὸ τότε ἡ βασιλεία τοῦ Θεοῦ
ε εὐαγγελίζεται, καὶ πᾶς τις αὐτὴν βιάζεται. εὐκοπώτερον δέ ἐστι τὸν 17
ρξε β οὐρανὸν καὶ τὴν γῆν παρελθεῖν ἢ τοῦ νόμου μίαν κεραίαν πεσεῖν. πᾶς 18
ὁ ἀπολύων τὴν γυναῖκα αὐτοῦ καὶ γαμῶν ἑτέραν μοιχεύει· καὶ πᾶς ὁ
ΝΘʹ ἀπολελυμένην ἀπὸ ἀνδρὸς γαμῶν μοιχεύει. ἄνθρωπος δέ τις ἦν πλού- 19
ρξϛ ι σιος καὶ ἐνεδιδύσκετο πορφύραν καὶ βύσσον, εὐφραινόμενος καθʼ ἡμέραν
λαμπρῶς. πτωχὸς δέ τις ἦν ὀνόματι Λάζαρος, ὃς ἐβέβλητο πρὸς τὸν 20
πυλῶνα αὐτοῦ ἡλκωμένος καὶ ἐπιθυμῶν χορτασθῆναι ἀπὸ τῶν πιπτόν- 21
των ψιχίων ἀπὸ τῆς τραπέζης τοῦ πλουσίου· ἀλλὰ καὶ οἱ κύνες
ἐρχόμενοι ἔλειχον τὰ ἕλκη αὐτοῦ. ἐγένετο δὲ ἀποθανεῖν τὸν πτωχόν, 22
καὶ ἀπενεχθῆναι αὐτὸν ὑπὸ τῶν ἀγγέλων εἰς τὸν κόλπον Ἀβραάμ·
ἀπέθανε δὲ καὶ ὁ πλούσιος, καὶ ἐτάφη. καὶ ἐν τῷ ᾅδῃ ἐπάρας τοὺς 23
ὀφθαλμοὺς αὐτοῦ, ὑπάρχων ἐν βασάνοις, ὁρᾷ τὸν Ἀβραὰμ ἀπὸ μακρό-
θεν καὶ Λάζαρον ἐν τοῖς κόλποις αὐτοῦ· καὶ αὐτὸς φωνήσας εἶπε, Πάτερ 24
Ἀβραάμ, ἐλέησόν με καὶ πέμψον Λάζαρον, ἵνα βάψῃ τὸ ἄκρον τοῦ
δακτύλου αὐτοῦ ὕδατος καὶ καταψύξῃ τὴν γλῶσσάν μου, ὅτι ὀδυνῶμαι ἐν
τῇ φλογὶ ταύτῃ. εἶπε δὲ Ἀβραάμ, Τέκνον, μνήσθητι ὅτι ἀπέλαβες 25
σὺ τὰ ἀγαθά σου ἐν τῇ ζωῇ σου, καὶ Λάζαρος ὁμοίως τὰ κακά· νῦν
δὲ ὅδε παρακαλεῖται, σὺ δὲ ὀδυνᾶσαι. καὶ ἐπὶ πᾶσι τούτοις, μεταξὺ 26
ἡμῶν καὶ ὑμῶν χάσμα μέγα ἐστήρικται, ἵνα οἱ θέλοντες διαβῆναι ἐντεῦ-
θεν πρὸς ὑμᾶς μὴ δύνωνται, μηδὲ οἱ ἐκεῖθεν πρὸς ἡμᾶς διαπερῶσιν.
εἶπε δέ, Ἐρωτῶ οὖν σε, πάτερ, ἵνα πέμψῃς αὐτὸν εἰς τὸν οἶκον 27
τοῦ πατρός μου· ἔχω γὰρ πέντε ἀδελφούς· ὅπως διαμαρτύρηται αὐτοῖς, 28
ἵνα μὴ καὶ αὐτοὶ ἔλθωσιν εἰς τόπον τοῦτον τῆς βασάνου. λέγει δὲ 29
αὐτῷ Ἀβραάμ, Ἔχουσι Μωσέα καὶ τοὺς προφήτας· ἀκουσάτωσαν
αὐτῶν. ὁ δὲ εἶπεν, Οὐχί, πάτερ Ἀβραάμ· ἀλλʼ ἐάν τις ἐκ νεκρῶν 30
πορευθῇ πρὸς αὐτούς, μετανοήσουσιν. εἶπε δὲ αὐτῷ, Εἰ Μωσέως 31
καὶ τῶν προφητῶν οὐκ ἀκούουσιν, οὐδὲ ἐάν τις ἐκ νεκρῶν ἀναστῇ
πεισθήσονται.
ρξζ β XVII. Εἶπε δὲ πρὸς τοὺς μαθητάς, Ἀνένδεκτόν ἐστι μὴ ἐλθεῖν

15 γινοσκει cod. **25** ὁμοίος (hoc accentu) cod.

118 131 209 ϛ **15** Θεου εστιν 118 ϛ **16** μεχρις] εως ϛ τις] εις ϛ **21** των ψιχιων των πιπτοντων 131 ϛ απελειχον ϛ **22** Ἀβρααμ 131 ϛ et sic infra quinquies **26** ινα] οπως ϛ **28** τον τοπον 118 131 209 ϛ **29** om δε ϛ **30** εκ] απο ϛ ηκουσανουσιν 118

2 τὰ σκάνδαλα· πλὴν οὐαὶ δι' οὗ ἔρχεται. λυσιτελεῖ αὐτῷ εἰ λίθος
μυλικὸς περίκειται περὶ τὸν τράχηλον αὐτοῦ, καὶ ἔρριπται εἰς τὴν
3 θάλασσαν, ἢ ἵνα σκανδαλίσῃ ἕνα τῶν μικρῶν τούτων. προσέχετε ἑαυ- ρξη ε
τοῖς. ἐὰν δὲ ἁμάρτῃ ὁ ἀδελφός σου, ἐπιτίμησον αὐτῷ· καὶ ἂν μὴ
4 μετανοήσῃ, ἄφες αὐτῷ. καὶ ἐὰν ἑπτάκις τῆς ἡμέρας ἁμάρτῃ εἰς σέ, ρξθ ε
καὶ ἑπτάκις τῆς ἡμέρας ἐπιστρέψῃ ἐπὶ σὲ λέγων, Μετανοῶ, ἀφήσεις
αὐτῷ.
5 6 Καὶ εἶπαν οἱ ἀπόστολοι τῷ Κυρίῳ, Πρόσθες ἡμῖν πίστιν. εἶπε δὲ σ ε
ὁ Κύριος, Εἰ ἔχετε πίστιν ὡς κόκκον σινάπεως, ἐλέγετε ἂν τῇ συκα-
μίνῳ ταύτῃ, Ἐκριζώθητι, καὶ φυτεύθητι ἐν τῇ θαλάσσῃ, καὶ ὑπήκουσεν
7 ἂν ὑμῖν. τίς δὲ ἐξ ὑμῶν δοῦλον ἔχων ἀροτριῶντα ἢ ποιμαίνοντα, ὃς σα ι
8 εἰσελθόντι ἐκ τοῦ ἀγροῦ ἐρεῖ αὐτῷ εὐθέως, Παρελθὼν ἀνάπεσαι, ἀλλ'
οὐκ ἐρεῖ αὐτῷ, Ἑτοίμασον τί δειπνήσω, καὶ περιζωσάμενος διακόνει
μοι ἕως φάγω καὶ πίω, καὶ μετὰ ταῦτα φάγεσαι καὶ πίεσαι καὶ σύ;
9 10 Μὴ χάριν ἔχει τῷ δούλῳ ἐκείνῳ, ὅτι ἐποίησε τὰ διαταχθέντα. οὕτως
καὶ ὑμεῖς, ὅταν ποιήσητε πάντα τὰ διαταχθέντα ὑμῖν, λέγετε, Δοῦλοι
ἀχρεῖοί ἐσμεν, ὃ ὠφείλομεν ποιῆσαι πεποιήκαμεν.
11 Καὶ ἐγένετο ἐν τῷ πορεύεσθαι αὐτὸν εἰς Ἱερουσαλήμ, καὶ αὐτὸς ξα′
12 διήρχετο ἀνὰ μέσον Σαμαρείας καὶ Γαλιλαίας· καὶ εἰσερχομένου αὐτοῦ
εἴς τινα κώμην ὑπήντησαν αὐτῷ δέκα λεπροὶ ἄνδρες, οἳ ἔστησαν πόρ-
13 ρωθεν· καὶ αὐτοὶ ἦραν φωνὴν λέγοντες, Ἰησοῦ, ἐπιστάτα, ἐλέησον ἡμᾶς.
14 καὶ ἰδὼν εἶπεν αὐτοῖς, Πορευθέντες ἐπιδείξατε ἑαυτοὺς τοῖς ἱερεῦσι. καὶ
15 ἐγένετο ὑπάγειν αὐτούς, ἐκαθαρίσθησαν. εἷς δὲ ἐξ αὐτῶν ἰδὼν ὅτι
16 ἰάθη ὑπέστρεψε, μετὰ φωνῆς μεγάλης δοξάζων τὸν Θεόν, καὶ ἔπεσεν
ἐπὶ πρόσωπον παρὰ τοὺς πόδας αὐτοῦ, εὐχαριστῶν αὐτῷ· καὶ αὐτὸς ἦν
17 Σαμαρείτης. καὶ ἀποκριθεὶς ὁ Ἰησοῦς εἶπεν, Οὐχὶ οἱ δέκα ἐκαθαρί-
18 σθησαν; οἱ δὲ ἐννέα ποῦ; οὐχ εὑρέθησαν ὑποστρέψαντες δοῦναι δόξαν
19 τῷ Θεῷ, εἰ μὴ ὁ ἀλλογενὴς οὗτος; καὶ εἶπεν αὐτῷ, Ἀναστὰς πορεύου·
ἡ πίστις σου σέσωκέ σε.
20 Ἐπερωτηθεὶς δὲ ὑπὸ τῶν Φαρισαίων πότε ἔρχεται ἡ βασιλεία τοῦ σβ ε
Θεοῦ, ἀπεκρίθη αὐτοῖς καὶ εἶπεν, Οὐκ ἔρχεται ἡ βασιλεία τοῦ Θεοῦ
21 μετὰ παρατηρήσεως, οὐδὲ ἐροῦσιν, Ἰδοὺ ὧδε, ἢ ἰδοὺ ἐκεῖ· ἰδοὺ γὰρ ἡ
22 βασιλεία τοῦ Θεοῦ ἐντὸς ὑμῶν ἐστιν. εἶπε δὲ πρὸς τοὺς μαθητάς, σγ ι
Ἐλεύσονται ἡμέραι ὅτε ἐπιθυμήσητε μίαν τῶν ἡμερῶν τοῦ υἱοῦ τοῦ

1 πλην ουαι] ουαι δε ς **2** μυλος ονικος ς **3** αμαρτη εις σε 118 ς 118 131 209 ς αν] εαν 118 131 ς om μη 118 131 ς **4** αμαρτηση 131 **5** ειπον 131 ς **6** ειχετε ς **7** om αυτω ς αναπεσε 131 **8** ουκ] ουχι ς om και 5° ς **9** διαταχθεντα]+αυτω; ου δοκω ς ουτω ς **10** λεγετε οτι ς εσμεν οτι ς **11** δια μεσου ς **12** απηντησαν ς **14** εν τω υπαγειν 118 131 209 ς **17** αποκριθεις δε ς **22** αι ημεραι 131 επιθυμησετε ς

σδ β ἀνθρώπου ἰδεῖν, καὶ οὐκ ὄψεσθε. καὶ ἐροῦσιν ὑμῖν, Ἰδοὺ ὧδε, μὴ 23
σε ε διώξητε· ἢ ἰδοὺ ἐκεῖ ὁ Χριστός· μὴ πιστεύσητε. ὥσπερ γὰρ ἡ 24
ἀστραπὴ ἀστράπτουσα ἐκ τῆς ὑπ' οὐρανὸν εἰς τὴν ὑπ' οὐρανὸν
σϛ β λάμπει, οὕτως ἔσται ὁ υἱὸς τοῦ ἀνθρώπου ἐν τῇ ἡμέρᾳ αὐτοῦ. πρῶτον 25
δὲ δεῖ αὐτὸν πολλὰ παθεῖν καὶ ἀποδοκιμασθῆναι ἀπὸ τῆς γενεᾶς ταύτης.
σζ ε καὶ καθὼς ἐγένετο ἐν ταῖς ἡμέραις τοῦ Νῶε, οὕτως ἔσται καὶ ἐν ταῖς 26
ἡμέραις τοῦ υἱοῦ τοῦ ἀνθρώπου· ἤσθιον, ἔπινον, ἐγάμουν, ἐξεγαμίζοντο, 27
ἄχρι ἧς ἡμέρας εἰσῆλθε Νῶε εἰς τὴν κιβωτόν, καὶ ἦλθεν ὁ κατα-
ση ι κλυσμὸς καὶ ἀπώλεσεν ἅπαντας. ὁμοίως καὶ ὡς ἐγένετο ἐν ταῖς ἡμέ- 28
ραις Λώτ· ἤσθιον, ἔπινον, ἠγόραζον, ἐπώλουν, ἐφύτευον, ᾠκοδόμουν· ᾗ 29
δὲ ἡμέρᾳ ἐξῆλθε Λὼτ ἀπὸ Σοδόμων, ἔβρεξε πῦρ καὶ θεῖον ἀπ' οὐρανοῦ
καὶ ἀπώλεσεν ἅπαντας· κατὰ ταῦτα ἔσται ᾗ ἡμέρᾳ ὁ υἱὸς τοῦ ἀνθρώπου 30
σθ β ἀποκαλύπτεται. ἐν ἐκείνῃ τῇ ἡμέρᾳ, ὃς ἔσται ἐπὶ τοῦ δώματος καὶ τὰ 31
σκεύη αὐτοῦ ἐν τῇ οἰκίᾳ, μὴ καταβάτω ἆραι αὐτά· καὶ ὁ ἐν τῷ ἀγρῷ
σι ι ὁμοίως μὴ ἐπιστρεψάτω εἰς τὰ ὀπίσω. μνημονεύετε τῆς γυναικὸς Λώτ. 32
σια ὃς ἐὰν ζητήσῃ τὴν ψυχὴν αὐτοῦ σῶσαι, ἀπολέσει αὐτήν· καὶ ὃς ἐὰν 33
γ ἀπολέσῃ, σώσει αὐτήν. λέγω ὑμῖν, ταύτῃ τῇ νυκτὶ ἔσονται δύο ἐπὶ 34
σιβ ε κλίνης μιᾶς· ὁ εἷς παραληφθήσεται καὶ ὁ ἕτερος ἀφεθήσεται· δύο 35
ἔσονται ἀλήθουσαι ἐπὶ τὸ αὐτό· ἡ μία παραληφθήσεται καὶ ἡ ἑτέρα
σιγ ε ἀφεθήσεται. καὶ ἀποκριθέντες λέγουσιν αὐτῷ, Ποῦ, κύριε; ὁ δὲ εἶπεν, 36
Ὅπου τὸ σῶμα, ἐκεῖ συναχθήσονται οἱ ἀετοί.
ΞΑ' XVIII. Ἔλεγε δὲ καὶ παραβολὴν αὐτοῖς πρὸς τὸ δεῖν πάντοτε
σιδ ι προσεύχεσθαι καὶ μὴ ἐκκακεῖν, Κριτής τις ἦν ἔν τινι πόλει τὸν Θεὸν 2
μὴ φοβούμενος καὶ ἄνθρωπον μὴ ἐντρεπόμενος. χήρα δέ τις ἦν ἐν τῇ 3
πόλει ἐκείνῃ, καὶ ἤρχετο πρὸς αὐτὸν λέγουσα, Ἐκδίκησόν με ἀπὸ τοῦ
ἀντιδίκου μου. καὶ οὐκ ἤθελεν ἐπὶ χρόνον· μετὰ δὲ ταῦτα εἶπεν ἐν 4
ἑαυτῷ, Εἰ καὶ τὸν Θεὸν οὐ φοβοῦμαι καὶ ἄνθρωπον οὐκ ἐντρέπομαι,
διά γε τὸ παρέχειν μοι κόπους τὴν χήραν ταύτην ἐκδικήσω αὐτήν, 5
ἵνα μὴ εἰς τέλος ἐρχομένη ὑπωπιάζῃ με. καὶ εἶπεν ὁ Κύριος, Ἀκού- 6
σατε τί ὁ κριτὴς τῆς ἀδικίας λέγει· ὁ δὲ Θεὸς οὐ μὴ ποιήσει τὴν 7
ἐκδίκησιν τῶν ἐκλεκτῶν αὐτοῦ τῶν βοώντων πρὸς αὐτὸν ἡμέρας καὶ
νυκτός, καὶ μακροθυμεῖ ἐπ' αὐτοῖς; λέγω ὑμῖν ὅτι ποιήσει τὴν ἐκδί- 8

34 ταυτη] αὐτῃ cod.

118 131 209 ϛ **23** om μη διωξητε ϛ om η 131 om ο Χριστος ϛ πιστευσητε] διωξητε 131, απελθητε μηδε διωξητε ϛ **24** η αστραπτουσα ϛ εσται και ϛ **26** om του 1° 131 **33** απολεση] απολεσει 131, +αυτην ϛ σωσει] ζωογονησει ϛ **36** ειπεν αυτοις ϛ σωμα] πτωμα 131

2 κριτης] pr λεγων ϛ **3** om τις ϛ **4** ηθελησεν ϛ **5** κοπους] κοπον ϛ **6** ειπε δε ϛ **8** μακροθυμων 118² 131 ϛ επ αυτοις] ab his verbis usque ad ειπε XIX 9 deest 118* sed 118² duas paginas amissas supplevit

κησιν αὐτῶν ἐν τάχει. πλὴν ὁ υἱὸς τοῦ ἀνθρώπου ἐλθὼν ἆρα εὑρήσει
τὴν πίστιν ἐπὶ τῆς γῆς;
9 Εἶπε δὲ καὶ πρός τινας τοὺς πεποιθότας ἐφ' ἑαυτοῖς ὅτι εἰσὶ δίκαιοι, ΞΒ'
10 καὶ ἐξουθενοῦντας τοὺς λοιπούς, τὴν παραβολὴν ταύτην· Ἄνθρωποι δύο
ἀνέβησαν εἰς τὸ ἱερὸν προσεύξασθαι, ὁ εἷς Φαρισαῖος καὶ ὁ ἕτερος
11 τελώνης. ὁ Φαρισαῖος σταθεὶς ταῦτα πρὸς ἑαυτὸν προσηύξατο,
Ὁ Θεός, εὐχαριστῶ σοι ὅτι οὐκ εἰμὶ ὥσπερ οἱ λοιποὶ τῶν ἀνθρώπων,
12 ἅρπαγες, ἄδικοι, μοιχοί, ἢ καὶ ὡς οὗτος ὁ τελώνης· νηστεύω δὶς τοῦ
13 σαββάτου, ἀποδεκατῶ πάντα ὅσα κτῶμαι. καὶ ὁ τελώνης μακρόθεν
ἑστὼς οὐκ ἤθελεν οὐδὲ τοὺς ὀφθαλμοὺς εἰς τὸν οὐρανὸν ἐπᾶραι, ἀλλ'
ἔτυπτε τὸ στῆθος, λέγων, Ὁ Θεός, ἱλάσθητί μοι τῷ ἁμαρτωλῷ.
14 λέγω ὑμῖν, κατέβη οὗτος δεδικαιωμένος εἰς τὸν οἶκον αὐτοῦ, πὰρ σιε/ε
ἐκεῖνον· ὅτι πᾶς ὁ ὑψῶν ἑαυτὸν ταπεινωθήσεται, καὶ ὁ ταπεινῶν
ἑαυτὸν ὑψωθήσεται.
15 Προσέφερον δὲ αὐτῷ καὶ βρέφη, ἵνα αὐτῶν ἅπτηται· ἰδόντες δὲ σις/β
16 οἱ μαθηταὶ ἐπετίμων αὐτοῖς. ὁ δὲ Ἰησοῦς προσεκαλεῖτο αὐτὰ
λέγων, Ἄφετε τὰ παιδία ἔρχεσθαι πρός με, καὶ μὴ κωλύετε αὐτά·
17 τῶν γὰρ τοιούτων ἐστὶν ἡ βασιλεία τοῦ Θεοῦ. ἀμὴν λέγω ὑμῖν, ὃς σιζ/β
ἐὰν μὴ δέξηται τὴν βασιλείαν τοῦ Θεοῦ ὡς παιδίον, οὐ μὴ εἰσέλθῃ
εἰς αὐτήν.
18 Καὶ ἐπηρώτησέν αὐτόν τις ἄρχων, λέγων, Διδάσκαλε ἀγαθέ, τί ΞΓ'
19 ποιῶν ζωὴν αἰώνιον κληρονομήσω; εἶπε δὲ αὐτῷ ὁ Ἰησοῦς, Τί με σιη/β
20 λέγεις ἀγαθόν; οὐδεὶς ἀγαθὸς εἰ μὴ εἷς, ὁ Θεός. τὰς ἐντολὰς οἶδας,
Μὴ μοιχεύσῃς, μὴ φονεύσῃς, μὴ κλέψῃς, μὴ ψευδομαρτυρήσῃς, τίμα
21 τὸν πατέρα σου καὶ τὴν μητέρα. ὁ δὲ εἶπε, Ταῦτα πάντα ἐφύλαξα
22 ἐκ νεότητός μου. ἀκούσας δὲ ὁ Ἰησοῦς εἶπεν αὐτῷ, Ἔτι ἓν σοι σιθ/β
λείπει· πάντα ὅσα ἔχεις πώλησον καὶ δὸς πτωχοῖς, καὶ ἕξεις θησαυρὸν
23 ἐν οὐρανῷ· καὶ δεῦρο, ἀκολούθει μοι. ὁ δὲ ἀκούσας ταῦτα περίλυπος σκ/β
24 ἐγένετο· ἦν γὰρ πλούσιος σφόδρα. ἰδὼν δὲ αὐτὸν ὁ Ἰησοῦς εἶπε,
Πῶς δυσκόλως οἱ τὰ χρήματα ἔχοντες εἰσελεύσονται εἰς τὴν βασιλείαν
25 τοῦ Θεοῦ. εὐκοπώτερον γάρ ἐστι κάμηλον διὰ τρυμαλιᾶς βελόνης
26 διελθεῖν, ἢ πλούσιον εἰς τὴν βασιλείαν τοῦ Θεοῦ εἰσελθεῖν. εἶπον

14 *ουτος*] *ουστος* cod.

10 *ανευησαν* 131 **11** *προς εαυτον ταυτα προσηυχετο* 118² ς **13** *ετυπτεν εις* ς *στηθος αυτου* 131 ς **14** *παρ εκεινον*] *η γαρ εκεινος* 118² 131, *η εκεινος* ς *και ο*] *ο δε* ς **15** *τα βρεφη* ς *επετιμησαν* ς **16** *προσκαλεσαμενος* ς *λεγων*] *ειπεν* ς **18** *τις αρχων αυτον* 131, *τις αυτον αρχων* 118² ς *ποιησας* 118² ς **20** *μητερα σου* 131 ς **21** *εφυλαξαμην* 118² 131 ς **22** *δε*]+*ταυτα* 118² ς *διαδος* 118² ς **24** *Ιησους*] +*περιλυπον γενομενον* 118² ς **25** *βελονης*] *ραφιδος* 118² 131 ς *διελθειν*] *εισελθειν* 131 ς 118 131 209 ς

δὲ οἱ ἀκούοντες, Καὶ τίς δύναται σωθῆναι; ὁ δὲ εἶπε, Τὰ ἀδύνατα 27
παρὰ ἀνθρώποις δυνατὰ παρὰ τῷ Θεῷ ἐστιν. εἶπε δὲ ὁ Πέτρος, 28
σκα β Ἰδοὺ πάντα τὰ ἴδια ἀφέντες ἠκολουθήσαμέν σοι. ὁ δὲ εἶπεν 29
αὐτοῖς, Ἀμὴν λέγω ὑμῖν, ὅτι οὐδείς ἐστιν ὃς ἀφῆκεν οἰκίαν ἢ γονεῖς
ἢ ἀδελφοὺς ἢ γυναῖκα ἢ τέκνα ἕνεκεν τῆς βασιλείας τοῦ Θεοῦ, ὃς 30
οὐχὶ μὴ ἀπολάβῃ πολλαπλασίονα ἐν τῷ καιρῷ τούτῳ, καὶ ἐν τῷ αἰῶνι
τῷ ἐρχομένῳ ζωὴν αἰώνιον.

σκβ β Παραλαβὼν δὲ τοὺς δώδεκα εἶπε πρὸς αὐτούς, Ἰδοὺ ἀναβαίνομεν 31
εἰς Ἱεροσόλυμα, καὶ τελεσθήσεται πάντα τὰ γεγραμμένα διὰ τῶν
προφητῶν τῷ υἱῷ τοῦ ἀνθρώπου. παραδοθήσεται γὰρ τοῖς ἔθνεσι, καὶ 32
ἐμπαιχθήσεται καὶ ὑβρισθήσεται καὶ ἐμπτυσθήσεται, καὶ μαστιγώσαντες 33
σκγ ι ἀποκτενοῦσιν αὐτόν· καὶ τῇ τρίτῃ ἡμέρᾳ ἀναστήσεται. καὶ αὐτοὶ 34
οὐδὲν τούτων συνῆκαν, ἀλλ' ἦν τὸ ῥῆμα κεκρυμμένον ἀπ' αὐτῶν,
καὶ οὐκ ἐγίνωσκον τὰ λεγόμενα.

ΞΔ' σκδ β Ἐγένετο δὲ ἐν τῷ ἐγγίζειν αὐτὸν εἰς Ἱεριχώ, τυφλός τις ἐκάθητο 35
παρὰ τὴν ὁδὸν προσαιτῶν, ἀκούσας δὲ ὄχλου διαπορευομένου ἐπυνθάνετο 36
τί ἂν εἴη τοῦτο. ἀπήγγειλαν δὲ αὐτῷ ὅτι Ἰησοῦς ὁ Ναζαρηνὸς 37
παρέρχεται. καὶ ἐβόησε λέγων, Ἰησοῦ, υἱὲ Δαβίδ, ἐλέησόν με. καὶ 38 39
οἱ προάγοντες ἐπετίμων αὐτῷ ἵνα σιωπήσῃ· αὐτὸς δὲ πολλῷ μᾶλλον
ἔκραζεν, Ἰησοῦ, υἱὲ Δαβίδ, ἐλέησόν με. σταθεὶς δὲ ὁ Ἰησοῦς ἐκέλευ- 40
σεν αὐτὸν ἀχθῆναι· ἐγγίσαντος δὲ αὐτοῦ ἐπηρώτησεν αὐτὸν λέγων, Τί 41
σοι θέλεις ποιήσω; ὁ δὲ εἶπε, Κύριε, ἵνα ἀναβλέψω. καὶ ὁ Κύριος 42
εἶπεν αὐτῷ, Ἀνάβλεψον· ἡ πίστις σου σέσωκέ σε. καὶ παραχρῆμα 43
ἀνέβλεψε, καὶ ἠκολούθει αὐτῷ δοξάζων τὸν Θεόν· καὶ πᾶς ὁ λαὸς ἰδὼν
ἔδωκεν αἶνον τῷ Θεῷ.

ΞΕ' σκε ι XIX. Καὶ εἰσελθὼν διήρχετο τὴν Ἱεριχώ· καὶ ἰδοὺ ἀνὴρ ὀνόματι 2
καλούμενος Ζακχαῖος, καὶ αὐτὸς ἦν ἀρχιτελώνης, καὶ αὐτὸς πλούσιος·
καὶ ἐζήτει ἰδεῖν τὸν Ἰησοῦν, τίς ἐστι, καὶ οὐκ ἠδύνατο ἀπὸ τοῦ ὄχλου, 3
ὅτι τῇ ἡλικίᾳ μικρὸς ἦν. καὶ προδραμὼν ἔμπροσθεν ἀνέβη ἐπὶ συκο- 4
μωρέαν, ἵνα ἴδῃ αὐτόν· ὅτι δι' ἐκείνης ἔμελλε παρέρχεσθαι. καὶ 5
ὡς ἦλθεν ἐπὶ τὸν τόπον, ἀναβλέψας ὁ Ἰησοῦς εἶπε πρὸς αὐτόν, Ζακχαῖε,
σπεύσας κατάβηθι· σήμερον γὰρ ἐν τῷ οἴκῳ σου δεῖ με μεῖναι. καὶ 6

118 131 209 ς **26** ακουσαντες ς **27** εστι παρα τω θεω ς **28** ιδου]+ημεις 118² 131 209 ς αφηκαμεν παντα και ς **29** η αδελφους η γονεις 131 **30** ουχι] ου 118² ς **33** τη ημερα τη τριτη ς **34** και ην 118² ς ρημα τουτο 118² ς κεκρυμενον 131 **36** om αν 118² ς **37** Ναζωραιος 118² ς **39** om Ιησου 118² 209 ς **40** αχθηναι προς αυτον 118² ς **42** Κυριος] Ιησους 118² 131 ς

2 αυτος 2°] ουτος ην 118² 209 ς **4** συκομορεαν 209, συκομοραιαν 118², συκομωραιαν ς ημελλε ς διερχεσθαι 118² ς **5** ειπε] pr ειδεν αυτον και ς

7 σπεύσας κατέβη, καὶ ὑπεδέξατο αὐτὸν χαίρων. καὶ ἰδόντες ἅπαντες
διεγόγγυζον, λέγοντες ὅτι Παρὰ ἁμαρτωλῷ ἀνδρὶ εἰσῆλθε καταλῦσαι.
8 σταθεὶς δὲ ὁ Ζακχαῖος εἶπε πρὸς τὸν Κύριον, Ἰδοὺ τὰ ἡμίση μου
τῶν ὑπαρχόντων, Κύριε, τοῖς πτωχοῖς δίδωμι· καὶ εἴ τινός τι
9 ἐσυκοφάντησα, ἀποδίδωμι τετραπλοῦν. εἶπε δὲ πρὸς αὐτὸν ὁ Ἰησοῦς
ὅτι Σήμερον σωτηρία τῷ οἴκῳ τούτῳ ἐγένετο, καθότι καὶ αὐτὸς υἱὸς
10 Ἀβραάμ ἐστιν· ἦλθε γὰρ ὁ υἱὸς τοῦ ἀνθρώπου ζητῆσαι καὶ σῶσαι σκϛ ε
τὸ ἀπολωλός.
11 Ἀκουόντων δὲ αὐτῶν ταῦτα προσθεὶς εἶπε παραβολήν, διὰ τὸ σκζ ι
αὐτὸν ἐγγὺς εἶναι Ἱερουσαλήμ, καὶ δοκεῖν αὐτοὺς ὅτι παρα-
12 χρῆμα μέλλει ἡ βασιλεία τοῦ Θεοῦ ἀναφαίνεσθαι· εἶπεν οὖν, ΞϚʹ
Ἄνθρωπός τις εὐγενὴς ἐπορεύθη εἰς χώραν μακράν, λαβεῖν ἑαυτῷ βασι- σκη β
13 λείαν καὶ ὑποστρέψαι. καλέσας δὲ δέκα δούλους ἑαυτοῦ ἔδωκεν αὐτοῖς ΞΖʹ σκθ
14 δέκα μνᾶς, καὶ εἶπε πρὸς αὐτούς, Πραγματεύεσθε ἐν ᾧ ἔρχομαι. οἱ ε
δὲ πολῖται αὐτοῦ ἐμίσουν αὐτόν, καὶ ἀπέστειλαν πρεσβείαν ὀπίσω αὐτοῦ
15 λέγοντες, Οὐ θέλομεν τοῦτον βασιλεῦσαι ἐφ' ἡμᾶς. καὶ ἐγένετο ἐν τῷ
ἐπανελθεῖν αὐτὸν λαβόντα τὴν βασιλείαν, καὶ εἶπε φωνηθῆναι αὐτῷ τοὺς
δούλους οἷς δεδώκει τὸ ἀργύριον, ἵνα γνῷ τίς τί διεπραγματεύσατο.
16 παρεγένετο δὲ ὁ πρῶτος λέγων, Κύριε, ἡ μνᾶς σου δέκα προσειρ-
17 γάσατο μνᾶς. καὶ εἶπεν αὐτῷ, Εὖ, δοῦλε ἀγαθέ· ὅτι ἐν ἐλαχίστῳ
18 πιστὸς ἐγένου, ἴσθι ἐξουσίαν ἔχων ἐπάνω δέκα πόλεων. καὶ ἦλθεν ὁ
19 δεύτερος λέγων, Κύριε, ἡ μνᾶς σου ἐποίησε πέντε μνᾶς. εἶπε δὲ
20 καὶ τούτῳ, Καὶ σὺ ἐπάνω γίνου πέντε πόλεων. καὶ ἕτερος ἦλθε
λέγων, Κύριε, ἰδοὺ ἡ μνᾶς σου, ἣν εἶχον ἀποκειμένην ἐν σουδαρίῳ·
21 ἐφοβούμην γάρ σε, ὅτι ἄνθρωπος αὐστηρὸς εἶ· αἴρεις ὃ οὐκ ἔθηκας καὶ
22 θερίζεις ὃ οὐκ ἔσπειρας. λέγει αὐτῷ, Ἐκ τοῦ στόματός σου κρινῶ
σε, πονηρὲ δοῦλε. ᾔδεις ὅτι ἐγὼ ἄνθρωπος αὐστηρός εἰμι, αἴρων ὃ οὐκ
23 ἔθηκα καὶ θερίζων ὃ οὐκ ἔσπειρα· καὶ διατί οὐκ ἔδωκας τὸ ἀργύριόν
24 μου ἐπὶ τράπεζαν, καὶ ἐγὼ ἐλθὼν σὺν τόκῳ ἂν ἔπραξα αὐτό; καὶ
τοῖς παρεστῶσιν εἶπεν, Ἄρατε ἀπ' αὐτοῦ τὴν μνᾶν, καὶ δότε τῷ

7 παντες 118[2] 8 om ο 118[2] ϛ Κυριον] 118[corr] $\overline{\kappa\nu}$ in $\overline{\iota\nu}$ mutavit 118 1:
των υπαρχοντων μου 131 ϛ, των υπαρχοντων μοι 118[2] διδωμι τοις πτωχοις 209 ,
118[2] 131 ϛ εις το τετραπλουν 209 9 δε] hic rursus inc. 118* Ἀβρααμ
131 ϛ 11 ταυτα αυτων 118 209 εγγυς αυτον ειναι Ιερουσαλημ ϛ, εγγυς
Ιερουσαλημ ειναι αυτον 118 209 η βασιλεια του Θεου παραχρημα μελλει
φαινεσθαι 131 13 εαυτου] αυτου 118 209, om 131 πραγματευσασθε ϛ
εν ω] εως ϛ 15 δουλους τουτους ϛ οις] ους 131 εδωκε 118 209 ϛ
16 μνα 131 ϛ προσειργασατο δεκα ϛ 17 αγαθε δουλε ϛ 18 μνα
131 ϛ 19 γινου επανω ϛ 20 om ιδου 131 μνα 131 ϛ
21 συδαριω 209 22 λεγει δε ϛ ο bis] οπου bis 131 23 την
τραπεζαν ϛ

ἔχοντι τὰς δέκα μνᾶς (καὶ εἶπον αὐτῷ, Κύριε, ἔχει δέκα μνᾶς)· 25
σλ λέγω ὑμῖν Παντὶ τῷ ἔχοντι δοθήσεται, ἀπὸ δὲ τοῦ μὴ ἔχοντος καὶ 26
β ὃ ἔχει ἀρθήσεται ἀπ' αὐτοῦ. πλὴν τοὺς ἐχθρούς μου ἐκείνους τοὺς 27
σλα ε μὴ θέλοντάς με βασιλεῦσαι ἐπ' αὐτοὺς ἀγάγετε ὧδε, καὶ κατασφάξατε
σλβ ἔμπροσθέν μου. καὶ εἰπὼν ταῦτα ἐπορεύετο ἔμπροσθεν ἀναβαίνων εἰς 28
β Ἱεροσόλυμα.

ΞΗ' Καὶ ἐγένετο ὡς ἤγγισεν εἰς Βηθφαγὴν καὶ Βηθανίαν, πρὸς τὸ 29
ὄρος τὸ καλούμενον Ἐλαιῶν, ἀπέστειλε δύο τῶν μαθητῶν αὐτοῦ εἰπών, 30
Ὑπάγετε εἰς τὴν κατέναντι κώμην, ἐν ᾗ εἰσπορευόμενοι εὑρήσετε πῶλον
δεδεμένον, ἐφ' ὃν οὐδεὶς πώποτε ἀνθρώπων κεκάθικε· λύσαντες αὐτὸν
ἀγάγετε. καὶ ἐάν τις ὑμᾶς ἐρωτᾷ, Διατί λύετε; οὕτως ἐρεῖτε αὐτῷ, 31
σλγ β ὅτι Ὁ κύριος αὐτοῦ χρείαν ἔχει. ἀπελθόντες δὲ οἱ ἀπεσταλμένοι εὗρον 32
καθὼς εἶπεν αὐτοῖς· λυόντων δὲ αὐτῶν τὸν πῶλον εἶπον οἱ κύριοι αὐτοῦ 33
πρὸς αὐτούς, Τί λύετε τὸν πῶλον; οἱ δὲ εἶπον ὅτι Ὁ κύριος αὐτοῦ 34
χρείαν ἔχει. καὶ ἤγαγον αὐτὸν πρὸς τὸν Ἰησοῦν, καὶ ἐπερρίψαν 35
αὐτῶν τὰ ἱμάτια ἐπὶ τὸν πῶλον καὶ ἐπεβίβασαν τὸν Ἰησοῦν· πορευο- 36
σλδ α μένου δὲ αὐτοῦ ὑπεστρώννυον τὰ ἱμάτια αὐτῶν ἐν τῇ ὁδῷ. ἐγγίζοντος 37
δὲ αὐτοῦ ἤδη πρὸς τῇ καταβάσει τοῦ ὄρους τῶν Ἐλαιῶν ἤρξαντο
ἅπαν τὸ πλῆθος τῶν μαθητῶν χαίροντες αἰνεῖν τὸν Θεὸν φωνῇ μεγάλῃ
περὶ πασῶν ὧν εἶδον δυνάμεων, λέγοντες, Εὐλογημένος ὁ ἐρχόμενος 38
βασιλεὺς ἐν ὀνόματι Κυρίου· εἰρήνη ἐν οὐρανῷ, καὶ δόξα ἐν ὑψίστοις.
σλε ε καί τινες τῶν Φαρισαίων ἀπὸ τοῦ ὄχλου εἶπον πρὸς αὐτόν, Διδάσκαλε, 39
ἐπιτίμησον τοῖς μαθηταῖς σου. καὶ ἀποκριθεὶς εἶπεν αὐτοῖς, Λέγω 40
σλϛ ι ὑμῖν καὶ ἐὰν οὗτοι σιωπήσωσιν, οἱ λίθοι κεκράξονται. καὶ ὡς ἤγγισεν, 41
ἰδὼν τὴν πόλιν ἔκλαυσεν ἐπ' αὐτήν, λέγων ὅτι Εἰ ἔγνως καὶ σύ, καί 42
γε ἐν τῇ ἡμέρᾳ ταύτῃ, τὰ πρὸς εἰρήνην σου· νῦν δὲ ἐκρύβη ἀπὸ
ὀφθαλμῶν σου· ὅτι ἥξουσιν ἡμέραι ἐπὶ σέ, καὶ περιβαλοῦσιν οἱ 43
ἐχθροί σου χάρακά σοι καὶ περικυκλώσουσί σε καὶ συνέξουσί σε πάν-
σλζ β τοθεν, καὶ ἐδαφιοῦσί σε καὶ τὰ τέκνα σου ἐν σοί, καὶ οὐκ ἀφήσουσι 44
λίθον ἐπὶ λίθον ἐν ὅλῃ σοί, ἀνθ' ὧν οὐκ ἔγνως τὸν καιρὸν τῆς
ἐπισκοπῆς σου.

25 δεκα] δέ cod.

118 131 209 ϛ **24** *τας δεκα μνας εχοντι* ϛ **25** *υμιν*] *γαρ υμιν οτι* ϛ **27** *θελησαντας* 131 ϛ **29** Βηθσφαγη 131 209*, Βηθσφαγην 118 209², Βηθφαγη ϛ Βηθανια 131 **30** *εκαθισε* ϛ om *αυτον* 131 **34** om *οτι* ϛ **35** *επιρριψαντες* ϛ *εαυτων* 131 ϛ om *και* 3° ϛ **36** *εαυτων* 131 **37** *ηρξατο* 118 209 **39** *τους μαθητας* 131 **40** *και* 2°] *οτι* 118 209 ϛ. **41** *αυτην*] *αυτη* ϛ **42** om *ει* 131 *ημερα σου* ϛ **43** *περιβαλλουσιν* 131 **44** *αφησουσιν εν σοι* ϛ *λιθον* 2°] *λιθω* ϛ om *εν ολη σοι* ϛ, *ος* 131 (sic)

45 Καὶ εἰσελθὼν εἰς τὸ ἱερὸν ἤρξατο ἐκβάλλειν τοὺς πωλοῦντας, σλη
46 λέγων αὐτοῖς, Γέγραπται, Καὶ ἔσται ὁ οἶκός μου οἶκος προσευχῆς· α
ὑμεῖς δὲ αὐτὸν ἐποιήσατε σπήλαιον λῃστῶν.

47 Καὶ ἦν διδάσκων τὸ καθ' ἡμέραν ἐν τῷ ἱερῷ· οἱ δὲ ἀρχιερεῖς καὶ οἱ σλθ
48 γραμματεῖς ἐζήτουν αὐτὸν ἀπολέσαι, καὶ οἱ πρῶτοι τοῦ λαοῦ· καὶ α
οὐχ ηὕρισκον τί ποιήσωσιν· ὁ λαὸς γὰρ ἅπας ἐξεκρέματο αὐτοῦ
ἀκούων.

XX. Καὶ ἐγένετο ἐν μιᾷ τῶν ἡμερῶν, διδάσκοντος αὐτοῦ τὸν ξθ′
λαὸν ἐν τῷ ἱερῷ καὶ εὐαγγελιζομένου, ἐπέστησαν οἱ ἀρχιερεῖς καὶ οἱ σμ β
2 γραμματεῖς σὺν τοῖς πρεσβυτέροις, λέγοντες πρὸς αὐτόν, Εἰπὸν
ἡμῖν, ἐν ποίᾳ ἐξουσίᾳ ταῦτα ποιεῖς, ἢ τίς ἐστιν ὁ δούς σοι τὴν ἐξου-
3 σίαν ταύτην; ἀποκριθεὶς δὲ εἶπε πρὸς αὐτούς, Ἐρωτήσω ὑμᾶς καὶ
4 ἐγὼ λόγον, καὶ εἴπατέ μοι· Τὸ βάπτισμα Ἰωάννου ἐξ οὐρανοῦ ἦν, ἢ
5 ἐξ ἀνθρώπων; οἱ δὲ διελογίσαντο πρὸς ἑαυτοὺς λέγοντες ὅτι Ἐὰν
6 εἴπωμεν, Ἐξ οὐρανοῦ, ἐρεῖ, Διατί οὖν οὐκ ἐπιστεύσατε αὐτῷ; ἐὰν δὲ
εἴπωμεν, Ἐξ ἀνθρώπων, ὁ λαὸς ἅπας καταλιθάσει ἡμᾶς· πεπει-
7 σμένος γάρ ἐστιν Ἰωάννην προφήτην εἶναι. καὶ ἀπεκρίθησαν μὴ
8 εἰδέναι πόθεν. καὶ ὁ Ἰησοῦς εἶπεν αὐτοῖς, Οὐδὲ ἐγὼ λέγω ὑμῖν ἐν
ποίᾳ ἐξουσίᾳ ταῦτα ποιῶ.

9 Ἤρξατο δὲ πρὸς τὸν λαὸν λέγειν τὴν παραβολὴν ταύτην· Ἄνθρω- ο′
πος ἐφύτευσεν ἀμπελῶνα, καὶ ἐξέδοτο αὐτὸν γεωργοῖς, καὶ ἀπεδήμησε σμα β
10 χρόνους ἱκανούς. καὶ τῷ καιρῷ ἀπέστειλε πρὸς τοὺς γεωργοὺς δοῦλον,
ἵνα ἀπὸ τοῦ καρποῦ τοῦ ἀμπελῶνος δῶσιν αὐτῷ· οἱ δὲ γεωργοὶ δείραντες
11 αὐτὸν ἐξαπέστειλαν κενόν. καὶ προσέθετο πέμψαι ἕτερον δοῦλον· οἱ δὲ
12 κἀκεῖνον δείραντες καὶ ἀτιμάσαντες ἐξαπέστειλαν κενόν. καὶ προσέθετο
13 πέμψαι τρίτον· οἱ δὲ καὶ τοῦτον τραυματίσαντες ἐξέβαλον. εἶπε δὲ ὁ
κύριος τοῦ ἀμπελῶνος, Τί ποιήσω; πέμψω τὸν υἱόν μου τὸν ἀγαπητόν·
14 ἴσως τοῦτον ἐντραπήσονται. ἰδόντες δὲ αὐτὸν οἱ γεωργοὶ διελογίζοντο
πρὸς ἀλλήλους λέγοντες, Οὗτός ἐστιν ὁ κληρονόμος· ἀποκτείνωμεν
15 αὐτόν, καὶ ἡμῶν ἔσται ἡ κληρονομία. καὶ ἐκβαλόντες αὐτὸν ἔξω τοῦ
ἀμπελῶνος ἀπέκτειναν. τί οὖν ποιήσει αὐτοῖς ὁ κύριος τοῦ ἀμπελῶνος;

45 πωλουντας] + εν αυτω και αγοραζοντας 118 131 ϛ (sed επ αυτω 131) 118 131 209 ϛ
46 om και εσται ϛ προσευχης] + εστι ϛ **48** om και οι πρωτοι του λαου 118 209 ευρισκον 118 131 209 ϛ το τι ϛ ποιησουσιν 118 209 ακουων] ακουειν 131

1 ημερων εκεινων ϛ και ειπον προς αυτον λεγοντες ϛ ειπον] ειπε 118 131 209 **3** καγω ϛ ενα λογον ϛ **5** συνελογισαντο ϛ **6** πας ο λαος ϛ καταδικασει 131 **9** om την 131 om ταυτην 131 ανθρωπος τις ϛ **10** τω] εν ϛ **12** εξεβαλλον 118 131 209 ϛ **13** τουτον] + ιδοντες ϛ **14** αλληλους] εαυτους ϛ αποκτεινωμεν] pr δευτε ϛ ινα ημων γενηται ϛ

ἐλεύσεται καὶ ἀπολέσει τοὺς γεωργοὺς ἐκείνους, καὶ δώσει τὸν ἀμπε- 16
λῶνα ἄλλοις. ἀκούσαντες δὲ εἶπον, Μὴ γένοιτο. ὁ δὲ ἐμβλέψας 17
αὐτοῖς αὐτοῖς εἶπε, Τί οὖν ἐστι τὸ γεγραμμένον τοῦτο, Λίθον ὃν
ἀπεδοκίμασαν οἱ οἰκοδομοῦντες, οὗτος ἐγενήθη εἰς κεφαλὴν γωνίας; πᾶς 18
ὁ πεσὼν ἐπ' ἐκεῖνον τὸν λίθον συνθλασθήσεται· ἐφ' ὃν δ' ἂν πέσῃ,
ΟΑ' λικμήσει αὐτόν. καὶ ἐζήτησαν οἱ γραμματεῖς καὶ οἱ ἀρχιερεῖς 19
σμβ α ἐπιβαλεῖν ἐπ' αὐτὸν τὰς χεῖρας ἐν αὐτῇ τῇ ὥρᾳ, καὶ ἐφοβήθησαν τὸν
λαόν· ἔγνωσαν γὰρ ὅτι πρὸς αὐτοὺς τὴν παραβολὴν ταύτην εἶπε.
σμγ β Καὶ παρατηρήσαντες ἀπέστειλαν ἐγκαθέτους, ὑποκρινομένους ἑαυτοὺς 20
δικαίους εἶναι, ἵνα ἐπιλάβωνται αὐτοῦ λόγου, εἰς τὸ παραδοῦναι αὐτὸν
τῇ ἀρχῇ καὶ τῇ ἐξουσίᾳ τοῦ ἡγεμόνος. καὶ ἐπηρώτησαν αὐτὸν λέγοντες, 21
Διδάσκαλε, οἴδαμεν ὅτι ὀρθῶς λέγεις καὶ διδάσκεις, καὶ οὐ λαμβάνεις
πρόσωπον, ἀλλ' ἐπ' ἀληθείας τὴν ὁδὸν τοῦ Θεοῦ διδάσκεις. ἔξεστιν 22
ἡμῖν Καίσαρι φόρον δοῦναι, ἢ οὔ; κατανοήσας δὲ αὐτῶν τὴν παν- 23
ουργίαν εἶπε πρὸς αὐτούς, Ἐπιδείξατέ μοι δηνάριον· οἱ δὲ ἔδειξαν. 24
καὶ εἶπε, Τίνος ἔχει εἰκόνα καὶ ἐπιγραφήν; ἀποκριθέντες εἶπον,
Καίσαρος. ὁ δὲ εἶπεν πρὸς αὐτούς, Ἀπόδοτε τοίνυν τὰ Καίσαρος 25
Καίσαρι, καὶ τὰ τοῦ Θεοῦ τῷ Θεῷ. καὶ οὐκ ἴσχυσαν ἐπιλαβέσθαι 26
αὐτοῦ ῥήματος ἐναντίον τοῦ λαοῦ· καὶ θαυμάσαντες ἐπὶ τῇ ἀποκρίσει
αὐτοῦ ἐσίγησαν.
ΟΒ' Προσελθόντες δέ τινες τῶν Σαδδουκαίων, οἱ λέγοντες ἀνάστασιν 27
μὴ εἶναι, ἐπηρώτησαν αὐτὸν λέγοντες, Διδάσκαλε, Μωσῆς ἔγραψεν ἡμῖν, 28
ἐάν τινος ἀδελφὸς ἀποθάνῃ ἔχων γυναῖκα, καὶ οὗτος ἄτεκνος ᾖ, ἵνα
λάβῃ ὁ ἀδελφὸς αὐτοῦ τὴν γυναῖκα καὶ ἐξαναστήσῃ σπέρμα τῷ ἀδελφῷ
αὐτοῦ. ἑπτὰ οὖν ἀδελφοὶ ἦσαν· καὶ ὁ πρῶτος λαβὼν γυναῖκα ἀπέθανεν 29
ἄτεκνος· καὶ ἔλαβεν ὁ δεύτερος τὴν γυναῖκα, καὶ οὗτος ἀπέθανεν ἄτεκνος· 30
καὶ ὁ τρίτος ἔλαβεν αὐτήν, ὡσαύτως δὲ καὶ οἱ ἑπτά· καὶ οὐ κατέλιπον 31
τέκνα· ὕστερον δὲ καὶ ἡ γυνὴ ἀπέθανεν. ἐν τῇ ἀναστάσει οὖν 32 33
τίνος αὐτῶν ἔσται γυνή; οἱ γὰρ ἑπτὰ ἔσχον αὐτὴν γυναῖκα. καὶ 34
ἀποκριθεὶς εἶπεν αὐτοῖς ὁ Ἰησοῦς, Οἱ υἱοὶ τοῦ αἰῶνος τούτου γαμοῦσι
καὶ γαμίζονται· οἱ δὲ καταξιωθέντες τοῦ αἰῶνος ἐκείνου τυχεῖν καὶ 35
τῆς ἀναστάσεως τῆς ἐκ νεκρῶν οὔτε γαμοῦσιν οὔτε γαμίζονται· οὔτε 36
γὰρ ἀποθανεῖν δύνανται· ἰσάγγελοι γάρ εἰσι, καὶ υἱοὶ τοῦ Θεοῦ, τῆς

118 131 209 ϛ

16 εκεινους] τουτους ϛ **17** om αυτοις 1° 118 131 209 **18** πεσει 131 **19** οι αρχιερεις και οι γραμματεις ϛ **23** αυτους] + τι με πειραζετε ϛ **24** om οι δε εδειξαν και ειπε ϛ αποκριθεντες δε ϛ **25** προς αυτους] αυτοις ϛ **27** αντιλεγοντες ϛ **28** η] αποθανη ϛ **31** τεκνα] + και απεθανον ϛ **32** υστερον δε παντων ϛ απεθανε και η γυνη 118 209 ϛ **33** ουν αναστασει ϛ εσται] γινεται ϛ **34** εκγαμισκονται ϛ **35** εκγαμισκονται ϛ **36** αποθανειν ετι 131 ϛ υιοι εισι ϛ

37 ἀναστάσεως υἱοὶ ὄντες. ὅτι δὲ ἐγείρονται οἱ νεκροί, καὶ Μωσῆς ἐμνη-
μόνευσεν ἐπὶ τῆς βάτου, ὡς λέγει Κύριον τὸν Θεὸν Ἀβραὰμ καὶ
38 τὸν Θεὸν Ἰσαὰκ καὶ τὸν Θεὸν Ἰακώβ. Θεὸς δὲ οὐκ ἔστι νεκρῶν,
39 ἀλλὰ ζώντων· πάντες γὰρ αὐτῷ ζῶσιν. ἀποκριθέντες δέ τινες τῶν
40 γραμματέων εἶπον, Διδάσκαλε, καλῶς λέγεις. οὐκ ἔτι δὲ ἐτόλμων σμδ β
ἐπερωτῆσαι αὐτὸν οὐδὲ ἕν.
41 Εἶπε δὲ πρὸς αὐτούς, Πῶς λέγουσι τὸν Χριστὸν υἱὸν Δαβὶδ εἶναι; ΟΓ′
42 αὐτὸς γὰρ Δαβὶδ λέγει ἐν βίβλῳ ψαλμῶν, Εἶπεν ὁ Κύριος τῷ κυρίῳ σμε β
43 μου, Κάθου ἐκ δεξιῶν μου ἕως ἂν θῶ τοὺς ἐχθρούς σου ὑποπόδιον
44 τῶν ποδῶν σου. Δαβὶδ οὖν κύριον αὐτὸν καλεῖ, καὶ πῶς αὐτοῦ υἱός
45 46 ἐστιν; ἀκούοντος δὲ παντὸς τοῦ λαοῦ εἶπε τοῖς μαθηταῖς αὐτοῦ, Προσ- σμϛ β
έχετε ἀπὸ τῶν γραμματέων τῶν θελόντων ἐν στολαῖς περιπατεῖν,
καὶ φιλούντων ἀσπασμοὺς ἐν ταῖς ἀγοραῖς καὶ πρωτοκαθεδρίας ἐν ταῖς
47 συναγωγαῖς καὶ πρωτοκλισίας ἐν τοῖς δείπνοις· οἳ κατεσθίουσι τὰς σμζ η
οἰκίας τῶν χηρῶν καὶ προφάσει μακρὰ προσεύχονται· οὗτοι λήψονται
περισσότερον κρῖμα.

XXI. Ἀναβλέψας δὲ εἶδε τοὺς βάλλοντας εἰς τὸ γαζοφυλάκιον ΟΔ′
2 τὰ δῶρα αὐτῶν πλουσίους· εἶδε δέ τινα καὶ χήραν πενιχρὰν βαλοῦ-
3 σαν ἐκεῖ δύο λεπτά, καὶ εἶπεν, Ἀληθῶς λέγω ὑμῖν ὅτι ἡ χήρα ἡ
4 πτωχὴ αὕτη πλεῖον πάντων ἔβαλεν· ἅπαντες γὰρ οὗτοι ἐκ τοῦ περισ-
σεύματος αὐτοῖς ἔβαλον εἰς τὰ δῶρα, αὕτη δὲ ἐκ τοῦ ὑστερήματος
αὐτῆς ἅπαντα τὸν βίον ὃν εἶχεν ἔβαλε.
5 Καί τινων λεγόντων περὶ τοῦ ἱεροῦ, ὅτι λίθοις καλοῖς καὶ ἀναθή- σμη β
6 μασι κεκόσμηται, εἶπε, Ταῦτα ἃ θεωρεῖτε, ἐλεύσονται ἡμέραι ἐν αἷς οὐκ
7 ἀφεθήσεται ὧδε λίθος ἐπὶ λίθον, ὃς οὐ καταλυθήσεται. ἐπηρώτησαν σμθ β
δὲ αὐτὸν λέγοντες, Διδάσκαλε, πότε ταῦτα ἔσται; καὶ τί τὸ σημεῖον
ὅτε μέλλει ταῦτα γίνεσθαι;
8 Ὁ δὲ εἶπε, Βλέπετε μὴ πλανηθῆτε· πολλοὶ γὰρ ἐλεύσονται ἐπὶ τῷ ΟΕ′
ὀνόματί μου, λέγοντες ὅτι Ἐγώ εἰμι, καί, Ὁ καιρὸς ἤγγικε. μὴ οὖν
9 πορευθῆτε ὀπίσω αὐτῶν. ὅταν δὲ ἀκούσητε πολέμους καὶ ἀκαταστα-
σίας, μὴ πτοηθῆτε· δεῖ γὰρ ταῦτα γενέσθαι πρῶτον, ἀλλ' οὐκ εὐθέως

37 εμηνυσεν ϛ   'Αβρααμ 131 ϛ   **39** λεγεις] ειπας ϛ, ειπας και λεγεις 131   118 131 209 ϛ   **40** επερωταν ϛ   ουδεν 131 ϛ   **42** αυτος γαρ] και αυτος ϛ   **44** υιος αυτου 131 ϛ   **46** περιπατειν εν στολαις ϛ   **47** μακραν 131

1 τα δωρα αυτων εις το γαζοφυλακιον ϛ   **2** και τινα ϛ   βαλλουσαν 131 ϛ   **3** εβαλλεν 118 131 209   **4** περισσευοντος ϛ   αυτοις] αυτων plene script. 131, ἀυ̅τ̅ 209 quod αυτων significare potest sed idem αυτοις significare nolo omnino negare, αυτο spat. rel. 118   εβαλλον 118 131 209   δωρα του θεου ϛ   εβαλλε 118 131 209   **6** om ωδε ϛ   λιθον] λιθω ϛ   **7** ποτε ουν ϛ   οταν μελλη ϛ

τὸ τέλος. τότε ἔλεγεν αὐτοῖς, Ἐγερθήσεται ἔθνος ἐπ' ἔθνος καὶ βασι- 10
λεία ἐπὶ βασιλείαν, σεισμοί τε μεγάλοι κατὰ τόπους καὶ λιμοὶ καὶ 11
λοιμοὶ ἔσονται, φόβητρά τε καὶ ἀπ' οὐρανοῦ σημεῖα μεγάλα ἔσται.
σν/α πρὸ δὲ τούτων πάντων ἐπιβαλοῦσιν ἐφ' ὑμᾶς τὰς χεῖρας αὐτῶν καὶ 12
διώξουσι, παραδιδόντες εἰς συναγωγὰς καὶ φυλακάς, ἀπαγομένους ἐπὶ
βασιλεῖς καὶ ἡγεμόνας, ἕνεκεν τοῦ ὀνόματός μου. ἀποβήσεται δὲ ὑμῖν 13
σνα/β εἰς μαρτύριον· θέσθε οὖν ἐν ταῖς καρδίαις ὑμῶν μὴ προμελετᾶν ἀπο- 14
λογηθῆναι· ἐγὼ γὰρ δώσω ὑμῖν στόμα καὶ σοφίαν, ᾗ οὐ δυνήσονται 15
ἀντειπεῖν οὐδὲ ἀντιστῆναι πάντες οἱ ἀντικείμενοι ὑμῖν. παραδοθήσεσθε 16
δὲ καὶ ὑπὸ γονέων καὶ ἀδελφῶν συγγενέων καὶ φίλων, καὶ θανατώ-
σουσιν ἐξ ὑμῶν, καὶ ἔσεσθε μισούμενοι ὑπὸ πάντων διὰ τὸ ὄνομά μου· 17
καὶ θρὶξ ἐκ τῆς κεφαλῆς ὑμῶν οὐ μὴ ἀπόληται. ἐν τῇ ὑπομονῇ ὑμῶν 18 19
σνβ/ι κτήσασθε τὰς ψυχὰς ὑμῶν. ὅταν δὲ ἴδητε κυκλουμένην ὑπὸ στρατο- 20
πέδων τὴν Ἱερουσαλήμ, τότε γινώσκετε ὅτι ἤγγισεν ἡ ἐρήμωσις
σνγ/β αὐτῆς. τότε οἱ ἐν τῇ Ἰουδαίᾳ φευγέτωσαν εἰς τὰ ὄρη, καὶ οἱ ἐν μέσῳ 21
αὐτῆς ἐκχωρείτωσαν, καὶ οἱ ἐν ταῖς χώραις μὴ εἰσερχέσθωσαν εἰς αὐτήν·
ὅτι ἡμέραι ἐκδικήσεως αὗταί εἰσι, τοῦ πληρωθῆναι πάντα τὰ γεγραμ- 22
σνδ/β μένα. οὐαὶ δὲ ταῖς ἐν γαστρὶ ἐχούσαις καὶ ταῖς θηλαζούσαις ἐν ἐκείναις 23
σνε/β ταῖς ἡμέραις· ἔσται γὰρ τότε ἀνάγκη μεγάλη ἐπὶ τῆς γῆς, καὶ ὀργὴ
τῷ λαῷ τούτῳ· καὶ πεσοῦνται στόματι μαχαίρας, καὶ αἰχμαλωτισθή- 24
σνϛ/ι σονται εἰς πάντα τὰ ἔθνη· καὶ Ἱερουσαλὴμ ἔσται πατουμένη ὑπὸ ἐθνῶν,
σνζ/β ἄχρι πληρωθῶσι καιροὶ ἐθνῶν. καὶ ἔσται σημεῖα ἐν ἡλίῳ καὶ σελήνῃ 25
καὶ ἄστροις, καὶ ἐπὶ τῆς γῆς συνοχὴ ἐθνῶν, ἐν ἀπορίᾳ ἠχοῦς θαλάσσης
καὶ σάλου, ἀποψυχόντων ἀνθρώπων ἀπὸ φόβου καὶ προσδοκίας τῶν ἐπερ- 26
χομένων τῇ οἰκουμένῃ· αἱ γὰρ δυνάμεις τῶν οὐρανῶν σαλευθήσονται.
σνη/β καὶ τότε ὄψονται τὸν υἱὸν τοῦ ἀνθρώπου ἐρχόμενον ἐν νεφέλῃ μετὰ 27
δυνάμεως καὶ δόξης πολλῆς.

Ἀρχομένων δὲ τούτων γίνεσθαι, ἀνακαλύψατε καὶ ἐπάρατε τὰς 28
κεφαλὰς ὑμῶν, ὅτι ἤγγικεν ἡ ἀπολύτρωσις ὑμῶν.

Καὶ εἶπε παραβολὴν αὐτοῖς, Ἴδετε τὴν συκῆν καὶ πάντα τὰ δένδρα· 29
ὅταν προβάλωσιν ἤδη, βλέποντες ἀφ' ἑαυτῶν γινώσκετε ὅτι ἤδη ἐγγὺς 30
τὸ θέρος ἐστίν. οὕτω καὶ ὑμεῖς, ὅταν ἴδητε ταῦτα γινόμενα, γινώσκετε 31
ὅτι ἐγγύς ἐστιν ἡ βασιλεία τοῦ Θεοῦ. ἀμὴν λέγω ὑμῖν, οὐ μὴ παρ- 32
έλθῃ ἡ γενεὰ αὕτη, ἕως ἂν πάντα γένηται. ὁ οὐρανὸς καὶ ἡ γῆ 33

27 πολλης] πολης cod. **30** γινοσκετε cod.

118 131 209 ς **10** επ] επι 131 ς **11** σημεια απ ουρανου 118 131 209 ς **12** απαντων ς επιβαλλουσιν 131 αγομενους ς **14** εις τας καρδιας ς **16** και συγγενων 131 ς, om 118 209 **20** γνωτε ς ηγγικεν ς **23** om τοτε ς τω] pr εν ς **25** ηχους] ηχουσης 131 ς **28** ανακυψατε ς διοτι εγγιζει ς **32** υμιν] + οτι ς

34 παρελεύσεται, οἱ δὲ λόγοι μου οὐ μὴ παρέλθωσι. προσέχετε σνθ/ι
ἑαυτοῖς, μήποτε βαρηθῶσιν ὑμῶν αἱ καρδίαι ἐν κραιπάλῃ καὶ μέθῃ
καὶ μερίμναις βιωτικαῖς, καὶ αἰφνιδίως ἐφ' ὑμᾶς ἐπιστῇ ἡ ἡμέρα
35 ἐκείνη· ὡς παγὶς γὰρ ἐπελεύσεται ἐπὶ πάντας τοὺς καθημένους ἐπὶ
36 προσώπου τῆς γῆς. ἀγρυπνεῖτε οὖν ἐν παντὶ καιρῷ δεόμενοι ἵνα
κατισχύσητε ἐκφυγεῖν ταῦτα πάντα τὰ μέλλοντα γίνεσθαι, καὶ σταθῆ-
ναι ἔμπροσθεν τοῦ υἱοῦ τοῦ ἀνθρώπου.
37 Ἦν δὲ τὰς ἡμέρας ἐν τῷ ἱερῷ διδάσκων· τὰς δὲ νύκτας ἐξερχόμενος
38 ηὐλίζετο εἰς τὸ ὄρος τῶν Ἐλαιῶν. καὶ πᾶς ὁ λαὸς ὤρθριζε πρὸς αὐτὸν
ἐν τῷ ἱερῷ ἀκούειν αὐτοῦ.

XXII. Ἤγγιζε δὲ ἡ ἑορτὴ τῶν ἀζύμων, ἡ λεγομένη πάσχα. ΟϚ'/σξ/α
2 καὶ ἐζήτουν οἱ ἀρχιερεῖς καὶ οἱ γραμματεῖς τὸ πῶς ἀνέλωσιν αὐτόν·
ἐφοβοῦντο γὰρ τὸν λαόν. σξα/α
3 Εἰσῆλθε δὲ Σατανᾶς εἰς Ἰούδαν τὸν ἐπικαλούμενον Ἰσκαριώτην, σξβ/θ
4 ὄντα ἐκ τοῦ ἀριθμοῦ τῶν δώδεκα· καὶ ἀπελθὼν συνελάλησε τοῖς ἀρχιε-
5 ρεῦσι καὶ στρατηγοῖς τὸ πῶς αὐτὸν παραδῷ αὐτοῖς. καὶ συνέθεντο σξγ/β
6 αὐτῷ ἀργύριον δοῦναι· καὶ ἐξωμολόγησε, καὶ ἐζήτει εὐκαιρίαν τοῦ
παραδοῦναι αὐτὸν αὐτοῖς ἄτερ ὄχλου.
7 8 Ἦλθε δὲ ἡ ἡμέρα τῶν ἀζύμων, ἐν ᾗ ἔδει θύεσθαι τὸ πάσχα· καὶ
ἀπέστειλε Πέτρον καὶ Ἰωάννην, εἰπών, Πορευθέντες ἑτοιμάσατε ἡμῖν τὸ
9 πάσχα, ἵνα φάγωμεν. οἱ δὲ εἶπον αὐτῷ, Ποῦ θέλεις ἑτοιμάσομεν;
10 ὁ δὲ εἶπεν αὐτοῖς, Ἰδού, εἰσελθόντων ὑμῶν εἰς τὴν πόλιν, συναντήσει
ὑμῖν ἄνθρωπος κεράμιον ὕδατος βαστάζων· ἀκολουθήσατε αὐτῷ εἰς τὴν
11 οἰκίαν οὗ εἰσπορεύεται· καὶ ἐρεῖτε τῷ οἰκοδεσπότῃ τῆς οἰκίας, Λέγει
σοι ὁ διδάσκαλος, Ποῦ ἐστι τὸ κατάλυμα, ὅπου τὸ πάσχα μετὰ τῶν
12 μαθητῶν μου φάγω; κἀκεῖνος ὑμῖν δείξει ἀνώγεον μέγα ἐστρωμένον·
13 ἐκεῖ ἑτοιμάσατε. ἀπελθόντες δὲ εὗρον καθὼς εἴρηκεν αὐτοῖς, καὶ ἡτοί-
μασαν τὸ πάσχα.
14 Καὶ ὅτε ἐγένετο ἡ ὥρα, ἀνέπεσε, καὶ οἱ δώδεκα ἀπόστολοι σὺν
15 αὐτῷ. καὶ εἶπε πρὸς αὐτούς, Ἐπιθυμίᾳ ἐπεθύμησα τοῦτο τὸ πάσχα σξδ/ι
16 φαγεῖν μεθ' ὑμῶν πρὸ τοῦ με παθεῖν· λέγω γὰρ ὑμῖν ὅτι οὐ μὴ
17 φάγω αὐτὸ ἕως οὗ πληρωθῇ ἐν τῇ βασιλείᾳ τοῦ Θεοῦ. καὶ δεξά- σξε/β

12 ανωγεον] sic lego, sed Tischendorfio αναγεον scriptum esse videtur

33 παρελευσονται ϛ **34** προσεχετε δε ϛ βαρυνθωσιν ϛ αιφνιδιος ϛ ημερᾳ εκεινῃ 118 **35** προσωπον 118 131 209 ϛ πασης της 118 209 ϛ **36** κατισχησητε 118, καταξιωθητε ϛ **37** των] το καλουμενον ϛ 118 131 209 ϛ

3 ο Σατανας 131 ϛ **4** τοις στρατηγοις 131 ϛ **5** και 1°] pr και εχαρησαν ϛ **9** ετοιμασωμεν 118 131 ϛ **12** αναγαιον 131 **15** παθειν] απελθειν 131 **16** ουκετι ου μη 118 131 209 ϛ αυτο] εξ αυτου ϛ οὗ] οτου ϛ

μενος ποτήριον εὐχαριστήσας εἶπε, Λάβετε τοῦτο καὶ διαμερίσατε εἰς
ἑαυτούς· λέγω γὰρ ὑμῖν, Ἀπὸ τοῦ νῦν οὐ μὴ πίω ἀπὸ τοῦ γενή- 18
σξϛ α ματος τῆς ἀμπέλου ἕως οὗ ἡ βασιλεία τοῦ Θεοῦ ἔλθῃ. καὶ λαβὼν 19
ἄρτον εὐχαριστήσας ἔκλασε, καὶ ἔδωκεν αὐτοῖς λέγων, Τοῦτό ἐστι τὸ
σῶμά μου τὸ ὑπὲρ ὑμῶν διδόμενον· τοῦτο ποιεῖτε εἰς τὴν ἐμὴν ἀνά-
σξζ β μνησιν. ὡσαύτως καὶ τὸ ποτήριον μετὰ τὸ δειπνῆσαι, λέγων, Τοῦτο 20
τὸ ποτήριον ἡ καινὴ διαθήκη ἐν τῷ αἵματί μου, τὸ ὑπὲρ ὑμῶν ἐκχυ-
σξη β νόμενον. πλὴν ἰδοὺ ἡ χεὶρ τοῦ παραδιδόντος με μετ' ἐμοῦ ἐπὶ τῆς 21
τραπέζης. καὶ ὁ μὲν υἱὸς τοῦ ἀνθρώπου πορεύεται κατὰ τὸ ὡρισμένον· 22
σξθ α πλὴν οὐαὶ τῷ ἀνθρώπῳ ἐκείνῳ, δι' οὗ παραδίδοται. καὶ αὐτοὶ ἤρξαντο 23
συζητεῖν πρὸς ἑαυτοὺς τὸ τίς ἄρα ἐστὶν ἐξ αὐτῶν ὁ τοῦτο μέλλων
ΟΖ' πράσσειν. ἐγένετο δὲ καὶ φιλονεικία ἐν αὐτοῖς, τὸ τίς αὐτῶν δοκεῖ 24
σο β εἶναι μείζων. ὁ δὲ εἶπεν αὐτοῖς, Οἱ βασιλεῖς τῶν ἐθνῶν κυριεύουσιν 25
αὐτῶν, καὶ οἱ ἐξουσιάζοντες αὐτῶν εὐεργέται καλοῦνται. ὑμεῖς δὲ οὐχ 26
οὕτως· ἀλλ' ὁ μείζων ἐν ὑμῖν γινέσθω ὡς ὁ νεώτερος· καὶ ὁ ἡγού-
σοα ι μενος ὡς ὁ διακονῶν. τίς γὰρ μείζων, ὁ ἀνακείμενος ἢ ὁ διακονῶν; 27
οὐχ ὁ ἀνακείμενος; ἐγὼ δέ εἰμι ἐν μέσῳ ὑμῶν ὡς ὁ διακονῶν. ὑμεῖς 28
δέ ἐστε οἱ διαμεμενηκότες μετ' ἐμοῦ ἐν τοῖς πειρασμοῖς μου· κἀγὼ 29
διατίθημι ὑμῖν, καθὼς διέθετό μοι ὁ πατήρ μου, βασιλείαν, ἵνα 30
ἐσθίητε καὶ πίνητε ἐπὶ τῆς τραπέζης μου ἐν τῇ βασιλείᾳ μου, καὶ
σοβ ε καθήσεσθε ἐπὶ θρόνων κρίνοντες τὰς δώδεκα φυλὰς τοῦ Ἰσραήλ.
ΟΗ' εἶπε δὲ ὁ Κύριος, Σίμων, Σίμων, ἰδοὺ ὁ Σατανᾶς ἐξῃτήσατο ὑμᾶς, τοῦ 31
σογ ι σινιάσαι ὡς τὸν σῖτον· ἐγὼ δὲ ἐδεήθην περὶ σοῦ, ἵνα μὴ ἐκλίπῃ ἡ 32
σοδ θ πίστις σου· καὶ σύ ποτε ἐπιστρέψας στήρισον τοὺς ἀδελφούς σου.
σοε α ὁ δὲ εἶπεν αὐτῷ, Κύριε, μετὰ σοῦ ἕτοιμός εἰμι καὶ εἰς φυλακὴν 33
καὶ εἰς θάνατον πορεύεσθαι. ὁ δὲ εἶπε, Λέγω σοι, Πέτρε, οὐ μὴ 34
σοϛ ι φωνήσει σήμερον ἀλέκτωρ πρὶν ἢ τρὶς ἀπαρνήσῃ με εἰδέναι. καὶ 35
εἶπεν αὐτοῖς, Ὅτε ἀπέστειλα ὑμᾶς ἄτερ βαλλαντίου καὶ πήρας καὶ
ὑποδημάτων, μή τινος ὑστερήθη; οἱ δὲ εἶπον, Οὐδενός. εἶπεν οὖν, 36
Ἀλλὰ νῦν ὁ ἔχων βαλλάντιον ἀράτω, ὁμοίως καὶ πήραν· καὶ ὁ μὴ
σοζ ε ἔχων πωλησάτω τὸ ἱμάτιον αὐτοῦ καὶ ἀγορασάτω μάχαιραν. λέγω 37
γὰρ ὑμῖν ὅτι τοῦτο τὸ γεγραμμένον δεῖ τελεσθῆναι ἐν ἐμοί, τό, Καὶ

118 131 209 ϛ

17 εις εαυτους] εαυτοις ϛ **18** απο του νυν] οτι ϛ γεννηματος ϛ ου] οτου ϛ **21** om με 131 **23** εστιν] ειη ϛ **24** το] ὁ sed sine spiritu 118 **26** γενεσθω ϛ **27** ουχι ϛ **29** διατιθεμαι ϛ διεθετο] εθετο 131 **30** καθισεσθε 118 131 209, καθισησθε ϛ **32** εκλειπη 131 ϛ στηριξον 118 131^2 209 ϛ **34** λεγω] ου μη 131 φωνηση 131 μη ειδεναι 131, μ ειδεναι spat. rel. 118, μη ειδεναι με ϛ **35** om και ειπεν αυτοις 131 βαλαντιου 118 209 ϛ **35** υστερηθητε 118 131 209, υστερησατε ϛ ουθενος 131 **36** ουν]+αυτοις 118 209 ϛ βαλαντιον 118 209 ϛ τα ιματια 131 **37** ετι τουτο 131 ϛ

38 μετὰ ἀνόμων ἐλογίσθη· καὶ γὰρ τὸ περὶ ἐμοῦ τέλος ἔχει. οἱ δὲ εἶπον, σοη
Κύριε, ἰδοὺ μάχαιραι ὧδε δύο. ὁ δὲ εἶπεν, Ἱκανόν ἐστι. ι
39 Καὶ ἐξελθὼν ἐπορεύθη κατὰ τὸ ἔθος εἰς τὸ ὄρος τῶν Ἐλαιῶν· σοθ α
40 ἠκολούθησαν δὲ αὐτῷ καὶ οἱ μαθηταί. γενόμενος δὲ ἐπὶ τοῦ τόπου σπ
41 εἶπεν αὐτοῖς, Προσεύχεσθε μὴ εἰσελθεῖν εἰς πειρασμόν. καὶ αὐτὸς β
ἀπεσπάσθη ἀπ' αὐτῶν ὡσεὶ λίθου βολήν, καὶ θεὶς τὰ γόνατα προσ- σπα α
42 ηύχετο λέγων, Πάτερ, παρένεγκε τὸ ποτήριον τοῦτο ἀπ' ἐμοῦ· πλὴν σπβ α
43 μὴ τὸ θέλημά μου, ἀλλὰ τὸ σὸν γινέσθω. ὤφθη δὲ αὐτῷ ἄγγελος σπγ
44 ἀπ' οὐρανοῦ ἐνισχύων αὐτόν. καὶ γενόμενος ἐν ἀγωνίᾳ ἐκτενέστερον ι
προσηύχετο. καὶ ἐγένετο ὁ ἱδρὼς αὐτοῦ ὡσεὶ θρόμβοι αἵματος κατα-
45 βαίνοντες ἐπὶ τὴν γῆν. καὶ ἀναστὰς ἀπὸ τῆς προσευχῆς, ἐλθὼν πρὸς σπδ β
46 τοὺς μαθητὰς αὐτοῦ εὗρεν αὐτοὺς κοιμωμένους ἀπὸ τῆς λύπης, καὶ εἶπεν
αὐτοῖς, Τί καθεύδετε; ἀναστάντες προσεύχεσθε, ἵνα μὴ εἰσέλθητε εἰς
πειρασμόν.
47 Ἔτι αὐτοῦ λαλοῦντος, ἰδοὺ ὄχλος, καὶ ὁ καλούμενος Ἰούδας, εἷς σπε
τῶν δώδεκα, προῆγεν αὐτοὺς καὶ ἤγγισε τῷ Ἰησοῦ φιλῆσαι αὐτόν. α
48 ὁ δὲ Ἰησοῦς εἶπεν αὐτῷ, Ἰούδα, φιλήματι τὸν υἱὸν τοῦ ἀνθρώπου παρα- σπς β
49 δίδως; ἰδόντες δὲ οἱ περὶ αὐτὸν τὸ ἐσόμενον εἶπον αὐτῷ, Κύριε, εἰ σπζ
50 πατάξομεν ἐν μαχαίρᾳ; καὶ ἐπάταξεν εἷς τις ἐξ αὐτῶν τὸν δοῦλον α
51 τοῦ ἀρχιερέως, καὶ ἀφεῖλεν αὐτοῦ τὸ οὖς τὸ δεξιόν. ἀποκριθεὶς δὲ ὁ σπη
Ἰησοῦς εἶπεν, Ἐᾶτε ἕως τούτου. καὶ ἁψάμενος τοῦ ὠτίου ἰάσατο ι
52 αὐτόν. εἶπε δὲ πρὸς τοὺς παραγενομένους ἐπ' αὐτὸν ἀρχιερεῖς καὶ σπθ
στρατηγοὺς τοῦ ἱεροῦ καὶ πρεσβυτέρους, Ὡς ἐπὶ λῃστὴν ἐξήλθετε α
53 μετὰ μαχαιρῶν καὶ ξύλων; καθ' ἡμέραν ὄντος μου μεθ' ὑμῶν ἐν τῷ
ἱερῷ οὐκ ἐξετείνατε χεῖρας ἐπ' ἐμέ. ἀλλ' αὕτη ὑμῶν ἐστιν ἡ ὥρα
καὶ ἡ ἐξουσία τοῦ σκότους.
54 Συλλαβόντες δὲ αὐτὸν ἤγαγον εἰς τὴν οἰκίαν τοῦ ἀρχιερέως· σϟ α
55 ὁ δὲ Πέτρος ἠκολούθει μακρόθεν. ἁψάντων δὲ πυρὰν ἐν μέσῳ τῆς σϟα
αὐλῆς καὶ περικαθισάντων αὐτῶν, ἐκάθητο ὁ Πέτρος μέσος αὐτῶν. α
56 ἰδοῦσα δὲ αὐτὸν παιδίσκη τις καθήμενον πρὸς τὸ φῶς καὶ ἀτενίσασα
57 αὐτῷ εἶπε, Καὶ οὗτος σὺν αὐτῷ ἦν. ὁ δὲ ἠρνήσατο λέγων, Γύναι, σϟβ
58 οὐκ οἶδα αὐτόν. καὶ μετὰ βραχὺ ἕτερος ἰδὼν αὐτὸν ἔφη, Καὶ σὺ α

37 το 3°] τα ς **38** ειπεν αυτοις ς **39** και 2°] om 118 μαθηται αυτου ς **42** ει βουλει παρενεγκειν ς γενεσθω 118 209 ς **44** εγενετο δε ς **47** ετι δε 131 ς καλουμενος] λεγομενος ς προηγεν αυτους] προηρχετο αυτων ς **49** παταξωμεν 131 **51** ωτιου αυτου ς **52** δε] +ο Ιησους ς εξεληλυθατε ς **53** τας χειρας ς η εξουσια και η ωρα 131 **54** ηγαγον]+και εισηγαγον αυτον 131 ς τον οικον ς **55** πυραν] πυρ 131 ς συγκαθισαντων ς om ο Πετρος ς μεσος] εν μεσω 131 ς **56** ατενισας 131 **57** ηρνησατο αυτον ς **58** αυτον ιδων 131 118 131 209 ς

ἐξ αὐτῶν εἶ. ὁ δὲ Πέτρος εἶπεν, Ἄνθρωπε, οὐκ εἰμί. καὶ διαστάσης 59
ὡσεὶ ὥρας μιᾶς ἄλλος τις διϊσχυρίζετο λέγων, Ἐπ' ἀληθείας καὶ
οὗτος μετ' αὐτοῦ ἦν· καὶ γὰρ Γαλιλαῖός ἐστιν. εἶπε δὲ ὁ Πέτρος, 60
Ἄνθρωπε, οὐκ οἶδα ὃ λέγεις. καὶ παραχρῆμα ἔτι αὐτοῦ λαλοῦντος
σλγ ἐφώνησεν ἀλέκτωρ· καὶ στραφεὶς ὁ Ἰησοῦς ἐνέβλεψε τῷ Πέτρῳ· καὶ 61
β ὑπεμνήσθη ὁ Πέτρος τοῦ λόγου τοῦ Κυρίου, ὡς εἶπεν αὐτῷ ὅτι Πρὶν
ἀλέκτορα φωνῆσαι ἀπαρνήσῃ με τρίς. καὶ ἐξελθὼν ἔξω ἔκλαυσε 62
πικρῶς.

σλδ α Καὶ οἱ ἄνδρες οἱ συνέχοντες τὸν Ἰησοῦν ἐνέπαιζον αὐτῷ δέροντες, 63
καὶ περικαλύψαντες αὐτοῦ τὸ πρόσωπον, ἐπηρώτων αὐτὸν λέγοντες, 64
Προφήτευσον τίς ἐστιν ὁ παίσας σε. καὶ ἕτερα πολλὰ βλασφη- 65
μοῦντες ἔλεγον εἰς αὐτόν.

σλε β Καὶ ὡς ἡμέρα ἐγένετο, συνήχθη τὸ πρεσβυτέριον τοῦ λαοῦ, ἀρχιε- 66
ρεῖς καὶ γραμματεῖς, καὶ ἀνήγαγον αὐτὸν εἰς τὸ συνέδριον ἑαυτῶν
σλϛ ι λέγοντες, Εἰ σὺ εἶ ὁ Χριστός, εἰπὲ ἡμῖν. εἶπε δὲ αὐτοῖς, Ἐὰν ὑμῖν 67
εἴπω, οὐ μὴ πιστεύσητε· ἐὰν δὲ καὶ ἐρωτήσω, οὐ μὴ ἀποκριθῆτέ μοι. 68
σλζ α ἀπὸ τοῦ νῦν ἔσται ὁ υἱὸς τοῦ ἀνθρώπου καθήμενος ἐκ δεξιῶν τῆς δυνά- 69
σλη ι μεως τοῦ Θεοῦ. εἶπον οὖν πάντες, Σὺ οὖν εἶ ὁ υἱὸς τοῦ Θεοῦ; ὁ δὲ 70
πρὸς αὐτοὺς ἔφη, Ὑμεῖς λέγετε ὅτι ἐγώ εἰμι. οἱ δὲ εἶπον, Τί ἔτι 71
σλθ β χρείαν ἔχομεν μαρτυρίας; αὐτοὶ γὰρ ἠκούσαμεν ἐκ τοῦ στόματος
αὐτοῦ.

τ α XXIII. Καὶ ἀναστὰν ἅπαν τὸ πλῆθος αὐτῶν ἤγαγον αὐτὸν ἐπὶ
τα ι τὸν Πιλάτον. ἤρξατο δὲ κατηγορεῖν αὐτοῦ λέγοντες, Τοῦτον εὕραμεν 2
διαστρέφοντα Καίσαρι φόρους διδόναι, λέγοντα ἑαυτὸν Χριστὸν
τβ α βασιλέα εἶναι. ὁ δὲ Πιλάτος ἐπηρώτησεν αὐτὸν λέγων, Σὺ εἶ ὁ βασι- 3
τγ θ λεὺς τῶν Ἰουδαίων; ὁ δὲ ἀπεκρίθη αὐτῷ, Σὺ λέγεις. ὁ δὲ Πιλάτος 4
εἶπε πρὸς τοὺς ἀρχιερεῖς καὶ τοὺς ὄχλους, Οὐδὲν εὑρίσκω αἴτιον ἐν τῷ
ἀνθρώπῳ τούτῳ.

61 αλεκτωρα cod. 63 συνεχοντες] συνεοτες cod.

118 131 209 ς

59 ἀλλ ὅστις 118, ἄλλός τις 209 αυτων 131 **60** λαλουντος αυτου ς ο αλεκτωρ ς **61** Ιησους] Κυριος ς om αυτω 131 τρις απαρνηση με 131 εξω]+ο Πετρος ς κλαυσεν 131 **63** περικαλυψαντες]+αυτον ετυπτον ς προσωπον]+και ς, +ετυπτον αυτον και 131 **64** προφητευσον ημιν χριστε 131 **65** εις] προς 131 **66** εγενετο ημερα ς και 2°] τε και 118 131 209 ς αυτων 118 209 **68** εαν δε] eras. 118 μοι]+η απολυσητε ς **70** ουν] δε ς **71** μαρτυριας] μαρτυρων 118 εκ] απο ς om του 118

1 ηγαγεν ς **2** ηρξαντο 131 ς ευρομεν 131 ς διαστρεφοντα]+το εθνος 209 ς, +το εθνος ημων 118 131 Καισαρι] pr και κωλυοντα 118 131 209 ς **3** αποκριθεις αυτω εφη ς

5 Οἱ δὲ ἐπίσχυον λέγοντες ὅτι Ἀνασείει τὸν λαόν, διδάσκων καθ' τδ ι
6 ὅλης τῆς Ἰουδαίας, ἀρξάμενος ἀπὸ τῆς Γαλιλαίας ἕως ὧδε. Πιλάτος
7 δὲ ἀκούσας Γαλιλαίαν ἐπηρώτησεν εἰ ὁ ἄνθρωπος Γαλιλαῖός ἐστι· καὶ
ἐπιγνοὺς ὅτι ἐκ τῆς ἐξουσίας Ἡρώδου ἐστίν, ἀνέπεμψεν αὐτὸν πρὸς
Ἡρώδην, ὄντα καὶ αὐτὸν ἐν Ἱεροσολύμοις ἐν ταῖς ἡμέραις ταύταις.
8 ὁ δὲ Ἡρώδης ἰδὼν τὸν Ἰησοῦν ἐχάρη λίαν· ἦν γὰρ θέλων ἐξ ἱκανοῦ
χρόνου ἰδεῖν αὐτόν, διὰ τὸ ἀκούειν περὶ αὐτοῦ, καὶ ἤλπιζέ τι σημεῖον
9 ἰδεῖν ὑπ' αὐτοῦ γινόμενον. ἐπηρώτα δὲ αὐτὸν ἐν λόγοις ἱκανοῖς· αὐτὸς
10 δὲ οὐδὲν ἀπεκρίνατο αὐτῷ. εἱστήκεισαν δὲ οἱ ἀρχιερεῖς καὶ οἱ γραμ- τε β
11 ματεῖς εὐτόνως κατηγοροῦντες αὐτοῦ. ἐξουθενήσας δὲ αὐτὸν ὁ Ἡρώδης ΟΘ'
σὺν τοῖς στρατεύμασιν αὐτοῦ καὶ ἐμπαίξας, περιβαλὼν αὐτὸν ἐσθῆτα τς ι
12 λαμπράν, ἀνέπεμψεν αὐτὸν τῷ Πιλάτῳ. ἐγένετο δὲ φίλοι ὅ τε
Πιλάτος καὶ ὁ Ἡρώδης μετ' ἀλλήλων ἐν ἐκείνῃ τῇ ἡμέρᾳ· προϋ-
13 πῆρχον γὰρ ἐν ἔχθρᾳ ὄντες πρὸς ἑαυτούς. Πιλάτος δὲ συγκαλεσάμενος τζ θ
14 τοὺς ἀρχιερεῖς καὶ τοὺς ἄρχοντας καὶ τὸν λαὸν εἶπε πρὸς αὐτούς,
Προσηνέγκατέ μοι τὸν ἄνθρωπον τοῦτον ὡς διαστρέφοντα τὸν λαόν·
καὶ ἰδοὺ ἐνώπιον ὑμῶν ἀνακρίνας οὐθὲν εὗρον ἐν τῷ ἀνθρώπῳ τούτῳ
15 ὧν κατηγορεῖτε αὐτοῦ· ἀλλ' οὐδὲ Ἡρώδης· ἀνέπεμψα γὰρ ὑμᾶς πρὸς τη ι
16 αὐτόν, καὶ ἰδοὺ οὐδὲν ἄξιον θανάτου ἐστὶ πεπραγμένον αὐτῷ. παιδεύσας
17 οὖν αὐτὸν ἀπολύσω. ἀνάγκην δὲ εἶχεν ἀπολύειν αὐτοῖς κατὰ ἑορτὴν τθ β
18 ἕνα. ἀνέκραξαν δὲ παμπληθεὶ λέγοντες, Αἶρε τοῦτον, ἀπόλυσον δὲ τι
19 ἡμῖν τὸν Βαραββᾶν, ὅστις ἦν διὰ στάσιν τινὰ γενομένην ἐν τῇ α
20 πόλει καὶ φόβον βεβλημένος εἰς τὴν φυλακήν. πάλιν οὖν ὁ Πιλάτος τια α
21 προσεφώνησε, θέλων ἀπολῦσαι αὐτόν. οἱ δὲ ἐπεφώνουν, λέγοντες,
22 Σταύρωσον, σταύρωσον αὐτόν. ὁ δὲ τρίτον εἶπε πρὸς αὐτούς, Τί γὰρ τιβ θ
κακὸν ἐποίησεν οὗτος; οὐδὲν γὰρ αἴτιον θανάτου εὗρον ἐν αὐτῷ· παιδεύ-
23 σας οὖν αὐτὸν ἀπολύσω. οἱ δὲ ἐπέκειντο φωναῖς μεγάλαις αἰτούμενοι τιγ α
αὐτὸν σταυρωθῆναι· καὶ κατίσχυνον αἱ φωναὶ αὐτῶν καὶ τῶν ἀρχιε-
24 25 ρέων. ὁ δὲ Πιλάτος ἐπέκρινε γενέσθαι τὸ αἴτημα αὐτῶν· ἀπέλυσε δὲ τιδ α
αὐτοῖς τὸν Βαραββᾶν τὸν διὰ στάσιν καὶ φόβον βεβλημένον εἰς τὴν
φυλακήν, ὃν ᾐτοῦντο, τὸν δὲ Ἰησοῦν παρέδωκε τῷ θελήματι αὐτῶν.
26 Καὶ ὡς ἀπήγαγον αὐτόν, ἐπιλαβόμενοι Σίμωνός τινος Κυρηναίου τιε α

19 φοβον] cod. nunc habet φονον, β in ν per rasuram mutato

7 ταυταις ταις ημεραις ς 8 om χρονου ς ακουειν πολλα ς 118 131 209 ς
12 εγενοντο 118 131 ς εν αυτη τη ημερα μετ αλληλων ς 13 om τους 2° 131 14 αποστρεφοντα ς ιδου] + εγω ς ουθεν] ουδεν 118 209 ς τουτω] + αιτιον ς κατ αυτου ς 18 Βαραβαν 131 et sic infra 19 φονον 131 ς om την ς 20 αυτον] τον Ιησουν ς 22 om γαρ 2° ς 23 κατισχυον 118 209 ς, κατισχυων 131 24 om τον Βαραββαν ς 25 φονον 118 131 209 ς

ἐρχομένου ἀπ' ἀγροῦ, ἐπέθηκαν αὐτῷ τὸν σταυρὸν φέρειν ὄπισθεν
Π' αὐτοῦ. ἠκολούθει δὲ αὐτῷ πολὺ πλῆθος τοῦ λαοῦ, καὶ γυναικῶν αἳ 27
τις/ι καὶ ἐκόπτοντο καὶ ἐθρήνουν αὐτόν. στραφεὶς δὲ πρὸς αὐτὰς ὁ Ἰησοῦς 28
εἶπε, Θυγατέρες Ἱερουσαλήμ, μὴ κλαίετε ἐπ' ἐμέ, πλὴν ἐφ' ἑαυτὰς
κλαίετε καὶ ἐπὶ τὰ τέκνα ὑμῶν. ὅτι ἰδοὺ ἔρχονται ἡμέραι ἐν αἷς ἐροῦσι, 29
Μακάριαι αἱ στεῖραι καὶ αἱ κοιλίαι αἳ οὐκ ἐγέννησαν καὶ μαστοὶ οἳ
οὐκ ἐξέθρεψαν. τότε ἄρξονται λέγειν τοῖς ὄρεσι, Πέσετε ἐφ' ἡμᾶς, 30
καὶ τοῖς βουνοῖς, Καλύψατε ἡμᾶς· ὅτι, εἰ ἐν τῷ ὑγρῷ ξύλῳ ταῦτα 31
τιζ/α ποιοῦσιν, ἐν τῷ ξηρῷ τί γένηται; ἤγοντο δὲ καὶ ἕτεροι δύο κακοῦργοι 32
σὺν αὐτῷ ἀναιρεθῆναι.

τιη/α Καὶ ὅτε ἀπῆλθον ἐπὶ τὸν τόπον τὸν καλούμενον Κρανίον, ἐκεῖ 33
τιθ/α ἐσταύρωσαν αὐτὸν καὶ τοὺς κακούργους, ὃν μὲν ἐκ δεξιῶν, ὃν δὲ ἐξ
ἀριστερῶν. ὁ δὲ Ἰησοῦς ἔλεγε, Πάτερ, ἄφες αὐτοῖς· οὐ γὰρ οἴδασι 34
τκ/ι τί ποιοῦσι. διαμεριζόμενοι δὲ τὰ ἱμάτια αὐτοῦ ἔβαλλον κλήρους. καὶ 35
τκα/α εἱστήκει ὁ λαὸς θεωρῶν. ἐξεμυκτήριζον δὲ αὐτὸν οἱ ἄρχοντες σὺν αὐτοῖς,
τκβ/β λέγοντες, Ἄλλους ἔσωσε, σωσάτω ἑαυτόν, εἰ οὗτός ἐστιν ὁ Χριστὸς
τοῦ Θεοῦ ὁ ἐκλεκτός. ἐνέπαιζον δὲ αὐτῷ καὶ οἱ στρατιῶται, προσερ- 36
τκγ/β χόμενοι καὶ ὄξος προσφέροντες αὐτῷ καὶ λέγοντες, Σὺ εἶ ὁ βασιλεὺς 37
τκδ/α τῶν Ἰουδαίων, σῶσον σεαυτόν. ἦν δὲ ἐπιγραφὴ γεγραμμένη ἐπ' αὐτῷ 38
γράμμασιν Ἑλληνικοῖς καὶ Ῥωμαϊκοῖς καὶ Ἑβραϊκοῖς, Οὗτός ἐστιν
Ἰησοῦς ὁ βασιλεὺς τῶν Ἰουδαίων.

τκε/β Εἷς δὲ τῶν κρεμασθέντων κακούργων ἐβλασφήμει αὐτὸν λέγων, Εἰ 39
ΠΑ' σὺ εἶ ὁ Χριστός, σῶσον σεαυτὸν καὶ ἡμᾶς. ἀποκριθεὶς δὲ ὁ ἕτερος 40
τκς/ι ἐπετίμα αὐτῷ λέγων, Οὐδὲ φοβῇ σὺ τὸν Θεόν, ὅτι ἐν τῷ αὐτῷ κρίματι
εἶ; καὶ ἡμεῖς μὲν δικαίως· ἄξια γὰρ ὧν ἐπράξαμεν ἀπολαμβάνομεν· 41
οὗτος δὲ οὐδὲν ἄτοπον ἔπραξε. καὶ ἔλεγε τῷ Ἰησοῦ, Μνήσθητί μου, 42
Κύριε, ὅταν ἔλθῃς ἐν τῇ βασιλείᾳ σου. καὶ εἶπεν αὐτῷ ὁ Ἰησοῦς, 43
Ἀμὴν λέγω σοι, σήμερον μετ' ἐμοῦ ἔσῃ ἐν τῷ παραδείσῳ.

τκζ/β Ἦν δὲ ὡσεὶ ὥρα ἕκτη, καὶ σκότος ἐγένετο ἐφ' ὅλην τὴν γῆν ἕως 44
τκη/β ὥρας ἐνάτης· καὶ ἐσκοτίσθη ὁ ἥλιος, ἐσχίσθη δὲ τὸ καταπέτασμα 45
τοῦ ναοῦ μέσον· καὶ φωνήσας φωνῇ μεγάλῃ ὁ Ἰησοῦς εἶπε, Πάτερ, εἰς 46
τκθ/α χεῖράς σου παρατίθημι τὸ πνεῦμά μου· καὶ ταῦτα εἰπὼν ἐξέπνευσεν.

30 *ημας* 2°] 1* primum *υμας* scripsit sed ipse correxit

118 131 209 ς

26 *του ερχομενου* ς *αυτου*] *του Ιησου* ς **27** *ακολουθει* 118 **29** om *αι* 2° ς *μασθοι* 118 209 *εξεθρεψαν*] *εθρεψαν* 131, *εθηλασαν* ς **30** *αρχονται* 118 209 **34** *αυτου τα ιματια* 131 *εβαλον κληρον* ς **35** *δε*] + *και* ς om *αυτον* ς *Χριστος*] + *ο υιος* 131, + *ο* ς om *ο* 2° ς **37** *συ*] pr *ει* ς **38** *επιγραφη*] pr *και* ς, pr *και η* 131 om *Ιησους* ς **39** *αυτον*] *αυτω* 131 **44** *ενvατης* 118 209 ς **45** *και εσχισθη* 118 209 ς **46** *παραθησομαι* ς

47 ἰδὼν δὲ ὁ ἑκατοντάρχης τὸ γενόμενον ἐδόξασε τὸν Θεὸν λέγων, Ὄντως τλ β
48 ὁ ἄνθρωπος οὗτος δίκαιος ἦν. καὶ πάντες οἱ παραγενόμενοι ὄχλοι τλα
ἐπὶ τὴν θεωρίαν ταύτην, θεωροῦντες τὰ γενόμενα, τύπτοντες τὰ στήθη ι
49 ὑπέστρεφον. εἱστήκεισαν δὲ πάντες οἱ γνωστοὶ αὐτοῦ ἀπὸ μακρόθεν,
καὶ γυναῖκες αἱ συνακολουθήσασαι αὐτῷ ἀπὸ τῆς Γαλιλαίας, ὁρῶσαι
ταῦτα.
50 Καὶ ἰδοὺ ἀνὴρ ᾧ ὄνομα Ἰωσήφ, βουλευτὴς ὑπάρχων, ἀνὴρ ἀγαθὸς ΠΒ′
51 καὶ δίκαιος (οὗτος οὐκ ἦν συγκατατιθέμενος τῇ βουλῇ καὶ τῇ πράξει τλβ α
αὐτῶν), ἀπὸ Ἀριμαθαίας πόλεως τῶν Ἰουδαίων, ὃς προσεδέχετο καὶ
52 αὐτὸς τὴν βασιλείαν τοῦ Θεοῦ, οὗτος προσελθὼν τῷ Πιλάτῳ ᾐτήσατο
53 τὸ σῶμα τοῦ Ἰησοῦ. καὶ καθελὼν αὐτὸ ἐνετύλιξεν σινδόνι, καὶ τλγ α
54 ἔθηκεν ἐν μνήματι λαξευτῷ, οὗ οὐκ ἦν οὐδεὶς οὔπω κείμενος. καὶ τλδ
ἡμέρα ἦν παρασκευή, καὶ σάββατον ἐπέφωσκε. ι
55 Κατακολουθήσασαι δὲ αἱ γυναῖκες, αἵτινες ἦσαν συνεληλυθυῖαι αὐτῷ
ἐκ τῆς Γαλιλαίας, ἐθεάσαντο τὸ μνημεῖον, καὶ ὡς ἐτέθη τὸ σῶμα αὐτοῦ·
56 ὑποστρέψασαι δὲ ἡτοίμασαν ἀρώματα. καὶ τὸ μὲν σάββατον ἡσύ- τλε η
χασαν κατὰ τὴν ἐντολήν· XXIV. τῇ δὲ μιᾷ τῶν σαββάτων ὄρθρου τλϛ
βαθέος ἦλθον ἐπὶ τὸ μνῆμα φέρουσαι ἃ ἡτοίμασαν ἀρώματα, καί τινες α
σὺν αὐταῖς.
2 3 Εὗρον δὲ τὸν λίθον ἀποκεκυλισμένον ἀπὸ τοῦ μνημείου, εἰσελθοῦσαι
4 δὲ οὐχ εὗρον τὸ σῶμα τοῦ κυρίου Ἰησοῦ. καὶ ἐγένετο ἐν τῷ διαπορεῖν
αὐτὰς περὶ τούτου, καὶ ἰδοὺ ἄνδρες δύο ἐπέστησαν αὐταῖς ἐν ἐσθή-
5 σεσιν ἀστραπτούσαις. ἐμφόβων δὲ γενομένων αὐτῶν καὶ κλινουσῶν τὰ τλζ β
πρόσωπα εἰς τὴν γῆν, εἶπον πρὸς αὐτάς, Τί ζητεῖτε τὸν ζῶντα μετὰ
6 τῶν νεκρῶν; οὐκ ἔστιν ὧδε, ἀλλ' ἠγέρθη· μνήσθητε ὡς ἐλάλησεν ὑμῖν
7 ἔτι ὢν ἐν τῇ Γαλιλαίᾳ, λέγων ὅτι Δεῖ τὸν υἱὸν τοῦ ἀνθρώπου παρα-
δοθῆναι εἰς χεῖρας ἀνθρώπων ἁμαρτωλῶν καὶ σταυρωθῆναι καὶ τῇ
8 9 τρίτῃ ἡμέρᾳ ἀναστῆναι. καὶ ἐμνήσθησαν τῶν ῥημάτων αὐτοῦ, καὶ ὑπο- τλη β
στρέψασαι ἀπὸ τοῦ μνημείου ἀπήγγειλαν ταῦτα πάντα τοῖς ἕνδεκα καὶ
10 πᾶσι τοῖς λοιποῖς. ἦν δὲ ἡ Μαγδαληνὴ Μαριὰμ καὶ Ἰωάννα καὶ τλθ η
Μαριὰμ ἡ Ἰακώβου, καὶ αἱ λοιπαὶ σὺν αὐταῖς, ἔλεγον πρὸς τοὺς

47 *οντως*] *οντος* m. p., *οντως* corr. recent. **7** *χειρας*] *χηρας* cod.

47 *εκατονταρχος* ϛ **48** *συμπαραγενομενοι* ϛ *τυπτοντες*]+*εαυτων* ϛ **49** om *απο* ϛ **50** *ω ονομα*] *ονοματι* ϛ **51** *συγκατατεθειμενος* ϛ *ος*]+*και* ϛ **52** om *τω* 131 **53** *σινδονι*] pr *αυτο* ϛ *εθηκεν αυτο* ϛ *ουδεις ουπω*] *ουδεις ουδεπω* 131, *ουδεπω ουδεις* ϛ **54** *ην ημερα* 131 **55** *αι*] *και* ϛ **56** om *δε* 118 209 *αρωματα και μυρα* 118 209 ϛ **3** *και εισελθουσαι* 131 ϛ **4** *διαπορεισθαι* 118 ϛ om *και* 2° 131 *δυο ανδρες* ϛ **5** *το προσωπον* 118 131 209 ϛ **7** *παραδιδοναι* 131 **10** *ην*] *ησαν* ϛ *Μαρια* bis 118 131 ϛ, primo loco tantum 209 om *η* 2° 131 ϛ *ελεγον*] pr *αι* 131 ϛ 118 131 209 ϛ

ἀποστόλους ταῦτα. καὶ ἐφάνησαν αὐτῶν ὡσεὶ λῆρος τὰ ῥήματα αὐτῶν, 11
καὶ ἠπίστουν αὐταῖς. ὁ δὲ Πέτρος ἀναστὰς ἔδραμεν ἐπὶ τὸ μνημεῖον, 12
καὶ παρακύψας βλέπει τὰ ὀθόνια κείμενα μόνα· καὶ ἀπῆλθε πρὸς ἑαυτὸν
θαυμάζων τὸ γεγονός.

πγ' Καὶ ἰδοὺ δύο ἐξ αὐτῶν ἦσαν πορευόμενοι ἐν αὐτῇ τῇ ἡμέρᾳ 13
εἰς κώμην ἀπέχουσαν σταδίους ἑξήκοντα ἀπὸ Ἱερουσαλήμ, ᾗ ὄνομα
Ἐμμαούς· καὶ αὐτοὶ ὡμίλουν πρὸς ἀλλήλους περὶ πάντων τῶν συμ- 14
βεβηκότων τούτων. καὶ ἐγένετο ἐν τῷ ὁμιλεῖν αὐτοὺς καὶ συζητεῖν, 15
καὶ αὐτὸς ὁ Ἰησοῦς ἐγγίσας συνεπορεύετο αὐτοῖς· οἱ δὲ ὀφθαλμοὶ αὐτῶν 16
ἐκρατοῦντο τοῦ μὴ ἐπιγνῶναι αὐτόν. εἶπε δὲ πρὸς αὐτούς, Τίνες οἱ 17
λόγοι οὗτοι οὓς ἀντιβάλλετε πρὸς ἀλλήλους περιπατοῦντες, καί ἐστε
σκυθρωποί; ἀποκριθεὶς δὲ εἷς, ᾧ ὄνομα Κλεόπας, εἶπε πρὸς αὐτόν, 18
Σὺ μόνος παροικεῖς Ἱερουσαλὴμ καὶ οὐκ ἔγνως τὰ γενόμενα ἐν αὐτῇ
ἐν ταῖς ἡμέραις ταύταις; καὶ εἶπεν αὐτοῖς, Ποῖα; οἱ δὲ εἶπον, Τὰ 19
περὶ Ἰησοῦ τοῦ Ναζωραίου, ὃς ἐγένετο ἀνὴρ προφήτης, δυνατὸς ἐν ἔργῳ
καὶ λόγῳ ἐναντίον τοῦ Θεοῦ καὶ παντὸς τοῦ λαοῦ, ὅπως τε αὐτὸν 20
παρέδωκαν οἱ ἀρχιερεῖς καὶ οἱ ἄρχοντες ἡμῶν εἰς κρῖμα θανάτου,
καὶ ἐσταύρωσαν αὐτόν· ἡμεῖς δὲ ἠλπίζομεν ὅτι αὐτός ἐστιν ὁ μέλλων 21
λυτροῦσθαι τὸν Ἰσραήλ. ἀλλά γε καὶ σὺν πᾶσι τούτοις τρίτην ταύτην
ἡμέραν ἄγει ἀφ' οὗ ταῦτα ἐγένετο. ἀλλὰ καὶ γυναῖκές τινες ἐξ ἡμῶν 22
ἐξέστησαν ἡμᾶς, γενόμεναι ὀρθριναὶ ἐπὶ τὸ μνημεῖον· καὶ μὴ εὑροῦσαι 23
τὸ σῶμα αὐτοῦ ἦλθον λέγουσαι καὶ ὀπτασίαν ἀγγέλων ἑωρακέναι, οἳ
λέγουσιν αὐτὸν ζῆν. καὶ ἀπῆλθόν τινες τῶν σὺν ἡμῖν ἐπὶ τὸ μνη- 24
μεῖον, καὶ εὗρον οὕτως καθὼς καὶ αἱ γυναῖκες εἶπον, αὐτὸν δὲ οὐκ
εἶδον. καὶ αὐτὸς εἶπε πρὸς αὐτούς, Ὦ ἀνόητοι καὶ βραδεῖς τῇ καρδίᾳ 25
τοῦ πιστεύειν ἐπὶ πᾶσιν οἷς ἐλάλησαν οἱ προφῆται· οὐχὶ ταῦτα ἔδει 26
παθεῖν τὸν Χριστόν, καὶ εἰσελθεῖν εἰς τὴν δόξαν αὐτοῦ; καὶ ἀρξάμενος 27
ἀπὸ Μωσέως καὶ ἀπὸ πάντων τῶν προφητῶν διερμήνευεν αὐτοῖς τί
ἦν ἐν πάσαις ταῖς γραφαῖς τὰ περὶ αὐτοῦ. καὶ ἤγγισαν εἰς τὴν 28
κώμην οὗ ἐπορεύοντο· καὶ αὐτὸς προσεποιήσατο πορρωτέρω πορεύ-
εσθαι· καὶ παρεβιάσαντο αὐτὸν λέγοντες, Μεῖνον μεθ' ἡμῶν, ὅτι πρὸς 29
ἑσπέραν ἐστὶ καὶ κέκλικεν ἤδη ἡ ἡμέρα. καὶ εἰσῆλθε τοῦ μεῖναι
σὺν αὐτοῖς. καὶ ἐγένετο ἐν τῷ κατακλιθῆναι αὐτὸν μετ' αὐτῶν, λαβὼν 30

23 *αυτου*] *υ* in rasura sed a prima manu

118 131 209 ϛ **11** *ενωπιον αυτων* 118 131 ϛ **18** *ο εις* 118 ϛ *εν Ιερουσαλημ* 131 ϛ **19** *ειπον αυτω* 131 ϛ **20** *παρεδωκαν αυτον* 118 131 209 ϛ om *εις κριμα θανατου* 131 **21** om *και* 118 131 209 ϛ *αγει σημερον* 118 131 209 ϛ **22** *ορθριαι* 118 131 209 ϛ *ζην*] *ζη* 131, pr spat. 118 **24** *ουτω* ϛ **25** *του*] + *μη* suprascr. 209 **27** *διηρμηνευεν* ϛ om *τι ην* 118 131 209 ϛ *εαυτου* 131 ϛ **28** *προσεποιειτο* 118 131 209 ϛ **29** *κεκληκεν* 131 om *ηδη* 118 209 ϛ

31 τὸν ἄρτον εὐλόγησε, καὶ κλάσας ἐπεδίδου αὐτοῖς. αὐτῶν δὲ διενοί-
χθησαν οἱ ὀφθαλμοί, καὶ ἐπέγνωσαν αὐτόν· καὶ αὐτὸς ἄφαντος ἐγένετο
32 ἀπ᾽ αὐτῶν. καὶ εἶπον πρὸς ἀλλήλους, Οὐχὶ ἡ καρδία ἡμῶν καιομένη
ἦν ἐν ἡμῖν, ὡς ἐλάλει ἡμῖν ἐν τῇ ὁδῷ, καὶ ὡς διήνοιγεν ἡμῖν τὰς
33 γραφάς; καὶ ἀναστάντες αὐτῇ τῇ ὥρᾳ ὑπέστρεψαν εἰς Ἱερουσαλήμ,
34 καὶ εὗρον συνηθροισμένους τοὺς ἕνδεκα καὶ τοὺς σὺν αὐτοῖς, λέγοντας
35 ὅτι Ὄντως ἠγέρθη ὁ Κύριος, καὶ ὤφθη Σίμωνι. καὶ αὐτοὶ ἐξηγοῦντο
τὰ ἐν τῇ ὁδῷ, καὶ ὡς ἐγνώσθη αὐτοῖς ἐν τῇ κλάσει τοῦ ἄρτου.
36 Ταῦτα δὲ αὐτῶν λαλούντων αὐτὸς ὁ Ἰησοῦς ἔστη ἐν μέσῳ αὐτῶν, τμ θ
37 καὶ λέγει αὐτοῖς, Εἰρήνη ὑμῖν. πτοηθέντες δὲ καὶ ἔντρομοι γενόμενοι
38 ἐδόκουν πνεῦμα θεωρεῖν. καὶ εἶπεν αὐτοῖς, Τί τεταραγμένοι ἐστέ; καὶ
39 διατί διαλογισμοὶ ἀναβαίνουσιν ἐν ταῖς καρδίαις ὑμῶν; ἴδετε τὰς χεῖράς
μου καὶ τοὺς πόδας, ὅτι αὐτὸς ἐγώ εἰμι· ψηλαφήσατέ με καὶ ἴδετε·
ὅτι πνεῦμα σάρκα καὶ ὀστέα οὐκ ἔχει, καθὼς ἐμὲ θεωρεῖτε ἔχοντα.
40 41 καὶ τοῦτο εἰπὼν ἔδειξεν αὐτοῖς τὰς χεῖρας καὶ τοὺς πόδας. ἔτι δὲ τμα θ
ἀπιστούντων αὐτῶν ἀπὸ τῆς χαρᾶς καὶ θαυμαζόντων, εἶπεν αὐτοῖς,
42 Ἔχετέ τι βρώσιμον ἐνθάδε; οἱ δὲ ἐπέδωκαν αὐτῷ ἰχθύος ὀπτοῦ μέρος
43 44 καὶ ἀπὸ μελισσίου κηρίου· καὶ λαβὼν ἐνώπιον αὐτῶν ἔφαγεν. εἶπε τμβ ι
δὲ αὐτοῖς, Οὗτοι οἱ λόγοι, οὓς ἐλάλησα πρὸς ὑμᾶς ἔτι ὢν σὺν ὑμῖν,
ὅτι δεῖ πληρωθῆναι πάντα τὰ γεγραμμένα ἐν τῷ νόμῳ Μωσέως καὶ
45 προφήταις περὶ ἐμοῦ. τότε διήνοιξεν αὐτῶν τὸν νοῦν τοῦ συνιέναι
46 τὰς γραφάς· καὶ εἶπεν αὐτοῖς ὅτι Οὕτως γέγραπται, καὶ οὕτως ἔδει
47 παθεῖν τὸν Χριστὸν καὶ ἀναστῆναι ἐκ νεκρῶν τῇ τρίτῃ ἡμέρᾳ, καὶ
κηρυχθῆναι ἐπὶ τῷ ὀνόματι αὐτοῦ μετάνοιαν καὶ ἄφεσιν ἁμαρτιῶν εἰς
48 πάντα τὰ ἔθνη, ἀρξάμενον ἀπὸ Ἱερουσαλήμ. ὑμεῖς δέ ἐστε μάρτυρες
49 τούτων. καὶ ἐγὼ ἰδοὺ ἀποστέλλω τὴν ἐπαγγελίαν τοῦ πατρός μου
ἐφ᾽ ὑμᾶς· ὑμεῖς δὲ καθίσατε ἐν τῇ πόλει Ἱηρουσαλήμ, ἕως ὅτου ἐνδύ-
σασθε δύναμιν ἐξ ὕψους.
50 Ἐξήγαγε δὲ αὐτοὺς ἕως πρὸς Βηθανίαν· καὶ ἐπάρας τὰς χεῖρας
51 αὐτοῦ εὐλόγησεν αὐτούς. καὶ ἐγένετο ἐν τῷ εὐλογεῖν αὐτὸν αὐτούς,
52 διέστη ἀπ᾽ αὐτῶν καὶ ἀνεφέρετο εἰς τὸν οὐρανόν. καὶ αὐτοὶ προσκυνή-
53 σαντες αὐτὸν ὑπέστρεψαν εἰς Ἱερουσαλὴμ μετὰ χαρᾶς μεγάλης· καὶ ἦσαν
διαπαντὸς ἐν τῷ ἱερῷ, αἰνοῦντες καὶ εὐλογοῦντες τὸν Θεόν.

30 ηυλογησε 131 **34** οντως post Κυριος 118 209 ς **37** εντρομοι] εμφοβοι 131 ς 118 131 209 ς **39** ποδας μου 118 131 209 ς **40** επεδειξεν ς **42** κηριουν 131 sed ν punctis damnatum est **44** προφηταις] + και ψαλμοις 118 131 209 ς **46** ουτω ς **47** επι] εν 118 sed ν delevit et πι imperfecte scripsit **49** ιδου εγω 118 131 209 ς ου ενδυσησθε 118 131 209 ς **50** εως] pr εξω 118 131 209 ς προς] εις 118 131 209 ς **53** Θεον] + αμην 118 131 209 ς ad finem evangelii haec addita sunt:—※ ευαγγελιον κατα

Λουκαν εξεδοθη μετα χρονους ιε του Χριστου αναληψεως δια στιχων ,βω κεφαλαιων τμβ 118², *ιστεον οτι μετα χρονους δεκαπεντε της του κυριου ημων και θεου Ιησου Χριστου εκ νεκρων αναστασεως και εις ουρανους αναληψεως εγραφη το κατα Λουκαν αγιον ευαγγελιον* 209², *στιχοι ,βω.* ✠ *τελος του κατα Λουκαν ευαγγελιον* 131 qui post *κεφαλαια* ad Johannis evangelium addidit ·:· *το κατα Λουκαν ευαγγελιον εξεδοθη μετα χρονους ιε της του Χριστου αναληψεως* et hos iambos

> *Λουκας ο Χριστου φερτατος μυστογραφος*
> *το θειον ευαγγελιον αυ εσκεμμενως*
> *γραψας βροτοις ωπασεν ως μεγα κλεος*

post quos ima pagina 131² (eodem fere tempore) addidit ✝*επι ετει ,ϛωια ινδικτ. α εγινετο χειμεριος καιρος πανυ και εχιωνησεν ολος ομωρεας ιουμαριω εις την ζ και επεκρατησεν ο χιων ημερας β και μετα ταυτα επεσεν λαυρος νετος και εγινετο θνησι απειρος εις τα κτηνι* :—

ΕΥΑΓΓΕΛΙΟΝ ΚΑΤΑ ΙΩΑΝΝΗΝ

I. Ἐν ἀρχῇ ἦν ὁ λόγος, καὶ ὁ λόγος ἦν πρὸς τὸν Θεόν, καὶ α
2 3 Θεὸς ἦν ὁ λόγος. οὗτος ἦν ἐν ἀρχῇ πρὸς τὸν Θεόν. πάντα δι' αὐτοῦ γ
4 ἐγένετο, καὶ χωρὶς αὐτοῦ ἐγένετο οὐδέν, ὃ γέγονεν. ἐν αὐτῷ ζωὴ ἦν,
5 καὶ ἡ ζωὴ ἦν τὸ φῶς τῶν ἀνθρώπων· καὶ τὸ φῶς ἐν τῇ σκοτίᾳ φαίνει,
καὶ ἡ σκοτία αὐτὸ οὐ κατέλαβεν.
6 Ἐγένετο ἄνθρωπος ἀπεσταλμένος παρὰ Θεοῦ, ὄνομα αὐτῷ Ἰωάννης. β
7 οὗτος ἦλθεν εἰς μαρτυρίαν, ἵνα μαρτυρήσῃ περὶ τοῦ φωτός, ἵνα πάντες γ
8 πιστεύσωσι δι' αὐτοῦ. οὐκ ἦν ἐκεῖνος τὸ φῶς, ἀλλ' ἵνα μαρτυρήσῃ
9 περὶ τοῦ φωτός. ἦν τὸ φῶς τὸ ἀληθινόν, ὃ φωτίζει πάντα ἄνθρωπον γ
10 ἐρχόμενον εἰς τὸν κόσμον. ἐν τῷ κόσμῳ ἦν, καὶ ὁ κόσμος δι' αὐτοῦ γ
11 ἐγένετο, καὶ ὁ κόσμος αὐτὸν οὐκ ἔγνω. εἰς τὰ ἴδια ἦλθε, καὶ οἱ ἴδιοι δ
12 αὐτὸν οὐ παρέλαβον. ὅσοι δὲ ἔλαβον αὐτόν, ἔδωκεν αὐτοῖς ἐξουσίαν ι
13 τέκνα Θεοῦ γενέσθαι, τοῖς πιστεύουσιν εἰς τὸ ὄνομα αὐτοῦ· οἳ οὐκ ἐξ
αἱμάτων, οὐδὲ ἐκ θελήματος σαρκός, οὐδὲ ἐκ θελήματος ἀνδρός, ἀλλ' ἐκ
Θεοῦ ἐγεννήθησαν.
14 Καὶ ὁ λόγος σὰρξ ἐγένετο καὶ ἐσκήνωσεν ἐν ἡμῖν (καὶ ἐθεασάμεθα ε
τὴν δόξαν αὐτοῦ, δόξαν ὡς μονογενοῦς παρὰ πατρός), πλήρης χάριτος γ
καὶ ἀληθείας.
15 Ἰωάννης μαρτυρεῖ περὶ αὐτοῦ καὶ κέκραγε λέγων, Οὗτος ἦν ὃν εἶπον, ς
Ὁ ὀπίσω μου ἐρχόμενος ἔμπροσθέν μου γέγονεν· ὅτι πρῶτός μου ἦν. α
16 καὶ ἐκ τοῦ πληρώματος αὐτοῦ ἡμεῖς πάντες ἐλάβομεν καὶ χάριν ἀντὶ ζ
17 χάριτος· ὅτι ὁ νόμος διὰ Μωσέως ἐδόθη, ἡ χάρις καὶ ἡ ἀλήθεια διὰ ι
18 Ἰησοῦ Χριστοῦ ἐγένετο. Θεὸν οὐδεὶς ἑώρακε πώποτε· ὁ μονογενὴς υἱὸς η
19 ὁ ὢν εἰς τὸν κόλπον τοῦ πατρός, ἐκεῖνος ἐξηγήσατο. καὶ αὕτη ἐστὶν γ θ
ἡ μαρτυρία Ἰωάννου, ὅτε ἀπέστειλαν οἱ Ἰουδαῖοι ἐξ Ἱεροσολύμων ι

10 αυτον] αυτου cod.

Titul. το κατα Ιωαννην αγιον ευαγγελιον 209 ς, om 118 — 118 209 ς
2 εν] ε spat. rel. in quo rasura 118 — 3 ουδεν] ουδε εν 118 209 ς
19 του Ιωαννου ς

ἱερεῖς καὶ Λευΐτας, ἵνα ἐρωτήσωσιν αὐτόν, Σὺ τίς εἶ; καὶ ὡμολόγησε 20
καὶ οὐκ ἠρνήσατο· ὡμολόγησεν ὅτι Οὐκ εἰμὶ ἐγὼ ὁ Χριστός. καὶ 21
ἠρώτησαν αὐτόν, Τί οὖν; Ἠλίας εἶ σύ; καὶ λέγει, Οὐκ εἰμί. Ὁ
προφήτης εἶ σύ; ἀπεκρίθη, Οὔ. εἶπον οὖν, Τίς εἶ; ἵνα ἀπόκρισιν 22
ι/α δῶμεν τοῖς πέμψασιν ἡμᾶς· τί λέγεις περὶ σεαυτοῦ; ἔφη, Ἐγὼ φωνὴ 23
βοῶντος ἐν τῇ ἐρήμῳ, Εὐθύνατε τὴν ὁδὸν Κυρίου, καθὼς εἶπεν Ἡσαΐας
ια/ι ὁ προφήτης. καὶ οἱ ἀπεσταλμένοι ἦσαν ἐκ τῶν Φαρισαίων· καὶ ἠρώ- 24 25
τησαν αὐτὸν καὶ εἶπον αὐτῷ, Τί οὖν βαπτίζεις, εἰ σὺ οὐκ εἶ ὁ Χριστός,
ιβ/α οὐδὲ Ἠλίας, οὐδὲ ὁ προφήτης; ἀπεκρίθη αὐτοῖς ὁ Ἰωάννης, Ἐγὼ 26
βαπτίζω ἐν ὕδατι· μέσος δὲ ὑμῶν στήκει ὃν ὑμεῖς οὐκ οἴδατε· ὁ ὀπίσω 27
μου ἐρχόμενος, οὗ ἐγὼ οὐκ εἰμὶ ἄξιος ἵνα λύσω αὐτοῦ τὸν ἱμάντα τοῦ
ιγ/ι ὑποδήματος. ταῦτα ἐν Βηθαβαρᾳ̣ ἐγένετο πέραν τοῦ Ἰορδάνου, ὅπου 28
ἦν Ἰωάννης βαπτίζων.

Τῇ ἐπαύριον βλέπει τὸν Ἰησοῦν ἐρχόμενον πρὸς αὐτόν, καὶ λέγει, 29
ιδ/α Ἴδε ὁ ἀμνὸς τοῦ Θεοῦ ὁ αἴρων τὴν ἁμαρτίαν τοῦ κόσμου. οὗτός ἐστι 30
περὶ οὗ ἐγὼ εἶπον, Ὀπίσω μου ἔρχεται ἀνήρ, ὃς ἔμπροσθέν μου γέγονεν,
ὅτι πρῶτός μου ἦν. κἀγὼ οὐκ ᾔδειν αὐτόν· ἀλλ' ἵνα φανερωθῇ τῷ 31
ιε/α Ἰσραήλ, διὰ τοῦτο ἦλθον ἐγὼ ἐν ὕδατι βαπτίζων. καὶ ἐμαρτύρησεν 32
Ἰωάννης λέγων ὅτι Τεθέαμαι τὸ Πνεῦμα καταβαῖνον ὡσεὶ περιστερὰν
ἐκ τοῦ οὐρανοῦ, καὶ ἔμεινεν ἐπ' αὐτόν. κἀγὼ οὐκ ᾔδειν αὐτόν· ἀλλ' ὁ 33
πέμψας με βαπτίζειν ἐν τῷ ὕδατι, ἐκεῖνός μοι εἶπεν, Ἐφ' ὃν ἂν ἴδῃς
τὸ Πνεῦμα καταβαῖνον καὶ μένον ἐπ' αὐτόν, οὗτός ἐστιν ὁ βαπτίζων
ἐν Πνεύματι Ἁγίῳ. κἀγὼ ἑώρακα, καὶ μεμαρτύρηκα ὅτι οὗτός ἐστιν 34
ὁ υἱὸς τοῦ Θεοῦ.

ις/ι Τῇ ἐπαύριον πάλιν εἱστήκει ὁ Ἰωάννης καὶ ἐκ τῶν μαθητῶν αὐτοῦ 35
δύο· καὶ ἐμβλέψας τῷ Ἰησοῦ περιπατοῦντι λέγει, Ἴδε ὁ ἀμνὸς τοῦ 36
Θεοῦ. ἤκουσαν αὐτοῦ οἱ δύο μαθηταὶ λαλοῦντος, καὶ ἠκολούθησαν 37
τῷ Ἰησοῦ. στραφεὶς δὲ ὁ Ἰησοῦς καὶ θεασάμενος αὐτοὺς ἀκολου- 38
θοῦντας λέγει αὐτοῖς, Τί ζητεῖτε; οἱ δὲ εἶπον αὐτῷ, Ῥαββί, (ὃ 39
ἑρμηνεύεται Διδάσκαλε) ποῦ μένεις; λέγει αὐτοῖς, Ἔρχεσθε καὶ 40
ὄψεσθε. ἦλθον καὶ εἶδον ποῦ μένει· καὶ παρ' αὐτῷ ἔμειναν τὴν ἡμέραν
ἐκείνην· ὥρα ἦν ὡς δεκάτη. ἦν Ἀνδρέας ὁ ἀδελφὸς Σίμωνος Πέτρου 41

28 Βηθαβαρᾳ̣] θ in rasura esse videtur

118 209 ς **20** και ωμολογησεν ς **21** και απεκριθη ς **22** ουν]+αυτω 118 ς **25** ουδε bis] ουτε bis ς **26** Ιωαννης]+λεγων 118 ς στηκει] εστηκεν 118 209 ς **27** ο] pr αυτος εστιν 118 ς ερχομενος]+ος εμπροθεν μου γεγονεν 118 ς **28** Βηθανια 118 209 **29** βλεπει]+ο Ιωαννης ς **31** τω υδατι ς **32** εκ του] εξ ς **33** om τω ς **37** και ηκουσαν 118 209 ς **39** ραββει 118 sed ραββι 118[2] ερμηνευεται] λεγεται ερμηνευομενον ς **40** οψεσθε] ιδετε ς ωρα δε ς

εἷς ἐκ τῶν δύο τῶν ἀκουσάντων παρὰ Ἰωάννου καὶ ἀκολουθησάντων
42 αὐτῷ. εὑρίσκει οὗτος πρῶτον τὸν ἀδελφὸν τὸν ἴδιον Σίμωνα, καὶ λέγει ιζ
αὐτῷ, Εὑρήκαμεν τὸν Μεσσίαν (ὅ ἐστι μεθερμηνευόμενον Χριστός). α
43 οὗτος ἤγαγεν αὐτὸν πρὸς τὸν Ἰησοῦν. ἐμβλέψας αὐτῷ ὁ Ἰησοῦς
εἶπε, Σὺ εἶ Σίμων υἱὸς Ἰωνᾶ· σὺ κληθήσῃ Κηφᾶς· ὃ ἑρμηνεύεται
Πέτρος.
44 Τῇ ἐπαύριον ἠθέλησεν ἐξελθεῖν εἰς τὴν Γαλιλαίαν· καὶ εὑρίσκει ιη
45 Φίλιππον καὶ λέγει αὐτῷ ὁ Ἰησοῦς, Ἀκολούθει μοι. ἦν δὲ ὁ Φίλιππος ι
46 ἀπὸ Βηθσαϊδά, ἐκ τῆς πόλεως Ἀνδρέου καὶ Πέτρου. εὑρίσκει Φίλιππος
τὸν Ναθαναὴλ καὶ λέγει αὐτῷ, Ὃν ἔγραψε Μωσῆς ἐν τῷ νόμῳ καὶ οἱ
προφῆται, εὑρήκαμεν, Ἰησοῦν τὸν υἱὸν τοῦ Ἰωσὴφ τὸν ἀπὸ Ναζαρέθ.
47 καὶ εἶπεν αὐτῷ Ναθαναήλ, Ἐκ Ναζαρὲθ δύναταί τι ἀγαθὸν εἶναι;
48 λέγει αὐτῷ Φίλιππος, Ἔρχου καὶ ἴδε. εἶδεν ὁ Ἰησοῦς τὸν Ναθαναὴλ
ἐρχόμενον πρὸς αὐτόν, καὶ λέγει περὶ αὐτοῦ, Ἴδε ἀληθῶς Ἰσραηλίτης,
49 ἐν ᾧ δόλος οὐκ ἔστι. λέγει αὐτῷ Ναθαναήλ, Πόθεν με γινώσκεις;
ἀπεκρίθη ὁ Ἰησοῦς καὶ εἶπεν αὐτῷ, Πρὸ τοῦ σε Φίλιππον φωνῆσαι,
50 ὄντα ὑπὸ τὴν συκῆν εἶδόν σε. ἀπεκρίθη Ναθαναὴλ καὶ λέγει αὐτῷ,
Ῥαββί, σὺ εἶ ὁ υἱὸς τοῦ Θεοῦ, σὺ βασιλεὺς εἶ τοῦ Ἰσραήλ.
51 ἀπεκρίθη Ἰησοῦς καὶ εἶπεν αὐτῷ, Ὅτι εἶπόν σοι, Εἶδόν σε ὑποκάτω
52 τῆς συκῆς, πιστεύεις; μείζω τούτων ὄψει. καὶ λέγει αὐτῷ, Ἀμὴν
ἀμὴν λέγω ὑμῖν, ἀπ' ἄρτι ὄψεσθε τὸν οὐρανὸν ἀνεῳγότα, καὶ τοὺς
ἀγγέλους τοῦ Θεοῦ ἀναβαίνοντας καὶ καταβαίνοντας ἐπὶ τὸν υἱὸν τοῦ
ἀνθρώπου.

II. Καὶ τῇ ἡμέρᾳ τῇ τρίτῃ γάμος ἐγένετο ἐν Κανᾷ τῆς Γαλιλαίας· Α'
2 καὶ ἦν ἡ μήτηρ τοῦ Ἰησοῦ ἐκεῖ· ἐκλήθη δὲ καὶ ὁ Ἰησοῦς καὶ οἱ
3 μαθηταὶ αὐτοῦ εἰς τὸν γάμον. καὶ ὑστερήσαντος οἴνου λέγει ἡ μήτηρ
4 τοῦ Ἰησοῦ πρὸς αὐτόν, Οἶνον οὐκ ἔχουσι. λέγει αὐτῇ ὁ Ἰησοῦς, Τί
5 ἐμοὶ καὶ σοί, γύναι; οὔπω ἥκει ἡ ὥρα μου. λέγει ἡ μήτηρ αὐτοῦ
6 τοῖς διακόνοις, Ὅ τι ἐὰν λέγῃ ὑμῖν, ποιήσατε. ἦσαν δὲ ἐκεῖ ὑδρίαι
λίθιναι ἓξ κείμεναι κατὰ τὸν καθαρισμὸν τῶν Ἰουδαίων, χωροῦσαι ἀνὰ
7 μετρητὰς δύο ἢ τρεῖς. λέγει αὐτοῖς ὁ Ἰησοῦς, Γεμίσατε τὰς ὑδρίας
8 ὕδατος. καὶ ἐγέμισαν αὐτὰς ἕως ἄνω. καὶ λέγει αὐτοῖς, Ἀντλήσατε
9 νῦν καὶ φέρετε τῷ ἀρχιτρικλίνῳ. οἱ δὲ ἤνεγκαν. ὡς δὲ ἐγεύσατο ὁ

6 *μετριτας* cod.

42 *πρωτον*] *πρωτ°ν* 118 (*πρωτ°* semper significat *πρωτος*), *πρωτος* ς 118 209
ο Χριστος ς **43** *ουτος*] *και* 118 ς *εμβλεψας δε* ς *ο υιος* 118 ς ς
44 *ηθελησεν*] + *ο Ιησους* ς om *ο Ιησους* ς **46** *Ναζαρετ* 118 ς
47 *Ναζαρετ* 118 209 ς **50** *ει ο βασιλευς* 118 209 ς
5 *εαν*] *αν* ς **9** *οι δε*] *και* ς

ἀρχιτρίκλινος τὸ ὕδωρ οἶνον γεγενημένον, καὶ οὐκ ᾔδει πόθεν ἐστίν
(οἱ δὲ διάκονοι ᾔδεισαν οἱ ἠντληκότες τὸ ὕδωρ), φωνεῖ τὸν νυμφίον ὁ
ἀρχιτρίκλινος καὶ λέγει αὐτῷ, Πᾶς ἄνθρωπος πρῶτον τὸν καλὸν οἶνον 10
τίθησι, καὶ ὅταν μεθυσθῶσι, τότε τὸν ἐλάσσω· σὺ τετήρηκας τὸν καλὸν
οἶνον ἕως ἄρτι. ταύτην ἐποίησεν ἀρχὴν τῶν σημείων ὁ Ἰησοῦς ἐν 11
Κανᾷ τῆς Γαλιλαίας, καὶ ἐφανέρωσε τὴν δόξαν αὐτοῦ· καὶ ἐπίστευσαν
εἰς αὐτὸν οἱ μαθηταὶ αὐτοῦ.

ιθ Μετὰ τοῦτο κατέβη ὁ Ἰησοῦς εἰς Καπερναοὺμ αὐτὸς καὶ ἡ μήτηρ 12
ς αὐτοῦ καὶ οἱ ἀδελφοὶ αὐτοῦ καὶ οἱ μαθηταὶ αὐτοῦ· καὶ ἐκεῖ ἔμεινεν
κ α οὐ πολλὰς ἡμέρας. καὶ ἐγγὺς ἦν τὸ πάσχα τῶν Ἰουδαίων, καὶ ἀνέβη 13
Β′ εἰς Ἱεροσόλυμα ὁ Ἰησοῦς. καὶ εὗρεν ἐν τῷ ἱερῷ τοὺς πωλοῦντας βόας 14
κα α καὶ πρόβατα καὶ περιστεράς, καὶ τοὺς κερματιστὰς καθημένους. καὶ 15
ποιήσας ὡς φραγέλλιον ἐκ σχοινίων πάντας ἐξέβαλεν ἐκ τοῦ ἱεροῦ, τά
τε πρόβατα καὶ τοὺς βόας· καὶ τῶν κολλυβιστῶν τὸ κέρμα ἐξέχεε,
καὶ τὰς τραπέζας ἀνέστρεψε· καὶ τοῖς τὰς περιστερὰς πωλοῦσιν εἶπεν, 16
Ἄρατε ταῦτα ἐντεῦθεν· καὶ μὴ ποιεῖτε τὸν οἶκον τοῦ πατρός μου οἶκον
κβ ι ἐμπορίου. ἐμνήσθησαν δὲ οἱ μαθηταὶ αὐτοῦ ὅτι γεγραμμένον ἐστίν, 17
Ὁ ζῆλος τοῦ οἴκου σου καταφάγεταί με. ἀπεκρίθησαν οὖν οἱ 18
κγ δ Ἰουδαῖοι καὶ εἶπον αὐτῷ, Τί σημεῖον δεικνύεις ἡμῖν, ὅτι ταῦτα ποιεῖς;
κδ ι ἀπεκρίθη ὁ Ἰησοῦς καὶ εἶπεν αὐτοῖς, Λύσατε τὸν ναὸν τοῦτον, καὶ ἐν 19
τρισὶν ἡμέραις ἐγερῶ αὐτόν. εἶπον οὖν οἱ Ἰουδαῖοι, Τεσσαράκοντα καὶ 20
ἓξ ἔτεσιν ᾠκοδομήθη ὁ ναὸς οὗτος, καὶ σὺ ἐν τρισὶν ἡμέραις ἐγερεῖς
αὐτόν; ἐκεῖνος δὲ ἔλεγε περὶ τοῦ ναοῦ τοῦ σώματος αὐτοῦ. ὅτε οὖν 21 22
ἠγέρθη ἐν νεκρῶν, ἐμνήσθησαν οἱ μαθηταὶ αὐτοῦ ὅτι τοῦτο ἔλεγεν,
καὶ ἐπίστευσαν τῇ γραφῇ καὶ τῷ λόγῳ ᾧ εἶπεν ὁ Ἰησοῦς. ὡς δὲ ἦν 23
ἐν τοῖς Ἱεροσολύμοις ἐν τῷ πάσχα, ἐν τῇ ἑορτῇ, πολλοὶ ἐπίστευσαν
εἰς τὸ ὄνομα αὐτοῦ, θεωροῦντες τὰ σημεῖα ἃ ἐποίει. αὐτὸς δὲ ὁ 24
Ἰησοῦς οὐκ ἐπίστευεν ἑαυτὸν αὐτοῖς, διὰ τὸ αὐτὸν γινώσκειν πάντας,
καὶ ὅτι οὐ χρείαν εἶχεν ἵνα τις μαρτυρήσῃ περὶ τοῦ ἀνθρώπου· αὐτὸς 25
γὰρ ἐγίνωσκε τί ἦν ἐν τῷ ἀνθρώπῳ.

Γ′ III. Ἦν δὲ ἄνθρωπος ἐκ τῶν Φαρισαίων, Νικόδημος ὄνομα αὐτῷ,
ἄρχων τῶν Ἰουδαίων. οὗτος ἦλθε πρὸς αὐτὸν νυκτός, καὶ εἶπεν αὐτῷ, 2
Ῥαββί, οἴδαμεν ὅτι ἀπὸ Θεοῦ ἐλήλυθας διδάσκαλος· οὐδεὶς γὰρ ταῦτα
τὰ σημεῖα δύναται ποιῆσαι, ἐὰν μὴ ᾖ ὁ Θεὸς μετ᾽ αὐτοῦ. ἀπεκρίθη 3
Ἰησοῦς καὶ εἶπεν αὐτῷ, Ἀμὴν ἀμὴν λέγω σοι, ἐὰν μή τις γεννηθῇ

118 209 ς 11 την αρχην 118 209 ς 12 om ο Ιησους 118 209 ς εμειναν ς
15 om ως ς εξεχεε το κερμα ς 16 om και 2° ς 17 κατεφαγε ς
22 ελεγεν αυτοις ς 23 om τοις ς θεωρουντες] + αυτου ς
2 αυτον] τον Ιησουν ς ποιησαι] ποιειν α συ ποιεις ς 3 ο Ιησους
118 209 ς

4 ἄνωθεν, οὐ δύναται ἰδεῖν τὴν βασιλείαν τοῦ Θεοῦ. λέγει πρὸς αὐτὸν
ὁ Νικόδημος, Πῶς δύναται ἄνθρωπος γεννηθῆναι γέρων ὤν; μὴ δύναται
εἰς τὴν κοιλίαν τῆς μητρὸς αὐτοῦ δεύτερον εἰσελθεῖν καὶ γεννηθῆναι;
5 ἀπεκρίθη Ἰησοῦς, Ἀμὴν ἀμὴν λέγω σοι, ἐὰν μή τις γεννηθῇ ἐξ ὕδατος
6 καὶ Πνεύματος, οὐ δύναται εἰσελθεῖν εἰς τὴν βασιλείαν τοῦ Θεοῦ. τὸ
γεγεννημένον ἐκ τῆς σαρκὸς σάρξ ἐστι· καὶ τὸ γεγεννημένον ἐκ τοῦ
7 πνεύματος πνεῦμά ἐστι. μὴ θαυμάσῃς ὅτι εἶπόν σοι, Δεῖ ὑμᾶς γεν-
8 νηθῆναι ἄνωθεν. τὸ πνεῦμα ὅπου θέλει πνεῖ, καὶ τὴν φωνὴν αὐτοῦ
ἀκούεις, ἀλλ' οὐκ οἶδας πόθεν ἔρχεται καὶ ποῦ ὑπάγει· οὕτως ἐστὶ πᾶς
9 ὁ γεγεννημένος ἐκ τοῦ πνεύματος. ἀπεκρίθη Νικόδημος καὶ εἶπεν αὐτῷ,
10 Πῶς δύναται ταῦτα γενέσθαι; ἀπεκρίθη Ἰησοῦς καὶ εἶπεν αὐτῷ, Σὺ
11 εἶ ὁ διδάσκαλος τοῦ Ἰσραήλ, καὶ ταῦτα οὐ γινώσκεις; ἀμὴν ἀμὴν
λέγω σοι ὅτι ὃ οἴδαμεν λαλοῦμεν, καὶ ὃ ἑωράκαμεν μαρτυροῦμεν· καὶ
12 τὴν μαρτυρίαν ἡμῶν οὐ λαμβάνετε. εἰ τὰ ἐπίγεια εἶπον ὑμῖν καὶ οὐ
13 πιστεύετε, πῶς ἐὰν εἴπω ὑμῖν τὰ ἐπουράνια πιστεύσητε; καὶ οὐδεὶς
ἀναβέβηκεν εἰς τὸν οὐρανόν, εἰ μὴ ὁ ἐκ τοῦ οὐρανοῦ καταβάς, ὁ υἱὸς
14 τοῦ ἀνθρώπου ὁ ὢν ἐν τῷ οὐρανῷ· καὶ καθὼς Μωσῆς ὕψωσε τὸν ὄφιν
15 ἐν τῇ ἐρήμῳ, οὕτως ὑψωθῆναι δεῖ τὸν υἱὸν τοῦ ἀνθρώπου, ἵνα πᾶς ὁ
16 πιστεύων εἰς αὐτὸν ἔχῃ ζωὴν αἰώνιον. οὕτως γὰρ ἠγάπησεν ὁ Θεὸς
τὸν κόσμον, ὥστε τὸν υἱὸν αὐτοῦ τὸν μονογενῆ ἔδωκεν, ἵνα πᾶς ὁ
17 πιστεύων εἰς αὐτὸν μὴ ἀπόληται ἀλλ' ἔχῃ ζωὴν αἰώνιον. οὐ γὰρ ἀπέ-
στειλεν ὁ Θεὸς τὸν υἱὸν εἰς τὸν κόσμον ἵνα κρίνῃ τὸν κόσμον, ἀλλ'
18 ἵνα σωθῇ ὁ κόσμος δι' αὐτοῦ. ὁ πιστεύων εἰς αὐτὸν οὐ κρίνεται· ὁ δὲ
μὴ πιστεύων ἤδη κέκριται, ὅτι μὴ πεπίστευκεν εἰς τὸ ὄνομα τοῦ μονο-
19 γενοῦς υἱοῦ τοῦ Θεοῦ. αὕτη δέ ἐστιν ἡ κρίσις, ὅτι τὸ φῶς ἐλήλυθεν
εἰς τὸν κόσμον, καὶ ἠγάπησαν μᾶλλον οἱ ἄνθρωποι τὸ σκότος ἢ τὸ
20 φῶς· ἦν γὰρ αὐτῶν πονηρὰ τὰ ἔργα. πᾶς γὰρ ὁ φαῦλα πράσσων
μισεῖ τὸ φῶς, καὶ οὐκ ἔρχεται πρὸς τὸ φῶς, ἵνα μὴ ἐλεγχθῇ αὐτοῦ
21 τὰ ἔργα· ὁ δὲ ποιῶν τὴν ἀλήθειαν ἔρχεται πρὸς τὸ φῶς, ἵνα φανερωθῇ
αὐτοῦ τὰ ἔργα ὅτι ἐν Θεῷ ἐστιν εἰργασμένα.

22 Μετὰ ταῦτα ἦλθεν ὁ Ἰησοῦς καὶ οἱ μαθηταὶ αὐτοῦ εἰς τὴν Ἰουδαίαν
23 γῆν· καὶ ἐκεῖ διέτριβε μετ' αὐτῶν καὶ ἐβάπτιζεν. ἦν δὲ καὶ Ἰωάννης κε
ὁ βαπτίζων ἐν Αἰνὼν ἐγγὺς τοῦ Σαλήμ, ὅτι ὕδατα πολλὰ ἦν ἐκεῖ· γ
24 καὶ παρεγίνοντο καὶ ἐβαπτίζοντο· οὔπω γὰρ ἦν βεβλημένος εἰς κϛ δ
25 φυλακὴν ὁ Ἰωάννης. ἐγένετο οὖν ζήτησις ἐκ τῶν μαθητῶν Ἰωάννου Δ' κζ ι

5 ο Ιησους ς **7** υμας] ημας 118 209 **8** και πας 118 209 118 209 ς
10 ο Ιησους ς **12** πιστευσετε ς **15** αυτον]+μη αποληται αλλ ς
16 ουτω ς **17** υιον αυτου ς **19** οι ανθρωποι μαλλον ς πονηρα αυτων
118 ς **20** τα εργα αυτου 118 ς **23** om ο ς Σαλειμ ς παρε-
γενοντο 118 **24** την φυλακην ς

μετὰ Ἰουδαίων περὶ καθαρισμοῦ· καὶ ἦλθον πρὸς Ἰωάννην καὶ εἶπον 26
αὐτῷ, Ῥαββί, ὃς ἦν μετὰ σοῦ πέραν τοῦ Ἰορδάνου, ᾧ σὺ μεμαρτύ-
ρηκας, ἰδοὺ οὗτος βαπτίζει, καὶ πάντες ἔρχονται πρὸς αὐτόν. ἀπεκρίθη 27
Ἰωάννης καὶ εἶπεν, Οὐ δύναται ἄνθρωπος λαμβάνειν οὐδέν, ἐὰν μὴ
κη *ᾖ δεδομένον αὐτῷ ἐκ τοῦ οὐρανοῦ. αὐτοὶ ὑμεῖς ἐμοὶ μαρτυρεῖτε ὅτι* 28
α *εἶπον, Οὐκ εἰμὶ ἐγὼ ὁ Χριστός, ἀλλ' ὅτι ἀπεσταλμένος εἰμὶ ἔμπροσθεν*
κθ *ἐκείνου. ὁ ἔχων τὴν νύμφην νυμφίος ἐστίν· ὁ δὲ φίλος τοῦ νυμφίου,* 29
ι *ὁ ἑστηκὼς καὶ ἀκούων αὐτοῦ, χαρᾷ χαίρει διὰ τὴν φωνὴν τοῦ νυμφίου.*
αὕτη οὖν ἡ χαρὰ ἡ ἐμὴ πεπλήρωται. ἐκεῖνον δεῖ αὐξάνειν, ἐμὲ δὲ 30
ἐλαττοῦσθαι. ὁ ἄνωθεν ἐρχόμενος ἐπάνω πάντων ἐστίν. ὁ ὢν ἐκ τῆς 31
γῆς ἐκ τῆς γῆς ἐστι καὶ ἐκ τῆς γῆς λαλεῖ· ὁ ἐκ τοῦ οὐρανοῦ ἐρχό-
μενος, ὃ ἑώρακε καὶ ἤκουσε μαρτυρεῖ· καὶ τὴν μαρτυρίαν αὐτοῦ 32
οὐδεὶς λαμβάνει. ὁ λαβὼν αὐτοῦ τὴν μαρτυρίαν ἐσφράγισεν ὅτι ὁ Θεὸς 33
ἀληθής ἐστιν. ὃν γὰρ ἀπέστειλεν ὁ Θεός, τὰ ῥήματα τοῦ Θεοῦ λαλεῖ· 34
λ γ *οὐ γὰρ ἐκ μέτρου δίδωσι τὸ Πνεῦμα. ὁ πατὴρ ἀγαπᾷ τὸν υἱόν, καὶ* 35
λα *πάντα δέδωκεν ἐν τῇ χειρὶ αὐτοῦ. ὁ πιστεύων εἰς τὸν υἱὸν ἔχει ζωὴν* 36
ι *αἰώνιον· ὁ δὲ ἀπειθῶν τῷ υἱῷ οὐκ ὄψεται ζωήν, ἀλλ' ἡ ὀργὴ τοῦ Θεοῦ*
μένει ἐπ' αὐτόν.

IV. *Ὡς οὖν ἔγνω ὁ Ἰησοῦς ὅτι ἤκουσαν οἱ Φαρισαῖοι ὅτι Ἰησοῦς*
πλείονας μαθητὰς ποιεῖ καὶ βαπτίζει ἢ Ἰωάννης (καίτοιγε Ἰησοῦς αὐτὸς 2
λβ *οὐκ ἐβάπτιζεν, ἀλλ' οἱ μαθηταὶ αὐτοῦ), ἀφῆκε δὲ τὴν Ἰουδαίαν γῆν* 3
ς λγ *καὶ ἀπῆλθε πάλιν εἰς τὴν Γαλιλαίαν. ἔδει δὲ αὐτὸν διέρχεσθαι διὰ* 4
ι Ε' *τῆς Σαμαρείας. ἔρχεται οὖν εἰς πόλιν τῆς Σαμαρείας λεγομένην Συχάρ,* 5
πλησίον τοῦ χωρίου οὗ ἔδωκεν Ἰακὼβ Ἰωσὴφ τῷ υἱῷ αὐτοῦ. ἦν δὲ 6
ἐκεῖ πηγὴ τοῦ Ἰακώβ. ὁ οὖν Ἰησοῦς κεκοπιακὼς ἐκ τῆς ὁδοιπορίας
ἐκαθέζετο ἐπὶ τῇ πηγῇ. ὥρα ἦν ὡσεὶ ἕκτη. ἔρχεται γυνὴ ἐκ τῆς 7
Σαμαρείας ἀντλῆσαι ὕδωρ. λέγει αὐτῇ ὁ Ἰησοῦς, Δός μοι πιεῖν. οἱ 8
γὰρ μαθηταὶ αὐτοῦ ἀπελύθεισαν εἰς τὴν πόλιν, ἵνα τροφὰς ἀγορά-
σωσι. λέγει αὐτῷ ἡ γυνὴ ἡ Σαμαρεῖτις, Πῶς σὺ Ἰουδαῖος ὢν παρ' 9
ἐμοῦ πιεῖν αἰτεῖς, οὔσης γυναικὸς Σαμαρείτιδος; οὐ γὰρ συγχρῶνται
Ἰουδαῖοι Σαμαρείταις. ἀπεκρίθη Ἰησοῦς καὶ εἶπεν αὐτῇ, Εἰ ᾔδεις τὴν 10
δωρεὰν τοῦ Θεοῦ, καὶ τίς ἐστιν ὁ λέγων σοι, Δός μοι πιεῖν, σὺ ἂν
ᾔτησας αὐτόν, καὶ ἔδωκεν ἄν σοι ὕδωρ ζῶν. λέγει αὐτῷ ἡ γυνή, Κύριε, 11
οὔτε ἄντλημα ἔχεις, καὶ τὸ φρέαρ ἐστὶ βαθύ· πόθεν οὖν ἔχεις τὸ ὕδωρ
τὸ ζῶν; μὴ σὺ μείζων εἶ τοῦ πατρὸς ἡμῶν τοῦ Ἰακώβ, ὃς ἔδωκεν 12

118 209 ς **26** *τον Ιωαννην* ς *ιδε* ς **28** *εμοι*] *μοι* ς **31** *ερχομενος*]+*επανω παντων εστι· και* ς **32** *τουτο μαρτυρει* ς **34** *διδωσιν ο Θεος* 118 ς
1 *Ιησους*] *Κυριος* ς **3** om *δε* 118 209 ς om *γην* ς **5** *ου*] *ο* ς **6** *εκαθεζετο*]+*ουτως* ς **8** *απελυθησαν* 118 209, *απεληλυθεισαν* ς **9** *λεγει ουν* 118 ς **12** *του* 2°] om 118 ς

ἡμῖν τὸ φρέαρ, καὶ αὐτὸς ἐξ αὐτοῦ ἔπιε καὶ οἱ υἱοὶ αὐτοῦ καὶ τὰ
13 θρέμματα αὐτοῦ; ἀπεκρίθη Ἰησοῦς καὶ εἶπεν αὐτῇ, Πᾶς ὁ πίνων ἐκ
14 τοῦ ὕδατος τούτου διψήσει πάλιν· ὃς δ' ἂν πίῃ ἐκ τοῦ ὕδατος οὗ ἐγὼ
δώσω αὐτῷ, οὐ μὴ διψήσει εἰς τὸν αἰῶνα· ἀλλὰ τὸ ὕδωρ ὃ δώσω
αὐτῷ, γενήσεται ἐν αὐτῷ πηγὴ ὕδατος ἁλλομένου εἰς ζωὴν αἰώνιον.
15 λέγει πρὸς αὐτὸν ἡ γυνή, Κύριε, δός μοι τοῦτο τὸ ὕδωρ, ἵνα μὴ διψῶ
16 μηδὲ ἔρχωμαι ἐνθάδε ἀντλεῖν. λέγει αὐτῇ Ἰησοῦς, Ὕπαγε, φώνησον
17 τὸν ἄνδρα σου, καὶ ἐλθὲ ἐνθάδε. ἀπεκρίθη ἡ γυνὴ καὶ εἶπεν, Οὐκ
ἔχω ἄνδρα. λέγει αὐτῇ ὁ Ἰησοῦς, Καλῶς εἶπας ὅτι Ἄνδρα οὐκ ἔχω·
18 πέντε γὰρ ἄνδρας ἔσχες· καὶ νῦν ὃν ἔχεις, οὐκ ἔστι σου ὁ ἀνήρ· τοῦτο
19 ἀληθὲς εἴρηκας. λέγει αὐτῷ ἡ γυνή, Κύριε, θεωρῶ ὅτι προφήτης εἶ
20 σύ. οἱ πατέρες ἡμῶν ἐν τῷ ὄρει τούτῳ προσεκύνησαν· καὶ ὑμεῖς
21 λέγετε ὅτι ἐν Ἱεροσολύμοις ἐστὶν ὁ τόπος ὅπου δεῖ προσκυνεῖν. λέγει
αὐτῇ ὁ Ἰησοῦς, Γύναι, πίστευέ μοι ὅτι ἔρχεται ὥρα, ὅτε οὔτε ἐν τῷ
22 ὄρει τούτῳ οὔτε ἐν Ἱεροσολύμοις προσκυνήσητε τῷ πατρί. ὑμεῖς
προσκυνεῖτε ὃ οὐκ οἴδατε· ἡμεῖς προσκυνοῦμεν ὃ οἴδαμεν, ὅτι ἡ σωτη-
23 ρία ἐκ τῶν Ἰουδαίων ἐστίν. ἀλλ' ἔρχεται ὥρα καὶ νῦν ἐστιν, ὅτε οἱ
ἀληθινοὶ προσκυνηταὶ προσκυνήσουσι τῷ πατρὶ ἐν τῷ πνεύματι καὶ
24 ἀληθείᾳ. πνεῦμα ὁ Θεός· καὶ τοὺς προσκυνοῦντας αὐτὸν ἐν πνεύματι
25 καὶ ἀληθείᾳ δεῖ προσκυνεῖν. λέγει αὐτῷ ἡ γυνή, Οἶδα ὅτι Μεσσίας
ἔρχεται (ὁ λεγόμενος Χριστός)· ὅταν ἔλθῃ ἐκεῖνος, ἀναγγελεῖ ἡμῖν
26 27 ἅπαντα. λέγει αὐτῇ ὁ Ἰησοῦς, Ἐγώ εἰμι, ὁ λαλῶν σοι. καὶ ἐπὶ
τούτῳ ἦλθον οἱ μαθηταὶ αὐτοῦ, καὶ ἐθαύμαζον ὅτι μετὰ γυναικὸς
ἐλάλει· οὐδεὶς μέντοι εἶπε, Τί ζητεῖς; ἤ, Τί λαλεῖς μετ' αὐτῆς;
28 Ἀφῆκεν οὖν τὴν ὑδρίαν αὐτῆς ἡ γυνὴ καὶ ἀπῆλθεν εἰς τὴν πόλιν,
29 καὶ λέγει τοῖς ἀνθρώποις, Δεῦτε ἴδετε ἄνθρωπον ὃς εἶπέ μοι πάντα ὅσα
30 ἐποίησα· μήτι οὗτός ἐστιν ὁ Χριστός; ἐξῆλθον οὖν ἐκ τῆς πόλεως,
καὶ ἤρχοντο πρὸς αὐτόν.
31 Ἐν δὲ τῷ μεταξὺ ἠρώτων αὐτὸν οἱ μαθηταὶ λέγοντες, Ῥαββί, φάγε.
32 33 ὁ δὲ εἶπεν αὐτοῖς, Ἐγὼ βρῶσιν ἔχω φαγεῖν ἣν ὑμεῖς οὐκ οἴδατε. ἔλεγον
34 οὖν οἱ μαθηταὶ πρὸς ἀλλήλους, Μή τις ἤνεγκεν αὐτῷ φαγεῖν; λέγει
αὐτοῖς ὁ Ἰησοῦς, Ἐμὸν βρῶμά ἐστιν ἵνα ποιήσω τὸ θέλημα τοῦ
35 πέμψαντός με καὶ τελειώσω αὐτοῦ τὸ ἔργον. οὐχ ὑμεῖς λέγετε ὅτι

20 τουτω] τούτο cod. **31** αυτον] αυτων cod.

13 ο Ιησους ς **14** διψηση 118 209 ς **16** ο Ιησους 118 ς 118 209 ς
18 ανηρ sine ο 118 ς **20** τουτω τω ορει 209 ς **21** πιστευσον ς
προσκυνησετε ς **23** om τω 2° 118 209 ς αληθεια] + και γαρ ο πατηρ
τοιουτους ζητει τους προσκυνουντας αυτον ς **25** Μεσιας 118 209 παντα ς
27 εθαυμασαν ς, εθαυμαζσαν 118 **34** ποιησω] ποιω 118 ς

ἔτι τετράμηνός ἐστι καὶ ὁ θερισμὸς ἔρχεται; ἐπάρατε τοὺς ὀφθαλ-
μοὺς ὑμῶν καὶ θεάσασθε τὰς χώρας, ὅτι λευκαί εἰσι πρὸς θερισμὸν
ἤδη. καὶ ὁ θερίζων μισθὸν λαμβάνει, καὶ συνάγει καρπὸν εἰς ζωὴν 36
αἰώνιον, ἵνα ὁ σπείρων ὁμοῦ χαίρῃ καὶ ὁ θερίζων. ἐν γὰρ τούτῳ 37
ὁ λόγος ἐστὶν ἀληθής, ὅτι ἄλλος ἐστὶν ὁ σπείρων καὶ ἄλλος ὁ
θερίζων. ἐγὼ ἀπέστειλα ὑμᾶς θερίζειν ὃ οὐχ ὑμεῖς κεκοπιάκατε· 38
ἄλλοι κεκοπιάκασι, καὶ ὑμεῖς εἰς τὸν κόπον αὐτῶν εἰσεληλύθατε. ἐκ 39
δὲ τῆς πόλεως ἐκείνης πολλοὶ ἐπίστευσαν τῶν Σαμαρειτῶν εἰς
αὐτὸν διὰ τὸν λόγον τῆς γυναικὸς μαρτυρούσης ὅτι Εἶπέ μοι πάντα
ὅσα ἐποίησα. ὡς οὖν ἦλθον πρὸς αὐτὸν οἱ Σαμαρεῖται, ἠρώτων αὐτὸν 40
μεῖναι παρ' αὐτοῖς· καὶ ἔμεινεν ἐκεῖ δύο ἡμέρας. καὶ πολλῷ πλείους 41
ἐπίστευσαν διὰ τὸν λόγον αὐτοῦ, τῇ τε γυναικὶ ἔλεγον ὅτι Οὐκέτι διὰ 42
τὴν σὴν λαλιὰν πιστεύομεν· αὐτοὶ γὰρ ἀκηκόαμεν παρ' αὐτοῦ, καὶ
οἴδαμεν ὅτι οὗτός ἐστιν ἀληθῶς ὁ σωτὴρ τοῦ κόσμου, ὁ Χριστός.
λδ/ς Μετὰ δὲ τὰς δύο ἡμέρας ἐξῆλθεν ἐκεῖθεν καὶ ἀπῆλθεν εἰς τὴν 43
λε/α Γαλιλαίαν. αὐτὸς γὰρ Ἰησοῦς ἐμαρτύρησεν ὅτι προφήτης ἐν τῇ ἰδίᾳ 44
πατρίδι τιμὴν οὐκ ἔχει. ὅτε οὖν ἦλθεν εἰς τὴν Γαλιλαίαν, ἐδέξαντο 45
λϛ/ι αὐτὸν οἱ Γαλιλαῖοι, πάντα ἑωρακότες ὅσα ἐποίησεν ἐν Ἱεροσολύμοις
ἐν τῇ ἑορτῇ· καὶ αὐτοὶ γὰρ ἦλθον εἰς τὴν ἑορτήν.
ϛ' Ἦλθεν οὖν πάλιν ὁ Ἰησοῦς εἰς τὴν Κανᾶ τῆς Γαλιλαίας, ὅπου 46
λζ/γ ἐποίησε τὸ ὕδωρ οἶνον. καὶ ἦν τις βασιλικός, οὗ ὁ υἱὸς ἠσθένει ἐν
Καπερναούμ. οὗτος ἀκούσας ὅτι Ἰησοῦς ἥκει ἐκ τῆς Ἰουδαίας εἰς τὴν 47
Γαλιλαίαν, ἦλθε πρὸς αὐτόν, καὶ ἠρώτα αὐτὸν ἵνα καταβῇ καὶ ἰάσηται
αὐτοῦ τὸν υἱόν· ἤμελλε γὰρ ἀποθνήσκειν. εἶπεν οὖν ὁ Ἰησοῦς πρὸς 48
αὐτόν, Ἐὰν μὴ σημεῖα καὶ τέρατα ἴδητε, οὐ μὴ πιστεύσητε. λέγει 49
πρὸς αὐτὸν ὁ βασιλικός, Κύριε, κατάβηθι πρὶν ἀποθανεῖν τὸ παιδίον.
λέγει αὐτῷ ὁ Ἰησοῦς, Πορεύου· ὁ υἱός σου ζῇ. καὶ ἐπίστευσεν ὁ 50
ἄνθρωπος τῷ λόγῳ ᾧ εἶπεν αὐτῷ Ἰησοῦς, καὶ ἐπορεύετο. ἤδη δὲ 51
αὐτοῦ καταβαίνοντος, οἱ δοῦλοι ὑπήντησεν αὐτῷ καὶ ἀνήγγειλαν
λέγοντες ὅτι Ὁ παῖς σου ζῇ. ἐπύθετο οὖν τὴν ὥραν παρ' αὐτῶν 52
ἐν ᾗ κομψότερον ἔσχεν· εἶπον οὖν αὐτῷ ὅτι Χθὲς ὥραν ἑβδόμην

46 παλιν] παλι cod.

118 209 ϛ **35** τετραμηνον ϛ επαρατε] pr ιδου λεγω υμιν ϛ **36** ινα] + και ϛ **37** αληθης] ο αληθινος ϛ εστιν 2°...θεριζων haec in rasura scripsit 209* sed quae erasa sint legere non possum **39** εις αυτον των Σαμαρειτων ϛ **42** om παρ αυτου ϛ **44** ο Ιησους ϛ **45** οσα] α ϛ **46** ο Ιησους παλιν ϛ **47** απηλθε ϛ εμελλε 118 **49** πριν η 118 209 παιδιον μου ϛ **50** ο Ιησους 118 209 ϛ **51** δουλοι αυτου ϛ απηντησαν ϛ απηγγειλαν ϛ **52** παρ αυτων την ωραν ϛ ειπον ουν] και ειπον 118 209 ϛ

53 ἀφῆκεν αὐτὸν ὁ πυρετός. ἔγνω οὖν ὁ πατὴρ ὅτι ἐκείνῃ τῇ ὥρᾳ ἐν
ᾗ εἶπεν αὐτῷ ὁ Ἰησοῦς, Ὁ υἱός σου ζῇ· καὶ ἐπίστευσεν αὐτὸς καὶ ἡ
54 οἰκία αὐτοῦ ὅλη. τοῦτο πάλιν δεύτερον σημεῖον ἐποίησεν ὁ Ἰησοῦς,
ἐλθὼν ἐκ τῆς Ἰουδαίας εἰς τὴν Γαλιλαίαν.
V. Μετὰ ταῦτα ἦν ἡ ἑορτὴ τῶν Ἰουδαίων, καὶ ἀνέβη ὁ Ἰησοῦς λη
2 εἰς Ἱεροσόλυμα. ἔστι δὲ ἐν τοῖς Ἱεροσολύμοις ἐπὶ τῇ προβατικῇ α
κολυμβήθρα, ἡ λεγομένη Ἑβραϊστὶ Βηθεσδά, πέντε στοὰς ἔχουσα.
3 ἐν ταύταις κατέκειτο πλῆθος πολὺ τῶν ἀσθενούντων, τυφλῶν, χωλῶν,
4 ξηρῶν, ἐκδεχομένων τὴν τοῦ ὕδατος κίνησιν. ἄγγελος γὰρ κατὰ καιρὸν
κατέβαινεν ἐν τῇ κολυμβήθρᾳ καὶ ἐτάρασσε τὸ ὕδωρ· ὁ οὖν πρῶτος
ἐμβὰς μετὰ τὴν ταραχὴν τοῦ ὕδατος ὑγιὴς ἐγίνετο, ᾧ δήποτε κατεί-
5 χετο νοσήματι. ἦν δέ τις ἄνθρωπος ἐκεῖ τριάκοντα καὶ ὀκτὼ ἔτη Z'
6 ἔχων ἐν τῇ ἀσθενείᾳ αὐτοῦ. τοῦτον ἰδὼν ὁ Ἰησοῦς κατακείμενον, καὶ
γνοὺς ὅτι πολὺν χρόνον ἤδη ἔχει, λέγει αὐτῷ, Θέλεις ὑγιὴς γενέ-
7 σθαι; ἀπεκρίθη αὐτῷ ὁ ἀσθενῶν, Κύριε, ἄνθρωπον οὐκ ἔχω, ἵνα ὅταν
ταραχθῇ τὸ ὕδωρ, βάλῃ με εἰς τὴν κολυμβήθραν· ἐν ᾧ δὲ ἔρχομαι
8 ἐγώ, ἄλλος πρὸ ἐμοῦ καταβαίνει. λέγει αὐτῷ ὁ Ἰησοῦς, Ἔγειρε,
9 ἆρον τὸν κράβαττόν σου καὶ περιπάτει. καὶ εὐθέως ὑγιὴς ἐγένετο
ὁ ἄνθρωπος, καὶ ἐγερθεὶς ἦρε τὸν κράβαττον αὐτοῦ καὶ περιεπάτει. ἦν
10 δὲ σάββατον ἐν ἐκείνῃ τῇ ἡμέρᾳ. ἔλεγον οὖν οἱ Ἰουδαῖοι τῷ τεθερα-
πευμένῳ, Σάββατόν ἐστιν καὶ οὐκ ἔξεστί σοι ἆραι τὸν κράβαττον.
11 ἀπεκρίθη αὐτοῖς, Ὁ ποιήσας με ὑγιῆ, ἐκεῖνός μοι εἶπεν, Ἆρον τὸν λθ
12 κράβαττόν σου καὶ περιπάτει. ἠρώτησαν οὖν αὐτόν, Τίς ἐστιν ὁ ἄν- ι
13 θρωπος ὁ εἰπών σοι, Ἆρον τὸν κράβαττόν σου καὶ περιπάτει; ὁ δὲ
ἰαθεὶς οὐκ ᾔδει τίς ἐστιν· ὁ γὰρ Ἰησοῦς ἐξένευσεν, ὄχλου ὄντος ἐν τῷ
14 τόπῳ. μετὰ ταῦτα εὑρίσκει αὐτὸν ὁ Ἰησοῦς ἐν τῷ ἱερῷ, καὶ εἶπεν
αὐτῷ, Ἴδε ὑγιὴς γέγονας· μηκέτι ἁμάρτανε, ἵνα μὴ χεῖρόν τί σοι γένη-
15 ται. ἀπῆλθεν ὁ ἄνθρωπος, καὶ ἀνήγγειλε τοῖς Ἰουδαίοις ὅτι Ἰησοῦς
ἐστιν ὁ ποιήσας με ὑγιῆ.
16 Καὶ διὰ τοῦτο ἐδίωκον τὸν Ἰησοῦν οἱ Ἰουδαῖοι, ὅτι ταῦτα ἐποίει
17 ἐν σαββάτῳ. ὁ δὲ Ἰησοῦς ἀπεκρίνατο αὐτοῖς, Ὁ πατήρ μου ἕως ἄρτι
18 ἐργάζεται, κἀγὼ ἐργάζομαι. διὰ τοῦτο οὖν μᾶλλον ἐζήτουν αὐτὸν οἱ
Ἰουδαῖοι ἀποκτεῖναι, ὅτι οὐ μόνον ἔλυε τὸ σάββατον, ἀλλὰ καὶ πατέρα
19 ἴδιον ἔλεγε τὸν Θεόν, ἴσον ἑαυτὸν ποιῶν τῷ Θεῷ. ἀπεκρίνατο οὖν ὁ

53 εν εκεινη 118 ϛ οτι ο υιος 118 ϛ 118 209 ϛ
1 om η ϛ **2** επιλεγομενη ϛ **4** εγενετο 118 **5** τριακοντα-οκτω ϛ om αυτου ϛ **6** ηδη χρονον ϛ **7** βαλη με] βαλλη με ϛ, βαλημα 118*, βαλημαι 118[2] **8** εγειραι 118 209 ϛ κραββατον 118 209 ϛ et sic passim **9** εγενετο υγιης ϛ om εγερθεις ϛ **10** om και ϛ **15** με] αυτον ϛ **16** Ιουδαιοι] + και εζητουν αυτον αποκτειναι 118 ϛ

Ἰησοῦς καὶ λέγει αὐτοῖς, Ἀμὴν ἀμὴν λέγω ὑμῖν, οὐ δύναται ὁ υἱὸς
ποιεῖν ἀφ' ἑαυτοῦ οὐδὲ ἕν, ἐὰν μή τι βλέπῃ τὸν πατέρα ποιοῦντα· ἃ
γὰρ ἂν ἐκεῖνος ποιῇ, ταῦτα καὶ ὁ υἱὸς ὁμοίως ποιεῖ. ὁ γὰρ πατὴρ 20
φιλεῖ τὸν υἱόν, καὶ πάντα δείκνυσιν αὐτῷ ἃ αὐτὸς ποιεῖ· καὶ μείζονα
τούτων δείξει αὐτῷ ἔργα, ἵνα ὑμεῖς θαυμάζητε. ὥσπερ γὰρ ὁ πατὴρ 21
ἐγείρει τοὺς νεκροὺς καὶ ζωοποιεῖ, οὕτω καὶ ὁ υἱὸς οὓς θέλει ζωοποιεῖ.
οὐδὲ γὰρ ὁ πατὴρ κρίνει οὐδένα, ἀλλὰ τὴν κρίσιν πᾶσαν δέδωκε τῷ 22
μ α υἱῷ, ἵνα πάντες τιμῶσι τὸν υἱὸν καθὼς τιμῶσι τὸν πατέρα. ὁ μὴ 23
μα τιμῶν τὸν υἱὸν οὐ τιμᾷ τὸν πατέρα τὸν πέμψαντα αὐτόν. ἀμὴν ἀμὴν 24
ι λέγω ὑμῖν ὅτι ὁ τὸν λόγον μου ἀκούων καὶ πιστεύων τῷ πέμψαντί
με ἔχει ζωὴν αἰώνιον, καὶ εἰς κρίσιν οὐκ ἔρχεται, ἀλλὰ μεταβέβηκεν
ἐκ τοῦ θανάτου εἰς τὴν ζωήν. ἀμὴν ἀμὴν λέγω ὑμῖν ὅτι ἔρχεται ὥρα 25
καὶ νῦν ἐστιν, ὅτε οἱ νεκροὶ ἀκούσωσι τῆς φωνῆς τοῦ υἱοῦ τοῦ
Θεοῦ, καὶ οἱ ἀκούσαντες ζήσουσιν. ὥσπερ γὰρ ὁ πατὴρ ἔχει ζωὴν ἐν 26
ἑαυτῷ, καὶ ἐξουσίαν ἔδωκεν αὐτῷ καὶ κρίσιν ποιεῖν, ὅτι υἱὸς ἀνθρώπου 27
ἐστί. μὴ θαυμάζετε τοῦτο· ὅτι ἔρχεται ὥρα ἐν ᾗ πάντες οἱ ἐν τοῖς 28
μνημείοις ἀκούσονται τῆς φωνῆς αὐτοῦ καὶ ἐκπορεύσονται, οἱ τὰ ἀγαθὰ 29
ποιήσαντες εἰς ἀνάστασιν ζωῆς, οἱ δὲ τὰ φαῦλα πράξαντες εἰς ἀνά-
στασιν κρίσεως. οὐ δύναμαι ἐγὼ ποιεῖν ἀπ' ἐμαυτοῦ οὐδέν· καθὼς 30
μβ α ἀκούω, κρίνω· καὶ ἡ κρίσις ἡ ἐμὴ δικαία ἐστίν· ὅτι οὐ ζητῶ τὸ θέλημα
μγ τὸ ἐμόν, ἀλλὰ τὸ θέλημα τοῦ πέμψαντός με. ἐὰν ἐγὼ μαρτυρῶ περὶ 31
ι ἐμαυτοῦ, ἡ μαρτυρία μου οὐκ ἔστιν ἀληθής. ἄλλος ἐστὶν ὁ μαρτυ- 32
ρῶν περὶ ἐμοῦ, καὶ οἶδα ὅτι ἀληθής ἐστιν ἡ μαρτυρία ἣν μαρτυρεῖ
περὶ ἐμοῦ.

Ὑμεῖς ἀπεστάλκατε πρὸς Ἰωάννην, καὶ μεμαρτύρηκε τῇ ἀληθείᾳ· 33
ἐγὼ δὲ οὐ παρὰ ἀνθρώπου τὴν μαρτυρίαν λαμβάνω, ἀλλὰ ταῦτα λέγω 34
ἵνα ὑμεῖς σωθῆτε. ἐκεῖνος ἦν ὁ λύχνος ὁ καιόμενος καὶ φαίνων, ὑμεῖς 35
δὲ ἠθελήσατε ἀγαλλιασθῆναι πρὸς ὥραν ἐν τῷ φωτὶ αὐτοῦ. ἐγὼ 36
δὲ ἔχω τὴν μαρτυρίαν μείζω τοῦ Ἰωάννου· τὰ γὰρ ἔργα ἃ δέδωκέ
μοι ὁ πατὴρ ἵνα τελειώσω αὐτά, αὐτὰ τὰ ἔργα ἃ ποιῶ μαρτυρεῖ περὶ
ἐμοῦ ὅτι ὁ πατήρ με ἀπέσταλκε· καὶ ὁ πέμψας με πατὴρ αὐτὸς μεμαρ- 37
μδ γ τύρηκε περὶ ἐμοῦ. οὔτε φωνὴν αὐτοῦ ἀκηκόατε πώποτε, οὔτε εἶδος
με ι αὐτοῦ ἑωράκατε· καὶ τὸν λόγον αὐτοῦ οὐκ ἔχετε ἐν ὑμῖν μένοντα, 38

26 εαυτω] scriba vel idem vel ejusdem fere temporis addidit in marg. ουτως εδωκε και τω υιω ζωην εχειν εν εαυτω

118 209 ς **19** λεγει] ειπεν ς ουδε εν] ουδεν ς **21** ουτως 118 209 **25** ακουσονται 118 209 ς ζησονται 118 209 ς **26** εαυτω] + ουτως εδωκε και τω υιω ζωην εχειν εν εαυτω 118 209 ς **30** με] + πατρος 118 corr recent ς **35** αγαλλιασθηναι ς **36** εδωκε ς εγω ποιω 118 209 ς **38** μενοντα εν υμιν ς

39 ὅτι ὃν ἀπέστειλεν ἐκεῖνος, τούτῳ ὑμεῖς οὐ πιστεύετε. ἐρευνᾶτε τὰς
γραφάς, ὅτι ὑμεῖς δοκεῖτε ἐν αὐταῖς ζωὴν αἰώνιον ἔχειν, καὶ ἐκεῖναί
40 εἰσιν αἱ μαρτυροῦσαι περὶ ἐμοῦ· καὶ οὐ θέλετε ἐλθεῖν πρός με ἵνα
41 42 ζωὴν ἔχητε. δόξαν παρὰ ἀνθρώπων οὐ λαμβάνω· ἀλλ' ἔγνωκα ὑμᾶς
43 ὅτι τὴν ἀγάπην τοῦ Θεοῦ οὐκ ἔχετε ἐν ἑαυτοῖς. ἐγὼ ἐλήλυθα ἐν τῷ
ὀνόματι τοῦ πατρός μου, καὶ οὐ λαμβάνετέ με· ἐὰν ἄλλος ἔλθῃ ἐν
44 τῷ ὀνόματι τῷ ἰδίῳ, ἐκεῖνον λήψεσθε. πῶς δύνασθε ὑμεῖς πιστεύειν,
δόξαν παρ' ἀλλήλων λαμβάνοντες, καὶ τὴν δόξαν τὴν παρὰ τοῦ μόνου
45 Θεοῦ οὐ ζητεῖτε; μὴ δοκεῖτε ὅτι ἐγὼ κατηγορήσω ὑμῶν πρὸς τὸν
46 πατέρα· ἔστιν ὁ κατηγορῶν ὑμῶν Μωσῆς, εἰς ὃν ὑμεῖς ἠλπίκατε. εἰ
γὰρ ἐπιστεύετε Μωσεῖ, ἐπιστεύετε ἂν ἐμοί· περὶ γὰρ ἐμοῦ ἐκεῖνος
47 ἔγραψεν. εἰ δὲ τοῖς ἐκείνου γράμμασιν οὐ πιστεύετε, πῶς τοῖς ἐμοῖς
ῥήμασι πιστεύσητε;

VI. Μετὰ ταῦτα ἀπῆλθεν ὁ Ἰησοῦς πέραν τῆς θαλάσσης τῆς μς
2 Γαλιλαίας τῆς Τιβεριάδος· ἠκολούθει δὲ αὐτῷ ὄχλος πολύς, ὅτι α
3 ἑώρων τὰ σημεῖα ἃ ἐποίει ἐπὶ τῶν ἀσθενούντων. ἀνῆλθεν οὖν εἰς τὸ μζ
4 ὄρος ὁ Ἰησοῦς, καὶ ἐκάθητο ἐκεῖ μετὰ τῶν μαθητῶν αὐτοῦ. ἦν δὲ γ
5 ἐγγὺς τὸ πάσχα, ἡ ἑορτὴ τῶν Ἰουδαίων. ἐπάρας οὖν τοὺς ὀφθαλμοὺς μη α
ὁ Ἰησοῦς, καὶ θεασάμενος ὅτι πολὺς ὄχλος ἔρχεται πρὸς αὐτόν, λέγει Η′ μθ
πρὸς τὸν Φίλιππον, Πόθεν ἀγοράσωμεν ἄρτους ἵνα φάγωσιν οὗτοι; α
6 τοῦτο δὲ ἔλεγε πειράζων αὐτόν· αὐτὸς γὰρ ᾔδει τί ἤμελλε ποιεῖν.
7 ἀπεκρίθη αὐτῷ Φίλιππος, Διακοσίων δηναρίων ἄρτοι οὐκ ἀρκοῦσιν
8 αὐτοῖς, ἵνα ἕκαστος αὐτῶν βραχύ τι λάβῃ. λέγει αὐτῷ εἷς ἐκ τῶν
9 μαθητῶν αὐτοῦ, Ἀνδρέας ὁ ἀδελφὸς Σίμωνος Πέτρου, Ἔστι παιδά-
ριον ὧδε, ὃ ἔχει πέντε ἄρτους κριθίνους καὶ δύο ὀψάρια· ἀλλὰ ταῦτα
10 τί ἐστιν εἰς τοσούτους; εἶπε δὲ ὁ Ἰησοῦς, Ποιήσατε τοὺς ἀνθρώ-
πους ἀναπεσεῖν. ἦν δὲ χόρτος πολὺς ἐν τῷ τόπῳ. ἀνέπεσαν οὖν
11 ἄνδρες τὸν ἀριθμὸν ὡσεὶ πεντακισχίλιοι. καὶ λαβὼν τοὺς ἄρτους
ὁ Ἰησοῦς καὶ εὐχαριστήσας διέδωκε τοῖς ἀνακειμένοις· ὁμοίως καὶ ἐκ
12 τῶν ὀψαρίων ὅσον ἤθελον. ὡς δὲ ἐπλήσθησαν, λέγει τοῖς μαθηταῖς
αὐτοῦ, Συναγάγετε τὰ περισσεύσαντα κλάσματα, ἵνα μή τι ἀπόληται.
13 συνήγαγον οὖν, καὶ ἐγέμισαν δώδεκα κοφίνους κλασμάτων ἐκ τῶν πέντε
14 ἄρτων τῶν κριθίνων, ἃ ἐπερίσσευσε τοῖς βεβρωκόσιν. οἱ οὖν ἄνθρωποι ν
ἰδόντες ὃ ἐποίησε σημεῖον ὁ Ἰησοῦς ἔλεγον ὅτι Οὗτός ἐστιν ἀληθῶς ὁ ι

44 πιστευσαι ς   παρ] παρα ς   **46** Μωση ς   **47** πιστευσετε ς   118 209
2 και ηκολουθει ς   τα] pr αυτου ς   **3** ουν] δε ς   εκει εκαθητο ς   ς
5 ο Ιησους τους οφθαλμους ς   αγορασομεν 118 209 ς   **6** εμελλε ς
9 παιδαριον εν ς   **10** ανεπεσον ς   οι ανδρες ς   **11** και λαβων]
ελαβε δε ς   διεδωκε]+τοις μαθηταις οι δε μαθηται 118^2 in mg ς   **12** ενε-
πλησθησαν ς

προφήτης ὁ ἐρχόμενος εἰς τὸν κόσμον. Ἰησοῦς οὖν, γνοὺς ὅτι μέλλου- 15
σιν ἔρχεσθαι καὶ ἁρπάζειν αὐτὸν ἵνα ποιήσωσι βασιλέα, ἀνεχώρησε
πάλιν εἰς τὸ ὄρος αὐτὸς μόνος.
θ' Ὡς δὲ ὀψία ἐγένετο, κατέβησαν οἱ μαθηταὶ αὐτοῦ ἐπὶ τὴν θάλασ- 16
να δ σαν, καὶ ἐμβάντες εἰς τὸ πλοῖον ἤρχοντο πέραν τῆς θαλάσσης εἰς 17
Καπερναούμ. καὶ σκοτία ἤδη ἐγεγόνει, καὶ οὐκ ἐληλύθει πρὸς αὐτοὺς
ὁ Ἰησοῦς, ἥ τε θάλασσα ἀνέμου μεγάλου πνέοντος διηγείρετο. ἐληλα- 18 19
κότες οὖν ὡσεὶ σταδίους εἰκοσιπέντε ἢ τριάκοντα θεωροῦσι τὸν Ἰησοῦν
περιπατοῦντα ἐπὶ τῆς θαλάσσης καὶ ἐγγὺς τοῦ πλοίου γινόμενον· καὶ
ἐφοβήθησαν. ὁ δὲ λέγει αὐτοῖς, Ἐγώ εἰμι· μὴ φοβεῖσθε. ἤθελον οὖν 20 21
λαβεῖν αὐτὸν εἰς τὸ πλοῖον, καὶ εὐθέως ἐγένετο τὸ πλοῖον ἐπὶ τῆς
γῆς εἰς ἣν ὑπῆγον.
νβ ι Τῇ ἐπαύριον ὁ ὄχλος ὁ ἑστηκὼς πέραν τῆς θαλάσσης, ἰδὼν ὅτι 22
πλοιάριον ἄλλο οὐκ ἦν ἐκεῖ εἰ μὴ ἕν, καὶ ὅτι οὐ συνεισῆλθε τοῖς
μαθηταῖς αὐτοῦ ὁ Ἰησοῦς εἰς τὸ πλοῖον, ἀλλὰ μόνοι οἱ μαθηταὶ
αὐτοῦ ἀπῆλθον· ἄλλα δὲ ἦλθον πλοιάρια ἐκ Τιβεριάδος ἐγγὺς τοῦ 23
τόπου ὅπου ἔφαγον τὸν ἄρτον τοῦ Κυρίου εὐχαριστήσαντος· ὅτε 24
οὖν εἶδεν ὁ ὄχλος ὅτι Ἰησοῦς οὐκ ἔστιν ἐκεῖ οὐδὲ οἱ μαθηταὶ
αὐτοῦ, ἀνέβησαν καὶ αὐτοὶ εἰς τὰ πλοῖα καὶ ἦλθον εἰς Καπερναοὺμ
ζητοῦντες τὸν Ἰησοῦν, καὶ εὑρόντες αὐτὸν πέραν τῆς θαλάσσης εἶπον 25
αὐτῷ, Ῥαββί, πότε ὧδε γέγονας; ἀπεκρίθη αὐτοῖς ὁ Ἰησοῦς καὶ εἶπεν, 26
Ἀμὴν ἀμὴν λέγω ὑμῖν, ζητεῖτέ με, οὐχ ὅτι εἴδετε σημεῖα, ἀλλ' ὅτι
ἐφάγετε ἐκ τῶν ἄρτων καὶ ἐχορτάσθητε. ἐργάζεσθε μὴ τὴν βρῶσιν 27
τὴν ἀπολλυμένην, ἀλλὰ τὴν βρῶσιν τὴν μένουσαν εἰς ζωὴν αἰώνιον,
ἣν ὁ υἱὸς τοῦ ἀνθρώπου ὑμῖν δώσει· τοῦτον γὰρ ὁ πατὴρ ἐσφράγισεν
ὁ Θεός. εἶπον οὖν πρὸς αὐτόν, Τί ποιῶμεν, ἵνα ἐργαζώμεθα τὰ 28
ἔργα τοῦ Θεοῦ; ἀπεκρίθη ὁ Ἰησοῦς καὶ εἶπεν αὐτοῖς, Τοῦτό ἐστι τὸ 29
νγ δ ἔργον τοῦ Θεοῦ, ἵνα πιστεύητε εἰς ὃν ἀπέστειλεν ἐκεῖνος. εἶπον οὖν 30
αὐτῷ, Τί οὖν ποιεῖς σὺ σημεῖον, ἵνα ἴδωμεν καὶ πιστεύσωμέν σοι;
νδ ι τί ἐργάζῃ; οἱ πατέρες ἡμῶν τὸ μάννα ἔφαγον ἐν τῇ ἐρήμῳ, καθὼς 31
γέγραπται, Ἄρτον ἐκ τοῦ οὐρανοῦ ἔδωκεν αὐτοῖς φαγεῖν. εἶπεν οὖν 32
αὐτοῖς ὁ Ἰησοῦς, Ἀμὴν ἀμὴν λέγω ὑμῖν, Οὐ Μωσῆς δέδωκεν ὑμῖν τὸν
ἄρτον ἐκ τοῦ οὐρανοῦ· ἀλλ' ὁ πατήρ μου δίδωσιν ὑμῖν τὸν ἄρτον ἐκ
τοῦ οὐρανοῦ τὸν ἀληθινόν· ὁ γὰρ ἄρτος τοῦ Θεοῦ ἐστιν ὁ καταβαίνων 33
ἐκ τοῦ οὐρανοῦ καὶ διδοὺς τῷ κόσμῳ. εἶπον οὖν πρὸς αὐτόν, Κύριε, 34

118 209 ς 15 ποιησωσιν αυτον 118 ς 19 ως ς 21 το πλοιον εγενετο ς
22 εν] + εκεινο εις ο ενεβησαν οι μαθηται αυτου 118 ς sed ανεβησαν 118
πλοιον] πλοιαριον ς 23 ηλθε ς ευχαριστησαντος του Κυριου ς
24 ενεβησαν ς 28 ποιουμεν 118 209 ς 29 πιστευσητε ς 31 εστι
γεγραμμενον ς 33 διδους] + ζωην 118, pr ζωην ς

35 πάντοτε δὸς ἡμῖν τὸν ἄρτον τοῦτον. εἶπε δὲ αὐτοῖς ὁ Ἰησοῦς, Ἐγώ νε α
εἰμι ὁ ἄρτος τῆς ζωῆς· ὁ ἐρχόμενος πρός με οὐ μὴ πεινάσει, καὶ ὁ
36 πιστεύων εἰς ἐμὲ οὐ μὴ διψήσει πώποτε. ἀλλ' εἶπον ὑμῖν ὅτι καὶ
37 ἑωράκατέ με, καὶ οὐ πιστεύετε. πᾶν ὃ δίδωσί μοι ὁ πατὴρ πρός με νς ι
38 ἥξει· καὶ τὸν ἐρχόμενον πρός με οὐ μὴ ἐκβάλω ἔξω· ὅτι καταβέβηκα νζ
ἐκ τοῦ οὐρανοῦ, οὐχ ἵνα ποιῶ τὸ θέλημα τὸ ἐμόν, ἀλλὰ τὸ θέλημα α
39 τοῦ πέμψαντός με. τοῦτο δέ ἐστι τὸ θέλημα τοῦ πέμψαντός με, ἵνα νη ι
πᾶν ὃ δέδωκέ μοι, μὴ ἀπολέσω ἐξ αὐτοῦ, ἀλλ' ἀναστήσω αὐτὸ τῇ
40 ἐσχάτῃ ἡμέρᾳ. τοῦτο γάρ ἐστι τὸ θέλημα τοῦ πατρός μου, ἵνα
πᾶς ὁ θεωρῶν τὸν υἱὸν καὶ πιστεύων εἰς αὐτὸν ἔχῃ ζωὴν αἰώνιον, καὶ
41 ἀναστήσω αὐτὸν τῇ ἐσχάτῃ ἡμέρᾳ. ἐγόγγυζον οὖν οἱ Ἰουδαῖοι περὶ νθ α
42 αὐτοῦ, ὅτι εἶπεν, Ἐγώ εἰμι ὁ ἄρτος ὁ καταβὰς ἐκ τοῦ οὐρανοῦ· καὶ
ἔλεγον, Οὐχ οὗτός ἐστιν ὁ Ἰησοῦς ὁ υἱὸς Ἰωσήφ, οὗ ἡμεῖς οἴδαμεν
τὸν πατέρα καὶ τὴν μητέρα; πῶς οὖν λέγει ὅτι Ἐκ τοῦ οὐρανοῦ
43 καταβέβηκα; ἀπεκρίθη οὖν ὁ Ἰησοῦς καὶ εἶπεν αὐτοῖς, Μὴ γογγύ- ξ ι
44 ζετε μετ' ἀλλήλων. οὐδεὶς δύναται ἐλθεῖν πρός με, ἐὰν μὴ ὁ πατὴρ
ὁ πέμψας με ἑλκύσῃ αὐτόν, κἀγὼ ἀναστήσω αὐτὸν ἐν τῇ ἐσχάτῃ
45 ἡμέρᾳ. ἔστι γεγραμμένον ἐν τοῖς προφήταις, Καὶ ἔσονται πάντες
διδακτοὶ Θεοῦ. πᾶς οὖν ὁ ἀκούσας παρὰ τοῦ πατρὸς καὶ μαθὼν ἔρχε-
46 ται πρός με· οὐχ ὅτι τὸν πατέρα τις ἑώρακεν, εἰ μὴ ὁ ὢν ἐκ τοῦ ξα γ
47 Θεοῦ, οὗτος ἑώρακε τὸν πατέρα. ἀμὴν ἀμὴν λέγω ὑμῖν, ὁ πιστεύων ξβ ι
48 49 εἰς ἐμὲ ἔχει ζωὴν αἰώνιον. ἐγώ εἰμι ὁ ἄρτος τῆς ζωῆς. οἱ πατέρες
50 ὑμῶν ἔφαγον τὸ μάννα ἐν τῇ ἐρήμῳ, καὶ ἀπέθανον· οὗτός ἐστιν ὁ ξγ α
ἄρτος ὁ ἐκ τοῦ οὐρανοῦ καταβαίνων, ἵνα τις ἐξ αὐτοῦ φάγῃ καὶ μὴ ξδ ι
51 ἀποθάνῃ. ἐγώ εἰμι ὁ ἄρτος ὁ ζῶν, ὁ ἐκ τοῦ οὐρανοῦ καταβάς· ἐάν ξε α
τις φάγῃ ἐκ τούτου τοῦ ἄρτου, ζήσεται εἰς τὸν αἰῶνα. καὶ ὁ ἄρτος
δὲ ὃν ἐγὼ δώσω ἡ σάρξ μου ἐστίν, ἣν ἐγὼ δώσω ὑπὲρ τῆς τοῦ κόσμου
52 ζωῆς. ἐμάχοντο οὖν οἱ Ἰουδαῖοι πρὸς ἀλλήλους λέγοντες, Πῶς ξς ι
53 δύναται ἡμῖν οὗτος δοῦναι τὴν σάρκα φαγεῖν; εἶπεν οὖν αὐτοῖς ὁ
Ἰησοῦς, Ἀμὴν ἀμὴν λέγω ὑμῖν, ἐὰν μὴ φάγητε τὴν σάρκα τοῦ υἱοῦ
τοῦ ἀνθρώπου καὶ πίητε αὐτοῦ τὸ αἷμα, οὐκ ἔχετε ζωὴν ἐν ἑαυτοῖς.
54 ὁ τρώγων μου τὴν σάρκα καὶ πίνων μου τὸ αἷμα ἔχει ζωὴν αἰώνιον,
55 κἀγὼ ἀναστήσω αὐτὸν τῇ ἐσχάτῃ ἡμέρᾳ. ἡ γὰρ σάρξ μου ἀληθής ξζ α

35 πινασῃ 209, πεινασῃ 118 ς διψησῃ 118 209 ς **37** εμε 118 209 ς 118 209 ς εκβαλλω 118 209 sed 209 primum εκβαλω tum autem λ alterum scripsisse videtur **39** με] + πατρος 118² 209 ς, 118* ni fallor spatium reliquit αλλα ς εν τῃ ς **40** γαρ] δε ς πατρος μου] πεμψαντος με ς εν τῃ 118, εγω τῃ ς **42** om ο 1° ς λεγει ουτος ς **43** om ο 118 209 **44** και εγω 118 ς om εν ς **45** του Θεου ς **46** εκ] παρα ς **52** προς αλληλους οι Ιουδαιοι ς ουτος ημιν ς **54** και εγω 118 ς **55** αληθως bis ς

ξη ἔστι βρῶσις, καὶ τὸ αἷμά μου ἀληθής ἐστι πόσις. ὁ τρώγων μου 56
ι τὴν σάρκα καὶ πίνων μου τὸ αἷμα ἐν ἐμοὶ μένει, κἀγὼ ἐν αὐτῷ. καθὼς 57
ἀπέστειλέ με ὁ ζῶν πατήρ, κἀγὼ ζῶ διὰ τὸν πατέρα, καὶ ὁ τρώγων
με, κἀκεῖνος ζήσεται δι' ἐμέ. οὗτός ἐστιν ὁ ἄρτος ὁ ἐκ τοῦ 58
οὐρανοῦ καταβάς· οὐ καθὼς ἔφαγον οἱ πατέρες ὑμῶν τὸ μάννα, καὶ
ἀπέθανον· ὁ τρώγων τοῦτον τὸν ἄρτον ζήσει εἰς τὸν αἰῶνα. ταῦτα 59
ἐλάλησεν ἐν συναγωγῇ διδάσκων ἐν Καπερναούμ.

Πολλοὶ οὖν ἀκούσαντες ἐκ τῶν μαθητῶν αὐτοῦ εἶπον, Σκληρός ἐστιν 60
ὁ λόγος οὗτος· τίς δύναται αὐτοῦ ἀκούειν; εἰδὼς δὲ ὁ Ἰησοῦς ἐν 61
ἑαυτῷ ὅτι γογγύζουσι περὶ τούτου οἱ μαθηταὶ αὐτοῦ, εἶπεν αὐτοῖς,
ξθ Τοῦτο ὑμᾶς σκανδαλίζει; ἐὰν οὖν θεωρῆτε τὸν υἱὸν τοῦ ἀνθρώπου 62
α ἀναβαίνοντα ὅπου ἦν τὸ πρότερον; τὸ πνεῦμά ἐστι τὸ ζωοποιοῦν, ἡ 63
ο δ σὰρξ οὐκ ὠφελεῖ οὐδέν· τὰ ῥήματα ἃ ἐγὼ λελάληκα ὑμῖν πνεῦμά
οα ι ἐστι καὶ ζωή ἐστιν. ἀλλ' εἰσὶν ἐξ ὑμῶν τινες οἳ οὐ πιστεύουσιν. 64
οβ ἤδει γὰρ ἐξ ἀρχῆς ὁ Ἰησοῦς τίνες εἰσὶν οἱ μὴ πιστεύοντες, καὶ τίς
δ ἐστιν ὁ παραδώσων αὐτόν. καὶ ἔλεγε, Διὰ τοῦτο εἴρηκα ὑμῖν ὅτι οὐδεὶς 65
ογ ι δύναται ἐλθεῖν πρός με, ἐὰν μὴ ᾖ δεδομένον αὐτῷ ἐκ τοῦ πατρός μου.
ἐκ τούτου πολλοὶ ἐκ τῶν μαθητῶν αὐτοῦ ἀπῆλθον εἰς τὰ ὀπίσω, 66
καὶ οὐκέτι μετ' αὐτοῦ περιεπάτουν. εἶπεν οὖν ὁ Ἰησοῦς τοῖς δώδεκα, 67
οδ Μὴ καὶ ὑμεῖς θέλετε ὑπάγειν; ἀπεκρίθη αὐτῷ Σίμων Πέτρος, Κύριε, 68
α πρὸς τίνα ἀπελευσόμεθα; ῥήματα ζωῆς αἰωνίου ἔχεις· καὶ ἡμεῖς πεπι- 69
στεύκαμεν καὶ ἐγνώκαμεν ὅτι σὺ εἶ ὁ Χριστὸς ὁ υἱὸς τοῦ Θεοῦ.
οε ἀπεκρίθη αὐτοῖς ὁ Ἰησοῦς, Οὐκ ἐγὼ ὑμᾶς τοὺς δώδεκα ἐξελεξάμην, καὶ 70
ι ἐξ ὑμῶν εἷς διάβολός ἐστιν; ἔλεγε δὲ Ἰούδαν Σίμωνος Ἰσκαριώτην· 71
οὗτος γὰρ ἔμελλεν αὐτὸν παραδιδόναι εἷς ὢν ἐκ τῶν δώδεκα.

VII. Καὶ μετὰ ταῦτα περιεπάτει ὁ Ἰησοῦς ἐν τῇ Γαλιλαίᾳ·
οὐ γὰρ ἤθελεν ἐν τῇ Ἰουδαίᾳ περιπατεῖν, ὅτι ἐζήτουν αὐτὸν οἱ Ἰουδαῖοι
ἀποκτεῖναι. ἦν δὲ ἐγγὺς ἡ ἑορτὴ τῶν Ἰουδαίων ἡ σκηνοπηγία. εἶπον 2 3
οὖν πρὸς αὐτὸν οἱ ἀδελφοὶ αὐτοῦ, Μετάβηθι ἐντεῦθεν καὶ ὕπαγε εἰς
τὴν Ἰουδαίαν, ἵνα καὶ οἱ μαθηταί σου θεωρήσωσι τὰ ἔργα ἃ σὺ ποιεῖς·
οὐδεὶς γὰρ ἐν κρυπτῷ τι ποιεῖ, καὶ ζητεῖ αὐτὸς ἐν παρρησίᾳ εἶναι. εἰ 4
ταῦτα ποιεῖς, φανέρωσον σεαυτὸν τῷ κόσμῳ. οὐδὲ γὰρ οἱ ἀδελφοὶ 5
αὐτοῦ ἐπίστευον εἰς αὐτόν. λέγει οὖν αὐτοῖς ὁ Ἰησοῦς, Ὁ καιρὸς ὁ 6

67 ουν] pr rasura in qua nihil legi potest
69 Θεου] m. recen. add. in marg. του ζωντος

118 209 **57** om ο τρωγων με κακεινος ζησεται δι εμε 209 **58** ζησεται ς
ς **59** ελαλησεν] ειπεν 118 ς **60** ουτος ο λογος ς **63** λαλω ς
66 απηλθον των μαθητων αυτου ς **68** απεκριθη ουν ς **69** Θεου]+του
ζωντος 118[rubr] in mg ς **71** τον Ιουδαν ς ημελλεν ς
1 περιεπατει ο Ιησους μετα ταυτα ς **3** α συ] σου α ς

ἐμὸς οὔπω πάρεστιν· ὁ δὲ καιρὸς ὁ ὑμέτερος πάντοτέ ἐστιν ἕτοιμος.
7 οὐ δύναται ὁ κόσμος μισεῖν ὑμᾶς· ἐμὲ δὲ μισεῖ, ὅτι ἐγὼ μαρτυρῶ περὶ
8 αὐτοῦ ὅτι τὰ ἔργα αὐτοῦ πονηρά ἐστιν. ὑμεῖς ἀνάβητε εἰς τὴν ἑορτήν·
ἐγὼ οὔπω ἀναβαίνω εἰς τὴν ἑορτὴν ταύτην, ὅτι ὁ ἐμὸς καιρὸς οὔπω
9 πεπλήρωται. ταῦτα εἰπὼν αὐτὸς ἔμεινεν ἐν τῇ Γαλιλαίᾳ.
10 Ὡς δὲ ἀνέβησαν οἱ ἀδελφοὶ αὐτοῦ, τότε καὶ αὐτὸς ἀνέβη εἰς τὴν
11 ἑορτήν, οὐ φανερῶς, ἀλλ' ὡς ἐν κρυπτῷ. οἱ οὖν Ἰουδαῖοι ἐζήτουν
12 αὐτὸν ἐν τῇ ἑορτῇ καὶ ἔλεγον, Ποῦ ἐστιν ἐκεῖνος; καὶ γογγυσμὸς
πολὺς περὶ αὐτοῦ ἦν ἐν τοῖς ὄχλοις. οἱ μὲν ἔλεγον ὅτι Ἀγαθός
13 ἐστιν· ἄλλοι δὲ ἔλεγον ὅτι Ἀλλὰ πλανᾷ τὸν ὄχλον. οὐδεὶς μέντοι
παρρησίᾳ ἐλάλει περὶ αὐτοῦ διὰ τὸν φόβον τῶν Ἰουδαίων.
14 Ἤδη δὲ τῆς ἑορτῆς μεσαζούσης, ἀνέβη ὁ Ἰησοῦς εἰς τὸ ἱερόν,
15 καὶ ἐδίδασκε. ἐθαύμαζον οὖν οἱ Ἰουδαῖοι λέγοντες, Πῶς οὗτος γράμ-
16 ματα οἶδε μὴ μεμαθηκώς; ἀπεκρίθη αὐτοῖς ὁ Ἰησοῦς καὶ εἶπεν,
17 Ἡ ἐμὴ διδαχὴ οὐκ ἔστιν ἐμή, ἀλλὰ τοῦ πέμψαντός με· ἐάν τις θέλῃ
τὸ θέλημα αὐτοῦ ποιεῖν, γνώσεται περὶ τῆς διδαχῆς, πότερον ἐκ τοῦ
18 Θεοῦ ἐστιν ἢ ἐγὼ ἀπ' ἐμαυτοῦ λαλῶ. ὁ ἀφ' ἑαυτοῦ λαλῶν τὴν δόξαν
τὴν ἰδίαν ζητεῖ· ὁ δὲ ζητῶν τὴν δόξαν τοῦ πέμψαντος αὐτόν, οὗτος
19 ἀληθής ἐστι, καὶ ἀδικία ἐν αὐτῷ οὐκ ἔστιν. οὐ Μωσῆς δέδωκεν
ὑμῖν τὸν νόμον, καὶ οὐδεὶς ἐξ ὑμῶν ποιεῖ τὸν νόμον; τί με ζητεῖτε
20 ἀποκτεῖναι; ἀπεκρίθη αὐτῷ ὁ ὄχλος καὶ εἶπε, Δαιμόνιον ἔχεις· τίς σε
21 ζητεῖ ἀποκτεῖναι; ἀπεκρίθη Ἰησοῦς καὶ εἶπεν αὐτοῖς, Ἓν ἔργον
22 ἐποίησα, καὶ πάντες θαυμάζετε. διὰ τοῦτο Μωσῆς δέδωκεν ὑμῖν τὴν
περιτομήν (οὐχ ὅτι ἐκ τοῦ Μωσέως ἐστίν, ἀλλ' ἐκ τῶν πατέρων),
23 καὶ ἐν σαββάτῳ περιτέμνετε ἄνθρωπον. εἰ περιτομὴν λαμβάνει
ἄνθρωπος ἐν σαββάτῳ ἵνα μὴ λυθῇ ὁ νόμος Μωσέως, ἐμοὶ χολᾶτε
24 ὅτι ὅλον ἄνθρωπον ὑγιῆ ἐποίησα ἐν σαββάτῳ; μὴ κρίνετε κατ'
25 ὄψιν, ἀλλὰ τὴν δικαίαν κρίσιν κρίνατε. ἔλεγον οὖν τινες ἐκ τῶν
26 Ἱεροσολυμιτῶν, Οὐχ οὗτός ἐστιν ὃν ζητοῦσιν ἀποκτεῖναι; καὶ ἴδε παρ-
ρησίᾳ λαλεῖ, καὶ οὐδὲν αὐτῷ λέγουσι. μήποτε ἀληθῶς ἔγνωσαν οἱ
27 ἄρχοντες, ὅτι οὗτός ἐστιν ὁ Χριστός; ἀλλὰ τοῦτον οἴδαμεν πόθεν
28 ἐστίν· ὁ δὲ Χριστὸς ὅταν ἔρχηται, οὐδεὶς γινώσκει πόθεν ἐστίν. ἔκραξεν ος
οὖν ὁ Ἰησοῦς ἐν τῷ ἱερῷ διδάσκων καὶ λέγων, Κἀμὲ οἴδατε, καὶ οἴδατε γ
πόθεν εἰμί· καὶ ἀπ' ἐμαυτοῦ οὐκ ἐλήλυθα, ἀλλ' ἔστιν ἀληθινὸς ὁ πέμψας
29 με, ὃν ὑμεῖς οὐκ οἴδατε· ἐγὼ δὲ οἶδα αὐτόν, ὅτι παρ' αὐτοῦ εἰμι, κἀκεῖ-

8 εορτην ταυτην ς ο καιρος ο εμος ς **9** ταυτα δε ς αυτος] αυτοις ς 118 209
12 om δε 118 209 οτι] ου 118 209 ς **14** μεσουσης ς **15** και ς
εθαυμαζον ς, εθαυμαζον δε 118 209 οιδε γραμματα 118 209 μεθαθηκως 118
20 om αυτω ς **21** ο Ιησους ς **22** περιτεμνεται ανθρωπος 118 209
26 εστιν αληθως ς **27** ποθεν] ὅθεν 118* sed postea ipse π supra ὅ scripsit
28 ο Ιησους post διδασκων ς

οζ/α νός με ἀπέστειλεν. ἐζήτουν οὖν αὐτὸν πιάσαι· καὶ οὐδεὶς ἐπέβαλεν 30
ἐπ' αὐτὸν τὰς χεῖρας, ὅτι οὔπω ἐληλύθει ἡ ὥρα αὐτοῦ. ἐκ τοῦ ὄχλου 31
οη/ι οὖν πολλοὶ ἐπίστευσαν εἰς αὐτὸν καὶ ἔλεγον, Ὁ Χριστὸς ὅταν ἔλθῃ,
μὴ πλείονα σημεῖα ποιήσει ὧν οὗτος ἐποίησεν; ἤκουσαν οὖν οἱ 32
οθ/α Φαρισαῖοι τοῦ ὄχλου γογγύζοντος περὶ αὐτοῦ· καὶ ἀπέστειλαν οἱ
π/ι ἀρχιερεῖς καὶ οἱ Φαρισαῖοι ὑπηρέτας, ἵνα πιάσωσιν αὐτόν. εἶπεν 33
οὖν αὐτοῖς ὁ Ἰησοῦς, Ἔτι μικρὸν χρόνον μεθ' ὑμῶν εἰμι, καὶ ὑπάγω
πα/ι πρὸς τὸν πέμψαντά με. ζητήσετέ με, καὶ οὐχ εὑρήσετε· καὶ ὅπου εἰμὶ 34
ἐγὼ ὑμεῖς οὐ δύνασθε ἐλθεῖν. εἶπον οὖν οἱ Ἰουδαῖοι πρὸς ἑαυτούς, 35
Ποῦ οὗτος μέλλει πορεύεσθαι, ὅτι ἡμεῖς οὐχ εὑρήσομεν αὐτόν; μὴ εἰς
τὴν διασπορὰν τῶν Ἑλλήνων μέλλει πορεύεσθαι, καὶ διδάσκειν τοὺς
Ἕλληνας; τίς ἐστιν ὁ λόγος οὗτος ὃν εἶπε, Ζητήσετέ με, καὶ οὐχ 36
εὑρήσετέ με, καί, Ὅπου εἰμὶ ἐγὼ ὑμεῖς οὐ δύνασθε ἐλθεῖν;

Ἐν δὲ τῇ ἐσχάτῃ ἡμέρᾳ τῇ μεγάλῃ τῆς ἑορτῆς εἱστήκει ὁ Ἰησοῦς 37
καὶ ἔκραζε λέγων, Ἐάν τις διψᾷ, ἐρχέσθω πρός με καὶ πινέτω· ὁ 38
πιστεύων εἰς ἐμέ, καθὼς εἶπεν ἡ γραφή, ποταμοὶ ἐκ τῆς κοιλίας αὐτοῦ
ῥεύσουσιν ὕδατος ζῶντος. τοῦτο δὲ εἶπε περὶ τοῦ Πνεύματος οὗ ἔμελ- 39
λον λαμβάνειν οἱ πιστεύοντες εἰς αὐτόν· οὔπω γὰρ ἦν Πνεῦμα Ἅγιον,
πβ/ζ ὅτι Ἰησοῦς οὐδέπω ἐδοξάσθη. ἐκ τοῦ ὄχλου οὖν ἀκούσαντες τῶν 40
λόγων τούτων ἔλεγον, Οὗτός ἐστιν ἀληθῶς ὁ προφήτης. ἄλλοι δὲ 41
πγ/ζ ἔλεγον, Οὗτός ἐστιν ὁ Χριστός. οἱ δὲ ἔλεγον, Μὴ γὰρ ἐκ τῆς
Γαλιλαίας ὁ Χριστὸς ἔρχεται; οὐχὶ ἡ γραφὴ εἶπεν ὅτι ἐκ σπέρματος 42
Δαβίδ, καὶ ἀπὸ Βηθλεὲμ τῆς κώμης ὅπου ἦν Δαβίδ, ὁ Χριστὸς ἔρχεται;
πδ/ι σχίσμα οὖν ἐν τῷ ὄχλῳ ἐγένετο δι' αὐτόν. τινὲς δὲ ἤθελον ἐξ αὐτῶν 43 44
πε/α πιάσαι αὐτόν, ἀλλ' οὐδεὶς ἐπέβαλεν ἐπ' αὐτὸν τὰς χεῖρας. ἦλθον οὖν 45
οἱ ὑπηρέται πρὸς τοὺς ἀρχιερεῖς καὶ Φαρισαίους· καὶ εἶπον αὐτοῖς ἐκεῖνοι,
πϛ/ι Διατί οὐκ ἠγάγετε αὐτόν; ἀπεκρίθησαν οἱ ὑπηρέται, Οὐδέποτε οὕτως 46
ἐλάλησεν ἄνθρωπος ὡς οὗτος ὁ ἄνθρωπος. ἀπεκρίθησαν αὐτοῖς οἱ 47
Φαρισαῖοι, Μὴ καὶ ὑμεῖς πεπλάνησθε; μή τις ἐκ τῶν ἀρχόντων ἐπί- 48
στευσεν εἰς αὐτὸν ἢ ἐκ τῶν Φαρισαίων; ἀλλ' ὁ ὄχλος οὗτος ὁ μὴ 49
γινώσκων τὸν νόμον ἐπάρατοί εἰσι. λέγει Νικόδημος πρὸς αὐτούς, 50
ὁ ἐλθὼν νυκτὸς πρὸς αὐτὸν τὸ πρότερον, εἷς ὢν ἐξ αὐτῶν, Μὴ ὁ 51

118 209 ς

30 πιασαι αυτον 118 209 την χειρα ς **31** πολλοι δε εκ του οχλου ς ελεγον οτι ς μη] μη 118 209 ς σημεια] + τουτων ς, pr τουτων 118 209 **32** αυτου] + ταυτα ς οι Φαρισαιοι και οι αρχιερεις ς, haec om 118 209 **36** ουτος ο λογος ς om με 2° 118 209 ς **37** εκραξε ς **39** ο Ιησους ς **40** εκ] pr πολλοι ουν ς ουν] om ς, + πολλοι 118 τον λογον ς τουτων om ς **41** δε 1°] om ς οι] αλλοι ς **42** του σπερματος ς **47** απεκριθησαν ουν 118 ς **49** επικαταραγοι 118 209 ς **50** om το προτερον ς

νόμος ἡμῶν κρίνει τὸν ἄνθρωπον, ἐὰν μὴ ἀκούσῃ παρ' αὐτοῦ πρῶτον
52 καὶ γνῷ τί ποιεῖ; ἀπεκρίθησαν καὶ εἶπον αὐτῷ, Μὴ καὶ σὺ ἐκ τῆς
Γαλιλαίας εἶ; ἐρεύνησον καὶ ἴδε ὅτι προφήτης ἐκ τῆς Γαλιλαίας οὐκ
ἐγείγερται.

12 VIII. Πάλιν οὖν ἐλάλησεν αὐτοῖς ὁ Ἰησοῦς λέγων, Ἐγώ εἰμι
τὸ φῶς τοῦ κόσμου· ὁ ἀκολουθῶν ἐμοὶ οὐ μὴ περιπατήσει ἐν τῇ σκοτίᾳ,
13 ἀλλ' ἕξει τὸ φῶς τῆς ζωῆς. οἱ οὖν Φαρισαῖοι εἶπον αὐτῷ, Σὺ
14 περὶ σεαυτοῦ μαρτυρεῖς· ἡ μαρτυρία σου οὐκ ἔστιν ἀληθής. ἀπεκρίθη
Ἰησοῦς καὶ εἶπεν αὐτοῖς, Κἂν ἐγὼ μαρτυρῶ περὶ ἐμαυτοῦ, ἀληθής ἐστιν
ἡ μαρτυρία μου, ὅτι οἶδα πόθεν ἦλθον καὶ ποῦ ὑπάγω· ὑμεῖς δὲ οὐκ
15 οἴδατε πόθεν ἔρχομαι ἢ ποῦ ὑπάγω· ὑμεῖς κατὰ τὴν σάρκα κρίνετε· ἐγὼ
16 οὐ κρίνω οὐδένα· καὶ ἐὰν κρίνω δὲ ἐγώ, ἡ κρίσις ἡ ἐμὴ ἀληθής ἐστιν,
17 ὅτι μόνος οὐκ εἰμί, ἀλλ' ἐγὼ καὶ ὁ πέμψας με πατήρ. καὶ ἐν τῷ
νόμῳ δὲ τῷ ὑμετέρῳ γέγραπται ὅτι δύο ἀνθρώπων ἡ μαρτυρία ἀληθής
18 ἐστιν· ἐγώ εἰμι ὁ μαρτυρῶν περὶ ἐμαυτοῦ, καὶ μαρτυρεῖ περὶ ἐμοῦ
19 ὁ πέμψας με πατήρ. ἔλεγον οὖν αὐτῷ, Ποῦ ἐστιν ὁ πατήρ σου; πζ
ἀπεκρίθη Ἰησοῦς, Οὔτε ἐμὲ οἴδατε, οὔτε τὸν πατέρα μου· εἰ ἐμὲ γ
20 ᾔδειτε, καὶ τὸν πατέρα μου ἂν ᾔδειτε. ταῦτα τὰ ῥήματα ἐλάλησεν ὁ πη
Ἰησοῦς ἐν τῷ γαζοφυλακίῳ διδάσκων ἐν τῷ ἱερῷ· καὶ οὐδεὶς ἐπίασεν α
αὐτόν, ὅτι οὔπω ἐληλύθει ἡ ὥρα αὐτοῦ.

21 Εἶπεν οὖν πάλιν αὐτοῖς ὁ Ἰησοῦς, Ἐγὼ ὑπάγω, καὶ ζητήσετέ με, πθ
καὶ οὐχ εὑρήσετέ με, καὶ ἐν τῇ ἁμαρτίᾳ ὑμῶν ἀποθανεῖσθε· καὶ ι
22 ὅπου ἐγὼ ὑπάγω ὑμεῖς οὐ δύνασθε ἐλθεῖν. ἔλεγον οὖν οἱ Ἰουδαῖοι,
Μήτι ἀποκτενεῖ ἑαυτόν, ὅτι λέγει, Ὅπου ἐγὼ ὑπάγω ὑμεῖς οὐ δύνασθε
23 ἐλθεῖν; καὶ εἶπεν αὐτοῖς, Ὑμεῖς ἐκ τῶν κάτω ἐστέ, ἐγὼ ἐκ τῶν ἄνω
εἰμί· ὑμεῖς ἐκ τοῦ κόσμου τούτου ἐστέ, ἐγὼ οὐκ εἰμὶ ἐκ τοῦ κόσμου
24 τούτου. εἶπον οὖν ὑμῖν ὅτι ἀποθανεῖσθε ἐν ταῖς ἁμαρτίαις ὑμῶν· ἐὰν
γὰρ μὴ πιστεύσητε ὅτι ἐγώ εἰμι, ἀποθανεῖσθε ἐν ταῖς ἁμαρ-
25 τίαις ὑμῶν. ἔλεγον οὖν αὐτῷ, Σὺ τίς εἶ; εἶπεν αὐτοῖς ὁ Ἰησοῦς,
26 Τὴν ἀρχὴν ὅ τι καὶ λαλῶ ὑμῖν. πολλὰ ἔχω περὶ ὑμῶν λαλεῖν καὶ
κρίνειν· ἀλλ' ὁ πέμψας με ἀληθής ἐστι, κἀγὼ ἃ ἤκουσα παρ' αὐτοῦ,

51 *πρωτον*] *προτερον* ς 52 *εγηγερται* 209 ς 53—VIII 11 hanc pericopen hoc loco praebent 118 209 ς; post finem evangelii 1; primo omisit 209*, verbis *παλιν ουν ελαλησεν ο Ιησους* scriptis et postea erasis. textum cum variis lectionibus invenies sub fine evangelii. (118 209 ς) 13 *ειπον ουν αυτω οι Φαρισαιοι* 118 209 ς om *ουκ εστιν* 118 14 *ἡ*] *και* ς 19 *ο Ιησους* ς *αν*] post *ηδειτε* 118 ς, om 209 21 om *και ουχ ευρησετε με* ς om *με* 2° 118 om *και* 2° 118 209 ς 22 *εαυτον*] *αυτον* 118 24 *εαν...υμων*] om 118* 209* sed add. 209² in marg. et 118* errore detecto quae omiserat in textu ipse scripsit 25 *και ειπεν* ς

ταῦτα λαλῶ εἰς τὸν κόσμον. οὐκ ἔγνωσαν ὅτι τὸν πατέρα αὐτοῖς 27
ἔλεγεν. εἶπεν οὖν ὁ Ἰησοῦς, Ὅταν ὑψώσητε τὸν υἱὸν τοῦ ἀνθρώπου, 28
τότε γνώσεσθε ὅτι ἐγώ εἰμι· καὶ ἀπ' ἐμαυτοῦ ποιῶ οὐδέν, ἀλλὰ καθὼς
ἐδίδαξέ με ὁ πατήρ μου, ταῦτα λαλῶ. καὶ ὁ πέμψας με μετ' ἐμοῦ 29
ἐστιν· καὶ οὐκ ἀφῆκέ με μόνον, ὅτι ἐγὼ τὰ ἀρεστὰ αὐτῷ ποιῶ πάντοτε.
ταῦτα αὐτοῦ λαλοῦντος πολλοὶ ἐπίστευσαν εἰς αὐτόν. 30
Ἔλεγεν οὖν ὁ Ἰησοῦς πρὸς τοὺς πεπιστευκότας αὐτῷ Ἰουδαίους, 31
Ἐὰν ὑμεῖς μείνητε ἐν τῷ λόγῳ τῷ ἐμῷ, ἀληθῶς μαθηταί μού ἐστε,
καὶ γνώσεσθε τὴν ἀλήθειαν, καὶ ἡ ἀλήθεια ἐλευθερώσει ὑμᾶς. ἀπεκρί- 32 33
θησαν αὐτῷ καὶ εἶπον, Σπέρμα Ἀβραάμ ἐσμεν, καὶ οὐδενὶ δεδουλεύ-
καμεν πώποτε· πῶς σὺ λέγεις, Ἐλεύθεροι γενήσεσθε; ἀπεκρίθη αὐτοῖς 34
ὁ Ἰησοῦς, Ἀμὴν ἀμὴν λέγω ὑμῖν ὅτι πᾶς ὁ ποιῶν τὴν ἁμαρτίαν δοῦλός
ἐστι τῆς ἁμαρτίας· ὁ δὲ δοῦλος οὐ μένει ἐν τῇ οἰκίᾳ εἰς τὸν αἰῶνα· 35
ὁ υἱὸς μένει εἰς τὸν αἰῶνα· ἐὰν οὖν ὁ υἱὸς ὑμᾶς ἐλευθερώσῃ, ὄντως 36
ἐλεύθεροι ἔσεσθε. οἶδα ὅτι σπέρμα Ἀβραάμ ἐστε· ἀλλὰ ζητεῖτέ με 37
ἀποκτεῖναι, ὅτι ὁ λόγος ὁ ἐμὸς οὐ χωρεῖ ἐν ὑμῖν. ὃ ἐγὼ ἑώρακα παρὰ 38
τῷ πατρί μου λαλῶ· καὶ ὑμεῖς οὖν ἃ ἠκούσατε παρὰ τοῦ πατρὸς
ὑμῶν ποιεῖτε. ἀπεκρίθησαν καὶ εἶπον αὐτῷ, Ὁ πατὴρ ἡμῶν Ἀβραάμ 39
ἐστι. λέγει αὐτοῖς ὁ Ἰησοῦς, Εἰ τέκνα τοῦ Ἀβραὰμ ἦτε, τὰ ἔργα
τοῦ Ἀβραὰμ ἐποιεῖτε ἄν. νῦν δὲ ζητεῖτέ με ἀποκτεῖναι, ἄνθρωπον 40
ὃς τὴν ἀλήθειαν ὑμῖν λελάληκα, ἣν ἤκουσα παρὰ τοῦ Θεοῦ· τοῦτο
Ἀβραὰμ οὐκ ἐποίησεν. ὑμεῖς δὲ ποιεῖτε τὰ ἔργα τοῦ πατρὸς ὑμῶν. 41
εἶπον αὐτῷ, Ἡμεῖς ἐκ πορνείας οὐ γεγεννήμεθα· ἕνα πατέρα ἔχομεν
τὸν Θεόν. εἶπεν αὐτοῖς ὁ Ἰησοῦς, Εἰ ὁ Θεὸς πατὴρ ὑμῶν ἦν, ἠγαπᾶτε 42
ἂν ἐμέ· ἐγὼ γὰρ ἐκ τοῦ Θεοῦ ἐξῆλθον καὶ ἥκω· οὐδὲ γὰρ ἀπ' ἐμαυτοῦ
ἐλήλυθα, ἀλλ' ἐκεῖνός με ἀπέστειλε. διατί τὴν λαλιὰν τὴν ἐμὴν οὐ 43
γινώσκετε; ὅτι οὐ δύνασθε ἀκούειν τὸν λόγον τὸν ἐμόν. ὑμεῖς ἐκ τοῦ 44
πατρὸς τοῦ διαβόλου ἐστέ, καὶ τὰς ἐπιθυμίας τοῦ πατρὸς ὑμῶν θέλετε
ποιεῖν. ἐκεῖνος ἀνθρωποκτόνος ἦν ἀπ' ἀρχῆς, καὶ ἐν τῇ ἀληθείᾳ οὐχ
ἕστηκεν· ὅτι οὐκ ἔστιν ἀλήθεια ἐν αὐτῷ. ὅταν λαλῇ τὸ ψεῦδος, ἐκ τῶν
ἰδίων λαλεῖ· ὅτι ψεύστης ἐστὶ καὶ ὁ πατὴρ αὐτοῦ. ἐγὼ δὲ ὅτι τὴν 45
ἀλήθειαν λέγω, οὐ πιστεύετέ μοι. τίς ἐξ ὑμῶν ἐλέγχει με περὶ ἁμαρ- 46
τίας; εἰ ἀλήθειαν λέγω, διατί ὑμεῖς οὐ πιστεύετέ μοι; ὁ ὢν ἐκ τοῦ 47

36 οντως] οτως cod. **42** ῆκω cod.

118 209 ς **26** λαλω] λεγω ς **27** και ουκ 118 209 **28** ουν αυτοις 118 209 ς **29** om και 118 209 ς μονον] + ο πατηρ 118 209 ς **33** om και ειπον 118 209 ς Ἀβρααμ ς et sic passim λεγεις οτι 118 209 ς **35** ο δε υιος 118 209 **38** εγω ο 118 209 ς α ηκουσατε] ο εωρακατε 118 209 ς τω πατρι 118 209 ς **41** om δε 118 209 ς ειπον ουν 118 209 ς **42** ειπεν ουν 118 209 ς **44** om του 1° ς **46** ει δε ς

Θεοῦ τὰ ῥήματα τοῦ Θεοῦ ἀκούει· διὰ τοῦτο ὑμεῖς οὐκ ἀκούετε, ὅτι ἐκ
48 τοῦ Θεοῦ οὐκ ἐστέ. ἀπεκρίθησαν οἱ Ἰουδαῖοι καὶ εἶπον αὐτῷ, Οὐ
49 καλῶς λέγομεν ἡμεῖς ὅτι Σαμαρείτης εἶ καὶ δαιμόνιον ἔχεις; ἀπεκρίθη
Ἰησοῦς καὶ εἶπεν, Ἐγὼ δαιμόνιον οὐκ ἔχω, ἀλλὰ τιμῶ τὸν πατέρα
50 μου, καὶ ὑμεῖς ἀτιμάζετέ με. ἐγὼ δὲ οὐ ζητῶ τὴν δόξαν τὴν ἐμήν·
51 ἔστιν ὁ ζητῶν καὶ κρίνων. ἀμὴν ἀμὴν λέγω ὑμῖν, ἐάν τις τὸν λόγον
52 τὸν ἐμὸν τηρήσῃ, θάνατον οὐ μὴ θεωρήσει εἰς τὸν αἰῶνα. εἶπον
οὖν αὐτῷ οἱ Ἰουδαῖοι, Νῦν ἐγνώκαμεν ὅτι δαιμόνιον ἔχεις. Ἀβραὰμ
ἀπέθανε καὶ οἱ προφῆται, καὶ σὺ λέγεις, Ἐάν τις τὸν λόγον μου
53 τηρήσῃ, οὐ μὴ γεύσηται θανάτου εἰς τὸν αἰῶνα. μὴ σὺ μείζων εἶ
τοῦ πατρὸς ἡμῶν Ἀβραάμ, ὅστις ἀπέθανε; καὶ οἱ προφῆται ἀπέθανον·
54 τίνα σεαυτὸν ποιεῖς; ἀπεκρίθη Ἰησοῦς, Ἐὰν ἐγὼ δοξάσω ἐμαυτόν,
ἡ δόξα μου οὐδέν ἐστιν· ἔστιν ὁ πατήρ μου ὁ δοξάζων με, ὃν ὑμεῖς
55 λέγετε ὅτι Θεὸς ἡμῶν ἐστι, καὶ οὐκ ἐγνώκατε αὐτόν, ἐγὼ δὲ οἶδα
αὐτόν· καὶ ἐὰν εἴπω ὅτι οὐκ οἶδα αὐτόν, ἔσομαι ὅμοιος ὑμῖν ψεύστης·
56 ἀλλ' οἶδα αὐτὸν καὶ τὸν λόγον αὐτοῦ τηρῶ. Ἀβραὰμ ὁ πατὴρ ὑμῶν
57 ἠγαλλιάσατο ἵνα ἴδῃ τὴν ἡμέραν τὴν ἐμήν, καὶ εἶδε καὶ ἐχάρην. εἶπον
οὖν οἱ Ἰουδαῖοι πρὸς αὐτόν, Πεντήκοντα ἔτη οὔπω ἔχεις, καὶ Ἀβραὰμ
58 ἑώρακας; εἶπεν οὖν αὐτοῖς ὁ Ἰησοῦς, Ἀμὴν ἀμὴν λέγω ὑμῖν, πρὶν
59 Ἀβραὰμ γενέσθαι ἐγώ εἰμι. ἦραν οὖν λίθους ἵνα βάλωσιν ἐπ' αὐτόν·
Ἰησοῦς δὲ ἐκρύβη καὶ ἐξῆλθεν ἐκ τοῦ ἱεροῦ διελθὼν διὰ μέσου αὐτῶν,
καὶ παρῆγεν οὕτως.

2 IX. Καὶ παράγων εἶδεν ἄνθρωπον τυφλὸν ἐκ γεννητῆς. καὶ Ι'
ἠρώτησαν αὐτὸν οἱ μαθηταὶ αὐτοῦ λέγοντες, Ῥαββί, τίς ἥμαρτεν, οὗτος
3 ἢ οἱ γονεῖς αὐτοῦ, ἵνα τυφλὸς γεννηθῇ; ἀπεκρίθη Ἰησοῦς καὶ εἶπεν
αὐτοῖς, Οὔτε οὗτος ἥμαρτεν οὔτε οἱ γονεῖς αὐτοῦ· ἀλλ' ἵνα φανερωθῇ
4 τὰ ἔργα τοῦ Θεοῦ ἐν αὐτῷ. ἐμὲ δεῖ ἐργάζεσθαι τὰ ἔργα τοῦ πέμψαντός
5 με ἕως ἡμέρα ἐστίν· ἔρχεται νύξ, ὅτε οὐδεὶς δύναται ἐργάζεσθαι. ὅταν
6 ὦ ἐν τῷ κόσμῳ, φῶς εἰμι τοῦ κόσμου. ταῦτα εἰπὼν ἔπτυσε χαμαὶ
καὶ ἐποίησε πηλὸν ἐκ τοῦ πτύσματος, καὶ ἐπέχρισεν αὐτοῦ τοὺς
7 ὀφθαλμούς, καὶ εἶπεν αὐτῷ, Ὕπαγε νίψαι εἰς τὴν κολυμβήθραν τοῦ
Σιλωάμ· ὃ ἑρμηνεύεται ἀπεσταλμένος. ἀπῆλθεν οὖν καὶ ἐνίψατο, καὶ
ἦλθε βλέπων.

57 πεντικοντα cod.

48 απεκριθησαν ουν ϛ   ει συ ϛ   **49** om και ειπεν ϛ   **50** την εμην] 118 209 μου ϛ   **51** τηρηση] 118* primum ποιηση scripsit postea autem ipse correxit   θεωρηση 118 209 ϛ   **52** μου τον λογον 118 209   γευσεται ϛ   **53** συ ποιεις ϛ   **54** δοξαζω ϛ   ημων] υμων ϛ   **55** υμιν] υμων ϛ   **56** εχαρη ϛ   **58** om ουν ϛ

1 γεννητοις 118, γενετης ϛ   **3** ο Ιησους ϛ   om και ειπεν αυτοις ϛ   **5** εν τω κοσμω ω ϛ   **6** επεχρισε τον πηλον επι τους οφθαλμους του τυφλου ϛ

Οἱ οὖν γείτονες καὶ οἱ θεωροῦντες αὐτὸν τὸ πρότερον ὅτι προσ- 8
αιτὴς ἦν, ἔλεγον, Οὐχ οὗτός ἐστιν ὁ καθήμενος καὶ προσαιτῶν; ἄλλοι 9
ἔλεγον ὅτι Οὗτός ἐστιν· ἄλλοι δέ, Οὐχὶ ἀλλ' ὅμοιος αὐτῷ ἐστιν.
ἐκεῖνος ἔλεγεν ὅτι Ἐγώ εἰμι. ἔλεγον οὖν αὐτῷ, Πῶς ἀνεῴχθησάν σου 10
οἱ ὀφθαλμοί; ἀπεκρίθη ἐκεῖνος, Ὁ ἄνθρωπος ὁ λεγόμενος Ἰησοῦς 11
πηλὸν ἐποίησε καὶ ἐπέχρισέ μου τοὺς ὀφθαλμούς, καὶ εἶπέ μοι, Ὕπαγε
εἰς τὸν Σιλωὰμ καὶ νίψαι. ἀπελθὼν οὖν καὶ νιψάμενος ἀνέβλεψα.
καὶ εἶπον αὐτῷ, Ποῦ ἐστιν ἐκεῖνος; λέγει, Οὐκ οἶδα. 12
Ἄγουσιν αὐτὸν πρὸς τοὺς Φαρισαίους, τόν ποτε τυφλόν· ἦν δὲ 13 14
σάββατον ὅτε τὸν πηλὸν ἐποίησεν ὁ Ἰησοῦς καὶ ἀνέῳξεν αὐτοῦ τοὺς
ὀφθαλμούς. πάλιν οὖν ἠρώτων αὐτὸν καὶ οἱ Φαρισαῖοι, πῶς ἀνέβλε- 15
ψεν. ὁ δὲ εἶπεν αὐτοῖς, Πηλὸν ἐποίησε καὶ ἐπέθηκέ μου ἐπὶ τοὺς
ὀφθαλμούς, καὶ ἐνιψάμην, καὶ βλέπω. ἔλεγον οὖν ἐκ τῶν Φαρισαίων 16
τινές, Οὗτος ὁ ἄνθρωπος οὐκ ἔστι παρὰ Θεοῦ, ὅτι τὸ σάββατον οὐ
τηρεῖ. ἄλλοι δὲ ἔλεγον, Πῶς δύναται ἄνθρωπος ἁμαρτωλὸς τοιαῦτα
σημεῖα ποιεῖν; καὶ σχίσμα ἦν ἐν αὐτοῖς. λέγουσιν οὖν τῷ τυφλῷ 17
πάλιν, Σὺ τί λέγεις περὶ αὐτοῦ, ὅτι ἀνέωξέ σου τοὺς ὀφθαλμούς; ὁ
δὲ εἶπεν ὅτι Προφήτης ἐστίν. οὐκ ἐπίστευσαν οὖν οἱ Ἰουδαῖοι περὶ 18
αὐτοῦ, ὅτι τυφλὸς ἦν καὶ ἀνέβλεψεν, ἕως ὅτου ἐφώνησαν τοὺς γονεῖς
αὐτοῦ καὶ ἠρώτησαν αὐτοὺς λέγοντες, Οὗτός ἐστιν ὁ υἱὸς ὑμῶν, ὃν 19
ὑμεῖς λέγετε ὅτι τυφλὸς ἐγεννήθη; πῶς οὖν ἄρτι βλέπει; ἀπεκρί- 20
θησαν αὐτοῖς οἱ γονεῖς αὐτοῦ καὶ εἶπον, Οἴδαμεν ὅτι οὗτός ἐστιν ὁ
υἱὸς ἡμῶν, καὶ ὅτι τυφλὸς ἐγεννήθη· πῶς δὲ νῦν βλέπει οὐκ οἴδαμεν· 21
ἢ τίς ἠνέωξεν αὐτοῦ τοὺς ὀφθαλμοὺς ἡμεῖς οὐκ οἴδαμεν· αὐτὸν ἐρω-
τήσατε, ἡλικίαν ἔχει· αὐτὸς περὶ ἑαυτοῦ λαλήσει. ταῦτα εἶπον οἱ 22
γονεῖς αὐτοῦ, ὅτι ἐφοβοῦντο τοὺς Ἰουδαίους· ἤδη γὰρ συνετέθειντο οἱ
Ἰουδαῖοι ἵνα, ἐάν τις αὐτὸν ὁμολογήσῃ Χριστόν, ἀποσυνάγωγος γένηται.
διὰ τοῦτο οἱ γονεῖς αὐτοῦ εἶπον ὅτι Ἡλικίαν ἔχει, αὐτὸν ἐρωτήσατε. 23
ἐφώνησαν οὖν ἐκ δευτέρου τὸν ἄνθρωπον ὃς ἦν τυφλός, καὶ εἶπον αὐτῷ, 24
Δὸς δόξαν τῷ Θεῷ· ἡμεῖς οἴδαμεν ὅτι ὁ ἄνθρωπος οὗτος ἁμαρτωλός
ἐστιν. ἀπεκρίθη ἐκεῖνος, Εἰ ἁμαρτωλός ἐστιν οὐκ οἶδα· ἓν οἶδα, ὅτι 25
τυφλὸς ἤμην καὶ ἄρτι βλέπω. εἶπον οὖν αὐτῷ πάλιν, Τί ἐποίησέ 26
σοι; πῶς ἀνέωξέ σου τοὺς ὀφθαλμούς; ἀπεκρίθη αὐτοῖς, Εἶπον ὑμῖν 27

118 209 8 προσαιτης] τυφλος ς 9 ουχι αλλ] οτι ς 11 εκεινος] + και
ς ειπεν ς om ο 1° ς om ο 2° ς εις τον] εις του 118 209, εις την κολυμβηθραν του ς ουν] δε ς 12 ειπον ουν ς 15 om εποιησε και ς μου post οφθαλμους ς 16 του Θεου ς om δε ς 17 om ουν ς ηνοιξε ς 18 αυτου]+του αναβλεψαντος ς 21 ηνοιξεν ς αυτος ηλικιαν εχει· αυτον ερωτησατε 118 209 ς εαυτου] αυτου ς 25 απεκριθη ουν ς εκεινος]+και ειπε ς ημην και] ων ς 26 ουν] δε ς ηνοιξε ς

ἤδη, καὶ οὐκ ἠκούσατε· τί πάλιν θέλετε ἀκούειν; μὴ καὶ ὑμεῖς θέλετε
28 αὐτοῦ μαθηταὶ γενέσθαι; οἱ δὲ ἐλοιδόρησαν αὐτὸν καὶ εἶπον, Σὺ
29 μαθητὴς εἶ ἐκείνου· ἡμεῖς δὲ τοῦ Μωσέως ἐσμὲν μαθηταί. ἡμεῖς
οἴδαμεν ὅτι Μωσεῖ λελάληκεν ὁ Θεός, τοῦτον δὲ οὐκ οἴδαμεν πόθεν
30 ἐστίν. ἀπεκρίθη ὁ ἄνθρωπος καὶ εἶπεν αὐτοῖς, Ἐν γὰρ τούτῳ τὸ
θαυμαστόν ἐστιν, ὅτι ὑμεῖς οὐκ οἴδατε πόθεν ἐστί, καὶ ἀνέῳξέ μου
31 τοὺς ὀφθαλμούς. οἴδαμεν ὅτι ἁμαρτωλῶν ὁ Θεὸς οὐκ ἀκούει· ἀλλ᾽
32 ἐάν τις θεοσεβὴς ᾖ καὶ τὸ θέλημα αὐτοῦ ποιῇ, τούτου ἀκούει. ἐκ τοῦ
αἰῶνος οὐκ ἠκούσθη ὅτι ἀνέῳξέ τις ὀφθαλμοὺς τυφλοῦ γεγεννημένου.
33 34 εἰ μὴ ἦν οὗτος παρὰ Θεοῦ, οὐκ ἠδύνατο ποιεῖν οὐδέν. ἀπεκρίθησαν
καὶ εἶπον αὐτῷ, Ἐν ἁμαρτίαις σὺ ἐγεννήθης ὅλως, καὶ σὺ διδάσκεις
35 ἡμᾶς; καὶ ἐξέβαλον αὐτὸν ἔξω. ἤκουσεν ὁ Ἰησοῦς ὅτι ἐξέβαλον αὐτὸν
ἔξω· καὶ εὑρὼν αὐτὸν εἶπεν αὐτῷ, Σὺ πιστεύεις εἰς τὸν υἱὸν τοῦ
36 Θεοῦ; ἀπεκρίθη ἐκεῖνος καὶ εἶπε, Καὶ τίς ἐστι, κύριε, ἵνα πιστεύσω
37 εἰς αὐτόν; εἶπε δὲ αὐτῷ ὁ Ἰησοῦς, Καὶ ἑώρακας αὐτόν, καὶ ὁ λαλῶν
38 μετὰ σοῦ ἐκεῖνός ἐστιν. ὁ δὲ ἔφη, Πιστεύω, κύριε· καὶ προσεκύνησεν
39 αὐτῷ. καὶ εἶπεν ὁ Ἰησοῦς, Εἰς κρῖμα ἐγὼ εἰς τὸν κόσμον τοῦτον
ἦλθον, ἵνα οἱ μὴ βλέποντες βλέπωσι καὶ οἱ βλέποντες τυφλοὶ γένων-
40 ται. ἤκουσαν οὖν ἐκ τῶν Φαρισαίων ταῦτα οἱ μετ᾽ αὐτοῦ ὄντες,
41 καὶ εἶπον αὐτῷ, Μὴ καὶ ἡμεῖς τυφλοί ἐσμεν; εἶπεν αὐτοῖς ὁ Ἰησοῦς,
Εἰ τυφλοὶ ἦτε, οὐκ ἂν εἴχετε ἁμαρτίαν· νῦν δὲ λέγετε ὅτι Βλέπομεν·
ἡ ἁμαρτία ὑμῶν μένει.

X. Ἀμὴν ἀμὴν λέγω ὑμῖν, ὁ μὴ εἰσερχόμενος διὰ τῆς θύρας εἰς
τὴν αὐλὴν τῶν προβάτων, ἀλλὰ ἀναβαίνων ἀλλαχόθεν, ἐκεῖνος κλέπτης
2 ἐστὶ καὶ λῃστής· ὁ δὲ εἰσερχόμενος διὰ τῆς θύρας ποιμήν ἐστι τῶν
3 προβάτων. τούτῳ ὁ θυρωρὸς ἀνοίγει, καὶ τὰ πρόβατα τῆς φωνῆς αὐτοῦ
4 ἀκούει, καὶ τὰ ἴδια πρόβατα φωνεῖ κατ᾽ ὄνομα καὶ ἐξάγει αὐτά. ὅταν
τὰ ἴδια πάντα ἐκβάλῃ, ἔμπροσθεν αὐτῶν πορεύεται, καὶ τὰ πρόβατα
5 αὐτῷ ἀκολουθεῖ, ὅτι οἴδασι τὴν φωνὴν αὐτοῦ. ἀλλοτρίῳ δὲ οὐ μὴ
ἀκολουθήσωσιν, ἀλλὰ φεύξονται ἀπ᾽ αὐτοῦ, ὅτι οὐκ οἴδασι τῶν ἀλλο-
6 τρίων τὴν φωνήν. ταύτην τὴν παροιμίαν εἶπεν αὐτοῖς ὁ Ἰησοῦς· ἐκεῖνοι
δὲ οὐκ ἔγνωσαν τίνα ἦν ἃ ἐλάλει αὐτοῖς.

7 Εἶπεν οὖν αὐτοῖς ὁ Ἰησοῦς, Ἀμὴν ἀμὴν λέγω ὑμῖν ὅτι ἐγώ εἰμι
8 ἡ θύρα τῶν προβάτων. πάντες ὅσοι πρὸ ἐμοῦ ἦλθον, κλέπται εἰσὶ

28 οι δε ελοιδορησαν] ελοιδορησαν ουν ς   ει μαθητης ς   **29** Μωση ς   118 209 ς
30 om το 118 209 ς   **31** οιδαμεν δε 118 209 ς   **32** ηνοιξε ς
34 ολος ς   **36** om και 2° ς   **40** και ηκουσαν ς   οντες μετ αυτου ς
41 η ουν αμαρτια 118 209 ς
3 φωνει] καλει ς   **4** και οταν 118 209 ς   παντα] προβατα 118 209 ς
7 παλιν αυτοις 118 ς   om ο 118

καὶ λησταί· ἀλλ' οὐκ ἤκουσαν αὐτῶν τὰ πρόβατα. ἐγώ εἰμι ἡ θύρα· 9
δι' ἐμοῦ ἐάν τις εἰσέλθῃ, σωθήσεται, καὶ εἰσελεύσεται καὶ ἐξελεύσεται
καὶ νομὴν εὑρήσει. ὁ κλέπτης οὐκ ἔρχεται εἰ μὴ ἵνα κλέψῃ καὶ θύσῃ 10
καὶ ἀπολέσῃ· ἐγὼ ἦλθον ἵνα ζωὴν ἔχωσι, καὶ περισσὸν ἔχωσιν. ἐγώ 11
εἰμι ὁ ποιμὴν ὁ καλός· ὁ ποιμὴν ὁ καλὸς τὴν ψυχὴν αὐτοῦ τίθησιν
ὑπὲρ τῶν προβάτων. ὁ μισθωτὸς καὶ οὐκ ὢν ποιμήν, οὗ οὐκ ἔστι 12
τὰ πρόβατα ἴδια, θεωρεῖ τὸν λύκον ἐρχόμενον, καὶ ἀφίησι τὰ πρόβατα
καὶ φεύγει· καὶ ὁ λύκος ἁρπάζει αὐτὰ καὶ σκορπίζει, ὅτι μισθωτός 13
ἐστι καὶ οὐ μέλει αὐτῷ περὶ τῶν προβάτων. ἐγώ εἰμι ὁ ποιμὴν ὁ 14
ζ̄ καλός· καὶ γινώσκω τὰ ἐμὰ καὶ γινώσκομαι ὑπὸ τῶν ἐμῶν, καθὼς 15
γ/ζα γινώσκει με ὁ πατὴρ κἀγὼ γινώσκω τὸν πατέρα· καὶ τὴν ψυχήν μου
δ/ζβ τίθημι ὑπὲρ τῶν προβάτων. καὶ ἄλλα πρόβατα ἔχω, ἃ οὐκ ἔστιν ἐκ 16
ι τῆς αὐλῆς ταύτης· κἀκεῖνα δεῖ μὲ ἀγαγεῖν, καὶ τῆς φωνῆς μου ἀκού-
σουσι, καὶ γενήσονται μία ποίμνη, εἷς ποιμήν. διὰ τοῦτο ὁ πατήρ 17
με ἀγαπᾷ, ὅτι ἐγὼ τίθημι τὴν ψυχήν μου, ἵνα πάλιν λάβω αὐτήν.
οὐδεὶς αἴρει αὐτὴν ἀπ' ἐμοῦ, ἀλλ' ἐγὼ τίθημι αὐτὴν ἀπ' ἐμαυτοῦ. 18
ἐξουσίαν ἔχω θεῖναι αὐτήν, καὶ ἐξουσίαν ἔχω πάλιν λαβεῖν αὐτήν.
ταύτην τὴν ἐντολὴν ἔλαβον παρὰ τοῦ πατρός μου. σχίσμα οὖν 19
ἐγένετο πάλιν ἐν τοῖς Ἰουδαίοις διὰ τοὺς λόγους τούτους. ἔλεγον 20
οὖν πολλοὶ ἐξ αὐτῶν, Δαιμόνιον ἔχει καὶ μαίνεται· τί αὐτοῦ ἀκούετε;
ἄλλοι ἔλεγον, Ταῦτα τὰ ῥήματα οὐκ ἔστι δαιμονιζομένου· μὴ δαιμόνιον 21
δύναται τυφλῶν ὀφθαλμοὺς ἀνοῖξαι;

Ἐγένετο τὰ ἐγκαίνια ἐν Ἱεροσολύμοις, χειμὼν ἦν· καὶ περι- 22 23
επάτει ὁ Ἰησοῦς ἐν τῷ ἱερῷ ἐν τῇ στοᾷ Σολομῶνος. ἐκύκλωσαν 24
οὖν αὐτὸν οἱ Ἰουδαῖοι, καὶ ἔλεγον αὐτῷ, Ἕως πότε τὴν ψυχὴν ἡμῶν
αἴρεις; εἰ σὺ εἶ ὁ Χριστός, εἰπὲ ἡμῖν παρρησίᾳ. ἀπεκρίθη αὐτοῖς ὁ 25
Ἰησοῦς, Εἶπον ὑμῖν, καὶ οὐ πιστεύετε. τὰ ἔργα ἃ ἐγὼ ποιῶ ἐν τῷ
ὀνόματι τοῦ πατρός μου, ταῦτα μαρτυρεῖ περὶ ἐμοῦ· ἀλλ' ὑμεῖς οὐ 26
πιστεύετε· ὅτι οὐκ ἐστὲ ἐκ τῶν προβάτων τῶν ἐμῶν, καθὼς εἶπον
ὑμῖν. τὰ πρόβατα τὰ ἐμὰ τῆς φωνῆς μου ἀκούει, κἀγὼ γινώσκω 27
αὐτά· καὶ ἀκολουθοῦσί μοι, κἀγὼ ζωὴν αἰώνιον δίδωμι αὐτοῖς, καὶ οὐ 28
μὴ ἀπόλωνται εἰς τὸν αἰῶνα, καὶ οὐχ ἁρπάσει τις αὐτὰ ἐκ τῆς χειρός
μου. ὁ πατήρ μου ὃς δέδωκέ μοι μείζων πάντων ἐστί, καὶ οὐδεὶς 29

16 *της* 2°] bis script.

118 209 ϛ **9** *θυρα*]+*των προβατων* 118 209 **12** *και* 1°] pr *δε* 118 209 ϛ *εισι* 118 209 ϛ *σκορπιζει*]+*τα προβατα* 118 209 ϛ **13** *οτι*] pr *ο δε μισθωτος φευγει* 118 209 ϛ **16** *με δει* 118 209 ϛ *γενησεται* 118 209 ϛ **17** *με ο πατηρ* 118 209 **19** *παλιν εγενετο* ϛ **20** *ουν*] *δε* ϛ **21** *ανοιγειν* ϛ **22** *εγενοντο* 118 209, *εγενετο δε* ϛ *τοις Ιεροσολυμοις και χειμων* 118 209 ϛ **23** *του Σολομωντος* 118 209 ϛ **26** *οτι ουκ*] *ου γαρ* ϛ

30 δύναται ἁρπάζειν ἐκ τῆς χειρὸς τοῦ πατρός μου. ἐγὼ καὶ ὁ πατὴρ
31 ἕν ἐσμεν. ἐβάστασαν οὖν πάλιν λίθους οἱ Ἰουδαῖοι, ἵνα λιθάσωσιν
32 αὐτόν. ἀπεκρίθη αὐτοῖς ὁ Ἰησοῦς, Πολλὰ ἔργα καλὰ ἔδειξα ὑμῖν
33 ἐκ τοῦ πατρός μου· διὰ ποῖον αὐτῶν ἔργον λιθάζετέ με; ἀπεκρίθησαν
αὐτῷ οἱ Ἰουδαῖοι, Περὶ καλοῦ ἔργου οὐ λιθάζομέν σε, ἀλλὰ περὶ
34 βλασφημίας, καὶ ὅτι σὺ ἄνθρωπος ὢν ποιεῖς σεαυτὸν Θεόν. ἀπεκρίθη
αὐτοῖς ὁ Ἰησοῦς, Οὐκ ἔστι γεγραμμένον ἐν τῷ νόμῳ ὑμῶν, Ἐγὼ εἶπα,
35 θεοί ἐστε; εἰ ἐκείνους εἶπε θεούς, πρὸς οὓς ὁ λόγος τοῦ Θεοῦ ἐγένετο,
36 καὶ οὐ δύναται λυθῆναι ἡ γραφή, ὃν ὁ πατὴρ ἡγίασε καὶ ἀπέστειλεν
εἰς τὸν κόσμον ὑμεῖς λέγετε ὅτι Βλασφημεῖς, ὅτι εἶπον, Υἱὸς τοῦ Θεοῦ
37 38 εἰμι; εἰ οὐ ποιῶ τὰ ἔργα τοῦ πατρός μου, μὴ πιστεύετέ μοι· εἰ δὲ
ποιῶ, κἂν ἐμοὶ μὴ πιστεύετε, τοῖς ἔργοις πιστεύετε· ἵνα γνῶτε καὶ
39 γινώσκητε ὅτι ἐν ἐμοὶ ὁ πατὴρ κἀγὼ ἐν αὐτῷ. ἐζήτουν οὖν αὐτὸν
πάλιν πιάσαι· καὶ ἐξῆλθεν ἐκ τῶν χειρῶν αὐτῶν.
40 Καὶ ἀπῆλθε πάλιν πέραν τοῦ Ἰορδάνου εἰς τὸν τόπον ὅπου ἦν ϟγ δ
41 Ἰωάννης τὸ πρῶτον βαπτίζων, καὶ ἔμεινεν ἐκεῖ. καὶ πολλοὶ ἦλθον
πρὸς αὐτόν, καὶ ἔλεγον ὅτι Ἰωάννης μὲν ἐποίησε σημεῖον οὐδὲ ϟδ ι
42 ἕν· πάντα δὲ ὅσα εἶπεν Ἰωάννης περὶ τούτου ἀληθῆ ἦν. καὶ πολλοὶ
ἐπίστευσαν εἰς αὐτὸν ἐκεῖ.

XI. Ἦν δέ τις ἀσθενῶν Λάζαρος ἀπὸ Βηθανίας, ἐκ τῆς κώμης ΙΑʹ
2 Μαρίας καὶ Μάρθας τῆς ἀδελφῆς αὐτῆς. ἦν δὲ Μαρία ἡ ἀλείψασα
τὸν Κύριον μύρῳ καὶ ἐκμάξασα τοὺς πόδας αὐτοῦ ταῖς θριξὶν αὐτῆς,
3 ἧς ὁ ἀδελφὸς Λάζαρος ἠσθένει. ἀπέστειλαν οὖν αἱ ἀδελφαὶ αὐτοῦ
4 πρὸς αὐτὸν λέγουσαι, Κύριε, ἴδε ὃν φιλεῖς ἀσθενεῖ. ἀκούσας δὲ ὁ
Ἰησοῦς εἶπεν, Αὕτη ἡ ἀσθένεια οὐκ ἔστι πρὸς θάνατον, ἀλλ' ὑπὲρ
5 τῆς δόξης τοῦ Θεοῦ, ἵνα δοξασθῇ ὁ υἱὸς τοῦ Θεοῦ δι' αὐτῆς. ἠγάπα
δὲ ὁ Ἰησοῦς τὴν Μαριὰν καὶ τὴν ἀδελφὴν αὐτῆς Μαρθὰν καὶ τὸν
6 Λάζαρον. ὡς οὖν ἤκουσεν ὅτι ἀσθενεῖ, τότε μὲν ἔμεινεν ἐν ᾧ ἦν τόπῳ
7 δύο ἡμέρας· ἔπειτα μετὰ τοῦτο λέγει τοῖς μαθηταῖς, Ἄγωμεν πάλιν
8 εἰς τὴν Ἰουδαίαν. λέγουσιν αὐτῷ οἱ μαθηταί, Ῥαββί, νῦν ἐζήτουν σε

38 μη] supra lineam scrips. m. prim. πιστευετε 1°] sic ni fallor primum scripsit m. prim. sed ipsa ad πιστευητε correxit
4 δι αυτης] δια τῆς cod. nec habet δια accentum

32 καλα εργα ϛ **33** Ιουδαιοι]+λεγοντες ϛ σεαυτον] εαυτον 118 sed sine spiritu **37** πιστευητε 118 209 **38** πιστευετε 1°] πιστευητε 118 209 ϛ πιστευετε 2°] πιστευσατε 118 209 ϛ γινωσκητε] πιστευσητε ϛ **39** παλιν αυτον ϛ της χειρος ϛ **41** σημειον εποιησεν ϛ ουδεν ϛ **42** επιστευσαν πολλοι ϛ εκει] om 118 209; ante εις αυτον ϛ
3 om αυτου ϛ **5** Μαριαν] Μαρθαν 118 209 ϛ om Μαρθαν 118 209 ϛ **7** om παλιν ϛ Ιουδαιαν]+παλιν ϛ 118 209 ϛ

οἱ Ἰουδαῖοι λιθάσαι, καὶ πάλιν ὑπάγεις ἐκεῖ; ἀπεκρίθη ὁ Ἰησοῦς, 9
Οὐχὶ δώδεκα ὧραί εἰσιν τῆς ἡμέρας; ἐάν τις περιπατῇ ἐν τῇ ἡμέρᾳ,
οὐ προσκόπτει, ὅτι τὸ φῶς τοῦ κόσμου τούτου βλέπει· ἐὰν δέ τις 10
περιπατῇ ἐν τῇ νυκτί, προσκόπτει, ὅτι τὸ φῶς οὐκ ἔστιν ἐν αὐτῷ.
ταῦτα εἶπε, καὶ μετὰ τοῦτο λέγει αὐτοῖς, Λάζαρος ὁ φίλος ἡμῶν κεκοί- 11
μηται· ἀλλὰ πορεύομαι ἵνα ἐξυπνίσω αὐτόν. εἶπον οὖν οἱ μαθηταὶ 12
αὐτοῦ, Κύριε, εἰ κεκοίμηται. εἰρήκει δὲ ὁ Ἰησοῦς περὶ τοῦ θανάτου 13
αὐτοῦ· ἐκεῖνοι δὲ ἔδοξαν ὅτι περὶ τῆς κοιμήσεως τοῦ ὕπνου λέγει. τότε 14
οὖν εἶπεν αὐτοῖς παρρησίᾳ ὁ Ἰησοῦς, Λάζαρος ἀπέθανε· καὶ χαίρω 15
δι' ὑμᾶς, ἵνα πιστεύσητε, ὅτι οὐκ ἤμην ἐκεῖ· ἀλλ' ἄγωμεν πρὸς αὐτόν.
εἶπεν οὖν Θωμᾶς ὁ λεγόμενος Δίδυμος τοῖς συμμαθηταῖς, Ἄγωμεν καὶ 16
ἡμεῖς, ἵνα ἀποθάνωμεν μετ' αὐτοῦ.

Ἐλθὼν οὖν ὁ Ἰησοῦς εὗρεν αὐτὸν τέσσαρας ἡμέρας ἤδη ἔχοντα 17
ἐν τῷ μνημείῳ. ἦν δὲ ἡ Βηθανία ἐγγὺς τῶν Ἱεροσολύμων, ὡς ἀπὸ 18
σταδίων δεκαπέντε· πολλοὶ οὖν ἐκ τῶν Ἰουδαίων ἐληλύθεισαν πρὸς τὰς 19
περὶ Μάρθαν καὶ Μαρίαν, ἵνα παραμυθήσωνται αὐτὰς περὶ τοῦ ἀδελφοῦ
αὐτῶν. ἡ οὖν Μάρθα ὡς ἤκουσεν ὅτι Ἰησοῦς ἔρχεται, ὑπήντησεν 20
αὐτῷ· Μαρία δὲ ἐν τῷ οἴκῳ ἐκαθέζετο. εἶπεν οὖν ἡ Μάρθα πρὸς τὸν 21
Ἰησοῦν, Κύριε, εἰ ἦς ὧδε, οὐκ ἂν ἀπέθανέ μου ὁ ἀδελφός. καὶ 22
νῦν οἶδα ὅτι ὅσα ἂν αἰτήσῃ τὸν Θεὸν δώσει σοι ὁ Θεός. λέγει αὐτῇ 23
ὁ Ἰησοῦς, Ἀναστήσεται ὁ ἀδελφός σου. λέγει αὐτῷ Μάρθα, Οἶδα ὅτι 24
ἀναστήσεται ἐν τῇ ἀναστάσει ἐν τῇ ἐσχάτῃ ἡμέρᾳ. εἶπε δὲ αὐτῇ 25
ὁ Ἰησοῦς, Ἐγώ εἰμι ἡ ἀνάστασις καὶ ἡ ζωή· ὁ πιστεύων εἰς ἐμέ,
κἂν ἀποθάνῃ, ζήσεται· καὶ πᾶς ὁ ζῶν καὶ πιστεύων εἰς ἐμὲ οὐ μὴ 26
ἀποθάνῃ εἰς τὸν αἰῶνα. πιστεύεις τοῦτο; λέγει αὐτῷ, Ναί, κύριε, 27
ἐγὼ πεπίστευκα ὅτι σὺ εἶ ὁ Χριστός, ὁ υἱὸς τοῦ Θεοῦ, ὁ εἰς τὸν
κόσμον ἐρχόμενος. καὶ ταῦτα εἰποῦσα ἀπῆλθε καὶ ἐφώνησε Μαρίαν 28
τὴν ἀδελφὴν αὐτῆς λάθρα εἰποῦσα, Ὁ διδάσκαλος πάρεστι καὶ φωνεῖ
σε. ἐκείνη ὡς ἤκουσεν, ἐγείρεται ταχὺ καὶ ἔρχεται πρὸς αὐτόν. οὔπω 29 30
δὲ ἐληλύθει ὁ Ἰησοῦς εἰς τὴν κώμην, ἀλλ' ἦν ἔτι ἐν τῷ τόπῳ ὅπου
ὑπήντησεν αὐτῷ ἡ Μάρθα. οἱ οὖν Ἰουδαῖοι οἱ ὄντες μετ' αὐτῆς ἐν 31
τῇ οἰκίᾳ καὶ παραμυθούμενοι αὐτήν, ἰδόντες τὴν Μαρίαν ὅτι ταχέως
ἀνέστη καὶ ἐξῆλθεν, ἠκολούθησαν αὐτῇ, δόξαντες ὅτι ὑπάγει εἰς τὸ

12 κεκοιμηται] m. recentiss. add. σοθησεται in marg.

118 209 ϛ 8 λιθασαι οι Ιουδαιοι ϛ 9 εισιν ωραι ϛ 12 κεκοιμηται] + σωθησεται 118 209 ϛ 14 ο Ιησους παρρησια ϛ 19 πολλοι ουν] και πολλοι ϛ 20 ο Ιησους ϛ 21 απεθανε] ετεθνηκει 118 209 ϛ ο αδελφος μου ουκ αν ετεθνηκει ϛ 22 αλλα και 118 ϛ 25 om δε ϛ 30 εις] προς 118 209 om ετι ϛ 31 δοξαντες] λεγοντες ϛ

32 μνημεῖον, ἵνα κλαύσῃ ἐκεῖ. ἡ οὖν Μαρία ὡς ἦλθεν ὅπου ἦν ὁ Ἰησοῦς
ἰδοῦσα αὐτὸν ἔπεσεν αὐτοῦ πρὸς τοὺς πόδας λέγουσα αὐτῷ, Κύριε,
33 εἰ ἦς ὧδε, οὐκ ἂν ἀπέθανέ μου ὁ ἀδελφός. Ἰησοῦς οὖν ὡς εἶδεν αὐτὴν
κλαίουσαν, καὶ τοὺς συνελθόντας αὐτῇ Ἰουδαίους κλαίοντας, ἐταράχθη
34 τῷ πνεύματι ὡς ἐμβριμώμενος, καὶ εἶπε, Ποῦ τεθείκατε αὐτόν;
35 36 λέγουσιν αὐτῷ, Κύριε, ἔρχου καὶ ἴδε. ἐδάκρυσεν ὁ Ἰησοῦς. ἔλεγον
37 οὖν οἱ Ἰουδαῖοι, Ἴδε πῶς ἐφίλει αὐτόν. τινὲς δὲ ἐξ αὐτῶν εἶπον, Οὐκ
ἠδύνατο οὗτος ὁ ἀνοίξας τοὺς ὀφθαλμοὺς τοῦ τυφλοῦ ποιῆσαι ἵνα καὶ
38 οὗτος μὴ ἀποθάνῃ; Ἰησοῦς οὖν πάλιν ἐμβριμώμενος ἐν ἑαυτῷ ἔρχεται
39 εἰς τὸ μνημεῖον. ἦν δὲ σπήλαιον, καὶ λίθος ἐπέκειτο ἐπ' αὐτῷ. λέγει
ὁ Ἰησοῦς, Ἄρατε τὸν λίθον. λέγει αὐτῷ ἡ ἀδελφὴ τοῦ τεθνηκότος
40 Μάρθα, Κύριε, ἤδη ὄζει· τεταρταῖος γάρ ἐστι. λέγει αὐτῇ Ἰησοῦς,
41 Οὐκ εἶπόν σοι ὅτι ἐὰν πιστεύσῃς, ὄψει τὴν δόξαν τοῦ Θεοῦ; ἦραν
οὖν τὸν λίθον, οὗ ἦν. ὁ οὖν Ἰησοῦς ἦρε τοὺς ὀφθαλμοὺς ἄνω καὶ
42 εἶπε, Πάτερ, εὐχαριστῶ σοι ὅτι ἤκουσάς μου. ἐγὼ δὲ ᾔδειν ὅτι
πάντοτέ μου ἀκούεις· ἀλλὰ διὰ τὸν ὄχλον τὸν περιεστῶτα εἶπον, ἵνα
43 πιστεύσωσιν ὅτι σύ με ἀπέστειλας. καὶ ταῦτα εἰπὼν φωνῇ μεγάλῃ
44 ἐκραύγασε, Λάζαρε, δεῦρο ἔξω. καὶ ἐξῆλθεν ὁ τεθνηκὼς δεδεμένος τοὺς
πόδας καὶ τὰς χεῖρας κηρίαις, καὶ ἡ ὄψις αὐτοῦ σουδαρίῳ περι-
εδέδετο. λέγει αὐτοῖς ὁ Ἰησοῦς, Λύσατε αὐτὸν καὶ ἄφετε ὑπάγειν.
45 Πολλοὶ οὖν τῶν Ἰουδαίων, οἱ ἐλθόντες πρὸς τὴν Μαρίαν καὶ
46 θεασάμενοι ὃ ἐποίησεν, ἐπίστευσαν εἰς αὐτόν. τινὲς δὲ ἐξ αὐτῶν
ἀπῆλθον πρὸς τοὺς Φαρισαίους καὶ εἶπον αὐτοῖς ἃ ἐποίησεν ὁ Ἰησοῦς.
47 συνήγαγον οὖν οἱ ἀρχιερεῖς καὶ οἱ Φαρισαῖοι συνέδριον, καὶ ἔλεγον,
48 Τί ποιοῦμεν; ὅτι οὗτος ὁ ἄνθρωπος πολλὰ σημεῖα ποιεῖ. ἐὰν ἀφῶμεν
αὐτὸν οὕτως, πάντες πιστεύσωσιν εἰς αὐτόν, καὶ ἐλεύσονται οἱ
49 Ῥωμαῖοι καὶ ἀροῦσιν ἡμῶν καὶ τὸν τόπον καὶ τὸ ἔθνος. εἷς δέ τις
ἐξ αὐτῶν ὀνόματι Καϊάφας ἀρχιερεὺς ὢν τοῦ ἐνιαυτοῦ ἐκείνου, εἶπεν
50 αὐτοῖς, Ὑμεῖς οὐκ οἴδατε οὐδέν, οὐδὲ λογίζεσθε ὅτι συμφέρει ἡμῖν ἵνα
εἷς ἄνθρωπος ἀποθάνῃ ὑπὲρ τοῦ λαοῦ, καὶ μὴ ὅλον τὸ ἔθνος ἀπόληται.
51 τοῦτο δὲ ἀφ' ἑαυτοῦ οὐκ εἶπεν, ἀλλ' ἀρχιερεὺς ὢν τοῦ ἐνιαυτοῦ ἐκείνου

38 δε] δαι cod.

32 αυτου post ποδας ς προς] εις ς **33** ενεβριμησατο τω πνευματι 118 209 ς και εταραξεν εαυτον 118 209 ς sed αυτον non εαυτον 118 209 **40** ο Ιησους 118 209 ς **41** ου] οπου 118 209 ην]+ο τεθνηκως κειμενος 118 209 ς ουν] δε 118 209 ς **44** τας χειρας και τους ποδας 118 209 κειριαις 118 209 ς **45** εκ των ς om και 118 209 ο] α 118 209 ς εποιησεν]+ο Ιησους 118 209 ς **48** ουτω ς πιστευσουσιν 118 209 ς **49** om ονοματι ς **50** διαλογιζεσθε ς **51** αλλα ς

προεφήτευσεν ὅτι ἤμελλεν Ἰησοῦς ἀποθνήσκειν ὑπὲρ τοῦ ἔθνους,
καὶ οὐχ ὑπὲρ τοῦ ἔθνους μόνον, ἀλλ' ἵνα καὶ τὰ τέκνα τοῦ Θεοῦ τὰ 52
ϟε δ διεσκορπισμένα συναγάγῃ εἰς ἕν. ἀπ' ἐκείνης οὖν τῆς ἡμέρας συν- 53
εβουλεύσαντο ἵνα ἀποκτείνουσιν αὐτόν. ὁ οὖν Ἰησοῦς οὐκ ἔτι 54
παρρησίᾳ περιεπάτει ἐν τοῖς Ἰουδαίοις, ἀλλ' ἀπῆλθεν ἐκεῖθεν εἰς
χώραν ἐγγὺς τῆς ἐρήμου, εἰς Ἐφραὶμ λεγομένην πόλιν, κἀκεῖ διέτριβε
ϟϛ α μετὰ τῶν μαθητῶν αὐτοῦ. ἦν δὲ ἐγγὺς τὸ πάσχα τῶν Ἰουδαίων· καὶ 55
ϟζ ι ἀνέβησαν πολλοὶ εἰς Ἱεροσόλυμα ἐκ τῆς χώρας πρὸ τοῦ πάσχα, ἵνα
ἁγνίσωσιν ἑαυτούς. ἐζήτουν οὖν τὸν Ἰησοῦν, καὶ ἔλεγον μετ' ἀλλήλων 56
ἐν τῷ ἱερῷ ἑστηκότες, Τί δοκεῖ ὑμῖν, ὅτι οὐ μὴ ἔλθῃ εἰς τὴν ἑορτήν;
δεδώκεισαν δὲ οἱ ἀρχιερεῖς καὶ οἱ Φαρισαῖοι ἐντολὰς ἵνα, ἐάν τις γνῷ 57
ποῦ ἐστι, μηνύσῃ, ὅπως πιάσωσιν αὐτόν.

XII. Ὁ οὖν Ἰησοῦς πρὸ ἓξ ἡμερῶν τοῦ πάσχα ἦλθεν εἰς Βηθανίαν,
ϟη α ὅπου ἦν Λάζαρος ὁ τεθνηκώς, ὃν ἤγειρεν ἐκ νεκρῶν. ἐποίησαν οὖν αὐτῷ 2
δεῖπνον ἐκεῖ, καὶ ἡ Μάρθα διηκόνει· ὁ δὲ Λάζαρος εἷς ἦν τῶν ἀνακει-
ΙΒ' μένων σὺν αὐτῷ. ἡ οὖν Μαριὰμ λαβοῦσα λίτραν μύρου νάρδου 3
πιστικῆς πολυτίμου ἤλειψε τοὺς πόδας τοῦ Ἰησοῦ, καὶ ταῖς θριξὶν
αὐτῆς ἐξέμαξεν· ἡ δὲ οἰκία ὅλη ἐπληρώθη ἐκ τῆς ὀσμῆς τοῦ μύρου.
ΙΓ' λέγει οὖν εἷς ἐκ τῶν μαθητῶν αὐτοῦ, Ἰούδας ὁ Ἰσκαριώτης ὁ μέλλων 4
αὐτὸν παραδιδόναι, Διατί τοῦτο τὸ μύρον οὐκ ἐπράθη τριακοσίων 5
δηναρίων καὶ ἐδόθη πτωχοῖς; εἶπε δὲ τοῦτο, οὐχ ὅτι περὶ τῶν πτωχῶν 6
ἔμελεν αὐτῷ, ἀλλ' ὅτι κλέπτης ἦν, καὶ τὸ γλωσσόκομον ἔχων καὶ
τὰ βαλλόμενα ἐβάσταζεν. εἶπεν οὖν ὁ Ἰησοῦς, Ἄφες αὐτήν· εἰς τὴν 7
ἡμέραν τοῦ ἐνταφιασμοῦ μου τετήρηκεν αὐτό. τοὺς πτωχοὺς γὰρ πάντοτε 8
ἔχετε μεθ' ἑαυτῶν, ἐμὲ δὲ οὐ πάντοτε ἔχετε.

ϟθ ι Ἔγνω οὖν ὄχλος πολὺς ἐκ τῶν Ἰουδαίων ὅτι ἐκεῖ ἐστι· καὶ ἦλθον 9
οὐ διὰ τὸν Ἰησοῦν μόνον, ἀλλ' ἵνα καὶ τὸν Λάζαρον ἴδωσιν, ὃν ἤγειρεν
ἐκ νεκρῶν. ἐβουλεύσαντο δὲ οἱ ἀρχιερεῖς ἵνα καὶ τὸν Λάζαρον ἀπο- 10
κτείνωσιν· ὅτι πολλοὶ δι' αὐτὸν ὑπῆγον τῶν Ἰουδαίων καὶ ἐπίστευον εἰς 11
τὸν Ἰησοῦν.

ρ α Τῇ ἐπαύριον ὄχλος πολὺς ὁ ἐλθὼν εἰς τὴν ἑορτήν, ἀκούσαντες ὅτι 12
ἔρχεται Ἰησοῦς εἰς Ἱεροσόλυμα, ἔλαβον τὰ βαΐα τῶν φοινίκων καὶ 13
ἐξῆλθον εἰς ὑπάντησιν αὐτῷ, καὶ ἔκραζον, λέγοντες Ὡσαννά· εὐλο-

118 209 ϛ **51** εμελλεν 118 209 ϛ ο Ιησους ϛ **52** το εν 118 **53** αποκτει-
νωσιν 118 209 ϛ **54** Ιησους ουν ϛ αλλα ϛ την χωραν ϛ
56 υμιν] ημιν 118 209 **57** δε και ϛ εντολην ϛ

2 συνανακειμενων αυτω ϛ **3** Μαρια 118 209 ϛ εξεμαξε ταις θριξιν αυτης τους ποδας αυτου ϛ om ολη ϛ **4** ο 1°] Σιμωνος ϛ **5** τριακοσιων] διακοσιων 118 209 **6** εμελλε 118 209 ειχε ϛ **12** ο Ιησους ϛ **13** om λεγοντες ϛ

γημένος ὁ ἐρχόμενος ἐν ὀνόματι Κυρίου, ὁ βασιλεὺς τοῦ Ἰσραήλ.
14 εὑρὼν δὲ ὁ Ἰησοῦς ὀνάριον ἐκάθισεν ἐπ᾽ αὐτό, καθώς ἐστι γεγραμμένον, ΙΔ'
15 Μὴ φοβοῦ, θύγατερ Σιών· ἰδοὺ ὁ βασιλεύς σου ἔρχεται καθήμενος ρα ζ
16 ἐπὶ πῶλον ὄνου. ταῦτα δὲ οὐκ ἔγνωσαν οἱ μαθηταὶ αὐτοῦ τὸ πρῶτον· ρβ ι
ἀλλ᾽ ὅτε ἐδοξάσθη Ἰησοῦς, τότε ἐμνήσθησαν ὅτι ταῦτα ἦν ἐπ᾽ αὐτῷ
17 γεγραμμένα, καὶ ταῦτα ἐποίησαν αὐτῷ. ἐμαρτύρει οὖν ὁ ὄχλος ὁ
ὢν μετ᾽ αὐτοῦ ὅτε τὸν Λάζαρον ἐφώνησεν ἐκ τοῦ μνημείου καὶ ἤγει-
18 ρεν αὐτὸν ἐκ νεκρῶν· διὰ τοῦτο καὶ ὑπήντησεν αὐτῷ ὁ ὄχλος, ὅτι
19 ἤκουσαν τοῦτο αὐτὸν πεποιηκέναι τὸ σημεῖον. οἱ οὖν Φαρισαῖοι εἶπον
πρὸς ἑαυτούς, Θεωρεῖτε ὅτι οὐκ ὠφελεῖτε οὐδέν; ἴδε ὁ κόσμος ὀπίσω
αὐτοῦ ἀπῆλθεν.
20 Ἦσαν δὲ Ἕλληνές τινες ἐκ τῶν ἀναβαινόντων ἵνα προσκυνήσω- ΙΕ'
21 σιν ἐν τῇ ἑορτῇ· οὗτοι οὖν προσῆλθον Φιλίππῳ τῷ ἀπὸ Βηθσαϊδὰ τῆς
Γαλιλαίας, καὶ ἠρώτησαν αὐτὸν λέγοντες, Κύριε, θέλομεν τὸν Ἰησοῦν
22 ἰδεῖν. ἔρχεται Φίλιππος καὶ λέγει τῷ Ἀνδρέᾳ, καὶ πάλιν Ἀνδρέας καὶ
23 Φίλιππος λέγουσι τῷ Ἰησοῦ. ὁ δὲ Ἰησοῦς ἀπεκρίνατο αὐτοῖς λέγων, ργ δ
24 Ἐλήλυθεν ἡ ὥρα ἵνα δοξασθῇ ὁ υἱὸς τοῦ ἀνθρώπου. ἀμὴν ἀμὴν λέγω ρδ ι
ὑμῖν, ἐὰν μὴ ὁ κόκκος τοῦ σίτου πεσὼν εἰς τὴν γῆν ἀποθάνῃ, αὐτὸς
25 μόνος μένει· ἐὰν δὲ ἀποθάνῃ, πολὺν καρπὸν φέρει. ὁ φιλῶν τὴν ψυχὴν ρε γ
αὐτοῦ ἀπολέσει αὐτήν· καὶ ὁ μισῶν τὴν ψυχὴν αὐτοῦ ἐν τῷ κόσμῳ
26 τούτῳ εἰς ζωὴν αἰώνιον φυλάξει αὐτήν. ἐάν τις ἐμοὶ διακονῇ, ἐμοὶ ρς ι
ἀκολουθείτω· καὶ ὅπου εἰμὶ ἐγώ, ἐκεῖ καὶ ὁ διάκονος ὁ ἐμὸς ἔσται· ἐάν
τις ἐμοὶ διακονῇ, τιμήσει αὐτὸν ὁ πατήρ.
27 Νῦν ἡ ψυχή μου τετάρακται· καὶ τί εἴπω; πάτερ, σῶσόν με ἐκ ρζ δ
28 τῆς ὥρας ταύτης· ἀλλὰ διὰ τοῦτο ἦλθον εἰς τὴν ὥραν ταύτην· πάτερ, ρη ι
δόξασόν σου τὸν υἱόν. ἦλθεν οὖν φωνὴ ἐκ τοῦ οὐρανοῦ, Καὶ ἐδόξασα,
29 καὶ πάλιν δοξάσω. ὁ οὖν ὄχλος ὁ ἑστὼς ἀκούων ἔλεγε βροντὴν
30 γεγονέναι. ἄλλοι ἔλεγον, Ἄγγελος αὐτῷ λελάληκεν. ἀπεκρίθη ὁ
Ἰησοῦς καὶ εἶπεν, Οὐ δι᾽ ἐμὲ ἡ φωνὴ αὕτη γέγονεν, ἀλλὰ δι᾽ ὑμᾶς.
31 νῦν κρίσις ἐστὶ τοῦ κόσμου τούτου· νῦν ὁ ἄρχων τοῦ κόσμου τούτου
32 ἐκβληθήσεται ἔξω· κἀγὼ ἐὰν ὑψωθῶ ἐκ τῆς γῆς, πάντας ἑλκύσω πρὸς
33 ἐμαυτόν. τοῦτο δὲ ἔλεγε σημαίνων ποίῳ θανάτῳ ἔμελλεν ἀποθνή-
34 σκειν. ἀπεκρίθη αὐτῷ ὁ ὄχλος, Ἡμεῖς ἠκούσαμεν ἐκ τοῦ νόμου ὅτι
ὁ Χριστὸς μένει εἰς τὸν αἰῶνα· καὶ πῶς σὺ λέγεις ὅτι Δεῖ ὑψωθῆναι

14 εκαθησεν cod.

13 Κυριου] + και 209 ni fallor sed non pro certo habeo **16** ο Ιησους ϛ 118 209 ϛ **18** ηκουσε ϛ τουτον 118* 209 sed 118 nunc habet ν erasum **20** τινες Ελληνες ϛ **21** ηρωτων ϛ **26** εμοι διακονη τις ϛ εαν 2°] και εαν ϛ **28** τον υιον] το ονομα ϛ **29** ακουων] και ακουσας ϛ **30** αυτη η φωνη ϛ **33** ημελλεν ϛ

τὸν υἱὸν τοῦ ἀνθρώπου; τίς ἐστιν οὗτος ὁ υἱὸς τοῦ ἀνθρώπου; εἶπεν 35
οὖν αὐτοῖς ὁ Ἰησοῦς, Ἔτι μικρὸν χρόνον τὸ φῶς ἐν ὑμῖν ἐστι. περι-
πατεῖτε ὡς τὸ φῶς ἔχετε, ἵνα μὴ ἡ σκοτία ὑμᾶς καταλάβῃ· καὶ ὁ
περιπατῶν ἐν τῇ σκοτίᾳ οὐκ οἶδε ποῦ ὑπάγει. ἕως τὸ φῶς ἔχετε, 36
πιστεύετε εἰς τὸ φῶς, ἵνα υἱοὶ φωτὸς γένησθε. ταῦτα ἐλάλησεν ὁ
Ἰησοῦς, καὶ ἀπελθὼν ἐκρύβη ἀπ' αὐτῶν.

Τοσαῦτα δὲ αὐτοῦ σημεῖα πεποιηκότος ἔμπροσθεν αὐτῶν οὐκ ἐπί- 37
στευον εἰς αὐτόν· ἵνα ὁ λόγος Ἡσαΐου τοῦ προφήτου πληρωθῇ, ὃν 38
εἶπε, Κύριε, τίς ἐπίστευσε τῇ ἀκοῇ ἡμῶν; καὶ ὁ βραχίων Κυρίου τίνι
ρθ α ἀπεκαλύφθη; διὰ τοῦτο οὐκ ἠδύνατο πιστεύειν, ὅτι πάλιν Ἡσαΐας, 39
Τετύφλωκεν αὐτῶν τοὺς ὀφθαλμοὺς καὶ πεπώρωκεν αὐτῶν τὴν καρδίαν, 40
ἵνα μὴ ἴδωσι τοῖς ὀφθαλμοῖς καὶ νοήσωσι τῇ καρδίᾳ καὶ ἐπιστραφῶσι,
ρι ι καὶ ἰάσωμαι αὐτούς. ταῦτα εἶπεν Ἡσαΐας, ὅτι εἶδε τὴν δόξαν αὐτοῦ 41
καὶ ἐλάλησε περὶ αὐτοῦ· ὅμως μέντοι καὶ ἐκ τῶν ἀρχόντων πολλοὶ 42
ἐπίστευσαν εἰς αὐτόν· ἀλλὰ διὰ τοὺς Φαρισαίους οὐχ ὡμολόγουν, ἵνα
μὴ ἀποσυνάγωγοι γένωνται. ἠγάπησαν γὰρ τὴν δόξαν τῶν ἀνθρώπων 43
μᾶλλον ὑπὲρ τὴν δόξαν τοῦ Θεοῦ.

ρια α Ἰησοῦς δὲ ἔκραξε καὶ εἶπεν, Ὁ πιστεύων εἰς ἐμὲ οὐ πιστεύει εἰς 44
ἐμέ, ἀλλ' εἰς τὸν πέμψαντά με· καὶ ὁ θεωρῶν ἐμὲ θεωρεῖ τὸν πέμψαντά 45
ριβ ι με. ἐγὼ φῶς εἰς τὸν κόσμον ἐλήλυθα, ἵνα πᾶς ὁ πιστεύων εἰς ἐμὲ 46
ἐν τῇ σκοτίᾳ μὴ μείνῃ. καὶ ἐάν τις μου ἀκούσῃ τῶν ῥημάτων καὶ μὴ 47
φυλάξῃ, ἐγὼ οὐ κρίνω αὐτόν· οὐ γὰρ ἦλθον ἵνα κρίνω τὸν κόσμον,
ἀλλ' ἵνα σώσω τὸν κόσμον. ὁ ἀθετῶν ἐμὲ καὶ μὴ λαμβάνων τὰ 48
ῥήματά μου ἔχει τὸν κρίνοντα αὐτόν· ὁ λόγος ὃν ἐλάλησα, ἐκεῖνος
κρινεῖ αὐτὸν ἐν τῇ ἐσχάτῃ ἡμέρᾳ· ὅτι ἐγὼ ἀπ' ἐμαυτοῦ οὐκ ἐλάλησα, 49
ἀλλ' ὁ πέμψας με πατὴρ αὐτὸς ἐντολήν μοι δέδωκε, τί εἴπω καὶ τί
λαλήσω· καὶ οἶδα ὅτι ἡ ἐντολὴ αὐτοῦ ζωὴ αἰώνιός ἐστιν. ἃ οὖν ἐγὼ 50
λαλῶ, καθὼς εἴρηκέ μοι ὁ πατήρ, οὕτως λαλῶ.

XIII. Πρὸ δὲ τῆς ἑορτῆς τοῦ πάσχα, εἰδὼς ὁ Ἰησοῦς ὅτι ἦλθεν
αὐτοῦ ἡ ὥρα ἵνα μεταβῇ ἐκ τοῦ κόσμου τούτου πρὸς τὸν πατέρα,
ἀγαπήσας τοὺς ἰδίους τοὺς ἐν τῷ κόσμῳ, εἰς τέλος ἠγάπησεν αὐτούς.
ριγ θ καὶ δείπνου γενομένου, τοῦ διαβόλου ἤδη βεβληκότος εἰς τὴν καρδίαν 2
ιϛ' Ἰούδα Σίμωνος Ἰσκαριώτου ἵνα αὐτὸν παραδῷ, εἰδὼς ὁ Ἰησοῦς ὅτι 3
ριδ γ πάντα ἔδωκεν αὐτῷ ὁ πατὴρ εἰς τὰς χεῖρας, καὶ ὅτι ἀπὸ τοῦ Θεοῦ
ριε ι ἐξῆλθε καὶ πρὸς τὸν Θεὸν ὑπάγει, ἐγείρεται ἐκ τοῦ δείπνου καὶ τίθησι 4

118 209 ς **35** μεθ υμων ς ως] εως 118 209 ς om η ς **39** ηδυναντο ς παλιν ειπε 118 ς **41** οτι] οτε 118 209 ς **43** ηπερ ς **47** φυλαξη] πιστευση ς **49** απ] εξ ς μοι εντολην εδωκε ς **50** λαλω εγω ς ουτω ς

1 ηλθεν] εληλυθεν ς **3** δεδωκεν 118 209 ς om του ς

5 τὰ ἱμάτια, καὶ λαβὼν λέντιον διέζωσεν ἑαυτόν· εἶτα βάλλει ὕδωρ εἰς
τὸν νιπτῆρα, καὶ ἤρξατο νίπτειν τοὺς πόδας τῶν μαθητῶν καὶ ἐκμάσ-
6 σειν τῷ λεντίῳ ᾧ ἦν διεζωσμένος. ἔρχεται οὖν πρὸς Σίμωνα Πέτρον·
7 καὶ λέγει αὐτῷ ἐκεῖνος, Κύριε, σύ μου νίπτεις τοὺς πόδας; ἀπεκρίθη
Ἰησοῦς καὶ εἶπεν αὐτῷ, Ὃ ἐγὼ πριῶ σὺ οὐκ οἶδας ἄρτι, γνώσῃ δὲ
8 μετὰ ταῦτα. λέγει αὐτῷ Πέτρος, Οὐ μή μου νίψεις τοὺς πόδας εἰς
τὸν αἰῶνα. ἀπεκρίθη αὐτῷ ὁ Ἰησοῦς, Ἐὰν μὴ νίψω σε, οὐκ ἔχεις
9 μέρος μετ' ἐμοῦ. λέγει αὐτῷ Σίμων Πέτρος, Κύριε, μὴ τοὺς πόδας
10 μου μόνον, ἀλλὰ καὶ τὰς χεῖρας καὶ τὴν κεφαλήν. λέγει αὐτῷ ὁ
Ἰησοῦς, Ὁ λελουμένος οὐ χρείαν ἔχει ἢ τοὺς πόδας νίψασθαι, ἀλλ'
ἔστι καθαρὸς ὅλος· καὶ ὑμεῖς καθαροί ἐστε, ἀλλ' οὐχὶ πάντες.
11 ᾔδει γὰρ τὸν παραδιδόντα αὐτόν· διὰ τοῦτο εἶπεν, Οὐχὶ πάντες καθα-
ροί ἐστε.

12 Ὅτε οὖν ἔνιψε τοὺς πόδας αὐτῶν καὶ ἔλαβε τὰ ἱμάτια αὐτοῦ, ἀνα-
13 πεσὼν πάλιν εἶπεν αὐτοῖς, Γινώσκετε τί πεποίηκα ὑμῖν; ὑμεῖς φωνεῖτέ ριϛ
14 με, Ὁ διδάσκαλος καὶ ὁ κύριος· καὶ καλῶς λέγετε, εἰμὶ γάρ. εἰ οὖν γ ριζ
ἐγὼ ἔνιψα ὑμῶν τοὺς πόδας, ὁ κύριος καὶ ὁ διδάσκαλος, καὶ ὑμεῖς ι
15 ὀφείλετε ἀλλήλων νίπτειν τοὺς πόδας· ὑπόδειγμα γὰρ δέδωκα ὑμῖν,
16 ἵνα καθὼς ἐγὼ ἐποίησα ὑμῖν καὶ ὑμεῖς ποιεῖτε. ἀμὴν ἀμὴν λέγω ριη
ὑμῖν, οὐκ ἔστι δοῦλος μείζων τοῦ κυρίου αὐτοῦ, οὐδὲ ἀπόστολος μείζων γ
17 τοῦ πέμψαντος αὐτόν. εἰ ταῦτα οἴδατε, μακάριοί ἐστε ἐὰν ποιῆτε
18 αὐτά. οὐ περὶ πάντων ὑμῶν λέγω· ἐγὼ οἶδα οὓς ἐξελεξάμην· ἀλλ' ριθ
ἵνα ἡ γραφὴ πληρωθῇ, Ὁ τρώγων μετ' ἐμοῦ ἐπῆρεν ἐπ' ἐμὲ τὴν ι
19 πτέρναν αὐτοῦ. ἀπ' ἄρτι λέγω ὑμῖν πρὸ τοῦ γενέσθαι, ἵνα ὅταν
20 γένηται πιστεύσητε ὅτι ἐγώ εἰμι. ἀμὴν ἀμὴν λέγω ὑμῖν, Ὁ λαμ- ρκ
βάνων ἐάν τινα πέμψω, ἐμὲ λαμβάνει· ὁ δὲ ἐμὲ λαμβάνων λαμβάνει α
τὸν ἀποστείλαντά με.

21 Ταῦτα εἰπὼν ὁ Ἰησοῦς ἐταράχθη τῷ πνεύματι, καὶ ἐμαρτύρησε καὶ ρκα
22 εἶπεν, Ἀμὴν ἀμὴν λέγω ὑμῖν ὅτι εἷς ἐξ ὑμῶν παραδώσει με. ἔβλεπον δ ρκβ
23 οὖν εἰς ἀλλήλους οἱ μαθηταί, ἀπορούμενοι περὶ τίνος λέγει. ἦν δὲ α ρκγ
ἀνακείμενος εἷς τῶν μαθητῶν αὐτοῦ ἐν τῷ κόλπῳ τοῦ Ἰησοῦ, ὃν ἠγάπα ι
24 ὁ Ἰησοῦς· νεύει οὖν τούτῳ Σίμων Πέτρος πυθέσθαι τίς ἂν εἴη περὶ
25 οὗ λέγει. ἐπιπεσὼν οὖν ἐκεῖνος ἐπὶ τὸ στῆθος τοῦ Ἰησοῦ λέγει αὐτῷ,
26 Κύριε, τίς ἐστιν; ἀποκρίνεται ὁ Ἰησοῦς, Ἐκεῖνός ἐστιν ᾧ ἂν ἐγὼ
ἐμβάψας τὸ ψωμίον ἐπιδώσω. καὶ ἐμβάψας τὸ ψωμίον δίδωσιν Ἰούδᾳ

18 επηρεν] επηρκεν cod. **25** του] το cod.

8 μου post ποδας ϛ νιψης 118 209 ϛ **10** om αλλ...ολος 209 118 209 ϛ
15 εδωκα ϛ ποιητε ϛ **18** εμου] + τον αρτον ϛ **20** αποστειλαντα]
πεμψαντα ϛ **25** ουν] δε ϛ **26** om αν ϛ βαψας ϛ

ρκδ/θ Σίμωνος Ἰσκαριώτῃ. καὶ μετὰ τὸ ψωμίον, τότε εἰσῆλθεν εἰς ἐκεῖνον 27
ρκε/ι ὁ Σατανᾶς. λέγει οὖν αὐτῷ ὁ Ἰησοῦς, Ὃ ποιεῖς, ποίησον τάχιον.
τοῦτο δὲ οὐδεὶς ἔγνω τῶν ἀνακειμένων πρὸς τί εἶπεν αὐτῷ. τινὲς γὰρ 28 29
ἐδόκουν, ἐπεὶ τὸ γλωσσόκομον εἶχεν Ἰούδας, ὅτι λέγει αὐτῷ, Ἀγό-
ρασον ὧν χρείαν ἔχομεν εἰς τὴν ἑορτήν· ἢ τοῖς πτωχοῖς ἵνα τι δῷ.
λαβὼν οὖν τὸ ψωμίον ἐκεῖνος εὐθέως ἐξῆλθεν· ἦν δὲ νύξ. 30
Ὅτε οὖν ἐξῆλθε λέγει ὁ Ἰησοῦς, Νῦν ἐδοξάσθη ὁ υἱὸς τοῦ ἀνθρώ- 31
που, καὶ ὁ Θεὸς ἐδοξάσθη ἐν αὐτῷ. καὶ ὁ Θεὸς δοξάσει αὐτὸν ἐν 32
ἑαυτῷ, καὶ εὐθὺς δοξάσει αὐτόν. τεκνία, ἔτι μικρὸν μεθ' ὑμῶν εἰμι. 33
ζητήσετέ με, καὶ καθὼς εἶπον τοῖς Ἰουδαίοις ὅτι Ὅπου ἐγὼ ὑπάγω
ὑμεῖς οὐ δύνασθε ἐλθεῖν, καὶ ὑμῖν λέγω ἄρτι. πλὴν ἐντολὴν καινὴν 34
δίδωμι ὑμῖν, ἵνα ἀγαπᾶτε ἀλλήλους· καθὼς ἠγάπησα ὑμᾶς ἵνα καὶ
ὑμεῖς ἀγαπᾶτε ἀλλήλους. ἐν τούτῳ γνώσονται πάντες ὅτι ἐμοὶ μαθηταί 35
ἐστε, ἐὰν ἀγάπην ἔχητε ἐν ἀλλήλοις. λέγει αὐτῷ Σίμων Πέτρος, 36
Κύριε, ποῦ ὑπάγεις; ἀπεκρίθη αὐτῷ ὁ Ἰησοῦς, Ὅπου ὑπάγω οὐ
ρκϛ/α δύνασαί μοι νῦν ἀκολουθῆσαι· ἀκολουθήσεις δὲ ὕστερον. λέγει 37
αὐτῷ ὁ Πέτρος, Κύριε, διατί οὐ δύναμαί σοι ἀκολουθῆσαι ἄρτι; τὴν
ψυχήν μου ὑπὲρ σοῦ θήσω. ἀποκρίνεται αὐτῷ ὁ Ἰησοῦς, Τὴν ψυχήν 38
σου ὑπὲρ ἐμοῦ θήσεις; ἀμὴν ἀμὴν λέγω σοι, οὐ μὴ ἀλέκτωρ φωνήσει
ἕως οὗ ἀρνήσῃ με τρίς.

ρκζ/ι XIV. Μὴ ταρασσέσθω ὑμῶν ἡ καρδία· πιστεύετε εἰς τὸν Θεόν,
καὶ εἰς ἐμὲ πιστεύετε. ἐν τῇ οἰκίᾳ τοῦ πατρός μου μοναὶ πολλαί 2
εἰσιν· εἰ δὲ μήγε, εἶπον ἂν ὑμῖν· καὶ ἐὰν πορευθῶ καὶ ἑτοιμάσω τόπον 3
ὑμῖν, πάλιν ἔρχομαι καὶ παραλήψομαι ὑμᾶς πρὸς ἐμαυτόν, ἵνα ὅπου
εἰμὶ ἐγὼ καὶ ὑμεῖς ἦτε. καὶ ὅπου ὑπάγω οἴδατε, καὶ τὴν ὁδὸν οἴδατε. 4
λέγει αὐτῷ Θωμᾶς, Κύριε, οὐκ οἴδαμεν ποῦ ὑπάγεις· καὶ πῶς δυνά- 5
μεθα τὴν ὁδὸν εἰδέναι; λέγει αὐτῷ ὁ Ἰησοῦς, Ἐγώ εἰμι ἡ ὁδὸς καὶ 6
ἡ ἀλήθεια καὶ ἡ ζωή· οὐδεὶς ἔρχεται πρὸς τὸν πατέρα, εἰ μὴ δι' ἐμοῦ.
εἰ ἐγνώκειτέ με, καὶ τὸν πατέρα μου ἂν ᾔδειτε· ἀπ' ἄρτι γινώσκετε 7
αὐτὸν καὶ ἑωράκατε αὐτόν. λέγει αὐτῷ Φίλιππος, Κύριε, δεῖξον ἡμῖν 8
τὸν πατέρα, καὶ ἀρκεῖ ἡμῖν. λέγει αὐτῷ ὁ Ἰησοῦς, Τοσοῦτον χρόνον 9

118 209 ς **29** ο Ιουδας ς αυτω] + ο Ιησους ς **32** και 1°] pr ει ο Θεος εδοξασθη εν αυτω 118 209 ς **33** υπαγω εγω ς **34** om πλην 118 209 ς **35** εν αλληλοις] μετ αλληλων 118 209 **36** οπου εγω 118 209 υστερον δε ακολουθησεις μοι 118 209 ς **37** om ο 118 209 **38** απεκριθη ς om αυτω 118 209 φωνηση 118* 209 sed 118 nunc habet φωνησε απαρνηση 118 209 ς

2 μηγε] μη 118 209 ς υμιν] + πορευομαι ετοιμασαι τοπον υμιν 118 209 ς **3** υμιν τοπον 118 209 ς **4** οπου εγω 118 209 ς **7** εγνωκητε 118 209 αν ηδειτε] εγνωκειτε αν και 118 209 ς sed εγνωκητε 118 209 non εγνωκειτε

μεθ' ὑμῶν εἰμι, καὶ οὐκ ἔγνωκάς με, Φίλιππε; ὁ ἑωρακὼς ἐμὲ ἑώρακε
10 τὸν πατέρα· καὶ πῶς σὺ λέγεις, Δεῖξον ἡμῖν τὸν πατέρα; οὐ πιστεύεις
ὅτι ἐγὼ ἐν τῷ πατρὶ καὶ ὁ πατὴρ ἐν ἐμοί ἐστι; τὰ ῥήματα ἃ ἐγὼ
λαλῶ ὑμῖν ἀπ' ἐμαυτοῦ οὐ λαλῶ· ὁ δὲ πατὴρ ὁ ἐν ἐμοὶ μένων αὐτὸς
11 ποιεῖ τὰ ἔργα. πιστεύετέ μοι ὅτι ἐγὼ ἐν τῷ πατρὶ καὶ ὁ πατὴρ ἐν
12 ἐμοί ἐστιν· εἰ δὲ μή, διὰ τὰ ἔργα αὐτὰ πιστεύετέ μοι. ἀμὴν ἀμὴν
λέγω ὑμῖν, ὁ πιστεύων εἰς ἐμέ, τὰ ἔργα ἃ ἐγὼ ποιῶ κἀκεῖνος ποιήσει,
13 καὶ μείζονα τούτων ποιήσει, ὅτι ἐγὼ πρὸς τὸν πατέρα πορεύομαι. καὶ ρκη δ
ὃ ἐὰν αἰτήσητε ἐν τῷ ὀνόματί μου, τοῦτο ποιήσω, ἵνα δοξασθῇ ὁ
πατὴρ ἐν τῷ υἱῷ.
15 16 Ἐὰν ἀγαπᾶτέ με, τὰς ἐντολὰς τὰς ἐμὰς τηρήσατε. κἀγὼ ἐρωτήσω
τὸν πατέρα, καὶ ἄλλον παράκλητον δώσει ὑμῖν, ἵνα μένῃ μεθ' ὑμῶν
17 εἰς τὸν αἰῶνα, τὸ πνεῦμα τῆς ἀληθείας, ὃ ὁ κόσμος οὐ δύναται λαβεῖν,
ὅτι οὐ θεωρεῖ αὐτὸ οὐδὲ γινώσκει αὐτό· ὑμεῖς δὲ γινώσκετε αὐτό, ὅτι
18 παρ' ὑμῖν μένει καὶ σὺν ὑμῖν ἐστιν. οὐκ ἀφήσω ὑμᾶς ὀρφανούς·
19 ἔρχομαι πρὸς ὑμᾶς. ἔτι μικρὸν καὶ ὁ κόσμος με οὐκ ἔτι θεωρεῖ· ὑμεῖς
20 δὲ θεωρεῖτέ με· ὅτι ἐγὼ ζῶ, καὶ ὑμεῖς ζήσεσθε. ἐν ἐκείνῃ τῇ ἡμέρᾳ
γνώσεσθε ὑμεῖς ὅτι ἐγὼ ἐν τῷ πατρί μου, καὶ ὑμεῖς ἐν ἐμοί, κἀγὼ
21 ἐν ὑμῖν. ὁ ἔχων τὰς ἐντολάς μου καὶ τηρῶν αὐτάς, ἐκεῖνός ἐστιν ὁ
ἀγαπῶν με· ὁ δὲ ἀγαπῶν με ἀγαπηθήσεται ὑπὸ τοῦ πατρός μου· κἀγὼ ρκθ α
22 ἀγαπήσω αὐτὸν καὶ ἐμφανίσω αὐτῷ ἐμαυτόν. λέγει αὐτῷ Ἰούδας (οὐχ ρλ
ὁ Ἰσκαριώτης), Κύριε, καὶ τί γέγονεν ὅτι ἡμῖν μέλλεις ἐμφανίζειν ι
23 σεαυτόν, καὶ οὐχὶ τῷ κόσμῳ; ἀπεκρίθη Ἰησοῦς καὶ εἶπεν αὐτῷ,
Ἐάν τις ἀγαπᾷ με, τὸν λόγον μου τηρήσει, καὶ ὁ πατήρ μου ἀγαπήσει
αὐτόν, καὶ πρὸς αὐτὸν ἐλευσόμεθα καὶ μονὴν παρ' αὐτῷ ποιησόμεθα.
24 ὁ μὴ ἀγαπῶν με τοὺς λόγους μου οὐ τηρεῖ· καὶ ὁ λόγος ὃν ἀκούετε ρλα α
οὐκ ἔστιν ἐμός, ἀλλὰ τοῦ πέμψαντός με πατρός.
25 26 Ταῦτα λελάληκα ὑμῖν παρ' ὑμῖν μένων· ὁ δὲ παράκλητος, τὸ Πνεῦμα ρλβ ι
τὸ Ἅγιον, ὃ πέμψει ὁ πατὴρ ἐν τῷ ὀνόματί μου, ἐκεῖνος ὑμᾶς διδάξει
27 πάντα καὶ ὑπομνήσει ὑμᾶς πάντα ὅσα εἶπον ὑμῖν. εἰρήνην ἀφίημι
ὑμῖν, εἰρήνην τὴν ἐμὴν δίδωμι ὑμῖν· οὐ καθὼς ὁ κόσμος δίδωσιν ἐγὼ
28 δίδωμι ὑμῖν. μὴ ταρασσέσθω ὑμῶν ἡ καρδία μηδὲ δειλιάτω. ἠκούσατε
ὅτι ἐγὼ εἶπον ὑμῖν, Ὑπάγω καὶ ἔρχομαι πρὸς ὑμᾶς. εἰ ἠγαπᾶτέ με,

9 *φιλππε* cod. **12** *μειζωνα* cod. **26** *η* a deauratore scriptum

10 *πατερα*] + *και αρκει ημιν* 118 209 om *ου* 118 209 **11** om *εστιν* 118 209 ς **12** *πατερα μου* 118 209 ς **13** *ο εαν*] *ο τι εαν* 118 209 ς om *ινα...υιω* 118 209 *υιω*] + *εαν τι αιτησητε εν τω ονοματι μου εγω ποιησω* ς **15** *τας εμας*] *μου* 118 209 **16** *και εγω* 118 ς **17** *συν*] *εν* 118 209 ς *εσται* 118 209 ς **21** *και εγω* 118 209 ς **22** om *και* 1° ς *σεαυτω* 118 209 **23** *ο* Ιησους ς *ποιησομεν* 118 209 ς **26** *η*] *ο* 118 209 ς *οσα*] *α* 118 209 ς

ἐχάρητε ἂν ὅτι πορεύομαι πρὸς τὸν πατέρα, ὅτι ὁ πατὴρ μείζων
μού ἐστι. καὶ νῦν εἴρηκα ὑμῖν πρὶν γενέσθαι, ἵνα ὅταν γένηται 29
πιστεύσητε.

Οὐκ ἔτι πολλὰ λαλήσω μεθ' ὑμῶν· ἔρχεται γὰρ ὁ ἄρχων τοῦ 30
κόσμου τούτου, καὶ ἐν ἐμοὶ οὐκ ἔχει οὐδέν, ἀλλ' ἵνα γνῷ ὁ κόσμος 31
ὅτι ἀγαπῶ τὸν πατέρα, καὶ ἔδωκέ μοι ὁ πατὴρ ἐντολήν, οὕτως
ποιῶ. ἐγείρεσθε, ἄγωμεν ἐντεῦθεν.

XV Ἐγώ εἰμι ἡ ἄμπελος ἡ ἀληθινή, καὶ ὁ πατήρ μου ὁ γεωργός
ἐστι. πᾶν κλῆμα ἐν ἐμοὶ μὴ φέρον καρπόν, αἴρει· καὶ πᾶν τὸ καρπὸν 2
φέρον, καθαίρει αὐτὸ ἵνα πλείονα καρπὸν φέρῃ. ἤδη ὑμεῖς καθαροί 3
ἐστε διὰ τὸν λόγον ὃν λελάληκα ὑμῖν. μείνατε ἐν ἐμοί, κἀγὼ ἐν ὑμῖν. 4
καθὼς τὸ κλῆμα οὐ δύναται καρπὸν φέρειν ἀφ' ἑαυτοῦ, ἐὰν μὴ μείνῃ
ἐν τῇ ἀμπέλῳ, οὕτως οὐδὲ ὑμεῖς, ἐὰν μὴ ἐν ἐμοὶ μείνητε. ἐγώ εἰμι 5
ἡ ἄμπελος, ὑμεῖς τὰ κλήματα. ὁ μένων ἐν ἐμοί, κἀγὼ ἐν αὐτῷ, οὗτος
φέρει καρπὸν πολύν· ὅτι χωρὶς ἐμοῦ οὐ δύνασθε ποιεῖν οὐδέν. ἐὰν 6
μή τις μείνῃ ἐν ἐμοί, ἐβλήθη ἔξω ὡς τὸ κλῆμα καὶ ἐξηράνθη, καὶ
ρλγ συνάγουσιν αὐτὸ καὶ εἰς τὸ πῦρ βάλλουσι, καὶ καίεται. ἐὰν μείνητε 7
δ ἐν ἐμοὶ καὶ τὰ ῥήματά μου ἐν ὑμῖν μείνῃ, ὃ ἐὰν θέλητε αἰτήσασθε,
ρλδ καὶ γενήσεται ὑμῖν. ἐν τούτῳ ἐδοξάσθη ὁ πατήρ μου, ἵνα καρπὸν 8
ι πολὺν φέρητε· καὶ γένησθε ἐμοὶ μαθηταί. καθὼς ἠγάπησέ με ὁ 9
πατήρ, κἀγὼ ὑμᾶς ἠγάπησα· μείνατε ἐν τῇ ἀγάπῃ τῇ ἐμῇ. ἐὰν 10
τὰς ἐντολάς μου τηρήσητε, μενεῖτε ἐν τῇ ἀγάπῃ μου· καθὼς ἐγὼ τὰς
ἐντολὰς τοῦ πατρός μου τετήρηκα καὶ μένω αὐτοῦ ἐν τῇ ἀγάπῃ. ταῦτα 11
λελάληκα ὑμῖν, ἵνα ἡ χαρὰ ἡ ἐμὴ ἐν ἡμῖν ᾖ καὶ ἡ χαρὰ ὑμῶν
πληρωθῇ. αὕτη ἐστὶν ἡ ἐντολὴ ἡ ἐμή, ἵνα ἀγαπᾶτε ἀλλήλους καθὼς 12
ρλε ἠγάπησα ὑμᾶς. μείζονα ταύτης ἀγάπην οὐδεὶς ἔχει, ἵνα τις τὴν ψυχὴν 13
δ αὐτοῦ θῇ ὑπὲρ τῶν φίλων αὐτοῦ. ὑμεῖς φίλοι μού ἐστε, ἐὰν ποιῆτε 14
ρλϛ ι ἃ ἐγὼ ἐντέλλομαι ὑμῖν. οὐκέτι ὑμᾶς λέγω δούλους, ὅτι ὁ δοῦλος οὐκ 15
οἶδε τί ποιεῖ αὐτοῦ ὁ κύριος· ὑμᾶς δὲ εἴρηκα φίλους, ὅτι πάντα ἃ

4 εαν 1°] εναν cod. ν 1° eras. m. recent. 6 εαν] εναν 1* sed ν 1° nunc eras. 11 ταῦτα] αῦτα cod. per incuriam deauratoris sed τ addidit m. recent.

118 209 ϛ 28 οτι 1°]+ειπον 118 209 ϛ πατηρ μου 118 209 ϛ 29 πριν η 118 209 30 ο του κοσμου αρχων 118 209, ο του κοσμου τουτου αρχων ϛ καθως ενετειλατο μοι ο πατηρ 118 209 ϛ ουτω ϛ

2 αιρει αυτο 118 209 ϛ 6 om μεινη 209 εκβληθη 118 209 αυτο] αυτα ϛ om το 2° ϛ 7 εαν] αν 209 αιτησεσθε 118 209 ϛ γενησεται] δοθησεται 118 209 8 γενησεσθε 118 209 ϛ ηγαπησα ημας 118 209 ϛ 11 12 εμη] εμοι 118 11 ημιν η] υμιν μεινη 118 209 ϛ 14 α] οσα 118 209 ϛ

16 ἤκουσα παρὰ τοῦ πατρὸς ἐγνώρισα ὑμῖν. οὐχ ὑμεῖς με ἐξελέξασθε,
ἀλλ' ἐγὼ ἐξελεξάμην ὑμᾶς, καὶ ἔθηκα ὑμᾶς ἵνα ὑμεῖς ὑπάγητε καὶ
καρπὸν φέρητε καὶ ὁ καρπὸς ὑμῶν μένῃ, ἵνα ὅ τι ἂν αἰτήσητε τὸν ρλζ δ
17 πατέρα ἐν τῷ ὀνόματί μου, δῷ ὑμῖν. ταῦτα ἐντέλλομαι ὑμῖν, ἵνα ρλη ι
ἀγαπᾶτε ἀλλήλους.
18 Εἰ ὁ κόσμος ὑμᾶς μισεῖ, γινώσκετε ὅτι ἐμὲ πρῶτον ὑμῶν μεμίσηκεν.
19 εἰ ἐκ τοῦ κόσμου ἦτε, ὁ κόσμος ἂν τὸ ἴδιον ἐφίλει· ὅτι δὲ ἐκ τοῦ
κόσμου οὐκ ἐστέ, ἀλλ' ἐγὼ ἐξελεξάμην ὑμᾶς ἐκ τοῦ κόσμου, διὰ τοῦτο
20 μισεῖ ὑμᾶς ὁ κόσμος. μνημονεύετε τοῦ λόγου οὗ ἐγὼ εἶπον ὑμῖν, ρλθ γ
Οὐκ ἔστι δοῦλος μείζων τοῦ κυρίου αὐτοῦ. εἰ ἐμὲ ἐδίωξαν, καὶ ὑμᾶς ρμ ι
διώξουσιν· εἰ τὸν λόγον μου ἐτήρησαν, καὶ τὸν ἡμέτερον τηρήσουσιν. ρμα α
21 ἀλλὰ ταῦτα πάντα ποιήσουσιν εἰς ὑμᾶς διὰ τὸ ὄνομά μου, ὅτι οὐκ
22 οἴδασι τὸν πέμψαντά με. εἰ μὴ ἦλθον καὶ ἐλάλησα αὐτοῖς, ἁμαρτίαν ρμβ γ
οὐκ εἴχοσαν· νῦν δὲ πρόφασιν οὐκ ἔχουσι περὶ τῆς ἁμαρτίας αὐτῶν. ρμγ ι
23 24 ὁ ἐμὲ μισῶν καὶ τὸν πατέρα μου μισεῖ. εἰ τὰ ἔργα μὴ ἐποίησα ἐν ρμδ ι
αὐτοῖς ἃ οὐδεὶς ἄλλος ἐποίησεν, ἁμαρτίαν οὐκ εἴχωσαν· νῦν δὲ καὶ
25 ἑωράκασι καὶ μεμισήκασι καὶ ἐμὲ καὶ τὸν πατέρα μου· ἀλλ' ἵνα πλη- ρμε ι
ρωθῇ ὁ λόγος ὁ ἐν τῷ νόμῳ αὐτῶν γεγραμμένος, ὅτι Ἐμίσησάν
26 με δωρεάν. ὅταν δὲ ἔλθῃ ὁ παράκλητος, ὃν ἐγὼ πέμψω ὑμῖν παρὰ ΙΖ'
τοῦ πατρός, τὸ πνεῦμα τῆς ἀληθείας ὃ παρὰ τοῦ πατρὸς ἐκπορεύεται,
27 ἐκεῖνος μαρτυρήσει περὶ ἐμοῦ· καὶ ὑμεῖς δὲ μαρτυρεῖτε, ὅτι ἐξ ἀρχῆς
μετ' ἐμοῦ ἐστε.
2 XVI. Ταῦτα λελάληκα ὑμῖν, ἵνα μὴ σκανδαλισθῆτε. ἀποσυνα- ρμϛ α
γώγους ποιήσουσιν ὑμᾶς· ἀλλ' ἔρχεται ὥρα, ἵνα πᾶς ὁ ἀποκτείνας ὑμᾶς
3 δόξῃ λατρείαν προσφέρειν τῷ Θεῷ. καὶ ταῦτα ποιήσουσιν ὑμῖν, ὅτι
4 οὐκ ἔγνωσαν τὸν πατέρα οὐδὲ ἐμέ. ἀλλὰ ταῦτα λελάληκα ὑμῖν, ἵνα
ὅταν ἔλθῃ ἡ ὥρα, μνημονεύειτε αὐτῶν, ὅτι ἐγὼ εἶπον ὑμῖν. ταῦτα
5 δὲ ὑμῖν ἐξ ὀρχῆς οὐκ εἶπον, ὅτι μεθ' ὑμῶν ἤμην· νῦν δὲ ὑπάγω πρὸς ρμζ ι
6 τὸν πέμψαντά με, καὶ οὐδεὶς ἐξ ὑμῶν ἐρωτᾷ με, Ποῦ ὑπάγεις; ἀλλ' ὅτι
7 ταῦτα λελάληκα ὑμῖν, ἡ λύπη πεπλήρωκεν ὑμῶν τὴν καρδίαν. ἀλλ' ἐγὼ
τὴν ἀλήθειαν λέγω ὑμῖν, συμφέρει ὑμῖν ἵνα ἐγὼ ἀπέλθω. ἐὰν γὰρ
μὴ ἀπέλθω, ὁ παράκλητος οὐκ ἐλεύσεται πρὸς ὑμᾶς· ἐὰν δὲ πορευθῶ,
8 πέμψω αὐτὸν πρὸς ὑμᾶς· καὶ ἐλθὼν ἐκεῖνος ἐλέγξει τὸν κόσμον περὶ

20 ετηρησαν] επηρησαν cod. **21** πεμψαντα με] πεψαντα μεο cod.

15 πατρος μου 118 209 ς **16** υπαγετε 118 209 **20** οτι ουκ 118 209 118 209 ς
υμετερον 118 209 ς **21** εις υμας] υμιν 118 209 ς **22** ειχον 118 209 ς
24 πεποιηκεν 118 209 ς ειχον 118 209 ς **25** γεγραμμενος εν τω νομω
αυτων 118 209 ς **27** εξ] απ 118 209 ς

3 εγνωσαν] οιδασι 118 209 **4** ωρα] + αυτων 118 209 μνημονευητε
118 209 ς υμιν 3º] post ειπον 118 **7** γαρ] + εγω 118 209

ἁμαρτίας καὶ περὶ δικαιοσύνης καὶ περὶ κρίσεως· περὶ ἁμαρτίας μέν, ὅτι 9
οὐ πιστεύουσιν εἰς ἐμέ· περὶ δικαιοσύνης δέ, ὅτι πρὸς τὸν πατέρα 10
ὑπάγω καὶ οὐκέτι θεωρεῖτέ με· περὶ δὲ κρίσεως, ὅτι ὁ ἄρχων τοῦ 11
κόσμου κέκριται.
Ἔτι πολλὰ ἔχω λέγειν ὑμῖν, ἀλλ' οὐ δύνασθε βαστάζειν ἄρτι· 12
ὅταν δὲ ἔλθῃ ἐκεῖνος, τὸ πνεῦμα τῆς ἀληθείας, ὁδηγήσει ὑμᾶς ἐν τῇ 13
ἀληθείᾳ πάσῃ· οὐ γὰρ λαλήσει ἀφ' ἑαυτοῦ, ἀλλ' ὅσα ἀκούσει
λαλήσει, καὶ τὰ ἐρχόμενα ἀναγγελεῖ ὑμῖν. ἐκεῖνος ἐμὲ δοξάσει, ὅτι 14
ρμη ἐκ τοῦ ἐμοῦ λήψεται καὶ ἀναγγελεῖ ὑμῖν. πάντα ὅσα ἔχει ὁ πατὴρ 15
γ ἐμά ἐστι· διὰ τοῦτο εἶπον, ὅτι ἐκ τοῦ ἐμοῦ λαμβάνει καὶ ἀναγγελεῖ
ρμθ ὑμῖν. μικρὸν καὶ οὐκέτι θεωρεῖτέ με, καὶ πάλιν μικρὸν καὶ ὄψεσθέ 16
ι με, ὅτι ὑπάγω πρὸς τὸν πατέρα. εἶπον οὖν ἐκ τῶν μαθητῶν αὐτοῦ 17
πρὸς ἀλλήλους, Τί ἐστι τοῦτο ὃ λέγει ἡμῖν, Μικρὸν καὶ οὐ θεωρεῖτέ
με, καὶ πάλιν μικρὸν καὶ ὄψεσθέ με; καί, Ὅτι ἐγὼ ὑπάγω πρὸς τὸν
πατέρα; ἔλεγον οὖν, Τί ἐστι τοῦτο, τὸ μικρόν; οὐκ οἴδαμεν τί 18
λαλεῖ. ἔγνω ὁ Ἰησοῦς ὅτι ἤθελον αὐτὸν ἐρωτᾶν, καὶ εἶπεν αὐτοῖς, 19
Περὶ τούτου ζητεῖτε μετ' ἀλλήλων, ὅτι εἶπον, Μικρὸν καὶ οὐ θεωρεῖτέ
με, καὶ πάλιν μικρὸν καὶ ὄψεσθέ με; ἀμὴν ἀμὴν λέγω ὑμῖν, ὅτι κλαύ- 20
σετε καὶ θρηνήσετε ὑμεῖς, ὁ δὲ κόσμος χαρήσεται· ὑμεῖς λυπηθήσεσθε,
ἀλλ' ἡ λύπη ὑμῶν εἰς χαρὰν γενήσεται. ἡ γυνὴ ὅταν τίκτῃ, λύπην 21
ἔχει, ὅτι ἦλθεν ἡ ὥρα αὐτῆς· ὅταν δὲ γεννήσῃ παιδίον, οὐκέτι μνη-
μονεύει τῆς θλίψεως, διὰ τὴν χαρὰν ὅτι ἐγεννήθη ἄνθρωπος εἰς τὸν
κόσμον. καὶ ὑμεῖς οὖν νῦν μὲν λύπην ἔχετε· πάλιν δὲ ὄψομαι ὑμᾶς, 22
καὶ χαρήσεται ὑμῶν ἡ καρδία, καὶ τὴν χαρὰν ὑμῶν οὐδεὶς αἴρει ἀφ'
ρν ὑμῶν. καὶ ἐν ἐκείνῃ τῇ ἡμέρᾳ ἐμὲ οὐκ ἐρωτήσετε οὐδέν. ἀμὴν ἀμὴν 23
δ λέγω ὑμῖν, ὅτι ὅσα ἂν αἰτήσητε τὸν πατέρα ἐν τῷ ὀνόματί μου,
δώσει ὑμῖν. ἕως ἄρτι οὐκ ᾐτήσατε οὐδὲν ἐν τῷ ὀνόματί μου· αἰτεῖτε, 24
ρνα καὶ λήψεσθε, ἵνα ἡ χαρὰ ὑμῶν ᾖ πεπληρωμένη. ταῦτα ἐν παροιμίαις 25
ι λελάληκα ὑμῖν· ἔρχεται ὥρα οὐκέτι ἐν παροιμίαις λαλήσω ὑμῖν,
ἀλλὰ παρρησίᾳ περὶ τοῦ πατρὸς ἀναγγελῶ ὑμῖν. ἐν ἐκείνῃ τῇ ἡμέρᾳ 26

11 κεσκριται cod.

118 209 ς

10 πατερα μου 118 209   11 κοσμου τουτου 118 209 ς   12 υμιν λεγειν 118 209   13 εις πασαν την αληθειαν 118 209 ς   οσα αν 118 209 ς ακουση 118 209 ς   14 αναγκελει 118   15 λαμβανει] ληψεται ς αναγκελει 118   16 ουκετι] ου 118 209 ς   εγω υπαγω ς   17 om και 4° 118 209   om εγω 118 209   18 τουτο τι εστιν ο λεγει 118 209 ς   19 εγνω ουν 118 209 ς   20 υμεις δε 118 209 ς   21 το παιδιον 118 209 ς   22 λυπην μεν νυν 118 209 ς   23 om εν τω ονοματι μου 118 209   25 αλλ ερχεται ωρα οτε 118 209 ς sed 209 οτι non οτε   παροιμιαις 2° hic desinit 118* quaeque m. post. supplevit indigna sunt quae conferantur

αἰτήσασθε ἐν τῷ ὀνόματί μου· καὶ οὐ λέγω ὑμῖν ὅτι ἐγὼ ἐρωτήσω
27 τὸν πατέρα περὶ ὑμῶν· αὐτὸς γὰρ ὁ πατὴρ φιλεῖ ὑμᾶς, ὅτι ὑμεῖς ἐμὲ
28 πεφιλήκατε καὶ πεπιστεύκατε ὅτι ἐγὼ παρὰ τοῦ Θεοῦ ἐξῆλθον. ἐξῆλθον
παρὰ τοῦ πατρὸς καὶ ἐλήλυθα εἰς τὸν κόσμον· πάλιν ἀφίημι τὸν κόσμον
καὶ πορεύομαι πρὸς τὸν πατέρα.
29 Λέγουσιν οἱ μαθηταὶ αὐτοῦ, Ἴδε νῦν παρρησίᾳ λαλεῖς, καὶ παροι-
30 μίαν οὐδεμίαν λέγεις. νῦν οἴδαμεν ὅτι οἶδας πάντα, καὶ οὐ χρείαν
ἔχεις ἵνα τίς σε ἐρωτᾷ. ἐν τούτῳ πιστεύομεν ὅτι ἀπὸ Θεοῦ ἐξῆλθες.
31 32 ἀπεκρίθη αὐτοῖς ὁ Ἰησοῦς, Ἄρτι πιστεύετε; ἰδοὺ ἔρχεται ὥρα καὶ νῦν ρνβ
ἐλήλυθεν, ἵνα σκορπισθῆτε ἕκαστος εἰς τὰ ἴδια κἀμὲ μόνον ἀφῆτε· δ
33 καὶ οὐκ εἰμὶ μόνος, ὅτι ὁ πατὴρ μετ' ἐμοῦ ἐστι. ταῦτα λελάληκα ὑμῖν, ριγ
ἵνα ἐν ἐμοὶ εἰρήνην ἔχητε. ἐν τῷ κόσμῳ θλῖψιν ἕξετε· ἀλλὰ θαρσεῖτε, ι
ἐγὼ νενίκηκα τὸν κόσμον.

XVII. Ταῦτα ἐλάλησεν ὁ Ἰησοῦς, καὶ ἐπάρας τοὺς ὀφθαλμοὺς
αὐτοῦ εἰς τὸν οὐρανὸν εἶπε, Πάτερ, ἐλήλυθεν ἡ ὥρα· δόξασόν σου
2 τὸν υἱόν, ἵνα ὁ υἱός σου δοξάσῃ σε· καθὼς ἔδωκας αὐτῷ ἐξουσίαν
πάσης σαρκός, ἵνα πᾶν ὃ δέδωκας αὐτῷ, δώσει αὐτῷ ζωὴν αἰώνιον.
3 αὕτη δέ ἐστιν ἡ αἰώνιος ζωή, ἵνα γινώσκωσί σε τὸν μόνον ἀληθινὸν
4 Θεόν, καὶ ὃν ἀπέστειλας Ἰησοῦν Χριστόν. ἐγώ σε ἐδόξασα ἐπὶ τῆς
5 γῆς τὸ ἔργον τελειώσας ὃ δέδωκάς μοι ἵνα ποιήσω· καὶ νῦν
δόξασόν με σύ, πάτερ, παρὰ σεαυτῷ, τῇ δόξῃ ᾗ εἶχον πρὸ τοῦ τὸν
6 κόσμον εἶναι παρὰ σοί. ἐφανέρωσά σου τὸ ὄνομα τοῖς ἀνθρώποις οὓς
δέδωκάς μοι ἐκ τοῦ κόσμου· σοὶ ἦσαν, κἀμοὶ αὐτοὺς δέδωκας, καὶ τὸν
7 λόγον σου τετηρήκασι. νῦν ἔγνωκαν ὅτι πάντα ὅσα ἔδωκάς μοι παρὰ
8 σοῦ ἐστιν· ὅτι τὰ ῥήματα ἃ δέδωκάς μοι δέδωκα αὐτοῖς· καὶ αὐτοὶ
ἔλαβον, καὶ ἔγνωσαν ἀληθῶς ὅτι παρὰ σοῦ ἐξῆλθον, καὶ ἐπίστευσαν
9 ὅτι σύ με ἀπέστειλας. ἐγὼ περὶ αὐτῶν ἐρωτῶ· οὐ περὶ τοῦ κόσμου
10 ἐρωτῶ, ἀλλὰ περὶ ὧν δέδωκάς μοι, ὅτι σοί εἰσι. καὶ τὰ ἐμὰ πάντα
11 σά ἐστι, καὶ τὰ σὰ ἐμά· καὶ δεδόξασμαι ἐν αὐτοῖς. καὶ οὐκ ἔτι εἰμὶ
ἐν τῷ κόσμῳ, καὶ οὗτοι ἐν τῷ κόσμῳ εἰσί, κἀγὼ πρός σε ἔρχομαι.
πάτερ ἅγιε, τήρησον αὐτοὺς ἐν τῷ ὀνόματί σου, ᾧ δέδωκάς μοι, ἵνα
12 ὦσιν ἓν καθὼς ἡμεῖς. ὅτε ἤμην μετ' αὐτῶν, ἐγὼ ἐτήρουν αὐτοὺς
ἐν τῷ ὀνόματί σου· οὓς δέδωκάς μοι ἐφύλαξα, καὶ οὐδεὶς ἐξ αὐτῶν

4 επι] linea altera ε desinit altera πι incipit qua re neglecta m. recent. ante πι ε add.

26 om αιτησασθε 209 ς μου]+αιτησεσθε 209 ς **29** λεγουσιν αυτω 209 ς 209 ς **32** σκορπισθη 209 και εμε 209 ς

1 επαρας] επηρε 209 ς και ειπε 209 ς ινα και 209 ς **2** δωση ς αυτω] αυτοις 209 ς **4** ετελειωσα 209 ς ποιησω αυτο 209 **6** και εμοι 209 ς **7** δεδωκας 209 ς σου] σοι 209 **11** και εγω 209 ς ω] ους 209 ς **12** αυτων εν τω κοσμω 209 ς καγω 209

ἀπώλετο, εἰ μὴ ὁ υἱὸς τῆς ἀπωλείας, ἵνα ἡ γραφὴ πληρωθῇ. νῦν δὲ 13
πρός σε ἔρχομαι, καὶ ταῦτα λαλῶ ἐν τῷ κόσμῳ, ἵνα ἔχωσι τὴν χαρὰν
τὴν ἐμὴν πεπληρωμένην ἐν αὐτοῖς. ἐγὼ δέδωκα αὐτοῖς τὸν λόγον σου, 14
καὶ ὁ κόσμος ἐμίσησεν αὐτούς, ὅτι οὐκ εἰσὶν ἐκ τοῦ κόσμου, καθὼς ἐγὼ
οὐκ εἰμὶ ἐκ τοῦ κόσμου. οὐκ ἐρωτῶ ἵνα ἄρῃς αὐτοὺς ἐκ τοῦ κόσμου, 15
ἀλλ' ἵνα τηρήσῃς αὐτοὺς ἐκ τοῦ πονηροῦ. ἐκ τοῦ κόσμου οὐκ εἰσί, 16
καθὼς ἐγὼ ἐκ τοῦ κόσμου οὐκ εἰμί. ἁγίασον αὐτοὺς ἐν τῇ ἀληθείᾳ· 17
ὁ λόγος ὁ σὸς ἀλήθειά ἐστι. καθὼς ἐμὲ ἀπέστειλας εἰς τὸν κόσμον, 18
κἀγὼ ἀπέστειλα αὐτοὺς εἰς τὸν κόσμον· καὶ ὑπὲρ αὐτῶν ἐγὼ ἁγιάζω 19
ἐμαυτόν, ἵνα ὦσιν καὶ αὐτοὶ ἡγιασμένοι ἐν ἀληθείᾳ. οὐ περὶ τούτων 20
δὲ ἐρωτῶ μόνον, ἀλλὰ καὶ περὶ πάντων τῶν πιστευόντων διὰ τοῦ
λόγου αὐτῶν εἰς ἐμέ, ἵνα πάντες ἓν ὦσι· καθὼς σύ, πάτερ, ἐν ἐμοὶ κἀγὼ 21
ἐν σοί, ἵνα καὶ αὐτοὶ ἐν ἡμῖν ἓν ὦσιν, ἵνα καὶ ὁ κόσμος πιστεύσῃ ὅτι
σύ με ἀπέστειλας. κἀγὼ τὴν δόξαν ἣν δέδωκάς μοι δέδωκα αὐτοῖς, 22
ἵνα ὦσιν ἓν καθὼς ἡμεῖς ἕν, ἐγὼ ἐν αὐτοῖς καὶ σὺ ἐν ἐμοί, ἵνα ὦσι 23
τετελειωμένοι εἰς ἕν, καὶ γινώσκῃ ὁ κόσμος ὅτι σύ με ἀπέστειλας
καὶ ἠγάπησας αὐτοὺς καθὼς ἐμὲ ἠγάπησας. πάτερ, οὓς δέδωκάς μοι, 24
θέλω ἵνα ὅπου εἰμὶ ἐγὼ κἀκεῖνοι ὦσι μετ' ἐμοῦ, ἵνα θεωρῶσι τὴν
δόξαν τὴν ἐμήν, ἣν δέδωκάς μοι, ὅτι ἠγάπησάς με πρὸ καταβολῆς
ρνδ κόσμου. πάτερ δίκαιε, καὶ ὁ κόσμος σε οὐκ ἔγνω, ἐγὼ δέ σε ἔγνων, 25
γ ρνε καὶ οὗτοι ἔγνωσαν ὅτι σύ με ἀπέστειλας· καὶ ἐγνώρισα αὐτοῖς τὸ 26
ι ὄνομά σου καὶ γνωρίσω· ἵνα ἡ ἀγάπη ἣν ἠγάπησάς με ἐν αὐτοῖς ᾖ,
κἀγὼ ἐν αὐτοῖς.

ρνϛ XVIII. Ταῦτα εἰπὼν ὁ Ἰησοῦς ἐξῆλθε σὺν τοῖς μαθηταῖς αὐτοῦ
α πέραν τοῦ χειμάρρου τῶν Κέδρων, ὅπου ἦν κῆπος, εἰς ὃν εἰσῆλθεν
ρνζ αὐτὸς καὶ οἱ μαθηταὶ αὐτοῦ. ᾔδει δὲ καὶ Ἰούδας ὁ παραδιδοὺς αὐτὸν 2
ι τὸν τόπον, ὅτι πολλάκις συνήχθη ὁ Ἰησοῦς ἐκεῖ μετὰ τῶν μαθητῶν
ρνη αὐτοῦ. ὁ οὖν Ἰούδας παραλαβὼν τὴν σπεῖραν, καὶ ἐκ τῶν ἀρχιερέων 3
α καὶ Φαρισαίων ὑπηρέτας, ἔρχεται ἐκεῖ μετὰ φανῶν καὶ λαμπάδων καὶ
ρνθ ὅπλων. Ἰησοῦς δὲ εἰδὼς πάντα τὰ ἐρχόμενα ἐπ' αὐτόν, ἐξῆλθε 4
ι καὶ λέγει αὐτοῖς, Τίνα ζητεῖτε; ἀπεκρίθησαν αὐτῷ, Ἰησοῦν τὸν 5
Ναζωραῖον. λέγει αὐτοῖς ὁ Ἰησοῦς, Ἐγώ εἰμι. εἱστήκει δὲ καὶ
Ἰούδας ὁ παραδιδοὺς αὐτὸν μετ' αὐτῶν. ὡς οὖν εἶπεν αὐτοῖς, Ἐγώ 6
εἰμι, ἀπῆλθον εἰς τὰ ὀπίσω καὶ ἔπεσαν χαμαί. πάλιν οὖν αὐτοὺς 7

209 ϛ **17** αληθεια 1°] αληθεια σου 209 ϛ **19** και αυτοι ωσιν 209 ϛ **20** om παντων 209 ϛ πιστευσοντων ϛ **21** om και 2° ϛ **22** και εγω ϛ εν εσμεν 209 ϛ **23** ινα γινωσκη 209 ϛ **24** και εκεινοι 209 δεδωκας 2°] εδωκας 209 ϛ **25** εγνω] εγνων 209

3 λαβων 209 ϛ **4** δε] ουν ϛ εξελθων ειπεν ϛ **6** οτι εγω ϛ επεσον 209 ϛ **7** om ουν 209

8 ἐπηρώτησε, Τίνα ζητεῖτε; οἱ δὲ εἶπον, Ἰησοῦν τὸν Ναζωραῖον. ἀπ-
εκρίθη αὐτοῖς ὁ Ἰησοῦς, Εἶπον ὑμῖν ὅτι ἐγώ εἰμι. εἰ οὖν ἐμὲ ζητεῖτε,
9 ἄφετε τούτους ὑπάγειν· ἵνα πληρωθῇ ὁ λόγος ὃν εἶπεν, ὅτι Οὓς δέδωκάς
10 μοι, οὐκ ἀπώλεσα ἐξ αὐτῶν οὐδένα. Σίμων οὖν Πέτρος ἔχων μάχαιραν ρξ
εἵλκυσεν αὐτὴν καὶ ἔπαισε τὸν τοῦ ἀρχιερέως δοῦλον καὶ ἀπέκοψεν α
11 αὐτοῦ τὸ ὠτίον τὸ δεξιόν· ἦν δὲ ὄνομα τῷ δούλῳ Μάλχος. εἶπεν ρξα
οὖν ὁ Ἰησοῦς τῷ Πέτρῳ, Βάλε τὴν μάχαιράν σου εἰς τὴν θήκην. τὸ α
ποτήριον ὃ δέδωκέ μοι ὁ πατήρ, οὐ μὴ πίω αὐτό;
12 Ἡ οὖν σπεῖρα καὶ ὁ χιλίαρχος καὶ οἱ ὑπηρέται τῶν Ἰουδαίων συν- ρξβ
13 έλαβον τὸν Ἰησοῦν καὶ ἔδησαν αὐτόν, καὶ ἀπήγαγον αὐτὸν πρὸς Ἄνναν α ρξγ
πρῶτον· ἦν γὰρ πενθερὸς τοῦ Καϊάφα, ὃς ἦν ἀρχιερεὺς τοῦ ἐνιαυτοῦ ι
14 ἐκείνου· ἦν δὲ Καϊάφας ὁ συμβουλεύσας τοῖς Ἰουδαίοις ὅτι συμφέρει
15 ἕνα ἄνθρωπον ἀποθανεῖν ὑπὲρ τοῦ λαοῦ. ἠκολούθει δὲ τῷ Ἰησοῦ ρξδ
Σίμων Πέτρος, καὶ ὁ ἄλλος μαθητής. ὁ δὲ μαθητὴς ἐκεῖνος ἦν γνωστὸς δ ρξε
τῷ ἀρχιερεῖ, καὶ συνεισῆλθε τῷ Ἰησοῦ εἰς τὴν αὐλὴν τοῦ ἀρχιερέως· ι
16 ὁ δὲ Πέτρος εἱστήκει πρὸς τῇ θύρᾳ ἔξω. ἐξῆλθεν οὖν ὁ μαθητὴς ὁ ρξϛ
ἄλλος ὃς ἦν γνωστὸς τῷ ἀρχιερεῖ, καὶ εἶπε τῇ θυρωρῷ, καὶ εἰσήγαγε α ρξζ
17 τὸν Πέτρον. λέγει οὖν ἡ παιδίσκη ἡ θυρωρὸς τῷ Πέτρῳ, Μὴ καὶ σὺ ι ρξη
ἐκ τῶν μαθητῶν εἶ τοῦ ἀνθρώπου τούτου; λέγει ἐκεῖνος, Οὐκ εἰμί. α
18 εἱστήκεισαν δὲ οἱ δοῦλοι καὶ οἱ ὑπηρέται ἀνθρακιὰν πεποιηκότες, ὅτι ρξθ
ψῦχος ἦν, ἦν δὲ καὶ ὁ Πέτρος μετ' αὐτῶν ἑστὼς καὶ θερμαινόμενος. ι
19 ὁ οὖν ἀρχιερεὺς ἠρώτησε τὸν Ἰησοῦν περὶ τῶν μαθητῶν αὐτοῦ καὶ
20 περὶ τῆς διδαχῆς αὐτοῦ. ἀπεκρίθη δὲ αὐτῷ ὁ Ἰησοῦς, Ἐγὼ παρρησίᾳ ρο
λελάληκα τῷ κόσμῳ· ἐγὼ πάντοτε ἐδίδαξα ἐν τῇ συναγωγῇ καὶ ἐν α
τῷ ἱερῷ, ὅπου πάντες οἱ Ἰουδαῖοι συνέρχονται, καὶ ἐν κρυπτῷ ἐλάλησα
21 οὐδέν. τί με ἐπερωτᾷς; ἐρώτησον τοὺς ἀκηκοότας, τί ἐλάλησα αὐτοῖς· ροα
22 ἴδε οὗτοι οἴδασιν ἃ εἶπον ἐγώ. ταῦτα δὲ αὐτοῦ εἰπόντος εἷς τῶν ὑπ- ι ροβ
ηρετῶν παρεστηκὼς ἔδωκε ῥάπισμα τῷ Ἰησοῦ, εἰπών, Οὕτως ἀποκρίνῃ α
23 τῷ ἀρχιερεῖ; ἀπεκρίθη αὐτῷ ὁ Ἰησοῦς, Εἰ κακῶς ἐλάλησα, μαρτύρησον ρογ
24 περὶ τοῦ κακοῦ· εἰ δὲ καλῶς, τί με δέρεις; ἀπέστειλεν οὖν αὐτὸν ὁ ι ροδ
Ἄννας δεδεμένον πρὸς Καϊάφαν τὸν ἀρχιερέα. α
25 Ἦν δὲ Σίμων Πέτρος ἑστὼς καὶ θερμαινόμενος· εἶπον οὖν αὐτῷ, ροε
Μὴ καὶ σὺ ἐκ τῶν μαθητῶν αὐτοῦ εἶ; ἠρνήσατο ἐκεῖνος καὶ εἶπεν, α
26 Οὐκ εἰμί. λέγει οὖν εἷς ἐκ τῶν δούλων τοῦ ἀρχιερέως, συγγενὴς ὢν

15 *συνεισηλθε*] *συνεισηλθενθεν* cod. sed *θεν* 2° damnavit m. recent.

8 om *αυτοις* ϛ **14** *αποθανειν*] *απολεσθαι* ϛ **15** *συνηλθε* 209 209 ϛ
18 *ην* 1°] + *και εθερμαινοντο* ϛ om *και* 2° ϛ *μετ αυτων ο Πετρος* ϛ
20 om *δε* ϛ *ελαλησα* ϛ *παντες*] *παντοτε* ϛ **21** *επερωτησον* ϛ
24 om *ουν* ϛ **26** om *ουν* ϛ

οὗ ἀπέκοψε Πέτρος τὸ ὠτίον, Οὐκ ἐγώ σε εἶδον ἐν τῷ κήπῳ μετ' αὐτοῦ;
πάλιν οὖν ἠρνήσατο Πέτρος, καὶ εὐθέως ἀλέκτωρ ἐφώνησεν. 27
ρος / α Ἄγουσιν οὖν τὸν Ἰησοῦν ἀπὸ τοῦ Καϊάφα εἰς τὸ πραιτώριον. ἦν 28
ρος / ι δὲ πρωΐ· καὶ αὐτοὶ οὐκ εἰσῆλθον εἰς τὸ πραιτώριον, ἵνα μὴ μιαν-
θῶσιν, ἀλλὰ ἵνα φάγωσι τὸ πάσχα. ἐξῆλθεν οὖν ὁ Πιλάτος ἔξω 29
πρὸς αὐτοὺς καὶ φησί, Τίνα κατηγορίαν φέρετε κατὰ τοῦ ἀνθρώπου
τούτου; ἀπεκρίθησαν καὶ εἶπον αὐτῷ, Εἰ μὴ ἦν οὗτος κακοποιός, οὐκ 30
ἄν σοι παρεδώκαμεν αὐτόν. εἶπεν οὖν αὐτοῖς ὁ Πιλάτος, Λάβετε αὐτὸν 31
ὑμεῖς, καὶ κατὰ τὸν νόμον ὑμῶν κρίνατε. εἶπον δὲ αὐτῷ οἱ Ἰουδαῖοι,
Ἡμῖν οὐκ ἔξεστιν οὐδένα ἀποκτεῖναι· ἵνα ὁ λόγος τοῦ Ἰησοῦ 32
πληρωθῇ, ὃν εἶπε σημαίνων ποίῳ θανάτῳ ἤμελλεν ἀποθνήσκειν.
ροη / α εἰσῆλθεν οὖν εἰς τὸ πραιτώριον πάλιν ὁ Πιλάτος, καὶ ἐφώνησε τὸν 33
ροθ / ι Ἰησοῦν καὶ εἶπεν αὐτῷ, Σὺ εἶ ὁ βασιλεὺς τῶν Ἰουδαίων; ἀπεκρί- 34
νατο Ἰησοῦς, Ἀφ' ἑαυτοῦ σὺ τοῦτο λέγεις, ἢ ἄλλοι σοι εἶπον περὶ
ἐμοῦ; ἀπεκρίθη ὁ Πιλάτος, Μὴ ἐγὼ Ἰουδαῖός εἰμι; τὸ ἔθνος τὸ σὸν 35
καὶ οἱ ἀρχιερεῖς παρέδωκάν σε ἐμοί· τί ἐποίησας; ἀπεκρίθη Ἰησοῦς, 36
Ἡ βασιλεία ἡ ἐμὴ οὐκ ἔστιν ἐκ τοῦ κόσμου τούτου· εἰ ἐκ τοῦ κόσμου
τούτου ἦν ἡ βασιλεία ἡ ἐμή, οἱ ὑπηρέται οἱ ἐμοὶ ἠγωνίζοντο ἄν, ἵνα
μὴ παραδοθῶ τοῖς Ἰουδαίοις· νῦν δὲ ἡ βασιλεία ἡ ἐμὴ οὐκ ἔστιν ἐν-
ρπ / δ τεῦθεν. εἶπεν οὖν αὐτῷ ὁ Πιλάτος, Οὐκοῦν βασιλεὺς εἶ σύ; ἀπεκρίθη 37
ρπα ὁ Ἰησοῦς, Σὺ λέγεις ὅτι βασιλεύς εἰμι. ἐγὼ εἰς τοῦτο γεγέννημαι
ι καὶ εἰς τοῦτο ἐλήλυθα εἰς τὸν κόσμον, ἵνα μαρτυρήσω τῇ ἀληθείᾳ.
πᾶς ὁ ὢν ἐκ τῆς ἀληθείας ἀκούει μου τῆς φωνῆς. λέγει αὐτῷ ὁ 38
Πιλάτος, Τί ἐστιν ἡ ἀλήθεια; καὶ τοῦτο εἰπὼν πάλιν ἐξῆλθε πρὸς
ρπβ / θ τοὺς Ἰουδαίους καὶ λέγει αὐτοῖς, Ἐγὼ οὐδεμίαν αἰτίαν εὑρίσκω ἐν
ρπγ αὐτῷ. ἔστι δὲ συνήθεια ὑμῖν ἵνα ἕνα ἀπολύσω ὑμῖν ἐν τῷ πάσχα· 39
δ / ρπδ βούλεσθε οὖν ἀπολύσω ὑμῖν τὸν βασιλέα τῶν Ἰουδαίων; ἐκραύ- 40
α γασαν οὖν πάντες, λέγοντες, Μὴ τοῦτον, ἀλλὰ τὸν Βαραββᾶν· ἦν δὲ
ρπε / δ ὁ Βαραββᾶς οὗτος λῃστής. XIX. Τότε οὖν ἔλαβεν ὁ Πιλάτος
τὸν Ἰησοῦν καὶ ἐμαστίγωσε. καὶ οἱ στρατιῶται πλέξαντες στέφανον 2
ἐξ ἀκανθῶν ἐπέθηκαν αὐτοῦ τῇ κεφαλῇ, καὶ ἱμάτιον πορφυροῦν περι-
έβαλον αὐτόν, καὶ ἔλεγον, Χαῖρε, ὁ βασιλεὺς τῶν Ἰουδαίων, καὶ 3

29 εξηλθεν] ξηλθεν cod. per incuriam deauratoris

209 ς **27** ο Πετρος 209 ς **28** πρωια ς αλλ 209 ς **29** om εξω ς φησι] ειπε ς **31** κρινατε αυτον ς δε] ουν ς αποκτειναι ουδενα ς **32** εμελλεν 209 **34** απεκριθη αυτω ς ο Ιησους 209 ς **35** μη] μητι ς **36** ο Ιησους ς αν ante οι εμοι 209 ς **37** ειμι εγω ς **38** om η 209 ς **39** υμιν απολυσω bis ς **40** παλιν παντες ς om ουτος 209 ς

4 ἐδίδοσαν αὐτῷ ῥαπίσματα. ἐξῆλθε πάλιν ἔξω ὁ Πιλάτος καὶ λέγει ρπϛ
αὐτοῖς, Ἴδε ἄγω ὑμῖν αὐτὸν ἔξω, ἵνα γνῶτε ὅτι οὐδεμίαν αἰτίαν εὑρίσκω θ
5 ἐν αὐτῷ. ἐξῆλθεν οὖν ἔξω ὁ Ἰησοῦς, ἔχων τὸν ἀκάνθινον στέφα- ρπζ
νον καὶ τὸ πορφυροῦν ἱμάτιον. καὶ λέγει αὐτοῖς, Ἰδοὺ ὁ ἄνθρωπος. δ
6 Ὅτ' ἂν εἶδον αὐτὸν οἱ ἀρχιερεῖς καὶ οἱ ὑπηρέται, ἐκραύγασαν λέγοντες, ρπη
Σταύρωσον, σταύρωσον. λέγει αὐτοῖς ὁ Πιλάτος, Λάβετε αὐτὸν ὑμεῖς α ρπθ
7 καὶ σταυρώσατε· ἐγὼ γὰρ οὐχ εὑρίσκω ἐν αὐτῷ αἰτίαν. ἀπεκρίθησαν ι ρϟ
οἱ Ἰουδαῖοι, Ἡμεῖς νόμον ἔχομεν, καὶ κατὰ τὸν νόμον ἡμῶν ὀφείλει θ ρϟα
ἀποθανεῖν, ὅτι υἱὸν Θεοῦ ἑαυτὸν ἐποίησεν. ι
8 Ὅτε οὖν ἤκουσεν ὁ Πιλάτος τοῦτον τὸν λόγον, μᾶλλον ἐφοβήθη, ρϟβ
9 καὶ εἰσῆλθεν εἰς τὸ πραιτώριον πάλιν, καὶ λέγει τῷ Ἰησοῦ, Πόθεν εἶ δ
10 σύ; ὁ δὲ Ἰησοῦς ἀπόκρισιν οὐκ ἔδωκεν αὐτῷ. λέγει οὖν αὐτῷ ὁ ρϟγ
Πιλάτος, Ἐμοὶ οὐ λαλεῖς; οὐκ οἶδας ὅτι ἐξουσίαν ἔχω σταυρῶσαί σε ι
11 καὶ ἐξουσίαν ἔχω ἀπολῦσαί σε; ἀπεκρίθη αὐτῷ ὁ Ἰησοῦς, Οὐκ εἶχες
ἐξουσίαν κατ' ἐμοῦ οὐδεμίαν, εἰ μὴ ἦν σοι δεδομένον ἄνωθεν· διὰ
12 τοῦτο ὁ παραδιδούς μέ σοι μείζονα ἁμαρτίαν ἔχει. ἐκ τούτου οὖν
ἐζήτει ὁ Πιλάτος ἀπολῦσαι αὐτόν. οἱ δὲ Ἰουδαῖοι ἐκραύγαζον λέ-
γοντες, Ἐὰν τοῦτον ἀπολύσῃς, οὐκ εἶ φίλος τοῦ Καίσαρος. πᾶς ὁ
13 βασιλέα ἑαυτὸν ποιῶν ἀντιλέγει Καίσαρι. ὁ οὖν Πιλάτος ἀκούσας
τούτων τῶν λόγων ἤγαγεν ἔξω τὸν Ἰησοῦν, καὶ ἐκάθισεν ἐπὶ βή-
ματος εἰς τόπον ὃς λέγεται Λιθόστρωτον, Ἑβραϊστὶ δὲ Καπφαθᾶ·
14 ἦν δὲ παρασκευὴ τοῦ πάσχα, ὥρα ἦν ὡσεὶ ἕκτη. καὶ λέγει τοῖς
15 Ἰουδαίοις, Ἴδε ὁ βασιλεὺς ὑμῶν. οἱ δὲ ἐκραύγασαν, Ἆρον, ἆρον, ρϟδ
σταύρωσον αὐτόν. λέγει αὐτοῖς ὁ Πιλάτος, Τὸν βασιλέα ὑμῶν σταυ- α ρϟε
ρώσω; ἀπεκρίθησαν οἱ ἀρχιερεῖς, Οὐκ ἔχομεν βασιλέα εἰ μὴ Καίσαρα. ι
16 τότε οὖν παρέδωκεν αὐτὸν αὐτοῖς ἵνα σταυρωθῇ. ρϟϛ
17 Οἱ δὲ παραλαβόντες αὐτὸν ἀπήγαγον· καὶ βαστάζων τὸν σταυ- α ρϟζ
ρὸν ἑαυτῷ ἐξῆλθεν εἰς τὸν λεγόμενον Κρανίου τόπον, ὃς λέγεται α
18 Ἑβραϊστὶ Γολγοθᾶ· ὅπου ἐσταύρωσαν αὐτόν, καὶ μετ' αὐτοῦ ἄλλους ρϟη
19 δύο ἐντεῦθεν καὶ ἐντεῦθεν, μέσον δὲ τὸν Ἰησοῦν. ἔγραψε δὲ καὶ τίτλον α ρϟθ
ὁ Πιλάτος καὶ ἔθηκεν ἐπὶ τοῦ σταυροῦ· ἦν δὲ γεγραμμένον, Ἰησοῦς α
20 ὁ Ναζωραῖος ὁ βασιλεὺς τῶν Ἰουδαίων. τοῦτον οὖν τὸν τίτλον πολλοὶ σ
ἀνέγνωσαν τῶν Ἰουδαίων, ὅτι ἐγγὺς ἦν τῆς πόλεως ὁ τόπος ὅπου ι

3 εδιδουν ϛ εξηλθεν ουν ϛ 4 εν αυτω ante ουδεμιαν ϛ 5 ο Ιησους 209
εξω ϛ εχων] φορων 209 ϛ ιδου] ιδε ϛ 6 οτ αν] οταν 209, οτε ϛ ϛ
7 απεκριθησαν αυτω ϛ εαυτον υιον Θεου ϛ 11 om αυτω ϛ ουδε-
μιαν κατ εμου 209 ϛ 12 om ουν ϛ εκραζον ϛ εαυτον] αυτον ϛ
τω Καισαρι 209 ϛ 13 τουτον τον λογον ϛ του βηματος ϛ ος λεγεται]
λεγομενον 209 ϛ Γαββαθα 209 ϛ 14 ην] δε ϛ 16 οι...αυτον]
παρελαβον δε τον Ιησουν και ϛ 17 εαυτω] αυτου ϛ αυτον εσταυρωσαν ϛ
20 ο τοπος της πολεως 209

ἐσταυρώθη ὁ Ἰησοῦς· καὶ ἦν γεγραμμένον Ἑβραϊστί, Ἑλληνιστί,
Ῥωμαϊστί. ἔλεγον οὖν τῷ Πιλάτῳ οἱ ἀρχιερεῖς τῶν Ἰουδαίων, Μὴ 21
γράφε, Ὁ βασιλεὺς τῶν Ἰουδαίων, ἀλλ' ὅτι ἐκεῖνος εἶπε, Βασιλεύς εἰμι
σα τῶν Ἰουδαίων. ἀπεκρίθη ὁ Πιλάτος, Ὃ γέγραφα, γέγραφα. οἱ οὖν 22 23
α στρατιῶται, ὅτε ἐσταύρωσαν τὸν Ἰησοῦν, ἔλαβον τὰ ἱμάτια αὐτοῦ, καὶ
ἐποίησαν τέσσαρα μέρη, ἑκάστῳ στρατιώτῃ μέρος, καὶ τὸν χιτῶνα. ἦν
δὲ ὁ χιτὼν ἄραφος, ἐκ τῶν ἄνωθεν ὑφαντὸς δι' ὅλου· εἶπον οὖν πρὸς 24
ἀλλήλους, Μὴ σχίσωμεν αὐτόν, ἀλλὰ λάχωμεν περὶ αὐτοῦ, τίνος ἔσται·
ἵνα ἡ γραφὴ πληρωθῇ ἡ λέγουσα, Διεμερίσαντο τὰ ἱμάτιά μου ἑαυτοῖς,
καὶ ἐπὶ τὸν ἱματισμόν μου ἔβαλον κλῆρον.

σβ ι Οἱ μὲν οὖν στρατιῶται ταῦτα ἐποίησαν. εἱστήκεισαν δὲ παρὰ τῷ 25
σταυρῷ τοῦ Ἰησοῦ ἡ μήτηρ καὶ ἡ ἀδελφὴ τῆς μητρὸς αὐτοῦ Μαριὰμ
ἡ τοῦ Κλωπᾶ καὶ Μαριὰμ ἡ Μαγδαληνή. Ἰησοῦς οὖν ὡς εἶδεν 26
τὴν μητέρα καὶ τὸν μαθητὴν παρεστῶτα ὃν ἠγάπα, λέγει τῇ μητρί,
Γύναι, ἰδοὺ ὁ υἱός σου. εἶτα λέγει τῷ μαθητῇ, Ἰδοὺ ἡ μήτηρ σου. 27
ἀπ' ἐκείνης οὖν τῆς ὥρας ἔλαβεν αὐτὴν ὁ μαθητὴς εἰς τὰ ἴδια.
σγ μετὰ τοῦτο εἰδὼς ὁ Ἰησοῦς ὅτι πάντα τετέλεσται, ἵνα ἡ γραφὴ 28
δ πληρωθῇ, λέγει, Διψῶ. σκεῦος οὖν ἔκειτο ὄξους μεστόν· σπόγγον 29
οὖν μεστὸν τοῦ ὄξους ὑσσώπῳ περιθέντες, προσήνεγκαν αὐτοῦ τῷ
σδ στόματι. ὅτε οὖν ἔλαβε τὸ ὄξος ὁ Ἰησοῦς, εἶπε, Τετέλεσται· καὶ κλίνας 30
α τὴν κεφαλὴν παρέδωκε τὸ πνεῦμα.

σε ι Οἱ οὖν Ἰουδαῖοι, ἐπεὶ παρασκευὴ ἦν, ἵνα μὴ μείνῃ ἐπὶ τοῦ 31
σταυροῦ τὰ σώματα ἐν τῷ σαββάτῳ, ἦν γὰρ μεγάλη ἡ ἡμέρα ἐκείνου
τοῦ σαββάτου, ἠρώτησαν τὸν Πιλάτον ἵνα κατεαγῶσιν αὐτῶν τὰ σκέλη,
καὶ ἀρθῶσιν. ἦλθον οὖν οἱ στρατιῶται καὶ τοῦ μὲν πρώτου κατέαξαν 32
τὰ σκέλη καὶ τοῦ ἄλλου τοῦ συσταυρωθέντος αὐτῷ· ἐπὶ δὲ τὸν Ἰησοῦν 33
ἐλθόντες ὡς εἶδον αὐτὸν ἤδη τεθνηκότα, οὐ κατέαξαν αὐτοῦ τὰ σκέλη·
ἀλλ' εἷς τῶν στρατιωτῶν λόγχῃ αὐτοῦ τὴν πλευρὰν ἔνυξε· καὶ εὐθὺς 34
ἐξῆλθεν αἷμα καὶ ὕδωρ. καὶ ὁ ἑωρακὼς μεμαρτύρηκε, καὶ ἀληθινὴ αὐτοῦ 35
ἐστιν ἡ μαρτυρία, καὶ ἐκεῖνος οἶδεν ὅτι ἀληθῆ λέγει, ἵνα καὶ ὑμεῖς
πιστεύσητε. ἐγένετο γὰρ ταῦτα, ἵνα ἡ γραφὴ πληρωθῇ, Ὀστοῦν 36

29 το στοματι cod. **35** αληληθινη cod.

209 ς **23** αρραφος ς **25** μητηρ αυτου 209 ς Μαρια bis 209 ς **26** ως ειδεν] ιδων 209 ς μητρι αυτου 209 ς ιδου] ιδε 209 **27** και απ 209 ς om ουν 209 ς μαθητης εκεινος 209 **28** ηδη τετελεσται ς τελειωθη η γραφη ς **29** σπογγον...οξους] οι δε πλησαντες σπογγον οξους 209 ς **31** επει παρασκευη ην post σαββατω ς om η 209 **34** ευθεως 209 **35** αυτου post μαρτυρια 209 κακεινος 209 ς om και 4° ς

37 οὐ συντριβήσεται αὐτοῦ. καὶ πάλιν ἑτέρα γραφή, Ὄψονται εἰς ὃν
ἐξεκέντησαν.
38 Μετὰ δὲ ταῦτα ἠρώτησε τὸν Πιλάτον Ἰωσὴφ ὁ ἀπὸ Ἀριματθαίας, ΙΗ'
ὢν μαθητὴς τοῦ Ἰησοῦ, κεκρυμμένος δὲ διὰ τὸν φόβον τῶν Ἰουδαίων, σϛ α
39 ἵνα ἄρῃ τὸ σῶμα τοῦ Ἰησοῦ· ἦλθε δὲ καὶ Νικόδημος ὁ ἐλθὼν πρὸς σζ ι
τὸν Ἰησοῦν νυκτὸς τὸ πρῶτον, φέρων μῖγμα σμύρνης καὶ ἀλόης ὡσεὶ
40 λίτρας ἑκατόν. ἔλαβον οὖν τὸ σῶμα τοῦ Ἰησοῦ, καὶ ἔδησαν αὐτὸ ση α
ὀθονίοις μετὰ τῶν ἀρωμάτων, καθὼς ἔθος ἐστὶ τοῖς Ἰουδαίοις ἐντα-
41 φιάζειν. ἦν δὲ ἐν τῷ τόπῳ ὅπου ἐσταυρώθη κῆπος, καὶ ἐν τῷ τόπῳ
42 μνημεῖον καινόν, ἐν ᾧ οὐδέπω οὐδεὶς ἐτέθη. ἐκεῖ οὖν διὰ τὴν παρασκευὴν
τῶν Ἰουδαίων, ὅτι ἐγγὺς ἦν τὸ μνημεῖον, ἔθηκαν τὸν Ἰησοῦν.
XX. Τῇ δὲ μιᾷ τῶν σαββάτων Μαριὰμ ἡ Μαγδαληνὴ ἔρχεται σθ α
πρωῒ σκοτίας ἔτι οὔσης εἰς τὸ μνημεῖον, καὶ βλέπει τὸν λίθον ἠρμένον
2 ἀπὸ τῆς θύρας τοῦ μνημείου. τρέχει οὖν καὶ ἔρχεται πρὸς Σίμωνα σι ι
Πέτρον καὶ πρὸς τὸν ἄλλον μαθητὴν ὃν ἐφίλει ὁ Ἰησοῦς, καὶ λέγει
αὐτοῖς, Ἦραν τὸν κύριον ἐκ τοῦ μνημείου, καὶ οὐκ οἴδαμεν ποῦ ἔθηκαν
3 αὐτόν. ἐξῆλθεν οὖν ὁ Πέτρος καὶ ὁ ἄλλος μαθητής, καὶ ἤρχοντο εἰς
4 τὸ μνημεῖον. ἔτρεχον δὲ οἱ δύο ὁμοῦ· καὶ ὁ ἄλλος μαθητὴς προέδραμε
5 τάχιον τοῦ Πέτρου καὶ ἦλθε πρῶτος εἰς τὸ μνημεῖον, καὶ παρακύψας
6 βλέπει τὰ ὀθόνια κείμενα, οὐ μέντοιγε εἰσῆλθεν. ἔρχεται οὖν
Σίμων Πέτρος ἀκολουθῶν αὐτῷ, καὶ εἰσῆλθεν εἰς τὸ μνημεῖον, καὶ
7 θεωρεῖ τὰ ὀθόνια κείμενα, καὶ τὸ σουδάριον ὃ ἦν ἐπὶ τῆς κεφαλῆς
αὐτοῦ, οὐ μετὰ τῶν ὀθονίων κείμενον, ἀλλὰ χωρὶς ἐντετυλιγμένον εἰς
8 ἕνα τόπον. τότε οὖν εἰσῆλθε καὶ ὁ ἄλλος μαθητὴς ὁ ἐλθὼν πρῶτος
9 εἰς τὸ μνημεῖον, καὶ εἶδε καὶ ἐπίστευσεν· οὐδέπω γὰρ ᾔδεισαν τὴν
10 γραφήν, ὅτι δεῖ αὐτὸν ἐκ νεκρῶν ἀναστῆναι. ἀπῆλθον οὖν πάλιν πρὸς
11 ἑαυτοὺς οἱ μαθηταί. Μαριὰμ δὲ εἱστήκει πρὸς τῷ μνημείῳ ἔξω σια α
12 κλαίουσα. ὡς οὖν ἔκλαιε, παρέκυψεν εἰς τὸ μνημεῖον, καὶ θεωρεῖ
δύο ἀγγέλους ἐν λευκοῖς, καθεζομένους ἕνα πρὸς τῇ κεφαλῇ καὶ ἕνα
13 πρὸς τοῖς ποσίν, ὅπου ἔκειτο τὸ σῶμα τοῦ Ἰησοῦ. καὶ λέγουσιν αὐτῇ σιβ ι
ἐκεῖνοι, Γύναι, τί κλαίεις; λέγει αὐτοῖς, Ὅτι ἦραν τὸν κύριόν μου,
14 καὶ οὐκ οἴδαμεν ποῦ ἔθηκαν αὐτόν. ταῦτα εἰποῦσα ἐστράφη εἰς τὰ

38 Ἰησοῦ 2°] nota 〃 addita est

1 ἠρμένον cod. 13 οιδαμεν] μεν nunc eras. sed accentus non mut.

37 γραφη λεγει 209 ϛ 38 ο Ιωσηφ ϛ Αριμαθαιας ϛ 209
Ιησου 2°]+και επετρεψεν ο Πιλατος. ηλθεν ουν και ηρε το σωμα του Ιησου ϛ ϛ
41 τοπω 2°] κηπω ϛ

1 Μαρια 209 ϛ ουσης ετι 209 απο της θυρας] εκ ϛ 2 τον
Σιμωνα 209 5 κειμενα τα οθονια ϛ μεντοι 209 ϛ 11 Μαρια ϛ
το μνημειον 209 ϛ κλαιουσα εξω 209 ϛ 13 οιδα ϛ 14 και ταυτα ϛ

ὀπίσω, καὶ θεωρεῖ τὸν Ἰησοῦν ἑστῶτα· καὶ οὐκ ᾔδει ὅτι Ἰησοῦς ἐστι.
λέγει αὐτῇ ὁ Ἰησοῦς, Γύναι, τί κλαίεις; τίνα ζητεῖς; ἐκείνη, δοκοῦσα 15
ὅτι ὁ κηπουρός ἐστι, λέγει αὐτῷ, Κύριε, εἰ σὺ ἐβάστασας αὐτόν,
εἰπέ μοι ποῦ ἔθηκας αὐτόν, κἀγὼ αὐτὸν ἀρῶ. λέγει αὐτῇ ὁ Ἰησοῦς, 16
Μαριάμ. στραφεῖσα ἐκείνη λέγει αὐτῷ, Ῥαββουνί, ὃ λέγεται Διδά-
σκαλε. λέγει αὐτῇ ὁ Ἰησοῦς, Μή μου ἅπτου, οὔπω γὰρ ἀναβέβηκα 17
πρὸς τὸν πατέρα μου· πορεύου δὲ πρὸς τοὺς ἀδελφούς μου, καὶ εἰπὲ
αὐτοῖς, Ἀναβαίνω πρὸς τὸν πατέρα μου καὶ πατέρα ὑμῶν καὶ Θεόν
μου καὶ Θεὸν ὑμῶν. ἔρχεται Μαριὰμ ἡ Μαγδαληνὴ ἀπαγγέλλουσα 18
τοῖς μαθηταῖς ὅτι ἑώρακε τὸν κύριον καὶ ταῦτα εἶπεν αὐτῇ.
σιγ θ Οὔσης οὖν ὀψίας τῇ ἡμέρᾳ ἐκείνῃ τῇ μιᾷ τῶν σαββάτων, καὶ τῶν 19
θυρῶν κεκλεισμένων ὅπου ἦσαν οἱ μαθηταὶ συνηγμένοι, διὰ τὸν φόβον
τῶν Ἰουδαίων, ἦλθεν ὁ Ἰησοῦς καὶ ἔστη εἰς τὸ μέσον, καὶ λέγει αὐτοῖς,
Εἰρήνη ὑμῖν. καὶ τοῦτο εἰπὼν ἔδειξεν αὐτοῖς τὰς χεῖρας καὶ τὴν 20
σιδ ι πλευράν. ἐχάρησαν δὲ οἱ μαθηταὶ ἰδόντες τὸν κύριον. εἶπεν οὖν 21
αὐτοῖς πάλιν ὁ Ἰησοῦς, Εἰρήνη ὑμῖν· καθὼς ἀπέσταλκέ με ὁ πατήρ,
κἀγὼ πέμπω ὑμᾶς. καὶ τοῦτο εἰπὼν ἐνεφύσησε, καὶ λέγει αὐτοῖς, 22
σιε ς Λάβετε Πνεῦμα Ἅγιον. ἄν τινων ἀφῆτε τὰς ἁμαρτίας, ἀφέωνται 23
σις ι αὐτοῖς· ἄν τινων κρατῆτε, κεκράτηνται. Θωμᾶς οὖν, εἷς ἐκ τῶν δώ- 24
δεκα, ὁ λεγόμενος Δίδυμος, οὐκ ἦν μετ' αὐτῶν ὅτε ἦλθεν ὁ Ἰησοῦς.
ἔλεγον οὖν αὐτῷ οἱ ἄλλοι μαθηταί, Ἑωράκαμεν τὸν κύριον. ὁ δὲ εἶπεν 25
αὐτοῖς, Ἐὰν μὴ ἴδω ἐν ταῖς χερσὶν αὐτοῦ τὸν τύπον τῶν ἥλων, καὶ
βάλω τὸν δάκτυλόν μου εἰς τὸν τύπον τῶν ἥλων, καὶ βάλω τὴν χεῖρα
σιζ θ εἰς τὴν πλευρὰν αὐτοῦ, οὐ μὴ πιστεύσω. καὶ μεθ' ἡμέρας ὀκτὼ πάλιν 26
ἦσαν ἔσω οἱ μαθηταί, καὶ Θωμᾶς μετ' αὐτῶν. ἔρχεται οὖν ὁ Ἰησοῦς,
τῶν θυρῶν κεκλεισμένων, καὶ ἔστη εἰς τὸ μέσον καὶ εἶπεν, Εἰρήνη
ὑμῖν. εἶτα λέγει τῷ Θωμᾷ, Φέρε τὸν δάκτυλόν σου ὧδε, καὶ ἴδε 27
τὰς χεῖράς μου, καὶ φέρε τὴν χεῖρά σου, καὶ βάλε εἰς τὴν πλευράν
σιη ι μου, καὶ μὴ γίνου ἄπιστος, ἀλλὰ πιστός. ἀπεκρίθη Θωμᾶς καὶ 28
εἶπεν αὐτῷ, Ὁ κύριός μου καὶ ὁ Θεός μου. λέγει αὐτῷ ὁ Ἰησοῦς, 29
Ὅτι ἑώρακάς με, πεπίστευκας· μακάριοι οἱ μὴ ἰδόντες καὶ πιστεύ-
σαντες.

Πολλὰ μὲν οὖν καὶ ἄλλα σημεῖα ἐποίησεν ὁ Ἰησοῦς ἐνώπιον τῶν 30
μαθητῶν αὐτοῦ, ἃ οὐκ ἔστι γεγραμμένα ἐν τῷ βιβλίῳ τούτῳ· ταῦτα δὲ 31

23 αφεωωται cod. sed ω 2° aliquis partim erasit forsitan ν scribendi causa

209 ς 14 ο Ιησους ς 15 om κυριε 209 αυτον εθηκας ς 16 Μαρια 209 ς 18 Μαρια 209 ς 20 πλευραν αυτου 209 ς δε] ουν ς 21 ο Ιησους παλιν 209 ς 23 αφιενται ς 24 ουν] δε 209 ς 25 χειρα μου 209[2] ς . 26 μαθηται αυτου 209 ς om ουν ς 28 και απεκριθη ς ο Θωμας ς 29 με]+Θωμα ς ιδοντες με 209

γέγραπται ἵνα πιστεύσητε ὅτι Ἰησοῦς ἐστιν ὁ Χριστὸς ὁ υἱὸς τοῦ
Θεοῦ, καὶ ἵνα πιστεύοντες ζωὴν ἔχητε ἐν τῷ ὀνόματι αὐτοῦ.

XXI. Μετὰ ταῦτα ἐφανέρωσεν ἑαυτὸν πάλιν ὁ Ἰησοῦς τοῖς μαθη- σιθ θ
2 ταῖς ἐπὶ τῆς θαλάσσης τῆς Τιβεριάδος· ἐφανέρωσε δὲ οὕτως. ἦσαν
ὁμοῦ Σίμων Πέτρος καὶ Θωμᾶς ὁ λεγόμενος Δίδυμος καὶ Ναθαναὴλ
ὁ ἀπὸ Κανᾶ τῆς Γαλιλαίας καὶ οἱ τοῦ Ζεβεδαίου καὶ ἄλλοι ἐκ τῶν
3 μαθητῶν αὐτοῦ δύο. λέγει αὐτοῖς Σίμων Πέτρος, Ὑπάγω ἁλιεύειν.
λέγουσιν αὐτῷ, Ἐρχόμεθα σὺν σοί. ἐξῆλθον καὶ ἐνέβησαν εἰς
4 τὸ πλοῖον, καὶ ἐν ἐκείνῃ τῇ νυκτὶ ἐπίασαν οὐδέν. πρωΐας δὲ ἤδη
γενομένης ἔστη ὁ Ἰησοῦς εἰς τὸν αἰγιαλόν· οὐ μέντοι ἤδεισαν οἱ
5 μαθηταὶ ὅτι Ἰησοῦς ἐστι. λέγει οὖν αὐτοῖς ὁ Ἰησοῦς, Παιδία, μή
6 τι προσφάγιον ἔχετε; ἀπεκρίθησαν αὐτῷ, Οὔ. ὁ δὲ εἶπεν αὐτοῖς,
Βάλετε εἰς τὰ δεξιὰ μέρη τοῦ πλοίου τὸ δίκτυον, καὶ εὑρήσετε.
ἔβαλον οὖν, καὶ οὐκ ἔτι ἑλκύσαι αὐτὸ ἴσχυον ἀπὸ τοῦ πλήθους
7 τῶν ἰχθύων. λέγει οὖν ὁ μαθητὴς ἐκεῖνος ὃν ἠγάπα ὁ Ἰησοῦς τῷ σκ ι
Πέτρῳ, Ὁ κύριός ἐστι. Σίμων οὖν Πέτρος ἀκούσας ὅτι ὁ κύριός ἐστι,
τὸν ἐπενδύτην διεζώσατο, ἦν γὰρ γυμνός, καὶ ἔβαλεν ἑαυτὸν εἰς τὴν
8 θάλασσαν. οἱ δε ἄλλοι μαθηταὶ τῷ πλοιαρίῳ ἦλθον, οὐ γὰρ ἦσαν
μακρὰν ἀπὸ τῆς γῆς, ἀλλ' ὡς ἀπὸ πηχῶν διακοσίων, σύραντες τὸ
9 δίκτυον τῶν ἰχθύων. ὡς οὖν ἀπέβησαν εἰς τὴν γῆν, βλέπουσιν ἀνθρα- σκα θ
10 κιὰν κειμένην καὶ ὀψάριον ἐπικείμενον καὶ ἄρτον. λέγει αὐτοῖς ὁ
11 Ἰησοῦς, Ἐνέγκατε ἀπὸ τῶν ὀψαρίων ὧν ἐπιάσατε νῦν. ἐνέβη οὖν σκβ θ
Σίμων Πέτρος καὶ εἵλκυσε τὸ δίκτυον ἐπὶ τὴν γῆν, μεστὸν μεγάλων
ἰχθύων ἑκατὸν πεντηκοντατριῶν· καὶ τοσούτων ὄντων οὐκ ἐσχίσθη τὸ
δίκτυον.

12 Λέγει αὐτοῖς ὁ Ἰησοῦς, Δεῦτε ἀριστήσατε. οὐδεὶς δὲ ἐτόλμα τῶν σκγ θ
13 μαθητῶν ἐξετάσαι αὐτόν, Σὺ τίς εἶ; εἰδότες ὅτι ὁ κύριός ἐστιν. ἔρχε- σκδ ι
ται ὁ Ἰησοῦς καὶ λαμβάνει τὸν ἄρτον καὶ δίδωσιν αὐτοῖς, καὶ τὸ σκε θ
14 ὀψάριον ὁμοίως. τοῦτο ἤδη τρίτον ἐφανερώθη ὁ Ἰησοῦς τοῖς μαθηταῖς σκϛ ι
ἐγερθεὶς ἐκ νεκρῶν.

15 Ὅτε οὖν ἠρίστησαν, λέγει τῷ Σίμωνι Πέτρῳ ὁ Ἰησοῦς, Σίμων σκζ θ
Ἰωνᾶ, ἀγαπᾷς με; λέγει αὐτῷ, Ναί, κύριε, σὺ οἶδας ὅτι φιλῶ σε.

6 δικτυων cod.

31 ο Ιησους 209 ϛ

3 ερχομεθα και ημεις 209 ϛ εξηλθον ουν 209 ανεβησαν ϛ πλοιον] +ευθυς ϛ **4** om η 209 εις] επι 209 **6** ο] οι 209 (sed non ειπον) βαλλετε 209 εβαλλον 209* αυτο ελκυσαι ισχυσαν 209 ϛ **7** εβαλλεν 209 **8** συροντες ϛ **11** ανεβη 209 ϛ om ουν 209 ϛ της γης ϛ ιχθυων μεγαλων 209 ϛ **13** ερχεται ουν 209 ϛ **14** μαθηταις αυτου 209 ϛ **15** με]+πλεον τουτων 209 ϛ 209 ϛ

σκη/ι λέγει αὐτῷ, Βόσκε τὰ ἀρνία μου. λέγει αὐτῷ πάλιν τὸ δεύτερον, 16
σκθ/θ Σίμων Ἰωνᾶ, ἀγαπᾷς με; λέγει αὐτῷ, Ναί, κύριε, σὺ οἶδας ὅτι φιλῶ
σλ σε. λέγει αὐτῷ τὸ τρίτον, Σίμων Ἰωνᾶ, φιλεῖς με; ἐλυπήθη ὁ 17
ι Πέτρος ὅτι εἶπεν αὐτῷ τὸ τρίτον, Φιλεῖς με; καὶ λέγει αὐτῷ, Κύριε,
σλα/θ σὺ πάντα οἶδας· σὺ γινώσκεις ὅτι φιλῶ σε. λέγει αὐτῷ, Βόσκε
σλβ/ι τὰ πρόβατά μου. ἀμὴν ἀμὴν λέγω σοι, ὅτε ἦς νεώτερος, ἐζώννυες 18
σεαυτὸν καὶ περιεπάτεις ὅπου ἤθελες· ὅταν δὲ γηράσῃς, ἐκτενεῖς τὰς
χεῖράς σου, καὶ ἄλλοι σε ζώσουσιν καὶ ἀποίσουσιν ὅπου οὐ
θέλεις. τοῦτο δὲ ἔλεγε σημαίνων ποίῳ θανάτῳ δοξάσει τὸν Θεόν. 19
καὶ τοῦτο εἰπὼν λέγει αὐτῷ, Ἀκολούθει μοι. ἐπιστραφεὶς δὲ Πέτρος 20
βλέπει τὸν μαθητὴν ὃν ἠγάπα ὁ Ἰησοῦς ἀκολουθοῦντα, ὃς καὶ ἀν-
έπεσεν ἐν τῷ δείπνῳ ἐπὶ τὸ στῆθος αὐτοῦ καὶ εἶπε, Κύριε, τίς ἐστιν
ὁ παραδιδούς σε; τοῦτον ἰδὼν ὁ Πέτρος λέγει τῷ Ἰησοῦ, Κύριε, οὗτος 21
δὲ τί; λέγει αὐτῷ ὁ Ἰησοῦς, Ἐὰν αὐτὸν θέλω μένειν ἕως ἔρχομαι, 22
τί πρός σε; σύ μοι ἀκολούθει. ἐξῆλθεν οὖν οὗτος ὁ λόγος εἰς 23
τοὺς ἀδελφούς, ὅτι ὁ μαθητὴς ἐκεῖνος οὐκ ἀποθνήσκει· καὶ οὐκ εἶπεν
αὐτῷ ὁ Ἰησοῦς, ὅτι οὐκ ἀποθνήσκει· ἀλλ', Ἐὰν αὐτὸν θέλω μένειν
ἕως ἔρχομαι.

Οὗτός ἐστιν ὁ μαθητὴς ὁ μαρτυρῶν περὶ τούτων καὶ γράψας ταῦτα· 24
καὶ οἴδαμεν ὅτι ἀληθής ἐστιν ἡ μαρτυρία αὐτοῦ. ἔστι δὲ καὶ ἄλλα 25
πολλὰ ὅσα ἐποίησεν ὁ Ἰησοῦς, ἅτινα ἐὰν γράφηται καθ' ἕν, οὐδ' αὐτὸν
οἶμαι τὸν κόσμον χωρῆσαι τὰ γραφόμενα βιβλία.

IC	XΣ
NI	KA

15 *βοσκε*] *β* in rasura m. recent. scripsit sed ni fallor et 1* *β* scripsit nec rasurae causam fingere possum

Ad fin. evang. rubr² scrips. *κε συγχωρησον τη* (?) *ψυχη* (?) *του δουλου σου* (?) *Μαλαχιου ιερομοναχου το τουτο γραφοντος*

209 ς 16 om *το* 209 ς *σε*]+*λεγει αυτω ποιμαινε τα προβατα μου* ς 17 *λεγει*] *ειπεν* ς *βοσκε*] pr *ο Ιησους* ς 18 *αλλος σε ζωσει και οισει* 209 ς 19 *ελεγε*] *ειπε* ς 20 *ο Πετρος* 209 ς 22 *ακολουθει μοι* 209 ς 23 *ο λογος ουτος* 209 ς *ερχομαι*]+*τι προς σε* 209 ς 25 *ουδ*] *ουδε* 209 ς *τον κοσμον*] 209* primum omisit, sed postea ad lineae finem *τον* et ad lineae alterius initium *κοσμον* addidit ita ut codex nunc habeat *τον κοσμον οιμαι* *βιβλια*]+*αμην* 209 ς

Ad finem evangelii in cod. 209 rasura est magna quam legere non possum

Τὸ περὶ τῆς μοιχαλίδος κεφάλαιον ἐν τῷ κατὰ Ἰωάννην εὐαγγελίῳ ὡς ἐν πλείοσιν ἀντιγράφοις μὴ κείμενον, μηδὲ παρὰ τῶν θείων πατέρων τῶν ἑρμηνευσάντων μνημονευθέν, φημὶ δὴ Ἰωάννου τοῦ χ̄ καὶ Κυρίλλου Ἀλεξανδρέας, οὐδὲ μὴν ὑπὸ Θεοδώρου Μωψουεστίας καὶ τῶν λοιπῶν, παρέλειψα κατὰ τὸν τόπον, κεῖται δὲ οὕτως μετ' ὀλίγα τῆς ἄρχης τοῦ π̄ϛ̄ κεφαλαίου, ἑξῆς τοῦ Ἐρεύνησον καὶ ἴδε ὅτι προφήτης ἐκ τῆς Γαλιλαίας οὐκ ἐγείρεται.

53 Καὶ ἐπορεύθησαν ἕκαστος εἰς τὸν τόπον αὐτοῦ, (VIII) Ἰησοῦς
2 δὲ ἐπορεύθη εἰς τὸ ὄρος τῶν Ἐλαιῶν. ὄρθρου δὲ πάλιν παρεγένετο
εἰς τὸ ἱερόν, καὶ πᾶς ὁ λαὸς ἤρχετο πρὸς αὐτόν, καὶ καθίσας ἐδίδασκεν
3 αὐτούς. ἄγουσι δὲ οἱ ἀρχιερεῖς καὶ οἱ Φαρισαῖοι γυναῖκα ἐπὶ
4 μοιχείᾳ κατειλημμένην, καὶ στήσαντες αὐτὴν ἐν μέσῳ λέγουσιν αὐτῷ
Διδάσκαλε, αὕτη ἡ γυνὴ κατείληπται ἐπ' αὐτοφώρῳ μοιχευομένη.
5 ἐν δὲ τῷ νόμῳ ἡμῖν Μωσῆς ἐνετείλατο τὰς τοιαύτας λιθάζειν· σὺ οὖν
6 τί λέγεις; τοῦτο δὲ ἔλεγον πειράζοντες αὐτόν, ἵνα εὕρωσι κατηγορεῖν
αὐτοῦ. ὁ δὲ Ἰησοῦς κάτω κύψας τῷ δακτύλῳ ἔγραφεν εἰς τὴν γῆν.
7 ὡς δὲ ἐπέμενον ἐπερωτῶντες αὐτόν, ἀνέκυψε καὶ εἶπεν αὐτοῖς Ὁ
8 ἀναμάρτητος ὑμῶν πρῶτος ἐπ' αὐτῇ βαλλέτω λίθον· καὶ πάλιν κατα-
9 κύψας ἔγραφεν εἰς τὴν γῆν. ἀκούσαντες δὲ ἐξήρχοντο εἷς ἕκαστος
ἀρξάμενοι ἀπὸ τῶν πρεσβυτέρων, καὶ κατελείφθη μόνος, καὶ ἡ γυνὴ
10 ἐν μέσῳ ἑστῶσα. ἀνακύψας δὲ ὁ Ἰησοῦς εἶπεν αὐτῇ Γύναι, ποῦ
11 εἰσίν; οὐδείς σε κατέκρινεν; ἡ δὲ εἶπεν Οὐδείς, κύριε. εἶπε δὲ ὁ
Ἰησοῦς Οὐδὲ ἐγώ σε κατακρίνω· πορεύου, καὶ ἀπὸ τοῦ νῦν μηκέτι
ἁμάρτανε.

το περι...εγειρεται om 118 209 ϛ (vide supra p. 173) 118 209 ϛ
53 *επορευθησαν*] *απηλθεν* 118 209, *επορευθη* ϛ *τοπον*] *οικον* 118 209 ϛ **1** *Ιησους δε*] *και ο Ιησους* 118 209 ϛ **2** *παλιν*] + *βαθεος* 118 209 *παρεγενετο*] *ηλθεν ο Ιησους* 118 209 **3** *αρχιερεις*] *γραμματεις* 118 209 ϛ *γυναικα*] pr *προς αυτον* 118 209 ϛ *εν μοιχεια* ϛ **4** *τω μεσω* 118 209 *λεγουσιν*] *ειπον* 118 209 *αυτη η γυνη*] *ταυτην* 118 209 *κατειληπται*] *ευρομεν* 118 209, *κατειληφθη* ϛ *μοιχευομενην* 118 209 **5** *ημιν Μωσης*] *Μωυσης* 118 209, *Μωσης ημιν* ϛ *λιθοβολεισθαι* ϛ **6** *ευρωσι*] *εχωσι* 118 209 ϛ *κατηγοριαν κατ αυτου* 118 209 **7** *ερωτωντες* ϛ *ανεκυψε και*] *αναβλεψας* 118 209, *ανακυψας* ϛ *αυτοις*] *προς αυτους* ϛ *επ αυτην* 118 209 *βαλετω* 118 209 ϛ *τον λιθον επ αυτη βαλετω* ϛ **8** *κατω κυψας* 118 209 ϛ **9** *οι δε ακουσαντες και υπο της συνειδησεως ελεγχομενοι εξηρχοντο εις καθεις* 118 209 ϛ *πρεσβυτερων*] + *εως των εσχατων* 118 209 ϛ *μονος*] + *ο Ιησους* 118 209 ϛ *εστωσα*] *ουσα* 118 209 **10** *Ιησους*] + *ειδεν αυτην και* 118 209, + *και μηδενα θεασαμενος πλην της γυναικος* ϛ om *αυτη* 118 209 *γυναι*] *η γυνη* ϛ *που εισιν*] om 118 209, + *εκεινοι οι κατηγοροι σου* ϛ **11** *δε*] + *αυτη* 118 209 ϛ *απο του νυν*] ante *και* 118 209, om ϛ

15807668R00160

Printed in Poland
by Amazon Fulfillment
Poland Sp. z o.o., Wrocław